KAPLAN) MEDICAL

medEssentials

High-Yield USMLE™ Step 1 Review

Second Edition

© 2008 by Kaplan, Inc.

Published by Kaplan Publishing, a division of Kaplan, Inc.
1 Liberty Plaza, 24th Floor
New York, NY 10006

Printed in the United States of America

September 2008
10 9 8 7 6

ISBN-13: 978-1-4277-9716-2

For more information about Kaplan Medical, contact us at 1-800-533-8850 or visit kaplanmedical.com

LEAD AUTHORS/EDITORS

Michael S. Manley, M.D.
Director, Basic Sciences and Step 1 Curriculum
Kaplan Medical

Leslie D. Manley, Ph.D.
Director, Basic Sciences and Step 1 Curriculum
Kaplan Medical

EXECUTIVE EDITORS

Sonia Reichert, M.D.

Rochelle Rothstein, M.D.
Chief Medical Officer

CONTRIBUTORS

Stuart Bentley Hibbert, M.D., Ph.D.
Resident in Radiology
New York Presbyterian Hospital
Weill Cornell Medical Center

Steven Daugherty, Ph.D.
Director of Education and Testing
Kaplan Medical
Rush Medical College

Douglas E. Fitzovich, Ph.D.
Associate Professor of Physiology
Pikeville College School of Osteopathic Medicine

Beth Forshee, Ph.D.
Assistant Professor of Physiology
Lake Erie College of Osteopathic Medicine

Robert F. Kissling III, M.D.

John A. Kriak, Pharm.D.
Director, Medical Education Conference Archives, Inc.

Mary J. Ruebush, Ph.D.
Adjunct Associate Professor of Medical Science
Montana State University

Nancy Standler, M.D., Ph.D.
Pathologist

James S. White, Ph.D.
Assistant Professor of Cell Biology
School of Osteopathic Medicine
University of Medicine and Dentistry of New Jersey
Adjunct Assistant Professor of Cell and Developmental Biology
University of Pennsylvania School of Medicine

Glenn Yiu, Ph.D.
Division of Health Sciences and Technology
Harvard Medical School/M.I.T.

REVIEWERS

Thomas H. Adair, Ph.D.
Professor
Department of Physiology and Biophysics
University of Mississippi Medical Center

April Apperson, M.S.
UCSD Tutorial Program
University of California, San Diego

Barbara Hansen, Ph.D.
Biochemistry Faculty, Kaplan Medical

KAPLAN MEDICAL PUBLISHING

Editors
Kate McGreevy
Director, Editorial
Kaplan Medical

Melissa Atkin
Managing Editor
Kaplan Medical

Layout Artist/Designer
Michael Wolff
Manager, Production
Kaplan Medical

Assistant Layout Artist
Andrea Repole

Cover Design
Maria Nicholas
Joanna Myllo

Online Interactive Component

Sonia Reichert, M.D.
Director of Curriculum
Kaplan Medical

Abraham Thengampallil, M.D.
Associate Director of Curriculum
Kaplan Medical

Dennis Morgan
Senior Manager, Online Producer
Kaplan Medical

Joseph Pasion, M.D.
Medical Curriculum Consultant
Kaplan Medical

CREATIVE/DESIGN

Maria Nicholas
Senior Creative Director
Brand Marketing
Kaplan Test Prep and Admissions

Christie Shin
Web Designer
Brand Marketing
Kaplan Test Prep and Admissions

ONLINE DEVELOPMENT

ACT360 Solutions
Kaptest Technology
Kaplan eLearning

Special thanks to Richard Friedland, D.P.M.

Contents

(A more comprehensive list appears on the first page of each chapter.)

(A more comprehensive list appears on the first page of each chapter.)

Welcome to Kaplan Medical. This **medEssentials** course includes a comprehensive high-yield review book with interactive online exercises covering both first and second year medical school subjects. These tools are an excellent adjunct to your medical school curriculum and an important resource for your board preparations.

The *medEssentials: High-Yield USMLE*™ *Step 1 Review* Book

The *medEssentials* review book, structured by organ system and in a compact, concise fashion, presents the most relevant and important basic medical principles with reference charts and corresponding images. Our design allows a unique level of integration between the disciplines. For example, rather than sequentially reviewing each discipline within an organ system (anatomy, physiology, pathology, and pharmacology), the book integrates important information across various disciplines for a given subtopic in one place—sometimes on a single page. This way of reviewing allows you to obtain a complete, comprehensive understanding of any given topic.

The first section of the book (General Principles) covers the general principles of pathology, pharmacology, physiology, behavioral science, biostatistics, biochemistry, molecular biology, cell biology, genetics, microbiology, immunology, embryology, and histology. These subjects precede the organ system chapters and serve as a fundamental foundation for the organ-specific facts that follow.

The second section of the book features the following organ systems: cardiovascular; respiratory; renal and urinary; hematologic and lymphoreticular; nervous; musculoskeletal, skin and connective tissue; gastrointestinal; endocrine; and reproductive. Each chapter includes high-yield information from the disciplines corresponding to the basic science courses taken during the first two years of medical school. Each organ system is viewed from histologic, embryologic, physiologic, pathologic, and pharmacologic perspectives.

medEssentials Online Exercises

To access your online assets for *medEssentials*, register at kaptest.com/medessentialsonline. Have your book handy because you will need it to complete the registration. You will be prompted for the serial number found on the lower left corner of the inside back cover. The web address is case sensitive, so enter it carefully. As soon as you've registered, you're ready to take advantage of the online learning system. This registration process protects your *medEssentials* online content so that your content remains exclusive to you.

Based on important concepts from the book, online exercises allow organ system–based and discipline-based interactivity via individual learning exercises. The interactive exercises support, reinforce, and assess the important concepts found in the book and are an invaluable tool in the active learning process. This tool is also designed to help track your integration of concepts. The method of scoring provides you with a visual snapshot of your strengths and any areas of weakness. This way, your online tool is customized to your personal performance over time.

Finally, we want to hear what you think of this course. Please share with us your feedback by emailing **medfeedback@kaplan.com**.

Study Techniques

Effective study techniques for medical school and ultimately for the board exams are about making choices. At each stage of your medical career, you need to choose study strategies that will lead you to success.

Many medical students fear that not knowing all of the details may affect their clinical performance. It is natural to feel this way, but rest assured: Your ability to treat patients in these coming years will grow from mastery of concepts and by practicing your clinical skills. Your "clinical eye" will grow in time. Understanding basic mechanisms and key principles is crucial to developing the ability to apply what you know to real patients.

One of the most effective strategies for studying the basic sciences is to apply the medical concepts you have learned to your imagined, future patients. For example, when studying muscle groups in anatomy, imagine yourself as a surgeon and how you would find the structures of interest. In physiology, imagine a patient asking you about cortisol, what it is and what it does. Practice explaining to a patient the biochemical differences between lipids, how they differ, and what this means medically. *By doing so, you are simplifying the concepts, making them more memorable and clinically relevant; you are learning actively.*

Active use of the material that you learn increases retention and facilitates recall. Repetition makes memories. Each instance of recall produces a new memory trace, linking concepts and increasing the chance of recall in the future. Recall actually changes neuronal structures. To be truly useful, a piece of information needs to be triangulated, connected to a number of other concepts, or better yet, experienced. In other words, mere memorization is not your goal, but rather the ability to process and apply that information in a fully integrated manner.

Rereading textbooks from cover to cover and underlining—yet again, in a different color—every line on every page is *not* an efficient way to learn. You need to focus on the material most likely to be on your exams and on the material that is considered high-yield.

Begin your studies by following this simple outline:

- Start every study session with a list of specific goals.
- Make your notes richer by color-highlighting, adding notes to the diagrams, and re-summarizing what you have learned. This is your book; personalize it to get the most out of it.
- After reviewing your intended subject for the session, imagine how you'd teach the same concepts to someone else.

Using the *medEssentials: High-Yield USMLE™ Step 1 Review* Book

1. Learn the basic definitions and concepts central to each discipline (Section I: General Principles). The book provides the core vocabulary to understand the content of those disciplines. Terms and definitions are learned by the use of *associational memory*.

2. Learn central concepts for each of the subject areas and how they integrate within an organ system (Section II: Organ System). Integration of concepts and disciplines within each major organ system is the key to success in both medical school and licensing exams. Your basic mental task here is reconstructive memory, learning to recall the concepts in terms of how things fit together within an organ system. At this stage, patterns begin to emerge. The diagrams, tables, and pictures in this book are specifically designed for this stage of learning.

3. Engage in active learning by applying the concepts to scenarios, clinical settings, and mini-case presentations. This is the hardest stage of preparation, and one that most students neglect. Your task at this level is reasoning, comprehension, and deduction, which your *medEssentials* Online Learning System will help you achieve.

Helping you get organized. Each time that you logon to the online *medEssentials*, you will create a session name. Naming each session helps you track your previous sessions. Make your session name memorable and descriptive, such as an objective or study plan.

Matrix Menu Page

The Matrix Menu page is where you'll manage your study sessions, select exercises, and create personalized study sessions. Each box on the menu represents the cross-section between organ system and discipline. When you click on a box within the matrix, another box containing a list of interactions pops up. You may select any number of exercises within this menu; in fact, you can choose any exercises from any other boxes within this matrix simultaneously.

You can choose to work through the exercises within an organ system by moving to each box within a particular column, or you can work through exercises within a certain discipline by working across the rows. You may even choose to organize your study sessions by using a combination of both methods. By selecting the check box for an interaction and clicking ADD, these interactions are added to "My Folder," which is found on the left-hand side.

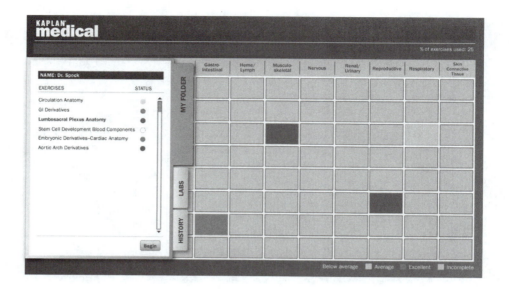

By moving your cursor to My Folder, the folder will expand and show the exercises you have already added to your study session. After you have selected all of the exercises you wish to work with, click BEGIN to start your session. You may reference all tabs at the left side of the screen at any time. The LABS tab provides the normal laboratory values, and the HISTORY tab displays your previous study sessions.

The beginning of each exercise provides learning objectives of that exercise and gives instructions on the type of exercise to follow. For each exercise, you have the option of taking that exercise in timed or untimed mode. (For more details, see "Timing and Scoring" on page xiv.)

Online exercises. There are seven different types of exercises:

1. *Labeling:*

    With options—You will be asked to label important structures with the correct word. Label images by dragging the correct label to the correct location on or near the image.

    Without options—You will be asked to label important structures with the correct word. You will be shown an image that can be labeled by clicking on the label box and typing the correct name with your keyboard.

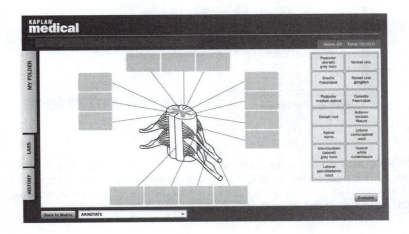

2. *Reaction Speed*—This exercise tests quick reaction to key concepts, terms, or associations in order to reinforce basic knowledge and subcategories of medical topics.

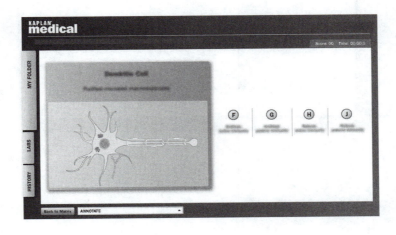

3. *Separating*—In this exercise you will be asked to separate relevant information into important subcategories. These exercises strengthen your ability to group important concepts for later recall.

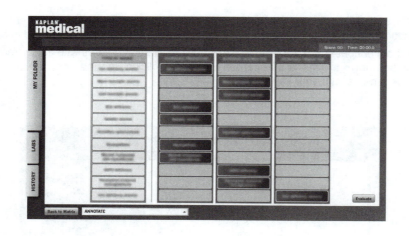

4. *Synaptic Match*—In this exercise, you will be making connections between a series of images and their corresponding labels, or a connection between a series of vignettes and their associated conditions. The labels are found to the right of the screen and are dragged with the cursor to the answer box.

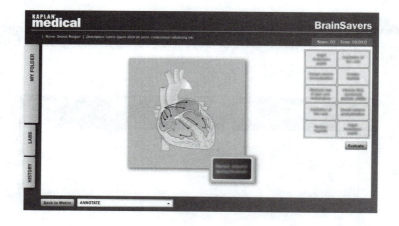

5. *Shooting Game*—In this exercise you will be asked to shoot an organism, disease, or condition with the most appropriate pharmacotherapy in an exciting, arcade-style game.

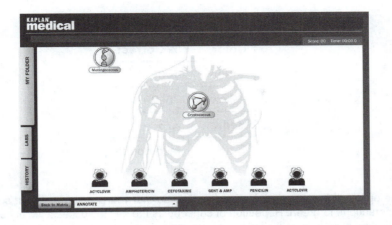

6. *Flashcards*—In this exercise, you will work through a series of flashcards that are grouped by a common topic or theme. The front side of the card will show an image or vignette. By clicking on the card, you will be shown the back, where you may view the question and answer choices. Once you have finished the deck of cards, you can review the explanations for each card.

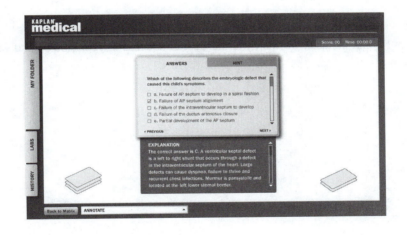

7. *Multiple choice questions*—USMLE® Step 1 exam-style questions. The series of questions in this type of exercise are at a level of difficulty that is representative of the USMLE Step 1 exam. They will help you become familiar with the level of questioning used in the boards and are also good practice as your Step 1 exam approaches.

Making Notes with the Annotation Button. You may make notes on anything you have learned within the exercise by clicking the ANNOTATE box at the bottom of the screen. A box will pop up in which you can make notes. The program automatically saves these notes for you to review the next time you access the exercise.

Timing and Scoring. Selecting a timed exercise allows you to track your performance by color medals in the matrix menu. Based on your percentage performance on each interaction, you will be assigned a green, yellow, red, or gray for that exercise.

Exercise Scoring Based on Percentage Correct

Color	% Correct
Green	100
Yellow	75–99
Red	<75
Gray	Incomplete

You have the option of redoing exercises at any time so that you can improve your score and turn all of your interactions to green. Repetition of concepts is the key to success; we encourage you to continue repeating exercises until all of them are green. Your last performance medal will be shown on the matrix menu pop-up box. The matrix menu box will show a summary performance medal, based on the performance of those attempted within the box.

In Summary

This online learning tool is designed to engage you actively in your learning process. By applying your growing knowledge base in this highly visual and interactive way, you are integrating concepts between organ systems and disciplines.

On behalf of Kaplan Medical, we wish you the best of success in your studies and your medical career!

General Principles

Behavioral Science

LEARNING AND BEHAVIOR THERAPY

CONDITIONING

Classic (Respondent or Pavlovian) Conditioning

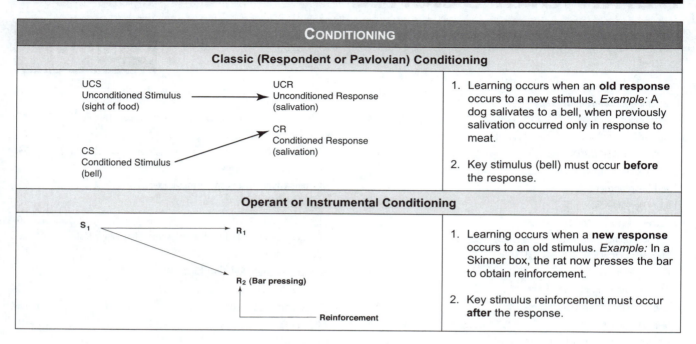

UCS
Unconditioned Stimulus
(sight of food)

UCR
Unconditioned Response
(salivation)

CR
Conditioned Response
(salivation)

CS
Conditioned Stimulus
(bell)

1. Learning occurs when an **old response** occurs to a new stimulus. *Example:* A dog salivates to a bell, when previously salivation occurred only in response to meat.

2. Key stimulus (bell) must occur **before** the response.

Operant or Instrumental Conditioning

S₁

R₁

R₂ (Bar pressing)

Reinforcement

1. Learning occurs when a **new response** occurs to an old stimulus. *Example:* In a Skinner box, the rat now presses the bar to obtain reinforcement.

2. Key stimulus reinforcement must occur **after** the response.

TYPES OF REINFORCEMENT

		Stimulus (S)	
		Add	**Remove**
Behavior (R)	**Stops**	Punishment	Extinction
	Increases	Positive reinforcement	Negative reinforcement

REINFORCEMENT SCHEDULES

		Contingency	
		Time	**Behaviors**
Schedule	**Constant**	Fixed interval (FI)	Fixed ratio (FR)
	Changing	Variable interval (VI)	Variable ratio (VR)

LEARNING-BASED THERAPIES	
On the Basis of Classic Conditioning	
Systematic desensitization	• Often used to treat anxiety and phobias **Step 1:** hierarchy of stimuli (least to most feared) **Step 2:** technique of muscle relaxation taught **Step 3:** patient relaxes in presence of each stimulus on the hierarchy • Works by replacing anxiety with relaxation, an incompatible response
Exposure (also flooding or implosion)	• Simple phobias treated by forced exposure to the feared object • Exposure maintained until fear response is extinguished
Aversive conditioning	• Properties of the original stimulus are changed to produce an aversive response • Can help reduce deviant behaviors
On the Basis of Operant Conditioning	
Shaping	• Achieves target behavior by reinforcing successive approximations of the desired response • Reinforcement gradually modified to move behaviors from general responses to specific responses desired
Extinction	• Discontinuing the reinforcement maintaining an undesired behavior • "Time out" with children or for test anxiety
Stimulus control	• Sometimes stimuli inadvertently acquire control over behavior; when this is true, removal of that stimulus can extinguish the response • *Example:* an insomniac only permitted in bed when he/she is so tired that sleep comes almost at once
Biofeedback	• Using external feedback to modify internal physiologic states; often uses electronic devices to present physiologic information, e.g., heart monitor to show heart rate • Works by means of trial-and-error learning and requires repeated practice to be effective
Fading	• Gradually removing the reinforcement while: *1)* without the subject discerning the difference and *2)* maintaining the desired response • *Example:* gradually replacing postoperative painkiller with a placebo

CHILD DEVELOPMENT

INFANT DEVELOPMENT

Evidenced at birth	• Reaching and grasping behavior • Ability to imitate facial expressions • Ability to synchronize limb movements with speech of others • Attachment behaviors, such as crying and clinging

Newborn characteristics	• Prefers:
	  – Large, bright objects with lots of contrast
	  – Moving objects
	  – Curves versus lines
	  – Complex versus simple designs
	  – Facial stimuli (girls more than boys)
	• Can discriminate between language and nonlanguage stimuli
	• At 1 week old, the infant responds differently to the smell of mother compared with father

Smiling	• The smile develops from an innate reflex present at birth (endogenous smile) • Shows exogenous smiling in response to a face at 8 weeks • A preferential social smile, e.g., to the mother's rather than another's face, appears about 12 to 16 weeks

FIGURES COPIED AND APPROXIMATE AGES

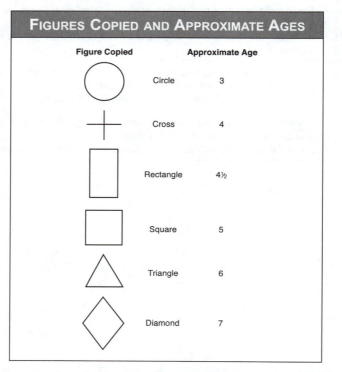

Figure Copied	Approximate Age
Circle	3
Cross	4
Rectangle	4½
Square	5
Triangle	6
Diamond	7

KEY DEVELOPMENTAL TERMS

Brain-growth spurt	• "Critical period" of great vulnerability to environmental influence • Extends from last trimester of pregnancy through first 14 postnatal months • Size of cortical cells and complexity of cell interconnections undergo their most rapid increase
Stranger anxiety	• Distress in the presence of unfamiliar people • Appears at 6 months, reaches peak at 8 months, then disappears after 12 months
Separation anxiety	• Distress of infant after separation from caretaker • Appears at 8 to 12 months; begins to disappear at 20 to 24 months • **Separation anxiety disorder** (school phobia) is failure to resolve separation anxiety • Treatment focuses on child's interaction with parents, not on activities in school

Children's Conceptions of Illness and Death

More than death, a preschool child is more likely to fear:	Separation from parents, punishment, mutilation (Freud's castration anxiety)
When they become ill:	May interpret illness or treatment as punishment Often have all sorts of misconceptions about what is wrong with them
Until age 5:	Children usually have no conception of death as an irreversible process
Only after age 8 or 9:	Child really understands that death is universal, inevitable, and irreversible

Child Development Milestones

Age	Physical and Motor Development	Social Development	Cognitive Development	Language Development
First year of life	• Puts everything in mouth • Sits with support (4 mo) • Stands with help (8 mo) • Crawls, fear of falling (9 mo) • Pincer grasp (12 mo) • Follows objects to midline (4 wk) • One-handed approach/grasp of toy • Feet in mouth (5 mo) • Bang and rattle stage • Changes hands with toy (6 mo)	• Parental figure central • Issues of trust are key • Stranger anxiety (6 mo) • Play is solitary and exploratory • Pat-a-cake, peek-a-boo (10 mo)	• Sensation/movement • Schemas • Assimilation and accommodation	• Laughs aloud (4 mo) • Repetitive responding (8 mo) • "mama, dada" (10 mo)
Year 1	• Walks alone (13 mo) • Climbs stairs alone (18 mo) • Emergence of hand preference (18 mo) • Kicks ball, throws ball • Pats pictures in book • Stacks three cubes (18 mo)	• Separation anxiety (12 mo) • Dependency on parental figure (rapprochement) • Onlooker and parallel play	• Achieves object permanence	• Great variation in timing of language development • Uses 10 words
Year 2	• High activity level • Walks backward • Can turn doorknob, unscrew lid jar • Scribbles with crayon • Able to aim to throw ball • Stands on tiptoes (30 mo) • Stacks six cubes (24 mo)	• Selfish and self-centered • Imitates mannerisms and activities • May be aggressive • "No" is favorite word	• A world of objects • Can use symbols • Transition objects • Strong egocentrism • Concrete use of objects	• Use of pronouns • Parents understand most words • Telegraphic sentences • Two-word sentences • Uses 250 words • Names body parts
Year 3	• Rides tricycle • Stacks 9 cubes (36 mo) • Alternates feet going upstairs • Bowel and bladder control (toilet training) • Draws recognizable figures • Catches ball with arms • Cuts paper with scissors • Unbuttons buttons	• Fixed gender identity • Sex-specific play • Understands "taking turns" • Knows sex and full names	—	• Completes sentences • Uses 900 words • Understands 4× that • Strangers can understand • Recognizes common objects in pictures

(Continued)

CHILD DEVELOPMENT MILESTONES *(CONT'D.)*

Age	Physical and Motor Development	Social Development	Cognitive Development	Language Development
Year 4	• Alternates feet going down stairs • Hops on one foot • Grooms self (brushes teeth)	• Imitation of adult roles • Curiosity about sex (playing doctor) • Nightmares and monster fears • Imaginary fears	• Points to and counts three objects • Repeats four digits • Names colors	• Can tell stories • Uses prepositions • Uses plurals • Compound sentences
Year 5	• Complete sphincter control • Brain at 75% of adult weight • Draws recognizable man with head, body, and limbs • Dresses and undresses self • Catches ball with two hands	• Conformity to peers important • Romantic feeling for others • Oedipal phase	• Counts 10 objects correctly	• Asks the meaning of words • Abstract words elusive
Years 6 to 12	• Boys heavier than girls • Refined motor skills • Rides bicycle • Gains athletic skill • Coordination increases	• "Rules of the game" are key • Organized sports possible • Being team member focal for many • Separation of the sexes • Demonstrating competence is key	• Abstracts from objects • Law of conservation achieved • Adherence to logic • No hypotheticals • Mnemonic strategies • Personal sense of right and wrong	• Shift from egocentric to social speech • Incomplete sentences decline • Vocabulary expands geometrically (50,000 words by age 12)
Years ≥12 (adolescence)	• Adolescent "growth spurt" (girls before boys) • Onset of sexual maturity (≥10 y) • Development of primary and secondary sexual characteristics	• Identity is critical issue • Conformity most important (11 to 12 y) • Organized sports diminish for many • Cross-gender relationships	• Abstracts from abstractions • Systematic problem-solving strategies • Can handle hypotheticals • Deals with past, present, future	• Adopts personal speech patterns • Communication becomes focus of relationships

TYPES OF ABUSE AND IMPORTANT ISSUES

	Child Abuse	Elder Abuse	Spousal Abuse
Annual cases	Over 2 million	5 to 10% in population	Over 4 million
Most common type	Physical battery/neglect	Neglect	Physical battery
Likely sex of victim	Before age 5: female After age 5: male	63% female	Female
Likely sex of perpetrator	Female	Male or female	Male
Mandatory reporting?	Yes	Yes	No
Physician's response	Protect and report	Protect and report	Counseling and information

SLEEP: PHYSIOLOGY AND DISORDERS

SLEEP PHYSIOLOGY

Types of Sleep

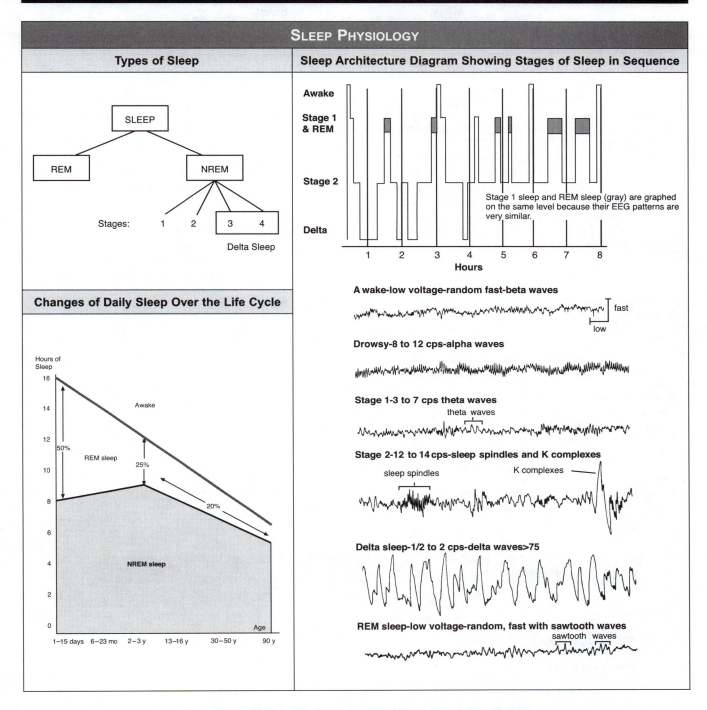

Sleep Architecture Diagram Showing Stages of Sleep in Sequence

Stage 1 sleep and REM sleep (gray) are graphed on the same level because their EEG patterns are very similar.

Awake-low voltage-random fast-beta waves

Drowsy-8 to 12 cps-alpha waves

Stage 1-3 to 7 cps theta waves

Stage 2-12 to 14 cps-sleep spindles and K complexes

Delta sleep-1/2 to 2 cps-delta waves>75

REM sleep-low voltage-random, fast with sawtooth waves

Changes of Daily Sleep Over the Life Cycle

CHANGES DURING THE FIRST 3 HOURS OF SLEEP	
Human growth hormone (HGH)	↑
Prolactin	↑
Dopamine	↓
Serotonin	↑
Thyroid-stimulating hormone (TSH)	↓

Sleep Disorders

Disorders	Signs, Symptoms, and Issues	Treatments
Narcolepsy	• Sleep attacks • Cataplexy • Hypnagogic hallucinations • Sleep paralysis • REM latency <10 minutes	• **Modafinil:** nonamphetamine alternative to CNS stimulants • Traditionally treated with CNS stimulants (e.g., amphetamines)
Sleep apnea syndromes	• Absence of respiration for extended periods during sleep • Patient often overweight • Risk of sudden death • Obstructive: rasping snoring • Central: Cheyne-Stokes	• Weight loss • Continuous positive airway pressure (CPAP) • Condition so sleeping position not on back • Surgery for severe cases
Sudden infant death syndrome (SIDS)	Unexplained death in children younger than 1 year	• Lay baby to sleep on back • Avoid overstuffed bedding and pillows • Rate higher if household member smokes • Fetal exposure to maternal smoking is strong risk factor
Insomnia	Causes: • Hypnotic medication abuse • Emotional problems • Conditioned poor sleep • Withdrawal from drugs	• Behavioral therapy best treatment • Pharmacology: acute relief by benzodiazepines, zolpidem, zaleplon, eszopiclone (no tolerance)
Somnambulism (sleepwalking)	• Stage 4 sleep • If wakened, person confused and disoriented	Identify anxiety issues
Enuresis (bedwetting)	• Delta sleep • Boys 2× more than girls • Defense mechanism of regression	Imipramine acutely
Bruxism (teeth grinding)	• Stage 2 sleep • Patient may be unaware unless told by others	Reduce anxiety, oral devices

Night Terrors Versus Nightmares

	Night Terrors	Nightmares
Sleep stage	Stage 4 (delta sleep)	REM
Physiologic arousal	Extreme	Elevated
Recall upon waking	No	Yes
Waking time anxiety	Yes, usually unidentified	Yes, often unidentified
Other issues	• Runs in families • More common in boys • Can be a precursor to temporal lobe epilepsy	• Common from ages 3 to 7 • Desensitization behavior therapy provides marked improvement

DEFENSE MECHANISMS

	COMMON FREUDIAN DEFENSE MECHANISMS	
Defense Mechanism	**Short Definition**	**Important Associations**
Projection	Attributing inner feelings to others	Paranoid behavior
Denial	Saying it is not so	Substance abuse, reaction to death
Splitting	The world composed of polar opposites	Borderline personality; good versus evil
Blocking	Transient inability to remember	Momentary lapse
Regression	Returning to an earlier stage of development	Enuresis, primitive behaviors
Somatization	Physical symptoms for psychological reasons	Somatoform disorders
Introjection	The outside becomes inside	Superego, being like parents
Displacement	Source stays the same, but target changes	Redirected emotion, phobias, scapegoat
Repression	Forgetting so it is nonretrievable	Forget and forget
Isolation of affect	Facts without feeling	Blunted affect, *la belle indifference*
Intellectualization	Affect replaced by academic content	Academic, not emotional, reaction
Acting out	Affect covered up by excessive action or sensation	Substance abuse, fighting, gambling
Rationalization	Why the unacceptable is okay in this instance	Justification, string of reasons
Reaction formation	The unacceptable transformed into its opposite	Manifesting the opposite; feel love but show hate: "Girls have cooties."
Undoing	Action to symbolically reverse the unacceptable	Fixing or repairing, obsessive–compulsive behaviors
Passive-aggressive	Passive nonperformance after promise	Unconscious, indirect hostility
Dissociation	Separating self from one's own experience	Fugue, depersonalization, amnesia, multiple personality
Humor	A pleasant release from anxiety	Laughter hides the pain
Sublimation	Moving an unacceptable impulse into an acceptable channel	Art, literature, mentoring
Suppression	Forgetting, but is retrievable	Forget and remember

SUBSTANCE ABUSE

ALCOHOL

Key Concepts

- Most costly health problem
- 10% of people are problem drinkers
- Heavy drinking increasing in younger people
- Accounts for 50% of auto accident deaths
- Leading known cause of mental retardation (fetal alcohol syndrome [FAS])
- Genetic vulnerability activated by environment and behavior
- Capacity to tolerate alcohol confers greatest risk

Medical Complications

Cirrhosis, alcoholic hepatitis, pancreatitis, gastric or duodenal ulcer, esophageal varices, middle-age onset of diabetes, gastrointestinal cancer, hypertension, peripheral neuropathies, myopathies, cardiomyopathy, cerebral vascular accidents, erectile dysfunction, gout, vitamin deficiencies, pernicious anemia, and brain disorders, including Wernicke-Korsakoff syndrome (mortality rate of untreated Wernicke is 50%; treatment is with thiamine)

Main Treatment: Alcoholics Anonymous

Twelve-step program, consists of meetings and sponsors; least expensive; believed to be most successful

Pharmacologic Treatment

Disulfiram (Antabuse®)	Inhibits **aldehyde dehydrogenase**; decreases alcohol consumption; produces symptoms of nausea, chest pain, hyperventilation, tachycardia, vomiting; effective for short-term treatment only
Acamprosate	Helps prevent relapse; hypothesized to decrease glutamate receptor sensitivity
Benzodiazepines	Helps prevent alcohol-related seizures
Naltrexone	Opiate-receptor antagonist; reduces cravings; helps patient to stop after first drink

Alcohol Effects and Metabolism

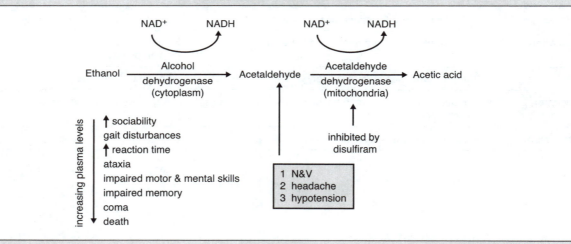

Withdrawal

- The chronic user can experience an alcohol withdrawal syndrome upon discontinuance of ethanol consumption. **Symptoms** include anxiety, tremor, insomnia, and possibly **delirium tremens (DTs)** and **life-threatening seizures**; arrhythmias, nausea/vomiting, and diarrhea may also occur.
- **Treatment** includes thiamine, sedative-hypnotics with gradual tapering; clonidine and propranolol are useful to correct the hyperadrenergic state of withdrawal.

DRUGS OF ABUSE				
Class/Agent	Mechanisms	Effects	Toxicity	Withdrawal
CNS stimulants				
Cocaine (crack is smokable form)	Blocks DA, NE, 5HT reuptake (also local anesthetic)	Euphoria, hypervigilance, anxiety, stereotyped behavior, grandiosity, tachycardia, pupillary dilation, ↓ appetite	Cardiac arrhythmias, myocardial infarction, stroke, hallucinations, paranoia, hyperthermia, seizures, death	Craving, depression, fatigue, ↑ sleep time, ↑ appetite
Amphetamines (speed, ice are smokable forms)	Releases DA, NE, 5HT, weak MAO inhibitor		*Treatment*: BZs, neuroleptics; control hyperthermia and CV effects, supportive care	
	Both: NE most important for peripheral effects; DA most important for central effects			
CNS depressants				
Benzodiazepines	↑ frequency of GABA$_A$ channel opening	Light to moderate CNS depression	Impaired judgment, slurred speech, uncoordination, unsteady gait, stupor, respiratory depression, death	Anxiety, delirium, insomnia, possible life-threatening seizures
Barbiturates	↑ duration of GABA$_A$ channel opening	Can produce light to severe CNS depression (EtOH, barbiturates)	*Treatment*: **flumazenil** for BZ overdose, supportive care	*Treatment*: long-acting BZ to suppress acute symptoms, taper dose
Ethanol (EtOH) (*see* previous table)		Cross-tolerance, additivity among drugs of this class		
Opioids				
(heroin, morphine, oxycodone)	Stimulate μ, κ, δ receptors; μ receptor most important in abuse	Euphoria, analgesia, sedation, cough suppression, miosis (except meperidine), constipation	**Respiratory depression**, nausea/vomiting, **miosis**, sedation, **coma**, death	Gooseflesh ("cold turkey"), diarrhea, rhinorrhea, lacrimation, sweating, yawning, muscle jerks ("kicking the habit"), very unpleasant but not life-threatening
			Treatment: naloxone (short half-life), naltrexone, supportive care	*Treatment*: methadone, LAAM, buprenorphine, clonidine

(Continued)

DRUGS OF ABUSE *(CONT'D.)*

Class/Agent	Mechanisms	Effects	Toxicity	Withdrawal
Cannabis (marijuana ["grass," hashish])	Binds CB_1 and CB_2 cannabinoid receptors	Euphoria, disinhibition, perceptual changes, reddened conjunctiva, dry mouth, ↑ appetite, antiemetic effects (**dronabinol** used as antiemetic)	Amotivational syndrome, respiratory effects	Mild irritability/anxiety
Hallucinogens (LSD, mescaline, psilocybin)	Interacts with 5HT receptors	Perceptual changes, synesthesias (i.e., hearing a smell), nausea	Panic reaction ("bad trip") possible, flashbacks	Minimal because of lack of physiologic dependence

Miscellaneous	
Phencyclidine (PCP, "angel dust")	• Assaultive, combative, impulsive, agitated, nystagmus, ataxia, muscle rigidity, ↓ response to pain, hyperacusis, paranoia, unpredictable violence, psychosis, hypertension, life-threatening seizures • **Ketamine**, a congener of PCP, also abused
MDMA ("ecstasy")	• 5HT releasers (amphetamine-like mechanism, except releases more 5HT than dopamine) • May cause damage to serotonergic neurons; causes hyperthermia; popular in "raves"
Anticholinergics	Deliriant effects, e.g., Jimson weed, scopolamine; psychotic and anticholinergic effects
Nicotine	• Tobacco use associated with cardiovascular, respiratory, and neoplastic disease • Nicotine patches and gum; bupropion used for cessation
Inhalants (glue, solvents)	Belligerence, impaired judgement, uncoordination; causes multiple organ damage

Definition of abbreviations: BZ, benzodiazepine; DA, dopamine; 5HT, serotonin; LAAM, levo-α-acetylmethadol; LSD, lysergic acid diethylamide; MDMA, methylenedioxymethamphetamine; NE, norepinephrine; CV, cardiovascular.

PSYCHOPATHOLOGY

FIVE MAJOR DIAGNOSTIC AXES

Axis I	Clinical disorders	• Includes schizophrenic, affective, anxiety, and somatoform disorders • Also includes anorexia nervosa, bulimia nervosa, sexual disorders, sleep disorders, and autism
Axis II	Personality disorders and mental retardation	Personality disorders and mental retardation
Axis III	Physical conditions and disorders	Any physical diagnosis
Axis IV	Psychosocial and environmental problems	Includes primary support group, social occupation, education, housing, economics, health care services, and legal issues
Axis V	Global assessment of functioning (GAF)	Scored on a descending scale of 100 to 1, where 100 represents superior functioning, 50 represents serious symptoms, and 10 represents persistent danger of hurting self or others

MENTAL RETARDATION

Level	IQ	Functioning
Mild	70 to 50	• Self-supporting with some guidance • 85% of retarded persons • Two times as many are male • Usually diagnosed first year in school
Moderate	49 to 35	• "Trainable" • Benefit from vocational training, but need supervision • Sheltered workshops
Severe	34 to 20	• Training not helpful • Can learn to communicate • Basic habits
Profound	Below 20	• Need highly structured environment, constant nursing care supervision

PERVASIVE DEVELOPMENTAL DISORDERS: AUTISM

General characteristics	• Usually diagnosed during age 2 • Male:female ratio—4:1 • 80% have IQs below 70
Clinical signs	• Problems with reciprocal social interaction • Abnormal/delayed language development, impaired verbal and nonverbal communication • No separation anxiety • Oblivious to external world • Fails to assume anticipatory posture, shrinks from touch • Preference for inanimate objects • Stereotyped behavior; decreased repertoire of activities and interests
Potential causes	• Association with prenatal and perinatal injury, e.g., rubella in first trimester • Possible role of environmental mercury exposure • Proposed mechanism: failure of apoptosis in cortex
Treatment	• Behavioral techniques (shaping)

ATTENTION DEFICIT/HYPERACTIVITY DISORDER (ADHD)	
General comments	• Male to female ratio—10:1 • Overtreatment is common; differentiate from child who is simply "overactive"
Clinical signs	• *Difficulty sustaining attention:* difficulty with organization, easily distracted, often does not listen when spoken to, doesn't complete tasks • *Hyperactivity:* fidgets, often leaves seat in classroom, difficulty playing quietly, talks excessively • *Impulsivity:* interrupts others, blurts out answers, difficulty waiting turn
Treatment	• Behavior therapy • Drug therapy: methylphenidate, dextroamphetamine, atomoxetine

SCHIZOPHRENIA	
Criteria	• Bizarre delusions • Auditory hallucinations (in 75%) • Blunted affect • Loose associations • Deficiency in reality testing, distorted perception; impaired functioning overall • Disturbances in behavior and form and content of language and thought • Changes in psychomotor behavior; loss of prosody • Symptoms for longer than 6 months
Epidemiology	• Onset: male, ages 15 to 24; female, ages 25 to 34 • Prevalence: 1% of population cross-culturally • More often in low social economic status • 50% patients attempt suicide; 10% succeed
Neurochemistry	• **"Dopamine hypothesis of schizophrenia"** suggests that symptoms arise because of a functional excess of dopamine activity in the CNS (mesolimbic/mesocortical pathways) • Serotonin and glutamate may also play roles
Subtypes	
Paranoid	• Delusions of **persecution** or **grandeur** • Often accompanied by hallucinations (voices)
Catatonic	• **Complete stupor** or pronounced decrease in spontaneous movements • Alternatively, **can be excited** and evidence extreme motor agitation
Disorganized	• Incoherent, primitive, uninhibited • Unorganized behaviors and speech • Active, but aimless • Pronounced thought disorder
Undifferentiated	• Psychotic symptoms but does not fit paranoid, catatonic, or disorganized diagnoses
Residual	• Previous episode, but no prominent psychotic symptoms at evaluation • Some lingering negative symptoms

ANTIPSYCHOTIC MEDICATIONS: AN OVERVIEW	
Clinical uses	Antipsychotics (neuroleptics) are used in a variety of clinical settings, including schizophrenia, schizoaffective disorders, mania (with lithium, initial management), Tourette syndrome (molindone), preoperative sedation (promethazine), drug or radiation emesis (prochlorperazine), and neuroleptic anesthesia (droperidol).
Anatomic targets	Antipsychotics unfortunately affect all dopaminergic tracts in the brain, including the **mesolimbic/mesocortical** (thought and mood), the **nigrostriatal** (extrapyramidal motor), and **tuberoinfundibular** (dopamine inhibits prolactin release) pathways. The goal is to block the mesolimbic/mesocortical pathways, but side effects result from blocking the nigrostriatal (extrapyramidal side effects [**EPS**]) and tuberoinfundibular (**hyperprolactinemia**) pathways.
Typical antipsychotics	This older group of antipsychotics falls into two general categories: **high potency** and **low potency** (see table below). Their mechanism of action is thought to be related primarily to their ability to block D_2 receptors.
Atypical antipsychotics	Newer group of antipsychotics; in general, weaker D_2 receptor antagonists and stronger **5HT$_2$** antagonists. They also have **less EPS**.

SIDE EFFECTS OF TYPICAL ANTIPSYCHOTIC MEDICATIONS

- The **high-potency** drugs block DA receptors well (cause more EPS), so a low drug dose can be used, minimizing other nonspecific side effects (α **blockade, antimuscarinic effects, sedation**).
- The **low-potency** drugs do not block DA receptors as well as high-potency drugs do, and a higher dose is required. Therefore, there is less EPS and more nonspecific side effects.
- The nonspecific side effects include orthostatic hypotension, male sexual dysfunction (α blockade); constipation, dry mouth, urinary retention, visual problems (muscarinic blockade); and sedation.
- **Hyperprolactinemia** may occur due to D_2-receptor blockade in the pituitary.
- **Neuroleptic malignant syndrome**, which is potentially life-threatening, may occur. Symptoms include extreme muscle rigidity, hyperthermia, and autonomic instability. Treatment may include **dantrolene** and **dopamine agonists**.
- Weight gain and a decrease in the seizure threshold may also occur.

Potency	EPS	Nonspecific Side Effects
High (haloperidol, fluphenazine)	High	Low
Low (chlorpromazine, thioridazine*)	Low	High

Definition of abbreviations: DA, dopamine; EPS, extrapyramidal side effects.

*Thioridazine can cause retinal deposits, leading to visual problems, and conduction defects that may result in fatal ventricular arrhythmias.

EXTRAPYRAMIDAL SIDE EFFECTS

Early Onset and Reversible

Dystonia	• Involuntary contraction primarily of the face, neck, tongue, and extraocular muscles • Responds to anticholinergics
Parkinsonism	• Akinesia, muscle rigidity, tremor, shuffling gait (typically appearing in that order)
Akathisia	• Motor restlessness and the urge to move

Late Onset and Irreversible

Tardive dyskinesia (TD)	• Diagnosis requires exposure to neuroleptics for at least 3 months, but often takes longer • Involuntary repetitive movements of lips, face, tongue, limbs • Try to prevent by using lowest possible dose of antipsychotic medication • Anticholinergics worsen TD • Try to reduce dose or discontinue medication if TD occurs (although increasing dose will temporarily mask symptoms) • Switch to an atypical antipsychotic

ATYPICAL ANTIPSYCHOTICS

Drugs	Characteristics	Side effects
Clozapine* Risperidone Olanzapine Quetiapine Ziprasidone Aripiprazole	• Generally good **5HT$_2$ antagonists** and weaker D$_2$ antagonists • Treats positive and negative symptoms of schizophrenia (typicals treat mostly positive) • **Less EPS** • Tend to be more expensive than typicals	• **Clozapine: agranulocytosis** • Ziprasidone: prolongs QT interval, may lead to torsades • Risperidone: some EPS

*Clozapine blocks D$_4$, rather than D$_2$, receptors.

MOOD DISORDERS: OVERVIEW

	Mild	Severe
Stable	Dysthymia	Unipolar (major depression)
Alternating	Cyclothymia	Bipolar (manic depression)

MOOD DISORDER SUBTYPES	
Types	**Characteristics**
Dysthymia	• Depressed mood • Loss of interest or pleasure • Chronic (at least 2 years)
Cyclothymia (nonpsychotic bipolar)	• Alternating states • Chronic • Often not recognized by affected person
Seasonal affective disorder (SAD)	• Depressive symptoms during winter months (shortest days, so least amount of light) • Caused by abnormal melatonin metabolism • Treat with bright light therapy
Unipolar depression (major depression)	• Symptoms for at least 2 weeks • Must be a change from previous functioning • May be associated with anhedonia, no motivation, feelings of worthlessness, decreased concentration, weight loss or gain, depressed mood, recurrent thoughts, insomnia or hypersomnia, psychomotor agitation or retardation, somatic complaints, delusions or hallucinations (mood congruent), loss of sex drive • Diurnal improvement as day progresses • Suicide: 60% of depressed patients have suicidal ideation; 15% die by suicide • Neurochemistry: "biogenic amine theory of depression"—caused by decreased NE/5HT • Sleep: ↑ REM in first half of sleep, ↓ REM latency, ↓ stage 4 sleep, ↑ REM time overall, early morning wakening

Bipolar disorder (manic-depression)	• Symptoms of major depression and symptoms of mania (period of abnormal and persistent elevated, expansive, or irritable mood)
	• Subtypes:
	  – **Bipolar I:** mania more prominent
	  – **Bipolar II:** recurrent depressive episodes, plus hypomanic episodes
	  – **"Rapidly cycling bipolar disorder":** if alternates within 48–72 hours
	• Manic symptoms: ↑ self-esteem or grandiosity, low frustration tolerance, ↓ need for sleep, flight of ideas, excessive involvement in activities, weight loss and anorexia, erratic and uninhibited behavior, ↑ libido

Definition of abbreviations: 5HT, serotonin; NE, norepinephrine; REM, rapid eye movement.

NORMAL GRIEF VERSUS DEPRESSION	
Normal Grief	**Depression**
Normal up to 1 year	Longer than 1 year, sooner if symptoms severe
Crying, ↓ libido, weight loss, insomnia	Same
Longing, wish to see loved one, may think they hear or see loved one in a crowd	Abnormal overidentification, personality change
Loss of other	Loss of self
Suicidal ideation rare	Suicidal ideation common
Self-limited, usually <6 months	Symptoms do not stop (may persist for years)
Antidepressants not helpful	Antidepressants helpful

ANTIDEPRESSANTS

Class/Agents	Mechanism	Side Effects and Comments
Tricyclic antidepressants (TCADs) (amitriptyline, imipramine, nortriptyline, desipramine)	Block reuptake of NE and 5HT	• Anticholinergic • Alpha blockade • Sedation • ↓ seizure threshold • **Overdose:** triad ("3 Cs"): coma, convulsions, cardiotoxicity • **Drug interactions:** do not mix with SSRIs and MAOIs; potentially fatal
Heterocyclics (amoxapine, bupropion, maprotiline, trazodone, mirtazapine, nefazodone, venlafaxine)	Mechanism varies	• Trazodone causes priapism, sedation • Amoxapine causes EPS (also dopamine receptor blocker) • Maprotiline, amoxapine: seizures, cardiotoxicity • Nefazodone, venlafaxine: P450 inhibitors • Bupropion used in smoking cessation
Selective serotonin reuptake inhibitors (SSRIs) (fluoxetine, sertraline, citalopram, fluvoxamine, paroxetine)	Blocks reuptake of 5HT	• Anxiety, agitation, insomnia • Nausea • Sexual dysfunction • **Serotonin syndrome** (muscle rigidity, hyperthermia, myoclonus, ANS instability), seizures occurs with **TCADs, MAOIs, meperidine, dextromethorphan**
MAO inhibitors (MAOIs) (phenelzine, tranylcypromine, isocarboxazid)	Interferes with metabolism of NE and 5HT by blocking monoamine oxidase (MAO) types A and B	• Orthostatic hypotension, weight gain • **Hypertensive crisis** if patient consumes food with **tyramine** and other indirect-acting sympathomimetics • **Serotonin syndrome** when combined with SSRIs

ELECTROCONVULSIVE THERAPY (ECT)

- **Common uses:**
  - Depression (80%)
  - Schizoaffective disorder (10%)
  - Bipolar disorder
- 90% show some immediate improvement
- Usually requires 5 to 10 treatments
- Treats depressive episodes, not for prophylaxis

- **Side effects:**
  - Anesthesia eliminates fractures and anticipatory anxiety
  - Memory loss and headache common, returns to normal in several weeks
  - Serious complications <1:1,000
- Contraindication: ↑ cranial pressure (e.g., tumor)

LITHIUM

- Used in **bipolar disorder**
- Mechanism not well understood but may inhibit the recycling of neuronal **phosphoinositides**
- Used in conjunction with antidepressants
- Neuroleptics and/or benzodiazepines may be used initially because lithium has very slow onset
- **Very narrow therapeutic index**
- Side effects: sedation, ataxia, tremor, reversible nephrogenic diabetes insipidus, edema, acne, leukocytosis
- Neonatal toxicity if administered to pregnant women
- **Valproic acid** and **olanzapine** are also used in bipolar disorder

EATING DISORDERS

Characteristics	Anorexia Nervosa	Bulimia Nervosa
Sex	F > M	F > M
Age	Mid-teenage years	Late adolescence/early adulthood
Socioeconomic status (SES)	May be high or low	May be high or low
Weight	>15% ideal body weight loss	Varies, usually normal or > normal
Neurotransmitters	Serotonin/norepinephrine?	Serotonin/norepinephrine?
Binge/purge	Yes	Yes
Laxative/diuretics	Yes	Yes
Sexual adjustment	Poor	Good
Medical complications	• Amenorrhea • Lanugo • High mortality • Dental cavities • Electrolyte imbalances • Cardiac abnormalities	• Dental cavities • Calluses on hands/fingers • Enlarged parotid glands • Electrolyte imbalances • Cardiac abnormalities

ANXIETY DISORDERS

Generalized anxiety disorder	• Symptoms exhibited more days than not for longer than a 6-month period
	  – Motor tension (fidgety, jumpy)
	  – Autonomic hyperactivity (heart pounding, sweating, chest pains), hyperventilation
	  – Apprehension (fear, worry, rumination), difficulty concentrating
	  – Vigilance and scanning (impatient, hyperactive, distracted)
	  – Fatigue and sleep disturbances common, especially insomnia and restlessness
	• **Treatment:** benzodiazepines, buspirone

Specific phobias (fear of specific object, e.g., spiders, snakes)	• Anxiety when faced with identifiable object • Phobic object avoided • Persistent and disabling fear
Agoraphobia (fear of open spaces)	• Also sense of helplessness or humiliation • Manifest anxiety, panic-like symptoms • Travel restricted
Social phobia (fear of feeling or being stupid, shameful)	• Leads to dysfunctional circumspect behavior, e.g., inability to urinate in public washrooms • May accompany avoidant personality disorder • Discrete performance anxiety (stage fright): most common phobia; treat with paroxetine (SSRI) or atenolol or propranolol (beta blocker) • **Treatment:** paroxetine (SSRI) or atenolol or propranolol (beta blocker); for generalized social anxiety, use phenelzine (MAO inhibitor) or paroxetine
Obsessive–compulsive disorder	• **Obsession:** focusing on one thought, usually to avoid another • **Compulsion:** repetitive action shields person from thoughts, action "fixes" bad thought • Primary concern of patient is to not lose control • ↑ frontal lobe metabolism, ↑ activity in the caudate nucleus • **Treatment:** fluoxetine, fluvoxamine, or other SSRI, clomipramine

Panic disorder	• Three attacks in 3-week period with no clear circumscribed stimulus
	• Abrupt onset of symptoms, peak within 10 minutes
	• **Clinical signs:**
	  – Great apprehension and fear
	  – Palpitations, trembling, sweating
	  – Fear of dying or going crazy
	  – Hyperventilation, "air hunger"
	  – Sense of unreality
	• **Treatment:** alprazolam, clonazepam, imipramine

SEDATIVE-HYPNOTIC DRUGS

Class	Notes	
Benzodiazepines	• Used as anxiolytics, hypnotics, anticonvulsants (diazepam, lorazepam, clonazepam), muscle relaxants, for anesthesia (e.g., midazolam) • Binds GABA$_A$ receptor and increases frequency of Cl$^-$ ion channel opening • Dose-dependent CNS depression occurs (not as much as barbiturates when used alone) • Differ in half-life and metabolism • Three BZs are not metabolized in liver: ("Out The Liver: **O**xazepam, **T**emazepam, **L**orazepam)	
Barbiturates	• Used as anticonvulsants (phenobarbital, long-acting), to induce anesthesia (thiopental, short-acting) • Binds GABA$_A$ receptor and increases duration of Cl$^-$ ion channel opening	
Miscellaneous	**Zolpidem, zaleplon,** and **eszopiclone**—nonbenzodiazepines (used for sleep) **Buspirone**—nonbenzodiazepine (anxiolytic)	

IMPORTANT BENZODIAZEPINES

Generic Name	Common Uses
Alprazolam	Panic, anxiety
Chlordiazepoxide	Alcohol detoxification
Clonazepam	Panic, anxiety, seizures
Diazepam	Anxiety, insomnia, pre-op sedation, muscle relaxation
Flurazepam	Insomnia
Lorazepam	Anxiety, alcohol-related seizures
Midazolam*	Anesthesia
Oxazepam	Alcohol detoxification
Temazepam	Insomnia
Triazolam†	Insomnia

*Shortest acting
†Short acting

SOMATOFORM DISORDERS

Somatization disorder	• Set of eight or more symptoms (four pain, two gastrointestinal, one sexual, one pseudoneurologic) • Onset before age 30 • Symptoms usually occur over period of years • More common in women than in men (20 to 1)
Conversion disorder	• One or more symptoms • Altering of physical functioning, suggesting physical disorder • Usually skeletal, muscular, sensory, or some peripheral nonautonomic system, e.g., paralysis of the hand, loss of sight • Loss of functioning is real and unfeigned • Look for *la belle indifference*
Hypochondriasis	• Unrealistic interpretation of physical signs as abnormal • Preoccupation with illness or fear of illness when none present • Preoccupation persists in spite of reassurance • At least 6 months' duration • Treat by simple palliative care and fostering relationship
Somatoform pain disorder	• Severe, prolonged pain with no cause found • Pain disrupts day-to-day life • Look for secondary gain
Body dysmorphic disorder	• Preoccupation with unrealistic negative evaluation of personal attractiveness • Sees self as ugly or horrific when normal in appearance • Preoccupation disrupts day-to-day life • May seek multiple plastic surgeries or other extreme interventions

DIFFERENTIATING SOMATOFORM DISORDERS FROM FACTITIOUS DISORDERS AND MALINGERING*

	Somatoform	Factitious	Malingering
Symptom production	Unconscious	Intentional	Intentional
Motivation	Unconscious	Unconscious	Intentional

*All three may present with similar symptom profile. The key to the differential is level of patient awareness.

PERSONALITY DISORDERS			
Types	**Definition**	**Epidemiology**	**Associated Defenses**
Paranoid	Feelings of persecution; feels that others are conspiring to harm them; suspicious	• Men > women • Increased incidence in families with schizophrenia	Projection
Schizoid	Isolated lifestyle; has no longing for others ("loner")	• Men > women • Increased incidence in families with schizophrenia	—
Schizotypal	Eccentric behavior, thought, and speech	• Prevalence is 3% • Men > women	—
Histrionic	Excessive emotion and attention seeking	• Women > men • Underdiagnosed in men	• Regression • Somatization • Conversion • Dissociation
Narcissistic	Grandiose; overconcerned with issues of self-esteem	• Common	Fixation at subphase of separation/individualization
Borderline	Instability of mood, self-image, and relationships	• Women > men • ↑ mood disorders in families	• Splitting • Projective identification • Dissociation • Passive-aggression
Antisocial	Does not recognize the rights of others	Prevalence: 3% in men; 1% in women	Superego lacunae
Avoidant	Shy or timid; fears rejection	• Common • Possible deforming illness	Avoidance
Dependent	Dependent, submissive	• Common • Women > men • May end up as abused spouse	—
Obsessive-compulsive	Perfectionistic and inflexible, orderly, rigid	• Men > women • ↑ concordance in identical twins	• Isolation • Reaction formation • Undoing • Intellectualization

KAPLAN) MEDICAL

Delirium Versus Dementia

Characteristics	Delirium	Dementia
History	Acute, identifiable date	Chronic, cannot be dated
Onset	Rapid	Insidious
Duration	Days to weeks	Months to years
Course	Fluctuating	Chronically progressive
Level of consciousness	Fluctuating	Normal
Orientation	Impaired periodically	Disorientation to person
Memory	Recent memory markedly impaired	Remote memories seen as recent
Perception	Visual hallucinations	Hallucinations less common
Sleep	Disrupted sleep-wake cycle	Less sleep disruption
Reversibility	Reversible	Mostly irreversible
Physiologic changes	Prominent	Minimal
Attention span	Very short	Not reduced

Common Abnormalities on Neurologic Examination

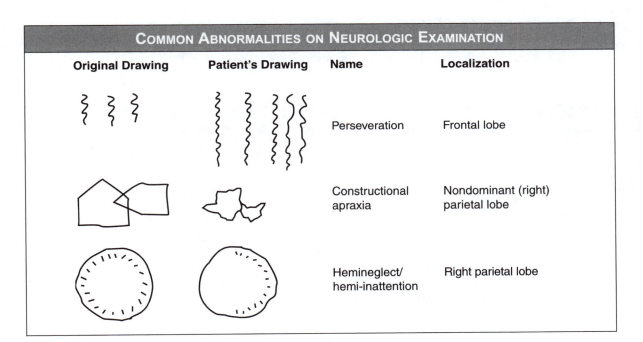

Original Drawing	Patient's Drawing	Name	Localization
		Perseveration	Frontal lobe
		Constructional apraxia	Nondominant (right) parietal lobe
		Hemineglect/ hemi-inattention	Right parietal lobe

SEXUAL DISORDERS

PARAPHILIAS	
Pedophilia	Sexual urges toward children; most common sexual assault
Exhibitionism	Recurrent desire to expose genitals to strangers
Voyeurism	Sexual pleasure from watching others who are naked, grooming, or having sex; begins early in childhood
Sadism	Sexual pleasure derived from others' pain
Masochism	Sexual pleasure derived from being abused or dominated
Fetishism	Sexual focus on objects, e.g., shoes, stockings *Variant:* transvestite fetishism (fantasies or actual dressing by heterosexual men in women's clothing for sexual arousal)
Frotteurism	Male rubbing of genitals against fully clothed woman to achieve orgasm; subways and buses
Zoophilia	Animals preferred in sexual fantasies or practices
Coprophilia	Combining sex and defecation
Urophilia	Combining sex and urination
Necrophilia	Preferring sex with cadavers
Hypoxyphilia	Altered state of consciousness secondary to hypoxia while experiencing orgasm *Variants:* autoerotic asphyxiation, poppers, amyl nitrate, nitric oxide

GENDER IDENTITY AND PREFERRED SEXUAL PARTNER OF A BIOLOGIC MALE		
Common Label	**Gender Identity**	**Preferred Sexual Partner**
Heterosexual	Male	Female
Transvestite fetishism	Male	Female
Gender identity disorder (transsexual)	Female	Male
Homosexual	Male	Male

SEXUAL DISORDERS	
Disorders of Sexual Desire	
Hypoactive	Deficiency or absence of fantasies or desires, 20% of population, more common in women
Sexual aversion	Aversion to all sexual contact
Sexual Arousal Disorders	
Female sexual arousal disorder	• As high as 33% of females; sometimes hormonally related • Antihistamine and anticholinergic medications ↓ vaginal lubrication

Male erectile disorder (impotence)	• *Primary:* never able to achieve erection
	• *Secondary:* once able to achieve erection
	  — Up to 20% lifetime prevalence; point prevalence 3%
	  — 50% of men treated for sexual disorders, incidence ↑ with age, more likely in smokers

Orgasm Disorders	
Anorgasmia (inhibited female orgasm)	• 5% of married women older than 35 have never achieved orgasm • Overall prevalence from all causes: 30% • Likelihood to have orgasm ↑ with age
Inhibited male orgasm (retarded ejaculation)	• Usually restricted to inability to orgasm in the vagina • 5% general prevalence • Differentiate from retrograde ejaculation
Premature ejaculation	• Male regularly ejaculates before or immediately after entering vagina • *Treatments:* stop and go technique, squeeze technique, SSRIs
Sexual Pain Disorders	
Dyspareunia	• Recurrent and persistent pain before, during, or after intercourse in either man or woman • More common in women • Chronic pelvic pain is a common complaint of women raped or sexually abused
Vaginismus	• Involuntary muscle constriction of the outer third of the vagina • Prevents penile insertion • *Treatment:* relaxation, Hegar dilators

PHYSICIAN–PATIENT RELATIONSHIPS

	GENERAL RULES	
Rule #1:	Always place the interests of the patient first.	Make it a point to ask about and know the patient's wishes.
Rule #2:	Always respond to the patient.	Respond to the emotional as well as the factual content of questions.
Rule #3:	Tell the patient everything, even if he or she does not ask.	• The patient should know what you know and when you know it. • Information should flow through the patient to the family, not the reverse.
Rule #4:	Work on long-term relationships with patients, not just short-term problems.	• Good relationships mean good medical practice. • Make eye contact; both patient and physician should both be sitting, if at all possible. Arrange the setting for comfortable, close communication. If patient is in room, talk to patient, not to colleagues. The patient is always the focus.
Rule #5:	Listening is better than talking.	• When patient talks, you are learning. • Take time to listen to the patient in front of you, even if other patients or colleagues are waiting. • Ask what the patient knows before explaining.
Rule #6:	The patient is the decision-maker.	Negotiate, do not order.
Rule #7:	Solve the problem presented; anticipate future problems.	• Find out what you need to; get the resources you need. • Change initial plans as information changes
Rule #8:	Admit to the patient when you make a mistake.	Take responsibility; don't blame the nursing staff or a medical student.
Rule #9:	Never "pass off" your patient to someone else.	• Refer to psychiatrist or other specialist only when beyond your expertise. • Provide instruction in aspects of care, e.g., nutrition, use of medications.
Rule #10:	Express empathy, then give control.	• "I'm sorry, what would you like to do?" • Important rule to remember when faced with grieving or angry patient or upset family members.
Rule #11:	Agree on the problem with the patient before moving to the solution.	Informed consent requires the patient to fully understand what is wrong before treatment options are presented.
Rule #12:	Be sure you understand what the patient is talking about before intervening.	Seek information before acting, clarify emotionally loaded words, begin with open-ended questions, then move to closed-ended questions.
Rule #13:	Patients do not get to select inappropriate treatments.	Patients select treatments, but only from presented, appropriate choices.
Rule #14:	Never lose sight of who your patient is.	Even if parent or surrogate is making decisions, patient is still the focus.
Rule # 15:	Never lie.	• Do not lie to patients, their families, or insurance companies. • Do not deceive to protect a colleague.
Rule #16:	Accept the health beliefs of patients and talk to them in those terms.	• Be accepting of benign folk medicine practices. Expect them. • Diagnoses need to be explained in the way patients can understand, even if not technically precise.
Rule #17:	Accept patients' religious beliefs and participate, if appropriate.	Religion is a source of comfort to many. Ask about a patient's religions beliefs if you are not sure.

(Continued)

Rule #18: Anything that increases communication is good.	• Take the time to talk with patients, even if others are waiting; ask why, not just what. • Seek information about the patient beyond the disease.
Rule #19: Be an advocate for the patient.	• Work to get the patient what he or she needs. • Need, not payment, should decide.
Rule #20: How you do it matters as much as what you do.	• Focus on the process, not just goals. Means, not just the ends. • Do the right thing, the right way. • Treat family members with courtesy and tact, but the wishes and interests of the patient come first.

ETHICAL AND LEGAL ISSUES

GENERAL RULES	
Rules	**Comments**
Rule #1: Competent patients have the right to refuse medical treatment.	• Patients have an almost absolute right to refuse. • Patients have almost absolute control over their own bodies.
Rule #2: Assume that the patient is competent unless clear behavioral evidence indicates otherwise.	Competence is a legal, not a medical issue. A diagnosis, by itself, tells you little about a patient's competence. Clear behavioral evidence would be: • Patient attempts suicide. • Patient is grossly psychotic and dysfunctional. • Patient's physical or mental state prevents simple communication.
Rule #3: Avoid going to court. Decision-making should occur in the clinical setting if possible.	Consider going to court only if: • There is intractable disagreement about a patient's competence, who should be the surrogate, or who should make the decision about life support. • You perceive a serious conflict of interest between surrogate and patient's interests. • Court approval of decision to terminate life support is, therefore, rarely required.

Rule #4: When surrogates make decisions for a patient, they should use the following criteria and in this order:	1. Subjective standard
	  • Actual intent, advance directive
	  • What did the patient say in the past?
	2. Substituted judgment
	  • Who best represents the patient?
	  • What would patient say if he or she could?
	3. Best interests standard
	  • Burdens versus benefits
	  • Interests of patient, not preferences of the decision-maker

Rule #5: If the patient is incompetent, physician may rely on advance directives.	• Advance directives can be oral. • Living will: written document expressing wishes • Health power of attorney: designating the surrogate decision-maker, "speaks with the patient's voice"
Rule #6: Feeding tube is a medical treatment and can be withdrawn at the patient's request.	A competent person can refuse even lifesaving hydration and nutrition.
Rule #7: Do nothing to actively assist the patient to die sooner.	• Passive, i.e., allowing to die is okay; active, i.e., killing is not okay • But do all you can to reduce the patient's suffering (e.g., giving pain medication).

(Continued)

Rule #8:	The physician decides when the patient is dead.	• What if there are no more treatment options (the patient is cortically dead), and the family insists on treatment? *If there are no options, there is nothing the physician can do; treatment must stop.* • What if the physician thinks continued treatment is futile (the patient has shown no improvement), but the surrogate insists on continued treatment? *The treatment should continue.*
Rule #9:	Never abandon a patient.	• Lack of financial resources or results are never reasons to stop the treatment of a patient. • An annoying or difficult patient is still your patient.

Rule #10:	Always obtain informed consent.	• The patient must receive and understand five pieces of information:
		  1. Nature of procedure
		  2. Purpose or rationale
		  3. Benefits
		  4. Risks
		  5. Availability of alternatives
		• Four exceptions to informed consent:
		  1. Emergency
		  2. Waiver by patient
		  3. Patient is incompetent
		  4. Therapeutic privilege

Rule #11:	Special rules apply with children.	• Children younger than 18 years are minors and are legally incompetent.
		• Exceptions: emancipated minors
		  – If patient is older than 13 years and taking care of self, i.e., living alone, treat as an adult.
		  – Marriage makes a child emancipated, as does serving in the military.
		  – Pregnancy or having a child, in most cases, does not.
		• Partial emancipation
		  – Generally age 14 and older
		  – Consent for certain issues only:
		     Substance drug treatment
		     Prenatal care
		     Sexually transmitted disease treatment
		     Birth control

Rule #12:	Parents cannot withhold life- or limb-saving treatment from their children.	If parents refuse permission to treat child: 1. If immediate emergency, go ahead and treat. 2. If not immediate, but still critical (e.g., juvenile diabetes), generally the child is declared a ward of the court and the court grants permission. 3. If not life- or limb-threatening (e.g., child needs minor stitches), listen to the parents.
Rule #13:	Organ donation should follow the patient's wishes.	The patient's advance directive should be decisive. Prior discussion with family members eliminates any confusion as to those wishes.

Rule #14:	Good Samaritan Laws limit liability in nonmedical settings.	• Physician is not required to stop and help.
		• If help offered, shielded from liability provided:
		  – Actions are within physician's competence.
		  – Only accepted procedures are performed.
		  – Physician remains at scene after starting therapy until relieved by competent personnel.
		  – No compensation changes hands.

(Continued)

Rule # 15: Confidentiality is absolute.	• Physicians cannot tell anyone anything about their patient without the patient's permission. • Physician must strive to ensure that others *cannot access* patient information. • Getting a consultation is permitted, as the consultant is bound by confidentiality, too. However, watch the location of the consultation. Be careful not to be overheard (e.g., in elevator or cafeteria). • If you receive a court subpoena, show up in court but do not divulge information about your patient. • If patient is a threat to self or others, the physician *must* break confidentiality.
Rule #16: Patients should be given the chance to state DNR (do not resuscitate) orders, and physicians should follow them.	• DNR refers only to cardiopulmonary resuscitation. • Continue with ongoing treatments. • DNR decisions can be made by the patient or surrogate. • Have DNR discussions as part of your first encounter with the patient.

Rule #17: Committed mentally ill patients retain their rights.	• Committed mentally ill adults are legally entitled to the following:
	  – They must have treatment available.
	  – They can refuse treatment.
	  – They can command a jury trial to determine "sanity."
	• They lose only the civil liberty to come and go.

Rule #18: Detain patients to protect them or others.	• Emergency detention can be effected by a physician and/or a law enforcement person for 48 hours, pending a hearing. • A physician can detain; only a judge can commit.
Rule #19: Remove from patient contact health care professionals who pose risk to patients.	Types of risks: • Infectious disease (TB) • Substance abuse • Depression (or other psychological issues) • Incompetence
Rule #20: Focus on what is the best ethical conduct, not simply the letter of the law.	The best conduct is both legal *and* ethical.

BIOSTATISTICS

INCIDENCE AND PREVALENCE

Incidence	$\text{Incidence rate} = \dfrac{\text{Number of \textbf{new events} in a specified period}}{\text{Number of persons exposed to risk of aquiring the condition during this period}} \times 10^n$
Prevalence	$\text{Prevalence rate} = \dfrac{\text{All cases of a disease at a given point/period}}{\text{Total population at risk for having the condition at a given point or period}} \times 10^n$

TYPES OF MORTALITY RATES

Crude mortality rate	Deaths ÷ population
Cause-specific mortality rate	Deaths from cause ÷ population
Cause-fatality rate	Deaths from cause ÷ number of persons with the disease/cause
Proportionate mortality rate (PMR)	Deaths from cause ÷ all deaths

SCREENING RESULTS IN A 2 × 2 TABLE

		Disease					
		Present		**Absent**		**Totals**	
Screening Test Results	**Positive**	TP	60	FP	70	TP + FP	
	Negative	FN	40	TN	30	TN + FN	
	Totals	TP + FN		TN + FP		TP + TN + FP + FN	

Sensitivity = TP/(TP + FN)	Detecting disease
Specificity = TN/(TN + FP)	Identifying healthy individuals
Positive predictive value = TP/(TP + FP)	What % of positive test results will be correct?
Negative predictive value = TN/(TN + FN)	What % of negative test results will be correct?
Accuracy = (TP + TN)/(TP + TN + FP + FN)	How good is the test overall?

Definition of abbreviations: FN, false negatives; FP, false positives; TN, true negatives; TP, true positives.

HEALTHY AND DISEASED POPULATIONS ALONG A SCREENING DIMENSION

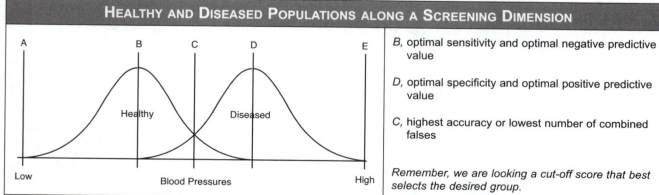

B, optimal sensitivity and optimal negative predictive value

D, optimal specificity and optimal positive predictive value

C, highest accuracy or lowest number of combined falses

Remember, we are looking a cut-off score that best selects the desired group.

Type of Bias in Research and Important Associations

Type of Bias	Definition	Important Associations	Solutions
Selection	Sample not representative	Berkson's bias, nonrespondent bias	Random, independent sample
Measurement	The process of gathering information distorts it	Hawthorne effect	Control group/placebo group
Experimenter expectancy	Researcher's beliefs affect outcome	Pygmalion effect	Double-blind design
Lead time	Early detection confused with increased survival	Benefits of screening	Measure "back end" survival
Recall	Subjects cannot remember accurately	Retrospective studies	Multiple sources to confirm information
Late-look	Severely diseased individuals are not uncovered	Early mortality	Stratify by severity
Confounding	Unanticipated factors obscure results	Hidden factors affect results	Multiple studies, good research design

Differentiating Observational Studies

Characteristic	Cross-Sectional Studies	Case-Control Studies	Cohort Studies
Time	One time point	Retrospective	Prospective
Incidence	No	No	Yes
Prevalence	Yes	No	No
Causality	No	Yes	Yes
Role of disease	Measure disease	Begin with disease	End with disease
Assesses	Association of risk factor and disease	Many risk factors for single disease	Single risk factor affecting many diseases
Data analysis	Chi-square to assess association	Odds ratio to estimate risk (Refer to Appendix A for equation.)	Relative and attributable risk to estimate risk (Refer to Appendix A for relative and attributable risk equations.)

Making Decisions Using p-Values

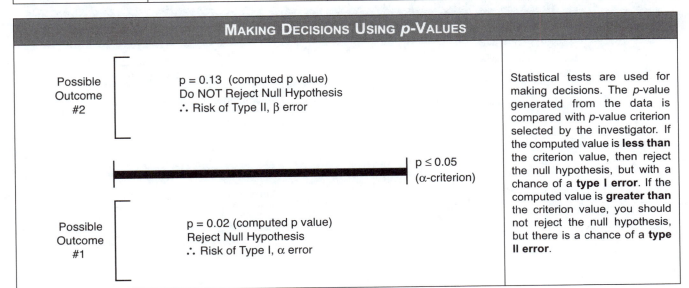

Possible Outcome #2

p = 0.13 (computed p value)
Do NOT Reject Null Hypothesis
∴ Risk of Type II, β error

p ≤ 0.05
(α-criterion)

Possible Outcome #1

p = 0.02 (computed p value)
Reject Null Hypothesis
∴ Risk of Type I, α error

Statistical tests are used for making decisions. The *p*-value generated from the data is compared with *p*-value criterion selected by the investigator. If the computed value is **less than** the criterion value, then reject the null hypothesis, but with a chance of a **type I error**. If the computed value is **greater than** the criterion value, you should not reject the null hypothesis, but there is a chance of a **type II error**.

CONFIDENCE INTERVALS

Confidence intervals (CI) estimate the **population** value based on the data from a **sample**. We give up precision, knowing exactly the population number, in exchange for confidence. Confidence intervals tell us that reality is most likely **within** the specified range.

Confidence interval of the mean	$$\overline{X} \pm Z\left(\frac{S}{\sqrt{N}}\right)$$	Where: $\overline{X}$ = sample mean Z = Z-score* S = standard deviation N = sample size *Z = 1.96 for 95% confidence Z = 2.58 for 99% confidence

Interpretation of Confidence Intervals		
Confidence intervals for the mean	If the CIs for two means overlap, then they could be the same. Therefore, we have no evidence that they are different. If the CIs do not overlap, then we usually assume that they are different (statistical significance). In general, any overlap in CIs indicates no difference.	
Confidence intervals for relative risk (RR) or odds ratios	If the CIs contain the number 1.0, then the population parameters compared in the ratio could be the same. Therefore, we cannot assume that they are different. If 1.0 is not included in the CI, then we assume that they are different (statistical significance). A 1.0 in the CI means that it is not significant.	

TYPES OF SCALES IN STATISTICS

Type of Scale	Description	Key Words	Examples
Nominal (categorical)	Different groups	"This" as opposed to "that"	Gender, comparing among treatment interventions
Ordinal	Groups in sequence	Comparative quality, rank order	Olympic medals, class rank in medical school
Interval	Exact differences among groups	Quantity, mean, and standard deviation	Height, weight, blood pressure, drug dosage
Ratio	Interval + true zero point	Zero means zero	Temperature measured in degrees Kelvin

TYPES OF SCALES AND BASIC STATISTICAL TESTS

Name of Statistical Test	Variables		Comment
	Interval	Nominal	
Pearson correlation	2	0	Is there a linear relationship?
Chi-square	0	2	Any number of groups
t-test	1	1	Two groups only
One-way ANOVA	1	1	Two or more groups
Matched pairs *t*-test	1	1	Two groups, linked data pairs, before and after
Repeated measures ANOVA	1	1	More than two groups, linked data

Biochemistry

GLYCOLYSIS

Glycolysis is a **cytoplasmic** pathway used by all cells to generate energy from glucose. **One** glucose molecule is converted into **2 pyruvate** molecules, generating a net of **2 ATPs** by substrate-level phosphorylation, and **2 NADHs**. When oxygen is present, NADH delivers electrons to the electron transport chain in mitochondria to generate ATP by oxidative phosphorylation. Under **anaerobic** conditions (e.g., short bursts of intense exercise) or in cells without mitochondria (e.g., RBCs), lactate is generated and the NADH is reoxidized into NAD^+.

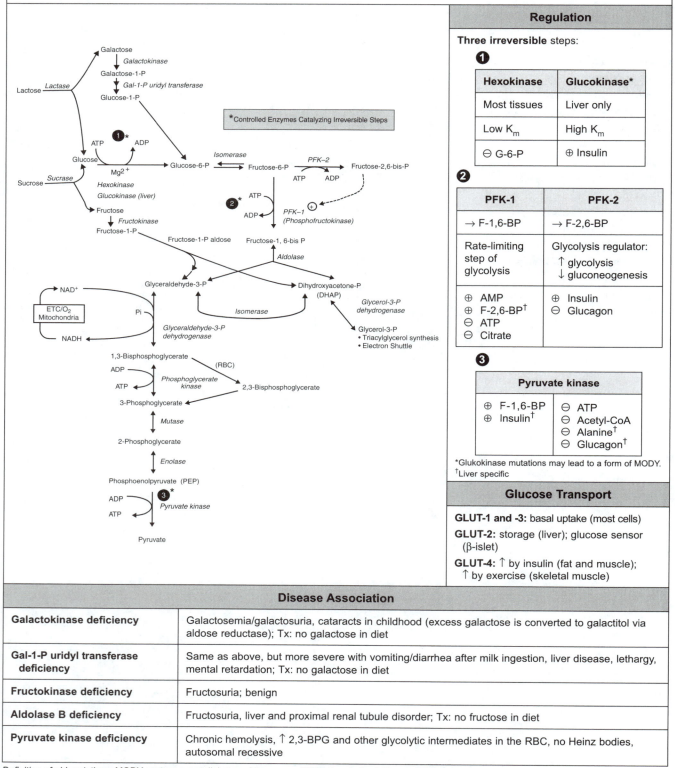

Regulation

Three irreversible steps:

❶

Hexokinase	Glucokinase*
Most tissues	Liver only
Low K_m	High K_m
$\ominus$ G-6-P	$\oplus$ Insulin

❷

PFK-1	PFK-2
→ F-1,6-BP	→ F-2,6-BP
Rate-limiting step of glycolysis	Glycolysis regulator: ↑ glycolysis ↓ gluconeogenesis
$\oplus$ AMP $\oplus$ F-2,6-BP† $\ominus$ ATP $\ominus$ Citrate	$\oplus$ Insulin $\ominus$ Glucagon

❸

Pyruvate kinase	
$\oplus$ F-1,6-BP $\oplus$ Insulin†	$\ominus$ ATP $\ominus$ Acetyl-CoA $\ominus$ Alanine† $\ominus$ Glucagon†

*Glukokinase mutations may lead to a form of MODY.
†Liver specific

Glucose Transport

GLUT-1 and -3: basal uptake (most cells)

GLUT-2: storage (liver); glucose sensor (β-islet)

GLUT-4: ↑ by insulin (fat and muscle); ↑ by exercise (skeletal muscle)

Disease Association

Galactokinase deficiency	Galactosemia/galactosuria, cataracts in childhood (excess galactose is converted to galactitol via aldose reductase); Tx: no galactose in diet
Gal-1-P uridyl transferase deficiency	Same as above, but more severe with vomiting/diarrhea after milk ingestion, liver disease, lethargy, mental retardation; Tx: no galactose in diet
Fructokinase deficiency	Fructosuria; benign
Aldolase B deficiency	Fructosuria, liver and proximal renal tubule disorder; Tx: no fructose in diet
Pyruvate kinase deficiency	Chronic hemolysis, ↑ 2,3-BPG and other glycolytic intermediates in the RBC, no Heinz bodies, autosomal recessive

Definition of abbreviations: MODY, mature-onset diabetes of the young; PFK, phosphofructokinase; RBC, red blood cell; Tx, treatment.

THE CITRIC ACID CYCLE

The citric acid cycle (**tricarboxylic acid cycle**) is a **mitochondrial** pathway that occurs **only** under **aerobic conditions**. Each acetyl-CoA generated from pyruvate is used to produce **3 NADH**, **1 FADH$_2$**, and **1 GTP**. Both the NADH and FADH$_2$ deliver electrons to the electron transport chain (ETC) to generate energy by oxidative phosphorylation.

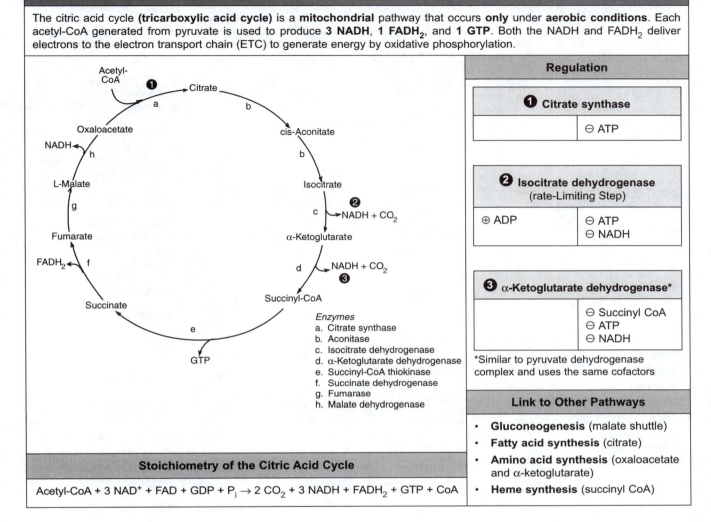

Enzymes
a. Citrate synthase
b. Aconitase
c. Isocitrate dehydrogenase
d. α-Ketoglutarate dehydrogenase
e. Succinyl-CoA thiokinase
f. Succinate dehydrogenase
g. Fumarase
h. Malate dehydrogenase

Regulation

❶ Citrate synthase

	⊖ ATP

❷ Isocitrate dehydrogenase
(rate-Limiting Step)

⊕ ADP	⊖ ATP
	⊖ NADH

❸ α-Ketoglutarate dehydrogenase*

	⊖ Succinyl CoA
	⊖ ATP
	⊖ NADH

*Similar to pyruvate dehydrogenase complex and uses the same cofactors

Link to Other Pathways

- **Gluconeogenesis** (malate shuttle)
- **Fatty acid synthesis** (citrate)
- **Amino acid synthesis** (oxaloacetate and α-ketoglutarate)
- **Heme synthesis** (succinyl CoA)

Stoichiometry of the Citric Acid Cycle

Acetyl-CoA + 3 NAD$^+$ + FAD + GDP + P$_i$ → 2 CO$_2$ + 3 NADH + FADH$_2$ + GTP + CoA

OXIDATIVE PHOSPHORYLATION

Electron transport and the coupled synthesis of ATP are known as oxidative phosphorylation. The **electron transport chain (ETC)** is a series of carrier enzymes in the **inner mitochondrial membrane** that pass electrons, in a stepwise fashion, from NADH and $FADH_2$ to **oxygen**, the final electron acceptor. These carriers create a proton gradient across the inner membrane, which drives the F_0/F_1 ATP synthase, with a net production of **3 ATPs** per **NADH** and **2 ATPs** per **$FADH_2$**.

Electron Transport Chain	Clinical Correlation

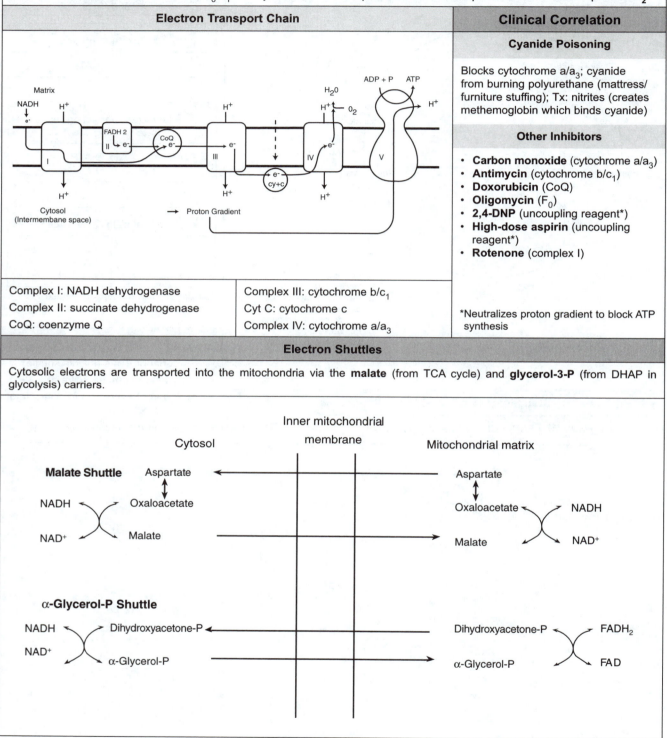

Clinical Correlation

Cyanide Poisoning

Blocks cytochrome a/a_3; cyanide from burning polyurethane (mattress/furniture stuffing); Tx: nitrites (creates methemoglobin which binds cyanide)

Other Inhibitors

- **Carbon monoxide** (cytochrome a/a_3)
- **Antimycin** (cytochrome b/c_1)
- **Doxorubicin** (CoQ)
- **Oligomycin** (F_0)
- **2,4-DNP** (uncoupling reagent*)
- **High-dose aspirin** (uncoupling reagent*)
- **Rotenone** (complex I)

Complex I: NADH dehydrogenase
Complex II: succinate dehydrogenase
CoQ: coenzyme Q

Complex III: cytochrome b/c_1
Cyt C: cytochrome c
Complex IV: cytochrome a/a_3

*Neutralizes proton gradient to block ATP synthesis

Electron Shuttles

Cytosolic electrons are transported into the mitochondria via the **malate** (from TCA cycle) and **glycerol-3-P** (from DHAP in glycolysis) carriers.

PYRUVATE METABOLISM

Lactate dehydrogenase: *Anaerobic tissues:* converts pyruvate to lactate, reoxidizing cytoplasmic NADH to NAD^+. *Liver:* converts lactate to pyruvate for gluconeogenesis or for metabolism to acetyl CoA

Alanine aminotransferase (ALT, GPT): *Muscle:* converts pyruvate to alanine to transport amino groups to the liver. *Liver:* converts alanine to pyruvate for gluconeogenesis and delivers the amino group for urea synthesis

Pyruvate carboxylase: produces oxaloacetate for gluconeogenesis and the citric acid cycle

Pyruvate dehydrogenase: generates acetyl-CoA for fatty acid synthesis and the citric acid cycle; complex of 3 enzymes

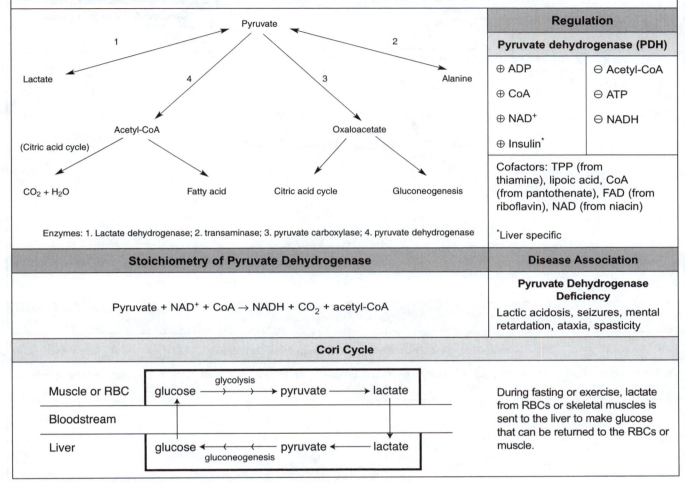

Enzymes: 1. Lactate dehydrogenase; 2. transaminase; 3. pyruvate carboxylase; 4. pyruvate dehydrogenase

Regulation

Pyruvate dehydrogenase (PDH)

⊕ ADP	⊖ Acetyl-CoA
⊕ CoA	⊖ ATP
⊕ NAD^+	⊖ NADH
⊕ Insulin*	

Cofactors: TPP (from thiamine), lipoic acid, CoA (from pantothenate), FAD (from riboflavin), NAD (from niacin)

*Liver specific

Stoichiometry of Pyruvate Dehydrogenase

$$Pyruvate + NAD^+ + CoA \rightarrow NADH + CO_2 + acetyl\text{-}CoA$$

Disease Association

Pyruvate Dehydrogenase Deficiency

Lactic acidosis, seizures, mental retardation, ataxia, spasticity

Cori Cycle

Muscle or RBC	glucose —glycolysis→ pyruvate —→ lactate
Bloodstream	
Liver	glucose ←gluconeogenesis← pyruvate ←— lactate

During fasting or exercise, lactate from RBCs or skeletal muscles is sent to the liver to make glucose that can be returned to the RBCs or muscle.

Definition of abbreviations: TCA, tricarboxylic acid; TPP, thiamine pyrophosphate.

Hexose Monophosphate Shunt

The **hexose monophosphate (HMP) shunt** (pentose phosphate pathway) is a **cytosolic** pathway that uses **glucose-6-phosphate** to synthesize **NADPH** and **ribose-5-P**. NADPH is important for fatty acid and steroid biosynthesis, maintenance of reduced glutathione to protect against reactive oxygen species (ROS), and bactericidal activity in polymorphonuclear leukocytes (PMNs). Ribose-5-P is required for nucleotide synthesis.

Regulation	
Glucose-6-P-dehydrogenase	
⊕ **NADP⁺**	⊖ NADPH

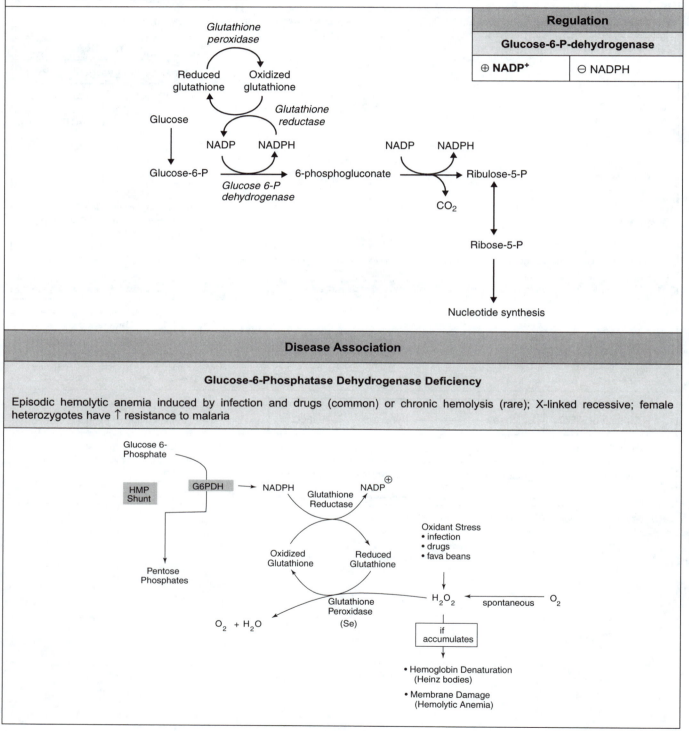

Disease Association

Glucose-6-Phosphatase Dehydrogenase Deficiency

Episodic hemolytic anemia induced by infection and drugs (common) or chronic hemolysis (rare); X-linked recessive; female heterozygotes have ↑ resistance to malaria

GLYCOGENESIS AND GLYCOGENOLYSIS

Glycogen is a branched polymer of glucose, stored primarily in liver and skeletal muscles, which can be mobilized during hypoglycemia (liver) or muscular contraction (muscles). Synthesis of glycogen (**glycogenesis**) is mediated by **glycogen synthase**, while its breakdown (**glycogenolysis**) is carried out by **glycogen phosphorylase**. Branching of the glycogen polymer occurs via a **branching enzyme**, which breaks an α-1,4-bond and transfers a block of glucosyl residues to create a new α-1,6-bond. This is reversed by a **debranching enzyme**.

Glycogen Metabolism

Regulation

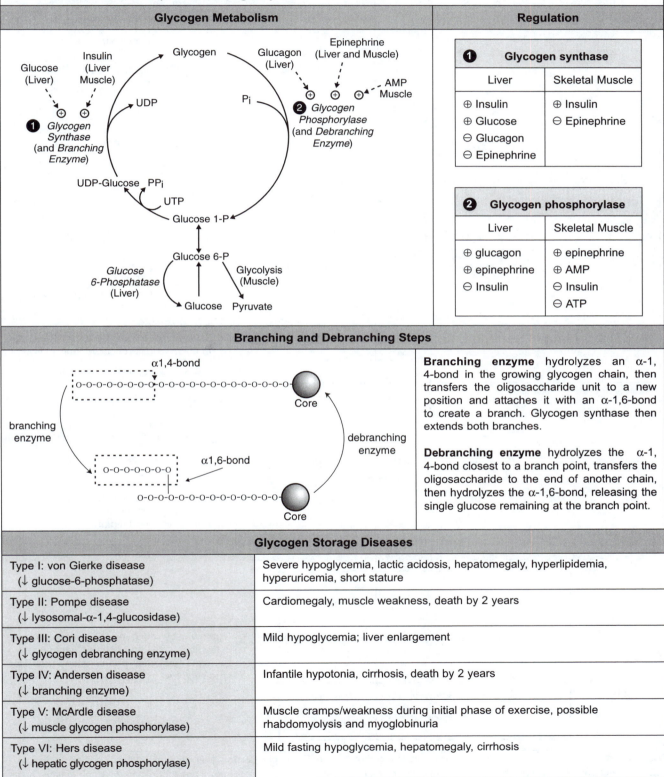

① Glycogen synthase	
Liver	Skeletal Muscle
⊕ Insulin	⊕ Insulin
⊕ Glucose	⊖ Epinephrine
⊖ Glucagon	
⊖ Epinephrine	

② Glycogen phosphorylase	
Liver	Skeletal Muscle
⊕ glucagon	⊕ epinephrine
⊕ epinephrine	⊕ AMP
⊖ Insulin	⊖ Insulin
	⊖ ATP

Branching and Debranching Steps

Branching enzyme hydrolyzes an α-1,4-bond in the growing glycogen chain, then transfers the oligosaccharide unit to a new position and attaches it with an α-1,6-bond to create a branch. Glycogen synthase then extends both branches.

Debranching enzyme hydrolyzes the α-1,4-bond closest to a branch point, transfers the oligosaccharide to the end of another chain, then hydrolyzes the α-1,6-bond, releasing the single glucose remaining at the branch point.

Glycogen Storage Diseases

Type I: von Gierke disease (↓ glucose-6-phosphatase)	Severe hypoglycemia, lactic acidosis, hepatomegaly, hyperlipidemia, hyperuricemia, short stature
Type II: Pompe disease (↓ lysosomal-α-1,4-glucosidase)	Cardiomegaly, muscle weakness, death by 2 years
Type III: Cori disease (↓ glycogen debranching enzyme)	Mild hypoglycemia; liver enlargement
Type IV: Andersen disease (↓ branching enzyme)	Infantile hypotonia, cirrhosis, death by 2 years
Type V: McArdle disease (↓ muscle glycogen phosphorylase)	Muscle cramps/weakness during initial phase of exercise, possible rhabdomyolysis and myoglobinuria
Type VI: Hers disease (↓ hepatic glycogen phosphorylase)	Mild fasting hypoglycemia, hepatomegaly, cirrhosis

GLUCONEOGENESIS

Gluconeogenesis is a pathway for de novo synthesis of **glucose** from **C3 and C4 precursors** using both **mitochondrial** and **cytosolic** enzymes. Occurring only in liver, kidney, and intestinal epithelium, this pathway functions to provide glucose for the body, especially the brain and RBCs, which require glucose for energy (the brain can also use ketone bodies during fasting conditions). Gluconeogenesis occurs during fasting, as glycogen stores become depleted. Important substrates for gluconeogenesis are gluconeogenic **amino acids** (protein from muscle), **lactate** (from RBCs and muscle during anaerobic exercise), and **glycerol-3-P** (from triacylglycerol from adipose tissues).

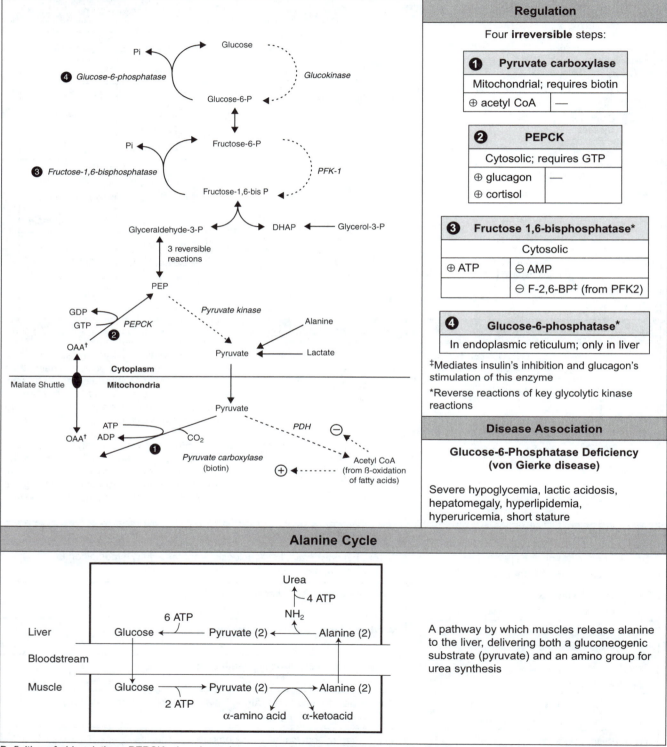

Regulation

Four **irreversible** steps:

❶	Pyruvate carboxylase	
Mitochondrial; requires biotin		
⊕ acetyl CoA	—	

❷	PEPCK	
Cytosolic; requires GTP		
⊕ glucagon	—	
⊕ cortisol	—	

❸	Fructose 1,6-bisphosphatase*	
Cytosolic		
⊕ ATP	⊖ AMP	
	⊖ F-2,6-BP‡ (from PFK2)	

❹	Glucose-6-phosphatase*	
In endoplasmic reticulum; only in liver		

‡Mediates insulin's inhibition and glucagon's stimulation of this enzyme

*Reverse reactions of key glycolytic kinase reactions

Disease Association

Glucose-6-Phosphatase Deficiency (von Gierke disease)

Severe hypoglycemia, lactic acidosis, hepatomegaly, hyperlipidemia, hyperuricemia, short stature

Alanine Cycle

A pathway by which muscles release alanine to the liver, delivering both a gluconeogenic substrate (pyruvate) and an amino group for urea synthesis

Definition of abbreviations: PEPCK, phosphoenolpyruvate carboxykinase; PFK2, phosphofructokinase 2; RBC, red blood cell.

†OAA is not transported across the membrane directly. Instead, it is transported as malate in exchange for asparate via the malate shuttle (*see* page 38).

AMINO ACID STRUCTURES

Hydrophobic Amino Acids

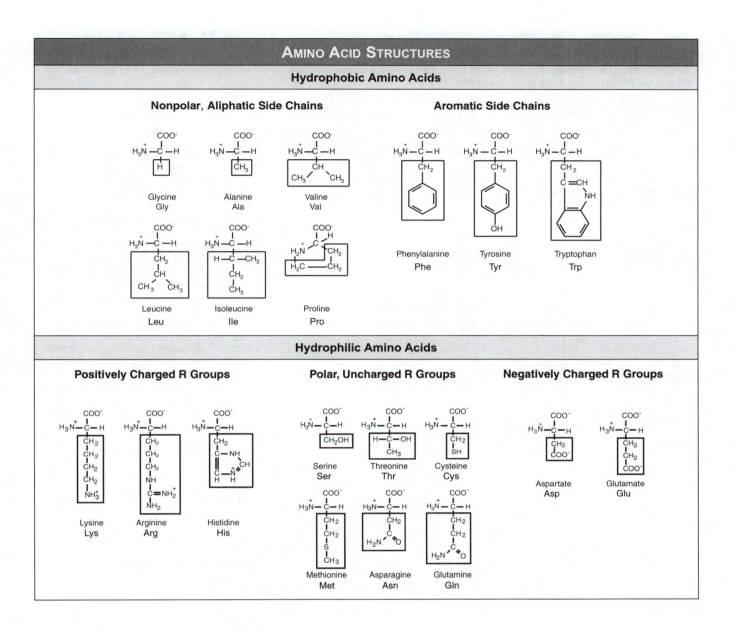

Nonpolar, Aliphatic Side Chains

Glycine
Gly

Alanine
Ala

Valine
Val

Leucine
Leu

Isoleucine
Ile

Proline
Pro

Aromatic Side Chains

Phenylalanine
Phe

Tyrosine
Tyr

Tryptophan
Trp

Hydrophilic Amino Acids

Positively Charged R Groups

Lysine
Lys

Arginine
Arg

Histidine
His

Polar, Uncharged R Groups

Serine
Ser

Threonine
Thr

Cysteine
Cys

Methionine
Met

Asparagine
Asn

Glutamine
Gln

Negatively Charged R Groups

Aspartate
Asp

Glutamate
Glu

AMINO ACID DERIVATIVES

Besides being the building blocks of proteins, amino acids are also precursors for various chemicals, such as **hormones**, **neurotransmitters**, and other small molecules.

Amino Acid	Product	Disease Association
Tyrosine	Thyroid hormones (T_3, T_4); melanin; catecholamines (dopamine, epinephrine)	**Albinism** Tyrosine hydroxylase (type I) or tyrosine transporter (type II) deficiency; ↓ pigmentation of skin, eyes, and hair, ↑ risk of skin cancer, visual defects

Tyrosine → (Tyrosine hydroxylase, O_2, THB → DHB) → DOPA → (Aromatic acid decarboxylase, CO_2) → Dopamine → (Dopamine-β-hydroxylase, O_2, Cu^+, Ascorbate) → Norepinephrine → (Phenylethanolamine-N-methyl transferase (PNMT), SAM → S-Adenosylhomocysteine) → Epinephrine

DOPA → Melanin

Amino Acid	Product	Disease Association
Tryptophan	Serotonin (5-HT); melatonin; NAD; NADP	**Carcinoid Syndrome** ↑ Serotonin excretion from gastrointestinal neuroendocrine tumors (carcinoid tumors); cutaneous flushing, venous telangiectasia, diarrhea, bronchospasm, cardiac valvular lesions

Tryptophan → (Tryptophan hydroxylase, O_2, THB → DHB) → 5-OH-Tryptophan → (Aromatic amino acid decarboxylase, CO_2) → Serotonin

Amino Acid	Product	Disease Association
Glycine	Heme	**Acute Intermittent Porphyria** Uroporphyrinogen-I synthase deficiency; episodic expression, acute abdominal pain, anxiety, confusion, paranoia, muscle weakness, no photosensitivity, port-wine urine in some patients, urine excretion of ALA and PBG; autosomal dominant

Glycine + Succinyl-CoA → (ALA synthase) → δ-Aminolevulinate → (ALA dehydratase) → Porphobilinogen → (Uroporphyrinogen-I synthase, Uro-III cosynthase) → Uroporphyrinogen-III → Protoporphyrin IX → (Heme synthase (ferrochelatase), Fe^{2+}) → Heme

Heme → (Heme oxygenase, NADPH, O_2) → Biliverdin → (Biliverdin reductase, NADPH) → Bilirubin → (UDP-glucuronyl transferase, UDP, UDP-glucuronate) → Bilirubin diglucuronide

Porphyria Cutanea Tarda

Uroporphyrinogen decarboxylase deficiency; photosensitivity, skin inflammation, and blistering; cirrhosis often associated

Lead Poisoning

Inhibits ALA dehydratase and ferrochelatase; microcytic sideroblastic anemia; basophilic stippling of erythrocytes; headache, nausea, memory loss, abdominal pain, diarrhea (lead colic), lead lines in gums, neuropathy (claw hand, wrist-drop), ↑ urine excretion of ALA; Tx: dimercaprol and EDTA

Amino Acid	Product
Glutamate	γ-aminobutyric acid (GABA)

Glutamate → (Glutamate decarboxylase) → γ-Aminobutyric acid (GABA)

Amino Acid	Product
Arginine	Nitric oxide (NO)

Arginine + O_2 → (NO synthase, ⊕ Ca^{2+}, NADPH → $NADP^+$) → Nitric oxide + citrulline

Hemolytic Crisis

Jaundice due to ↑ bilirubin from severe hemolysis; ↓ hemoglobin; ↑ reticulocytes; may result from:
(1) G6PD deficiency hemolysis
(2) Sickle cell crisis
(3) Rh disease of newborn

UDP-Glucuronyl Transferase Deficiency

Jaundice due to low bilirubin conjugation; may result from:
(1) Crigler-Najjar syndromes
(2) Gilbert syndrome
(3) Physiologic jaundice of newborn, especially premature infants

Amino Acid	Product
Histidine	Histamine

Histidine → (Histidine decarboxylase) → Histamine

Amino Acid	Product
Methionine	S-adenosylmethionine (SAM; methylating agent)
Arginine, glycine, SAM	Creatine

AMINO ACID SYNTHESIS AND METABOLISM

Amino acids are required for protein synthesis. Although some amino acids can be synthesized de novo (**nonessential**), others (**essential**) must be obtained from the digestion of dietary proteins. Nonessential amino acids are synthesized from intermediates of glycolysis and the citric acid cycle or from other amino acids. Degradation of amino acids occurs by transamination of the amino group to **glutamate**, while the remaining carbon skeletons of the amino acids may be oxidized to $CO_2 + H_2O$, or reverted to citric acid cycle intermediates for conversion to glucose (**glucogenic**) or ketones (**ketogenic**).

Genetic Deficiencies of Amino Acid Metabolism

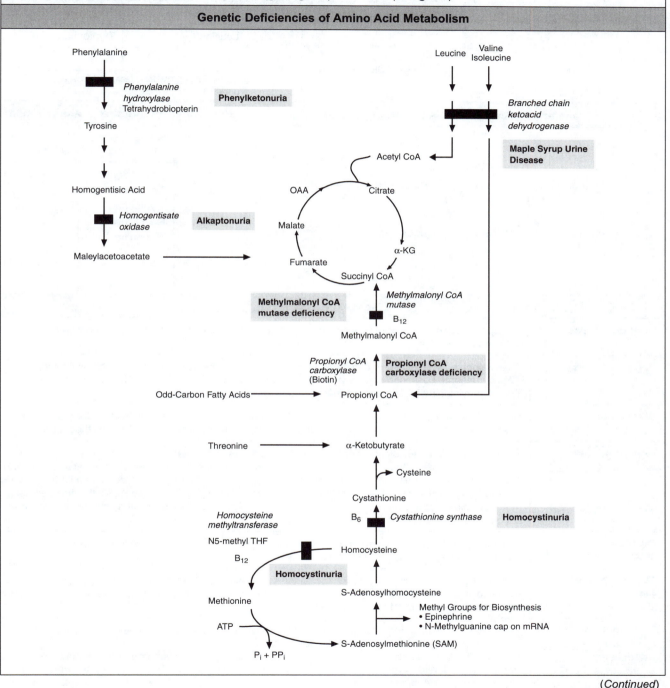

(Continued)

AMINO ACID SYNTHESIS AND METABOLISM (CONT'D.)

Precursors for Nonessential Amino Acids

| Glycolysis | | TCA cycle |

Glucose → Phosphoglycerate → Pyruvate → α-Ketoglutarate → Oxaloacetate

Phosphoglycerate ↓ Serine

Pyruvate ↓ Alanine

α-Ketoglutarate ↓ Glutamate

Oxaloacetate ↓ Aspartate

Serine ↙↘ Glycine   Cysteine

Glutamate ↙↘ Proline   Glutamine

Aspartate ↓ Asparagine

Essential Amino Acids*

Arginine†	Methionine
Histidine	Phenylalanine
Isoleucine	Threonine
Leucine	Tryptophan
Lysine	Valine

*Mnemonic: PVT. TIM HALL; †essential during periods of growth and pregnancy

Transfer of α-Amino Groups to α-Ketoglutarate

Amino acid

$$R-\underset{\underset{NH_2}{|}}{CH}-COOH$$

Enz-PLP

Glutamate

$$HOOC-CH_2-CH_2-\underset{\underset{NH_2}{|}}{CH}-COOH$$

$$R-\underset{\underset{O}{\|}}{C}-COOH$$

Enz-PLP | NH₂

$$HOOC-CH_2-CH_2-\underset{\underset{O}{\|}}{C}-COOH$$

α-Ketoacid

α-Ketoglutarate

Glucogenic and Ketogenic Amino Acids

Ketogenic	Ketogenic and Glucogenic	Glucogenic
Leucine Lysine	Phenylalanine Tyrosine Tryptophan Isoleucine Threonine	All others

Disease Association

Hartnup disease	Transport protein defect with ↑ excretion of neutral amino acids; symptoms similar to pellagra; autosomal recessive
Phenylketonuria	Phenylalanine hydroxylase or dihydrobiopterin reductase deficiency → buildup of phenylalanine; tyrosine becomes essential; musty body odor, mental retardation, microcephaly, autosomal recessive; Tx: ↓ phenylalanine in diet; avoid aspartame (Nutrasweet®)
Alkaptonuria	Homogentisate oxidase deficiency (for tyrosine degradation); ↑ homogentisic acid in blood and urine (darkens when exposed to air), ochronosis (dark pigment in cartilage), arthritis in adulthood; benign
Homocystinuria	↑ homocystine in urine. Classic homocystinuria, caused by a deficiency in cystathionine synthase, is associated with dislocated lens, deep venous thrombosis, stroke, atherosclerosis, mental retardation, and Marfan-like features. Deficiency of pyridoxine, folate, or vitamin B_{12} can produce a mild homocystinemia with elevated risk of atherosclerosis (previously listed symptoms absent). Methionine synthase (homocysteine methyltransferase) deficiency is extremely rare and is associated with megaloblastic anemia and mental retardation.
Cystinuria	Transport protein defect with ↑ excretion of lysine, arginine, cystine, and ornithine; excess cystine precipitates as kidney stones; Tx: acetazolamide
Maple syrup urine disease	Branched-chain ketoacid dehydrogenase deficiency; branched-chain ketoacidosis from infancy; weight loss, lethargy, alternating hypertonia/hypotonia, maple syrup odor of urine; ketosis/coma/death if untreated; Tx: ↓ valine, leucine, isoleucine in diet
Propionyl-CoA carboxylase deficiency **Methylmalonyl-CoA mutase deficiency**	Neonatal ketoacidosis from blocked degradation of valine, isoleucine, methionine, threonine, and odd-carbon fatty acids; Tx: ↓ these amino acids in diet *Propionyl-CoA carboxylase deficiency:* neonatal metabolic acidosis; hyperammonemia; elevated propionic acid, hydroxypropionic acid, and methylcitric acid; poor feeding, vomiting, lethargy, coma *Methylmalonyl-CoA mutase deficiency:* symptoms similar to propionyl CoA carboxylase deficiency, but accumulating metabolites differ (↑ methylmalonic acid)

Definition of abbreviation: PLP, pyridoxal-p, formed from vitamin B_6.

UREA CYCLE

Amino acids transported to the liver are transaminated to glutamate, which undergoes deamination to produce **NH4⁺** or transamination to make **aspartate**. Both of these are used for synthesis of urea in the liver for excretion via the **urea cycle**.

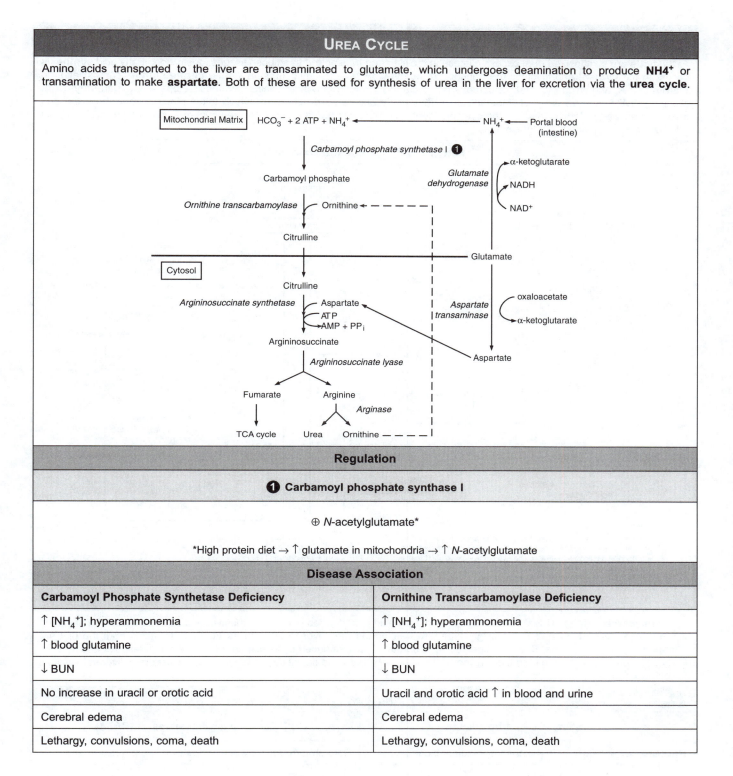

Regulation

❶ Carbamoyl phosphate synthase I

⊕ *N*-acetylglutamate*

*High protein diet → ↑ glutamate in mitochondria → ↑ *N*-acetylglutamate

Disease Association

Carbamoyl Phosphate Synthetase Deficiency	Ornithine Transcarbamoylase Deficiency
↑ [NH$_4^+$]; hyperammonemia	↑ [NH$_4^+$]; hyperammonemia
↑ blood glutamine	↑ blood glutamine
↓ BUN	↓ BUN
No increase in uracil or orotic acid	Uracil and orotic acid ↑ in blood and urine
Cerebral edema	Cerebral edema
Lethargy, convulsions, coma, death	Lethargy, convulsions, coma, death

LIPID SYNTHESIS AND METABOLISM

Fatty acids are synthesized from excess glucose in the liver and transported to adipose tissues for storage. Fatty acid **synthesis** occurs in the **cytosol** and involves the transport of **acetyl-CoA** from the mitochondria via the **citrate shuttle**, carboxylation to **malonyl CoA**, and linking together 2 carbons per cycle to form long fatty acid chains. Synthesis stops at C_{16} **palmitoyl-CoA**, requiring **7 ATP** and **14 NADPH**. Metabolism of fatty acids occurs by **β-oxidation**, which takes place in **mitochondria**, and involves transport of fatty acids from the cytosol via the **carnitine shuttle**, then oxidative removal of 2 carbons per cycle to yield **1 NADH**, **1 FADH$_2$**, and **1 acetyl-CoA**.

Fatty Acid Synthesis and Oxidation

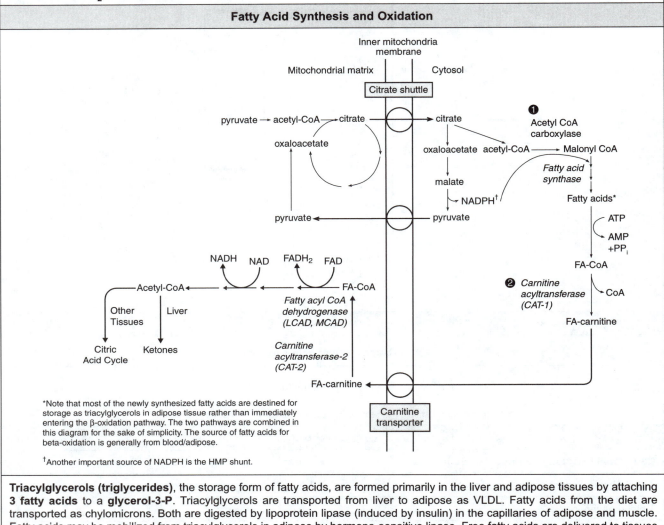

*Note that most of the newly synthesized fatty acids are destined for storage as triacylglycerols in adipose tissue rather than immediately entering the β-oxidation pathway. The two pathways are combined in this diagram for the sake of simplicity. The source of fatty acids for beta-oxidation is generally from blood/adipose.

†Another important source of NADPH is the HMP shunt.

Triacylglycerols (triglycerides), the storage form of fatty acids, are formed primarily in the liver and adipose tissues by attaching **3 fatty acids** to a **glycerol-3-P**. Triacylglycerols are transported from liver to adipose as VLDL. Fatty acids from the diet are transported as chylomicrons. Both are digested by lipoprotein lipase (induced by insulin) in the capillaries of adipose and muscle. Fatty acids may be mobilized from triacylglycerols in adipose by hormone-sensitive lipase. Free fatty acids are delivered to tissues for beta oxidation.

Regulation

❶ Acetyl-CoA carboxylase		❷ Carnitine acyltransferase-1 (CAT-1)
Rate-limiting for fatty acid synthesis; requires biotin		**Rate-limiting for fatty acid oxidation**
⊕ insulin ⊕ citrate	⊖ glucagon ⊖ palmitoyl-CoA	⊖ malonyl-CoA

Disease Association

Myopathic CAT/CPT Deficiency	Medium Chain Acyl-Dehydrogenase (MCAD) Deficiency
Muscle aches/weakness, myoglobulinuria provoked by prolonged exercise, ↑ muscle triacylglycerols	Fasting hypoglycemia, no ketone bodies, dicarboxylic acidemia, C8–C10 acyl carnitines in blood, vomiting, coma, death

(Continued)

Triacylglycerol (Triglyceride) Synthesis

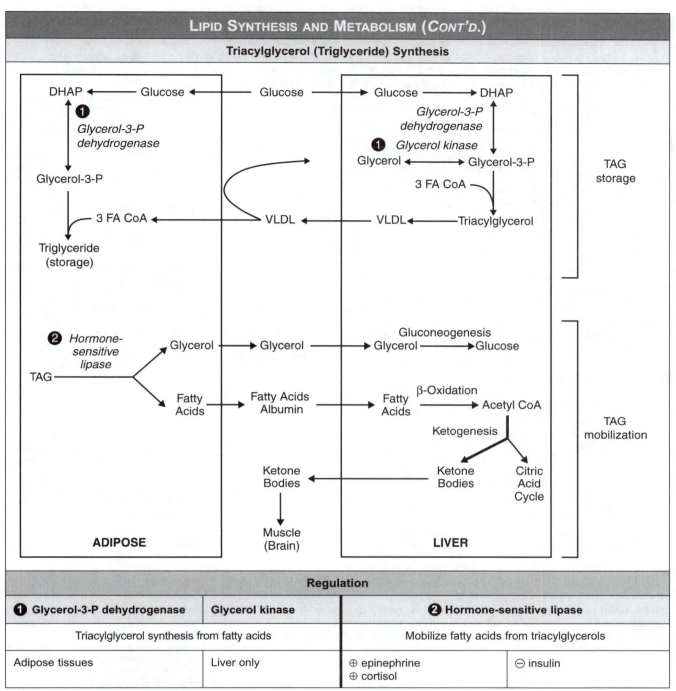

Regulation			
❶ **Glycerol-3-P dehydrogenase**	**Glycerol kinase**	❷ **Hormone-sensitive lipase**	
Triacylglycerol synthesis from fatty acids		Mobilize fatty acids from triacylglycerols	
Adipose tissues	Liver only	⊕ epinephrine ⊕ cortisol	⊖ insulin

Definition of abbreviations: CAT, carnitine acyltransferase (a.k.a. CPT, carnitine palmitoyl transferase); L/MCAD, long/medium chain acyl-dehydrogenase; TAG, triacylglycerols.

Diabetic ketoacidosis results from overactive hormone-sensitive lipase often in the context of stress, trauma, or infection.

KETONE BODY METABOLISM

During fasting, the liver converts excess acetyl-CoA from beta-oxidation of fatty acids into ketone bodies, **acetoacetate**, and **β-hydroxybutyrate**, which can be used by muscle and brain tissues. Ketosis represents a normal and advantageous response to fasting/starvation, whereas ketoacidosis is a pathologic condition associated with diabetes and other diseases.

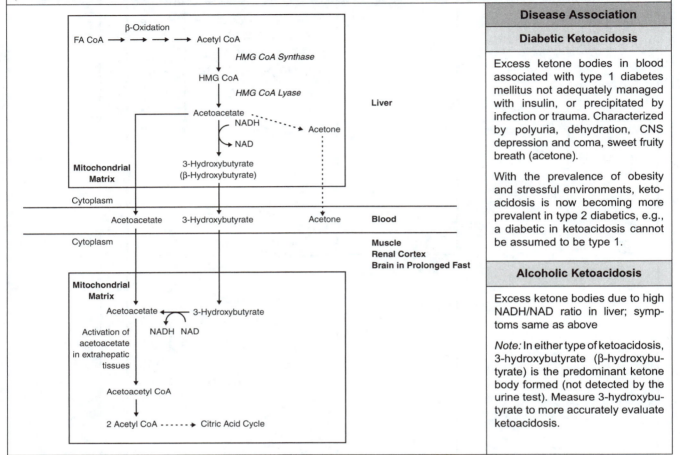

Disease Association

Diabetic Ketoacidosis

Excess ketone bodies in blood associated with type 1 diabetes mellitus not adequately managed with insulin, or precipitated by infection or trauma. Characterized by polyuria, dehydration, CNS depression and coma, sweet fruity breath (acetone).

With the prevalence of obesity and stressful environments, keto-acidosis is now becoming more prevalent in type 2 diabetics, e.g., a diabetic in ketoacidosis cannot be assumed to be type 1.

Alcoholic Ketoacidosis

Excess ketone bodies due to high NADH/NAD ratio in liver; symptoms same as above

Note: In either type of ketoacidosis, 3-hydroxybutyrate (β-hydroxybutyrate) is the predominant ketone body formed (not detected by the urine test). Measure 3-hydroxybutyrate to more accurately evaluate ketoacidosis.

CHOLESTEROL SYNTHESIS

Cholesterol is obtained from diet (about 20%) or synthesized de novo (about 80%). Synthesis occurs primarily in the liver for storage and bile acid synthesis, but also in adrenal cortex, ovaries, and testes for steroid hormone synthesis. Cholesterol may also be esterified into **cholesterol esters** by acyl-cholesterol acyl-transferase (**ACAT**) in cells for storage.

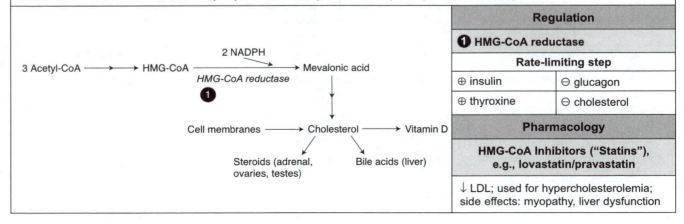

Regulation

❶ HMG-CoA reductase	
Rate-limiting step	
⊕ insulin	⊖ glucagon
⊕ thyroxine	⊖ cholesterol

Pharmacology

HMG-CoA Inhibitors ("Statins"), e.g., lovastatin/pravastatin

↓ LDL; used for hypercholesterolemia; side effects: myopathy, liver dysfunction

LIPOPROTEIN TRANSPORT AND METABOLISM

Free fatty acids are transported by serum albumin, whereas neutral lipids (triacylglycerols and cholesterol esters) are transported by **lipoproteins**. Lipoproteins consist of a hydrophilic shell and a hydrophobic core and are classified by their density into **chylomicrons**, **VLDL**, **LDL**, and **HDL**.

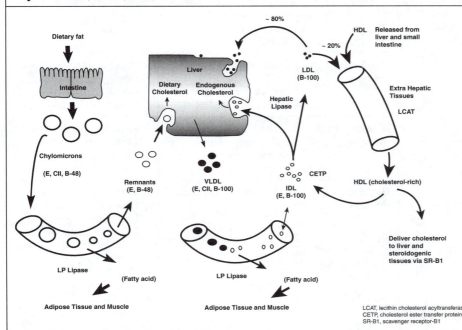

LCAT, lecithin cholesterol acyltransferase
CETP, cholesterol ester transfer protein
SR-B1, scavenger receptor-B1

Regulation

❶ Lipoprotein lipase

Hydrolyzes fatty acids from triacylglycerols from chylomicrons and VLDL

⊕ insulin

Hyperlipidemias

Type I Hypertriglyceridemia

Lipoprotein lipase deficiency; ↑ triacylglycerols and chylomicrons; orange-red eruptive xanthomas, fatty liver, acute pancreatitis, abdominal pain after fatty meal; autosomal recessive

Type II Hypercholesterolemia

LDL receptor deficiency; ↑ risk of atherosclerosis and CAD, xanthomas of Achilles tendon, tuberous xanthomas on elbows, xanthelasma (lipid in eyelid), corneal arcus, homozygotes die <20 years; autosomal dominant

Pharmacology

Cholestyramine/Colestipol

↑ Elimination of bile salts leads to ↑ LDL receptor expression, leading to ↓ LDL; for hypercholesterolemia; side effect: GI discomfort

Gemfibrozil/Clofibrate ("Fibrates")

↑ elimination of VLDL leads to ↓ triacylglycerols and ↑ HDL; for hypercholesterolemia; side effect: muscle toxicity

Nicotinic Acid

↓ VLDL synthesis leads to ↓ LDL; for hypercholesterolemia; side effects: GI irritation; hyperuricemia, hyperglycemia, flushing, pruritus

CLASSES OF LIPOPROTEINS AND IMPORTANT APOPROTEINS			
Lipoprotein	**Functions**	**Apoproteins**	**Functions**
Chylomicrons	Transport dietary triglyceride and cholesterol from intestine to tissues	apoB-48 apoC-II apoE	Secreted by epithelial cells Activates lipoprotein lipase Uptake by liver
VLDL	Transports triglyceride from liver to tissues	apoB-100 apoC-II apoE	Secreted by liver Activates lipoprotein lipase Uptake of remnants by liver
LDL	Delivers cholesterol into cells	apoB-100	Uptake by liver and other tissues via LDL receptor (apoB-100 receptor)
IDL (VLDL remnants)	Picks up cholesterol from HDL to become LDL Picked up by liver	apoE	Uptake by liver
HDL	Picks up cholesterol accumulating in blood vessels Delivers cholesterol to liver and steroidogenic tissues via scavenger receptor (SR-B1) Shuttles apoC-II and apoE in blood	apoA-1	Activates LCAT to produce cholesterol esters

Definition of abbreviations: CAD, coronary artery disease; CETP, cholesterol ester transfer protein; HDL, high-density lipoprotein; LCAT, lecithin-cholesterol acyl transferase; LDL, low-density lipoprotein; SR-B1, scavenger receptor B1; triglyceride, triacylglycerol; VLDL, very-low-density lipoprotein.

LIPID DERIVATIVES

Important lipid derivatives include **phospholipids**, **sphingolipids**, and **eicosanoids** (prostaglandins, thromboxanes, and leukotrienes).

Synthesis of Sphingolipids

From Serine → Sphingosine
From Fatty Acid →

Fatty Acyl CoA

Ceramide

CDP-Choline | UDP-Glucose UDP-Galactose

P-Choline

Sphingomyelin (phospholipid)

Cerebrosides

UDP-Sugars

CMP-Sialic Acid (N-acetylneuraminic acid, NANA)

Gangliosides (glycolipid)

Eicosanoid Metabolism

Membrane Phospholipids
↓ Phospholipase A₂ ⊖ — Corticosteroids
Arachidonic Acid
NSAIDs ⊖
Cyclooxygenases   Lipoxygenase ⊖ — Zileuton
COX1
COXibs ⊖ → COX2
Endoperoxides   Hydroperoxides
PGI₂   TXA₂   Leukotrienes
PGE₁ PGE₂   Receptors blocked by – Lukasts
PGF₂α

Lysosomal Storage Diseases

Disease	Deficiency and Accumulated Substrate	Features	
Tay-Sachs disease	↓ Hexosaminidase A ↑ GM₂ ganglioside *(whorled membranes in lysosomes)*	• Psychomotor retardation • Cherry red spots in macula • Death <2 years	AR*
Niemann-Pick disease	↓ Sphingomyelinase ↑ Sphingomyelin *(zebra bodies in lysosomes)*	• Hepatosplenomegaly • Microcephaly • Mental retardation • Foamy macrophages	AR*
Gaucher disease	↓ β-glucocerebrosidase ↑ Glucocerebroside	• Three clinical subtypes; type 1 is most common • Hepatosplenomegaly • Bone involvement, including fractures and bone pain • Neurologic defects (rare, types 2 and 3) • Mental retardation • Gaucher cells (enlarged macrophages with fibrillary cytoplasm)	AR
Fabry disease	↓ α-galactosidase A ↑ Ceramide trihexoside	• Renal failure • Telangiectasias • Angiokeratomas • Peripheral neuropathy with pain in extremities	XR
Metachromatic leukodystrophy	↓ arylsulfatase A ↑ sulfatide	• Ataxia • Dementia • Seizures	AR
Hurler syndrome (MPSI)	↓ α-L-iduronidase ↑ dermatan sulfate ↑ heparan sulfate	• Coarse facial features • Corneal clouding • Hepatosplenomegaly • Skeletal deformities • Upper airway obstruction • Recurrent ear infections • Hearing loss • Hydrocephalus • Mental retardation • Death <10 years	AR
Hunter syndrome (MPSII)	↓ L-iduronate-2-sulfatase ↑ dermatan sulfate ↑ heparan sulfate	• Both mild and severe forms • Severe similar to Hurler but retinal degeneration instead of corneal clouding, aggressive behavior, and death <15 years • Mild form compatible with long life	XR

Definition of abbreviations: AR, autosomal recessive; COX, cyclooxygenase; NSAIDs, nonsteroidal anti-inflammatory drugs; XR, X-linked recessive.
*Common in Ashkenazi Jews

ENZYME KINETICS

Whereas the thermodynamic equilibrium of a chemical reaction is determined by its **free energy** (ΔG), the rate at which the reaction reaches equilibrium is determined by its **activation energy** ($\Delta G^{\ddagger}$). Enzymes increase the rate of a reaction by reducing the energy of activation without affecting the equilibrium constant.

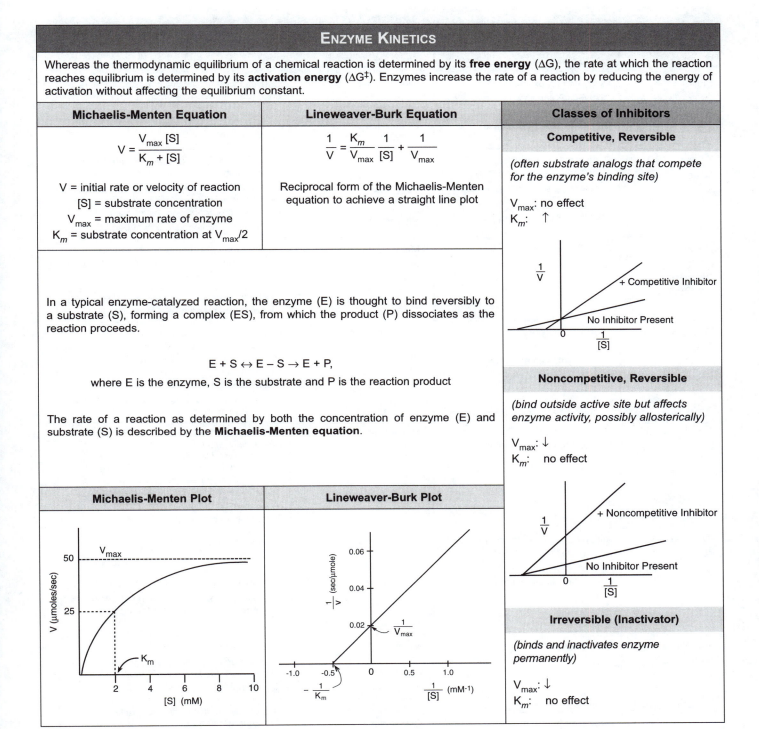

Michaelis-Menten Equation

$$V = \frac{V_{max}\,[S]}{K_m + [S]}$$

V = initial rate or velocity of reaction
[S] = substrate concentration
V_{max} = maximum rate of enzyme
K_m = substrate concentration at $V_{max}/2$

In a typical enzyme-catalyzed reaction, the enzyme (E) is thought to bind reversibly to a substrate (S), forming a complex (ES), from which the product (P) dissociates as the reaction proceeds.

$$E + S \leftrightarrow E - S \rightarrow E + P,$$

where E is the enzyme, S is the substrate and P is the reaction product

The rate of a reaction as determined by both the concentration of enzyme (E) and substrate (S) is described by the **Michaelis-Menten equation**.

Lineweaver-Burk Equation

$$\frac{1}{V} = \frac{K_m}{V_{max}}\frac{1}{[S]} + \frac{1}{V_{max}}$$

Reciprocal form of the Michaelis-Menten equation to achieve a straight line plot

Classes of Inhibitors

Competitive, Reversible

(often substrate analogs that compete for the enzyme's binding site)

V_{max}: no effect
K_m: ↑

Noncompetitive, Reversible

(bind outside active site but affects enzyme activity, possibly allosterically)

V_{max}: ↓
K_m: no effect

Irreversible (Inactivator)

(binds and inactivates enzyme permanently)

V_{max}: ↓
K_m: no effect

Michaelis-Menten Plot

Lineweaver-Burk Plot

Vitamin or Coenzyme	Enzyme	Pathway	Deficiency
Biotin	Pyruvate carboxylase Acetyl-CoA carboxylase Propionyl-CoA carboxylase	Gluconeogenesis Fatty acid synthesis Odd-carbon fatty acids, Val, Met, Ile, Thr	Causes (rare): excessive consumption of raw eggs (contain avidin, a biotin-binding protein) Alopecia (hair loss), bowel inflammation, muscle pain
Thiamine (B$_1$)	Pyruvate dehydrogenase α-Ketoglutarate dehydrogenase Transketolase	PDH TCA cycle HMP shunt	Causes: alcoholism (alcohol interferes with absorption) Wernicke (ataxia, nystagmus, ophthalmoplegia) Korsakoff (confabulation, psychosis) High-output cardiac failure (wet beri-beri)
Niacin (B$_3$) NAD(H) NADP(H)	Dehydrogenases	Many	Pellagra may also be related to deficiency of tryptophan (corn major dietary staple), which supplies a portion of the niacin requirement Pellagra: diarrhea, dementia, dermatitis, and, if not treated, death
Folic acid THF	Thymidylate synthase Purine synthesis enzymes	Thymidine (pyrimidine) synthesis Purine synthesis	Causes: alcoholics and pregnancy (body stores depleted in 3 months) Homocystinemia with risk of deep vein thrombosis and atherosclerosis Megaloblastic (macrocytic) anemia Deficiency in early pregnancy causes neural tube defects in fetus
Cyanocobalamin (B$_{12}$)	Homocysteine methyltransferase Methyl-malonyl-CoA mutase	Methionine, SAM Odd-carbon fatty acids, Val, Met, Ile, Thr	Causes: pernicious anemia. Also in aging, especially with poor nutrition, bacterial overgrowth of terminal ileum, resection of the terminal ileum secondary to Crohn disease, chronic pancreatitis, and, rarely, vegans, or infection with *Diphyllobothrium latum* Megaloblastic (macrocytic) anemia Progressive peripheral neuropathy
Pyridoxine (B$_6$) PLP	Aminotransferases (transaminase): AST (SGOT), ALT (SGPT) δ-Aminolevulinate synthase	Protein catabolism Heme synthesis	Causes: isoniazid therapy Sideroblastic anemia Cheilosis or stomatitis (cracking or scaling of lip borders and corners of the mouth) Convulsions
Riboflavin (B$_2$) FAD(H$_2$)	Dehydrogenases	Many	Corneal neovascularization Cheilosis or stomatitis (cracking or scaling of lip borders and corners of the mouth) Magenta-colored tongue
Ascorbate (C)	Prolyl and lysyl hydroxylases Dopamine β-hydroxylase	Collagen synthesis Catecholamine synthesis Absorption of iron in GI tract	Causes: diet deficient in citrus fruits and green vegetables Scurvy: poor wound healing, easy bruising (perifollicular hemorrhage), bleeding gums, increased bleeding time, painful glossitis, anemia
Pantothenic acid CoA	Fatty acid synthase Fatty acyl CoA synthetase Pyruvate dehydrogenase α-Ketoglutarate dehydrogenase	Fatty acid metabolism PDH TCA cycle	Rare

Definition of abbreviations: ALT, alanine aminotransferase; AST, aspartate aminotransferase; CoA, coenzyme A; FAD(H$_2$), flavin adenine dinucleotide; HMP, hexose monophosphate shunt; NAD(H); nicotinamide adenine dinucleotide; NADP(H), nicotinamide adenine dinucleotide phosphate; PDH, pyruvate dehydrogenase; PLP, pyridoxal phosphate, SAM, S-adenosylmethionine; TCA, tricarboxylic acid cycle; THF, tetrahydrofolate.

LIPID-SOLUBLE VITAMINS		
Vitamin	**Important Functions**	**Deficiency**
D (cholecalciferol)	In response to hypocalcemia, helps normalize serum calcium levels	Rickets (in childhood): skeletal abnormalities (especially legs), muscle weakness After epiphysial fusion: osteomalacia
A (carotene)	Retinoic acid and retinol act as growth regulators, especially in epithelium Retinal is important in rod and cone cells for vision	Night blindness, metaplasia of corneal epithelium, dry eyes, bronchitis, pneumonia, follicular hyperkeratosis
K	Carboxylation of glutamic acid residues in many Ca^{2+}-binding proteins, importantly coagulation factors II, VII, IX, and X, as well as proteins C and S	Easy bruising, bleeding Increased prothrombin time Associated with fat malabsorption, long-term antibiotic therapy, breast-fed newborns, infants of mothers who took anticonvulsants during pregnancy
E (α-tocopherol)	Antioxidant in the lipid phase; protects membrane lipids from peroxidation and helps prevent oxidation of LDL particles thought to be involved in atherosclerotic plaque formation	Hemolysis, neurologic problems, retinitis pigmentosa

Molecular Biology, Genetics, and Cell Biology

NUCLEIC ACID STRUCTURE

Nucleic acids, including **DNA** and **RNA**, are assembled from **nucleotides**, which contain a five-carbon sugar, a nitrogenous base, and phosphate. The sugar may be **ribose** (RNA) or **deoxyribose** (DNA). The base can be a **purine** (adenine or guanine) or **pyrimidine** (cytosine, uracil, thymidine). Phosphate groups link the 3′ carbon of one sugar to the 5′ carbon of the next, forming phosphate bonds. Base sequences are conventionally written in a **5′ → 3′** direction. Nucleotides lacking phosphate groups are called **nucleosides**. In eukaryotes, RNA is generally single-stranded, while DNA is generally double-stranded in an **antiparallel** orientation, with two hydrogen bonds between base pairs **A and T** and three between **G and C**. Nuclear DNA forms a **double-helix**, which undergoes **supercoiling** via **topoisomerase** activity, and is generally associated with **histones** and other proteins to form **nucleosomes**, the basic packaging unit of **chromatin**.

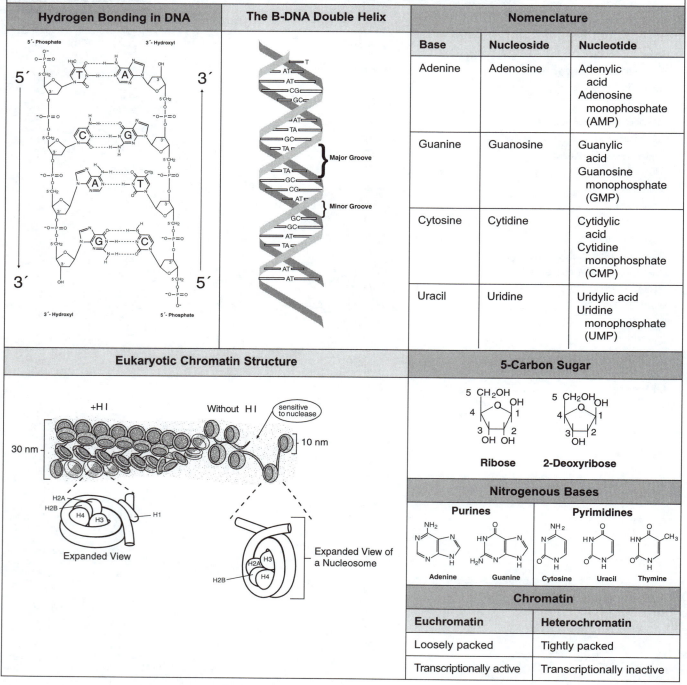

Hydrogen Bonding in DNA

The B-DNA Double Helix

Nomenclature

Base	Nucleoside	Nucleotide
Adenine	Adenosine	Adenylic acid Adenosine monophosphate (AMP)
Guanine	Guanosine	Guanylic acid Guanosine monophosphate (GMP)
Cytosine	Cytidine	Cytidylic acid Cytidine monophosphate (CMP)
Uracil	Uridine	Uridylic acid Uridine monophosphate (UMP)

Eukaryotic Chromatin Structure

5-Carbon Sugar

Ribose   2-Deoxyribose

Nitrogenous Bases

Purines: Adenine, Guanine

Pyrimidines: Cytosine, Uracil, Thymine

Chromatin

Euchromatin	Heterochromatin
Loosely packed	Tightly packed
Transcriptionally active	Transcriptionally inactive

Nucleotides for DNA and RNA synthesis can be generated by de novo synthesis or salvage pathways, both of which require **PRPP** generated from ribose-5-phosphate derived from the HMP shunt. **De novo synthesis** occurs mainly in the liver and generates new purine and pyrimidine bases from precursors. In contrast, **salvage pathways** reuse preformed bases derived from nucleotides during normal RNA turnover or released from dying cells or transported from the liver. Ribonucleotides are converted to deoxyribonucleotides for DNA synthesis by **ribonucleotide reductase**. Excretion of purine bases occurs in the form of **uric acid** from the kidneys.

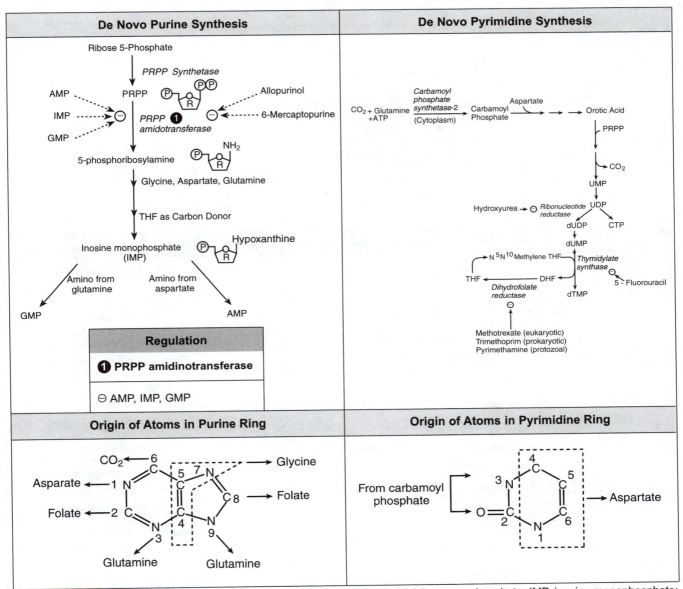

Definition of abbreviations: AMP, adenosine monophosphate; dTMP, deoxythymidine monophosphate; IMP, inosine monophosphate; dUDP, deoxyuridine diphosphate; CTP, cytosine triphosphate; THF, tetrahydrofolate.

(Continued)

Disease Association
Adenosine Deaminase Deficiency
• SCID (no B- or T-cell function) • Multiple infections in children • Autosomal recessive • Tx: enzyme replacement, bone marrow transplant
Gout
↑ production or ↓ excretion of uric acid by kidneys
Lesch-Nyhan Syndrome
• HGPRT deficiency • Mental retardation (mild) • Spastic cerebral palsy • Self-mutilation • Hyperuricemia • X-linked recessive

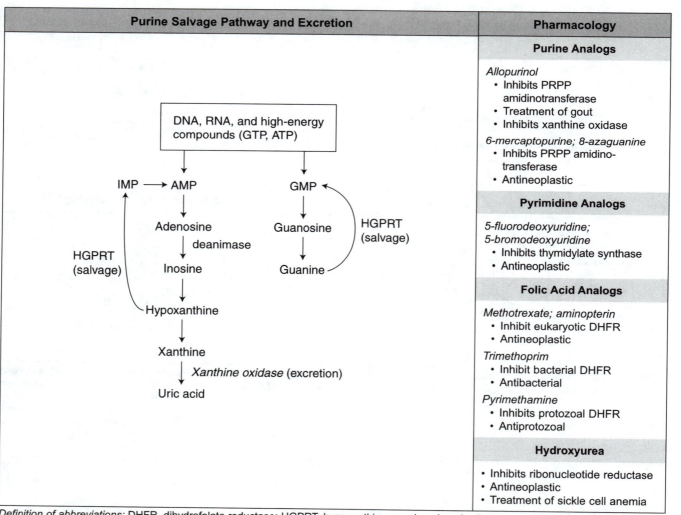

Purine Salvage Pathway and Excretion

DNA, RNA, and high-energy compounds (GTP, ATP)

IMP → AMP   GMP

Adenosine   Guanosine

deanimase   HGPRT
                                       (salvage)
Inosine   Guanine

HGPRT
(salvage)

Hypoxanthine

Xanthine

Xanthine oxidase (excretion)

Uric acid

Pharmacology

Purine Analogs

Allopurinol
• Inhibits PRPP amidinotransferase
• Treatment of gout
• Inhibits xanthine oxidase

6-mercaptopurine; 8-azaguanine
• Inhibits PRPP amidino-transferase
• Antineoplastic

Pyrimidine Analogs

5-fluorodeoxyuridine; 5-bromodeoxyuridine
• Inhibits thymidylate synthase
• Antineoplastic

Folic Acid Analogs

Methotrexate; aminopterin
• Inhibit eukaryotic DHFR
• Antineoplastic

Trimethoprim
• Inhibit bacterial DHFR
• Antibacterial

Pyrimethamine
• Inhibits protozoal DHFR
• Antiprotozoal

Hydroxyurea

• Inhibits ribonucleotide reductase
• Antineoplastic
• Treatment of sickle cell anemia

Definition of abbreviations: DHFR, dihydrofolate reductase; HGPRT, hypoxanthine-guanine phosphoribosyl pyrophosphate transferase; NSAID, nonsteroidal anti-inflammatory drug; PRPP, phosphoribosylpyrophosphate; THF, tetrahydrofolate; SCID, severe combined immunodeficiency disorder.

DNA REPLICATION

DNA replication involves the synthesis of new DNA molecules in a 5′ → 3′ direction by **DNA polymerase** using the double-stranded DNA template. One strand (**leading strand**) is made continuously, while the other (**lagging strand**) is synthesized in segments. **Prokaryotic** chromosomes are closed, double-stranded circular DNA molecules with a single origin of replication that separate into two replication forks moving away in opposite directions. **Eukaryotic** chromosomes are double-stranded and linear with multiple origins of replication.

DNA Replication by a Semiconservative, Bidirectional Mechanism

Prokaryotes

Origin of Replication

Eukaryotes

Multiple Origins of Replication

Centromere

Sister Chromatids Are Separated During Mitosis

Events at the Replication Fork

5′ 3′ Single-strand binding proteins

Helicase

Primase

DNA pol III (holo)

DNA pol I

Ligase

Okazaki fragment

3′

5′

Lagging strand

5′

3′

Lagging strand

Regulation		
	Prokaryote	**Eukaryote**
Recognizing replication origin	dna A	Unknown
Unwinding double helix	Helicase	Helicase
Strand stabilization	SSB	SSB
RNA primer synthesis	Primase	Primase
Leading strand synthesis	DNA pol III	DNA pol δ
Lagging strand synthesis	DNA pol III	DNA pol α
RNA primer removal	DNA pol I (5′→ 3′ exonuclease)	Unknown
Replacing RNA with DNA	DNA pol I	Unknown
Joining of Okazaki fragments	DNA ligase (use NAD)	DNA ligase (use ATP)
Removing positive supercoils ahead of replication fork	DNA topo II (DNA gyrase)	DNA topo II
Telomere synthesis	Not required	Telomerase

Pharmacology
Pyrimidine Analogs

Cytosine arabinoside
- Incorporation stops chain elongation
- Antineoplastic

Definition of abbreviations: DNA, deoxyribonucleic acid; DNA pol, DNA polymerase; DNA topo, DNA topoisomerase; RNA, ribonucleic acid; SSB, single-stranded DNA-binding protein.

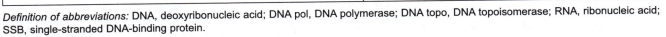

DNA REPAIR

DNA sequence and structure may be altered either during replication or by exposure to chemicals or radiation. Mutations include point mutations such as **insertion** or **deletion** of bases, or **substitution** of one base with another. Substitution mutations in the third position of a codon (**wobble position**) are usually benign because several codons code for the same amino acid. Other types of mutations include (1) large segment deletions (e.g., unequal crossover during meiosis), (2) mutations of 5′ or 3′ splice sites, or (3) triplet repeat expansion, which can lead to a longer, more unstable protein product (e.g., Huntington disease).

Damage	Cause	Recognition/ Excision Enzyme	Repair Enzymes	Types of Mutations		
Thymine dimers (G_1)	UV radiation	Excision endonuclease (deficient in xeroderma pigmentosum)	DNA polymerase DNA ligase	**Transition:** A:T → G:C or G:C → A:T **Transversion:** A:T → T:A or G:C → C:G		
Cytosine deamination (G_1)	Spontaneous/ chemicals	Uracil glycosylase AP endonuclease	DNA polymerase DNA ligase	**Silent**	No change in AA	Sub
Apurination or apyrimidination (G_1)	Spontaneous/ heat	AP endonuclease	DNA polymerase DNA ligase	**Missense**	Change AA to another	Sub
Mismatched base (G_2)	DNA replication errors	A mutation on one of two genes, *hMSH2* or *hMLH1*, initiates defective repair of DNA mismatches, resulting in a condition known as hereditary nonpolyposis colorectal cancer—HNPCC.	DNA polymerase DNA ligase	**Nonsense**	Early stop codon	Sub or Ins/Del
				Frameshift	Misreading of all codons downstream	Ins/Del

Thymine Dimer Repair

Thymine dimer

Incision step
Nicking by UV-specific endonuclease

Removal by associated helicase
5′ ⟶ 3′

DNA polymerase I synthesizes new DNA
P

Ligation by DNA ligase

DNA Repair Defects

Xeroderma Pigmentosum

(defect in nucleotide excision-repair)
- Extreme UV sensitivity
- Excessive freckling
- Multiple skin cancers
- Corneal ulcerations
- Autosomal recessive

Ataxia Telangiectasia

(defect in ATM gene product, a member of PI-3 kinase family involved in mitogenic signal transduction, detection of DNA damage, and cell cycle control)
- Sensitivity to ionizing radiation
- Degenerative ataxia
- Dilated blood vessels
- Chromosomal aberrations
- Lymphomas
- Autosomal recessive

HNPCC

(defect in mismatch repair; usually hMSH2 or hMLH1 gene)
- Colorectal cancer
- $2/3$ occur in right colon
- Autosomal dominant

Definition of abbreviations: AA, amino acid; HNPCC, hereditary nonpolyposis colorectal cancer; Ins/Del, insert or deletion; Sub, substitution

TRANSCRIPTION AND RNA PROCESSING

Transcription involves the synthesis of an RNA in a 5′ → 3′ direction by an RNA polymerase using DNA as a template. An important class of RNA is messenger RNA (mRNA). Initiation of transcription occurs from a promoter region, which is the binding site of RNA polymerase, and stops at a termination signal. In **prokaryotes**, a single mRNA transcript can encode several genes (**polycistronic**), and no RNA processing is required, allowing transcription and translation to proceed simultaneously. In **eukaryotes**, all mRNAs are **monocistronic**, but often include coding segments (**exons**) interrupted by noncoding regions (**introns**). Eukaryotic mRNAs must therefore undergo extensive processing, including a 5′ cap, a 3′ tail, and **splicing** of introns. Ribosomal RNA (rRNA) and transfer RNA (tRNA) are also produced by transcription.

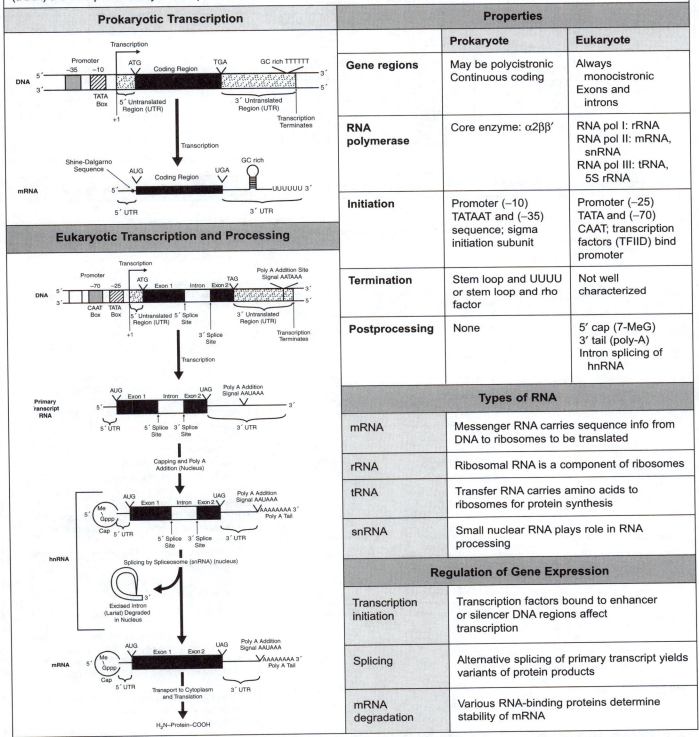

Prokaryotic Transcription

Eukaryotic Transcription and Processing

Properties

	Prokaryote	Eukaryote
Gene regions	May be polycistronic Continuous coding	Always monocistronic Exons and introns
RNA polymerase	Core enzyme: $\alpha 2\beta\beta'$	RNA pol I: rRNA RNA pol II: mRNA, snRNA RNA pol III: tRNA, 5S rRNA
Initiation	Promoter (−10) TATAAT and (−35) sequence; sigma initiation subunit	Promoter (−25) TATA and (−70) CAAT; transcription factors (TFIID) bind promoter
Termination	Stem loop and UUUU or stem loop and rho factor	Not well characterized
Postprocessing	None	5′ cap (7-MeG) 3′ tail (poly-A) Intron splicing of hnRNA

Types of RNA

mRNA	Messenger RNA carries sequence info from DNA to ribosomes to be translated
rRNA	Ribosomal RNA is a component of ribosomes
tRNA	Transfer RNA carries amino acids to ribosomes for protein synthesis
snRNA	Small nuclear RNA plays role in RNA processing

Regulation of Gene Expression

Transcription initiation	Transcription factors bound to enhancer or silencer DNA regions affect transcription
Splicing	Alternative splicing of primary transcript yields variants of protein products
mRNA degradation	Various RNA-binding proteins determine stability of mRNA

Definition of abbreviations: hnRNA, heterogenous nuclear RNA; 7-MeG, 7-methylguanosine; RNA pol, RNA polymerase; UTR, untranslated region.

PROTEIN TRANSLATION

Translation involves the synthesis of protein from mRNA templates in **ribosomes** (complexes of proteins and ribosomal RNAs [**rRNA**]). Protein synthesis begins from an initiation codon (**AUG** = methionine) and ends at a stop codon (**UAA, UGA,** or **UAG**). Elongation involves transfer RNAs (**tRNA**), which have an anticodon region at one end to recognize the codon on the mRNA and an amino acid attached at the other end for covalent linkage to the growing polypeptide chain. Several ribosomes can simultaneously transcribe an mRNA, forming a polyribosome, or **polysome**.

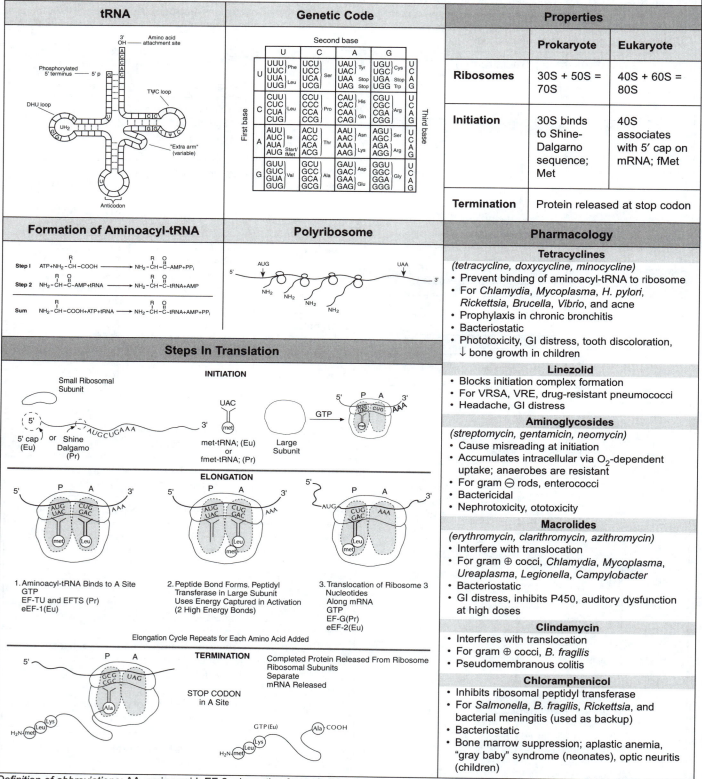

tRNA

Genetic Code

Properties

	Prokaryote	Eukaryote
Ribosomes	30S + 50S = 70S	40S + 60S = 80S
Initiation	30S binds to Shine-Dalgarno sequence; Met	40S associates with 5′ cap on mRNA; fMet
Termination	Protein released at stop codon	

Formation of Aminoacyl-tRNA

Polyribosome

Pharmacology

Tetracyclines
(tetracycline, doxycycline, minocycline)
- Prevent binding of aminoacyl-tRNA to ribosome
- For *Chlamydia, Mycoplasma, H. pylori, Rickettsia, Brucella, Vibrio,* and acne
- Prophylaxis in chronic bronchitis
- Bacteriostatic
- Phototoxicity, GI distress, tooth discoloration, ↓ bone growth in children

Linezolid
- Blocks initiation complex formation
- For VRSA, VRE, drug-resistant pneumococci
- Headache, GI distress

Aminoglycosides
(streptomycin, gentamicin, neomycin)
- Cause misreading at initiation
- Accumulates intracellular via O_2-dependent uptake; anaerobes are resistant
- For gram ⊖ rods, enterococci
- Bactericidal
- Nephrotoxicity, ototoxicity

Macrolides
(erythromycin, clarithromycin, azithromycin)
- Interfere with translocation
- For gram ⊕ cocci, *Chlamydia, Mycoplasma, Ureaplasma, Legionella, Campylobacter*
- Bacteriostatic
- GI distress, inhibits P450, auditory dysfunction at high doses

Clindamycin
- Interferes with translocation
- For gram ⊕ cocci, *B. fragilis*
- Pseudomembranous colitis

Chloramphenicol
- Inhibits ribosomal peptidyl transferase
- For *Salmonella, B. fragilis, Rickettsia,* and bacterial meningitis (used as backup)
- Bacteriostatic
- Bone marrow suppression; aplastic anemia, "gray baby" syndrome (neonates), optic neuritis (children)

Steps In Translation

INITIATION

ELONGATION

1. Aminoacyl-tRNA Binds to A Site GTP EF-TU and EFTS (Pr) eEF-1(Eu)

2. Peptide Bond Forms. Peptidyl Transferase in Large Subunit Uses Energy Captured in Activation (2 High Energy Bonds)

3. Translocation of Ribosome 3 Nucleotides Along mRNA GTP EF-G(Pr) eEF-2(Eu)

Elongation Cycle Repeats for Each Amino Acid Added

TERMINATION

Completed Protein Released From Ribosome Ribosomal Subunits Separate mRNA Released

STOP CODON in A Site

Definition of abbreviations: AA, amino acid; EF-2, elongation factor 2; fMet, formylmethionine; Met, methionine; VRE, vancomycin-resistant enterococci; VRSA, vancomycin-resistant *Staphylococcus aureus*.

POST-TRANSLATIONAL MODIFICATIONS

Whereas cytoplasmic proteins are translated on free cytoplasmic ribosomes, secreted proteins, membrane proteins, and lysosomal enzymes have an *N*-terminal hydrophobic signal sequence and are translated on ribosomes associated with the rough endoplasmic reticulum (RER). After translation, proteins acquire more complex structures by being folded with the help of molecular **chaperones**. Misfolded proteins are targeted for destruction by **ubiquitin** and digested in cytoplasmic protein-digesting complexes called **proteasomes**.

Co- and Postranslational Covalent Modifications		Protein Structure	
Glycosylation	Addition of oligosaccharides	**Primary**	Amino acid sequence
Phosphorylation	Addition of phosphate groups by protein kinases	**Secondary**	α-Helix or β-sheets
γ-carboxylation (vitamin K dependent)	Creation of Ca^{2+} binding sites	**Tertiary**	Higher order 3D structure
Prenylation	Addition of farnesyl/geranyl lipid groups to membrane proteins	**Quaternary**	Multiple subunits
Mannose phosphorylation	Addition of phosphates onto mannose residues to target protein to lysosomes		

Synthesis of Secretory, Membrane, and Lysosomal Proteins

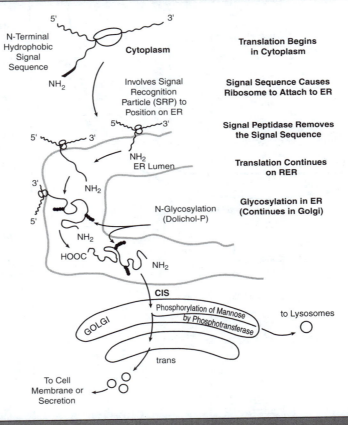

Disease Association

I-Cell Disease

(defect in mannose phosphorylation, causing lysosomal enzyme release into extracellular space)

- Coarse facial features, gingival hyperplasia, macroglossia
- Craniofacial abnormalities, joint immobility, club-foot, claw-hand, scoliosis
- Psychomotor and growth retardation
- Cardiorespiratory failure
- Death in first decade
- 10–20-fold increase in lysosomal enzyme activity in serum

COLLAGEN SYNTHESIS

Collagen is a structural protein composed of a triple helix of amino acid chains containing a repeating tripeptide Gly-X-Y-Gly-X-Y, where the unique amino acids **hydroxyproline** and **hydroxylysine** are frequently found in the X position. Hydroxylation of proline and lysine requires ascorbate (vitamin C), deficiency of which leads to scurvy.

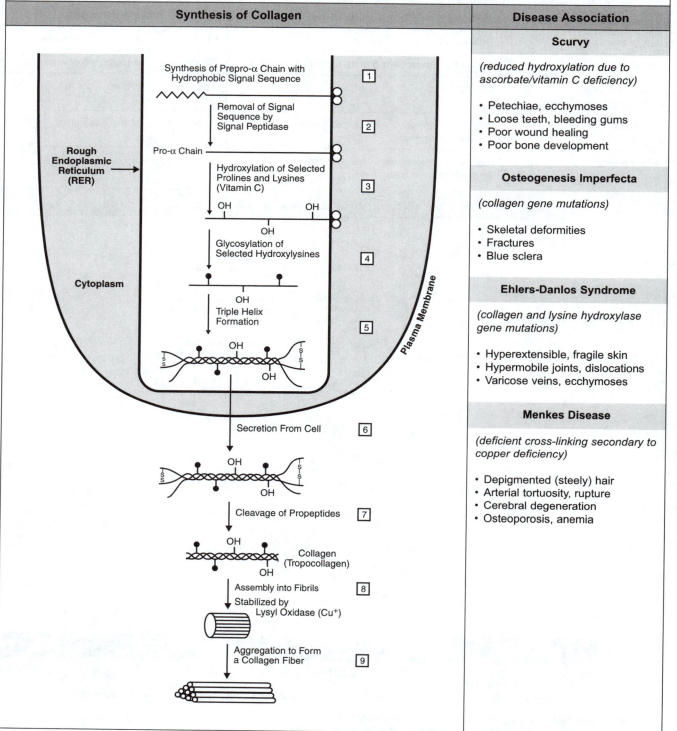

Synthesis of Collagen

Synthesis of Prepro-α Chain with Hydrophobic Signal Sequence [1]

Removal of Signal Sequence by Signal Peptidase [2]

Pro-α Chain

Hydroxylation of Selected Prolines and Lysines (Vitamin C) [3]

Glycosylation of Selected Hydroxylysines [4]

Triple Helix Formation [5]

Rough Endoplasmic Reticulum (RER)

Cytoplasm

Plasma Membrane

Secretion From Cell [6]

Cleavage of Propeptides [7]

Collagen (Tropocollagen)

Assembly into Fibrils Stabilized by Lysyl Oxidase (Cu⁺) [8]

Aggregation to Form a Collagen Fiber [9]

Disease Association

Scurvy

(reduced hydroxylation due to ascorbate/vitamin C deficiency)

- Petechiae, ecchymoses
- Loose teeth, bleeding gums
- Poor wound healing
- Poor bone development

Osteogenesis Imperfecta

(collagen gene mutations)

- Skeletal deformities
- Fractures
- Blue sclera

Ehlers-Danlos Syndrome

(collagen and lysine hydroxylase gene mutations)

- Hyperextensible, fragile skin
- Hypermobile joints, dislocations
- Varicose veins, ecchymoses

Menkes Disease

(deficient cross-linking secondary to copper deficiency)

- Depigmented (steely) hair
- Arterial tortuosity, rupture
- Cerebral degeneration
- Osteoporosis, anemia

RECOMBINANT DNA

Recombinant DNA technology allows DNA fragments to be copied, manipulated, and analyzed in vitro. Eukaryotic DNA fragments may be **genomic DNA** containing both introns and exons, or **complementary DNA (cDNA)**, which is reverse-transcribed from mRNA and contains exons only. DNA fragments may be amplified by **polymerase chain reaction (PCR)**, cut with specific **restriction endonucleases**, and ligated into a **DNA vector**. These vectors can then be used for further manipulation or amplification of the DNA to produce genomic DNA or cDNA (expression) libraries, to generate recombinant proteins, or for incorporation into humans (**gene therapy**) or other animals (**transgenic animals**).

Formation of a Recombinant Plasmid	Polymerase Chain Reaction

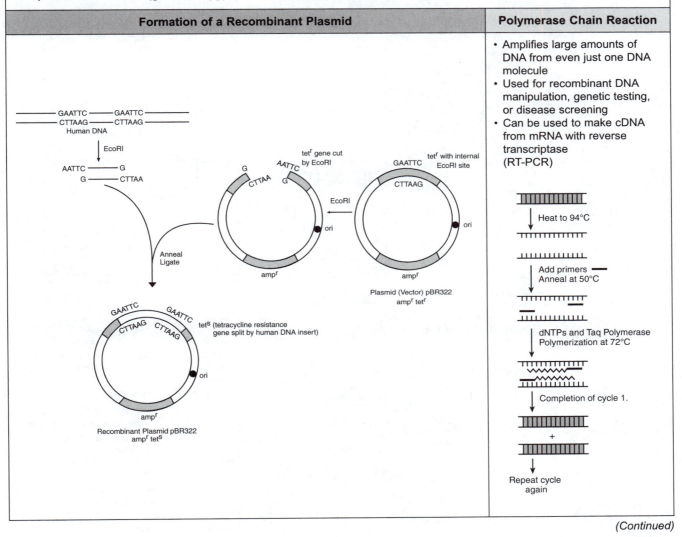

Polymerase Chain Reaction

- Amplifies large amounts of DNA from even just one DNA molecule
- Used for recombinant DNA manipulation, genetic testing, or disease screening
- Can be used to make cDNA from mRNA with reverse transcriptase (RT-PCR)

(Continued)

RECOMBINANT DNA (*Cont'd.*)

Screening a DNA Library

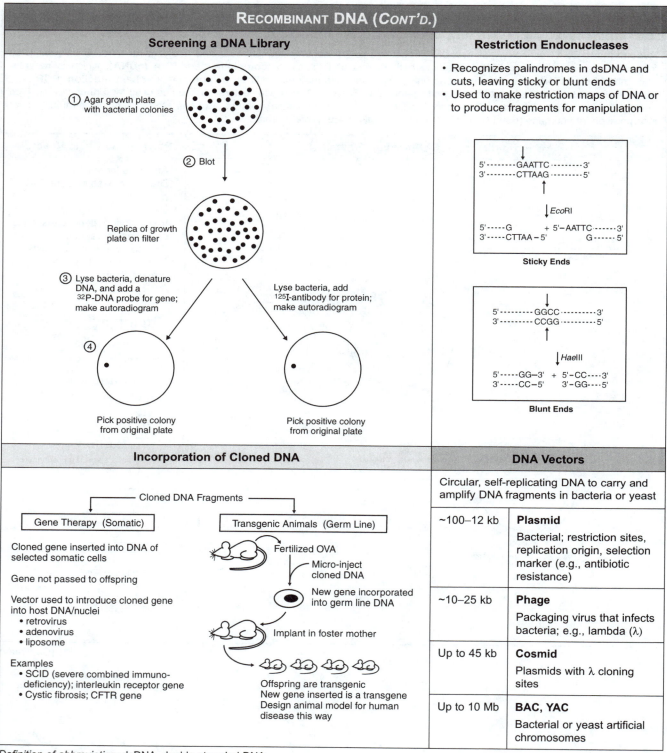

① Agar growth plate with bacterial colonies

② Blot

Replica of growth plate on filter

③ Lyse bacteria, denature DNA, and add a ^{32}P-DNA probe for gene; make autoradiogram

Lyse bacteria, add ^{125}I-antibody for protein; make autoradiogram

④

Pick positive colony from original plate

Pick positive colony from original plate

Restriction Endonucleases

- Recognizes palindromes in dsDNA and cuts, leaving sticky or blunt ends
- Used to make restriction maps of DNA or to produce fragments for manipulation

```
5' -------- GAATTC -------- 3'
3' -------- CTTAAG -------- 5'
           ↓EcoRI
5' ----- G        + 5'-AATTC ----- 3'
3' ----- CTTAA - 5'         G ----- 5'
```

Sticky Ends

```
5' -------- GGCC -------- 3'
3' -------- CCGG -------- 5'
           ↓HaeIII
5' ----- GG-3'  + 5'-CC ---- 3'
3' ----- CC-5'    3'-GG ---- 5'
```

Blunt Ends

Incorporation of Cloned DNA

Cloned DNA Fragments

Gene Therapy (Somatic)

Cloned gene inserted into DNA of selected somatic cells

Gene not passed to offspring

Vector used to introduce cloned gene into host DNA/nuclei
- retrovirus
- adenovirus
- liposome

Examples
- SCID (severe combined immunodeficiency); interleukin receptor gene
- Cystic fibrosis; CFTR gene

Transgenic Animals (Germ Line)

Fertilized OVA

Micro-inject cloned DNA

New gene incorporated into germ line DNA

Implant in foster mother

Offspring are transgenic
New gene inserted is a transgene
Design animal model for human disease this way

DNA Vectors

Circular, self-replicating DNA to carry and amplify DNA fragments in bacteria or yeast

~100–12 kb	**Plasmid** Bacterial; restriction sites, replication origin, selection marker (e.g., antibiotic resistance)
~10–25 kb	**Phage** Packaging virus that infects bacteria; e.g., lambda (λ)
Up to 45 kb	**Cosmid** Plasmids with λ cloning sites
Up to 10 Mb	**BAC, YAC** Bacterial or yeast artificial chromosomes

Definition of abbreviation: dsDNA, double-stranded DNA.

GENETIC TESTING

The presence of specific DNA, RNA, and proteins can be identified by first separating these molecules by **gel electrophoresis**, transferring to a membrane by **blotting**, and finally detecting with radioactive nucleic acid probes (for DNA and RNA) or antibodies (for proteins). Direct detection in cells or tissues can also be performed using similar tools to identify mRNA (**in situ hybridization**) or proteins (**immunostaining**). In vitro detection of proteins can also be achieved by enzyme-linked immunosorbent assay (**ELISA**). Using these methods of detection, diversity between individuals or genetic mutations manifested by different restriction endonuclease sites (restriction fragment length polymorphisms [**RFLP**]) or expansion of highly repetitive sequences (e.g., **satellites**, **minisatellites**, and **microsatellites**) may be employed for genetic testing.

	DNA	RNA	Protein		Repeated Unit	Length of Repeat
Separation	Gel electrophoresis			**Satellites**	20–175 bp	0.1–1 Mb
Blotting (probe)	Southern (^{32}P-DNA)	Northern (^{32}P-DNA)	Western (^{125}I or antibody)	**Minisatellites**	20–70 bp	Up to 20 kb
Other detection	—	In situ hybridization	Immunostaining or ELISA	**Microsatellites**	2–4 bp	<150 bp

Sickle Cell Disease (Southern Blot; RFLP)

*Mst*II restriction digest of patient sample, followed by Southern blotting using a probe against β-globin gene, allows identification of either the normal or sickle allele.

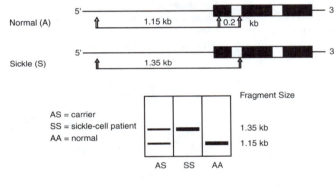

Mst II Restriction Map of the β-Globin Gene

Normal (A) 1.15 kb 0.2 kb

Sickle (S) 1.35 kb

AS = carrier
SS = sickle-cell patient
AA = normal

Fragment Size
1.35 kb
1.15 kb

AS SS AA

Paternity Testing (PCR; Microsatellite)

PCR amplification of microsatellite sequences can be used to match the banding pattern to each parent. The child should share one allele with each parent.

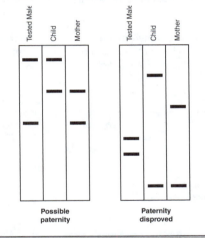

Possible paternity

Paternity disproved

Cystic Fibrosis (PCR; ASO Dot Blot)

The most common CF mutation, ΔF508, can be detected by comparing PCR product sizes by gel electrophoresis or hybridization with allele-specific oligonucleotide (ASO) probes on a dot blot (a simplified form of Southern blot).

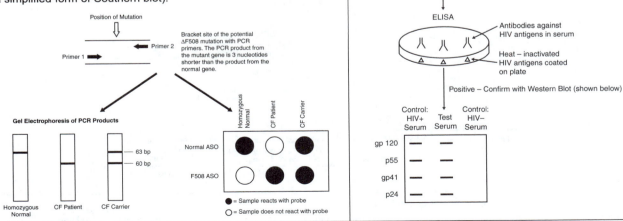

Position of Mutation

Bracket site of the potential ΔF508 mutation with PCR primers. The PCR product from the mutant gene is 3 nucleotides shorter than the product from the normal gene.

Primer 1   Primer 2

Gel Electrophoresis of PCR Products

63 bp
60 bp

Homozygous Normal   CF Patient   CF Carrier

Normal ASO
F508 ASO

● = Sample reacts with probe
○ = Sample does not react with probe

HIV Detection (ELISA and Western Blot)

Serum antibodies to HIV are first detected by ELISA and then confirmed by Western blot.

Serum to Test for HIV Infection

ELISA

Antibodies against HIV antigens in serum

Heat – inactivated HIV antigens coated on plate

Positive – Confirm with Western Blot (shown below)

Control: HIV+ Serum   Test Serum   Control: HIV– Serum

gp 120
p55
gp41
p24

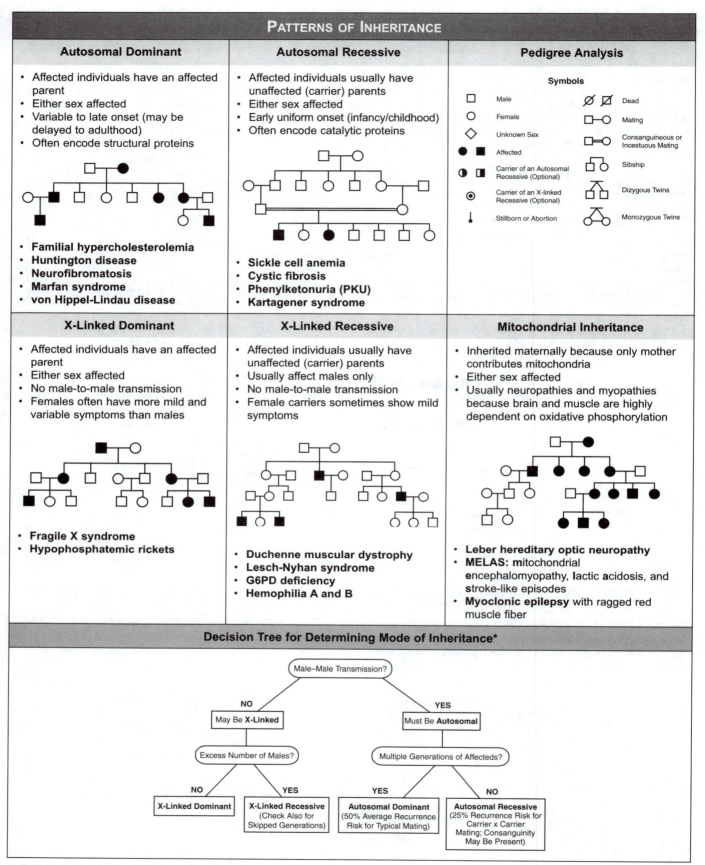

PATTERNS OF INHERITANCE

Autosomal Dominant

- Affected individuals have an affected parent
- Either sex affected
- Variable to late onset (may be delayed to adulthood)
- Often encode structural proteins

- **Familial hypercholesterolemia**
- **Huntington disease**
- **Neurofibromatosis**
- **Marfan syndrome**
- **von Hippel-Lindau disease**

Autosomal Recessive

- Affected individuals usually have unaffected (carrier) parents
- Either sex affected
- Early uniform onset (infancy/childhood)
- Often encode catalytic proteins

- **Sickle cell anemia**
- **Cystic fibrosis**
- **Phenylketonuria (PKU)**
- **Kartagener syndrome**

Pedigree Analysis

Symbols

□	Male	⌀ ⌀	Dead
○	Female	□—○	Mating
◇	Unknown Sex	□═○	Consanguineous or Incestuous Mating
● ■	Affected		Sibship
◑ ◨	Carrier of an Autosomal Recessive (Optional)		Dizygous Twins
⊙	Carrier of an X-linked Recessive (Optional)		Monozygous Twins
↓	Stillborn or Abortion		

X-Linked Dominant

- Affected individuals have an affected parent
- Either sex affected
- No male-to-male transmission
- Females often have more mild and variable symptoms than males

- **Fragile X syndrome**
- **Hypophosphatemic rickets**

X-Linked Recessive

- Affected individuals usually have unaffected (carrier) parents
- Usually affect males only
- No male-to-male transmission
- Female carriers sometimes show mild symptoms

- **Duchenne muscular dystrophy**
- **Lesch-Nyhan syndrome**
- **G6PD deficiency**
- **Hemophilia A and B**

Mitochondrial Inheritance

- Inherited maternally because only mother contributes mitochondria
- Either sex affected
- Usually neuropathies and myopathies because brain and muscle are highly dependent on oxidative phosphorylation

- **Leber hereditary optic neuropathy**
- **MELAS:** mitochondrial encephalomyopathy, lactic acidosis, and stroke-like episodes
- **Myoclonic epilepsy** with ragged red muscle fiber

Decision Tree for Determining Mode of Inheritance*

Male–Male Transmission?

- **NO** → May Be **X-Linked**
  - Excess Number of Males?
    - **NO** → **X-Linked Dominant**
    - **YES** → **X-Linked Recessive** (Check Also for Skipped Generations)
- **YES** → Must Be **Autosomal**
  - Multiple Generations of Affecteds?
    - **YES** → **Autosomal Dominant** (50% Average Recurrence Risk for Typical Mating)
    - **NO** → **Autosomal Recessive** (25% Recurrence Risk for Carrier x Carrier Mating; Consanguinity May Be Present)

Definition of abbreviation: G6PD, glucose-6-phosphate dehydrogenase.

Note: If transmission occurs only through affected mothers and never through affected sons, the pedigree is likely to reflect mitochondrial inheritance.

SINGLE-GENE DISORDERS		
Neurofibromatosis (NF) Type 1 (von Recklinghausen Disease)	**von Hippel-Lindau Disease**	**Features**
(mutation in NF1 tumor-suppressor gene on chromosome 17) • Multiple neurofibromas • Café-au-lait spots (pigmented skin lesions) • Lisch nodules (pigmented iris hamartomas) • Increased risk of meningiomas and pheochromocytoma • 90% of NF cases • Autosomal dominant	*(mutation in tumor-suppressor gene on chromosome 3)* • Hemangioblastomas in CNS and retina • Renal cell carcinoma • Cysts in internal organs • Autosomal dominant	**Variable expression—** differences in severity of symptoms for same genotype; allelic heterogeneity can contribute to variable expression **Incomplete penetrance—** some individuals with disease genotype do not have disease phenotype
Neurofibromatosis (NF) Type 2 (Bilateral Acoustic Neurofibromatosis)	**Cystic Fibrosis**	**Delayed age of onset—** individuals do not manifest phenotype until later in life
(mutation in NF2 tumor-suppressor gene on chromosome 22) • Bilateral acoustic neuromas • Neurofibromas and café-au-lait spots • Increased risk of meningiomas and pheochromocytoma • 10% of NF cases • Autosomal dominant	*(mutation in CFTR chloride channel gene on chromosome, leading to thick secretion of mucus plugs)* • Recurrent pulmonary infections (*P. aeruginosa* and *S. aureus*) • Pneumonia, bronchitis, bronchiectasis • Pancreatic insufficiency; steatorrhea • Fat-soluble vitamin deficiency • Male infertility • Biliary cirrhosis • Meconium ileus • Most common mutation: ΔF508 • Dx: ↑ NaCl in sweat; PCR and ASO probes • Tx: *N*-acetylcysteine, respiratory therapy, enzyme replacement, vitamin supplement • Autosomal recessive	**Pleiotropy—** single disease mutation affects multiple organ systems **Locus heterogeneity—** same disease phenotype from mutations in different loci **Anticipation—** earlier age of onset and increased disease severity with each generation **Imprinting—** symptoms depend on whether mutant gene was inherited from father or mother; due to different DNA methylation patterns of parents (e.g., Prader-Willi versus Angelman syndrome)
Marfan Syndrome		
(mutation of fibrillin gene on chromosome 15) • Skeletal abnormalities (tall build with hyperextensible joints) • Subluxation of lens • Cardiovascular defects (cystic medial necrosis, dissecting aortic aneurysm, valvular insufficiency) • Autosomal dominant		

Definition of abbreviations: ASO, allele-specific oligonucleotides; CFTR, cystic fibrosis transmembrane conductance regulator; CNS, central nervous system; Dx, diagnosis; PCR, polymerase chain reaction; Tx, treatment.

CHROMOSOMAL ABNORMALITIES

Aneuploidy refers to having a chromosome number that is not a multiple of the haploid number. It is the most common type of chromosomal disorder, and its incidence is related to increasing maternal age. Most arise from a **nondisjunction** event, when chromosomes fail to segregate during cell division. Nondisjunction during either phase of meiosis usually leads to spontaneous abortion, but sometimes results in live birth, often with severe physical deformities and mental retardation. Trisomies are the most common genetic cause of pregnancy loss. Nondisjunction during mitosis in the developing embryo can lead to cells in a single individual carrying different karyotypes, a condition known as **mosaicism**. Based on the **Lyon hypothesis**, females are naturally mosaics for genes on the X chromosome because one X chromosome in every cell is randomly inactivated to form a **Barr body**. Fluorescence in situ hybridization (FISH) can detect DNA sequences to identify deletions, translocations, and aneuploidies.

Nondisjunction During Meiosis I	Autosomal Trisomies

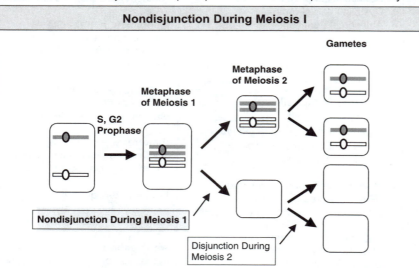

This figure shows the result of nondisjunction of one homologous pair (for example, chromosome 21) during meiosis 1. All other homologs segregate (disjoin) normally in the cell. Two of the gametes are diploid for chromosome 21. When fertilization occurs, the conception will be a trisomy 21 with Down syndrome. The other gametes with no copy of chromosome 21 will result in conceptions that are monosomy 21, a condition incompatible with a live birth.

Trisomy 21 (Down Syndrome)

- Most common chromosomal disorder
- Epicanthal folds, brachycephaly, flat nasal bridge, low-set ears, and short, broad hands with single transverse palmar crease
- Mental retardation
- Early-onset Alzheimer disease
- Congenital septal defects in heart
- ↑ risk of acute leukemia
- Incidence: 1/800 births (1/25 if age >45 years)
- 95% nondisjunction; 4% Robertsonian translocation

Trisomy 18 (Edwards Syndrome)

- Intrauterine growth retardation
- Mental retardation
- Failure to thrive
- Short sternum, small pelvis, rocker-bottom feet
- Cardiac, renal, and intestinal defects
- Usually death <1 year
- Incidence: 1/8,000 births

Trisomy 13 (Patau Syndrome)

- Microcephaly and abnormal brain development
- Cleft lip and palate, polydactyly
- Cardiac dextroposition and septal defects
- Incidence: 1/25,000 births

Nondisjunction During Meiosis II

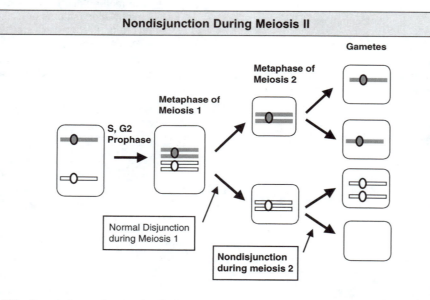

This figure shows the result of nondisjunction during meiosis 2. In this case, the sister chromatids of a chromosome (for example, chromosome 21) fail to segregate (disjoin). The sister chromatids of all other chromosomes segregate normally. One of the gametes is diploid for chromosome 21. When fertilization occurs, the conception will be a trisomy 21 with Down syndrome. One gamete has no copy of chromosome 21 and will result in a conception that is a monosomy 21. The remaining two gametes are normal haploid ones.

Sex Chromosome Aneuploidy

Turner Syndrome (45,XO)

- Short stature, webbed neck, shield chest
- Primary amenorrhea, infertility
- Coarctation of aorta
- Incidence: 1/6,000 female births

Klinefelter Syndrome (47,XXY)

- Eunuchoid body with lack of male secondary sex characteristics
- Hypogonadism, testicular atrophy
- Incidence: 1/2,000 male births

XYY Syndrome

- Excessively tall with severe acne
- ↑ risk of behavioral problems
- Incidence: 1/1,000 male births

In addition to aneuploidy, large segments of chromosomes may undergo structural aberrations, including deletions, inversions, and translocations. **Deletions** occur when a chromosome loses a segment because of breakage. **Inversions** are rearrangements of the gene order within a single chromosome due to incorrect repair of two breaks. An inversion that includes a centromere is called a **pericentric** inversion, whereas one that does not involve the centromere is **paracentric**. Finally, **translocations** involve the exchange of chromosomal material between nonhomologous chromosomes. **Reciprocal translocations** result when two nonhomologous chromosomes exchange pieces, and **Robertsonian translocations** involve any two acrocentric chromosomes that break near the centromeres and rejoin with a fusion of the q arms at the centromere and loss of the p arms.

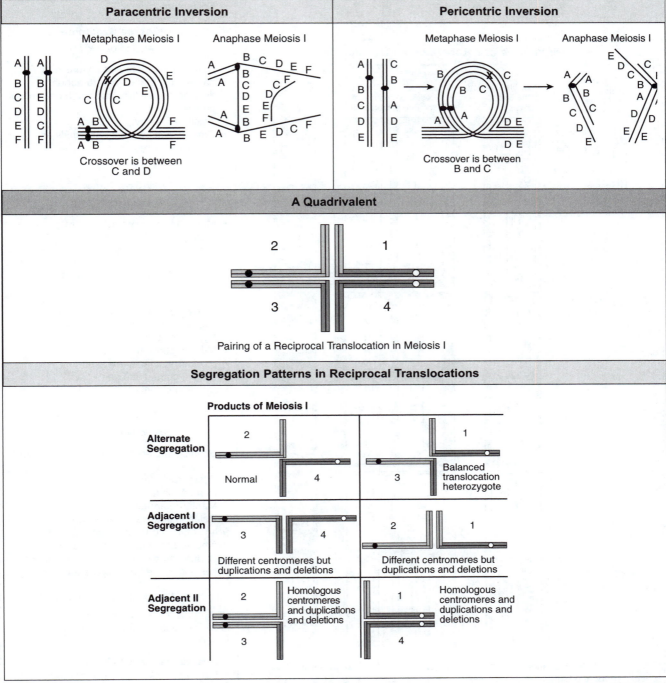

Paracentric Inversion

Metaphase Meiosis I   Anaphase Meiosis I

Crossover is between
C and D

Pericentric Inversion

Metaphase Meiosis I   Anaphase Meiosis I

Crossover is between
B and C

A Quadrivalent

Pairing of a Reciprocal Translocation in Meiosis I

Segregation Patterns in Reciprocal Translocations

Products of Meiosis I

Alternate Segregation — Normal / Balanced translocation heterozygote

Adjacent I Segregation — Different centromeres but duplications and deletions / Different centromeres but duplications and deletions

Adjacent II Segregation — Homologous centromeres and duplications and deletions / Homologous centromeres and duplications and deletions

(Continued)

Formation of a Robertsonian Translocation	Disease Association

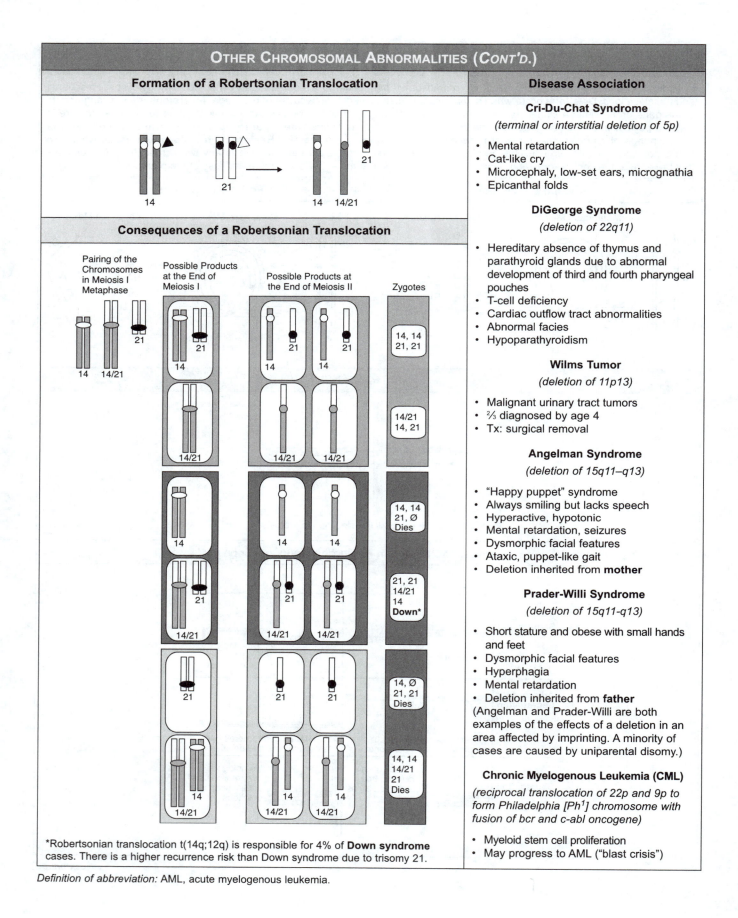

Consequences of a Robertsonian Translocation

Pairing of the Chromosomes in Meiosis I Metaphase

Possible Products at the End of Meiosis I

Possible Products at the End of Meiosis II

Zygotes

Cri-Du-Chat Syndrome
(terminal or interstitial deletion of 5p)

- Mental retardation
- Cat-like cry
- Microcephaly, low-set ears, micrognathia
- Epicanthal folds

DiGeorge Syndrome
(deletion of 22q11)

- Hereditary absence of thymus and parathyroid glands due to abnormal development of third and fourth pharyngeal pouches
- T-cell deficiency
- Cardiac outflow tract abnormalities
- Abnormal facies
- Hypoparathyroidism

Wilms Tumor
(deletion of 11p13)

- Malignant urinary tract tumors
- ⅔ diagnosed by age 4
- Tx: surgical removal

Angelman Syndrome
(deletion of 15q11–q13)

- "Happy puppet" syndrome
- Always smiling but lacks speech
- Hyperactive, hypotonic
- Mental retardation, seizures
- Dysmorphic facial features
- Ataxic, puppet-like gait
- Deletion inherited from **mother**

Prader-Willi Syndrome
(deletion of 15q11-q13)

- Short stature and obese with small hands and feet
- Dysmorphic facial features
- Hyperphagia
- Mental retardation
- Deletion inherited from **father**

(Angelman and Prader-Willi are both examples of the effects of a deletion in an area affected by imprinting. A minority of cases are caused by uniparental disomy.)

Chronic Myelogenous Leukemia (CML)
(reciprocal translocation of 22p and 9p to form Philadelphia [Ph[1]] chromosome with fusion of bcr and c-abl oncogene)

- Myeloid stem cell proliferation
- May progress to AML ("blast crisis")

*Robertsonian translocation t(14q;12q) is responsible for 4% of **Down syndrome** cases. There is a higher recurrence risk than Down syndrome due to trisomy 21.

Definition of abbreviation: AML, acute myelogenous leukemia.

POPULATION GENETICS

The **Hardy-Weinberg equilibrium** states that under certain conditions, if the population is large and randomly mating, the genotypic frequencies of the population will remain stable from generation to generation.

Hardy-Weinberg Conditions	Factors Affecting Equilibrium
1. No mutations 2. No selection against a genotype 3. No migration or immigration of the population 4. Random mating	**Natural Selection**
	Increases frequencies of genes that promote survival or fertility (e.g., malaria protection in sickle cell heterozygotes)
If: frequency of A allele = p frequency of a allele = q	**Genetic Drift**
	Gene frequency change due to finite population size
Then: allele frequencies can be expressed as:	**Gene Flow**
$$p + q = 1$$	Gene exchange between different populations
genotypic frequencies at that locus can be expressed as:	**Linkage Disequilibrium**
$$p^2 + 2pq + q^2 = 1$$ where p^2 = frequency of genotype AA $2pq$ = frequency of genotype Aa q^2 = frequency of genotype aa	Preferential association of an allele at one locus with another allele at a nearby locus more frequently than by chance alone

In contrast to simple prokaryotic cells which have a cell wall but no membrane-bound nucleus or organelles, eukaryotic cells are, in general, larger and lack a cell wall, but are composed of various subcellular membranous organelles with distinct functions.

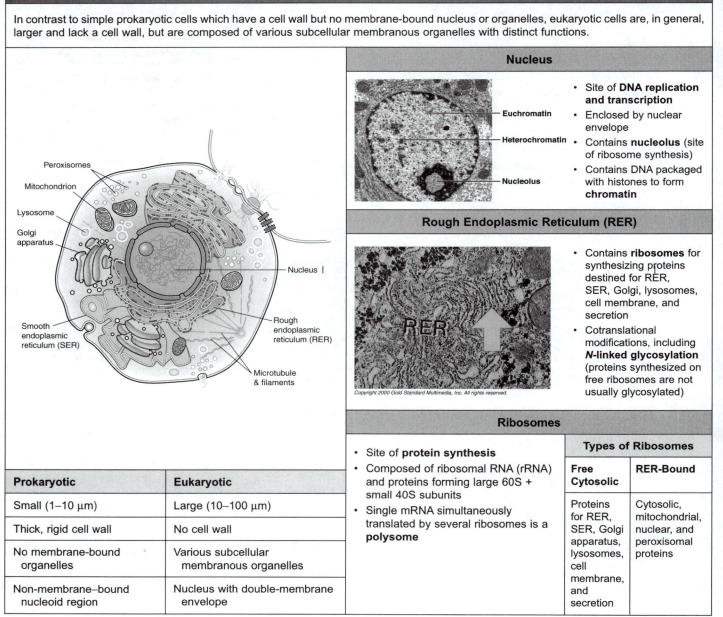

Nucleus

- Site of **DNA replication and transcription**
- Enclosed by nuclear envelope
- Contains **nucleolus** (site of ribosome synthesis)
- Contains DNA packaged with histones to form **chromatin**

Rough Endoplasmic Reticulum (RER)

- Contains **ribosomes** for synthesizing proteins destined for RER, SER, Golgi, lysosomes, cell membrane, and secretion
- Cotranslational modifications, including **N-linked glycosylation** (proteins synthesized on free ribosomes are not usually glycosylated)

Ribosomes

- Site of **protein synthesis**
- Composed of ribosomal RNA (rRNA) and proteins forming large 60S + small 40S subunits
- Single mRNA simultaneously translated by several ribosomes is a **polysome**

Types of Ribosomes	
Free Cytosolic	**RER-Bound**
Proteins for RER, SER, Golgi apparatus, lysosomes, cell membrane, and secretion	Cytosolic, mitochondrial, nuclear, and peroxisomal proteins

Prokaryotic	Eukaryotic
Small (1–10 μm)	Large (10–100 μm)
Thick, rigid cell wall	No cell wall
No membrane-bound organelles	Various subcellular membranous organelles
Non-membrane–bound nucleoid region	Nucleus with double-membrane envelope

(Continued)

Golgi Apparatus

- Site of **post-translational modifications and protein sorting**
- Consists of disk-shaped cisternae in stacks
- *Cis* (forming) face associated with RER
- *Trans* (maturing) face oriented toward plasma membrane

Smooth Endoplasmic Reticulum (SER)

- Involved in detoxification reactions, including **phase I hydroxylation** (via cytochrome P450) and **phase II conjugation** (addition of polar groups)
- Synthesis of phospholipids, lipoproteins, and sterols
- Known as **sarcoplasmic reticulum** in striated muscles, and sequesters calcium stores

Mitochondria

- Major function is ATP synthesis
- Similar to bacteria in size and shape; self-replicating
- Contain their own double-stranded circular DNA
- Smooth, permeable outer membrane; heavily infolded, impermeable inner membrane

Lysosomes

- Enzymatic degradation of extracellular or intracellular macromolecules
- Primary lysosome fuses with phagosomes or cellular organelles to form secondary lysosomes
- Acidic hydrolytic enzymes with optimal activity at pH 5
- Degradation of intracellular organelles known as **autophagy**

Endosomes

- Formed from endocytosed vesicles acquired by receptor-mediated endocytosis involving **clathrin-coated pits**
- Can fuse with primary lysosomes to form secondary lysosomes to degrade extracellular materials

Peroxisomes

- Synthesis and degradation of hydrogen peroxide
- β-oxidation of very long chain fatty acids ($>C_{24}$)
- Phospholipid exchange reactions
- Bile acid synthesis

PLASMA MEMBRANE

The **plasma membrane** of a cell is a bilayer of lipids and proteins. The lipids include phospholipids, unesterified cholesterol, and glycolipids and are **amphipathic** (polar head to interact with aqueous environment, and nonpolar tail to interact with the bilayer interior). Proteins may act as adhesion molecules, receptors, transporters, channels, or enzymes. Proteins embedded in the bilayer are **integral proteins**, whereas those loosely associated with the membrane are **peripheral proteins**. In general, **N-glycosylation** of proteins and lipids is associated with location on the external surface, whereas **N-myristoylation**, **prenylation**, and **palmitoylation** of proteins are associated with location on the cytoplasmic face of the plasma membrane.

Structure of Biologic Membranes

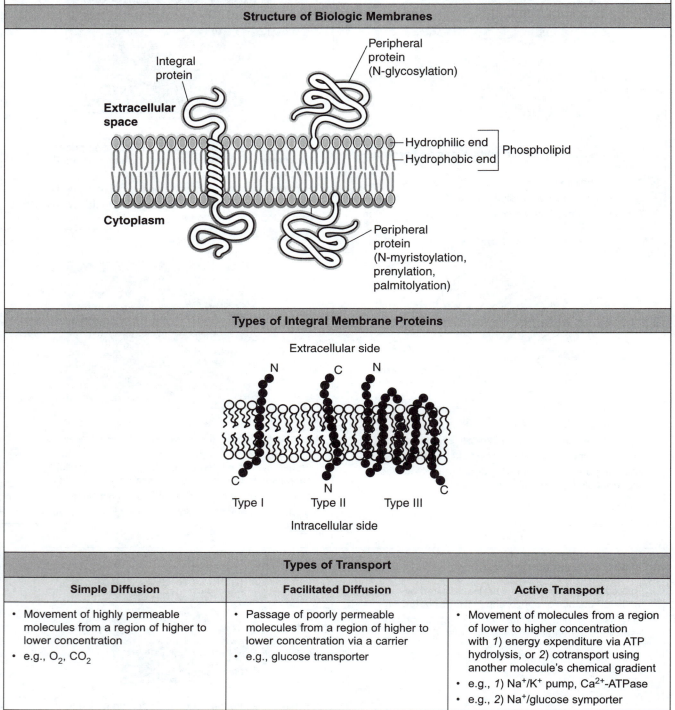

Types of Integral Membrane Proteins

Types of Transport

Simple Diffusion	Facilitated Diffusion	Active Transport
• Movement of highly permeable molecules from a region of higher to lower concentration • e.g., O_2, CO_2	• Passage of poorly permeable molecules from a region of higher to lower concentration via a carrier • e.g., glucose transporter	• Movement of molecules from a region of lower to higher concentration with *1)* energy expenditure via ATP hydrolysis, or *2)* cotransport using another molecule's chemical gradient • e.g., *1)* Na^+/K^+ pump, Ca^{2+}-ATPase • e.g., *2)* Na^+/glucose symporter

KAPLAN MEDICAL

CYTOSKELETON

The cytoskeleton consists of a supportive network of tubules and filaments in the cytoplasm of eukaryotic cells. It is a dynamic structure responsible for cellular movement, changes in cell shape, and the contraction of muscle cells. It also provides the machinery for intracellular movement of organelles. The cytoskeleton is composed of three types of supportive structures: **microtubules*, intermediate filaments**, and **microfilaments**.

Microtubules*	Intermediate Filaments	Microfilaments
Tubulin (hollow cylindrical polymer of tubulin dimers)	• **Keratin** (epithelium) • **Vimentin** (nonepithelial) • **Neurofilament** (neurons)	**Actin** (double-stranded polymer twisted in helical pattern)

Function		
• Movement of chromosomes in mitosis or meiosis • Intracellular transport via motor proteins • Ciliary and flagellar motility	Structural	• Structural • Muscle contraction via interaction with myosin

Axoneme Structure

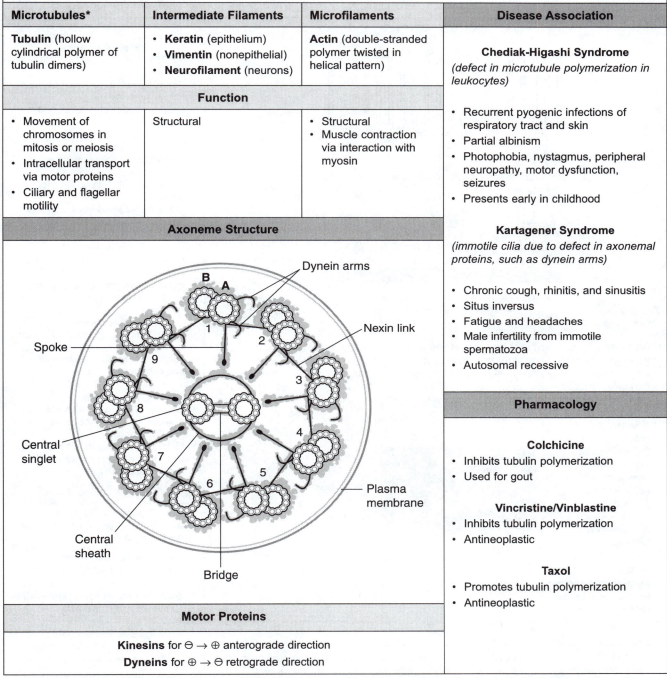

Motor Proteins

Kinesins for $\ominus \rightarrow \oplus$ anterograde direction

Dyneins for $\oplus \rightarrow \ominus$ retrograde direction

Disease Association

Chediak-Higashi Syndrome
(defect in microtubule polymerization in leukocytes)

• Recurrent pyogenic infections of respiratory tract and skin
• Partial albinism
• Photophobia, nystagmus, peripheral neuropathy, motor dysfunction, seizures
• Presents early in childhood

Kartagener Syndrome
(immotile cilia due to defect in axonemal proteins, such as dynein arms)

• Chronic cough, rhinitis, and sinusitis
• Situs inversus
• Fatigue and headaches
• Male infertility from immotile spermatozoa
• Autosomal recessive

Pharmacology

Colchicine
• Inhibits tubulin polymerization
• Used for gout

Vincristine/Vinblastine
• Inhibits tubulin polymerization
• Antineoplastic

Taxol
• Promotes tubulin polymerization
• Antineoplastic

*Microtubules are polarized structures with assembly/disassembly occurring at the $\oplus$ ends, which are oriented toward the cell's periphery.

CELL ADHESION

A cell must physically interact via cell surface molecules with its external environment, whether it be the extracellular matrix or **basement membrane**. The basement membrane is a sheet-like structure underlying virtually all epithelia, which consists of **basal lamina** (made of type VI collagen, glycoproteins [e.g., laminin], and proteoglycans [e.g., heparin sulfate]), and **reticular lamina** (composed of reticular fibers). Cell junctions anchor cells to each other, seal boundaries between cells, and form channels for direct transport and communication between cells. The three types of junctional complexes include **anchoring, tight,** and **gap junctions**.

Cell Junctions

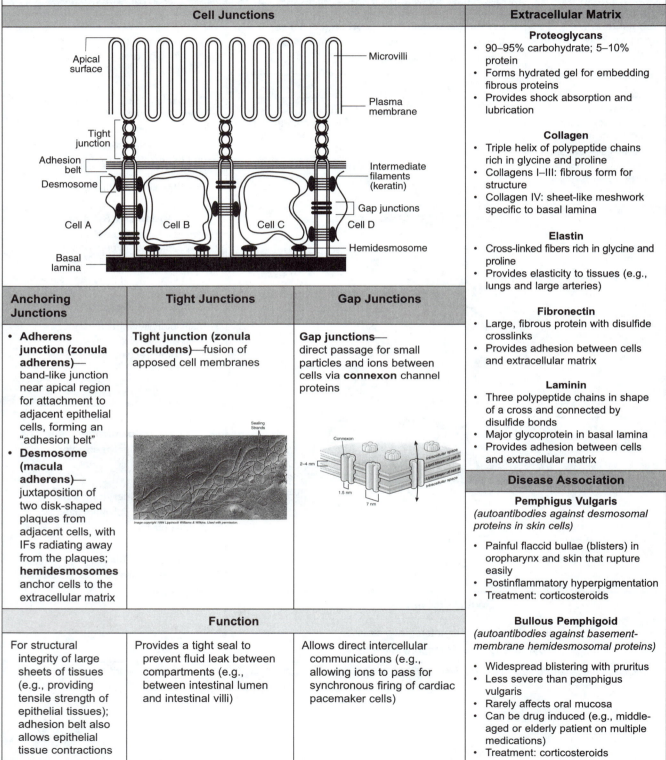

Extracellular Matrix

Proteoglycans
- 90–95% carbohydrate; 5–10% protein
- Forms hydrated gel for embedding fibrous proteins
- Provides shock absorption and lubrication

Collagen
- Triple helix of polypeptide chains rich in glycine and proline
- Collagens I–III: fibrous form for structure
- Collagen IV: sheet-like meshwork specific to basal lamina

Elastin
- Cross-linked fibers rich in glycine and proline
- Provides elasticity to tissues (e.g., lungs and large arteries)

Fibronectin
- Large, fibrous protein with disulfide crosslinks
- Provides adhesion between cells and extracellular matrix

Laminin
- Three polypeptide chains in shape of a cross and connected by disulfide bonds
- Major glycoprotein in basal lamina
- Provides adhesion between cells and extracellular matrix

Disease Association

Pemphigus Vulgaris
(autoantibodies against desmosomal proteins in skin cells)

- Painful flaccid bullae (blisters) in oropharynx and skin that rupture easily
- Postinflammatory hyperpigmentation
- Treatment: corticosteroids

Bullous Pemphigoid
(autoantibodies against basement-membrane hemidesmosomal proteins)

- Widespread blistering with pruritus
- Less severe than pemphigus vulgaris
- Rarely affects oral mucosa
- Can be drug induced (e.g., middle-aged or elderly patient on multiple medications)
- Treatment: corticosteroids

Anchoring Junctions	Tight Junctions	Gap Junctions
- **Adherens junction (zonula adherens)**—band-like junction near apical region for attachment to adjacent epithelial cells, forming an "adhesion belt" - **Desmosome (macula adherens)**—juxtaposition of two disk-shaped plaques from adjacent cells, with IFs radiating away from the plaques; **hemidesmosomes** anchor cells to the extracellular matrix	**Tight junction (zonula occludens)**—fusion of apposed cell membranes	**Gap junctions**—direct passage for small particles and ions between cells via **connexon** channel proteins

Function

For structural integrity of large sheets of tissues (e.g., providing tensile strength of epithelial tissues); adhesion belt also allows epithelial tissue contractions	Provides a tight seal to prevent fluid leak between compartments (e.g., between intestinal lumen and intestinal villi)	Allows direct intercellular communications (e.g., allowing ions to pass for synchronous firing of cardiac pacemaker cells)

Definition of abbreviations: IF, intermediate filament.

CELL CYCLE

The cell cycle consists of the mitosis phase (M), the presynthetic gap (G_1), the DNA synthesis phase (S), and the postsynthetic gap (G_2). Mitosis is the shortest phase, consisting of **prophase, metaphase, anaphase**, and **telophase**. Both G_1 and G_2 phases are variable in duration, with most cells spending much of their time in a stable, nondividing G_0 phase. Cells in G_2 have twice the amount of DNA as those in G_1.

Phases of Mitosis

Prophase	
	• Chromosomes coil • Nuclear envelope disappears • Spindle apparatus forms
Metaphase	
	Chromosomes align
Anaphase	
	Chromatids separate
Telophase	
	• Chromosomes uncoil • Nuclear envelope reappears • Spindle apparatus disassemble • Cell divides in two (cytokinesis)

Regulators of the Cell Cycle

Cyclins	**Cyclin** levels rise and fall with stages of cell cycle.
CDKs	**Cyclin-dependent kinases** with various substrates promote cell-cycle progression.
APC	**Anaphase-promoting complex** triggers chromatid separation; degrades M-phase cyclins.
SPF	**S-phase promoting factor** includes CDKs and cyclins, which prepare cell for DNA replication.
MPF	**M-phase/maturation-promoting factor** includes CDKs and cyclins, which promote assembly of mitotic spindle and nuclear envelope breakdown.
p53	**p53** is a tumor suppressor that blocks cell cycle if DNA is damaged.
RB	**Retinoblastoma susceptibility protein** is a substrate of CDKs that promote cell division.
p21	**p21** is a CDK inhibitor that also blocks cell-cycle progression.

Disease Association

Retinoblastoma

(mutation in the RB1 tumor-suppressor gene on chromosome 13)

- Most common childhood eye tumor
- Leukocoria (white reflex in pupil)
- Strabismus
- "Two-hit model" of carcinogenesis:
  1) inherited mutation of one allele
  2) somatic mutation of second allele

Cell Signaling

In order to act on a cell, external molecules, such as hormones and neurotransmitters, must interact with a **receptor**. In general, small hydrophobic molecules (e.g., cortisol, sex hormones, thyroid hormone, and retinoids) can readily penetrate the plasma membrane to bind **intracellular receptors**, which often act as transcription factors to affect gene expression. Most other molecules bind to cell surface receptors, which include **ion-channel–linked receptors** (e.g., transmitter-gated channels), **G-protein–linked receptors** (the largest family), and **enzyme-linked receptors** (e.g., tyrosine kinase receptors). These cell surface receptors (i.e., the "first messenger") usually transmit their signal via a number of downstream **second messengers**, leading to a **signal transduction cascade**. One exception is the gaseous **nitric oxide** (NO), which readily diffuses across the plasma membrane to activate soluble **guanylate cyclase**, generate **cGMP**, and promote smooth muscle relaxation.

G-Protein–Coupled Receptor Systems

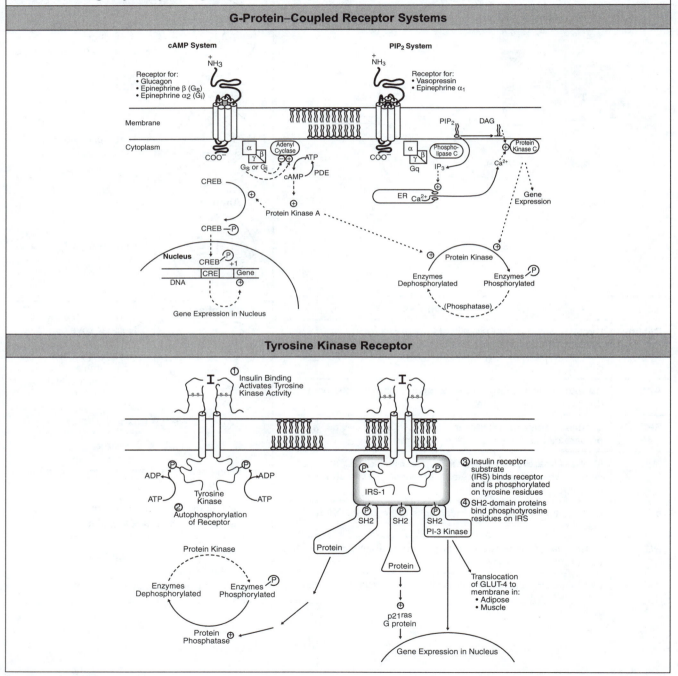

Tyrosine Kinase Receptor

Definition of abbreviations: See next page.

(Continued)

CELL SIGNALING (CONT'D.)

Guanylate Cyclase

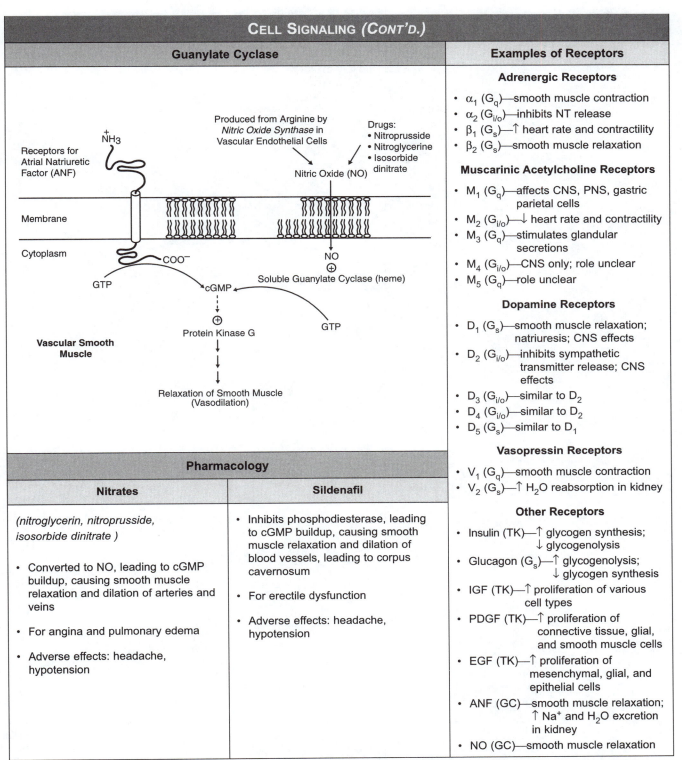

Receptors for Atrial Natriuretic Factor (ANF)

$\overset{+}{NH_3}$

Produced from Arginine by *Nitric Oxide Synthase* in Vascular Endothelial Cells

Drugs:
• Nitroprusside
• Nitroglycerine
• Isosorbide dinitrate

Nitric Oxide (NO)

Membrane

Cytoplasm

COO⁻

GTP

cGMP

NO
⊕
Soluble Guanylate Cyclase (heme)

GTP

⊕
Protein Kinase G

Vascular Smooth Muscle

Relaxation of Smooth Muscle (Vasodilation)

Examples of Receptors

Adrenergic Receptors

• α_1 (G_q)—smooth muscle contraction
• α_2 ($G_{i/o}$)—inhibits NT release
• β_1 (G_s)—↑ heart rate and contractility
• β_2 (G_s)—smooth muscle relaxation

Muscarinic Acetylcholine Receptors

• M_1 (G_q)—affects CNS, PNS, gastric parietal cells
• M_2 ($G_{i/o}$)—↓ heart rate and contractility
• M_3 (G_q)—stimulates glandular secretions
• M_4 ($G_{i/o}$)—CNS only; role unclear
• M_5 (G_q)—role unclear

Dopamine Receptors

• D_1 (G_s)—smooth muscle relaxation; natriuresis; CNS effects
• D_2 ($G_{i/o}$)—inhibits sympathetic transmitter release; CNS effects
• D_3 ($G_{i/o}$)—similar to D_2
• D_4 ($G_{i/o}$)—similar to D_2
• D_5 (G_s)—similar to D_1

Vasopressin Receptors

• V_1 (G_q)—smooth muscle contraction
• V_2 (G_s)—↑ H_2O reabsorption in kidney

Other Receptors

• Insulin (TK)—↑ glycogen synthesis; ↓ glycogenolysis
• Glucagon (G_s)—↑ glycogenolysis; ↓ glycogen synthesis
• IGF (TK)—↑ proliferation of various cell types
• PDGF (TK)—↑ proliferation of connective tissue, glial, and smooth muscle cells
• EGF (TK)—↑ proliferation of mesenchymal, glial, and epithelial cells
• ANF (GC)—smooth muscle relaxation; ↑ Na^+ and H_2O excretion in kidney
• NO (GC)—smooth muscle relaxation

Pharmacology

Nitrates	Sildenafil
(nitroglycerin, nitroprusside, isosorbide dinitrate) • Converted to NO, leading to cGMP buildup, causing smooth muscle relaxation and dilation of arteries and veins • For angina and pulmonary edema • Adverse effects: headache, hypotension	• Inhibits phosphodiesterase, leading to cGMP buildup, causing smooth muscle relaxation and dilation of blood vessels, leading to corpus cavernosum • For erectile dysfunction • Adverse effects: headache, hypotension

Definition of abbreviations: ANF, atrial natriuretic factor; ATP, adenosine triphosphate; cGMP, cyclic guanosine monophosphate; DAG, diacylglycerol; EGF, epidermal growth factor; ER, endoplasmic reticulum; GC, guanylate cyclase–coupled receptor; $G_{i/o}$, cAMP-inhibiting GPCR; G_q, PLC-activating GPCR; G_s, cAMP-activating GPCR; IGF, insulin-like growth factor; PDE, phosphodiesterase; PDGF, platelet-derived growth factor; PIP_2, phosphoinositol biphosphate; PLC, phospholipase C; NO, nitric oxide; TK, tyrosine kinase receptor.

Immunology

Chapter 4

OVERVIEW OF THE IMMUNE SYSTEM

CHARACTERISTICS OF INNATE VERSUS ADAPTIVE IMMUNITY

The immune system can be divided into **two** complementary arms: the **innate** (native, natural) immune system and the **adaptive** (acquired, specific) immune system. These two arms work in concert with each other through soluble substances, such as antibodies, complement, and cytokines.

Characteristics	Innate	Adaptive
Specificity	For structures shared by groups of microbes	For specific antigens of microbial and nonmicrobial agents
Diversity	Limited	**High**
Memory	No	**Yes**
Self-reactivity	No	No
Components	**Innate**	**Adaptive**
Anatomic and chemical barriers	Skin, mucosa, chemicals (lysozyme, interferons α and β), temperature, pH	Lymph nodes, spleen, mucosal-associated lymphoid tissues
Blood proteins	**Complement**	**Antibodies**
Cells	**Phagocytes and NK cells**	**Lymphocytes** (other than NK cells)

OVERVIEW OF THE IMMUNE RESPONSE

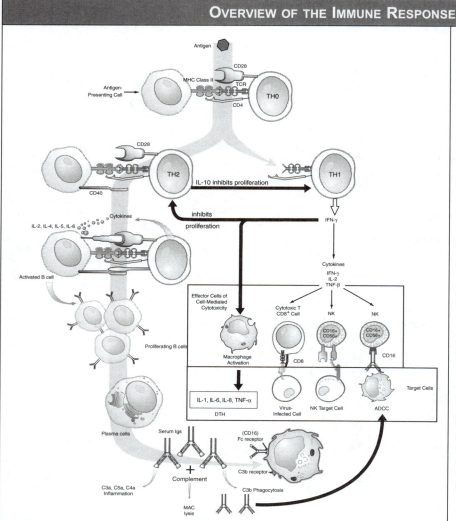

Foreign materials introduced into the body must be processed and presented to TH cells. Processed peptides presented in the MHC class II groove of the antigen-presenting cell are recognized via complementarity with the specific TCR.

Extracellular pathogens stimulate production of TH2 cells, which provide the CD40L costimulatory signal and cytokines to induce B cells to differentiate into plasma cells, which produce antibody. Antibody may assist in phagocytosis (opsonization) or complement-mediated lysis.

Intracellular pathogens stimulate production of TH1 cells, which stimulate the effector cells of cell-mediated immunity. Macrophages are induced to become more effective intracellular killers of the bacteria they ingest. Cytotoxic T cells kill virus-infected cells by recognition of peptides presented in the MHC class I molecule.

Natural killer (NK) cells kill cells devoid of MHC class I that are infected with some viruses or have undergone malignant transformation. In antibody-dependent cell-mediated cytotoxicity (ADCC), abnormal surface molecules on infected or transformed cells are recognized by antibodies and targeted for extracellular lysis by NK cells, eosinophils, neutrophils, or macrophages.

Definition of abbreviations: MHC, major histocompatibility complex; TCR, T cell receptor; TH, T helper.

CELLS OF THE IMMUNE SYSTEM

Myeloid Cell	Location	Identifying Features	Function
Monocyte	Bloodstream, 0–900/µL	**Horseshoe-shaped** nucleus	**Phagocytic**, differentiate into tissue macrophages
Macrophage	Tissues	Ruffled membrane, cytoplasm with vacuoles and vesicles	**Phagocytosis**, secretion of **cytokines**
Dendritic cell	Epithelia, tissues	Long, cytoplasmic arms	**Antigen capture**, transport, and presentation (There are also plasmacytoid dendritic cells that look like plasma cells and produce interferon-α.)
Neutrophil	Bloodstream, 1,800–7,800/µL	**Multilobed** nucleus; **small pink** granules	**Phagocytosis** and activation of bactericidal mechanisms
Eosinophil	Bloodstream, 0–450/µL	**Bilobed** nucleus; **large pink** granules	**Killing of antibody-coated parasites**
Basophil	Bloodstream, 0–200/µL	**Bilobed** nucleus; **large blue** granules	**Nonphagocytic**, release pharmacologically active substances during **allergy**
Mast cell	Tissues, mucosa, and epithelia	**Small** nucleus; **cytoplasm** packed with **large blue** granules	Release of granules containing histamine, etc., during **allergy**

(Continued)

CELLS OF THE IMMUNE SYSTEM *(CONT'D.)*

Lymphoid Cell	Location	Identifying Features	Function
Lymphocyte	Bloodstream, 1,000–4,000/µL, lymph nodes, spleen, submucosa, and epithelia	**Large, dark** nucleus, small rim of cytoplasm	**B cells produce antibody** **TH cells regulate immune responses** **Cytotoxic T cells (CTLs) kill altered or infected cells**
Natural killer (NK) lymphocyte	Bloodstream, ≤10% of lymphocytes	**Lymphocytes** with **large cytoplasmic** granules	**Kill tumor/virus cell** targets or antibody-coated target cells
Plasma cell	Lymph nodes, spleen, mucosal-associated lymphoid tissues, and bone marrow	**Small dark** nucleus, **intensely staining Golgi** apparatus	End cell of B-cell differentiation, **produce antibody**

CHARACTERISTICS OF LYMPHOID CELLS
Comparison of B- and T-lymphocyte Antigen Receptors

Property	B-Cell Antigen Receptor	T-Cell Antigen Receptor
Idiotypes/lymphocyte	1	1
Isotypes/lymphocyte	2 (**IgM and IgD**)	1 (α/β)
Is secretion possible?	**Yes**	**No**
Number of combining sites/molecules	2	1
Mobility	**Flexible** (hinge region)	**Rigid**
Signal transduction molecules	Ig-α, Ig-β, **CD19, CD21**	**CD3**

GENERATION OF RECEPTOR DIVERSITY IN B AND T LYMPHOCYTES

Mechanism	Cell in Which Expressed
Existence in genome of multiple V, D, J segments	B and T cells
VDJ recombination (gene segments are selected and recombined randomly to generate unique variable domains)	**B and T cells**
N-nucleotide addition (TdT adds nucleotides randomly where V, D, and J are joined)	**B cells (only heavy chain), T cells (both chains)**
Combinatorial association of heavy and light chains	B and T cells
Somatic hypermutation (mutations in variable domain coding occur during blastogenesis, and natural selection causes affinity maturation)	**B cells only,** after **Ag stimulation**

Definition of abbreviation: Tdt, terminal deoxyribonucleotidyl transferase.

	MHC Class I	MHC Class II

Names	HLA-A, HLA-B, HLA-C	HLA-DP, HLA-DQ, HLA-DR
Tissue distribution	**All nucleated cells**, platelets	**B and T lymphocytes, antigen-presenting cells**
Recognized by	Cytotoxic T cells **(CD8+)**	Helper T cells **(CD4+)**
Peptides bound	Endogenously **synthesized**	Exogenously **processed**
Function	**Elimination of abnormal (infected) host cells** by cytotoxic T cells	**Presentation of foreign antigen** to helper T cells
Invariant chain	No	**Yes**
β_2-**microglobulin**	**Yes**	No

SUPERANTIGENS
(Staphylococcal Enterotoxins, Toxic-Shock Syndrome Toxin-1, and Streptococcal Pyrogenic Exotoxins)

Superantigens act by cross-linking the variable β domain of a T-cell receptor to an α chain of a class II MHC molecule. They activate many clones of T cells in the absence of antigen-specificity and can cause life-threatening **overproduction of inflammatory cytokines (IL-1, IL-6, IFN-γ, and TNF-α)**.

T-Helper Cells

Naive TH cells (TH0) differentiate into TH1 cells when a strong initial innate immune response leads to production of IL-12 from macrophages or IFN-γ from NK cells. Differentiation of a TH0 cell into a TH2 cell occurs in the absence of an innate immune response. TH1 cells secrete IFN-γ, TNF-β, and IL-2. TH2 cells produce IL-2, IL-4, IL-5, IL-6, and IL-10. IFN-γ, produced by TH1, inhibits TH2. IL4 and IL10, produced by TH2, inhibit TH1.

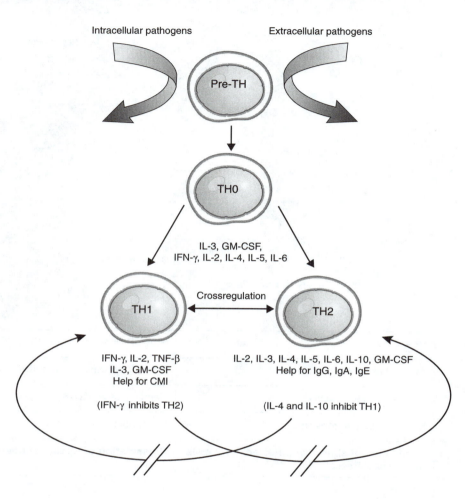

Effector Cells in Cell-Mediated Immunity

Effector Cell	CD Markers	Antigen Recognition	MHC Recognition Required for Killing	Effector Molecules
CTL	TCR, CD3, **CD8**, CD2	**Specific**, TCR	Yes, **class I**	**Perforin, cytokines** (TNF-β, IFN-γ)
NK cell	**CD16, CD56**, CD2	ADCC: specific by IgG, otherwise recognizes lectins	No, **MHC I recognition inhibits**	**Perforin, cytokines** (TNF-β, IFN-γ)
Macrophage	**CD14**	**Nonspecific**	No	**Intracellular** mechanisms

KEY CD MARKERS

CD Designation	Cellular Expression	Known Functions
CD2 (LFA-2)	T cells, thymocytes, NK cells	Adhesion molecule
CD3	**T cells**, thymocytes	Signal transduction by the TCR
CD4	**TH cells**, thymocytes, monocytes, and macrophages	Coreceptor for **MHC class II** TH-cell activation, **receptor for HIV**
CD8	**CTLs**, some thymocytes	Coreceptor for **MHC class I**–restricted T cells
CD14 (LPS receptor)	Monocytes, macrophages, granulocytes	Binds LPS
CD16 (Fc receptor)	**NK cells**, macrophages, mast cells	Immune complex-induced cellular activation, ADCC
CD19 and 20	**B cells**	Coreceptor with CD21 for B-cell activation
CD21 (CR2, C3d receptor)	Mature B cells, follicular dendritic cells	Receptor for complement fragment C3d, forms coreceptor complex with CD19, **Epstein-Barr virus** receptor
CD28	T cells	T-cell receptor for costimulatory molecule B7
CD40	B cells, macrophages, dendritic cells, endothelial cells	Binds CD40L, **starts isotype switch**
CD56	**NK cells**	Not known

Definition of abbreviations: ADCC, antibody-dependent cell-mediated cytotoxicity; CTL, cytotoxic T lymphocytes; LPS, endotoxin (lipopolysaccharide); NK, natural killer; TCR, T-cell receptor.

CYTOKINES

Cytokine	Source	Activity
Interleukin-1	Monocytes, macrophages	Stimulates cells, **endogenous pyrogen**
Interleukin-2	TH cells	**Induces proliferation**, enhances activity
Interleukin-3	TH cells, NK cells	Supports growth and differentiation of **myeloid cells**
Interleukin-4	TH2 cells	Stimulates activation, differentiation, class switch to IgG1 and **IgE**
Interleukin-5	TH2 cells	Stimulates proliferation and differentiation, class switch to **IgA**
Interleukin-6	Monocytes, macrophages, TH2 cells	Second endogenous pyrogen, promotes differentiation into plasma cells, **induces acute phase response**
Interleukin-7	Primary lymphoid organs	**Stimulates progenitor B- and T-cell production in bone marrow**
Interleukin-8	Macrophages, endothelial cells	**Chemokine** (chemotactic for neutrophils)
Interleukin-10	**TH2 cells**	Suppresses cytokine production of TH1 cells
Interleukin-12	Macrophages	**Stimulates CMI**
Interferon-α and -β	Leukocytes, fibroblasts	**Inhibits viral protein synthesis** by acting on uninfected cells
Interferon-γ	**TH1**, CTLs, NK cells	**Stimulates CMI, Inhibits TH2**, increases expression of class I and II MHC
Tumor necrosis factor-α and -β	CMI cells	Enhances CMI
Granulocyte and granulocyte-monocyte colony-stimulating factors (G-CSF and GM-CSF)	Macrophages and TH cells	Induce proliferation in bone marrow; counteract neutropenia following ablative chemotherapy

Definition of abbreviation: CMI, cell-mediated immunity.

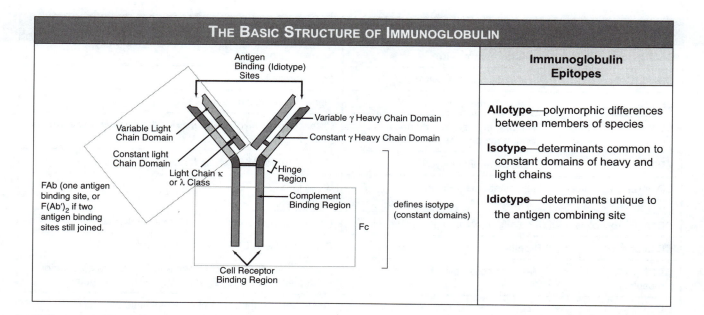

THE BASIC STRUCTURE OF IMMUNOGLOBULIN

Antigen Binding (Idiotype) Sites

Variable Light Chain Domain
Constant light Chain Domain
Variable γ Heavy Chain Domain
Constant γ Heavy Chain Domain
Light Chain κ or λ Class
Hinge Region
Complement Binding Region
Cell Receptor Binding Region
Fc
defines isotype (constant domains)

FAb (one antigen binding site, or F(Ab')₂ if two antigen binding sites still joined.

Immunoglobulin Epitopes

Allotype—polymorphic differences between members of species

Isotype—determinants common to constant domains of heavy and light chains

Idiotype—determinants unique to the antigen combining site

SUMMARY OF THE BIOLOGIC FUNCTIONS OF THE ANTIBODY ISOTYPES					
	IgM	IgG	IgA	IgD	IgE
Heavy chain	μ	γ	α	δ	ε
Adult serum levels	40–345 mg/dL	650–1,500 mg/dL	75–390 mg/dL	Trace	Trace
Functions					
Complement activation, classic pathway	+	+	–	–	–
Opsonization	–	+	–	–	–
Antibody-dependent, cell-mediated cytotoxicity (ADCC)	–	+	–	–	–
Placental transport	–	+	–	–	–
Naive B-cell antigen receptor	+	–	–	+	–
Memory B-cell antigen receptor (one only)	–	+	+	–	+
Trigger mast cell granule release	–	–	–	–	+

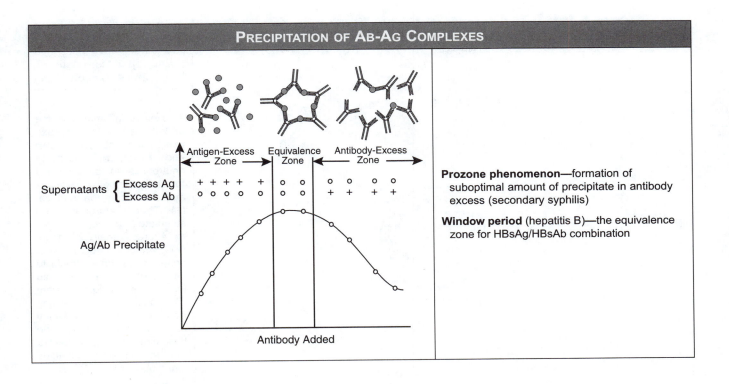

Prozone phenomenon—formation of suboptimal amount of precipitate in antibody excess (secondary syphilis)

Window period (hepatitis B)—the equivalence zone for HBsAg/HBsAb combination

INFLAMMATION

ACUTE INFLAMMATION

Acute inflammation is an immediate response to injury, associated with redness, heat, swelling, pain, and loss of function. Understand the sequence of events of acute inflammation (extravasation, chemotaxis, phagocytosis, intracellular killing) and how these events set the stage for the subsequent adaptive immune response.

Hemodynamic changes	• Transient initial vasoconstriction, followed by massive dilation (mediated by histamine, bradykinin, and prostaglandins) • Increased vascular permeability (due to endothelial cell contraction and/or injury)—histamine, serotonin, bradykinin, leukotrienes (e.g., LTC_4, LTD_4, LTE_4) • Blood stasis due to increased viscosity allows neutrophils to marginate

Cellular response	• **Neutrophils:** (segmented) polymorphonuclear leukocytes (PMNs) are important mediators in acute inflammation
	 • Neutrophils have **primary (azurophilic)** and **secondary (specific) granules:**
	    – **Primary granules contain:** myeloperoxidase, phospholipase A2, lysozyme, acid hydrolases, elastase, defensins, and bactericidal permeability increasing protein (BPI)
	    – **Secondary granules contain:** phospholipase A2, lysozyme, leukocyte alkaline phosphatase (LAP), collagenase, lactoferrin, vitamin B_{12}–binding proteins

NEUTROPHIL MARGINATION AND EXTRAVASATION

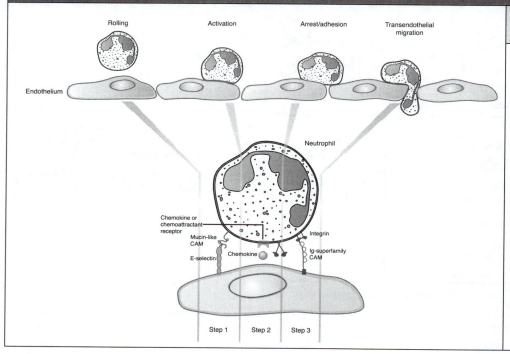

Neutrophil Margination and Adhesion

At sites of inflammation, the endothelial cells increase expression of **E-selectin** and **P-selectin**, allowing neutrophils to bind weakly to the endothelial selectins and roll along the surface. (1) Then neutrophils are stimulated by chemokines to express their integrins, (2) which mediate firm adherence of the neutrophil to the endothelial cell. (3) Then leukocytes emigrate from the vasculature by moving between the endothelial cells, migrating through the basement membrane toward the inflammatory stimulus (chemotaxis).

NEUTROPHIL MIGRATION/CHEMOTAXIS

Chemoattractive Molecule	Origin
Chemokines (**IL-8**)	Tissue mast cells, platelets, neutrophils, monocytes, macrophages, eosinophils, basophils, lymphocytes
Complement split product **C5a**	Endothelial damage → activation Hageman factor → plasmin activation
Fibrinopeptides	Endothelial damage → activation Hageman factor → thrombin → fibrin clot degradation
Leukotriene B$_4$	Membrane phospholipids of macrophages, monocytes, neutrophils, mast cells → arachidonic acid cascade → lipoxygenase pathway
Formyl methionyl peptides	Released from **microorganisms**

OTHER CHEMICAL MEDIATORS OF INFLAMMATION

Monoamine	Sources	Effects	Triggers for Release
Histamine	Basophils, platelets, and mast cells	Vasodilation and increased vascular permeability	• IgE-mediated mast cell reactions • Physical injury • Anaphylatoxins (C3a and C5a) • Cytokines (IL-1)
Serotonin	Platelets		Platelet aggregation

Enzyme	Arachidonic Acid Product	Effects	Comments
Cyclooxygenase	Thromboxane A_2	Vasoconstriction, platelet aggregation	Produced by platelets
	Prostacyclin (PGI_2)	**Vasodilation** and inhibits platelet aggregation	Produced by vascular endothelium
	PGE_2	Pain	—
	PGE_2, PGD_2, PGF_2	Vasodilation	—
Lipoxygenase	LTB_4	Neutrophil chemotaxis, **increased vascular permeability, vasoconstriction or vasodilation***	—
	LTC_4, LTD_4, LTE_4	**Bronchoconstriction, increased vascular permeability, vasoconstriction or vasodilation***	Slow-reacting substance of anaphylaxis

Kinin System

- Bradykinin—vasoactive peptide produced from kininogen by family of enzymes called kallikreins; degraded by different peptidases, including angiotensin-converting enzyme (ACE)
- Activated **Hageman factor (factor XII)** converts prekallikrein → kallikrein
- Kallikrein cleaves high molecular weight kininogen (HMWK) → **bradykinin** (produces increased vascular permeability, pain, vasodilation, bronchoconstriction)

*Can be tissue specific (e.g., vasoconstriction in kidneys and heart; vasodilation in skin and nasal mucosa)

PHAGOCYTOSIS

There are several steps to phagocytosis: engulfment, fusion of the phagosome and lysosome, and digestion. There are **three** mechanisms of intracellular killing, as shown in the figure: NADPH oxidase-dependent, myeloperoxidase-dependent, and lysosome-dependent. **Opsonization** is the enhancement of phagocytosis with IgG and/or C3b.

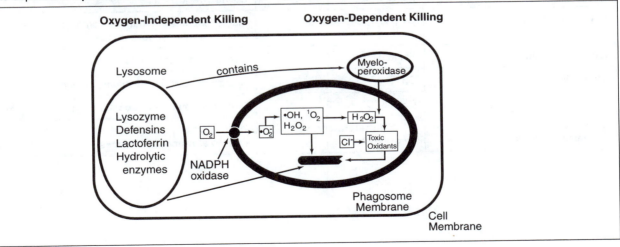

DEFECTS OF PHAGOCYTIC CELLS

Disease	Molecular Defect(s)	Symptoms
Chronic granulomatous disease (CGD)	Deficiency of **NADPH oxidase** (any one of four component proteins); failure to generate superoxide anion, other O_2 radicals	Recurrent infections with **catalase-positive** bacteria and fungi
Chédiak-Higashi syndrome	Granule structural defect	Recurrent infection with bacteria: chemotactic and degranulation defects; **absent NK** activity, **partial albinism**
Leukocyte adhesion deficiency	**Absence of CD18**—common β chain of the leukocyte integrins	Recurrent and chronic infections, failure to form pus, **does not reject umbilical cord** stump

COMPLEMENT CASCADE

The complement system is a set of interacting serum proteins that enhance inflammation (C3a, C4a, C5a) and opsonization (C3b) and cause lysis of particles (e.g., gram-negative bacteria) via C5b-9. The **alternative** pathway is initiated by **surfaces of pathogens**. The **classical** pathway is activated by **Ag/Ab complexes**.

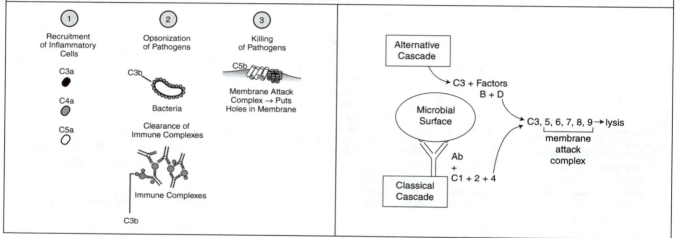

DEFICIENCIES OF COMPLEMENT OR ITS REGULATION

Deficiencies in Complement Components	Deficiency	Signs/Diagnosis
Classical pathway	C1q, C1r, C1s, C2, C4	Marked increase in immune complex diseases, increased infections with pyogenic bacteria
Alternative pathway	Factor B, properdin	Increased neisserial infections
Both pathways	C3	Recurrent bacterial infections, immune complex disease
	C5, C6, C7, or C8	**Recurrent meningococcal and gonococcal infections**
Deficiencies in complement regulatory proteins	C1-INH (**hereditary angioedema**)	Overuse of C1, C2, C4 **Edema at mucosal surfaces**

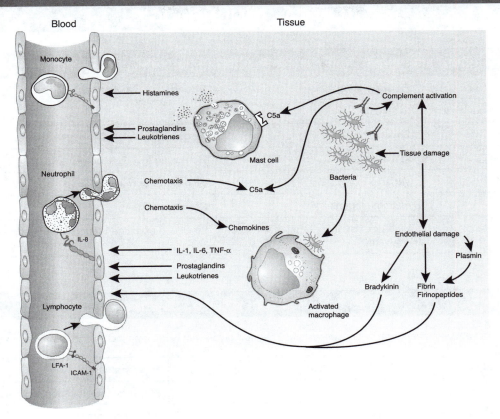

Blood — Tissue

CHRONIC INFLAMMATION	
Causes	**Important Cell Types**
	Macrophages

• Following a bout of acute inflammation
 	
• Persistent infections
 	
• Infections with certain organisms (viruses, mycobacteria, parasites, fungi)
 	
• Autoimmune diseases
 	
• Response to foreign material
	Derived from blood monocytes. During inflammation, macrophages are mainly recruited from the blood (circulating monocytes). Macrophages contain acid hydrolases, elastase, and collagenase, secrete monokines.
	    Chemotactic factors: C5a, MCP-1, MIP-1-α, PDGF, TGF-α
	    Tissue-based macrophages:
	      • Connective tissue (histiocyte)
	      • Lung (pulmonary alveolar macrophages)
	      • Liver (Kupffer cells)
	      • Bone (osteoclasts)
	      • Brain (microglia)
	      • Kidney (mesangial cells)

	Lymphocytes (e.g., B cells, plasma cells)
	• T cells • Lymphocyte chemokine: lymphotaxin
	Eosinophils

	Play an important role in parasitic infections and IgE-mediated allergic reactions
	    • Eosinophilic chemokine: eotaxin
	    • Granules contain major basic protein, which is toxic to parasites

	Basophils
	• Tissue-based basophils are called mast cells, present in high numbers in the lung and skin • Play an important role in IgE-mediated reactions (allergies and anaphylaxis), release histamine

CLINICAL IMMUNOLOGY

COMPARISON OF THE PRIMARY AND SECONDARY IMMUNE RESPONSES

Feature	Primary Response	Secondary Response
Time lag after immunization	5–10 days	1–3 days
Peak response	Small	Large
Antibody isotype	IgM then IgG	Increasing IgG, IgA, or IgE
Antibody **affinity**	Variable to low	High (**affinity maturation**)
Inducing agent	All immunogens	**Protein antigens**
Immunization protocol	High dose of antigen (often with adjuvant)	Low dose of antigen (often without adjuvant)

TYPES OF IMMUNIZATION USED IN MEDICINE

Adjuvants increase immunogenicity nonspecifically. They are given with weak immunogens to enhance the response.

Type of Immunity	Acquired Through	Examples
Natural	Passive means	Placental IgG transport, colostrum
Natural	Active means	Recovery from infection
Artificial	Passive means	Immunoglobulins or immune cells given
Artificial	Active means	Vaccination

DEFECTS OF HUMORAL IMMUNITY

Disease	Molecular Defect	Symptoms/Signs
Bruton X-linked hypogammaglobulinemia	Deficiency of a tyrosine kinase blocks B-cell maturation	Low immunoglobulin of all classes, **no circulating B cells**, **pre-B cells in bone marrow in normal numbers**, normal cell-mediated immunity
Selective IgA deficiency	Deficiency of IgA (most common)	Repeated **sinopulmonary and gastrointestinal infections**
X-linked hyper-IgM syndrome	Deficiency of **CD40L** on activated T cells	**High serum titers of IgM without other isotypes** Normal B- and T-cell numbers, susceptibility to extracellular bacteria and opportunists
Common variable immunodeficiency	B-cell maturation defect and **hypogammaglobulinemia**	Both sexes affected, childhood onset, recurrent bacterial infections and increased susceptibility to *Giardia* Increased risk later in life to autoimmune disease, lymphoma, or gastric cancer

DEFECTS OF T CELLS AND SEVERE COMBINED IMMUNODEFICIENCIES

Category	Disease	Defect	Clinical Manifestation
Selective T-cell deficiency	**DiGeorge syndrome**	Failure of formation of third and fourth pharyngeal pouches, **thymic aplasia**	Facial abnormalities, hypoparathyroidism, cardiac malformations, depression of T-cell numbers and absence of T-cell responses
	MHC class I deficiency	Failure of TAP 1 molecules to transport peptides to endoplasmic reticulum	**CD8+ T cells deficient**, CD4+ T cells normal, recurring viral infections, normal DTH, normal Ab production
Combined partial B- and T-cell deficiency	**Wiskott-Aldrich syndrome**	Defect in cytoskeletal glycoprotein, X-linked	Defective responses to bacterial polysaccharides and depressed IgM, gradual loss of humoral and cellular responses, **thrombocytopenia and eczema**
	Ataxia telangiectasia	Defect in kinase involved in the cell cycle	Ataxia (gait abnormalities), telangiectasia (capillary distortions in the eye), deficiency of IgA and IgE production
Complete functional B- and T-cell deficiency	Severe combined immunodeficiency (SCID)	Defects in common γ chain of IL-2 receptor (also present in receptors for IL-4, -7, -9, -15) X-linked	Chronic diarrhea; skin, mouth, and throat lesions; opportunistic (**fungal**) infections; low levels of circulating lymphocytes; cells unresponsive to mitogens
		Adenosine deaminase deficiency (results in toxic metabolic products in cells)	
		Defect in signal transduction from T-cell IL-2 receptors	
		Bare lymphocyte syndrome/MHC class II deficiency	T cells present and responsive to nonspecific mitogens, no GVHD, **deficient in CD4+ T cells,** hypogammaglobulinemia

ACQUIRED IMMUNODEFICIENCY SYNDROME (AIDS)

Diagnosis	When a patient is HIV-positive with CD4 count less than 200/mm³ *or* HIV-positive with an AIDS-defining disease

Transmission	• Sexual contact: homosexual > heterosexual in U.S.
	  – Cofactors: herpes and syphilis
	• Parenteral transmission:
	  – Intravenous drug abuse
	  – Hemophiliacs
	  – Blood transfusions
	  – Accidental needle sticks in hospital workers
	• Vertical transmission (mother to child)

Pathogenesis	• Human immunodeficiency virus (HIV; an enveloped retrovirus containing reverse transcriptase)
	• HIV infects CD4+ cells (gp120 binds to CD4)
	  – CD4+ T cells
	  – Macrophages
	  – Lymph node follicular dendritic cells
	  – Langerhans cells
	• Entry into cell by fusion requires gp41 and coreceptors
	  – CCR5 (β-chemokine receptor 5)
	  – CXCR4 (α-chemokine receptor)

Diagnosis	• HIV antibody ELISA test • Western blot confirmation
Monitoring	• CD4 count • HIV-1 RNA viral load by PCR
Treatment	• Combination antiretroviral treatment • Reverse transcriptase inhibitors • Protease inhibitors • Prophylaxis for opportunistic infections based on CD4 count

OPPORTUNISTIC INFECTION AND COMMON SITES OF INFECTION IN AIDS PATIENTS

Opportunistic Infection	Common Sites of Infection
Pneumocystis jiroveci (carinii)	Lung (pneumonia), bone marrow
Mycobacterium tuberculosis	Lung, disseminated
Mycobacterium avium-intracellulare	Lung, gastrointestinal tract, disseminated
Coccidioides immitis	Lung, disseminated
Histoplasma capsulatum	Lung, disseminated
Cytomegalovirus	Lung, retina, adrenals, and gastrointestinal tract
Giardia lamblia	Gastrointestinal tract
Cryptosporidium parvum	Gastrointestinal tract
Herpes simplex virus	Esophagus and CNS (encephalitis)
Candida albicans	Oropharynx and esophagus
Aspergillus spp.	CNS, lungs, blood vessels
Toxoplasma gondii	CNS
Cryptococcus neoformans	CNS (meningitis)
JC virus	CNS (progressive multifocal leukoencephalopathy)

Other Complications of AIDS

Hairy leukoplakia	Associated with Epstein-Barr virus (EBV)
Kaposi sarcoma	Associated with human herpes virus 8 (HHV8) Common sites: skin, GI tract, lymph nodes, and lungs
Non-Hodgkin lymphoma	Tend to be high-grade B-cell lymphomas Extranodal CNS lymphomas common
Miscellaneous	Cervical cancer HIV wasting syndrome AIDS nephropathy AIDS dementia complex

HIV Therapies

Anti-HIV therapy usually involves three or more antiretroviral agents, including antimetabolite inhibitors of retroviral reverse transcriptase and viral protease. These aggressive drug combinations (highly active antiretroviral therapy, HAART) are typically initiated early after HIV infection and will often reduce viral load, preserve CD4 counts, and limit opportunistic infections. Drug combinations, as opposed to monotherapy, also slow the resistance to drugs.

Drug	Mechanism of Action	Side Effects and Comments
Nucleoside Reverse Transcriptase Inhibitors (NRTIs)		
NRTIs are generally prodrugs that are converted to active forms via phosphorylation. Prevent conversion of viral RNA into dsDNA. Mechanisms and resistance mechanisms similar. Some cross-resistance occurs. Drugs differ in toxicity profiles (major side effects are listed below) and can cause lactic acidemia.		
Zidovudine (ZDV, formerly AZT)	Inhibits reverse transcriptase	• Used in HAART and in prophylaxis following needlesticks or to prevent maternal/fetal transmission • **Bone marrow suppression**—dose limiting, may require transfusions
Didanosine (ddI)		**Pancreatitis** (dose limiting)
Zalcitabine (ddC)		Peripheral neuropathy
Stavudine (d4T)		Peripheral neuropathy
Lamivudine (3TC)		• Fewer side effects—mild GI distress, headache • Also useful in treating hepatitis B
Nonnucleoside Reverse Transcriptase Inhibitors (NNRTIs)		
Do not require metabolic activation; no cross-resistance		
Nevirapine	Inhibits reverse transcriptase	Prevents maternal/fetal transmission
Delavirdine		Major drug interactions, possible teratogen
Efavirenz		Major drug interactions, possible teratogen
Protease Inhibitors		
Inhibition of aspartate protease (HIV-1 protease); a pol gene product; prevents viral assembly		
Indinavir Ritonavir Saquinavir Nelfinavir Amprenavir Lopinavir	Inhibits aspartate protease	GI distress, hyperglycemia, hyperlipidemia, altered fat distribution, nephrolithiasis (maintain hydration, indinavir), thrombocytopenia (indinavir)
Fusion Inhibitor		
Enfuvirtide	Binds gp41, preventing fusion of viral and cellular membranes	

HYPERSENSITIVITY REACTIONS

Type	Antibody	Complement	Effector Cells	Examples
I (immediate)	**IgE**	No	**Basophil, mast cell**	Hay fever, atopic dermatitis, **insect venom sensitivity**, **anaphylaxis** to drugs, some food allergies, allergy to animals and animal products, **asthma**
II (cytotoxic)	IgG, IgM	Yes	PMN, macrophages, NK cells	Autoimmune or drug-induced hemolytic anemia, transfusion reactions, **HDNB**, hyperacute graft rejection, **Goodpasture disease**, **rheumatic fever**
II (noncytotoxic)	IgG	**No**	None	Myasthenia gravis, Graves disease, type 2 diabetes mellitus
III (immune complex)	IgG, IgM	Yes	PMN, macrophages	**SLE, RA**, polyarteritis nodosa, poststreptococcal glomerulonephritis, Arthus reaction, serum sickness
IV (delayed, DTH)	None	No	CTL, TH1, macrophages	**Tuberculin test**, tuberculosis, leprosy, Hashimoto thyroiditis, poison ivy (**contact dermatitis**), acute graft rejection, **GVHD**, IDDM

Definition of abbreviations: GVHD, graft-versus-host disease; HDNB, hemolytic disease of the newborn; IDDM, insulin-dependent diabetes mellitus; RA, rheumatoid arthritis; SLE, systemic lupus erythematosus.

IMPORTANT AUTOIMMUNE DISEASES

Autoantibodies	Clinical Features	Comments
Systemic lupus erythematosus: chronic systemic autoimmune disease characterized by a loss of self-tolerance and production of autoantibodies		
Antinuclear antibody (ANA) (>95%): **Anti-dsDNA** (40–60%) **Anti-Sm** (20–30%)	• Hemolytic anemia, thrombocytopenia, leukopenia • Arthritis • Skin rashes (including classic "malar" rash) • Renal disease • Libman-Sacks endocarditis • Serositis • Neurologic symptoms	• Females >> Males (M:F = 1:9), peak age 20–45 years, African American > Caucasian • Mechanism of injury: type II and III hypersensitivity reactions • Treatment: steroids and other immunosuppressants
Sjögren syndrome: an autoimmune disease characterized by destruction of the lacrimal and salivary glands, resulting in the inability to produce saliva or tears		
Antiribonucleoprotein antibodies: Anti-SS-A (Ro) Anti-SS-B (La)	• Keratoconjuctivitis sicca (dry eyes) and corneal ulcers • Xerostomia (dry mouth) • Mikulicz syndrome: enlargement of the salivary and lacrimal glands	• Females > males; age range: 30–50 years • Often associated with rheumatoid arthritis and other autoimmune diseases (e.g., SLE) • Increased risk of developing lymphoma

(Continued)

IMPORTANT AUTOIMMUNE DISEASES (CONT'D.)

Autoantibodies	Clinical Features	Comments
Scleroderma (progressive systemic sclerosis): characterized by fibroblast stimulation and deposition of collagen in the skin and internal organs; females > males; age range: 20–55 years; activation of fibroblasts by growth factors/cytokines leads to fibrosis		
Diffuse Scleroderma		
Anti-DNA topoisomerase I antibodies (Scl-70) (70%)	Widespread skin involvement Early involvement of the visceral organs • Esophagus—dysphagia • GI tract—malabsorption • Pulmonary fibrosis—dyspnea on exertion • Cardiac fibrosis—arrhythmias • Kidney fibrosis—renal insufficiency	Raynaud phenomenon is seen in almost all patients and often preceeds other symptoms. **Treatment:** vasodilators, ACE inhibitors, NSAIDs, steroids, d-penicillamine
Limited scleroderma (e.g., CREST syndrome)		
Anticentromere antibodies	• Skin involvement of the face and hands • Late involvement of visceral organs (relatively benign clinical course)	(**C**alcinosis, **R**aynaud phenomenon, **E**sophageal dysmotility, **S**clerodactyly, **T**elangiectasia)

TRANSPLANTATION IMMUNOLOGY

GRAFTS USED IN MEDICINE

Grafts	Definition
Autologous (**autografts**)	Tissue is moved from one location to another in the same individual
Syngeneic	Transplants between genetically identical individuals (monozygotic twins)
Allogeneic	Transplants between genetically different members of the same species
Xenogeneic	Transplants between members of different species

GRAFT REJECTION REACTIONS

Type of Rejection	Time Taken	Cause
Hyperacute	Minutes to hours	Preformed anti-donor antibodies and complement
Accelerated	Days	Reactivation of sensitized T cells
Acute	Days to weeks	Primary activation of T cells
Chronic	Months to years	Causes are unclear: antibodies, immune complexes, slow cellular reaction, recurrence of disease
Graft versus host	Weeks to months	Grafted bone marrow T cells attack host

IMMUNOLOGY TECHNIQUES IN DIAGNOSIS

FLUORESCENCE ACTIVATED CELL SORTER

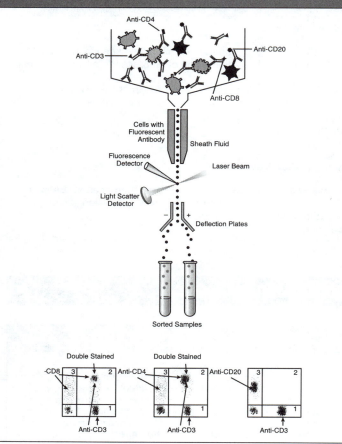

Complex mixtures of cells are treated with fluorescent dye-labeled antibodies and run through the apparatus. The fluorescence activated cell sorter (FACS) separates the cells into populations based on their level of fluorescence with a particular dye. A computer-generated diagram is created. Each dot on these diagrams represents a cell that has bound to a fluorescent-labeled antibody. Increasing fluorescence intensity with one dye is represented as a rise on the *y*-axis, and increasing fluorescence with the other dye occurs as you move right on the *x*-axis. Double-labeled cells are always found in the upper right quadrant. Cells that have only background fluorescence with either dye are found in the lower left quadrant.

The results of flow cytometry are often shown for question analysis. Be sure to know the key CD markers and the biologic functions of the cells that possess them.

IMMUNOPHARMACOLOGY

RECOMBINANT CYTOKINES AND CLINICAL USES

Cytokine	Clinical Uses
Aldesleukin (IL-2)	↑ Lymphocyte differentiation and ↑ NKs—used in renal cell cancer and metastatic melanoma
Oprelvekin (IL-11)	↑ Platelet formation—used in thrombocytopenia
Filgrastim (G-CSF)	↑ Granulocytes—used for bone marrow recovery
Sargramostim (GM-CSF)	↑ Granulocytes and macrophages—used for bone marrow recovery
Erythropoietin	Anemias, especially associated with renal failure
Thrombopoietin	Thrombocytopenia
Interferon-α	Hepatitis B and C, leukemias, malignant melanoma, Kaposi sarcoma
Interferon-β	Multiple sclerosis
Interferon-γ	Chronic granulomatous disease →↑ TNF

IMMUNOSUPPRESSANT AGENTS		
Drug	**Mechanism**	**Uses**
Azathioprine	Converted to mercaptopurine, whose metabolites inhibit purine metabolism Cytotoxic to proliferating lymphocytes (especially T cells)	Autoimmune diseases (e.g., SLE, rheumatoid arthritis) and immunosuppression in renal homografts
Corticosteroids	↓ synthesis of prostaglandins, leukotrienes, cytokines; inhibit T-cell proliferation; at immunosuppressive doses, they are cytotoxic to some T cells	Cancer, organ transplants
Cyclophosphamide	Cytotoxic to proliferating lymphocytes (especially B cells)	• Autoimmune diseases, bone marrow transplants • Similar cytotoxic drugs: cytarabine, dactinomycin, methotrexate, vincristine
Cyclosporine	Antibiotic that binds to cyclophilin → inhibits calcineurin (cytoplasmic phosphatase) → ↓ activation of T-cell transcription factors → ↓ IL-2, IL-3, and interferon-γ	• DOC in organ or tissue transplantation (± mycophenolate ± steroids ± cytotoxic drugs) • Side effects: peripheral neuropathy, nephrotoxicity, hyperglycemia, hypertension, hyperlipidemia, hirsutism, gingival overgrowth, cholelithiasis
Tacrolimus	Antibiotic that binds to FK-binding protein (FKBP); also inhibits calcineurin (similar to cyclosporine)	• Used alternatively to cyclosporine in renal and liver transplants • Side effects similar to cyclosporine
Mycophenolate	Inhibits de novo purine synthesis	• Kidney, liver, heart transplants • Used with cyclosporine in renal transplants to ↓ cyclosporine dose
RhD immune globulin (RhoGAM™)	Antibody to red cell RhD antigens	Administer to RhD ⊖ mother within 72 h of Rh ⊕ delivery to prevent hemolytic disease of newborn in subsequent pregnancy
Monoclonal antibodies	See dacliximab, infliximab, muromonab in table below	

MONOCLONAL ANTIBODIES (MABs) AND CLINICAL USES	
MAB	**Clinical Uses**
Abciximab	Antiplatelet (acute coronary symptoms, post-angioplasty)—antagonist of IIb/IIIa receptors
Dacliximab	Kidney transplants—blocks IL-2 receptors
Infliximab	Rheumatoid arthritis and Crohn disease—binds TNF-α
Muromonab	Allograft rejection block in renal transplants—binds the T3 (CD3) antigen on thymocytes
Palivizumab	Respiratory syncytial virus—blocks RSV protein
Rituximab	Non-Hodgkin lymphoma—binds to CD20 antigen on B-cell surface protein
Trastuzumab	Breast cancer—antagonist to HER2/neu receptor

Microbiology

GENERAL PRINCIPLES OF MICROBIOLOGY

COMPARISON OF MEDICALLY IMPORTANT MICROBIAL GROUPS

Characteristic	Viruses	Bacteria	Fungi	Parasites
Diameter	Minute (0.02–0.3 μ)	Small (0.3–2 μ)	3–10 μ	15–25 μ (trophozoites)
Cell type	**Acellular**—no nucleus	**Prokaryotic cells**	**Eukaryotic cells**	
	• DNA or RNA • 1 nucleocapsid, except in segmented or diploid viruses	• DNA and RNA • 1 chromosome • **No histones**	• DNA and RNA • More than one chromosome	
	Replicates in host cells	DNA replicates continuously	G and S phases	
		Exons, **no introns**	Introns and exons	
	Some have polycistronic mRNA and post-translational cleavage	**Mono- and polycistronic mRNA**	**Monocistronic RNA**	
	Uses host organelles; obligate intracellular parasites	**No membrane-bound organelles**	Mitochondria and other membrane-bound organelles	
	No ribosomes	**70S** ribosomes (30S+50S)	**80S** ribosomes (40S+60S)	
Cellular membrane	Some are enveloped, but no membrane function	Membranes have **no sterols, except** *Mycoplasma*, which have cholesterol	Membrane **ergosterol** is major sterol	Sterols, such as **cholesterol**
Cell wall	No cell wall	**Peptidoglycan**	Complex carbohydrate **cell wall: chitin,** glucans, or mannans	No cell wall
Replication	Make and assemble viral components	**Binary fission (asexual)**	Cytokinesis with mitosis/meiosis	Cytokinesis with mitosis/meiosis

BACTERIOLOGY

BACTERIAL GROWTH CURVE

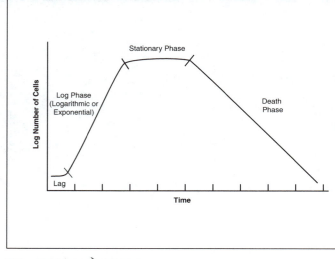

Lag Phase:

• Detoxifying medium
• Turning on enzymes to utilize medium

Log Phase:

• Rapid exponential growth
• Generation time—time it takes one cell to divide into two
• This is determined during log phase

Stationary Phase:

• Nutrients used up
• Toxic products begin to accumulate
• Number of new cells = the number of dying cells

Death Phase:

• Nutrients gone
• Toxic products kill cells
• Number of cells dying exceeds the number of cells dividing

FEATURES OF BACTERIA

Envelope Structure	Gram ⊕ or ⊖	Chemical Composition	Function
Capsule (nonessential) = slime = glycocalyx	Both Gram ⊕ and Gram ⊖	**Polysaccharide gel** (except *B. anthracis*)	• **Antiphagocytic** • **Immunogenic** (except *S. pyogenes* and *N. meningitidis*, type B)
Outer membrane	**Gram ⊖** only	Phospholipid/proteins LPS: • Lipid A • Polysaccharide	Hydrophobic membrane: • **LPS = endotoxin** • **Lipid A = toxic moiety** • PS = immunogenic portion
		Outer membrane proteins	Attachment, virulence, etc.
		Protein porins	Passive transport
Cell wall = peptidoglycan	Gram ⊕ (thick) Gram ⊖ (thin)	**Peptidoglycan**—open 3-D net of: • *N*-acetyl-glucosamine • *N*-acetyl-muramic acid • Amino acids (including DAP)	• Rigid support, cell shape, and protection from osmotic damage • Synthesis **inhibited by penicillins and** cephalosporins • **Confers Gram reaction**
	Gram ⊕ only	**Teichoic acids**	• Immunogenic, induces TNF-α, IL-1 • **Attachment**
	Acid-fast only	**Mycolic acids**	• Acid-fastness • **Resistance to drying and chemicals**
Periplasmic space	**Gram ⊖** only	"Storage space" between the inner and outer membranes	• Enzymes to break down large molecules (β-lactamases) • Aids regulation of osmolarity

Cytoplasmic membrane
= inner membrane
= cell membrane
= plasma membrane
	Gram ⊕
	Gram ⊖
		Phospholipid bilayer with many embedded proteins	• Hydrophobic cell "sac"
			• Selective permeability and active transport
			• **Carrier for enzymes** for:
			  – Oxidative metabolism
			  – Phosphorylation
			  – Phospholipid synthesis
			  – DNA replication
			  – Peptidoglycan cross linkage
			• **Penicillin binding proteins** (PBPs)

Definition of abbreviation: DAP, diaminopimelic acid; LPS, lipopolysaccharide.

NORMAL FLORA ORGANISMS

Most infectious disease vignettes begin with the necessity to rule out the normal flora organisms that are cultured from the patient. Make sure you know those organisms that can confound a simple Gram-stain type of diagnosis, e.g., notice in the oropharynx and vagina, normal flora organisms can be indistinguishable from pathogens by Gram stain alone!

Site	Common or Medically Important Organisms	Less Common but Notable Organisms
Blood, internal organs	None, generally sterile	—
Cutaneous surfaces	*Staphylococcus epidermidis*	*Staphylococcus aureus, Corynebacteria* (diphtheroids), streptococci, anaerobes, e.g., peptostreptococci, *Candida* spp.
Nose	*Staphylococcus aureus*	*S. epidermidis,* diphtheroids, assorted streptococci
Oropharynx	**Viridans streptococci**, including *Streptococcus mutans*	Assorted streptococci, **nonpathogenic *Neisseria*, nontypeable *Haemophilus influenzae***
Gingival crevices	Anaerobes: *Bacteroides, Prevotella, Fusobacterium, Streptococcus, Actinomyces*	—
Stomach	None	—
Colon (microaerophilic/ anaerobic)	Adult: ***Bacteroides**/Prevotella* (predominant organism), *Escherichia, Bifidobacterium*	*Eubacterium, Fusobacterium, Lactobacillus,* assorted gram-negative anaerobic rods *Enterococcus faecalis* and other streptococci
Vagina	**Lactobacillus**	Assorted streptococci, gram-negative rods, diphtheroids, yeasts

BACTERIAL TOXINS

Endotoxin

Endotoxin (lipopolysaccharide = LPS) is part of the gram-negative outer membrane.

- The toxic portion is lipid A. LPS is heat stable and not strongly immunogenic, so it cannot be converted to a toxoid.
- LPS activates macrophages, leading to release of TNF-α, IL-1, and IL-6. IL-1 is a major mediator of fever. Damage to the endothelium from bradykinin-induced vasodilation leads to shock. Coagulation (DIC) is mediated through the activation of Hageman factor.

Exotoxin

Exotoxins are protein toxins, generally quite toxic, and secreted by bacterial cells.

- Exotoxins can be modified by chemicals or heat to produce a toxoid that still is immunogenic, but no longer toxic, so it can be used as a vaccine.
- Most are A-B (or "two") component protein toxins. B component binds to specific cell receptors to facilitate the internalization of A (the active [toxic] component)

	Organism (Gram)	Toxin	Mode of Action	Role in Disease
MAJOR EXOTOXINS				
Protein synthesis inhibitors	*Corynebacterium diphtheriae* (⊕)	**Diphtheria toxin**	• ADP ribosyl transferase **inactivates EF-2** • *Targets:* **heart, nerves, epithelium**	Inhibits eukaryotic cell protein synthesis
	Pseudomonas aeruginosa (⊖)	**Exotoxin A**	• ADP ribosyl transferase **inactivates EF-2** • *Target:* **liver**	Inhibits eukaryotic cell protein synthesis
	Shigella dysenteriae (⊖)	**Shiga toxin**	**Interferes with 60S ribosomal subunit**	• Inhibits protein synthesis in eukaryotic cells • Enterotoxic, cytotoxic, and neurotoxic
	Enterohemorrhagic *E. coli* (EHEC) (⊖)	**Verotoxin** (shiga-like)	**Interferes with 60S ribosomal subunit**	Inhibits protein synthesis in eukaryotic cells
Neurotoxins	*Clostridium tetani* (⊕)	**Tetanus toxin**	**Blocks release of glycine and GABA**	Inhibits neurotransmission in inhibitory synapses
	Clostridium botulinum (⊕)	**Botulinum toxin**	**Blocks release of acetylcholine**	Inhibits cholinergic synapses
Endotoxin enhancers	*Staphylococcus aureus* (⊕)	**TSST-1**	• Pyrogenic, decreases liver clearance of LPS • **Superantigen**	Fever, increased susceptibility to LPS, rash, shock, capillary leakage
	Streptococcus pyogenes (⊕)	**Exotoxin A,** also called erythrogenic or pyrogenic toxin	**Similar to TSST-1**	Fever, increased susceptibility to LPS, rash, shock, capillary leakage, cardiotoxicity
cAMP inducers	Enterotoxigenic *Escherichia coli* (⊖)	Heat **labile toxin** (LT)	LT stimulates an adenylate cyclase by **ADP ribosylation of GTP-binding protein**	Both LT and ST promote secretion of fluid and electrolytes from intestinal epithelium
	Vibrio cholerae (⊖)	**Cholera toxin**	**Similar to *E. coli* LT**	Profuse, watery diarrhea
	Bacillus anthracis (⊕)	**Anthrax toxin (3 proteins make 2 toxins)**	• **EF = edema factor = adenylate cyclase** • **LF = lethal factor** • **PA = protective antigen (B component for both)**	• Decreases phagocytosis • Causes **edema, kills cells**
	Bordetella pertussis (⊖)	**Pertussis toxin**	**ADP ribosylates G$_i$,** the negative regulator of adenylate cyclase, leading to increased cAMP	• **Histamine sensitizing** • **Lymphocytosis promotion** • **Islet activation**
Cytolysins	*Clostridium perfringens* (⊕)	**Alpha toxin**	**Lecithinase**	• Damages cell membranes • **Myonecrosis**
	Staphylococcus aureus (⊕)	**Alpha toxin**	**Pore former**	Membrane becomes leaky

Important Pathogenic Factors and Diagnostic Enzymes

Factor	Function	Organisms
All **capsules**	**Antiphagocytic**	*S*treptococcus pneumoniae, *K*lebsiella pneumoniae, *H*aemophilus influenzae, *P*seudomonas aeruginosa, *N*eisseria meningitidis, *C*ryptococcus neoformans (mnemonic: **s**ome **k**illers **h**ave **p**retty **n**ice **c**apsules) and many more
M protein	Antiphagocytic	Group A streptococci
A protein	Antiphagocytic	*Staphylococcus aureus*
Lipoteichoic acid	Attachment to host cells	All **gram-positive** bacteria
All **pili**	Attachment	Many gram-negatives
Pili of *N. gonorrhoeae*	**Antiphagocytic, antigenic variation**	*N. gonorrhoeae*
Hyaluronidase	Hydrolysis of ground substance	Group A streptococci
Collagenase	Hydrolysis of collagen	*Clostridium perfringens, Prevotella melaninogenica*
Urease	Increases pH of locale, contributes to kidney stones	**P**roteus, **U**reaplasma, **N**ocardia, **C**ryptococcus, **H**elicobacter (mnemonic: **PUNCH**)
Kinases	Hydrolysis of fibrin	*Streptococcus, Staphylococcus*
Lecithinase	Destroys cell membranes	*Clostridium perfringens*
Heparinase	Thrombophlebitis	*Bacteroides*
Catalase	Destroys hydrogen peroxide (**major problem for CGD patients**)	• Most important: *Staphylococcus, Pseudomonas, Aspergillus, Candida,* Enterobacteriaceae • Most anaerobes lack catalase
IgA proteases	Destroy IgA, promote colonization of mucosal surfaces	*Neisseria, Haemophilus, Streptococcus pneumoniae*
Oxidase	Possession of cytochrome c oxidase	*Neisseria* and most gram-negatives, except the Enterobacteriaceae
Coagulase	Produces fibrin clot	***Staphylococcus aureus*** and *Yersinia pestis*

Unusual Growth Requirements

Requirements in Growth Media	Organism
Factors **X and V**	***Haemophilus***
Cholesterol	*Mycoplasma*
High salt	*Staphylococcus aureus*, group D **enterococci** and ***Vibrio***
Cysteine	***Francisella, Legionella, Brucella,* and *Pasteurella***

BACTERIAL GENETICS

Conjugation	The exchange of chromosomal or plasmid genes from one bacterium to another through conjugal bridge
Transduction	The delivery of bacterial genes from one bacterium to another via a virus vector
Transformation	The uptake and incorporation of free DNA from the environment
Lysogeny	The stable association between a bacterium and a temperate phage. It imparts the important traits: **O** = *Salmonella* O antigen, **B** = botulinum toxin, **E** = erythrogenic toxin of *Streptococcus pyogenes,* **D** = diphtheria toxin; mnemonic: **OBED** (or a little pregnant with phage)
Transposon	A mobile genetic element capable of transposition within a cell; these are responsible for the formation of multiple drug-resistance plasmids

ANTIBACTERIAL AGENTS

MECHANISMS OF ACTION OF ANTIMICROBIAL AGENTS

Mechanism of Action	Antimicrobial Agents
Inhibition of bacterial cell-wall synthesis	Penicillins, cephalosporins, imipenem/meropenem, aztreonam, vancomycin
Inhibition of bacterial protein synthesis	Aminoglycosides, chloramphenicol, macrolides, tetracyclines, streptogramins, linezolid
Inhibition of DNA replication or transcription	Fluoroquinolones, rifampin
Inhibition of nucleic acid synthesis	Trimethoprim, flucytosine
Inhibition of folic acid synthesis	Sulfonamides, trimethoprim, pyrimethamine
Disruption of cell membrane function	Azole and polyene antifungal agents

CELL WALL SYNTHESIS INHIBITORS

Class/Example	Mechanism of Action/ Resistance	Spectrum	Toxicity/Notes
Penicillins			
First generation: penicillin G, penicillin V **(narrow spectrum)**	**Mechanism:** inhibit cross-linking of peptidoglycan component of cell wall by transpeptidases; action mediated by binding of penicillin-binding proteins (PBPs) **Resistance:** production of β-lactamases, which cleave the β-lactam ring structure; change in PBPs; change in porins	Gram-positives *N. meningitidis* *Clostridia* Syphilis *Leptospira* Staph ubiquitously resistant	—
Second generation: methicillin, nafcillin **(β-lactam–resistant penicillins)**		Gram-positives, especially *S. aureus*	Resistant staph emerging "MRSA"
Third generation: ampicillin, amoxicillin **(wider spectrum)**		Gram-positives, enterococci, *H. influenzae* *L monocytogenes* *M. catarrhalis* *E. coli*	Activity may be augmented with penicillinase inhibitors (e.g., clavulanic acid and sulbactam)
Fourth generation: mezlocillin, piperacillin, carbenicillin, ticarcillin		• Gram-negatives, including **Pseudomonas** • Enterococci (mezlocillin and piperacillin)	—

(Continued)

CELL WALL SYNTHESIS INHIBITORS (CONT'D.)			
Class/Example	**Mechanism of Action/resistance**	**Spectrum**	**Toxicity/Notes**
Cephalosporins			
First generation: cefazolin, cephalexin	**Mechanism:** inhibition of cell wall formation similar to penicillins **Resistance:** same as penicillins	Gram-positives *Proteus mirabilis* *E. coli* *Klebsiella pneumoniae*	• Cross-allergenicity with penicillins occurs in 5% • Anaphylaxis, but not rash, a contraindication in penicillin-sensitive pt.
Second generation: cefotetan, cefoxitin, cefuroxime		Less gram-positive activity and more gram-negative activity than first generation • *B. fragilis* • *H. influenzae* • *M. catarrhalis* • *P. mirabilis* • *E. coli* • *K. pneumoniae* • *Neisseria, Enterobacter*	—
Third generation: ceftazidime, cefoperazone, cefotaxime		Less gram-positive activity and more gram-negative activity than second generation • *Serratia* sp. • *Borrelia burgdorferi* • *H. influenzae* • *Neisseria* • *Enterobacter* Some have anti-*Pseudomonas* activity	• Most penetrate **blood-brain** barrier (not cefoperazone) • Reserved for serious infections
Fourth generation: cefepime		More gram-negative activity while retaining first-generation gram-positive activity	More resistant to gram-negative penicillinases
Carbapenems and Monobactams			
Carbapenems (meropenem, imipenem)	Similar mechanism to penicillins	Gram positives, gram-negative rods, anaerobes	• **Nephrotoxic** • GI distress • Rash • CNS toxicity • **Cilastatin administered concurrently** with imipenem increases the drug's half-life and reduces nephrotoxicity • Beta-lactamase resistant
Monobactams (aztreonam)		Gram-negative rods	• GI distress with superinfection, vertigo, headache • Synergistic with aminoglycosides • Beta-lactamase resistant
Non-Beta Lactam Cell Wall Synthesis Inhibitors			
Vancomycin	Binds cell wall precursors, preventing polymerization	Drug resistant gram-positives, e.g., MRSA sepsis (IV) or *C. difficile* (oral [not absorbed from lumen])	• Chills, fever, ototoxicity, nephrotoxicity • Flushing or **"red man syndrome"** upon rapid infusion • Resistant strains emerging

Summary of Mechanisms of Protein Synthesis Inhibition

Event	Antibiotics and Binding Sites	Mechanism
Formation of initiation complex	Aminoglycosides (30S) Linezolid (50S)	Interfere with initiation codon functions—block association of 50S ribosomal subunit with mRNA-30S (bacteriostatic); misreading of code—incorporation of wrong amino acid (bactericidal)
Amino-acid incorporation	Tetracyclines (30S) Dalfopristin/quinupristin (50S)	Block the attachment of aminoacyl tRNA to acceptor site (bacteriostatic)
Formation of peptide bond	Chloramphenicol (50S)	Inhibit the activity of peptidyltransferase (bacteriostatic)
Translocation	Macrolides and clindamycin (50S)	Inhibit translocation of peptidyl tRNA from acceptor to donor site (bacteriostatic)

Protein Synthesis Inhibitors

Drug/Class	Site of Inhibition	Spectrum	Mechanisms of Resistance	Toxicities	Notes
Chloramphenicol	50S	Wide spectrum, including: <ul><li>*H. influenzae*</li><li>*N. meningitidis*</li><li>*Bacteroides*</li><li>*Rickettsia*</li><li>*Salmonella*</li></ul>	Plasmid-mediated acetyltransferases that inactivate the drug	<ul><li>**"Gray baby" syndrome** ($\downarrow$ glucuronyl transferase in neonates)</li><li>**Aplastic anemia**/bone marrow suppression</li><li>GI irritation</li></ul>	<ul><li>Toxicity limits clinical use</li><li>Reserved for severe *Salmonella* and bacterial meningitis in β-lactam–sensitive patients</li></ul>
Tetracyclines: <ul><li>tetracycline</li><li>doxycycline</li><li>minocycline</li></ul>	30S	Gram ⊕ and Gram ⊖: <ul><li>*Rickettsia*</li><li>*Chlamydia*</li><li>*Mycoplasma*</li><li>*H. pylori*</li><li>*Brucella*</li><li>*Vibrio*</li></ul>	Plasmid-mediated efflux pumps and reduced uptake via transport systems	<ul><li>GI irritation</li><li>**Tooth enamel dysplasia**</li><li>**Bone growth irregularities**</li><li>Hepatotoxic</li><li>**Photosensitivity**</li><li>Vestibular toxicity</li></ul>	<ul><li>**Fanconi syndrome** with expired tetracycline</li><li>Oral absorption limited by multivalent cations</li></ul>
Macrolides: <ul><li>erythromycin,</li><li>azithromycin</li><li>clarithromycin</li></ul>	50S	Gram ⊕, some Gram ⊖: <ul><li>*Chlamydia*</li><li>*Mycoplasma*</li><li>*Ureaplasma*</li><li>*Legionella*</li><li>*Campylobacter*</li></ul>	Methylation of binding site on 50S; increased efflux from multidrug exporters	<ul><li>**GI irritation**</li><li>Cholestasis</li><li>Hepatitis</li><li>Skin rashes</li><li>$\downarrow$ P-450</li></ul>	Useful in atypical pneumonia
Clindamycin	50S	Narrow spectrum: Gram ⊕, anaerobes	Methylation of binding site on 50S	<ul><li>GI irritation</li><li>Skin rash</li><li>***C. difficile* superinfection**</li></ul>	—
Aminoglycosides: <ul><li>gentamicin</li><li>neomycin</li><li>tobramycin</li><li>streptomycin</li></ul>	30S	Gram ⊖ rods	Plasmid-mediated **group transferases**	Ototoxicity, nephrotoxicity	Neomycin for bowel prep (stays in bowel lumen)
Oxazolidinones: <ul><li>linezolid</li></ul>	50S	Gram ⊕ cocci	Resistance rare	<ul><li>Thrombocytopenia, neutropenia, esp. in immunocompromised</li><li>MAO inhibition (dietary and drug restrictions)</li></ul>	No cross-resistance with other protein synthesis inhibitors, so often reserved for resistant infections

FOLIC ACID SYNTHESIS INHIBITORS

Pteridine + PABA

↓ Dihydropteroate Synthase ← Sulfonamides inhibit

Dihydropteroic Acid
+
Glutamate

↓

Dihydrofolic Acid

↓ Dihydrofolate Reductase ← Trimethoprim and pyrimethamine inhibit

Tetrahydrofolic Acid

Class/Drug	Mechanism of Action	Spectrum	Mechanism of Resistance	Toxicity	Notes
Sulfonamides	PABA antimetabolite inhibits bacterial dihydropteroate synthase, thus curbing folate synthesis	Gram ⊖, gram ⊕, *Chlamydia*, *Nocardia*	Decreased accumulation of drugs, decreased affinity of drug for **dihydropteroate synthase**	• Hypersensitivity • Hemolytic anemia in G6PD-deficient • Nephrotoxicity • Kernicterus in newborns	Combined with trimethoprim for increased efficacy
Trimethoprim	Inhibits bacterial dihydrofolate reductase, thus inhibiting folate synthesis	*H. influenzae* *M. catarrhalis*	Production of bacterial **dihydrofolate reductase** with decreased affinity for drug	• Megaloblastic anemia • Leukopenia • Granulocytopenia	• Adverse effects may be reduced by concurrent **folinic acid** • Good for UTIs because it is excreted in urine unchanged

DNA REPLICATION INHIBITORS

Class/drug	Mechanism of Action	Spectrum	Mechanism of Resistance	Toxicity	Notes
Fluoroquinolones: • ciprofloxacin • ofloxacin • levofloxacin	Interfere with bacterial DNA topoisomerase II and IV (DNA gyrase), resulting in inhibition of DNA synthesis	Gram ⊖ rods, *Neisseria*, occasional gram ⊕	• Decreased intracellular drug concentrations through efflux pumps and altered porins • Alteration of drug's binding site	• **GI distress** • Skin rash • Superinfection	Contraindicated in pregnancy due to cartilage formation abnormalities in animal studies

MISCELLANEOUS

Class/Drug	Mechanism of Action	Spectrum	Mechanism of Resistance	Toxicity	Notes
Metronidazole	When reduced, interferes with nucleic acid synthesis (bactericidal)	Anaerobes (except *Actinomyces*)	Rare plasma-mediated resistance	• GI distress • Disulfiram-like reaction with alcohol • Peripheral neuropathy, ataxia	• Strong metallic taste • DOC in pseudomembranous colitis

Definition of abbreviations: DOC, drug of choice; G6PD, glucose-6-phosphate dehydrogenase; PABA, para-aminobenzoic acid; UTI, urinary tract Infection.

PARASITES

OBLIGATE INTRACELLULAR PARASITES

- Cannot be cultured on inert media. Intracellular organisms (both obligate and facultative) protected from antibody and complement. Intracellular pathogens tend to elicit cell-mediated immune responses, so end pathologic lesion frequently a granuloma
- **All rickettsiae, chlamydiae, *Mycobacterium leprae***
- **All viruses**
- ***Plasmodium, Toxoplasma gondii, Babesia***, *Leishmania, Trypanosoma cruzi* (amastigotes in cardiac muscle)

FACULTATIVE INTRACELLULAR PARASITES

- Live inside phagocytic cells in the body, but can be cultured on inert media
- *Francisella tularensis*, **Listeria monocytogenes, Mycobacterium tuberculosis**, *Brucella* species, nontuberculous mycobacteria, *Salmonella typhi, Legionella pneumophila, Yersinia pestis, Nocardia, Borrelia burgdorferi*, **Histoplasma capsulatum**

PROTOZOANS

Common Name	Amebae	Flagellates	Ciliates	Apicomplexa (Intracellular)
Important genera	***Entamoeba*** *Naegleria* *Acanthamoeba*	LUMINAL (GUT, UG) ***Trichomonas*** ***Giardia*** HEMOFLAGELLATES *Leishmania* *Trypanosoma*	*Balantidium*	BLOOD/TISSUE ***Plasmodium*** ***Toxoplasma*** *Babesia* INTESTINAL ***Cryptosporidium*** *Isospora*

PROTOZOAN PARASITES

Species	Disease/Organs Most Affected	Form/Transmission	Diagnosis	Treatment
Entamoeba histolytica	• **Amebiasis:** dysentery • **Inverted, flask-shaped lesions** in large intestine with extension to peritoneum and liver, lungs, brain, and heart • Blood and pus in stool • Liver abscesses	• Cysts • Fecal-oral transmission: water, fresh fruits, and vegetables	• Trophozoites or cysts in stool • Nuclei have sharp central karyosome and fine chromatin "spokes" • Serology	Metronidazole followed by iodoquinol
Giardia lamblia	**Giardiasis:** Ventral sucking disk attaches to lining of duodenal wall, causing a **fatty**, foul-smelling diarrhea (diarrhea → **malabsorption** in duodenum, jejunum)	• Cysts • Fecal (human, beaver, muskrat, etc.), oral transmission: water, food, day care, oral-anal sex	• Trophozoites or cysts in stool or fecal antigen test (replaces "string" test) • "Falling leaf" motility	Metronidazole
Cryptosporidium **spp.**	Cryptosporidiosis: transient diarrhea in healthy; severe in immunocompromised hosts	• Cysts • Undercooked meat, water; not killed by chlorination	Acid fast oocysts in stool: biopsy shows dots (cysts) in intestinal glands	—
Balantidium coli	**Dysentery:** infection of colon with penetration	• Cysts • Contaminated food or water	Ciliated trophozoites, cysts in feces	Tetracycline
Trichomonas vaginalis (urogenital)	Trichomoniasis: often asymptomatic or frothy vaginal discharge	• Trophozoites • **Sexual**	Motile trophozoites in methylene blue wet mount	Metronidazole

FREE-LIVING AMEBAE THAT OCCASIONALLY INFECT HUMANS

Species	Disease/Locale	Form/Transmission	Diagnosis	Treatment
Naegleria	**Primary amebic meningoencephalitis** (PAM): severe prefrontal headache, nausea, high fever, often an altered sense of smell; often fatal	Free-living amebae picked up while swimming or **diving in very warm fresh water**	• Motile trophozoites in CSF • Culture on plates seeded with gram ⊖ bacteria; amebae will leave trails	Amphotericin B (rarely successful)
Acanthamoeba	**Keratitis; GAE** in immunocompromised patients; insidious onset but progressive to death	• Free-living amebae in contaminated **contact lens solution (airborne cysts)** • Not certain for GAE; inhalation or contact with contaminated soil or water	• Star-shaped cysts on biopsy; rarely seen in CSF • Culture as above	Keratitis: topical miconazole and propamidine isethionate GAE: sulfadiazine (rarely successful)

Definition of abbreviations: CSF, cerebrospinal fluid; GAE, granulomatous amaebic encephalitis.

PLASMODIUM LIFE CYCLE

Each *Plasmodium* has two distinct hosts:

- A vertebrate, such as the human, where asexual phase (schizogony) takes place in the liver and red blood cells
- An arthropod host (*Anopheles* mosquito), where gametogony (sexual phase) and sporogony take place

Disease is caused by a variety of mechanisms, including metabolism of hemoglobin and lysis of infected cells, leading to anemia and to agglutination of the infected RBCs. Paroxysms (chills, fever spike, and malarial rigors) occur when the infected RBCs are lysed, liberating a new crop of merozoites.

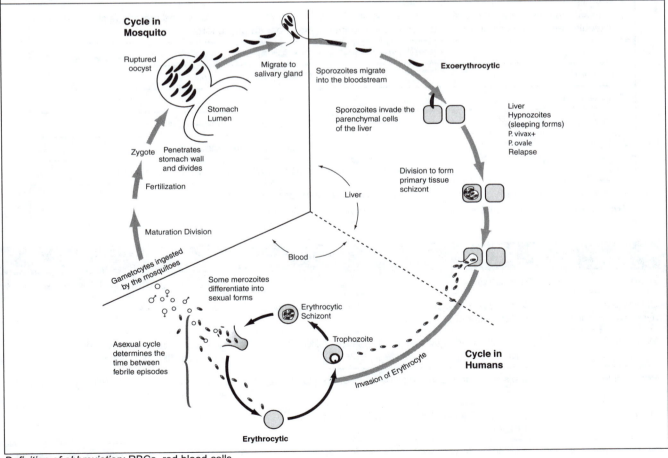

Definition of abbreviation: RBCs, red blood cells.

PLASMODIUM SPECIES

Species	Disease	Important Features	Blood Smears	Liver Stages	Treatment
Plasmodium vivax	Benign tertian	48-hour fever spikes	Enlarged host cells; ameboid trophozoites	Persistent hypnozoites Relapse*	Chloroquine PO$_4$ then primaquine
Plasmodium ovale	Benign tertian	48-hour fever spikes	Oval, jagged, infected RBCs	Persistent hypnozoites Relapse	Chloroquine PO$_4$ then primaquine
Plasmodium malariae	Quartan or malarial	72-hour fever spikes; recrudescence*	Bar and band forms; rosette schizonts	No persistent stage*	Chloroquine PO$_4$ (no radical cure necessary)
Plasmodium falciparum	Malignant tertian	Irregular fever spikes; causes cerebral malaria	Multiple ring forms crescent-shaped gametes	No persistent stage*	Chloroquine resistance a problem†

Definition of abbreviations: PO, by mouth; RBCs, red blood cells.

*Recrudescence is a recurrence of symptoms from low levels of organisms remaining in **red** cells. Relapse is an exacerbation from **l**iver stages (hypnozoites).

†Use quinine sulfate plus pyrimethamine-sulfadoxine.

ANTIMALARIAL DRUGS

1. Suppressive (to avoid infection)
2. Therapeutic (eliminate erythrocytic)
3. Radical cure (eliminate exoerythrocytic)
4. Gametocidal (destruction of gametocytes)

Successful treatment is accomplished with chloroquine followed by primaquine. Chloroquine therapy is suppressive, therapeutic, and gametocidal, whereas primaquine eliminates the exoerythrocytic form.

Chloroquine-Sensitive Malaria

P. falciparum	Chloroquine
P. malariae	Chloroquine
P. vivax	Chloroquine plus primaquine
P. ovale	Chloroquine plus primaquine

Chloroquine-Resistant Malaria

Prophylaxis: mefloquine; backup drugs: doxycycline, atovaquone-proguanil
Treatment: quinine ± either doxycycline, clindamycin, or pyrimethamine

ADVERSE EFFECTS OF ANTIMALARIAL DRUGS

Drug	Side Effects	Contraindications and Cautions
Chloroquine, hydroxychloroquine	GI distress, pruritus, headache, dizziness, hemolysis, ocular dysfunction	Avoid in psoriasis
Mefloquine	NVD, dizziness, syncope, extrasystoles, CNS effects (rare)	Avoid in seizures, psychiatric disorders, and in cardiac conduction defects
Primaquine	GI distress, headache, dizziness, neutropenia, hemolysis	Avoid in pregnancy, G6PD deficiency, and autoimmune disorders
Quinine	GI distress, cinchonism, CNS effects, hemolysis, hematotoxicity	Avoid in pregnancy

Definition of abbreviations: CNS, central nervous system; GI, gastrointestinal; G6PD, glucose-6-phosphate dehydrogenase; NVD, nausea, vomiting, diarrhea.

HEMOFLAGELLATES

Hemoflagellates (trypanosomes and leishmaniae) infect blood and tissues. They are found in:
- Human blood, as trypomastigotes with flagellum and undulating membrane
- Tissues, as **amastigotes (oval cells having neither the flagellum nor undulating membrane)**

Species	Disease	Vector/Form/ Transmission	Reservoirs	Diagnosis	Treatment
*Trypanosoma cruzi**	• **Chagas' disease** (American trypanosomiasis) • Latin America • Swelling around eye (**Romaña's sign**): common early sign • Cardiac muscle, liver, brain often involved	**Reduviid bug (kissing or cone bug**; genus *Triatoma*) passes trypomastigote (flagellated form) **in feces** as it bites; scratching implants in bite site	• Cats, dogs, armadillos, opossums • Poverty housing	Blood films, **trypomastigotes**	Nifurtimox
Trypanosoma brucei gambiense *Trypanosoma b. rhodesiense*	• **African sleeping sickness** (African trypanosomiasis) • **Antigenic variation**	Trypomastigote in saliva of **tsetse fly** contaminates bite	Humans, some wild animals	• **Trypomastigotes in blood films**, CSF • High immunoglobulin levels in CSF	• Acute: suramin • Chronic: melarsoprol
Leishmania donovani† complex	• **Visceral leishmaniasis** • Kala-azar	**Sandfly** bite	• Urban: humans • Rural: rodents and wild animals	**Amastigotes in macrophages** in bone marrow, liver, spleen	**Stibogluconate sodium** (from CDC)
Leishmania (about 15 different species)	Cutaneous leishmaniasis (Oriental sore, etc.)	**Sandfly** bite	• Urban: humans • Rural: rodents and wild animals	**Amastigotes in macrophages** in cutaneous lesions	Stibogluconate sodium
Leishmania braziliensis complex	Mucocutaneous leishmaniasis	**Sandfly** bite	• Urban: humans • Rural: rodents and wild animals	Same	Stibogluconate sodium

Definition of abbreviations: CDC, Center for Disease Prevention and Control; CSF, cerebrospinal fluid.

*T. cruzi: An estimated 0.5 million Americans are infected, creating some risk of transfusion transmission in the United States. In babies, acute infections are often serious and involve the CNS. In older children and adults, mild acute infections may become chronic with the risk of development of cardiomyopathy and heart failure.

† All *Leishmania*: intracellular, sandfly vector, stibogluconate

MISCELLANEOUS APICOMPLEXA INFECTING BLOOD OR TISSUES

Species	Disease/Locale of Origin	Transmission	Diagnosis	Treatment
Babesia (primarily a disease of cattle) Humans: *Babesia microti*, WA1 and MO1 strains	Babesiosis (hemolytic, **malaria-like**) Same range as Lyme: N.E., N. Central, California, and N.W. United States	• ***Ixodes* tick** • Coinfections with **Borrelia**	Giemsa stain of thin smear or hamster inoculation	Clindamycin plus quinine
Toxoplasma gondii	• Most common parasitic disease • Infections **after birth are most commonly asymptomatic** or mild; may mimic mononucleosis • Produces **severe disease in AIDS** or other immunocompromised • **Primary maternal infection during pregnancy may infect fetus:** – **Severe** congenital infections (intracerebral calcifications, chorioretinitis, hydro- or microcephaly, seizures) **if *Toxoplasma* crosses the placenta early** – **Later term congenital infection** may produce **progressive blindness**	**Cat** is **essential definitive** host; many other animals are intermediate hosts Mode: • Raw meat in U.S.; pork is #1 • Contact with cat feces	Serology: High IgM or rising IgM acute infection	Pyrimethamine plus sulfadiazine

MAJOR PROTOZOAL INFECTIONS AND DRUGS OF CHOICE

Infection	Drug of Choice	Comments
Amebiasis	Metronidazole	Diloxanide for noninvasive intestinal amebiasis
Giardiasis	Metronidazole or furazolidone	"Backpacker's diarrhea" from contaminated water or food
Trichomoniasis	Metronidazole	Treat both partners
Pneumocystosis	TMP-SMX	Atovaquone or pentamidine IV are backups
Toxoplasmosis	Pyrimethamine and sulfadiazine	TMP-SMX is also prophylactic against *Pneumocystis carinii* in AIDS
Leishmaniasis	Stibogluconate	—
Trypanosomiasis	• Nifurtimox (Chagas disease) • Arsenicals, pentamidine, suramin (African sleeping sickness)	—

METAZOANS: WORMS*

Phylum	Flat worms (Platyhelminthes)		Roundworms (Nemathelminthes)
Class (common name)	**Trematodes** (flukes)	**Cestodes** (tapeworms)	**Nematodes**[†] (roundworms)
Genera	*Fasciola* *Fasciolopsis* *Paragonimus* *Opisthorchis* (Clonorchis) *Schistosoma*	*Diphyllobothrium* *Hymenolepis* *Taenia* *Echinococcus*	**Necator** **Enterobius** (W)uchereria/Brugia **Ascaris** and **Ancylostoma** Toxocara, Trichuris, and Trichinella Onchocerca Dracunculus Eyeworm (Loa loa) Strongyloides

*Metazoans also include the Arthropoda, which serve mainly as intermediate hosts (the crustaceans) or as vectors of disease (the Arachnida and Insecta).

[†]Nematodes mnemonic (turn the "W" upsidedown)

TREMATODE (FLUKE) DISEASES

Trematodes:
- Are commonly called flukes, which are generally flat and fleshy, leaf-shaped worms
- Are hermaphroditic, except for *Schistosoma*, which has separate males and females
- Have complicated life cycles occurring in two or more hosts
- Have operculated eggs (except for *Schistosoma*), which contaminate water, perpetuating the life cycle, and which are also used to diagnose infections
- **The first intermediate hosts are snails**

Organism	Common Name	Reservoir Host	Acquisition	Progression in Humans	Important Ova	Treatment
Schistosoma mansoni *S. japonicum*	**Intestinal schistosomiasis**	Cats, dogs, cattle, etc.	Contact with water; skin penetration	Skin penetration (itching) → mature in veins of mesentery → eggs cause granulomas in liver (liver fibrosis in chronic cases)	—	Praziquantel
Schistosoma haematobium	**Vesicular schistosomiasis**	Primates	Contact with water; skin penetration	Skin penetration (itching) → mature in bladder veins; chronic infection has high association with **bladder carcinoma in Egypt and Africa**	—	Praziquantel
Nonhuman schistosomes	**Swimmer's itch**	Birds (Great Lakes, U.S.)	Contact with water; skin penetration	Penetrate skin, producing **dermatitis** without further development in humans; itching is most intense at 2 to 3 days	—	Trimeprazine, calamine, sedatives
Clonorchis sinensis	**Chinese liver fluke**	Dogs, cats, humans	Raw fish ingestion	—	Operculated eggs	Praziquantel
Fasciola hepatica	**Sheep liver fluke**	Sheep, cattle, humans	Ingestion of aquatic plants: watercress	—	Operculated eggs	Praziquantel
Fasciolopsis buski	**Giant intestinal fluke**	Pigs, dogs, rabbits, humans	Ingestion of aquatic plants: water chestnuts	—	Operculated eggs	Praziquantel
Paragonimus westermani	**Lung fluke**	Humans, cat family, canines, pigs	Raw crabs, crayfish	—	Operculated eggs	Praziquantel

GASTROINTESTINAL CESTODES (TAPEWORMS)

- Consist of three basic portions: the head or scolex; a "neck" section, which produces the proglottids; and the segments or proglottids, which mature as they move away from the scolex
- Are diagnosed by finding eggs or proglottids in the feces
- Have complex life cycles involving extraintestinal larval forms in intermediate hosts; when humans are intermediate host, these infections are generally more serious than intestinal infections with adult tapeworms

Cestode (Common Name)	Form/ Transmission	Human Host Type	Disease/Organ Involvement/Symptoms (Sx)	Diagnosis	Treatment
Taenia saginata (beef tapeworm) IH: cattle DH: humans	Ingestion of rare beef containing **cysticerci**	DH	• **Intestinal tapeworm**/small intestine • Sx: Asymptomatic or vague abdominal pains	**Proglottids** or **eggs** in feces	Praziquantel
Taenia solium (pork tapeworm) IH: swine; rare: humans	Water, vegetation, food contaminated with **eggs** Autoinfection	IH	**Cysticercosis**/eggs → larva develop in brain, eye, heart, lung, etc.	Biopsy	Praziquantel; surgery in some sites
DH: humans,developing and Slavic countries	Rare/raw pork containing the **cysticerci** ingested by humans	DH	• **Intestinal tapeworm** • Sx: same as for *Taenia saginata*	**Proglottids** or **eggs** in feces	Praziquantel
Diphyllobothrium latum (fish tapeworm) 2 IHs: crustaceans → fish; rare:, humans DH: humans/mammals; cool lake regions	Drinking pond water containing copepods (crustaceans) carrying the **larval** forms or frog/snake poultices	IH	**Sparganosis**/larvae penetrate intestinal wall and encyst	Biopsy	Praziquantel
	Rare, raw pickled fish containing a **sparganum**	DH	**Intestinal tapeworm** (up to 10 meters)/small intestine, **megaloblastic anemia**	Proglottids or eggs in feces	Praziquantel
Echinococcus granulosus IH: herbivores; rare: humans DH: carnivores in sheep-raising areas	Ingestion of eggs	IH	**Hydatid cyst disease;** liver and lung, where cysts containing blood capsules develop	Imaging, serology	Surgery, albendazole
Echinococcus multilocularis IH: rodents DH: canines and cats; Northern areas	Ingestion of eggs	IH	**Alveolar hydatid cyst disease**	Difficult, as above, but no protoscolices	Surgical resection

Definition of abbreviations: IH, intermediate host; DH, definitive host.

ROUNDWORMS (NEMATODES)

Roundworms are transmitted by:

- Ingestion of eggs (*Enterobius*, *Ascaris*, or *Trichuris*)
- Direct invasion of skin by larval forms (*Necator*, *Ancylostoma*, or *Strongyloides*)
- Ingestion of meat containing larvae (*Trichinella*)
- Infection involving insects transmitting the larvae with bites (*Wuchereria*, *Loa loa*, *Mansonella*, *Onchocerca*, and *Dracunculus*)

ROUNDWORMS (NEMATODES) TRANSMITTED BY EGGS

Species	Disease/Organs Most Affected	Form/ Transmission	Diagnosis	Treatment
Enterobius vermicularis (Most frequent helminth parasite in U.S.)	**Pinworms**, large intestine, perianal itching	• **Eggs**/person to person • **Autoinfection**	• Sticky swab of perianal area • Ova have flattened side with larvae inside	Albendazole Treat entire family
Trichuris trichiura	**Whipworm** cecum, appendicitis, and rectal prolapse	**Eggs** ingested	**Barrel-shaped eggs with bipolar plugs** in stools	Albendazole
Ascaris lumbricoides (Most common helminth worldwide; largest roundworm)	**Ascariasis** Ingest egg → larvae migrate through lungs (cough) and mature in small intestine; may obstruct intestine or bile duct	**Eggs** ingested	**Bile stained, knobby eggs** Adult 35 to 40 cm	• Supportive therapy during pneumonitis • Surgery for ectopic migrations • Albendazole
Toxocara canis or cati (Dog/cat ascarids)	**Visceral larva migrans** Larvae wander aimlessly until they die, cause inflammation	**Eggs** ingested/from handling puppies or from eating dirt in yard (pica)	Clinical findings and serology	Albendazole; self-limiting in most cases

ROUNDWORMS (NEMATODES) TRANSMITTED BY LARVAE

Species	Disease/Organs	Form/Transmission	Diagnosis	Treatment
Necator americanus (New World hookworm)	**Hookworm** infection Lung migration → pneumonitis Bloodsucking → anemia	Filariform **larva penetrates intact skin of bare feet**	Fecal larvae (up to 13 mm) and ova: oval, transparent with 2–8 cell-stage visible inside Fecal occult blood may be present	Mebendazole and iron therapy
Ancylostoma braziliense *Ancylostoma caninum* (dog and cat hookworms)	**Cutaneous larva migrans**/intense skin itching	Filariform larva penetrates intact skin but cannot mature in humans	Usually a presumptive diagnosis; exposure	Thiabendazole
Strongyloides stercoralis	**Threadworm** strongyloidiasis: *Early:* pneumonitis, abdominal pain, diarrhea *Later:* malabsorption, ulcers, bloody stools	Filariform **larva penetrates intact skin; autoinfection** leads to indefinite infections unless treated	Larvae in stool, serology	Thiabendazole
Trichinella spiralis	Trichinosis: larvae encyst in muscle → pain	**Viable encysted larvae in meat** are consumed: wildgame meat	Muscle biopsy; clinical findings: **fever, myalgia, splinter hemorrhages, eosinophilia**	Steroids for severe symptoms and mebendazole

VIROLOGY

DNA VIRUSES

Virus Family	DNA Type	Polymerase	Envelope	Area of Replication	Major Viruses
Parvovirus	**ssDNA**	No	**Naked**	Nucleus	**B19**
Papovavirus	dsDNA Circular	No	**Naked**	Nucleus	Papilloma Polyoma
Adenovirus	dsDNA Linear	No	**Naked**	Nucleus	Adenovirus
Herpesvirus	dsDNA Linear	No	Enveloped **Nuclear**	Nucleus, assembled in nucleus	**HSV, VZV, EBV, CMV**
Poxvirus	dsDNA Linear	**Yes**	Enveloped	**Cytoplasm**	Variola, vaccinia Molluscum contagiosum
Hepadnavirus	Partially dsDNA Circular	**Yes**	Enveloped	Nucleus via RNA intermediate	HBV

Definition of abbreviations: CMV, cytomegalovirus; ds, double-stranded; EBV, Epstein-Barr virus; HBV, hepatitis B virus; HSV, herpes simplex virus; ss, single-stranded; VZV, varicella-zoster virus.

DOUBLE-STRANDED RNA VIRUSES: REOVIRIDAE					
	RNA Structure	Polymerase	Envelope	Shape	Major viruses
Reovirus	• Linear dsRNA • **10–11 segments**	Yes	**Naked**	• Icosahedral • **Double shelled**	• Reovirus • **Rotavirus**

POSITIVE-SENSE RNA VIRUSES						
Family	RNA Structure	Polymerase	Envelope	Shape	Area of Replication	Major Viruses
Calicivirus	• ss⊕RNA, linear • Nonsegmented	No	**Naked**	Icosahedral	Cytoplasm	• Norwalk • **Cruise ship agent** • Hepatitis E
Picornavirus	• ss⊕RNA, linear • Nonsegmented	No	**Naked**	Icosahedral	Cytoplasm	• Polio, ECHO, Entero • Rhino, coxsackie • Hepatitis A
Flavivirus	• ss⊕RNA, linear • Nonsegmented	No	Enveloped	Icosahedral	Cytoplasm	Yellow fever, dengue, SLE, hepatitis C, **West Nile virus**
Togavirus	• ss⊕RNA, linear • Nonsegmented	No	Enveloped	Icosahedral	Cytoplasm	Rubella WEE, EEE, VEE
Coronavirus	• ss⊕RNA, linear • Nonsegmented	No	Enveloped	**Helical**	Cytoplasm	Coronaviruses **SARS agent**
Retrovirus	• **Diploid** • ss⊕RNA, linear • Nonsegmented	**RNA-dependent DNA polymerase**	Enveloped	Icosahedral or truncated conical	**Nucleus**	HIV HTLV Sarcoma

Definition of abbreviations: EEE, eastern equine encephalitis; HIV, human immunodeficiency virus; HTLV, human T-cell lymphocytotropic virus; VEE, Venezuelan equine encephalitis; WEE, western equine encephalitis.

Negative-Sense RNA Viruses

Virus	RNA	Polymerase	Envelope	Shape	Area Where Multiplies	Major Viruses
Paramyxovirus	• ss⊖RNA, linear • Nonsegmented	Yes	Yes	Helical	Cytoplasm	Mumps, measles RSV, parainfluenza
Rhabdovirus	• ss⊖RNA, linear • Nonsegmented	Yes	Yes	**Bullet-shaped**, helical	Cytoplasm	Rabies, VSV
Filovirus	• ss⊖RNA, linear • Nonsegmented	Yes	Yes	Helical	Cytoplasm	Marburg, Ebola
Orthomyxovirus	• ss⊖RNA, linear • **8 segments**	Yes	Yes	Helical	**Cytoplasm and nucleus**	Influenza
Bunyavirus	• ss⊖RNA, linear to circular • 3 segments, ambisense	Yes	Yes	Helical	Cytoplasm	California and LaCrosse encephalitis, Hantavirus
Arenavirus	• ss⊖RNA, circular, • 2 segments: 1 ⊖ sense, 1 ambisense	Yes	Yes	Helical	Cytoplasm	Lymphocytic choriomeningitis virus, Lassa fever

Definition of abbreviations: ds, double-stranded; RSV, respiratory syncytial virus; ss, single-stranded; VSV, vesicular stomatitis virus.

Viral Genetics

Phenotypic mixing	• Related viruses coinfect cell (virus A and virus B) • Resulting proteins on the surface are a mixture capsid of AB around nucleic acid of either A or B
Phenotypic masking	• Related viruses coinfect cell (virus A and virus B) • Capsid of proteins of virus A form around nucleic acid of B
Complementation	• Two related defective viruses infect the same cell; if they are defective in different genes, viral progeny (still with mutated DNA) will be formed • If they are defective in the same gene, no progeny will be formed • Coinfection of hepatitis B and D is a clinical example of complementation where HBV supplies the needed surface antigen for hepatitis D
Genetic reassortment (genetic shift)	• Two different strains of a segmented RNA virus infect the same cell. • Major new genetic combinations are produced through "shuffling," resulting in stable and dramatic changes
Genetic drift	• Minor antigenic changes from mutation • Occurs in many viruses, particularly RNA types • Most noted in HIV and influenza
Viral vectors	• Recombinant viruses are produced that have combinations of human replacement genes with the defective viral nucleic acid

ANTIVIRAL AGENTS

As viruses rely on host machinery to produce viral products, selectivity must be achieved by targeting minute differences in viral enzymes. This may be accomplished at any stage in the viral "life cycle," including adsorption, penetration, nucleic acid synthesis, late protein synthesis, protein processing, viral product packaging, and viral release.

Class/Agent	Mechanism of Action	Spectrum/Clinical Applications	Mechanism(s) of Resistance	Toxicity/Notes
Acyclovir	Acyclic guanosine analog activated by viral thymidine kinase to form a competitive substrate for viral DNA polymerase; chain terminator	HSV-1, HSV-2, VZV	Loss of thymidine kinase (enzyme needed for viral-specific phosphorylation and activation)	• Well-tolerated, occasional GI irritation, headache • IV use associated with seizure, delirium, nephrotoxicity
Famciclovir, valacyclovir	• Famciclovir—oral prodrug converted to penciclovir • Valacyclovir—oral prodrug of acyclovir • Mechanism of penciclovir same as acyclovir	HSV, especially VZV	*See* acyclovir	Famciclovir and valacyclovir have much greater oral bioavailability than acyclovir
Ganciclovir	• Phosphorylated by viral kinase; inhibits CMV DNA polymerase • Does not cause chain termination	• CMV (e.g., CMV retinitis) • HSV prophylaxis	Mutation in CMV DNA polymerase and/or activating viral kinase	• Diarrhea • Leukopenia and anemia • Toxicity limits use to life-threatening or vision-threatening infections
Foscarnet	Viral DNA polymerase inhibitor; viral RNA polymerase inhibitor	• CMV retinitis • Acyclovir-resistant mucocutaneous HSV in AIDS patients	Point mutations in DNA polymerase gene	Severe, including: • Nephrotoxicity • Anemia • Electrolyte disturbances • Genitourinary ulceration • Seizures
Amantadine and rimantadine	Blocks viral penetration/uncoating via interaction with viral M2 protein	• Influenza A (prophylaxis) • Amantadine also used in Parkinson disease to stimulate dopamine release	Amantadine resistance due to mutations in M2 protein	• Ataxia • Increased seizure activity • Dizziness and hypotension • Rimantadine better tolerated in elderly
Ribavirin	Inhibits viral RNA synthesis by altering the nucleotide pools and normal messenger RNA formation	• Influenza A and B parainfluenza • RSV • Paramyxoviruses • HCV (combined with α-interferon)	Unknown	Dose-dependent hemolytic anemia

Definition of abbreviations: CMV, cytomegalovirus; HCV, hepatitis C virus; HSV, herpes simplex virus; RSV, respiratory syncytial virus; VZV, varicella zoster virus.

(Continued)

Class/Agent	Mechanism of Action	Spectrum/Clinical Applications	Mechanism(s) of Resistance	Toxicity/Notes
Zidovudine	Converted to nucleoside triphosphate, which interferes with reverse transcriptase leading the inhibition of viral replication	Used for HIV disease in combination with at least two other agents	• Resistance via mutations in the reverse transcriptase gene • High level of resistance associated with multiple mutations	• Bone marrow suppression • Myalgia • Nausea • Fatigue • Headache • Abnormal liver function
Interferons	Interferons: • Class of related proteins with antiviral, antiproliferative, and immune-regulating activity • Induce synthesis of a number of antiviral proteins (e.g., RNAse and a protein kinase) that protect the cell against subsequent challenges by a variety of viruses	• Hepatitis B and C • Kaposi sarcoma • Leukemias • Malignant melanoma	Anti-interferon antibodies seen with prolonged use	• Interferons can cause influenza-like symptoms, especially in the first week of therapy • Bone marrow suppression • Profound fatigue, myalgia, weight loss, and increased susceptibility to bacterial infections • Depression seen in up to 20% of patients

Definition of abbreviations: HIV, human immunodeficiency virus.

FUNGI

FUNGI: OVERVIEW

Fungi are complex eukaryotic organisms with complex carbohydrate cell walls (the reason they frequently calcify in chronic infections) and ergosterol as their major membrane sterol (which are targeted with nystatin and the imidazoles). Morphologic and geographic clues are very important in determining the identity of the organism.

Fungi come in two basic forms	• **Hyphae**—filamentous forms may either have cross walls (septate) or lack them (aseptate) • **Yeasts**—single-celled oval/round forms • **Dimorphic fungi**—may convert from hyphal to yeast forms (key examples: *Histoplasma, Blastomyces, Coccidioides,* and *Sporothrix*)
Pseudohyphae	• Hyphae formed by budding off yeasts; formed by **Candida albicans**; the basis of the germ tube test for diagnosis of invasive *C. albicans*
Spores are used for reproduction and dissemination	• **Conidia**—asexual spores form off hyphae • **Blastoconidia**—asexual spores like buds on yeasts • **Arthroconidia**—asexual spores formed with joints between • **Spherules** with **endospores**—sexual spores in tissues (*Coccidioides*)

NONSYSTEMIC FUNGAL INFECTIONS

Organism	Disease	Notes
Malassezia furfur	**Pityriasis** or **tinea versicolor**	• Superficial infection of keratinized cells • **Hypopigmented spots on the chest/back** (blotchy suntan) • KOH mount of skin scales: "spaghetti and meatballs," yeast clusters and short, curved septate hyphae • Treatment is topical selenium sulfide; recurs.
	Fungemia	• In **premature infants**
Candida albicans, Candida spp.	**Cutaneous or mucocutaneous candidiasis**	• Causes oral thrush and vulvovaginitis in immunocompetent individuals • Source of opportunistic infections in hospitalized and immunocompromised (*see* Opportunistic Mycoses) Pseudohyphae Budding Yeasts Germ Tubes True Hyphae
Trichophyton, Microsporum, Epidermophyton	**Tinea** (capitis, barbae, corporis, cruris, pedis)	• Infects **skin, hair, and nails** • **Monomorphic** filamentous fungi • KOH mount shows **arthroconidia, hyphae** • **Pruritic lesions with serpiginous borders and central clearing**
Sporothrix schenckii (hyphae) (conidia)	• **Sporotrichosis (rose gardener's disease)** • **Pulmonary sporotrichosis** (in alcoholics/ homeless)	Dimorphic fungus: • Environmental form: hyphae with rosettes and sleeves of conidia • Tissue form: cigar-shaped yeast

SYSTEMIC FUNGAL INFECTIONS		
Organism	**Disease**	**Notes**
General Comments		
Histoplasma ***Coccidioides*** ***Blastomyces***	• Acute pulmonary (asymptomatic or self-resolving in about 95% of the cases) • Chronic pulmonary • Disseminated infections	**Diagnosis** (most people never see doctor): • Sputum cytology (calcofluor white staining helpful) • **Sputum cultures** on blood agar and **special fungal media** (inhibitory mold agar, Sabouraud's agar) • **Peripheral blood cultures are useful for** *Histoplasma* **because it circulates in RES cells**
Specific Organisms		

Histoplasma capsulatum
 	
	Fungus flu (a pneumonia)
	 • Asymptomatic or flu-like
	 • **Hepatosplenomegaly** may be present
	 • May **disseminate in AIDS patient**
	
		Dimorphic fungus:
		 • **Environmental form: hyphae** with **microconidia** and **tuberculate macroconidia**
		   – Endemic region: **Eastern Great Lakes, Ohio, Mississippi,** and **Missouri River beds**
		   – Found in **soil (dust) enriched with bird or bat feces** (caves, chicken coops)
		 • **Tissue form: small intracellular yeasts** with narrow neck on bud; **no capsule**
		 • **Facultative intracellular parasite** found in **RES cells** (tiny; can get 30 or so in a human cell)

Coccidioides immitis (endospores/spherules) (arthroconidia)	Coccidioidomycosis (San Joaquin Valley fever) 	• Dimorphic fungus • Asymptomatic to **self-resolving pneumonia** • Desert bumps (erythema nodosum) • **Pulmonary lesions may calcify** • **May disseminate in AIDS and immunocompromised** (meningitis, mucocutaneous lesions) • Has a tendency to **disseminate in third trimester of pregnancy**
Blastomyces dermatitidis 	Blastomycosis 	• Dimorphic fungus • Environmental form: hyphae with conidia • Tissue form: broad-based budding yeast • Pulmonary disease • Disseminated disease

Definition of abbreviations: RES, reticuloendothelial.

OPPORTUNISTIC FUNGI

Aspergillus fumigatus	• **Allergic bronchopulmonary aspergillosis**/asthma, allergies
	• **Fungus ball:** free in preformed lung cavities
	• **Invasive aspergillosis**/severe neutropenia, CGD, CF, burns
	  – Invades tissues, causing infarcts and hemorrhage
	  – Nasal colonization → **pneumonia or meningitis**
	  – **Cellulitis**/in burn patients; may also disseminate
		• **Dichotomously branching**
		• **Generally acute angles**
		• **Septate**
		• Compost pits, moldy marijuana
		• May cause disease in immunocompromised patients

Candida albicans (and other spp. of *Candida*)	• Involvement of the oral cavity and digestive tract • Septicemia, endocarditis in IV drug abusers • Mucocutaneous candidiasis	**Diagnosis:** • KOH: pseudohyphae, true hyphae, budding yeasts • Septicemia: culture lab identification: biochemical tests/formation of germ tubes **Treatment:** • Topical imidazoles or oral imidazoles; nystatin • Disseminated: amphotericin B or fluconazole

Cryptococcus neoformans	• **Meningitis/Hodgkin, AIDS (the dominant meningitis)**
	• **Acute pulmonary** (usually asymptomatic)/**pigeon breeders**
		• **Encapsulated yeast (monomorphic)**
		• **Environmental source:** Soil enriched with pigeon droppings
		• **Diagnosis of meningitis: CSF**
		  – Detect capsular antigen in CSF (by latex particle agglutination or counter immunoelectrophoresis)
		  – India ink mount (misses 50%) of CSF sediment to find budding yeasts with capsular "halos"
		  – Cultures (urease ⊕ yeast)
		• **Treatment:** amphotericin B plus flucytosine until afebrile and culture ⊖, then fluconazole

Mucor, Rhizopus, Absidia (Zygomycophyta family)	**Rhinocerebral infection** (mucormycosis) caused by *Mucor* (or other Zygomycophyta)	• Nonseptate, filamentous fungi • Characterized by paranasal swelling, necrotic tissues, hemorrhagic exudates from nose and eyes, mental lethargy • Occurs in **ketoacidotic diabetic patients** and **leukemic patients** • These fungi penetrate without respect to anatomic barriers, progressing rapidly from sinuses into brain tissue • **Diagnosis:** KOH of tissue; broad, ribbon-like nonseptate hyphae with about 90° angles on branches • **Treatment:** débride necrotic tissue and start amphotericin B fast; high fatality rate because of rapid growth and invasion
Pneumocystis carinii	Pneumonia in AIDS patients, malnourished babies, premature neonates, other immunocompromised	• An exudate with foamy or **honeycomb appearance on H & E stain** • **Silver stain shows cysts and trophozoites** • **Patchy infiltrative (ground-glass appearance) on x-ray** • **Diagnosis: silver-staining cysts** in bronchial alveolar lavage fluids or biopsy • Treatment: trimethoprim/sulfamethoxazole

Definition of abbreviations: CF, cystic fibrosis; CSF, cerebrospinal fluid; CGD, chronic granulomatous disease; KOH, potassium hydroxide.

ANTIFUNGAL AGENTS

Because fungi are eukaryotic, finding selectively toxic antifungal agents is difficult. Consequently, treating fungal infections poses a clinical challenge, especially in immunocompromised patients. Fungal cell membranes contain ergosterol, a sterol not found in mammalian tissue. Thus, this difference provides the basis for most systemically administered antifungal agents.

Class/Agent	Mechanism of Action	Spectrum/Clinical Use	Mechanism(s) of Resistance	Toxicity/Notes
Systemic Agents for Fungemia				
Amphotericin B	Binds ergosterol, causing formation of artificial pores, thus altering membrane permeability, killing the cell	Widest antifungal spectrum: *Aspergillus* *Coccidioides* *Blastomyces* *Candida albicans* *Cryptococcus* *Histoplasma* *Mucor* *Sporothrix schenckii*	Very uncommon; ↓ or structurally altered ergosterol	• Fever and chills ("cytokine storm") • **Nephrotoxicity** limits dosing (cumulative over lifetime) • Reversible anemia (secondary to ↓ erythropoietin) • Arrhythmias • IV only
Flucytosine	Permease allows entry, deaminated to 5-FU, then converted to 5-FdUMP (thymidylate synthase inhibitor)	Narrow spectrum: *Cryptococcus* *Candida albicans* (systemic)	Rapid if used as a single agent; ↓ activity of fungal permeases and deaminases	• Reversible **bone marrow suppression** • Alopecia • Typically **combined with amphotericin B** or fluconazole
Azoles: fluconazole, itraconazole, voriconazole, ketoconazole	Inhibit synthesis of ergosterol, leading to altered membrane permeability	Varies: *Candida* *Coccidioides* *Cryptococcus* *Aspergillus* *Histoplasma*	↓ sensitivity of target enzymes	• Vomiting and diarrhea • Skin rash • Hepatotoxicity (rare) • **Gynecomastia** • ↓ P450 inhibition
Echinocandin/ caspofungin	Inhibits synthesis of β-1,2 glycan, a component of fungal cell walls	*Candida* *Aspergillus*	—	• Not very toxic • Headache • Infusion-related reactions
Systemic Agents for Superficial Infections				
Griseofulvin	• Uptake by energy-dependent transport • Interferes with microtubule formation in dermatophytes • May inhibit polymerization of nucleic acids	• Dermatophytes of the hair and scalp • Accumulates in keratin	↓ in transport/uptake	• Confusion and vertigo • Headache • Blurred vision • Nausea/vomiting • ↑ P450 • GI irritation • **Disulfiram-like reaction** with ethanol
Terbinafine	Inhibits squalene epoxidase (for sterol biosynthesis)	Accumulates in keratin, used in onychomycosis		• GI irritation • Rash • Headache • Taste disturbance
Azoles (*see* Systemic Agents for Fungemia, above)	—	—	—	—
Topical Antifungals				
Nystatin	Disrupts membrane by binding ergosterol	*Candida*, especially in oral candidiasis (thrush)	Same as amphotericin B	• Contact dermatitis • Stevens-Johnson syndrome

Embryology

EARLY EMBRYOLOGY

Week 1

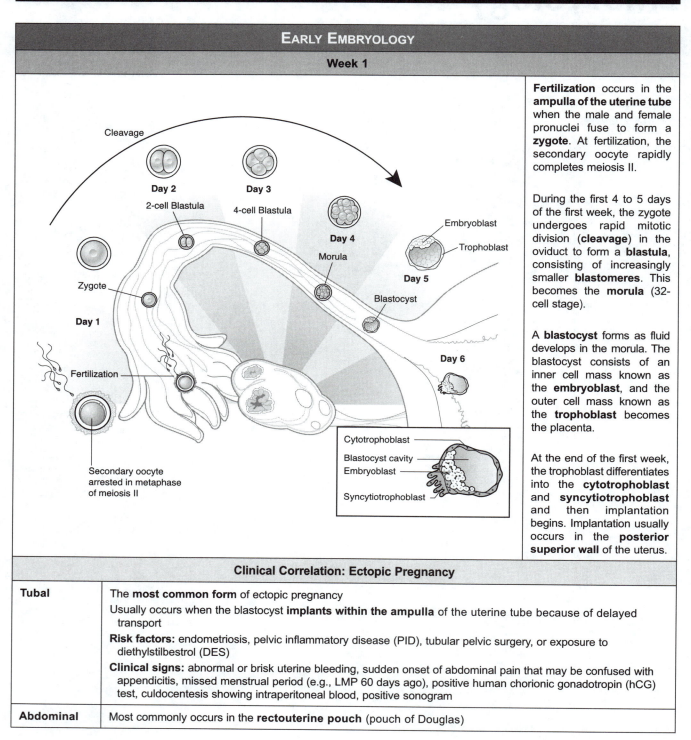

Cleavage

Day 2
2-cell Blastula

Day 3
4-cell Blastula

Day 4
Morula

Embryoblast
Trophoblast

Day 5
Blastocyst

Zygote

Day 1

Day 6

Fertilization

Secondary oocyte arrested in metaphase of meiosis II

Cytotrophoblast
Blastocyst cavity
Embryoblast
Syncytiotrophoblast

Fertilization occurs in the **ampulla of the uterine tube** when the male and female pronuclei fuse to form a **zygote**. At fertilization, the secondary oocyte rapidly completes meiosis II.

During the first 4 to 5 days of the first week, the zygote undergoes rapid mitotic division (**cleavage**) in the oviduct to form a **blastula**, consisting of increasingly smaller **blastomeres**. This becomes the **morula** (32-cell stage).

A **blastocyst** forms as fluid develops in the morula. The blastocyst consists of an inner cell mass known as the **embryoblast**, and the outer cell mass known as the **trophoblast** becomes the placenta.

At the end of the first week, the trophoblast differentiates into the **cytotrophoblast** and **syncytiotrophoblast** and then implantation begins. Implantation usually occurs in the **posterior superior wall** of the uterus.

Clinical Correlation: Ectopic Pregnancy

Tubal	The **most common form** of ectopic pregnancy Usually occurs when the blastocyst **implants within the ampulla** of the uterine tube because of delayed transport **Risk factors:** endometriosis, pelvic inflammatory disease (PID), tubular pelvic surgery, or exposure to diethylstilbestrol (DES) **Clinical signs:** abnormal or brisk uterine bleeding, sudden onset of abdominal pain that may be confused with appendicitis, missed menstrual period (e.g., LMP 60 days ago), positive human chorionic gonadotropin (hCG) test, culdocentesis showing intraperitoneal blood, positive sonogram
Abdominal	Most commonly occurs in the **rectouterine pouch** (pouch of Douglas)

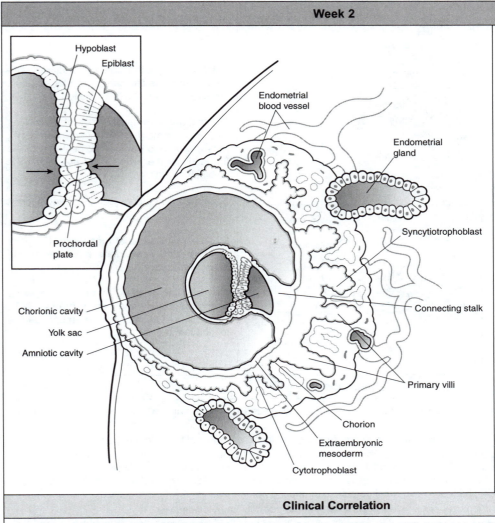

The embryoblast differentiates into the **epiblast** and **hypoblast**, forming a **bilaminar embryonic disk**.

The epiblast forms the **amniotic cavity**, and hypoblast cells migrate from the **primary yolk sac**.

The **prochordal plate**, formed from fusion of epiblast and hypoblast cells, is the site of the future **mouth**.

Extraembryonic mesoderm is derived from the epiblast. **Extraembryonic somatic meso- derm** lines the cytotrophoblast, forms the connecting stalk, and covers the amnion. **Extraembryonic visceral mesoderm** covers the yolk sac.

The connecting stalk suspends the conceptus within the chorionic cavity. The wall of the chorionic cavity is called the **chorion**, consisting of extraembryonic somatic mesoderm, the cytotrophoblast, and the syncytiotrophoblast.

Clinical Correlation

Human chorionic gonadotropin (hCG) is a glycoprotein produced by the syncytiotrophoblast. It stimulates progesterone production by the corpus luteum. hCG can be assayed in maternal blood or urine and is the basis for early pregnancy testing. hCG is detectable throughout pregnancy. **Low hCG** levels may predict a spontaneous abortion or ectopic pregnancy. **High hCG** levels may predict a multiple pregnancy, hydatidiform mole, or gestational trophoblastic disease.

Weeks 3 Through 8

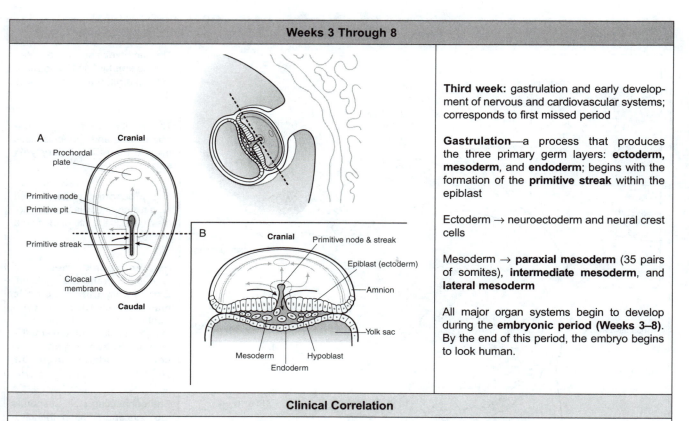

Third week: gastrulation and early development of nervous and cardiovascular systems; corresponds to first missed period

Gastrulation—a process that produces the three primary germ layers: **ectoderm, mesoderm,** and **endoderm**; begins with the formation of the **primitive streak** within the epiblast

Ectoderm → neuroectoderm and neural crest cells

Mesoderm → **paraxial mesoderm** (35 pairs of somites), **intermediate mesoderm,** and **lateral mesoderm**

All major organ systems begin to develop during the **embryonic period (Weeks 3–8).** By the end of this period, the embryo begins to look human.

Clinical Correlation

Sacrococcygeal teratoma: a tumor that arises from remnants of the primitive streak; often contains various types of tissue (bone, nerve, hair, etc).

Chordoma: a tumor that arises from remnants of the notochord, found either intracranially or in the sacral region

Caudal dysplasia (sirenomelia): a constellation of syndromes ranging from minor lesions of the lower vertebrae to complete fusion of lower limbs. Occurs as a result of abnormal gastrulation, in which migration of mesoderm is disturbed. Associated with VATER (vertebral defects, anal atresia, tracheoesophageal fistula, and renal defects) or VACTERL (vertebral defects, anal atresia, cardiovascular defects, tracheoesophageal fistula, renal defects, and upper limb defects)

Hydatidiform mole: results from the partial or complete replacement of the trophoblast by dilated villi

- **In a complete mole, there is no embryo;** a haploid sperm fertilizes a blighted ovum and reduplicates so that the karyotype is 46,XX, with all chromosomes of paternal origin. In a partial mole, there is a haploid set of maternal chromosomes and usually two sets of paternal chromosomes so that the typical karyotype is 69,XXY.
- **Molar pregnancies have high levels of hCG, and 20% develop into a malignant trophoblastic disease, including choriocarcinoma.**

GERM LAYER DERIVATIVES

Ectoderm	
Surface ectoderm	Epidermis, hair, nails, inner and external ear, tooth enamel, lens of eye, anterior pituitary (from Rathke pouch), parotid gland
Neuroectoderm	Neural tube: CNS, retina and optic nerve, pineal gland, neurohypophysis, astrocytes, oligodendrocytes
Neural crest	Adrenal medulla, ganglia (sensory, autonomic), melanocytes, Schwann cells, meninges (pia, arachnoid), pharyngeal arch cartilage, odontoblasts, parafollicular (C) cells, aorticopulmonary septum, endocardial cushions (abnormal development can lead to many congenital defects)
Mesoderm	Muscle (smooth, cardiac, skeletal), connective tissue, serous membranes, bone and cartilage, blood, lymph, cardiovascular organs, adrenal cortex, gonads and internal reproductive organs, spleen, kidney and ureter, dura mater
Endoderm	Epithelial parts: GI tract, tonsils, thymus, pharynx, larynx, trachea, bronchi, lungs, urinary bladder, urethra, tympanic cavity, auditory tube and other pharyngeal pouches Parenchyma: liver, pancreas, tonsils, thyroid, parathyroids, glands of GI tract, submandibular and sublingual glands

Physiology

PHYSIOLOGIC TERMINOLOGY	
Equilibrium	Equilibrium occurs when the balance of opposing forces has reached the **lowest free energy state**, and as a result, a given variable has reached a constant value.
Steady state	Steady state is a condition in which a variable is maintained within narrow limits by regulating an opposing activity. This process requires energy.
Negative feedback	This is a common system that acts to oppose changes in the internal environment. Negative feedback systems promote stability and act to restore steady-state function after a perturbation.
Positive feedback	This is a less common system (also called a vicious cycle) that acts to magnify a change in the internal environment; the initial change in a system is increased as a result of feedback activity. In a viable organism, any positive feedback system is ultimately overridden by one or more negative feedback systems.

Negative Feedback Example	Positive Feedback Example

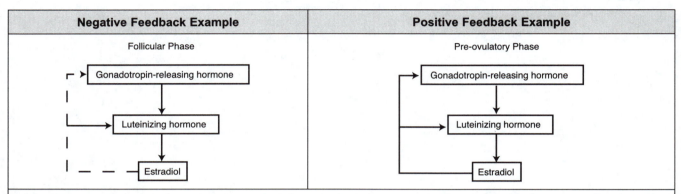

The figures above show the negative feedback relationship between estrogens and the gonadotropins that dominates during the follicular phase, which transforms into a positive feedback relationship, producing the LH surge prior to ovulation.

TRANSPORT				
Type of Transport	**Energy Source**	**Example**	**Other Characteristics**	**Clinical Correlation**
Simple diffusion	Passive	Pulmonary gases	—	Pulmonary edema decreases diffusion
Carrier-mediated or facilitated diffusion	Passive	Glucose uptake by muscle	• Insulin controls carrier population • Chemical specificity	Insulin-dependent glucose uptake impaired in diabetes mellitus
Primary active transport	Direct use of ATP	Na^+/K^+-ATPase H^+/K^+-ATPase	Antiport (countertransport)	Inhibition by cardiac glycosides
Secondary active transport	Electrochemical gradient for sodium is most common driving force	Na^+-glucose in kidney Na^+-H^+ exchange	Symport (cotransport) Antiport (countertransport)	Osmotic diuresis results when transporters saturated Renal tubular acidosis
Key Points				

- Passive processes are directly related to concentration gradients
- Active processes create or increase a concentration gradient and thus depend upon metabolic energy.
- Both carrier-mediated facilitated diffusion and active transport can be saturated; maximum transport rate depends on population and activity of transport molecules.
- Primary active transport proteins have an ATPase as part of their structure.
- Most secondary active transport depends upon the electrochemical gradient of sodium ions, which in turn depends on the activity of the primary active transporter, sodium-potassium ATPase.

DIFFUSION KINETICS

Simple diffusion	The rate is estimated by **Fick's law of diffusion**: $J = -DA(\Delta C/\Delta X)$ J = net flux, D = diffusion coefficient, A = surface area, ΔC = concentration or pressure gradient, ΔX = diffusion distance Changes in surface area or diffusion distance are most important in disease states (e.g., the decrease in surface area caused by destruction of alveoli in emphysema or the decreased diffusion of oxygen during pulmonary edema related to increased diffusion distance).
Carrier-mediated transport	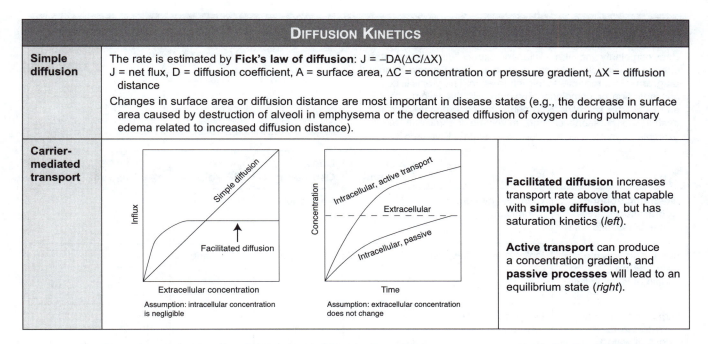 **Facilitated diffusion** increases transport rate above that capable with **simple diffusion**, but has saturation kinetics (*left*). **Active transport** can produce a concentration gradient, and **passive processes** will lead to an equilibrium state (*right*).

FLUID VOLUME COMPARTMENTS AND DISTRIBUTION

	% of Body Weight	Fraction of TBW	Markers Used to Measure Volume	Primary Cations	Primary Anions
Total body water (TBW)	60	1.0	Tritiated H_2O D_2O	—	—
Intracellular fluid volume (ICF)	40	⅔	TBW – ECF*	K^+	Organic phosphates; protein
Extracellular fluid volume (ECF)	20	⅓	Inulin Mannitol	Na^+	Cl^- HCO_3^-
Plasma	5	¹⁄₁₂ (¼ of ECF)	RISA Evans blue	Na^+	Cl^- HCO_3^- Plasma proteins
Interstitial fluid	15	¼ (¾ of ECF)	ECF-plasma volume*	Na^+	Cl^- HCO_3^-

Principles of Fluid Distribution

1. Osmolarity of the ICF and ECF are equal.
2. Intracellular volume changes only when extracellular osmolarity changes.
3. All substances enter or leave the body by passing through the extracellular compartment.

Measurement of Fluid Volumes

Volume = $\dfrac{\text{Mass}}{\text{Concentration}}$	*Example:* 100 mg of inulin is infused. After equilibration, its concentration = 0.01 mg/mL. What is patient's ECF volume? *Answer:* ECF = 100 mg/0.01 mg/mL = 10,000 mL, or 10 L

Osmolarity and Mass

1. Plasma osmolarity in mOsm/L can be quickly estimated as twice the plasma sodium concentration in mmol/L. More rigorously, plasma osmolarity (mOsm/L) = (2 × serum sodium [mEq/L]) + (BUN [mg/dL]/2.8) + (glucose [mg/dL]/18).
2. Mass of solutes in the TBW, ICF, or ECF in mOsm is calculated by the relevant volume multiplied by the osmolarity.

Definition of abbreviation: RISA, radio-iodinated serum albumin.
*Indirect measurement

SUMMARY OF VOLUME AND OSMOLARITY CHANGES OF BODY FLUIDS

Body osmolarity and intracellular and extracellular fluid volumes change in clinically relevant situations. The **Darrow-Yannet diagram** *(right)* represents this information. The *y*-axis is solute concentration or osmolarity. The *x*-axis is the volume of ICF and ECF. The *solid line* represents the control state, and the *dashed line* represents changes in volume or osmolarity. In this example, osmolarity ↓, ICF volume ↑, and ECF volume ↓.

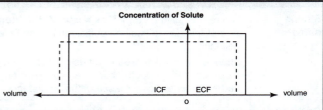

Type	Examples	ECF Volume	Body Osmolarity	ICF Volume	D-Y Diagram
Isosmotic volume contraction (loss of isotonic fluid)	Diarrhea, hemorrhage, vomiting	↓	No change	No change	
Isosmotic volume expansion (gain of isotonic fluid)	Isotonic saline infusion	↑	No change	No change	
Hyperosmotic volume contraction (loss of water)	Dehydration, diabetes insipidus	↓	↑	↓	
Hyperosmotic volume expansion (gain of NaCl)	Excessive NaCl intake, hypertonic mannitol	↑	↑	↓	
Hyposmotic volume contraction (loss of NaCl)	Adrenal insufficiency	↓	↓	↑	
Hyposmotic volume expansion (gain of water)	SIADH, water intoxication	↑	↓	↑	

Definiton of abbreviation: SIADH, syndrome of inappropriate antidiuretic hormone.

MEMBRANE POTENTIALS	
Equilibrium potential	Amount of voltage needed to balance the chemical force due to its concentration gradient The **Nernst equation** can determine this. For a monovalent cation: $$E_x = \frac{60\ mV}{Z}\ \log_{10} \frac{[X]_o}{[X]_i}\ ;\ E_x = \text{equilibrium potential, } [X] = \text{ion concentration (out and in), } Z = \text{charge}$$ ($Na^+ = 1$, $Cl^- = -1$, $Ca^{2+} = 2$)
Resting membrane (RM) potential	• RM is the potential difference across a cell membrane in millivolts (mV); −70 mV is typical. • RM occurs because of an **unequal distribution of ions** between the ICF and ECF and the **selective permeability** of the membrane to ions. **Proteins (anions)** in cells that do not diffuse help establish the electrical potential across the membrane. • The relative effect of an ion on the membrane potential is in proportion to the conductance or permeability of that ion. The **greater the conductance**, the closer the membrane will approach the **equilibrium potential** of that ion. • The resting potential of cells is negative inside. **Hyperpolarization** occurs when the membrane potential becomes more negative. **Depolarization** occurs when the membrane potential becomes less negative or even positive.
Chord conductance equation	$E_m = (g_K/\Sigma g \times E_K) + (g_{Na}/\Sigma g \times E_{Na}) + (g_{Cl}/\Sigma g \times E_{Cl})$ E_m = membrane potential in mV; g = conductance of individual ion; Σg = total conductance of cell membrane; E = equilibrium potential of individual ion from Nernst equation • Used to calculate membrane potential; useful to evaluate effects of ion conductance and concentrations; explains action potential, synaptic potentials, and electrolyte disorders
Properties of ions in a typical neuron	<table><tr><td>Ion</td><td>Extracellular (mM)</td><td>Intracellular (mM)</td><td>Equilibrium Potential (mV)</td><td>Conductance</td></tr><tr><td>Na⁺</td><td>150.0</td><td>15.0</td><td>+60</td><td>Very low</td></tr><tr><td>K⁺</td><td>5.5</td><td>150.0</td><td>−90</td><td>High</td></tr><tr><td>Cl⁻</td><td>125.0</td><td>9.0</td><td>−70</td><td>High</td></tr></table> • Because potassium and chloride have a high conductance, their equilibrium potentials dominate the membrane potential, so the inside of the cell is negative. • Changes in EC K⁺ can produce large changes in the membrane potential: ↑ EC K^+ → depolarization; ↓ EC K^+ → hyperpolarization. • Changes in EC Na⁺ have little effect on membrane potential, but an increase in Na⁺ conductance → depolarization.

Definition of abbreviation: EC, extracellular.

ACTION POTENTIAL

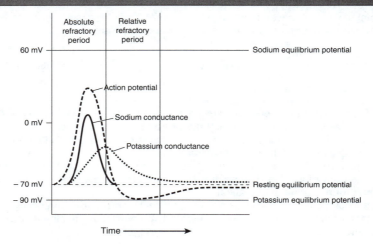

The action potentials (AP) of excitable cells involve the opening and closing of voltage-gated channels for sodium, potassium, and in some cells, calcium. The figure above shows a neuronal AP. The opening of a channel increases conductance. Steps are shown below.

- Inward currents depolarize the membrane potential to **threshold**.
- **Voltage-gated Na$^+$ channels open**, causing an **inward Na$^+$ current**. The membrane potential approaches the Na$^+$ equilibrium potential. These channels can be blocked by **tetrodotoxin**.
- These Na$^+$ channels close rapidly **(inactivation)**, even though the membrane is still depolarized.
- Depolarization slowly opens K$^+$ channels, **increasing K$^+$ conductance (outward current)**, leading to **repolarization**.
- **Absolute refractory period:** An AP cannot be elicited because Na$^+$ channels are closed.
- **Relative refractory period:** Only a greater than normal stimulus can produce an AP because the K$^+$ conductance is still higher than at rest.
- The **Na$^+$-K$^+$ pump** restores ion concentrations. It is **electrogenic** (3 Na$^+$ pumped out for every 2 K$^+$ pumped in).

Clinical Correlations

Calcium has a low resting conductance and does not contribute to the resting potential. It has a very positive equilibrium potential, so when conductance increases (e.g., cardiac and smooth muscle cells), **depolarization** occurs. Calcium concentration affects the action potentials and force of contraction of **cardiac and smooth muscle**.

Hypercalcemia stabilizes excitable membranes, leading to flaccid paralysis of skeletal muscle. **Hypocalcemia** destabilizes membranes, leading to spontaneous action potentials and spasms.

Abnormal increases and decreases of **extracellular potassium** have severe consequences for cardiac conduction and rhythm.

Renal and gastrointestinal disorders are likely to cause abnormalities of electrolytes and alteration of resting potentials and action potentials.

Pathology

Chapter 8

CELLULAR INJURY AND ADAPTATION

Changing conditions in the cell's environment can produce changes from adaptation to injury or even cell death. The cellular response to injury depends on the *type, duration*, and *severity* of injury, the *type of cell* injured, *metabolic state, and ability to adapt.*

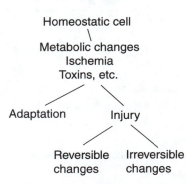

CAUSES	EXAMPLES
Hypoxia (most common)	• Ischemia (e.g., arteriosclerosis, thromboembolus) • Cardiopulmonary failure • Severe anemia
Infections	Viruses, bacteria, parasites, rickettsiae, fungi, prions
Immunologic reactions	• Hypersensitivity reactions • Autoimmune
Congenital/metabolic disorders	• Inborn errors of metabolism (e.g., phenylketonuria, galactosemia, glycogen storage diseases)
Chemical injury	• Drugs (e.g., therapeutic, drugs of abuse) • Poisons • Pollution • Occupational exposure (e.g., CCl_4, CO, asbestos)
Physical injury	Trauma, burns, frostbite, radiation
Nutritional or vitamin imbalance	• Inadequate calorie/protein intake (e.g., marasmus, kwashiorkor, anorexia nervosa) • Excess caloric intake (e.g., obesity, atherosclerosis) • Vitamin deficiencies • Hypervitaminosis

Important Mechanisms of Cell Injury

- Oxygen-free radicals (superoxide [$O_2^{\cdot-}$], hydroxyl radical [$OH\cdot$], hydrogen peroxide [H_2O_2]) damage DNA, proteins, lipid membranes, and circulating lipids (LDL) by peroxidation
- ATP depletion
- Increased cell-membrane permeability
- Influx of calcium—activates a wide spectrum of enzymes: proteases, ATPases, phospholipases, endonucleases
- Mitochondrial dysfunction, formation of mitochondrial permeability transition (MPT) channels
- Decreased oxidative phosphorylation
- Release of cytochrome c is a trigger for apoptosis

Protective Factors Against Free Radicals

1. *Antioxidants*—vitamins A, E, and C
2. *Superoxide dismutase*—superoxide → hydrogen peroxide
3. *Glutathione peroxidase*—hydroxyl ions or hydrogen peroxide → water
4. *Catalase*—hydrogen peroxide → oxygen and water

Direct and Indirect Results of Reversible Cell Injury

Direct Result	Consequences	Pathophysiologic Correlates
Decreased synthesis of ATP by oxidative phosphorylation	Decreased function of Na$^+$/K$^+$ ATPase → influx of Na$^+$ and water, efflux of K$^+$, and swelling of the ER	Cellular swelling (hydropic swelling), swelling of endoplasmic reticulum, membrane blebs, myelin figures
Increased glycolysis → glycogen depletion	Increased lactic acid production → decreased intracellular pH	Tissue acidosis
Ribosomes detach from rough ER	Decreased protein synthesis	Lipid deposition (fatty change)

As the Degree of Cellular Injury Worsens...

Severe plasma membrane damage	Massive influx of calcium, efflux of intracellular enzymes and proteins into the circulation	Markers of cellular damage detectable in serum (LDH, CK, ALT, AST, troponin, etc.)
Calcium influx into mitochondria	Irreparable damage to oxidative phosphorylation	Mitochondrial densities
Lysosomal contents leak out	Lysosomal hydrolases are activated intracellularly	Autolysis, heterolysis, nuclear changes (pyknosis, karyorrhexis, karyolysis)

Irreversible Injury and Cell Death

Morphologic Pattern	Characteristics
Coagulative necrosis	**Most common** (e.g., heart, liver, kidney) Proteins denatured, nucleus is lost, but cellular shape is maintained
Liquefactive necrosis	**Abscesses**, **brain infarcts**, pancreatic necrosis Cellular destruction by hydrolytic enzymes
Caseous necrosis	Seen in **tuberculosis** Combination of coagulation and liquefaction necrosis → soft, friable, and "cottage-cheese–like" appearance
Fat necrosis	Caused by the action of lipases on fatty tissue (e.g., with **pancreatic damage**) Chalky white appearance
Fibrinoid necrosis	Eosinophilic homogeneous appearance—resembles fibrin

Gangrenous necrosis	*Common sites:* lower limbs, gallbladder, GI tract, and testes
	  Dry gangrene—coagulative necrosis
	  Wet gangrene—liquefactive necrosis

Apoptosis	A specialized form of **programmed cell death**, an active process under genetic control Mediated by a cascade of **caspases** (digest nuclear and cytoskeletal proteins and activate endonucleases) Often affects only single cells or small groups of cells

Myocardial ischemia is a good example of cellular injury and death.

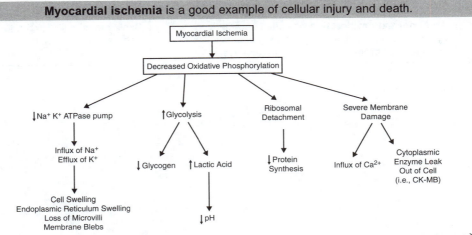

APOPTOSIS				
Morphology	**Stimuli for Apoptosis**	**Genetic Regulation**	**Physiologic Examples**	**Pathologic Examples**
• Cells shrink, cytoplasm is dense and eosinophilic • Nuclear chromatin condenses, then fragments • Cell membrane blebs • Cell fragments (apoptotic bodies) are phagocytized by adjacent cells or macrophages • **Lack of inflammatory response**	• Cell injury and DNA damage • Lack of hormones, cytokines, or growth factors • Receptor-ligand signals: – **Fas** binding to Fas ligand – Tumor necrosis factor (**TNF**) binding to TNF receptor 1 (TNFR1)	• *bcl-2* (inhibits apoptosis) • *p-53* (stimulates apoptosis)	• Embryogenesis— organogenesis and development • Hormone-dependent apoptosis (menstrual cycle) • Selective death of lymphocytes in thymus	• Viral hepatitis (Councilman body) • Graft versus host disease • Cystic fibrosis (CF)— duct obstruction and pancreatic atrophy

ADAPTIVE CELLULAR RESPONSES TO INJURY (POTENTIALLY REVERSIBLE)		
Types	**Definitions**	**Causes**
Atrophy	**Decrease in cell size and functional ability.** Cells shrink; lipofuscin granules can be seen microscopically. EM—autophagosomes	• Deceased workload/disuse • Ischemia • Lack of hormonal or neural stimulation • Malnutrition • Aging
Hypertrophy	**An increase in cell size and functional ability** mediated by growth factors, cytokines, and other trophic stimuli, leading to increased expression of genes and increased protein synthesis. May coexist with hyperplasia.	• Increased mechanical demand, e.g., striated muscle of weight lifters, cardiac muscle in hypertension • Increased endocrine stimulation, e.g., puberty, pregnancy, lactation
Hyperplasia	**An increase in the number of cells** in a tissue or organ, mediated by growth factors, cytokines, and other trophic stimuli. Increased expression of growth-promoting genes (proto-oncogenes), increased DNA synthesis, and cell division	**Physiologic causes:** • Compensatory (e.g., after partial hepatectomy) • Hormonal stimulation (e.g., breast development at puberty) • Antigenic stimulation (e.g., lymphoid hyperplasia) **Pathologic causes:** • Endometrial hyperplasia • Prostatic hyperplasia of aging
Metaplasia	**A reversible change of one cell type to another**	Irritation
Dysplasia	**An abnormal proliferation of cells** characterized by changes in cell size, shape, and loss of cellular organization; premalignant, e.g., cervical dysplasia	Similar to stimuli that produce cancer (e.g., HPV, esophageal reflux)

REGENERATION AND REPAIR

Wound healing involves **regeneration** of cells in a damaged tissue, along with repair of the connective tissue matrix.

CAPACITY OF CELLS TO REGENERATE

Cell Type	Properties	Examples
Labile	Regenerate throughout life	Skin and mucosal lining cells Hematopoietic cells Stem cells
Stable	Replicate at a low level throughout life Have the capacity to divide if stimulated by some initiating event	Hepatocytes Proximal tubule cells Endothelium
Permanent	Cannot replicate	Neurons and cardiac muscle

Growth Factors and Cytokines Involved in Growth Repair

- Transforming growth factor α (TGF-α)
- Platelet-derived growth factor (PDGF)
- Fibroblast growth factor (FGF)
- Vascular endothelial growth factor (VEGF)
- Epidermal growth factor (EGF)
- Tumor necrosis factor α (TNF-α) and IL-1

CONNECTIVE TISSUE COMPONENTS

Collagen production requires vitamin C (wound healing impaired in scurvy) and copper. Different types of collagen are found in different body sites.

- Type I collagen is the most common form.
- Type II collagen is found in cartilage.
- Type III collagen is an immature form found in granulation tissue.
- Type IV collage is found in basement membranes.

Other extracellular matrix components include:

- adhesion molecules
- proteoglycans
- glycosaminoglycans

WOUND HEALING

Primary Union (healing by first intention)

Occurs with clean wounds when there has been little tissue damage and wound edges are closely approximated, e.g., a surgical incision

Secondary Union (healing by second intention)

Occurs in wounds that have large tissue defects (the two skin edges are not in contact):

- Granulation tissue fills in the defects
- Often accompanied by significant wound contraction; may produce large residual scar

Keloids

Occur as result of excessive scar collagen deposition/hypertrophy, especially in dark-skinned people

Connective Tissue Diseases

Scurvy

Vitamin C deficiency first affecting collagen with highest hydroxyproline content, such as that found in blood vessels. Thus, an early symptom is bleeding gums.

Ehlers-Danlos (ED) Syndrome

Defect in collagen synthesis or structure. There are many types. ED type IV is a defect in type III collagen.

Osteogenesis Imperfecta

Defect in collagen type I

STAINING METHODS

Stain	Cell Type/Component
Hematoxylin (stains blue to purple)	Nuclei, nucleoli, bacteria, calcium
Eosin (stains pink to red)	Cytoplasm, collagen, fibrin, RBCs, thyroid colloid
Prussian blue	Iron
Congo red	Amyloid
Periodic acid-Schiff (PAS)	Glycogen, mucin, mucoprotein, glycoprotein, as well as fungi
Gram stain	Microorganisms
Trichrome	Collagen
Reticulin	Reticular fibers in loose connective tissue
Immunohistochemical (antibody) stains: • Cytokeratin • Vimentin • Desmin • Prostate-specific antigen (PSA) • S-100, neuron specific enolase, neurofilament • GFAP	 • Epithelial cells • Connective tissue • Muscle • Prostate • Neurons, neuronally derived, neural crest–derived growths • Glial cells (including astrocytes)

Definition of abbreviations: GFAP, glial fibrillary acidic protein.

AMYLOIDOSIS

An accumulation of various insoluble fibrillar in various tissues. It stains with **Congo red** and shows **apple-green birefringence** with polarized light.

Disease	Amyloid Type
Primary amyloidosis (e.g., plasma cell disorders)	AL (kappa or lambda chains)
Secondary amyloidosis (e.g., neoplasia, rheumatoid arthritis, SLE, TB, Crohn disease, osteomyelitis, familial Mediterranean fever)	AA (from serum amyloid A [SAA])
Renal hemodialysis	Amyloid protein $A\beta_2M$ and fibrillary protein β_2 microglobulin
Senile cerebral amyloidosis	Amyloid protein $A\beta$ and fibrillary protein β-amyloid precursor protein (βAPP)
Cardiac amyloidosis	Amyloid protein ATTR and fibrillary protein transthyretin
Medullary carcinoma of thyroid	Procalcitonin
Type 2 diabetes, pancreatic islet-cell tumors	Amylin

Definition of abbreviations: ATTR, amyloid transthyretin; SLE, systemic lupus erythematosus; TB, tuberculosis.

NEOPLASIA

Carcinogenesis is a multistep process involving multiple genetic changes from inherited germ-line mutations or acquired mutations, leading to monoclonal expansion of a mutated cell.

Progression of epithelial cancer: normal epithelium → atypical hyperplasia → dysplasia → carcinoma in situ → invasion, metastasis (collagenases, hydrolases aid in penetration of barriers, such as basement membrane)

BASIC TERMS

Anaplasia	Loss of cell differentiation and tissue organization
Atypical hyperplasia	Increased cell number with morphologic abnormalities
Carcinoma	Malignant tumor of epithelium
Carcinoma in situ	Malignant tumor of epithelium that does not penetrate basement membrane to underlying tissue
Desmoplasia	Excessive fibrous tissue formation in tumor stroma
Dysplasia	Abnormal atypical cellular proliferation
Metaplasia	Replacement of one type of adult cell or tissue by another (within the same germ cell line) that is not normally present in that site
Metastasis	Secondary, discontinuous malignant growth (spread), such as a lung metastasis of a colon carcinoma
Sarcoma	A nonepithelial (mesenchymal) malignant tumor

SELECTED RISK FACTORS FOR CANCER

Geographic/Racial	Stomach cancer (Japan); hepatocellular carcinoma (Asia)	
Occupational/Environmental exposures	**Aflatoxin:** hepatocellular carcinoma **Alkylating agents:** leukemia, lymphoma, other cancers **Aromatic "–amines" and "azo–" dyes:** hepatocellular carcinoma **Arsenic:** squamous cell carcinomas of skin and lung, angiosarcoma of liver **Asbestos:** bronchogenic carcinoma, mesothelioma **Benzene:** leukemia	**Chromium and nickel:** bronchogenic carcinoma **Cigarette smoke:** multiple malignancies **Ionizing radiation:** thyroid cancer, leukemia **Naphthylamine:** bladder cancer **Nitrosamines:** gastric cancer **Polycyclic aromatic hydrocarbons:** bronchogenic carcinoma **Ultraviolet exposure:** skin cancers **Vinyl chloride:** angiosarcoma of liver
Age	Increases risk of most cancers (exceptions: Wilms, etc.)	
Hereditary predisposition	Familial retinoblastoma; multiple endocrine neoplasia, familial polyposis coli	
Acquired risk factors	Cervical dysplasia, endometrial hyperplasia, cirrhosis, ulcerative colitis, chronic atrophic gastritis	

There are many proposed mechanisms of carcinogenesis. The most important mutations involve growth-promoting genes (proto-oncogenes), growth-inhibiting tumor suppressor genes, and genes regulating apoptosis.

Clinically Important Oncogenes			
Proto-oncogenes are normal cellular genes involved with growth and cellular differentiation. **Oncogenes** are derived from proto-oncogenes by changing the gene sequence (resulting in a new gene product, oncoprotein) or a loss of gene regulation → overexpression of the normal gene product. Oncogenes lack regulatory control and are overexpressed → unregulated cellular proliferation.			
Oncogene	**Tumor**	**Gene Product**	**Mechanism of Activation**
hst-1/int-2	Cancer of the stomach, breast, bladder, and melanoma	**Growth factor** Fibroblast growth factor	Overexpression
sis	Astrocytoma	Platelet-derived growth factor	Overexpression
erb-B1	SCC of lung	**Growth factor receptor** Epidermal growth factor receptor	Overexpression
erb-B2	Breast, ovary, lung	Epidermal growth factor receptor	Amplification
erb-B3	Breast	Epidermal growth factor receptor	Overexpression
ret	MEN II and III, familial thyroid (medullary) cancer	Glial neurotrophic factor receptor	Point mutation
abl	CML, ALL	**Signal transduction proteins** bcr-abl fusion protein with tyrosine kinase activity	Translocation t(9;22)
Ki-ras	Lung, pancreas, and colon	GTP-binding protein	Point mutation
c-myc	Burkitt lymphoma	Nuclear regulatory protein	Translocation t(8;14)
L-myc	Small cell lung carcinoma	Nuclear regulatory protein	Amplification
N-myc	Neuroblastoma	Nuclear regulatory protein	Amplification
bcl-1	Mantle cell lymphoma	**Cell-cycle regulatory proteins** Cyclin D protein	Translocation t(11;14)
CDK4	Melanoma, glioblastoma multiforme	Cyclin-dependent kinase	Amplification

Definition of abbreviations: ALL, acute lymphocytic leukemia; CML, chronic myelogenous leukemia; MEN, multiple endocrine neoplasia; SCC, squamous cell carcinoma.

Inactivation of Tumor Suppressor Genes

Tumor suppressor genes encode proteins that regulate and suppress cell proliferation by inhibiting progression through the cell cycle. Inactivation of these genes → uncontrolled cellular proliferation.

Chromosome	Gene	Tumors
3p25	VHL	Von Hippel-Lindau disease, renal cell carcinoma
11p13	WT-1	Wilms tumor
11p15	WT-2	Wilms tumor
13q14	Rb	Retinoblastoma, osteosarcoma
17q13.1	p53	Lung, breast, colon, etc.
17q12-21	BRCA-1	Hereditary breast and ovary cancers
13q12-13	BRCA-2	Hereditary breast cancer
5q21	APC	Adenomatous polyps and colon cancer
18q21	DCC	Colon cancer
17q11.2	NF-1	Neurofibromas
22q12	NF-2	Acoustic neuromas, meningiomas

Failure of Apoptosis Is Another Cause of Cancer

bcl-2

- **Prevents apoptosis**
- Overexpressed in follicular lymphomas t(14:18) (chromosome 14 [immunoglobulin heavy chain gene]; chromosome 18 [*bcl-2*])

bax, bad, bcl-xS, bid

- **Promote apoptosis**
- *p53* promotes apoptosis in mutated cells by stimulating *bax* synthesis; inactivation → failure of apoptosis

c-myc

- Promotes cellular proliferation
- When associated with *p53* → promotes apoptosis; when associated with *bcl-2* → inhibits apoptosis

ONCOGENIC VIRUSES

	RNA	DNA			
Specific virus	Human T-cell leukemia virus (HTLV-1)	Hepatitis B	Epstein-Barr	Human papilloma virus (types 16, 18)	Human herpesvirus 8
Associated disease	Adult T-cell leukemia/ lymphoma	Hepatocellular carcinoma	Burkitt lymphoma, B-cell lymphoma, nasopharyngeal carcinoma	Cervical cancer	Kaposi sarcoma

SERUM TUMOR MARKERS

These are usually normal cellular components that are increased in neoplasms but may also be elevated in non-neoplastic conditions. Can be used for screening, monitoring of treatment efficacy, and detecting recurrence.

Marker	Associated Cancers
α-fetoprotein (AFP)	Hepatocellular carcinoma, nonseminomatous testicular germ-cell tumors
β-human chorionic gonadotropin (hCG)	Trophoblastic tumors, choriocarcinoma
Calcitonin	Medullary carcinoma of the thyroid
Carcinoembryonic antigen (CEA)	Carcinomas of the lung, pancreas, stomach, breast, colon
CA-125	Ovarian cancer
CA19-9	Pancreatic cancer
Placental alkaline phosphatase	Seminoma
Prostatic acid phosphatase	Prostate cancer
PSA	Prostate cancer
S-100	Melanoma, neural-derived tumors, astrocytoma
Tartrate-resistant acid phosphatase (TRAP)	Hairy cell leukemia

PARANEOPLASTIC SYNDROMES

Tumor	Carcinoid tumor (metastatic, bronchial, ovarian)	Small cell carcinoma of lung	Squamous cell carcinoma of lung	Thymoma	Pancreatic carcinoma
Syndrome	Carcinoid syndrome, 5-HIAA produced	Ectopic ACTH secretion; SIADH	Hypercalcemia (PTH-like peptide)	Myasthenic syndrome	Migratory thrombophlebitis

Definition of abbreviations: ACTH, adrenocorticotropic hormone; 5-HIAA, 5-hydroxindolacetic acid; PTH, parathyroid hormone; SIADH, syndrome of inappropriate antidiuretic hormone.

GRADING AND STAGING

Grade	• An estimate of the cytologic malignancy of a tumor, including the degree of anaplasia and number of mitoses. • Nuclear size, chromatin content, nucleoli, and nuclear-to-cytoplasmic ratio are all used.
Stage	• The clinical estimate of the extent of spread of a malignant tumor. Low stage means a localized tumor. Stage rises as tumors spread locally then metastasize. • **TNM** is typically used; **T** = size of **t**umor; **N** = **n**ode involvement; **M** = **m**etastases

Pharmacology/Therapeutics

Chapter 9

PHARMACOKINETICS

KEY CONCEPTS

Volume of distribution (apparent)	$V_d = \dfrac{Dose}{C^0}$ C^0 = plasma concentration at time zero	• V_d estimates the fluid volume into which the drug has distributed (one needs to extrapolate plasma concentration at time zero). • The lower the C^0, the higher the V_d, and vice versa. • Drugs stored in nonfluid compartments like fat may have a V_d greater than TBW (e.g., lipid-soluble drugs, quinacrine). • Drugs that bind strongly to plasma proteins have a V_d that approaches plasma volume. • Approximate V_d values (weight 70 kg)—plasma volume (3 L), blood (5 L), extracellular fluid (12–14 L), TBW (40–42 L)
Clearance	$Cl = \dfrac{Rate\ of\ drug\ elimination}{Plasma\ drug\ concentration}$ $Cl = k_e \times V_d;$ k_e = elimination constant	Clearance is the theoretical volume of blood totally cleared of drug/unit time. It represents the ratio of drug elimination to its plasma concentration. For a drug with first-order elimination, clearance is constant.
Elimination	The rate of elimination of the active drug. It is not drug excretion because it may be metabolized before excretion.	

First-Order Elimination		**Zero-Order Elimination**	
	A constant **fraction** of drug is eliminated with time. Most drugs have first-order elimination.		A constant **amount** of drug is eliminated with time. Half-life is not applicable. *Examples:* ethanol (except at low blood levels), phenytoin, and aspirin (high doses)

Half-life	$t_{1/2} = \dfrac{0.7}{k_e}$ $t_{1/2} = \dfrac{0.7 \times V_d}{Cl}$	Half-life is the time it takes for the amount or concentration of a drug to fall to 50% of a previous estimate. It is constant for drugs eliminated by first-order kinetics.
Steady state	Plasma drug concentrations remain relatively constant over time. As a rule, it takes **4 to 5 half-lives** to achieve steady state. (Rise in concentration: 50% at 1 half-life; 75% at 2 half-lives; 87.5% at 3 half-lives; 93.75% at 4 half-lives. Decline in concentration is similar: 50% remains at 1 half-life; 25% at 2 half-lives; 12.5% at 3 half-lives; 6.25% at 4 half-lives.)	
Bioavailability (F)		The fraction of the administered drug that reaches the systemic circulation. $F = \dfrac{AUC_{PO}}{AUC_{IV}}$ (AUC = area under the curve, PO = oral, IV = intravenous) By definition, intravenous drug administration has an F of 1 (100%).

Definition of abbreviations: AUC, area under the curve; F, bioavailability; IV, intravenously; PO, by mouth; TBW, total body weight.

(Continued)

First-pass effect	With oral administration, drugs are absorbed into the portal circulation and initially distributed to the liver. For some drugs, their rapid hepatic metabolism decreases bioavailability. This can be avoided by giving the drug by an alternate route (e.g., sublingual, transdermal).	
Maintenance dose	$MD = \dfrac{Cl \times C_P}{F}$	A maintenance dose is given to maintain a relatively constant plasma concentration. It is equal to the rate of elimination.
Loading dose	$LD = \dfrac{V_d \times C_P}{F}$	If therapeutic plasma concentrations are needed quickly and the V_d is large, a loading dose may be given to produce the desired drug levels (fill up the V_d) without the typical delay of 4 to 5 half-lives.

Definition of abbreviation: C_P, desired plasma concentration

PHARMACODYNAMICS

KEY CONCEPTS	

Agonist	An agonist is a drug that binds to a receptor and activates it.	
Partial agonist	A partial agonist is a drug that binds to a receptor but does not elicit a 100% response. It will elicit a partial response when administered alone. When administered with a full agonist, it acts as an **antagonist** because it displaces the full agonist from the receptor.	
Graded dose–response curve		A graded dose–response curve depicts increasing responses to increasing drug doses.
		Potency: the measure of how much drug is required to produce a given effect. It is typically expressed as the concentration that can elicit a 50% response (EC_{50}). **Efficacy:** the maximal effect a drug can produce. It is also known as maximal efficacy. A partial agonist can be less potent (*C*) or more potent (*A*) than a full agonist (*B*). *(See figure to left.)*
Competitive antagonist		A competitive antagonist binds to the receptor without activating the effector system. It **can** be overcome by increasing the agonist dose. This is seen as a **parallel right shift** in the dose–response curve.
Noncompetitive antagonist		A noncompetitive antagonist binds to the receptor without activating the effector system. It **cannot** be overcome by increasing the agonist dose. This is seen as a **downward shift** in the dose–response curve.
K_d	The concentration of drug that binds to 50% of the receptors	
Spare receptors	These are "extra" receptors that do not need to be bound in order to produce a maximal response ($K_d > EC_{50}$).	
Quantal dose–response curve	A quantal dose–response curve depicts the dose of drug needed to produce a predetermined response in a population. It is the percent of population responding versus log (dose).	
Therapeutic index (TI)		The therapeutic index is the ratio of the drug dose required to produce a toxic or lethal effect to the dose needed for a therapeutic effect. $$TI = \frac{TD_{50}}{ED_{50}} \text{ or } \frac{LD_{50}}{ED_{50}}$$ ED_{50}, TD_{50}, and LD_{50} are the median effective, toxic, and lethal doses in 50% of the studied population, respectively. ↑ **TI, safe drug;** ↓ **TI, unsafe drug**

		SIGNAL TRANSDUCTION	

G-protein–coupled receptors

These receptors consist of one polypeptide with seven-transmembrane–spanning regions. When bound by an agonist, the trimeric (α, β, γ) GTP-binding protein (G protein) is activated. The α component usually interacts with the effector molecules.

The most common G proteins and their receptors are as follows:

G protein	Receptors	Effector	Second messenger response
G_s	β_1, β_2, D_1, H_2	Adenylyl cyclase	$\uparrow$ cAMP
G_i	α_2, M_2, D_2	Adenylyl cyclase	$\downarrow$ cAMP
G_q	α, M_1, M_3, H_1	Phospholipase C	$\uparrow$ IP$_3$ ($\uparrow$ Ca$_i^{2+}$), DAG

Ligand-gated channels

Activation of receptors within ion channels may directly open the channel, e.g., **nicotinic ACh** (Na$^+$/K$^+$), **GABA$_A$** (Cl$^-$), **NMDA** (Ca^{2+}/Na$^+$) receptors, or may regulate the ion channel's response to an agonist, e.g., benzodiazepine, barbiturate sites on the GABA$_A$ receptor.

Intracellular receptors

Lipid-soluble agents diffuse across the plasma membrane to bind intracellular receptors (e.g., **steroid** receptors, **thyroid** receptors). This permits receptor binding to nuclear DNA sequences that modify gene expression.

Ligand-regulated transmembrane enzymes

These receptors have extracellular ligand binding sites and intracellular catalytic sites. Ligand binding causes dimerization and activates the enzyme activity (often a **tyrosine kinase**). *Examples:* **insulin** and **growth factor** receptors.

Transmembrane receptors that activate a separate tyrosine kinase

These also form dimers when activated, then activate a separate cytoplasmic tyrosine kinase (Janus kinases; JAKs). The kinase phosphorylates STAT factors (signal transducers and activators of transcription). STAT dimers then regulate transcription. *Examples:* **cytokine** and **growth hormone** receptors.

TOXICOLOGY

SIGNS, SYMPTOMS, AND TREATMENTS FOR COMMON TOXIC SYNDROMES

Compounds	Signs and Symptoms	Treatment
AChE inhibitors	Miosis, salivation, sweating, GI cramps, diarrhea, seizures, anxiety/agitation, muscle fasciculations followed by muscle paralysis (including diaphragm), respiratory failure, coma	Respiratory support; atropine plus pralidoxime (2-PAM, AChE-reactivating agent for organophosphate inhibitors)
Atropine and muscarinic blockers	↑ HR, ↑ BP, hyperthermia (hot, dry skin), ↓ GI motility, urinary retention, delirium, hallucinations, seizures, coma	Control CV symptoms and hyperthermia plus physostigmine (crosses BBB)
Carbon monoxide (>10% carboxyHb)	Headache, dizziness, nausea/vomiting, shortness of breath, chest pain, ↑ HR, ↓ BP, arrhythmias, confusion, coma	Hyperbaric O_2 and decontamination
CNS stimulants	Anxiety/agitation, hyperthermia (warm, sweaty skin), mydriasis, ↑ HR, ↑ BP, psychosis, seizures	Control CV symptoms, hyperthermia, and seizures; BZs or antipsychotics may be beneficial
Opioid analgesics	Lethargy, sedation, coma, ↓ HR, ↓ BP, miosis, hypoventilation, respiratory failure, ↓ GI motility	Ventilatory support; naloxone at frequent intervals
Salicylates	Confusion, lethargy, hyperventilation, ototoxicity, hyperthermia, dehydration, hypokalemia, acid-base disturbances, seizures, coma	Correct acidosis and electrolytes, urinary alkalinization, possible hemodialysis
Sedative-hypnotics and ethanol	Disinhibition, lethargy, stupor, coma, ataxia, nystagmus, hypothermia, respiratory failure	Ventilatory support—flumazenil if BZs implicated
SSRIs	Agitation, confusion, coma, muscle rigidity, hyperthermia, seizures, autonomic instability	Control hyperthermia and seizures—possible use of cyproheptadine and BZs
Tricyclic antidepressants	Mydriasis, hyperthermia (hot, dry skin), 3 Cs (convulsions, coma, and cardiotoxicity)	Control seizures and hyperthermia, correct acidosis plus possible antiarrhythmics

Definition of abbreviations: AChE, acetylcholinesterase; BBB, blood–brain barrier; BP, blood pressure; BZs, benzodiazepines; CNS, central nervous system; CV, cardiovascular; GI, gastrointestinal; HR, heart rate; SSRIs, selective serotonin reuptake inhibitors.

SIGNS, SYMPTOMS, AND TREATMENTS FOR HEAVY METAL POISONING

Metals And Source	Signs and Symptoms	Treatment*
Arsenic (wood preservatives, insecticides, occupational, environmental)	**Acute:** GI distress, garlic breath, "rice water" stools, hypotension **Chronic:** paresthesias, stocking-glove neuropathy, pallor from anemia, skin **Arsine gas:** headache, N/V, abdominal pain, dyspnea, jaundice	Dimercaprol, penicillamine, succimer Supportive care
Iron (iron supplements, multivitamin supplements)	Occurs mainly in children; severe GI distress, GI bleeding, hepatocellular injury, seizures, shock, coma	Deferoxamine
Lead (tap water, leaded paint chips, glazed kitchenware, etc.)	**Acute:** abdominal (colic, N/V), CNS (headaches, ataxia, seizures, coma, encephalopathy) **Chronic:** anemia (inhibits heme synthesis), neuropathy (wristdrop), GI symptoms, nephropathy, developmental delays, growth retardation, decreased fertility, stillbirths	EDTA, dimercaprol, succimer
Mercury (dental amalgams, electroplating, batteries, wood preservatives, occupational, contaminated foods)	**Acute:** vapor inhalation (elemental)—chest pain, dyspnea, pneumonitis, confusion **Acute:** tremors, gingivitis, CNS disturbances, GI distress, renal failure **Chronic:** renal failure, dementia, acrodynia **Organic:** CNS (paresthesias, auditory and visual loss, movement disorders)	Dimercaprol, penicillamine, succimer

Definition of abbreviations: CNS, central nervous system; GI, gastrointestinal; EDTA, ethylenediaminetetraacetic acid; N/V, nausea and vomiting.
*Need to remove patient from source; decontamination is also important part of management.

SUMMARY OF ANTIDOTES	
Antidote	**Type of Poisoning**
Acetylcysteine	Acetaminophen
Atropine	AChE inhibitors
Deferoxamine	Iron
Digoxin antibodies	Digoxin
Dimercaprol (BAL)	Arsenic, mercury (inorganic, elemental), lead (with EDTA if severe poisoning); succimer and unithiol now used more frequently
EDTA	Primarily for lead poisoning
Esmolol	Theophylline, caffeine, β agonists
Ethanol	Methanol, ethylene glycol
Flumazenil	Benzodiazepines, zolpidem, suggested for zaleplon
Fomepizole	Methanol, ethylene glycol
Glucagon	β blockers
Naloxone	Opioid analgesics
Oxygen	Carbon monoxide
Penicillamine	Copper, Wilson disease, adjunctive in iron and arsenic intoxication
Physostigmine	Anticholinergics: atropine, antihistamine, antiparkinsonian—*not* tricyclic antidepressants
Pralidoxime (2-PAM)	Organophosphate cholinesterase inhibitors
Protamine	Heparins
Succimer	Lead, arsenic, mercury
Vitamin K	Warfarin and coumarin anticoagulants
Activated charcoal	Nonspecific: all oral poisonings except Fe, CN, Li, solvents, mineral acids, or corrosives

Definition of abbreviations: AChE, acetylcholinesterase; EDTA, edetate calcium disodium, ethylenediaminetetraacetic acid.

AUTACOIDS

Autacoids are endogenously produced substances that do not fit well in other classifications such as hormones or neurotransmitters. The autacoids include histamine, serotonin, vasoactive peptides, and prostaglandins (see page 52).

HISTAMINE

Synthesis	Histadine $\xrightarrow{\text{Histidine decarboxylase}}$ Histamine
Location	Circulating **basophils** and tissue **mast cells**, GI tract, skin, lung
Degranulation	• Liberation of histamine from mast cells via IgE-mediated hypersensitivity reactions, trauma, drugs, and venoms • $\downarrow$ cAMP favors release; $\uparrow$ cAMP (via β-adrenergic and glucocorticoid stimulation) $\downarrow$ release • Other substances released include kallikrein, kinins, prostaglandins, SRS-A

Histamine Receptors

Receptor	Second Messenger	Distribution	Action
H_1	G_q; $\uparrow$ IP$_3$, DAG	Smooth muscle	Vasodilation (via NO), $\uparrow$ bronchoconstriction, activates nociceptive receptors
H_2	G_s; $\uparrow$ cAMP	Stomach, smooth muscle	$\uparrow$ gastric acid secretion
H_3	G-protein	CNS	—

Pharmacologic Agents

Agent	Mechanism of Action	Clinical Uses	Notes/Toxicity

H$_1$ antagonists:
  Diphenhydramine
  Promethazine
  Chlorpheniramine
  Hydroxyzine
  Fexofenadine*
  Loratadine*
  Cetirizine*
	Competitively inhibit H_1 receptors	• Allergic reactions
		• Motion sickness
		• OTC: sleep aids and cold medications
			• Sedation
			• Dry mucosa

H$_2$ antagonists:
  Cimetidine
  Ranitidine
  Famotidine
  Nizatidine
	Competitively inhibit H_2 receptors $\rightarrow$ reduce gastric acid secretion†	• Peptic ulcer disease†
		• GERD
		• Zollinger Ellison syndrome
			Cimetidine: P450 inhibition, antiandrogen effect

Definition of abbreviations: GERD, gastroesophageal reflux disease; GI, gastrointestinal; IgE, immunoglobulin E; SRS-A, slow-reacting substance of anaphylaxis.

*No CNS entry (less sedating); loratadine (Claritin®), fexofenadine (Allegra®), cetirizine (Zyrtec®)

†Not as efficacious as proton pump inhibitors

SEROTONIN

Synthesis and degradation	Tryptophan $\xrightarrow{\text{Tryptophan hydroxylase}}$ 5HT $\xrightarrow{\text{MAO}}$ 5HIAA
Location	Enterochromaffin cells in the gut, CNS neurons, platelets (primarily just storage)

Serotonin Receptors

Receptor	Second Messenger	Action
$5HT_{1(A, B, D, E, F)}$	G_i; $\downarrow$ cAMP	• CNS • Behavioral effects (sleep, feeding, thermoregulation, anxiety) • Vasoconstriction
$5HT_{2(A, B, C)}$	G_q; $\uparrow$ IP_3, DAG	• CNS • Behavioral effects • Smooth muscle contraction • Platelet aggregation
$5HT_3$	Ion channel	• CNS (area postrema), PNS • Emesis • Anxiety
$5HT_4$	G_s; $\uparrow$ cAMP	• CNS: neuronal excitation • GI motility

Pharmacologic Agents

Agent	Mechanism of Action	Clinical Uses	Notes/Toxicity
Sumatriptan Naratriptan	$5HT_{1D}$ agonist	Migraine headaches	—
Buspirone	$5HT_{1A}$ partial agonist	Anxiety disorders	Lower addiction potential than other drugs like benzodiazepines
Ondansetron	$5HT_3$ antagonist	Emesis	Mainly for postoperative or chemotherapy-induced nausea and vomiting
SSRIs: Citalopram Fluoxetine Fluvoxamine Paroxetine Sertraline	Selectively block 5HT reuptake	• Anxiety disorders • Depression	• Sexual dysfunction • Interaction with MAOIs → **serotonin syndrome**
Ergot alkaloids: Ergonovine Ergotamine Methysergide Bromocriptine* Pergolide* LSD	Agonists, partial agonists, and antagonists at 5HT-and α-adrenergic receptors; some are agonists or partial agonists at DA receptors*	• Postpartum hemorrhage (ergonovine, ergotamine) • Migraine headaches (ergotamine [for acute attacks], methysergide [prophylaxis]) • Parkinson disease, hyperprolactinemia (bromocriptine, pergolide) • Abuse (LSD)	**Ergotism** ("St. Anthony's Fire"): – Mental disorientation – Hallucination – Convulsions – Muscle cramps – Dry gangrene of extremities
MAO inhibitors: Phenelzine Tranylcypromine	Inhibit metabolism of 5HT, NE, and DA by MAO	Depression	• Non-selective MAO inhibitors • Tyramine (red wine, cheese) ingestion → hypertensive crisis

Definition of abbreviations: DA, dopamine; 5-HT, 5-hydroxytrypamine; 5-HIAA, 5-hydroxyindoleacetic acid; LSD, D-Lysergic acid diethylamide; MAO, monoamine oxidase; SSRI, selective serotonin reuptake inhibitor.

ANGIOTENSIN II

Synthesis and Actions

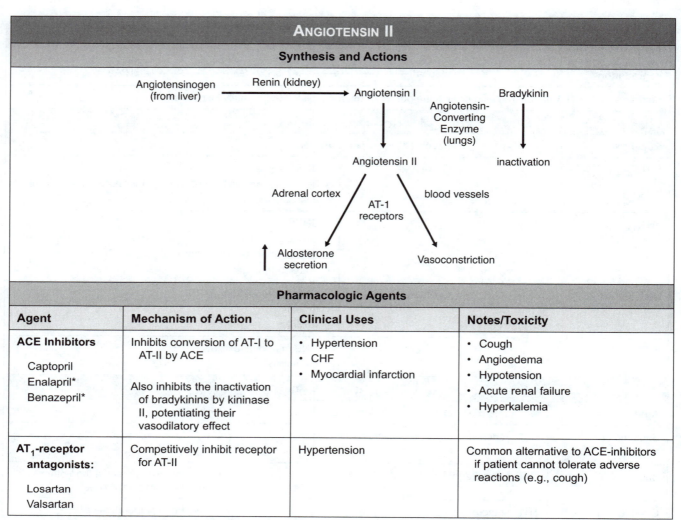

Pharmacologic Agents

Agent	Mechanism of Action	Clinical Uses	Notes/Toxicity
ACE Inhibitors Captopril Enalapril* Benazepril*	Inhibits conversion of AT-I to AT-II by ACE Also inhibits the inactivation of bradykinins by kininase II, potentiating their vasodilatory effect	• Hypertension • CHF • Myocardial infarction	• Cough • Angioedema • Hypotension • Acute renal failure • Hyperkalemia
AT$_1$-receptor antagonists: Losartan Valsartan	Competitively inhibit receptor for AT-II	Hypertension	Common alternative to ACE-inhibitors if patient cannot tolerate adverse reactions (e.g., cough)

Definition of abbreviations: ACE, angiotensin-converting enzyme; AT-I, angiotensin I; AT-II, angiotensin II; CHF, congestive heart failure.
*Ester prodrugs of ACE inhibitor converted to active form by liver

ANTINEOPLASTIC AGENTS

These agents are used to treat various neoplasms. Although the mechanism of action varies, each agent hinders cell replication in some way. Specificity relies on differential effect between neoplastic cells and normal tissue. The mechanism of action may be cell-cycle specific (affects cells in all stages except G_0) or cell-cycle nonspecific.

Class	Mechanism	Indications/Toxicities
Antimetabolites	**Cell-cycle specific (CCS).** Inhibit synthesis of nucleic acids and thus protein synthesis.	
Methotrexate	• A folic acid analog that inhibits dihydrofolate reductase; decreased dTMP levels hinder DNA and thus protein synthesis • **S-phase** specific	*Neoplastic indications:* leukemia, lymphomas, breast cancer, choriocarcinoma *Nonneoplastic indications:* rheumatoid arthritis, psoriasis, termination of pregnancy (e.g., ectopic)
		Toxicities: **suppresses bone marrow reversibly**; folinic acid (**leucovorin**) is used to **"rescue"**; fatty change in liver
5-Fluorouracil (5-FU)	• Pyrimidine antimetabolite is converted to **5-F-dUMP**, which when bound to folic acid, **inhibits thymidylate synthase.** This prevents dTMP synthesis, thus inhibiting DNA and protein synthesis. • **S-phase** specific	*Indications:* breast, ovarian, colon, head and neck cancers, basal cell carcinomas and keratoses (use topically)
		Toxicities: **irreversible myelosuppression** and **photosensitivity**, GI irritation, alopecia
Cytarabine (Ara-C)	• Pyrimidine antimetabolite • Inhibits DNA polymerases • **S-phase** specific	*Indications:* acute leukemias
		Toxicities: BMS, GI irritation, ↑ doses → neurotoxicity
6-Mercaptopurine (6-MP)	• Activated by hypoxanthine-guanine phosphoribosyltransferase (**HGPRT**) • **Inhibits purine synthesis**, inhibiting nucleic acid synthesis • **S-phase** specific	*Indications:* acute leukemias, CML, non-Hodgkin lymphoma
		Toxicities: • BMS, hepatotoxicity—coadministration with allopurinol increases toxicity (6-MP metabolized by xanthine oxidase) • Azathioprine forms 6-MP
Alkylating Agents	**Cell cycle-nonspecific (CCNS).** This class of agents causes alkylation of DNA, leading to cross-linking, abnormal base pairing, or DNA strand breakage.	
Busulfan	Alkylates DNA	*Indications:* CML
		Toxicities: **pulmonary fibrosis, hyperpigmentation,** and adrenal insufficiency
Cyclophosphamide	Alkylates DNA—attacks guanine N7, induces cross-linking	*Indications:* non-Hodgkin lymphoma; ovarian and breast cancers; neuroblastoma
		Toxicities: BMS and **hemorrhagic cystitis** (can be ↓ by **mesna**, which traps **acrolein**, a toxic metabolite)
Nitrosoureas (lomustine, carmustine)	• Alkylates DNA • Crosses blood–brain barrier	*Indications:* brain tumors
		Toxicities: **neurologic**

Definition of abbreviations: BMS, bone marrow suppression; CML, chronic myelogenous leukemia.

(Continued)

ANTINEOPLASTIC AGENTS (CONT'D.)

Class	Mechanism	Indications/Toxicities
Cisplatin, carboplatin	Alkylates DNA	*Indications:* testicular, bladder, lung, and ovarian carcinomas
		Toxicities: **nephrotoxic**, neurotoxicity (**deafness, tinnitus**)
Procarbazine	Alkylates DNA	*Indications:* Hodgkin disease (MOPP*)
		Toxicities: BMS, pulmonary toxicity, neurotoxic, leukemogenic
Antibiotics	Structurally dissimilar subclass of drugs. Mechanisms of action vary.	
Doxorubicin	Intercalates DNA, creating breaks. Hinders DNA replication and transcription.	*Indications:* Hodgkin lymphoma (ABVD†), breast, endometrial, lung, ovarian CAs, myeloma, sarcomas
		Toxicities: **cardiotoxic—dexrazoxane** (inhibits free radical formation may protect), BMS, alopecia, GI distress
Bleomycin	• Generates free radicals → DNA strand scission • **G₂ phase**	*Indications:* lymphomas, testicular, skin CA
		Toxicities: **pulmonary fibrosis**, mucocutaneous reactions (blisters, alopecia), hypersensitivity reactions
Hormones/ Hormone Antagonists	May inhibit hormone-dependent tumor growth.	
Prednisone	Induces apoptosis of lymphoid cells	*Indications:* chronic lymphocytic leukemia (CLL), Hodgkin lymphoma (MOPP*), autoimmune disease
		Toxicities: typical symptoms of glucocorticoid excess, including **Cushing syndrome**
Tamoxifen	**Selective estrogen receptor modulator (SERM)**. Prevents estrogen from binding estrogen receptor–positive breast CA cells, leading to involution of estrogen-dependent tumors.	*Indications:* breast cancer
		Toxicities: **hot flashes**, increased risk of **endometrial carcinoma**
Plant Alkaloids	Cell-cycle specific drugs that prevent the assembly of microtubules. Thus, mitotic spindle cannot form.	
Vinblastine	• Inhibits microtubule/spindle formation • **M-phase** specific	*Indications:* lymphoma, Wilms tumor, choriocarcinoma
		Toxicities: BMS
Vincristine	• Inhibits microtubule/spindle formation • **M-phase** specific	*Indications:* same as vinblastine, MOPP* (is Oncovin)
		Toxicities: neurotoxic, GI distress
Paclitaxel	• Stabilizes microtubules so that spindle cannot break down • **M-phase** specific	*Indications:* ovarian and breast carcinomas
		Toxicities: BMS
Etoposide	• Inhibits topoisomerase II, ↑ DNA degradation • **Late S/early G₂ phase**	*Indications:* small cell carcinoma, prostate cancer, testicular carcinoma
		Toxicities: BMS, GI irritation, alopecia

†ABVD: Adriamycin® (doxoribicin), bleomycin, vinblastine, decarbazine
*MOPP: mechlorethamine, vincristine (Oncovin®), procarbazine, prednisone

Organ Systems

The Nervous System

DEVELOPMENT OF THE NERVOUS SYSTEM

Neurulation

- **Neurulation** begins in the third week.
- The **notochord** induces the overlying ectoderm to form the neural plate.
- By end of the third week, **neural folds** grow over midline and fuse to form **neural tube**.
- During closure, **neural crest** cells form from neuroectoderm.

- **Neural tube** → brain and spinal cord (plus lower motoneurons, preganglionic neurons)
- Brain stem and spinal cord have an **alar** plate (**sensory**) and a **basal** plate (**motor**); plates are separated by the **sulcus limitans**.
- **Neural tube** → 3 primary vesicles → 5 primary vesicles

- **Neural crest** → sensory and postganglionic neurons

- **Peripheral NS (PNS):** cranial nerves (12 pairs) and spinal nerves (31 pairs)

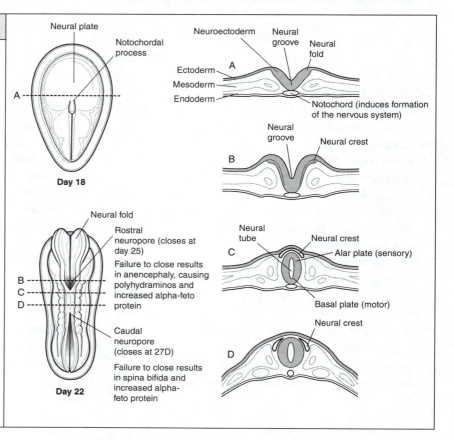

Neural plate
Notochordal process
A
Day 18

Neuroectoderm
Neural groove
Neural fold
Ectoderm
Mesoderm
Endoderm
A
Notochord (induces formation of the nervous system)

Neural groove
Neural crest
B

Neural fold
Rostral neuropore (closes at day 25)
Failure to close results in anencephaly, causing polyhydraminos and increased alpha-feto protein
Caudal neuropore (closes at 27D)
Failure to close results in spina bifida and increased alpha-feto protein
B
C
D
Day 22

Neural tube
Neural crest
Alar plate (sensory)
C
Basal plate (motor)

Neural crest
D

CENTRAL NERVOUS SYSTEM

5 secondary vesicles

Telencephalon
Diencephalon
Mesencephalon
Metencephalon
Myelencephalon
Brain stem
Spinal cord

3 primary vesicles

Forebrain
Midbrain
Hindbrain
Neural tube
Spinal cord

	Adult Derivatives		
	Structures		Ventricles
Telencephalon	Cerebral hemispheres, most of basal ganglia		Lateral ventricle
Diencephalon	Thalamus, hypothalamus, subthalamus, epithalamus (pineal gland), retina		Third ventricle
Mesencephalon	Midbrain		Cerebral aqueduct
Metencephalon	Pons, cerebellum		Fourth ventricle
Myelencephalon	Medulla		

CONGENITAL MALFORMATIONS OF THE NERVOUS SYSTEM

Condition	Types	Description
Anencephaly	—	Failure of **anterior neuropore** to close Brain does not develop Incompatible with life Increased AFP
Spina bifida	Failure of **posterior neuropore** to close	
	Spina bifida occulta **(Figure A)**	Mildest form **Vertebrae** fail to form around spinal cord **No** increase in **AFP** Asymptomatic
	Spina bifida with meningocele **(Figure B)**	**Meninges** protrude through vertebral defect Increase in AFP
	Spina bifida with meningomyelocele **(Figure C)**	**Meninges** and **spinal cord** protrude through vertebral defect Increase in AFP
	Spina bifida with myeloschisis **(Figure D)**	Most severe **Spinal cord** can be seen **externally** Increase in AFP

Condition	Types	Description
Arnold-Chiari malformation	Type I	Most common Mostly **asymptomatic** Downward displacement of cerebellar tonsils through foramen magnum
	Type II	More often **symptomatic** Downward displacement of **cerebellar vermis** and **medulla** through foramen magnum Compression of IV ventricle → obstructive **hydrocephaly** Frequent lumbar **meningomyelocele** Frequent association with **syringomyelia**
Dandy-Walker malformation		Failure of foramina of Luschka and Magendie to open → **dilation of IV ventricle** Agenesis of cerebellar vermis and splenium of the corpus callosum
Hydrocephalus		Most often caused by stenosis of cerebral aqueduct CSF accumulates in ventricles and subarachnoid space Increased head circumference
Holoprosencephaly		Incomplete separation of cerebral hemispheres One ventricle in telencephalon Seen in trisomy 13 (Patau)

Definition of abbreviation: AFP, α-fetoprotein.

PERIPHERAL NERVOUS SYSTEM

AUTONOMIC AND SOMATIC NERVOUS SYSTEMS

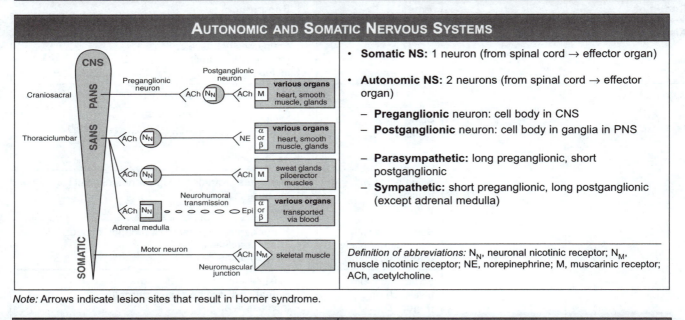

- **Somatic NS:** 1 neuron (from spinal cord → effector organ)

- **Autonomic NS:** 2 neurons (from spinal cord → effector organ)

  – **Preganglionic** neuron: cell body in CNS
  – **Postganglionic** neuron: cell body in ganglia in PNS

  – **Parasympathetic:** long preganglionic, short postganglionic
  – **Sympathetic:** short preganglionic, long postganglionic (except adrenal medulla)

Definition of abbreviations: N_N, neuronal nicotinic receptor; N_M, muscle nicotinic receptor; NE, norepinephrine; M, muscarinic receptor; ACh, acetylcholine.

Note: Arrows indicate lesion sites that result in Horner syndrome.

PARASYMPATHETIC NERVOUS SYSTEM | SYMPATHETIC NERVOUS SYSTEM

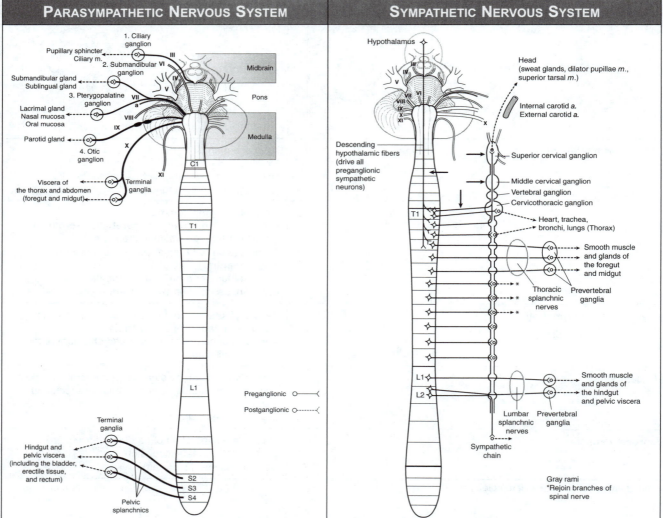

Note: Arrows indicate lesion sites that result in Horner syndrome.

PARASYMPATHETIC = CRANIOSACRAL OUTFLOW			SYMPATHETIC = THORACOLUMBAR OUTFLOW		
Origin	Site of Synapse	Innervation	Origin	Site of Synapse	Innervation
Cranial nerves III, VII, IX	4 cranial ganglia	Glands and smooth muscle of the head	Spinal cord levels T1–L2	Sympathetic chain ganglia (paravertebral ganglia)	Smooth and cardiac muscle and glands of body wall and limbs; head and thoracic viscera
Cranial nerve X	Terminal ganglia (in or near the walls of viscera)	Viscera of the neck, thorax, foregut, and midgut	Thoracic splanchnic nerves T5–T12	Prevertebral ganglia (collateral; e.g., celiac, aorticorenal superior mesenteric ganglia)	Smooth muscle and glands of the foregut and midgut
Pelvic splanchnic nerves (S2, S3, S4)	Terminal ganglia (in or near the walls of viscera)	Hindgut and pelvic viscera (including bladder and erectile tissue)	Lumbar splanchnic nerves L1, L2	Prevertebral ganglia (collateral; e.g., inferior mesenteric and pelvic ganglia)	Smooth muscle and glands of the pelvic viscera and hindgut

AUTONOMIC EFFECTS ON ORGAN SYSTEMS

As a general rule, the **sympathetic autonomic nervous system (SANS)** mediates **"fight or flight"** responses, such as increasing heart rate and contractility, dilating airways and pupils, inhibiting GI and GU functions, and directing blood flow away from skin and GI tract and toward skeletal muscles. In contrast, the **parasympathetic autonomic nervous system (PANS)** causes the body to **"rest and digest,"** reducing heart rate and contractility, contracting airways and pupils, inducing secretion from lacrimal and salivary glands, and promoting GI and GU motility. Blood vessels are solely innervated by SANS nerve fibers.

Organ	Sympathetic "Fight or Flight"		Parasympathetic "Rest and Digest"	
	Action	Receptor	Action	Receptor
Cardiovascular				
Heart				
SA node	↑ heart rate	$\beta_1, (\beta_2)$	↓ heart rate	M_2
Atria	↑ contractility		↓ contractility	
AV node	↑ conduction velocity and automaticity[1]		↓ conduction velocity and automaticity[1]	
Ventricles	↑ contractility		↓ contractility (slight)	
Arterioles[2]	Contract: ↑ resistance	α_1	—	$(M_3)[3]$
Veins	Contract: ↑ venous pressure	α_1	—	—
Kidney	Renin release	β_1	—	—
Respiratory				
Bronchiolar smooth muscle	Relax: ↓ resistance	β_2	Contract: ↑ resistance	M_3

(*Continued*)

[1]When acting as a pacemaker; otherwise, the SA node suppresses automaticity in these cells

[2]β_2 receptors that mediate relaxation and decrease resistance are also present on coronary arteries and arterioles. Low doses of epinephrine (or β_2 agonists) act selectively on β_2 receptors and can decrease systemic vascular resistance, but increased sympathetic tone increases systemic vascular resistance because vasoconstriction dominates.

[3]M_3 receptors are on vascular endothelium (not smooth muscle, like the adrenergic receptors) and cause vasodilation via nitric oxide (NO) generation; this has little physiologic significance because vasculature is not innervated by PANS, but is more important with muscarinic agonist administration.

AUTONOMIC EFFECTS ON ORGAN SYSTEMS (*CONT'D.*)				
	Sympathetic "Fight or Flight"		Parasympathetic "Rest and Digest"	
Organ	Action	Receptor	Action	Receptor
Gastrointestinal				
GI smooth muscle				
Walls	↓ GI motility	α_2,[4] β_2	↑ GI motility	M_3
Sphincters	Contracts	α_1	Relaxes	M_3
Glandular secretion	—	—	Increases	M_3
Liver	Gluconeogenesis	β_2, α	—	—
	Glycogenolysis	β_2, α	—	—
Fat cells	Lipolysis	β_3	—	—
Genitourinary				
Bladder				
Walls	Relaxes	β_2	Contracts	M_3
Sphincters	Contracts	α_1	Relaxes	M_3
Uterus, pregnant	Relaxes	β_2	—	—
	Contracts	α	Contracts	M_3
Penis, seminal vesicles	Ejaculation	α	Erection	M
Skin				
Sweat glands	Secretion	M,[5] α[6]	—	—
Eye				
Radial dilator muscle	Contracts (dilates pupil)	α_1	—	—
Pupillary sphincter muscle	—	—	Contracts (constricts pupil).	M_3
Ciliary muscle	Relaxes—far vision	β	Contracts—near vision	M_3

[4]Probably via inhibition of cholinergic nerve terminals
[5]Generalized
[6]Localized (e.g., palms of hands)

CHOLINERGIC TRANSMISSION

Acetylcholine (ACh) is synthesized from acetate and choline in synaptic nerve terminals via **choline acetyltransferase (ChAT)** and stored in synaptic vesicles and released by Ca^{2+} influx upon depolarization. The **uptake of choline** into the nerve terminal is the **rate-limiting step** of ACh synthesis and can be blocked by **hemicholinium**. ACh then binds to postsynaptic receptors to elicit somatic (N_M) or autonomic (N_N and M) effects. Signal termination occurs by degradation of ACh by **acetylcholinesterase (AChE)**.

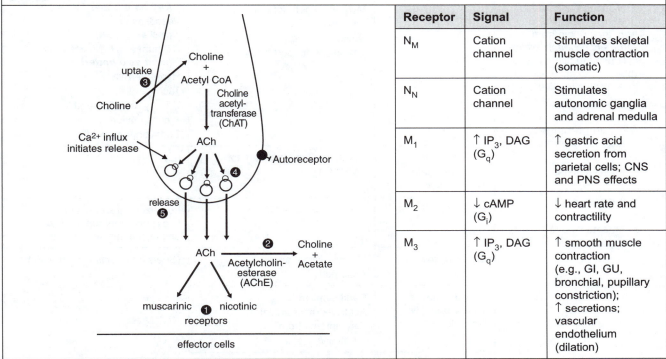

Receptor	Signal	Function
N_M	Cation channel	Stimulates skeletal muscle contraction (somatic)
N_N	Cation channel	Stimulates autonomic ganglia and adrenal medulla
M_1	↑ IP_3, DAG (G_q)	↑ gastric acid secretion from parietal cells; CNS and PNS effects
M_2	↓ cAMP (G_i)	↓ heart rate and contractility
M_3	↑ IP_3, DAG (G_q)	↑ smooth muscle contraction (e.g., GI, GU, bronchial, pupillary constriction); ↑ secretions; vascular endothelium (dilation)

Definition of abbreviations: DAG, diacylglycerol; GI, gastrointestinal; GU, genitourinary; IP_3, inositol triphosphate.

Note: The numbers in the figure correspond to the numbers in the table below.

CHOLINERGIC PHARMACOLOGY

Mechanism of Action	Agent	Clinical Uses	Other Notes and Toxicity
❶ ACh receptor			
Nicotinic (N_M) agonist/antagonists (skeletal muscle)	(*See* neuromuscular blockers, page 409.)		
Nicotinic (N_N) antagonists (ganglion blockers)	Hexamethonium Trimethaphan Mecamylamine	Rarely used due to toxicities	Blocks both SANS and PANS; effectively reduces predominant tone (*see table below*)
Cholinergic agonists M = muscarinic N = nicotinic B = both	Bethanechol (M)	Ileus (postop/neurogenic) Urinary retention	Heart block, cardiac arrest Syncope
	Methacholine (M)	Diagnosis of bronchial hyperreactivity in asthma	Partially sensitive to cholinesterase (others listed here are resistant)
	Pilocarpine (M)	Glaucoma (topical) Xerostomia	—
	Carbachol (B)	Glaucoma (topical)	—
	Nicotine (N)	Smoking deterrence	—

(Continued)

CHOLINERGIC PHARMACOLOGY (CONT'D.)

Mechanism of Action	Agent	Clinical Uses	Other Notes and Toxicity
Muscarinic antagonists Class known as "Belladonna" alkaloids (meaning "beautiful lady") from their origin from *Atropa belladonna*, which was used to dilate pupils (believed to make women look more attractive). Other drugs with anti-muscarinic effects: • Antihistamines • Tricyclics • Antipsychotics • Quinidine • Amantadine • Meperidine	Atropine	Counteracts cholinergic toxicity Antidiarrheal Mydriatic agent for eye exams Reversal of sinus bradycardia and heart block	Mydriasis and cycloplegia *(blind as a bat)* Decreased secretions *(dry as a bone)* Vasodilation *(red as a beet)* Delirium and hallucinations *(mad as a hatter)* Hyperthermia Tachycardia Urinary retention and constipation Sedation, amnesia
	Homatropine Cyclopentolate Tropicamide	Ophthalmology (topical), for mydriasis	—
	Ipratropium	Asthma and COPD	Localized effect because is a quaternary amine; few antimuscarinic side effects
	Scopolamine	Motion-sickness Antiemetic	*(See side effects for atropine.)*
	Benztropine Trihexyphenidyl Biperiden	Parkinsonism Acute extrapyramidal symptoms from antipsychotics	
	Glycopyrrolate Dicyclomine	Reduces hypermotility in GI and GU tracts	
❷ **Metabolism (AChE inhibitors)**			
Short-acting:	Edrophonium	Diagnosis of myasthenia gravis	Seizures
Tertiary amines:	Physostigmine	Glaucoma Reversal of atropine toxicity	Carbamylating inhibitor Seizures
Quaternary amines:	Neostigmine Pyridostigmine Ambenonium	Ileus, urinary retention Myasthenia gravis Reversal of nondepolarizing neuromuscular blockers	Carbamylating inhibitors
Lipid-soluble:	Donepezil Tacrine	Alzheimer disease	Hepatotoxicity GI bleeding

(Continued)

CHOLINERGIC PHARMACOLOGY (CONT'D.)			
Mechanism of Action	**Agent**	**Clinical Uses**	**Other Notes and Toxicity**
Organophosphates: (long-acting and irreversible) (causes time-dependent **aging**, which permanently inactivates AChE)	Echothiophate Malathion Parathion Sarin VX	Glaucoma Insecticide Nerve gas	**D**iarrhea **U**rination **M**iosis **B**radycardia **B**ronchoconstriction **E**xcitation (CNS and muscle) **L**acrimation, **s**alivation, **s**weating Mnemonic: **DUMBBELSS** Acute treatment with **atropine** and **pralidoxime (2-PAM)** to regenerate AChE before aging occurs
❸ **Reuptake inhibitors**	Hemicholinium	Only used in research settings	Blocks choline reuptake, slowing ACh synthesis
❹ **Vesicular transport inhibitors**	Vesamicol	Only used in research settings	Blocks ACh uptake into vesicles, preventing storage and leading to ACh depletion
❺ **Vesicle release inhibitors**	Botulinum toxin	Blepharospasm Strabismus/Hyperhydrosis Dystonia Cosmetics	Prevents fusion of cholinergic vesicles to membrane, thereby inhibiting ACh release

Definition of abbreviations: ACh, acetylcholine; AChE, acetylcholinesterase; ChAT, choline acetyltransferase; COPD, chronic obstructive pulmonary disorder.

PREDOMINANT TONE AND THE EFFECT OF GANGLIONIC BLOCKERS		
The effects of ganglionic blockers can be easily predicted if you know the predominant autonomic tone to a particular effector organ. The effect of the blockade will be the opposite of what the predominant tone causes. In general, the predominant tone to vessels is sympathetic, and most everything else is parasympathetic.		
Site	**Predominant Tone**	**Effect of Ganglionic Blockade**
Arterioles	Sympathetic	Dilation (↓ blood pressure)
Veins	Sympathetic	Dilation (↓ venous return)
Heart	Parasympathetic	↑ heart rate
GI tract	Parasympathetic	↓ motility and secretions
Eye	Parasympathetic	Pupillary dilation, focus to far vision
Urinary bladder	Parasympathetic	Urinary retention
Salivary glands	Parasympathetic	Dry mouth
Sweat glands	Sympathetic (cholinergic)	Anhidrosis

ADRENERGIC TRANSMISSION

Norepinephrine (NE), **epinephrine (EPI)**, and dopamine are part of the **catecholamine** family, which are synthesized from **tyrosine**. The first step of the synthetic pathway is carried out by **tyrosine hydroxylase**; it is also the **rate-limiting** step. NE levels inside the presynaptic terminal may also be regulated by metabolism by **monoamine oxidase (MAO)**. Once released, NE binds to various adrenergic receptors to transmit its signal. NE primarily binds α_1, α_2, and β_1 receptors, whereas EPI (released by the adrenal medulla) binds α_1, α_2, β_1, and β_2 receptors. **Reuptake** (especially uptake-1) and diffusion are most important in the termination of action of NE (and DA). Metabolism occurs via **catechol-O-methyltransferase ([COMT]** extracellular) and **MAO** (intracellular). Metabolites such as **metanephrine**, **normetanephrine**, **vanillylmandelic acid (VMA)** can be measured in the urine and are used in diagnosis diseases such as pheochromocytoma.

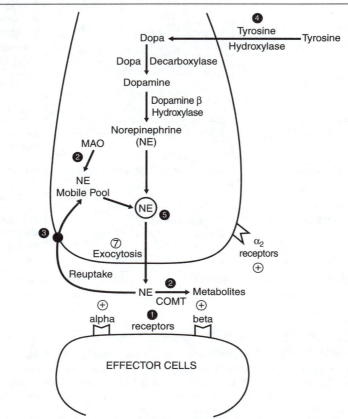

Receptor	Signal	Function
α_1	↑ IP_3, DAG (G_q)	↑ smooth muscle contraction (in vascular walls, radial dilator muscle [eye], and GI and bladder sphincters); ↑ glycogenolysis in liver
α_2	↓ cAMP (G_i)	Inhibits neurotransmitter release; inhibits insulin release and lipolysis
β_1	↑ cAMP (G_s)	↑ heart rate and contractility; ↑ AV conduction velocity; ↑ renin secretion
β_2		↑ smooth muscle relaxation (in vascular, bronchial, GI, and bladder walls); ↑ glycogenolysis in liver, ↑ insulin release
β_3		↑ lipolysis from adipose tissues
Mnemonic: You can get an adrenaline rush from a **QISSS** ($G_qG_iG_sG_sG_s$).		

Definition of abbreviations: DAG, diacylglycerol; GI, gastrointestinal; GU, genitourinary; IP_3, inositol triphosphate.

Note: The numbers in the figure correspond to the numbers in the table below.

ADRENERGIC PHARMACOLOGY

Mechanism of Action	Agent	Clinical Uses	Other Notes and Toxicity
❶ Adrenergic receptor			
α-adrenergic agonists	α_1: Phenylephrine	Nasal congestion Vasoconstriction Mydriasis (topical)	—
	α_1: Methoxamine	Paroxysmal supra-ventricular tachycardia	Bradycardia (vagal reflex)
	α_2: Clonidine Methyldopa	Hypertension	Decreases sympathetic outflow Methyldopa: prodrug converted to methylnorepinephrine
α-adrenergic antagonists	**Nonselective:** Phentolamine	Pheochromocytoma	**Reversible**, competitive inhibitor Postural hypotension, reflex tachycardia
	Nonselective: Phenoxybenzamine	Pheochromocytoma	**Irreversible** inhibitor Postural hypotension, reflex tachycardia
	α_1: Prazosin Doxazosin Terazosin Tamsulosin	Hypertension Benign prostatic hypertrophy	Postural hypotension on first dose
	α_2: Yohimbine	Impotence Postural hypotension	Clinical use limited
	α_2: Mirtazapine	Depression	May also block 5HT receptors
β-adrenergic agonists	$\beta_1 = \beta_2$: Isoproterenol	Bronchospasm Heart block and bradyarrhythmias	Clinical use limited ↓ BP, ↑ HR Arrhythmias
	$\beta_1 > \beta_2$: Dobutamine	Acute heart failure	—
	β_2: Albuterol Terbutaline Metaproterenol Salmeterol	Asthma	Tachycardia, skeletal muscle tremor Pulmonary delivery to minimize side effects Salmeterol is long-acting
	β_2: Ritodrine	Premature labor	—
β-adrenergic antagonists	β_1: Acebutolol Atenolol Esmolol Metoprolol	Hypertension Angina Chronic heart failure (carvedilol, labetalol, metoprolol) Arrhythmia (propanolol, acebutolol, esmolol) Glaucoma (timolol) Migraine, tremor, thyrotoxicosis (propanolol)	Sedation Decreases libido Bradycardia β_1 selectivity safer in asthma, diabetes, and vascular diseases Pindolol and acebutolol have intrinsic sympathomimetic activity (useful in asthmatics)
	Nonselective: Pindolol Propanolol Nadolol Timolol		
	α and β: Labetalol Carvedilol	CHF	Similar to above Liver damage (labetalol)

Definition of abbreviation: CHF, congestive heart failure.

(Continued)

ADRENERGIC PHARMACOLOGY (CONT'D.)

Mechanism of Action	Agent	Clinical Uses	Other Notes and Toxicity
❷ **Metabolism**			
MAO inhibitors MAO-A: mainly liver but <u>A</u>nywhere MAO-B: mainly in <u>B</u>rain	Phenelzine Tranylcypromine Isocarboxazid	Depression	Nonselective MAO-A/B inhibitors Tyramine (red wine, cheese) ingestion → hypertensive crisis Insomnia Postural hypotension MAO-AIs: moclobemide (reversible), clorgyline available in Europe
	Selegiline	Parkinson disease	Selective MAO-B inhibitor
COMT inhibitors	Entacapone Tolcapone	Parkinson disease	—
❸ **Reuptake inhibitors**	Cocaine	Local anesthesia Abuse	Inhibits monoamine reuptake Addiction
Tricyclic antidepressants	Amitriptyline Imipramine Desipramine Nortriptyline	Depression	Inhibits monoamine reuptake Sedation Postural hypotension Tachycardia Atropine-like effects
❹ **Synthesis inhibitors**	α-Methyltyrosine (metyrosine)	Hypertension	Inhibits tyrosine hydroxylase Only for hypertension associated with pheochromocytoma
❺ **Drugs affecting release**			
Adrenergic neuron blockers	Reserpine	Hypertension	Inhibits monoamine vesicular uptake, leading to neurotransmitter depletion Sedation, depression
	Guanethidine	Hypertension	Inhibits NE release from sympathetic nerve endings Requires neuronal uptake to work, so interferes with other drugs that require uptake carrier (e.g., cocaine, amphetamine, cyclic antidepressants)
Indirect-acting sympathomimetics	Amphetamine Methylphenidate	Narcolepsy and ADHD	Displaces NE from mobile pool Addiction Restlessness and rebound fatigue
	Ephedrine Pseudoephedrine	For vasoconstriction	Displaces NE from mobile pool Pseudoephedrine: OTC for nasal congestion

Definition of abbreviations: ADHD, attention deficit and hyperactivity disorder; COMT, catechol-O-methyltransferase; MAO, monoamine oxidase; NE, norepinephrine; OTC, over the counter.

MENINGES, VENTRICULAR SYSTEM, AND VENOUS DRAINAGE

MENINGES AND MENINGEAL SPACES

Meninges consist of three connective tissue membranes that surround the brain and spinal cord. Meningeal spaces are spaces or potential spaces adjacent to the meninges.

Meninges	Meningeal Space	Anatomic Description	Clinical Correlate
	Epidural space	Tight potential space between dura and skull Contains **middle meningeal artery**	**Epidural hematoma** Temporal bone fracture → rupture of **middle meningeal artery** **Lens-shaped biconvex** hematoma
Dura		Tough outer layer; dense connective tissue	
	Subdural space	Contains **bridging veins**	**Subdural hematoma** Rupture of bridging veins **Crescent-shaped** hematoma
Arachnoid		Delicate, nonvascular connective tissue	
	Subarachnoid space	Contains **CSF** Ends at S2 vertebra	**Subarachnoid hemorrhage** **"Worst headache of my life"** Often caused by **berry aneurysms** **Lumbar puncture** between L4, L5 discs
Pia		Thin, highly vascular connective tissue Adheres to brain and spinal cord	

MENINGITIS (INFECTION OF THE MENINGES, ESPECIALLY THE PIA AND ARACHNOID)

Acute purulent (bacterial) meningitis	• **Headache, fever, nuchal rigidity**, obtundation; coma may occur • Meninges opaque; neutrophilic exudate present • Sequelae: hydrocephalus, herniation, cranial nerve impairment
Acute aseptic (viral) meningitis	• Leptomeningeal inflammation (lymphomonocytic infiltrates) due to viruses (Enterovirus most frequent) • Fever, signs of meningeal irritation, depressed consciousness, but low mortality
Mycobacterial meningoencephalitis	• Can be caused by *Mycobacterium tuberculosis* or atypical mycobacteria • Usually involves the **basal surface** of the brain with tuberculomas within the brain and dura mater • Frequent in AIDS patients, particularly by *Mycobacterium avium-intracellulare* (MAI)
Fungal meningoencephalitis	• *Candida, Aspergillus, Cryptococcus*, and *Mucor* species most frequent agents • *Aspergillus* and *Mucor* attack blood vessels → vasculitis, rupture of blood vessels, and hemorrhage • *Cryptococcus* causes diffuse meningoencephalitis

ORGANISMS CAUSING BACTERIAL MENINGITIS BY AGE GROUP

Neonates	Infants/Children	Adolescents/Young Adults	Elderly
Group B streptococci ***Escherichia coli*** *Listeria monocytogenes*	***Haemophilus influenzae* B** (if not vaccinated) *Streptococcus pneumoniae* *Neisseria meningitidis*	***Neisseria meningitidis***	***Streptococcus pneumoniae*** *Listeria monocytogenes*

CSF Parameters in Meningitis

Condition	Cells/μl	Glucose (mg/dL)	Proteins (mg/dL)	Pressure (mm H$_2$O)
Normal values	<5 lymphocytes	45–85 (50–70% of blood glucose)	15–45	70–180
Purulent (bacterial)	Up to 90,000 neutrophils	Decreased (<45)	Increased (>50)	Markedly elevated
Aseptic (viral)	100–1,000 most lymphocytes	Normal	Increased (>50)	Slightly elevated
Granulomatous (mycobacterial/fungal)	100–1,000 most lymphocytes	Decreased (<45)	Increased (>50)	Moderately elevated

Viral Encephalitis

Pathology: perivascular cuffs, microglial nodules, neuron loss, and neuronophagia
Clinical: fever, headache, mental status changes, often progressing to coma

Arthropod-Borne	Herpes Simplex	Rabies	HIV
St. Louis, California, Eastern equine, Western equine, Venezuelan	Characteristic **hemorrhagic necrosis of temporal lobes**	**Negri bodies** in hippocampal and Purkinje neurons of the cerebellum	**Microglial nodules, multinucleated giant cells**

Ventricular System and Venous Drainage

The brain and spinal cord float within a protective bath of cerebrospinal fluid (CSF), which is produced by the lining of the ventricles, the choroid plexus. CSF circulation begins in the ventricles and then enters the subarachnoid space to surround the brain and spinal cord.

Ventricles and CSF Circulation

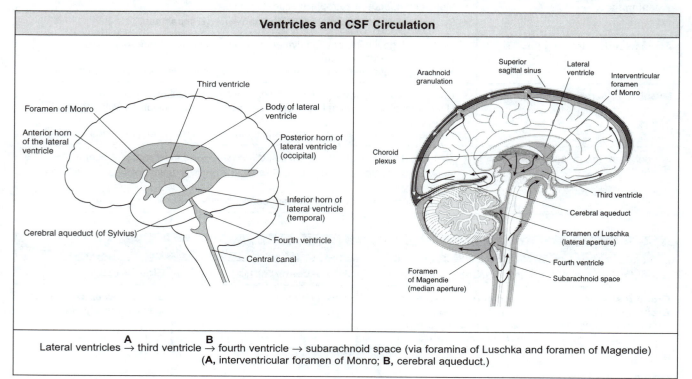

Lateral ventricles $\overset{A}{\rightarrow}$ third ventricle $\overset{B}{\rightarrow}$ fourth ventricle → subarachnoid space (via foramina of Luschka and foramen of Magendie)
(**A**, interventricular foramen of Monro; **B**, cerebral aqueduct.)

(Continued)

CSF Production and Barriers

Choroid plexus—contains **ependymal cells** and is in the lateral, third, and fourth ventricles. **Secretes CSF.** Tight junctions form **blood-CSF barrier**.

Blood-brain barrier—formed by capillary endothelium with tight junctions; astrocyte foot processes contribute.

Once CSF is in the subarachnoid space, it goes up over convexity of the brain and enters the venous circulation by passing through **arachnoid granulations** into the **superior sagittal sinus**.

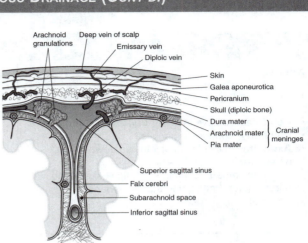

Sinuses

Superior sagittal sinus (in superior margin of falx cerebri)—drains into two **transverse sinuses**. Each of these drains blood from the **confluence of sinuses** into **sigmoid sinuses**. Each sigmoid sinus exits the skull (via **jugular foramen**) as the **internal jugular veins**.

Inferior sagittal sinus (in inferior margin of falx cerebri)—terminates by joining with the great cerebral vein of Galen to form the **straight sinus** at the falx cerebri and tentorium cerebelli junction. This drains into the confluence of sinuses.

Cavernous sinus—a plexus of veins on either side of the **sella turcica**. Surrounds internal carotid artery and cranial nerves III, IV, V, and VI. It drains into the transverse sinus (via the **superior petrosal sinus**) and the internal jugular vein (via the **inferior petrosal sinus**).

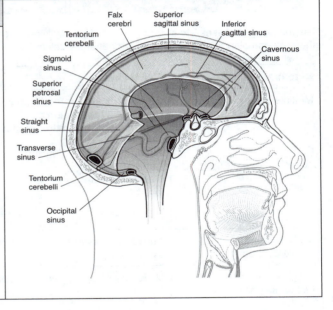

HYDROCEPHALUS
Excess Volume or Pressure of CSF, Leading to Dilated Ventricles

Noncommunicating	**Obstruction of flow within ventricles**; most commonly occurs at narrow points, e.g., foramen of Monro, cerebral aqueduct, fourth ventricle
Communicating	**Impaired CSF reabsorption** in arachnoid granulations or obstruction of flow in subarachnoid space
Normal pressure	CSF is not absorbed by arachnoid villi (a form of communicating hydrocephalus). CSF pressure is usually normal. Ventricles chronically dilated. Produces **triad** of **dementia, ataxic gait,** and **urinary incontinence**.
Hydrocephalus ex vacuo	Descriptive term referring to excess CSF in regions where brain tissue is lost due to atrophy, stroke, surgery, trauma, etc.

NEUROHISTOLOGY AND PATHOLOGIC CORRELATES

CELL TYPES OF THE NERVOUS SYSTEM

Neuron	Glia (non-neuronal cells of the nervous system)
Composed of: • **Dendrites:** receive info and transmit to the cell body • **Cell body:** contains organelles • **Axon:** transmits electrical impulse down to the nerve terminals • **Nerve terminals:** contain synaptic vesicles and release neurotransmitter into the synapse	• **Oligodendrocytes:** form **myelin** in the **CNS** (one cell myelinates many axons) • **Astrocytes:** control microenvironment of neurons and help maintain the blood/brain barrier with foot processes • **Schwann cells:** form **myelin** in the **PNS** (one cell myelinates one internode) • **Ependymal cells:** ciliated neurons that line the ventricles and central canal of the spinal cord • **Microglia:** are **phagocytic** and are part of the **mononuclear phagocyte system**

DISORDERS OF MYELINATION

Demyelinating diseases are acquired conditions involving selective damage to myelin. Other diseases (e.g., infectious, metabolic, inherited) can also affect myelin and are generally called **leukodystrophies**.

Disease	Symptoms	Notes
Multiple sclerosis (MS)	**Symptoms separated in space and time** Vision loss (**optic neuritis**) **Internuclear ophthalmoplegia** (MLF degeneration) Motor and sensory deficits Vertigo Neuropsychiatric	Occurs twice as often in **women** Onset often in **third or fourth decade** Higher prevalence in **temperate zones** **Relapsing–remitting course** is most common Well-circumscribed **demyelinated plaques** often in periventricular areas Chronic inflammation; axons initially preserved Increased IgG (**oligoclonal bands**) in CSF **Treatment:** high-dose steroids, interferon-beta, glatiramer (Copaxone®)
Metachromatic leukodystrophy	Varied neurologic and psychiatric symptoms	**Arylsulfatase A deficiency**
Progressive multifocal leukoencephalopathy (PML)	Varied neurologic symptoms, dementia	Caused by **JC virus** Affects **immunocompromised, especially AIDS** Demyelination, astrogliosis, lymphohistiocytosis
Central pontine myelinolysis (CPM)	**Pseudobulbar palsy** **Spastic quadriparesis** Mental changes May produce the "locked-in" syndrome Often fatal	Focal demyelination of central area of basis pontis (affects corticospinal, corticobulbar tracts) Seen in **severely malnourished, alcoholics, liver disease** Probably **caused by overly aggressive correction of hyponatremia**
Guillain-Barré syndrome	Acute symmetric ascending inflammatory neuropathy **Weakness begins in lower limbs and ascends; respiratory failure can occur** in severe cases Autonomic dysfunction may be prominent Cranial nerve involvement is common Sensory loss, pain, and paresthesias occur **Reflexes invariably decreased or absent**	Two-thirds of patients have **history of respiratory or GI illness 1–3 weeks prior to onset** Elevated CSF protein with normal cell count **(albuminocytologic dissociation)**

Definition of abbreviation: MLF, medial longitudinal fasciculus.

One half of brain and spinal cord tumors are metastatic. Some differences between primary and metastatic tumors are listed below:

Primary	Metastatic
Poorly circumscribed	Well circumscribed
Usually single	Often multiple
Location varies by specific type	Usually located at the junction between gray and white matter

PRIMARY TUMORS		
Tumor	**Features**	**Pathology**
Glioblastoma multiforme (grade IV astrocytoma)	• **Most common primary brain tumor** • **Highly malignant** • Usually lethal in 8–12 months	• Can cross the midline via the corpus callosum ("**butterfly glioma**") • Areas of necrosis surrounded by rows of neoplastic cells (**pseudopalisading necrosis**)
Astrocytoma (pilocytic)	• Benign tumor of children and young adults • Usually in **posterior fossa in children**	• **Rosenthal fibers** • Immunostaining with **GFAP**
Oligodendroglia	• Slow growing • Long survival (average 5–10 years)	• **"Fried-egg" appearance**—perinuclear halo
Ependymoma	• Ependymal origin • Can arise in IV ventricle and lead to **hydrocephalus**	Rosettes and pseudorosettes
Medulloblastoma	• Highly malignant cerebellar tumor • A type of primitive neuroectodermal tumors (PNET)	Blue, small, round cells with pseudorosettes
Meningioma	• Second most common primary brain tumor • Dural convexities; parasagittal region	• Attaches to the dura, compresses underlying brain without invasion • Microscopic—**psammoma bodies**
Schwannoma	• Third most common primary brain tumor • Most frequent location: **CN VIII at cerebellopontine angle** • **Hearing loss, tinnitus** • Good prognosis after surgical resection	• Antoni A (hypercellular) and B (hypocellular) areas • **Bilateral acoustic schwannomas— pathognomonic for neurofibromatosis type 2**
Retinoblastoma	• Sporadic—unilateral • **Familial—bilateral; associated with osteosarcoma**	Small, round, blue cells; may have rosettes
Craniopharyngioma	• Derived from odontogenic epithelium (remnants of **Rathke pouch**) • Usually children and young adults • Often calcified • Symptoms due to encroachment on pituitary stalk or optic chiasm • Benign but may recur	Histology resembles **adamantinoma** (most common tumor of tooth)

Definition of abbreviation: GFAP, glial fibrillary acidic protein.

SPINAL CORD

The spinal cord is divided internally into 31 segments that give rise to **31 pairs of spinal nerves** (from rostral to caudal): **8 cervical**, **12 thoracic**, **5 lumbar**, **5 sacral**, and **1 coccygeal**. Each segment is divided into an inner butterfly-like gray matter containing neuronal cell bodies and a surrounding area of white matter. The ventral horn contains alpha and gamma motoneurons; the intermediate horn contains preganglionic neurons and Clarke's nucleus; and the dorsal horn contains sensory neurons. The outer covering of the spinal cord is the white matter containing ascending and descending axons that form tracts located within funiculi.

GENERAL SPINAL CORD FEATURES	
Conus medullaris	Caudal end of the spinal cord (S3–S5). In adult, ends at the L2 vertebra
Cauda equina	Nerve roots of the lumbar, sacral, and coccygeal spinal nerves
Filum terminale	Slender pial extension that tethers the spinal cord to the bottom of the vertebral column
Doral root ganglia	Cell bodies of primary sensory neurons
Dorsal and ventral roots	Each segment has a pair
Dorsal	**In (sensory)**
Ventral	**Out (motor)**
Spinal nerve	Formed from dorsal and ventral roots (mixed nerve)
Cervical enlargement	(C4–T1) → branchial plexus → upper limbs
Lumbar enlargement	(L2–S3) → lumbar and sacral plexuses → lower limbs

The following figure shows additional features of the spinal cord, such as the gray and white communicating rami, which are part of the autonomic nervous system.

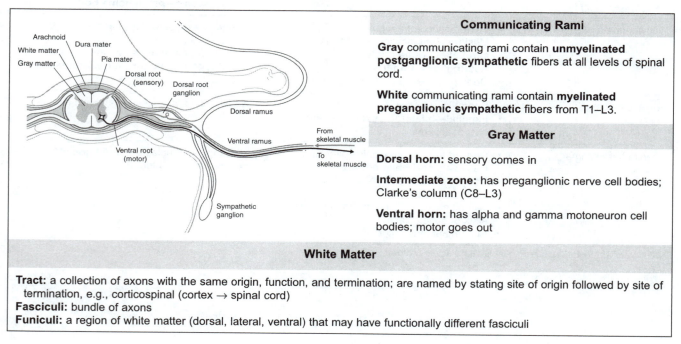

Communicating Rami

Gray communicating rami contain **unmyelinated postganglionic sympathetic** fibers at all levels of spinal cord.

White communicating rami contain **myelinated preganglionic sympathetic** fibers from T1–L3.

Gray Matter

Dorsal horn: sensory comes in

Intermediate zone: has preganglionic nerve cell bodies; Clarke's column (C8–L3)

Ventral horn: has alpha and gamma motoneuron cell bodies; motor goes out

White Matter

Tract: a collection of axons with the same origin, function, and termination; are named by stating site of origin followed by site of termination, e.g., corticospinal (cortex → spinal cord)
Fasciculi: bundle of axons
Funiculi: a region of white matter (dorsal, lateral, ventral) that may have functionally different fasciculi

The most essential descending pathway is that which mediates voluntary skilled motor activity. This is formed by the **upper motor neuron (UMN; corticospinal tract)** and the **lower motor neuron (LMN)**.

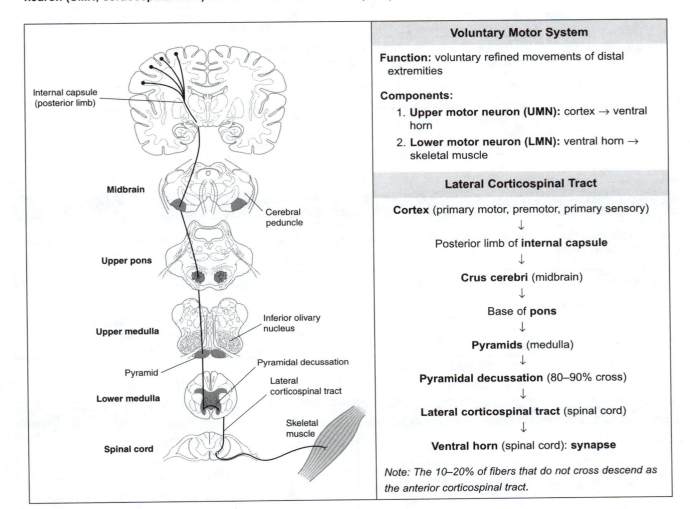

Voluntary Motor System

Function: voluntary refined movements of distal extremities

Components:

1. **Upper motor neuron (UMN):** cortex → ventral horn
2. **Lower motor neuron (LMN):** ventral horn → skeletal muscle

Lateral Corticospinal Tract

Cortex (primary motor, premotor, primary sensory)
↓
Posterior limb of **internal capsule**
↓
Crus cerebri (midbrain)
↓
Base of **pons**
↓
Pyramids (medulla)
↓
Pyramidal decussation (80–90% cross)
↓
Lateral corticospinal tract (spinal cord)
↓
Ventral horn (spinal cord): **synapse**

Note: The 10–20% of fibers that do not cross descend as the anterior corticospinal tract.

Diagram labels: Internal capsule (posterior limb), Midbrain, Cerebral peduncle, Upper pons, Upper medulla, Inferior olivary nucleus, Pyramid, Pyramidal decussation, Lateral corticospinal tract, Lower medulla, Skeletal muscle, Spinal cord

UPPER VERSUS LOWER MOTOR NEURON LESIONS

Clinical Signs	Upper Motor Neuron	Lower Motor Neuron
Paralysis	Spastic	Flaccid
Muscle tone	Hypertonia	Hypotonia
Muscle bulk	Disuse atrophy	Atrophy, fasciculations
Deep tendon reflexes	Hyperreflexia	Hyporeflexia
Pathologic reflexes	Babinski	None

Area of body involved:
    Size:
    Side:
	
	Large
	Contralateral if above decussation; ipsilateral if below decussation
		
		Small
		Ipsilateral

COMMONLY TESTED MUSCLE STRETCH REFLEXES

The **deep tendon (stretch, myotatic) reflex** is monosynaptic and ipsilateral. The **afferent limb** consists of a **muscle spindle receptor, Ia sensory neuron,** and **efferent limb (lower motor neuron)**. These reflexes are useful in the clinical exam.

Reflex	Cord Segment Involved	Muscle Tested
Knee (patellar)	L2–L4	Quadriceps
Ankle	S1	Gastrocnemius
Biceps	C5–C6	Biceps
Triceps	C7–C8	Triceps
Forearm	C5–C6	Brachioradialis

ASCENDING PATHWAYS

The two most important ascending pathways use a three-neuron system to convey sensory information to the cortex. Key general features are listed below.

Pathway	Function	Overview
Dorsal column–medial lemniscus	Discriminative touch, conscious proprioception, vibration, pressure	**3 neuron system:** 1° neuron: cell body in **DRG** 2° neuron: **decussates** 3° neuron: **thalamus (VPL) → cortex**
Anterolateral (spinothalamic)	Pain and temperature	

Definition of abbreviations: DRG, dorsal root ganglia; VPL, ventral posterolateral nucleus.

DORSAL COLUMN–MEDIAL LEMNISCUS

Pathway

1° neuron: cell body in **DRG**, synapses in **lower medulla**

- **Gracile fasciculus** from **lower** extremities; terminates in **gracile nucleus**
- **Cuneate fasciculus** from **upper** extremities; terminates in **cuneate nucleus**

2° neuron: decussates as **internal arcuate fibers**; ascends as **medial lemniscus**; synapses in **VPL** of the thalamus

3° neuron: VPL → somatosensory cortex

Clinical Correlation

If lesion is **above decussation** → **contralateral** loss of function

If lesion is in **spinal cord** → **ipsilateral** loss of function

Lesion can → **Romberg sign** (sways when standing, feet together, and eyes closed; swaying with eyes open indicates cerebellar dysfunction)

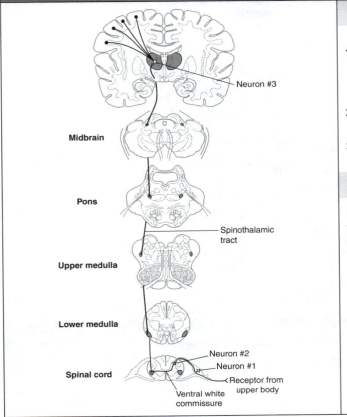

Pathway

1° neuron: cell body in **DRG**, enters cord via dorsolateral tract of Lissauer (ascends or descends one or two segments), **synapses in dorsal horn** of spinal cord. Fibers are **A-δ** (fast) or **C** (slow).

2° neuron: decussates as **ventral white commissure**; ascends in **lateral spinothalamic tract**; synapses in **VPL**

3° neuron: VPL → somatosensory cortex

Clinical Correlation

Lesion of lateral spinothalamic tract → loss of pain and temperature sensation on **contralateral** body, starting one or two segments below lesion

---

CLASSIC SPINAL CORD LESIONS

There are several classic and very testable spinal cord syndromes. An understanding of basic spinal cord anatomy makes the symptoms easy to predict.

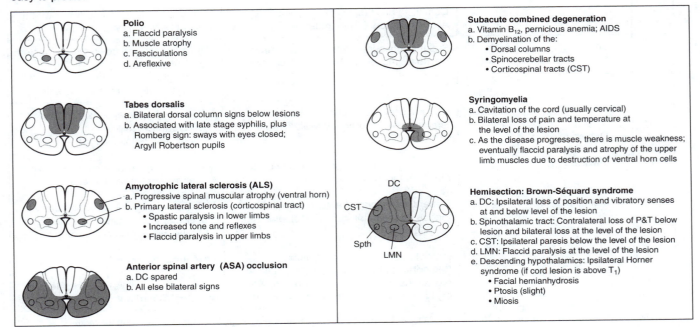

Polio
a. Flaccid paralysis
b. Muscle atrophy
c. Fasciculations
d. Areflexive

Tabes dorsalis
a. Bilateral dorsal column signs below lesions
b. Associated with late stage syphilis, plus Romberg sign: sways with eyes closed; Argyll Robertson pupils

Amyotrophic lateral sclerosis (ALS)
a. Progressive spinal muscular atrophy (ventral horn)
b. Primary lateral sclerosis (corticospinal tract)
  • Spastic paralysis in lower limbs
  • Increased tone and reflexes
  • Flaccid paralysis in upper limbs

Anterior spinal artery (ASA) occlusion
a. DC spared
b. All else bilateral signs

Subacute combined degeneration
a. Vitamin B₁₂, pernicious anemia; AIDS
b. Demyelination of the:
  • Dorsal columns
  • Spinocerebellar tracts
  • Corticospinal tracts (CST)

Syringomyelia
a. Cavitation of the cord (usually cervical)
b. Bilateral loss of pain and temperature at the level of the lesion
c. As the disease progresses, there is muscle weakness; eventually flaccid paralysis and atrophy of the upper limb muscles due to destruction of ventral horn cells

Hemisection: Brown-Séquard syndrome
a. DC: Ipsilateral loss of position and vibratory senses at and below level of the lesion
b. Spinothalamic tract: Contralateral loss of P&T below lesion and bilateral loss at the level of the lesion
c. CST: Ipsilateral paresis below the level of the lesion
d. LMN: Flaccid paralysis at the level of the lesion
e. Descending hypothalamics: Ipsilateral Horner syndrome (if cord lesion is above T₁)
  • Facial hemianhydrosis
  • Ptosis (slight)
  • Miosis

Definition of abbreviations: DC, dorsal column; LMN, lower motor neuron.

CRANIAL NERVES AND BRAIN STEM

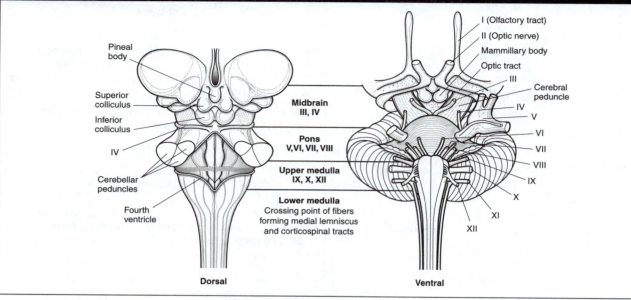

CRANIAL NERVES: FUNCTIONAL FEATURES				
CN	Name	Type	Function	Results of Lesions
I	Olfactory	Sensory	Smells	Anosmia
II	Optic	Sensory	Sees	Visual field deficits (anopsia) Loss of light reflex with III Only nerve to be affected by MS
III	Oculomotor	Motor	Innervates SR, IR, MR, IO extraocular muscles: adduction (MR) most important action Raises eyelid (levator palpebrae superioris) Constricts pupil (sphincter pupillae) Accommodates (ciliary muscle)	Diplopia, external strabismus Loss of parallel gaze Ptosis Dilated pupil, loss of light reflex with II Loss of near response
IV	Trochlear	Motor	Superior oblique—depresses and abducts eyeball (makes eyeball look down and out) Intorts	Weakness looking down with adducted eye Trouble going down stairs Head tilts away from lesioned side
V	Trigeminal Ophthalmic (V1) Maxillary (V2) Mandibular (V3)	Mixed	General sensation (touch, pain, temperature) of forehead/scalp/cornea General sensation of palate, nasal cavity, maxillary face, maxillary teeth General sensation of anterior two thirds of tongue, mandibular face, mandibular teeth Motor to muscles of mastication (temporalis, masseter, medial and lateral pterygoids) and anterior belly of digastric, mylohyoid, tensor tympani, tensor palati	V1—loss of general sensation in skin of forehead/scalp Loss of blink reflex with VII V2—loss of general sensation in skin over maxilla, maxillary teeth V3—loss of general sensation in skin over mandible, mandibular teeth, tongue, weakness in chewing Jaw deviation toward weak side Trigeminal neuralgia—intractable pain in V2 or V3 territory

Definition of abbreviations: IO, inferior oblique; MR, medial rectus; IR, inferior rectus; MS, multiple sclerosis; SR, superior rectus.

(Continued)

			CRANIAL NERVES: FUNCTIONAL FEATURES *(CONT'D.)*	
CN	**Name**	**Type**	**Function**	**Results of Lesions**
VI	Abducens	Motor	Lateral rectus—abducts eyeball	Diplopia, internal strabismus Loss of parallel gaze, "pseudoptosis"
VII	Facial	Mixed	To muscles of facial expression, posterior belly of digastric, stylohyoid, stapedius Salivation (submandibular, sublingual glands) Taste in anterior two thirds of tongue/palate Tears (lacrimal gland)	Corner of mouth droops, cannot close eye, cannot wrinkle forehead, loss of blink reflex, hyperacusis; Bell palsy—lesion of nerve in facial canal Alteration or loss of taste (ageusia) Eye dry and red
VIII	Vestibulocochlear	Sensory	Hearing Angular acceleration (head turning) Linear acceleration (gravity)	Sensorineural hearing loss Loss of balance, nystagmus
IX	Glossopharyngeal	Mixed	Sense of pharynx, carotid sinus/body Salivation (parotid gland) Taste and somatosensation of posterior one third of tongue Motor to one muscle—stylopharyngeus	Loss of gag reflex with X
X	Vagus	Mixed	To muscles of palate and pharynx for swallowing except tensor palati (V) and stylopharyngeus (IX) To all muscles of larynx (phonates) Sensory of larynx and laryngopharynx Sensory of GI tract To GI tract smooth muscle and glands in foregut and midgut	Nasal speech, nasal regurgitation Dysphagia, palate droop Uvula pointing away from affected side Hoarseness/fixed vocal cord Loss of gag reflex with IX Loss of cough reflex
XI	Accessory	Motor	Head rotation to opposite side (sternocleidomastoid) Elevates and rotates scapula (trapezius)	Weakness turning head to opposite side Shoulder droop
XII	Hypoglossal	Motor	Tongue movement (styloglossus, hyoglossus, genioglossus, and intrinsic tongue muscles—palatoglossus is by X)	Tongue pointing toward same (affected) side on protrusion

SKULL BASE ANATOMY

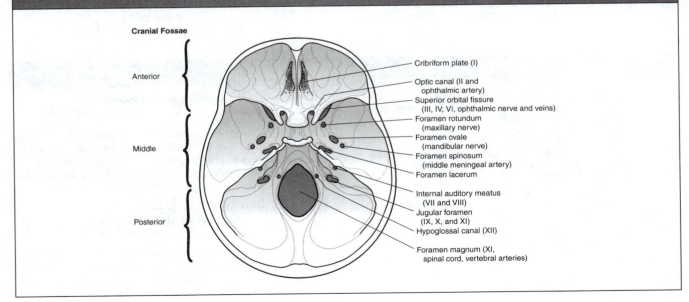

VISUAL SYSTEM

VISUAL FIELD DEFECTS

Defects

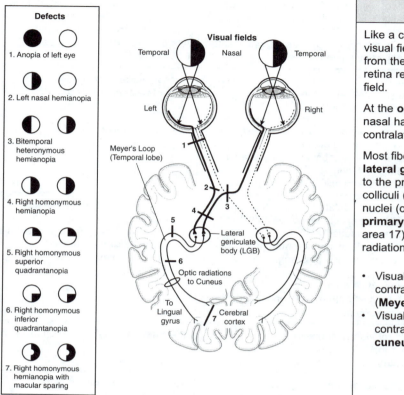

1. Anopia of left eye
2. Left nasal hemianopia
3. Bitemporal heteronymous hemianopia
4. Right homonymous hemianopia
5. Right homonymous superior quadrantanopia
6. Right homonymous inferior quadrantanopia
7. Right homonymous hemianopia with macular sparing

Visual fields

Temporal — Nasal — Temporal

Left — Right

Meyer's Loop (Temporal lobe)

Lateral geniculate body (LGB)

Optic radiations to Cuneus

To Lingual gyrus

Cerebral cortex

Notes

Like a camera, the lens inverts the image of the visual field, so the nasal retina receives information from the temporal visual field, and the temporal retina receives information from the nasal visual field.

At the **optic chiasm**, optic nerve fibers from the nasal half of each retina cross and project to the contralateral optic tract.

Most fibers from the **optic tract** project to the **lateral geniculate body (LGB)**; some also project to the pretectal area (light reflex), the superior colliculi (reflex gaze), and the suprachiasmatic nuclei (circadian rhythm). The LGB projects to the **primary visual cortex** (striate cortex, Brodmann area 17) of the occipital lobe via the optic radiations.

- Visual information from the lower retina (upper contralateral visual field) → temporal lobe (**Meyer loop**) → **lingual gyrus**
- Visual information from the upper retina (lower contralateral visual field) → parietal lobe → **cuneus gyrus**

Clinical Correlate (Some Causes of Lesions)

1. Optic neuritis, central retinal artery occlusion
2. Internal carotid artery aneurysm
3. Pituitary adenoma, craniopharyngioma

5. Middle cerebral artery (MCA) occlusion
6, 7. Posterior cerebral artery occlusion
Macula is spared in 7 due to collateral blood supply from MCA.

ANATOMY OF THE EYE AND GLAUCOMA

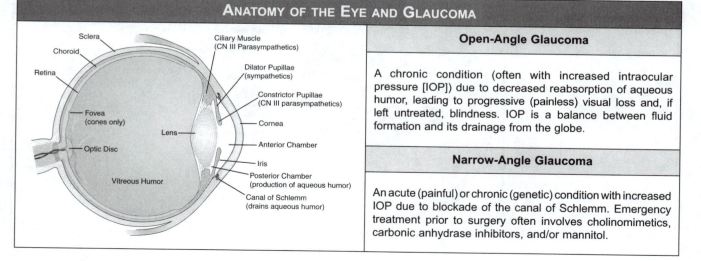

Sclera
Choroid
Retina
Fovea (cones only)
Optic Disc
Vitreous Humor
Ciliary Muscle (CN III Parasympathetics)
Dilator Pupillae (sympathetics)
Constrictor Pupillae (CN III parasympathetics)
Cornea
Lens
Anterior Chamber
Iris
Posterior Chamber (production of aqueous humor)
Canal of Schlemm (drains aqueous humor)

Open-Angle Glaucoma

A chronic condition (often with increased intraocular pressure [IOP]) due to decreased reabsorption of aqueous humor, leading to progressive (painless) visual loss and, if left untreated, blindness. IOP is a balance between fluid formation and its drainage from the globe.

Narrow-Angle Glaucoma

An acute (painful) or chronic (genetic) condition with increased IOP due to blockade of the canal of Schlemm. Emergency treatment prior to surgery often involves cholinomimetics, carbonic anhydrase inhibitors, and/or mannitol.

The eye is predominantly innervated by the parasympathetic nervous system. Therefore, application of muscarinic antagonists or ganglionic blockers has a large effect by blocking the parasympathetic nervous system.

Structure	Predominant Receptor	Receptor Stimulation	Receptor Blockade
Pupillary sphincter ms. (iris)	M_3 receptor (PANS)	Contraction → miosis	Relaxation → mydriasis
Radial dilator ms. (iris)	α receptor (SANS)	Contraction → mydriasis	Relaxation → miosis
Ciliary ms.	M_3 receptor (PANS)	Contraction → accommodation for near vision	Relaxation → focus for far vision
Ciliary body epithelium	β receptor (SANS)	Secretion of aqueous humor	Decreased aqueous humor production

Definition of abbreviations: ms., muscle; PANS, parasympathetic nervous system; SANS, sympathetic nervous system.

DRUGS USED TO TREAT GLAUCOMA

Drug Class	Drug	Mechanism
Cholinomimetics (miotics)	Pilocarpine (mAChR agonist) Carbachol (mAChR agonist) Physostigmine (AChEI) Echothiophate (AChEI)	Contracts ciliary muscle and opens trabecular meshwork, increasing the outflow of aqueous humor through the canal of Schlemm
Beta blockers	Timolol (nonselective) Betaxolol ($β_1$)	Blocks actions of NE at ciliary epithelium to ↓ aqueous humor secretion
Prostaglandins	Latanoprost ($PGF_{2α}$ analog)	↑ aqueous humor outflow
Alpha agonists	Epinephrine Dipivefrin	↑ aqueous humor outflow
Alpha-2 agonists	Apraclonidine Brimonidine	↓ aqueous humor secretion
Diuretics	Acetazolamide (oral; CAI) Dorzolamide (topical; CAI) Mannitol (for narrow-angle; osmotic)	CAI: ↓ HCO_3^- → ↓ aqueous humor secretion

Definition of abbreviations: AChEI, acetylcholinesterase inhibitor; CAI, carbonic anhydrase inhibitor; mAChR, muscarinic cholinergic receptor.

PUPILLARY LIGHT REFLEX PATHWAY

	Afferent Limb: CN II
Pretectal area Edinger-Westphal nucleus II III III II Pupil	Light stimulates ganglion retinal cells → impulses travel up **CNII**, which projects **bilaterally** to the **pretectal nuclei** (midbrain) The pretectal nucleus projects **bilaterally** → **Edinger-Westphal nuclei (CN III)**
	Efferent Limb: CN III
	Edinger-Westphal nucleus (preganglionic parasympathetic) → **ciliary ganglion** (postganglionic parasympathetic) → **pupillary sphincter ms.** → **miosis** *Note:* This is a simplified diagram; the ciliary ganglion is not shown.

Because cells in the pretectal area supply the Edinger-Westphal nuclei bilaterally, shining light in one eye → constriction in the ipsilateral pupil (direct light reflex) and the contralateral pupil (consensual light reflex).

Because this reflex does not involve the visual cortex, a person who is cortically blind can still have this reflex.

ACCOMMODATION–CONVERGENCE REACTION

When an individual focuses on a nearby object after looking at a distant object, three events occur:

1. Accommodation
2. Convergence
3. Pupillary constriction (miosis)

In general, stimuli from light → visual cortex → superior colliculus and pretectal nucleus → Edinger-Westphal nucleus (1, 3) and oculomotor nucleus (2).

Accommodation: Parasympathetic fibers contract the ciliary muscle, which relaxes suspensory ligaments, allowing the lens to increase its convexity (become more round). This increases the refractive index of the lens, thereby focusing a nearby object on the retina.

Convergence: Both medial rectus muscles contract, adducting both eyes.

Pupillary constriction: Parasympathetic fibers contract the pupillary sphincter muscle → miosis.

CLINICAL CORRELATIONS

Pupillary Abnormalities

Argyll Robertson pupil (pupillary light-near dissociation)	No direct or consensual light reflex; accommodation-convergence intact Seen in **neurosyphilis**, diabetes
Relative afferent (Marcus Gunn) pupil	Lesion of afferent limb of pupillary light reflex; diagnosis made with swinging flashlight Shine light in Marcus Gunn pupil → pupils do not constrict fully Shine light in normal eye → pupils constrict fully Shine light immediately again in affected eye → apparent dilation of both pupils because stimulus carried through that CN II is weaker; seen in multiple sclerosis
Horner syndrome	Caused by a lesion of the oculosympathetic pathway; syndrome consists of miosis, ptosis, apparent enophthalmos, and hemianhidrosis
Adie pupil	Dilated pupil that reacts sluggishly to light, but better to accommodation; often seen in women and often associated with loss of knee jerks
Transentorial (uncal) herniation	Increased intracranial pressure → leads to uncal herniation → CN III compression → fixed and dilated pupil, "down-and-out" eye, ptosis

Extraocular Muscles: Function and Innervation

CN III	**Medial rectus:** adducts eye **Superior rectus:** elevates, intorts, adducts eye **Inferior rectus:** depresses, extorts, adducts eye **Inferior oblique:** elevates, extorts, abducts eye	CN IV	**Superior oblique:** depresses, intorts, abducts eye
		CN VI	**Lateral rectus:** Abducts eye

Two important eye movements are **abduction** (away from nose, **CN VI**) and **adduction** (toward nose, **CN III**).

For the eyes to move together **(conjugate gaze)**, the oculomotor nuclei and abducens nuclei are interconnected by the **medial longitudinal fasciculus (MLF)**.

Horizontal gaze is controlled by two gaze centers:

1. **Frontal eye field** (contralateral gaze)
2. **PPRF** (paramedial pontine reticular formation, ipsilateral gaze)

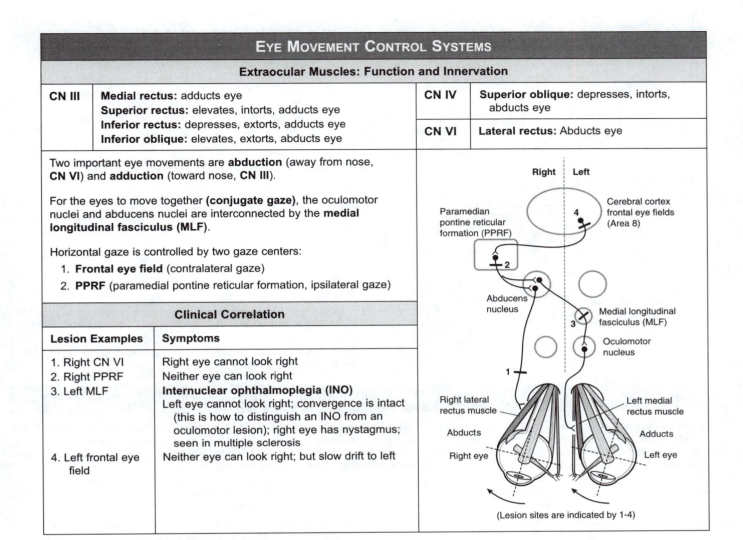

(Lesion sites are indicated by 1-4)

Clinical Correlation

Lesion Examples	Symptoms
1. Right CN VI	Right eye cannot look right
2. Right PPRF	Neither eye can look right
3. Left MLF	**Internuclear ophthalmoplegia (INO)** Left eye cannot look right; convergence is intact (this is how to distinguish an INO from an oculomotor lesion); right eye has nystagmus; seen in multiple sclerosis
4. Left frontal eye field	Neither eye can look right; but slow drift to left

TRIGEMINAL NERVE (V)	FACIAL NERVE (VII)

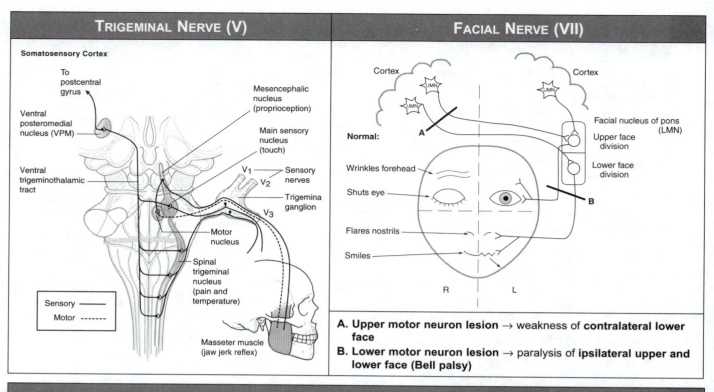

A. Upper motor neuron lesion → weakness of **contralateral lower face**

B. Lower motor neuron lesion → paralysis of **ipsilateral upper and lower face (Bell palsy)**

VESTIBULAR SYSTEM (VIII)

Three semicircular ducts respond to **angular acceleration and deceleration** of the head. The **utricle** and **saccule** respond to **linear acceleration** and the pull of **gravity**. There are four **vestibular nuclei** in the medulla and pons, which receive information from CN VIII. Fibers from the vestibular nuclei join the MLF and supply the motor nuclei of CNs III, IV, and VI, thereby regulating conjugate eye movements. Vestibular nuclei also receive and send information to the **flocculonodular lobe** of the cerebellum.

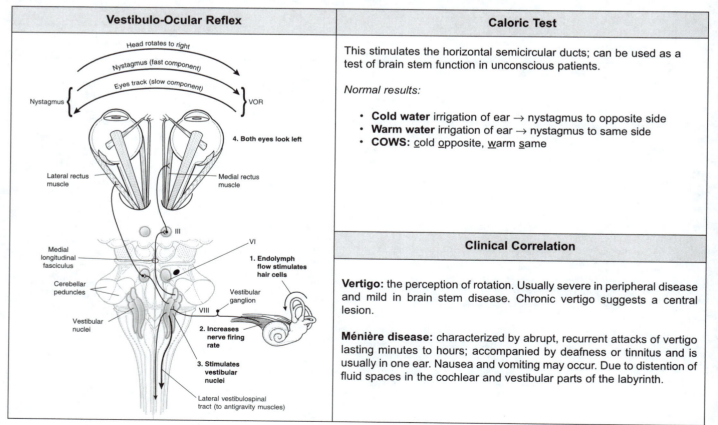

Vestibulo-Ocular Reflex

Caloric Test

This stimulates the horizontal semicircular ducts; can be used as a test of brain stem function in unconscious patients.

Normal results:

- **Cold water** irrigation of ear → nystagmus to opposite side
- **Warm water** irrigation of ear → nystagmus to same side
- **COWS:** cold opposite, warm same

Clinical Correlation

Vertigo: the perception of rotation. Usually severe in peripheral disease and mild in brain stem disease. Chronic vertigo suggests a central lesion.

Ménière disease: characterized by abrupt, recurrent attacks of vertigo lasting minutes to hours; accompanied by deafness or tinnitus and is usually in one ear. Nausea and vomiting may occur. Due to distention of fluid spaces in the cochlear and vestibular parts of the labyrinth.

AUDITORY SYSTEM (VIII)

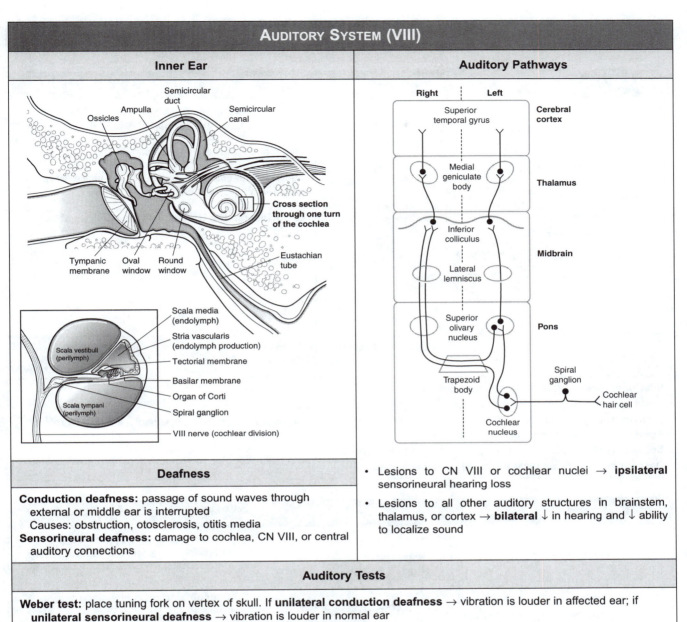

Inner Ear

- Ossicles
- Ampulla
- Semicircular duct
- Semicircular canal
- **Cross section through one turn of the cochlea**
- Tympanic membrane
- Oval window
- Round window
- Eustachian tube

- Scala media (endolymph)
- Stria vascularis (endolymph production)
- Tectorial membrane
- Basilar membrane
- Organ of Corti
- Spiral ganglion
- VIII nerve (cochlear division)
- Scala vestibuli (perilymph)
- Scala tympani (perilymph)

Auditory Pathways

Right | Left

- Superior temporal gyrus — **Cerebral cortex**
- Medial geniculate body — **Thalamus**
- Inferior colliculus — **Midbrain**
- Lateral lemniscus
- Superior olivary nucleus — **Pons**
- Trapezoid body
- Cochlear nucleus
- Spiral ganglion
- Cochlear hair cell

- Lesions to CN VIII or cochlear nuclei → **ipsilateral** sensorineural hearing loss
- Lesions to all other auditory structures in brainstem, thalamus, or cortex → **bilateral** ↓ in hearing and ↓ ability to localize sound

Deafness

Conduction deafness: passage of sound waves through external or middle ear is interrupted
  Causes: obstruction, otosclerosis, otitis media
Sensorineural deafness: damage to cochlea, CN VIII, or central auditory connections

Auditory Tests

Weber test: place tuning fork on vertex of skull. If **unilateral conduction deafness** → vibration is louder in affected ear; if **unilateral sensorineural deafness** → vibration is louder in normal ear
Rinne test: place tuning fork on mastoid process (bone conduction) until vibration is not heard, then place fork in front of ear (air conduction). If **unilateral conduction deafness** → no air conduction after bone conduction is gone; if **unilateral sensorineural deafness** → air conduction present after bone conduction is gone

BRAIN STEM LESIONS

MEDULLA

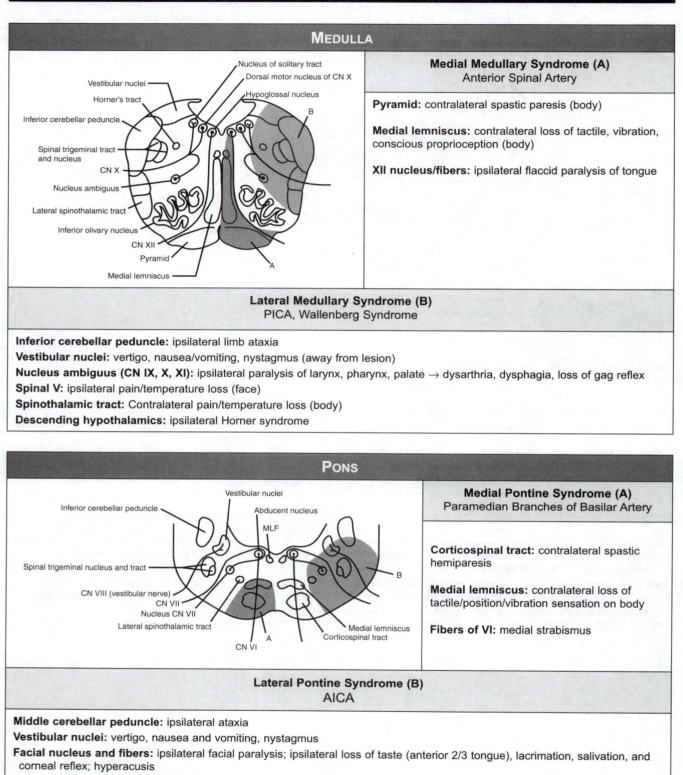

Medial Medullary Syndrome (A)
Anterior Spinal Artery

Pyramid: contralateral spastic paresis (body)

Medial lemniscus: contralateral loss of tactile, vibration, conscious proprioception (body)

XII nucleus/fibers: ipsilateral flaccid paralysis of tongue

Diagram labels (left figure):
Nucleus of solitary tract
Dorsal motor nucleus of CN X
Hypoglossal nucleus
Vestibular nuclei
Horner's tract
Inferior cerebellar peduncle
Spinal trigeminal tract and nucleus
CN X
Nucleus ambiguus
Lateral spinothalamic tract
Inferior olivary nucleus
CN XII
Pyramid
Medial lemniscus
B
A

Lateral Medullary Syndrome (B)
PICA, Wallenberg Syndrome

Inferior cerebellar peduncle: ipsilateral limb ataxia
Vestibular nuclei: vertigo, nausea/vomiting, nystagmus (away from lesion)
Nucleus ambiguus (CN IX, X, XI): ipsilateral paralysis of larynx, pharynx, palate → dysarthria, dysphagia, loss of gag reflex
Spinal V: ipsilateral pain/temperature loss (face)
Spinothalamic tract: Contralateral pain/temperature loss (body)
Descending hypothalamics: ipsilateral Horner syndrome

PONS

Medial Pontine Syndrome (A)
Paramedian Branches of Basilar Artery

Corticospinal tract: contralateral spastic hemiparesis

Medial lemniscus: contralateral loss of tactile/position/vibration sensation on body

Fibers of VI: medial strabismus

Diagram labels (lower figure):
Vestibular nuclei
Abducent nucleus
Inferior cerebellar peduncle
MLF
Spinal trigeminal nucleus and tract
CN VIII (vestibular nerve)
CN VII
Nucleus CN VII
Lateral spinothalamic tract
CN VI
A
B
Medial lemniscus
Corticospinal tract

Lateral Pontine Syndrome (B)
AICA

Middle cerebellar peduncle: ipsilateral ataxia
Vestibular nuclei: vertigo, nausea and vomiting, nystagmus
Facial nucleus and fibers: ipsilateral facial paralysis; ipsilateral loss of taste (anterior 2/3 tongue), lacrimation, salivation, and corneal reflex; hyperacusis
Spinal trigeminal nucleus/tract: ipsilateral pain/temperature loss (face)
Spinothalamic tract: contralateral pain/temperature loss (body)
Cochlear nucleus/VIII fibers: ipsilateral hearing loss
Descending sympathetics: ipsilateral Horner syndrome

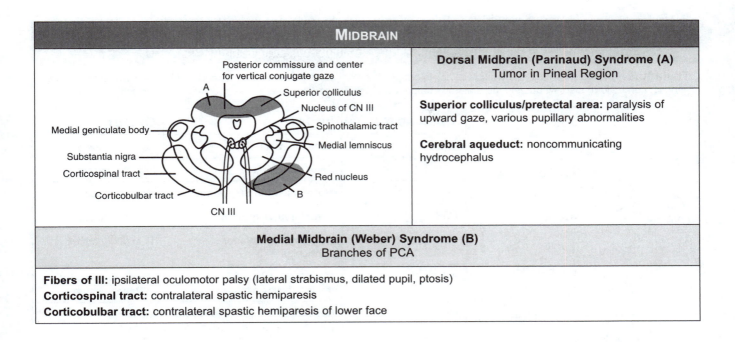

MIDBRAIN

Dorsal Midbrain (Parinaud) Syndrome (A)
Tumor in Pineal Region

Superior colliculus/pretectal area: paralysis of upward gaze, various pupillary abnormalities

Cerebral aqueduct: noncommunicating hydrocephalus

Medial Midbrain (Weber) Syndrome (B)
Branches of PCA

Fibers of III: ipsilateral oculomotor palsy (lateral strabismus, dilated pupil, ptosis)
Corticospinal tract: contralateral spastic hemiparesis
Corticobulbar tract: contralateral spastic hemiparesis of lower face

CEREBELLUM

The cerebellum controls posture, muscle tone, learning of repeated motor functions, and coordinates voluntary motor activity. Diseases of the cerebellum result in disturbances of gait, balance, and coordinated motor actions, but there is no paralysis or inability to start or stop movement.

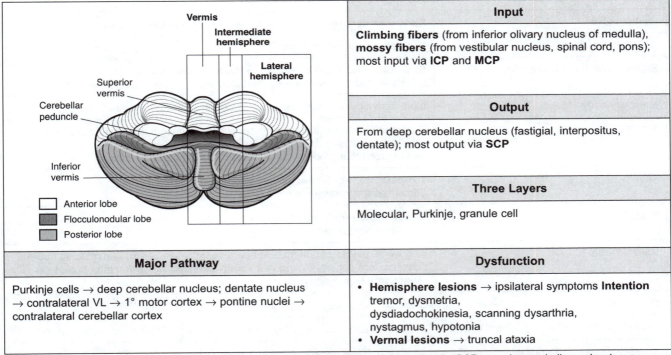

Input

Climbing fibers (from inferior olivary nucleus of medulla), **mossy fibers** (from vestibular nucleus, spinal cord, pons); most input via **ICP** and **MCP**

Output

From deep cerebellar nucleus (fastigial, interpositus, dentate); most output via **SCP**

Three Layers

Molecular, Purkinje, granule cell

Major Pathway

Purkinje cells → deep cerebellar nucleus; dentate nucleus → contralateral VL → 1° motor cortex → pontine nuclei → contralateral cerebellar cortex

Dysfunction

- **Hemisphere lesions** → ipsilateral symptoms **Intention** tremor, dysmetria, dysdiadochokinesia, scanning dysarthria, nystagmus, hypotonia
- **Vermal lesions** → truncal ataxia

Definition of abbreviations: ICP, inferior cerebellar peduncle; MCP, middle cerebellar peduncle; SCP, superior cerebellar peduncle; VL, ventral lateral nucleus.

DIENCEPHALON
Thalamus, Hypothalamus, Epithalamus, Subthalamus

Thalamus—serves as a major sensory relay for information that ultimately reaches the neocortex. Motor control areas (basal ganglia, cerebellum) also synapse in the thalamus before reaching the cortex. Other nuclei regulate states of consciousness.

Internal medullary lamina

THALAMIC NUCLEI	INPUT	OUTPUT
VPL	Sensory from **body**	Somatosensory cortex
VPM	Sensory from **face**	Somatosensory cortex
VA/VL	**Motor** info from BG, cerebellum	Motor cortices
LGB	**Visual** from optic tract	1° visual cortex
MGB	**Auditory** from inferior colliculus	1° auditory cortex
AN	Mamillary nucleus (via mamillothalamic tract)	Cingulate gyrus (part of **Papez** circuit)
MD	(Dorsomedial nucleus). Involved in **memory** Damaged in **Wernicke-Korsakoff** syndrome	
Pulvinar	Helps integrate somesthetic, visual, and auditory input	
Midline/intralaminar	Involved in **arousal**	

Hypothalamus—helps maintain homeostasis; has roles in the autonomic, endocrine, and limbic systems

HYPOTHALAMIC NUCLEI	FUNCTIONS AND LESIONS
Lateral hypothalamic	**Feeding center;** lesion → starvation
Ventromedial	**Satiety center;** lesion → hyperphagia, obesity, savage behavior
Suprachiasmatic	Regulates circadian rhythms
Supraoptic and paraventricular	Synthesizes **ADH** and **oxytocin; regulates water balance** Lesion → **diabetes insipidus**, characterized by polydipsia and polyuria
Mamillary body	Input from hippocampus; damaged in Wernicke encephalopathy
Arcuate	Produces hypothalamic releasing and inhibiting factors and gives rise to tuberohypophysial tract Has neurons that produce dopamine (prolactin-inhibiting factor)
Anterior	**Temperature regulation;** lesion → hyperthermia Stimulates the parasympathetic nervous system
Posterior	**Temperature regulation;** lesion → poikilothermia (inability to thermoregulate) Stimulates sympathetic nervous system
Preoptic area	Regulates release of gonotrophic hormones; contains sexually dimorphic nucleus Lesion before puberty → arrested sexual development; lesion after puberty → amenorrhea or impotence
Dorsomedial	Stimulation → savage behavior

Epithalamus—Consists of pineal body and habenular nuclei. The **pineal body** aids in the regulation of **circadian rhythms**.

Subthalamus—The **subthalamic nucleus** is involved in **basal ganglia** circuitry. Lesion → **hemiballismus** (contralateral flinging movements of one or both extremities)

Definition of abbreviations: ADH, antidiuretic hormone; AN, anterior nuclear group; BG, basal ganglia; LBG, lateral geniculate body; MD, mediodorsal nucleus; MGB, medial geniculate body; VA, ventral anterior nucleus; VL, ventral lateral nucleus; VLP, ventroposterolateral nucleus; VPM, ventroposteromedial nucleus.

BASAL GANGLIA

The basal ganglia initiate and provide gross control over skeletal muscle movements. The basal ganglia are sometimes called the **extrapyramidal** nervous system because they modulate the pyramidal (corticospinal) nervous system.

BASAL GANGLIA COMPONENTS	
Striatum (caudate and putamen)	**Subthalamic nucleus** (diencephalon)
Globus pallidus (external and internal segments)	**Lentiform nucleus** (globus pallidus and putamen)
Substantia nigra (midbrain)	**Corpus striatum** (lentiform nucleus and caudate)

Together with the cerebral cortex and **VA/VL** thalamic nuclei, these structures form two parallel but antagonistic circuits known as the **direct** and **indirect pathways**. The direct pathway increases cortical excitation and promotes movement, and the indirect pathway decreases cortical excitation and inhibits movement. Hypokinetic movement disorders (e.g., Parkinson disease) result in a lesion of the direct pathway, and hyperkinetic movement disorders (e.g., Huntington disease, hemiballismus) result from indirect pathway lesions.

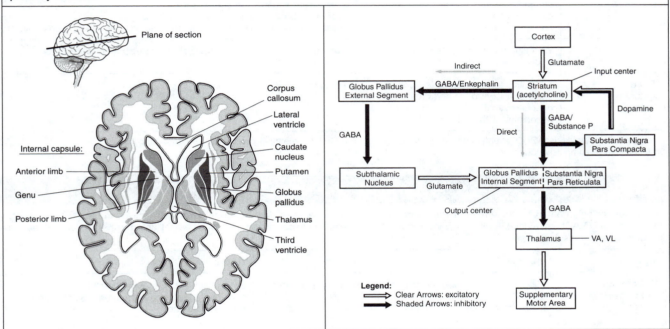

Definition of abbreviation: VA/VL, ventral anterior/ventral lateral thalamic nuclei.

DISEASES OF THE BASAL GANGLIA

Disease	Clinical Manifestations	Notes
Parkinson disease	Bradykinesia, cogwheel rigidity, pill rolling (resting) tremor, shuffling gate, stooped posture, masked facies, depression, dementia	**Loss of pigmented dopaminergic neurons from substantia nigra** **Lewy bodies:** intracytoplasmic eosinophilic inclusions, contain α-synuclein Known causes of parkinsonism: infections, vascular, and toxic insults (e.g., **MPTP**)
Huntington disease	Chorea (multiple, rapid, random movements), athetosis (slow writhing, movements), personality changes, dementia Onset: 20–40 years	**Degeneration** of GABAergic neurons in **neostriatum**, causing atrophy of neostriatum (and ventricular dilatation) **Autosomal dominant** **Unstable nucleotide repeat** on gene in chromosome 4, which codes for huntingtin protein Disease shows **anticipation** and **genomic imprinting** **Treatment:** antipsychotic agents, benzodiazepines, anticonvulsants
Wilson disease (hepatolenticular degeneration)	Tremor, asterixis, parkinsonian symptoms, chorea, neuropsychiatric symptoms; fatty change, hepatitis, or cirrhosis of liver	**Autosomal recessive defect in copper transport** Accumulation of copper in liver, brain, and eye (Descemet membrane, producing **Kayser-Fleischer ring**) Lesions in basal ganglia (especially putamen) **Treatment:** penicillamine (a chelator), zinc acetate (blocks absorption)
Hemiballism	Wild flinging movements of half the body	Hemorrhagic destruction of **contralateral subthalamic nucleus** Hypertensive patients
Tourette syndrome	Motor tics and vocal tics (e.g., snorting, sniffing, uncontrolled and often obscene vocalizations), commonly associated with OCD and ADHD	**Treatment:** Antipsychotic agents

Definition of abbreviations: ADHD, attention deficit hyperactivity disorder; MPTP, 1-methyl-4-phenyl-1,2,3,6-tetrahydropyridine; OCD, obsessive-compulsive disorder.

TREATMENT FOR PARKINSON DISEASE

The pharmacologic goal in the treatment of Parkinson disease is to **increase DA and/or decrease ACh** activity in the striatum, thereby correcting the DA/ACh imbalance. Additional treatment strategies include surgical intervention, such as pallidotomy, thalamotomy, deep brain stimulation, and transplantation.

Agents	Mechanism	Notes
Dopamine precursor: L-dopa	Dopamine precursor that crosses the blood–brain barrier (BBB) Converted to DA by DOPA decarboxylase (L-aromatic amino acid decarboxylase)	Side effects include on/off phenomena, dyskinesias, psychosis, postural hypotension, nausea/vomiting
DOPA decarboxylase inhibitor: carbidopa	Inhibits DOPA decarboxylase in the periphery, preventing L-dopa from being converted to dopamine in the periphery; instead, L-dopa crosses the BBB and is converted to dopamine in the brain	Often given in combination with L-dopa (Sinemet®)
DA agonists: bromocriptine pergolide pramipexole ropinirole	Stimulates D_2 receptors in the striatum	Pramipexole and ropinirole now considered first-line drugs in the initial management of PD
MAO B inhibitor: selegiline	Inhibits MAO type B, which preferentially metabolizes dopamine	Not to be taken with SSRIs (serotonin syndrome) or meperidine
Antimuscarinics: benztropine trihexyphenidyl	Blocks muscarinic receptors in the striatum	↓ tremor and rigidity, have little effect on bradykinesia Antimuscarinic side effects
COMT inhibitors: entacapone tolcapone	COMT inhibitors increase the efficacy of L-dopa. COMT metabolizes L-dopa to 3-O-methyldopa (3OMD), which competes with L-dopa for active transport into the CNS	Used as an adjunct to L-dopa/carbidopa, increases the "on" time
Amantadine	Increases dopaminergic neurotransmission, antimuscarinic; also an antiviral	Antimuscarinic effects, livedo reticularis

LIMBIC SYSTEM

The limbic system is involved in emotion, memory, attention, feeding, and mating behaviors. It consists of a core of cortical and diencephalic structures found on the medial aspect of the hemisphere. The limbic system modulates feelings, such as fear, anxiety, sadness, happiness, sexual pleasure, and familiarity.

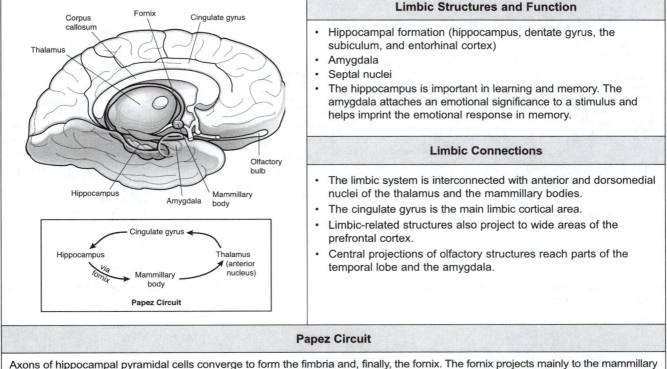

Limbic Structures and Function

- Hippocampal formation (hippocampus, dentate gyrus, the subiculum, and entorhinal cortex)
- Amygdala
- Septal nuclei
- The hippocampus is important in learning and memory. The amygdala attaches an emotional significance to a stimulus and helps imprint the emotional response in memory.

Limbic Connections

- The limbic system is interconnected with anterior and dorsomedial nuclei of the thalamus and the mammillary bodies.
- The cingulate gyrus is the main limbic cortical area.
- Limbic-related structures also project to wide areas of the prefrontal cortex.
- Central projections of olfactory structures reach parts of the temporal lobe and the amygdala.

Papez Circuit

Axons of hippocampal pyramidal cells converge to form the fimbria and, finally, the fornix. The fornix projects mainly to the mammillary bodies in the hypothalamus. The mammillary bodies project to the anterior nucleus of the thalamus (mammillothalamic tract). The anterior nuclei project to the cingulate gyrus, and the cingulate gyrus projects to the entorhinal cortex (via the cingulum). The entorhinal cortex projects to the hippocampus (via the perforant pathway).

CLINICAL CORRELATIONS

Anterograde Amnesia

Bilateral damage to the medial temporal lobes, including the **hippocampus**, results in a profound loss of the ability to acquire new information.

Wernicke Encephalopathy and Korsakoff Syndrome

Wernicke encephalopathy typically occurs in alcoholics who have a **thiamine deficiency**. Patients present with ocular palsies, confusion, and gait ataxia. If the thiamine deficiency is not corrected in time, patients can develop **Korsakoff syndrome**, characterized by **anterograde amnesia**, retrograde amnesia, and confabulation. Lesions are found in the **mammillary bodies** and the **dorsomedial nuclei of the thalamus**. Wernicke encephalopathy is reversible; Korsakoff syndrome is not.

Klüver-Bucy Syndrome

Klüver-Bucy syndrome results from bilateral lesions of the anterior temporal lobes, including the **amygdala**. Symptoms include placidity (decrease in aggressive behavior), psychic blindness (visual agnosia), increased oral exploratory behavior, hypersexuality and loss of sexual preference, hypermetamorphosis (visual stimuli are repeatedly approached as if they were new), and anterograde amnesia.

CEREBRAL CORTEX

The cerebral cortex is highly convoluted with bulges (**gyri**) separated by spaces (**sulci**). Several prominent sulci separate the cortex into four lobes: **frontal**, **parietal**, **temporal**, and **occipital**. The figures below show the lateral and medial views of the right cerebral hemispheres.

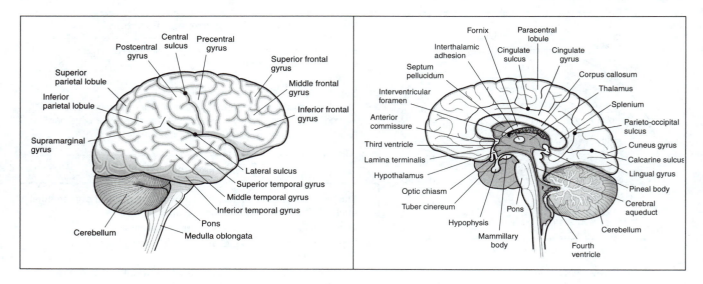

Most of the cortex has **six layers** (**neocortex**). The olfactory cortex and hippocampus have **three layers** (**allocortex**). The figure below shows the six-layered cortex:

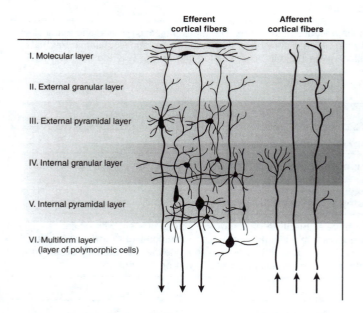

Key Afferents/Efferents
Layer IV receives thalamocortical inputs.
Layer V gives rise to corticospinal and corticobulbar tracts.

KEY FEATURES OF LOBES

Lobes	Important Regions	Deficit After Lesion
Frontal	Primary motor and premotor cortex	Contralateral spastic paresis (region depends on area of homunculus affected; see figure above)
	Frontal eye fields	Eyes deviate to ipsilateral side
	Broca speech area*	**Broca aphasia (expressive, nonfluent aphasia):** patient can understand written and spoken language, but speech and writing are slow and effortful; patients are aware of their problem; often associated with contralateral facial and arm weakness
	Prefrontal cortex	**Frontal lobe syndrome:** symptoms can include poor judgment, difficulty concentrating and problem solving, apathy, inappropriate social behavior
Parietal	Primary somatosensory cortex	Contralateral hemihypesthesia (region depends on area of homunculus affected)
	Superior parietal lobule	Contralateral astereognosis and sensory neglect, apraxia
	Inferior parietal lobule	**Gerstmann syndrome** (if dominant hemisphere): right/left confusion, dyscalculia and dysgraphia, finger agnosia, contralateral hemianopia or lower quadrantanopia
Temporal	Primary auditory cortex	Bilateral damage → deafness Unilateral leads to slight hearing loss
	Wernicke area*	**Wernicke aphasia (receptive, fluent aphasia):** patient cannot understand any form of language; speech is fast and fluent, but not comprehensible
	Hippocampus	Bilateral lesions lead to inability to consolidate short-term to long-term memory
	Amygdala	**Klüver-Bucy syndrome:** hyperphagia, hypersexuality, visual agnosia
	Olfactory bulb, tract, primary cortex	Ipsilateral anosmia
	Meyer loop (visual radiations)	Contralateral upper quadrantanopia ("pie in the sky")
Occipital	Primary visual cortex	Blindness

*In the dominant hemisphere. Eighty percent of people are left-hemisphere dominant.

ALZHEIMER DISEASE

- Alzheimer disease accounts for 60% of all cases of dementia. The incidence increases with age.
- **Clinical:** insidious onset, progressive memory impairment, mood alterations, disorientation, aphasia, apraxia, and progression to a bedridden state with eventual death
- Five to 10% of AD cases are hereditary, early onset, and transmitted as an autosomal dominant trait.

GENETICS OF ALZHEIMER DISEASE

Gene	Location	Notes
Amyloid precursor protein (*APP*) gene	Chromosome 21	Virtually all Down syndrome patients are destined to develop AD in their forties. Down patients have triple copies of the *APP* gene.
Presenilin-1 gene	Chromosome 14	Majority of hereditary AD cases—early onset
Presenilin-2 gene	Chromosome 1	Early onset
Apolipoprotein E gene	Chromosome 19	Three allelic forms of this gene: epsilon 2, epsilon 3, and epsilon 4 The allele epsilon 4 of apolipoprotein E (*ApoE*) increases the risk for AD, epsilon 2 confers relative protection

PATHOLOGY OF ALZHEIMER DISEASE

Lesions involve the neocortex, hippocampus, and subcortical nuclei, including forebrain cholinergic nuclei (i.e., basal nucleus of Meynert). These areas show atrophy, as well as characteristic microscopic changes. The earliest and most severely affected areas are the hippocampus and temporal lobe, which are involved in learning and memory.

Intra- and extracellular accumulation of abnormal proteins	**Aβ amyloid:** 42-residue peptide from a normal transmembrane protein, the amyloid precursor protein (APP) **Abnormal *tau*** (a microtubule-associated protein)
Senile plaques	Core of Aβ amyloid surrounded by dystrophic neuritic processes associated with microglia and astrocytes
Neurofibrillary tangles (NFT)	Intraneuronal aggregates of insoluble cytoskeletal elements, mainly composed of abnormally phosphorylated tau forming **paired helical filaments** (PHF)
Cerebral amyloid angiopathy (CAA)	Accumulation of Aβ amyloid within the media of small and medium-sized intracortical and leptomeningeal arteries; associated with intracerebral hemorrhage
Granulovacuolar degeneration (GVD) and Hirano bodies (HBs)	GVD and HBs develop in the hippocampus and are less significant diagnostically

TREATMENT OF ALZHEIMER DISEASE

AChE Inhibitors
(rivastigmine, donepezil, galantamine, tacrine)

These agents prevent the metabolism of ACh to counteract the depletion in ACh in the cerebral cortex and hippocampus. Rivastigmine and tacrine also inhibit BuChE. Indicated for mild to moderate AD.

NMDA Antagonist
(memantine)

This is the newest class of agents used for the treatment of AD. It is hypothesized that overstimulation of NMDA receptors contributes to the symptomatology of AD. Indicated for moderate to severe AD. Often used in combination with the AChEIs.

Definition of abbreviations: AChE, acetylcholinesterase; BuChE, butyrylcholinesterase; NMDA, *N*-methyl-D-aspartate.

CREUTZFELDT-JAKOB DISEASE (CJD)

Mechanism of Disease

Caused by a **prion protein** (PrP = 30-kD protein normally present in neurons encoded by gene on chromosome 20); PrP^c = normal conformation = alpha-helix; PrP^{sc} = abnormal conformation = beta-pleated sheet. PrP^{sc} facilitates conformational change of other PrP^c molecules into PrP^{sc}.

Spontaneous change from one form to another → sporadic cases (85% of total) of CJD

Mutations of PrP → hereditary cases (15% of total) of CJD

Pathology

Spongiform change: vacuolization of the neuropil in gray matter (especially cortex) due to large membrane-bound vacuoles within neuronal processes
- Associated with neuronal loss and astrogliosis
- **Kuru plaques** are deposits of amyloid of altered PrP protein

Clinical Manifestations

Rapidly progressive dementia, memory loss, startle myoclonus or other involuntary movements. EEG changes. Death within 6–12 months.

Variant CJD (vCJD)

Affects young adults. May be related to bovine spongiform encephalopathy (BSE; mad cow disease). Pathologically similar to CJD.

PICK DISEASE (LOBAR ATROPHY)

- Rare cause of dementia
- Striking **atrophy of frontal and temporal lobes** with sparing of posterior structures
- Microscopic: swollen neurons (Pick cells) or neurons containing **Pick bodies** (round to oval inclusions that stain with silver stains)

CNS TRAUMA

Concussion	Occurs with a change in momentum of the head (impact against a rigid surface) Loss of consciousness and reflexes, temporary respiratory arrest, and amnesia for the event
Contusion	Bruising to the brain resulting from impact of the brain against inner calvarial surfaces, especially along crests of orbital gyri (frontal lobe) and temporal poles Coup (site of injury) and contrecoup (site diametrically opposite) develop when the head is **mobile** at the time of impact.
Diffuse axonal injury	Injury to white matter due to acceleration/deceleration produces damage to axons at nodes of Ranvier with impairment of axoplasmic flow Poor prognosis, related to duration of coma

CEREBRAL HERNIATIONS

Subfalcine (cingulate)	Cingulate gyrus displaced underneath the falx to the opposite side with compression of anterior cerebral artery	
Transtentorial (uncal)	The uncus of the temporal lobe displaced over the free edge of the tentorium Compression of the third nerve, with pupillary dilatation on the same side Infarct in dependent territory Advanced stages: **Duret hemorrhage** within the central pons and midbrain	
Cerebellar tonsillar	Displacement of cerebellar tonsils through the foramen magnum Compression of medulla leads to cardiorespiratory arrest	

BLOOD SUPPLY

The blood supply of the cortex is supplied by branches of the **two internal carotid arteries** and **two vertebral arteries**.

- On the ventral surface of the brain, the anterior cerebral and middle cerebral branches of the internal carotid arteries connect with the posterior cerebral artery (derived from the basilar artery) and form the **circle of Willis**. This circle of vessels is completed by the anterior and posterior communicating arteries.

- The **middle cerebral artery** mainly supplies the lateral surface of the frontal, parietal, and upper aspect of the temporal lobe. Deep branches also supply part of the basal ganglia and internal capsule.

- The **anterior cerebral artery** supplies the medial aspect of the frontal and parietal lobes.

- The entire occipital lobe, lower aspect of temporal lobe, and the midbrain are supplied by the **posterior cerebral artery**.

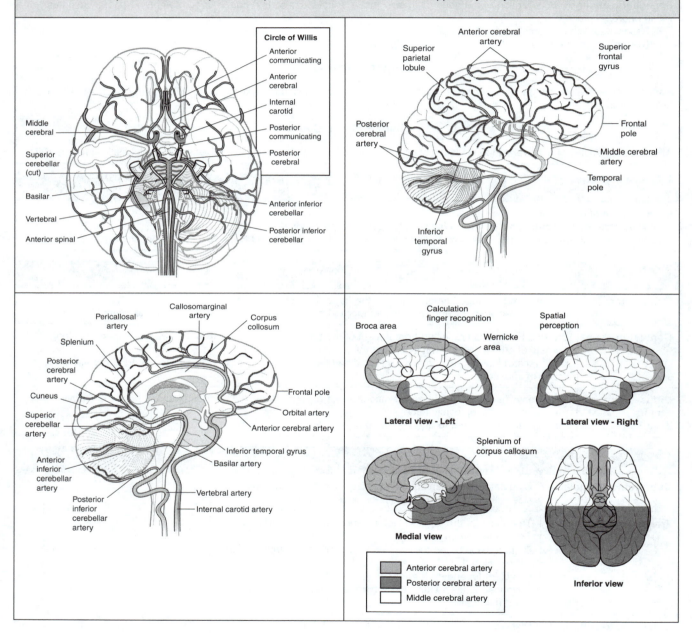

		BLOOD SUPPLY (CONT'D.)		
System	**Primary Arteries**	**Branches**	**Supplies**	**Deficits after Stroke**
Vertebrobasilar (posterior circulation)	**Vertebral arteries**	**Anterior spinal artery**	Anterior 2/3 of spinal cord	Dorsal columns spared; all else bilateral
		Posterior cerebellar (PICA)	Dorsolateral medulla	See brain stem lesions on pages 198–199.
	Basilar artery	Pontine arteries	Base of pons	
		Anterior inferior cerebral (AICA)	Inferior cerebellum, cerebellar nuclei	
		Superior cerebellar artery	Dorsal cerebellar hemispheres; superior cerebellar peduncle	
		Labyrinthine artery (sometimes arises from AICA)	Inner ear	
	Posterior cerebral arteries	—	Midbrain, thalamus, occipital lobe	**Contralateral hemianopia with macular sparing** Alexia without agraphia*
Internal carotid (anterior circulation)	Ophthalmic artery	Central artery of retina	Retina	Blindness
	Posterior communicating artery	—	—	Second most common **aneurysm** site (often with CN III palsy)
	Anterior cerebral artery	—	Primary motor and sensory cortex (leg/foot)	Contralateral spastic paralysis and anesthesia of **lower limb** Frontal lobe abnormalities
	Anterior communicating artery	—	—	Most common site of **aneurysm**
	Middle cerebral artery	Outer cortical	Lateral convexity of hemispheres	Contralateral spastic paralysis and anesthesia of **upper limb/face** **Gaze palsy** **Aphasia*** Gerstmann syndrome* Hemi inattention and neglect of contralateral body†
		Lenticulostriate	Internal capsule, caudate, putamen, globus pallidus	

*If dominant hemisphere is affected (usually the left).

†Right parietal lobe lesion

CEREBROVASCULAR DISORDERS		
Disorder	**Types**	**Key Concepts**
Cerebral infarcts	Thrombotic	**Anemic/pale** infarct; usually atherosclerotic complication
	Embolic	**Hemorrhagic/red** infarct; from heart or atherosclerotic plaques; **middle cerebral artery** most vulnerable to emboli
	Hypotension	**"Watershed"** areas and **deep cortical layers** most affected
	Hypertension	**Lacunar** infarcts; **basal ganglia** most affected
Hemorrhages	Epidural hematoma	Almost always traumatic Rupture of **middle meningeal artery** after skull fracture Lucid interval before loss of consciousness ("talk and die" syndrome)
	Subdural hematoma	Usually caused by trauma Rupture of **bridging veins** (connect brain and sagittal sinus)
	Subarachnoid hemorrhage	**Ruptured berry aneurysm** is most frequent cause Predisposing factors: Marfan syndrome, Ehlers-Danlos type 4, adult polycystic kidney disease, hypertension, smoking
	Intracerebral hemorrhage	Common causes: hypertension, trauma, infarction

SEIZURES AND ANTICONVULSANTS

SEIZURES

Partial	Occur in localized region of brain; can become secondarily generalized **Drugs of choice:** carbamazepine, phenytoin, valproic acid, phenobarbital in pregnancy and infants **Backup and adjuvants:** most newer drugs are also effective
Simple	• **Consciousness unaffected** • Can be motor, somatosensory or special sensory, autonomic, psychic
Complex	• Consciousness is impaired • The four "A"s: <u>a</u>ura, <u>a</u>lteration of consciousness, <u>a</u>utomatisms, <u>a</u>mnesia • Often called "psychomotor" or "temporal lobe seizures"
Generalized	Affects **entire brain**
Absence	• Impaired consciousness (usually abrupt onset and brief); automatisms sometimes occur • Begin in childhood, often end by age 20 • Also called **petit mal** • **Drugs of choice:** ethosuximide, valproic acid • **Backup and adjuvants:** clonazepam, lamotrigine, topiramate
Tonic-clonic	• Alternating tonic (stiffening) and clonic (movements); loss of consciousness • Also called grand mal • **Drugs of choice:** carbamazepine, phenytoin, valproic acid, phenobarbital in pregnancy and infants • **Backup and adjuvants:** some newer drugs are also effective
Myoclonic	Single or multiple myoclonic jerks • **Drug of choice:** valproic acid • **Backup and adjuvants:** clonazepam, felbamate
Status epilepticus	• Seizure activity (often tonic-clonic), continuous or intermittent (without recovery of consciousness) for at least 30 minutes; life-threatening • **Drugs of choice:** diazepam, lorazepam, phenytoin, fosphenytoin • **Backup and adjuvants:** phenobarbital, general anesthesia

ANTICONVULSANTS		
Drug	**Mechanism**	**Notes**
Benzodiazepines	↑ frequency of $GABA_A$ (Cl^-) receptor opening	Sedation, dependence, tolerance
Carbamazepine	Blocks Na^+ channels	Diplopia, ataxia, blood dyscrasias (agranulocytosis, aplastic anemia), enzyme induction, teratogenic
Ethosuximide	Blocks T-type Ca^{2+} channels (thalamus)	GI distress, headache, lethargy, hematotoxicity, Stevens-Johnson syndrome
Phenobarbital	↑ duration of $GABA_A$ (Cl^-) receptor opening	Induction of cytochrome P450, sedation, dependence, tolerance
Phenytoin	Blocks Na^+ channels	Gingival hyperplasia, hirsutism, sedation, anemia, nystagmus, diplopia, ataxia, teratogenic (fetal hydantoin syndrome), enzyme induction, zero-order kinetics
Valproic acid	Blocks Na^+ channels, inhibits GABA transaminase	GI distress, hepatotoxic (rare but can be fatal), inhibits drug metabolism, neural tube defects

NEWER AGENTS	
Drug	**Side Effects**
Felbamate	Aplastic anemia, hepatoxicity
Gabapentin	Sedation, dizziness
Lamotrigine	Life-threatening rash, Stevens-Johnson syndrome
Tiagabine	Sedation, dizziness
Topiramate	Sedation, dizziness, ataxia, anomia, renal stones, weight loss
Vigabatrin	Sedation, dizziness, visual field defects, psychosis

OPIOID ANALGESICS AND RELATED DRUGS

Opioid analgesics act by stimulating receptors for endogenous opioid peptides (e.g., enkephalins, β-endorphin, dynorphins). Opioid receptors are G-protein coupled, and the three major classes are μ **(mu)**, κ **(kappa)**, and δ **(delta)**. β-Endorphin has the greatest affinity for the μ receptor, dynorphins for the κ receptor, and enkephalins for the δ receptor. The effects of specific drugs depend on the receptor subtype with which they interact, and whether they act as full agonists, partial agonists, or antagonists. The μ receptor is primarily responsible for analgesia, respiratory depression, euphoria, and physical dependence.

INDIVIDUAL AGENTS		
Strong Agonists		
Morphine	Full μ agonist	Prototype of this class; poor oral bioavailability; histamine release
Methadone		Orally active; long duration; useful in maintenance
Meperidine		Muscarinic antagonist (no miosis or smooth muscle contraction); forms normeperidine → possible seizures; do not combine with MAO inhibitors or SSRIs
Additional strong agonists: fentanyl, heroin (schedule 1), levorphanol		
Moderate Agonists		
Codeine	Partial μ agonist	Antitussive, often given in combination with NSAIDs
Additional moderate agonists: oxycodone, hydrocodone		
Weak Agonists		
Propoxyphene	Partial μ agonist	Analgesia weaker than codeine; toxic in overdose; large doses → drug dependence
Mixed Agonist–Antagonists		
Pentazocine **Nalbuphine** **Butorphanol**	κ agonist/weak μ agonist	In general, less analgesia than morphine Can cause hallucinations and nightmares Has less respiratory depression and abuse liability than the pure agonists
Buprenorphine	Partial μ agonist/ weak κ and δ antagonist	Binds tightly to receptor, so is more resistant to naloxone reversal
Antitussives		
Codeine **Dextromethorphan**	Codeine is by prescription; dextromethorphan is available OTC	
Antidiarrheals		
Diphenoxylate **Loperamide**	Diphenoxylate used in combination with atropine to prevent abuse Loperamide available OTC	
Antagonists		
Naloxone (IV) **Naltrexone (PO)** **Nalmefene (IV)**	All are used in the management of acute opioid overdose. Naloxone has a short half-life and may require multiple doses. Naltrexone ↓ craving for ethanol and is used in alcohol dependency programs.	

CHARACTERISTICS OF OPIOID ANALGESICS

Effects and Side Effects

- Analgesia
- Sedation
- Respiratory depression
- Constipation
- Smooth muscle: (except meperidine)
  ↑ tone: biliary tract (biliary colic), bladder, ureter
  ↓ tone: uterus (prolongs labor), vascular

- Euphoria
- Cough suppression
- Nausea and vomiting
- Pupillary miosis (except meperidine)
- Cardiovascular:
  Cerebrovascular dilation (esp. with ↑ Pco_2) leads to ↑ intracranial pressure
  ↓ BP may occur; bradycardia

Clinical Uses

Analgesia, cough suppression, treatment of diarrhea, preoperative medications and adjunct to anesthesia, management of pulmonary edema

Chronic Effects

- Pharmacodynamic tolerance (tolerance does not develop to constipation or miosis)
- **Dependence:** Psychological and physical
- **Abstinence syndrome (withdrawal):** anxiety, hostility, GI distress (cramps and diarrhea) gooseflesh ("cold turkey"), muscle cramps and spasms ("kicking the habit"), rhinorrhea, lacrimation, sweating, yawning
- Abstinence syndrome can be precipitated in tolerant individuals by administering an opioid antagonist

Overdose

- **Classic triad:** Respiratory depression, miosis (pinpoint pupils), coma
- Diagnosis confirmed with naloxone (short duration, may need repeat dosing); give supportive care

Contraindications and Cautions

- Use of full agonists with weak partial agonists. Weak agonists can precipitate withdrawal from the full agonist.
- Use in patients with pulmonary dysfunction (acute respiratory failure). Exception: pulmonary edema
- Use in patients with head injuries (possible increased intracranial pressure)

- Use in patients with hepatic/renal dysfunction (drug accumulation)
- Use in patients with adrenal or thyroid deficiencies (prolonged and exaggerated responses)
- Use in pregnant patients (possible neonatal depression or dependence)

LOCAL ANESTHETICS

Local anesthetics **block voltage-gated sodium channels**, preventing sensory information from being transmitted from a local area to the brain. These agents are initially uncharged and diffuse across the axonal membrane to enter the cytoplasm. Once inside, they become ionized and block the Na^+ channels from the **inside**. These agents bind best to channels that are open or recently inactivated, rather than resting, and therefore work better in rapidly firing fibers (**use-dependence**). Infection leads to a more acidic environment, making the basic local anesthetic more likely to be ionized, therefore higher doses may be required. **Order of blockade:** small fibers > larger fibers; myelinated fibers > unmyelinated fibers. **Modality blocked:** autonomic and pain > touch/pressure > motor. There are two main classes: **amides** and **esters**.

Amides (metabolized in **liver**)		Esters (metabolized by **plasma cholinesterases**)		Side Effects
Bupivacaine	(L)	Tetracaine	(L)	1. **Neurotoxicity:** lightheadedness, nystagmus, restlessness, convulsions
Etidocaine	(L)	Cocaine	(M)†	
Ropivacaine	(L)	Procaine	(S)	2. **Cardiovascular toxicity**: ↓ CV parameters (except cocaine which ↑ HR and BP); bupivacaine especially notable for CV toxicity
Lidocaine	(M)*	Benzocaine‡		
Mepivacaine	(M)			
Prilocaine	(M)			3. **Allergic reaction:** esters via PABA formation; switch to amides if allergic to esters
Notes				
Duration of action can be increased by coadministration of a vasoconstrictor (e.g., epinephrine) to limit blood flow				
Hint: <u>Amide</u> drugs have two "i"s, and <u>ester</u> drugs have one "i" in their names.				

Definition of abbreviations: L, long acting; M, medium acting; S, short acting.

*Also a IB antiarrhythmic

†Primarily used topically; sympathomimetic; drug of abuse (schedule II)

‡Topical only

GENERAL ANESTHETICS

The ideal general anesthetic produces unconsciousness, analgesia, skeletal muscle relaxation, loss of reflexes, and amnesia. There are two broad classes of general anesthetics: **inhalational** and **intravenous**.

INHALATIONAL ANESTHETICS

Definitions

- **Solubility:** blood:gas partition coefficient
- **Minimum alveolar anesthetic concentration (MAC):** the minimal alveolar concentration at which 50% of patients do not response to a standardized painful stimulus. **MAC $\propto$ 1/potency**

General Principles

- Drugs with a $\uparrow$ **solubility** have **slow induction and recovery times** (if it is soluble in blood, then it takes longer to achieve the partial pressure required for anesthesia).
- Drugs with a $\downarrow$ **solubility** have **rapid induction and recovery times** (if it is not very soluble in blood, it quickly achieves the partial pressure required for anesthesia).
- Anesthesia is **terminated by redistribution** of the agent from the brain to the blood.
- Anesthetics that undergo **hepatic metabolism** tend be **more toxic**.

General Side Effects

- Sometimes when administered with muscle relaxants (especially succinylcholine) $\rightarrow$ **malignant hyperthermia**. Treat with dantrolene.
- Most $\downarrow$ BP moderately.

Anesthetic	Solubility	MAC (%)	Metabolism (%)	Unique Side Effects/Properties
Nitrous oxide	0.5	>100	0	Low potency; because the **MAC is >100**, it cannot provide complete anesthesia; good for induction; **good analgesia and amnesia**
Desflurane	0.4	6.5	<0.1	**Pulmonary irritant**
Sevoflurane	0.7	2.0	3	—
Isoflurane	1.4	1.3	0.2	—
Enflurane	1.8	1.7	8	**Proconvulsant**
Halothane	2.3	0.8	20	**Halothane hepatitis; sensitizes heart to arrhythmogenic effects of catecholamines**
Methoxyflurane	12	0.2	> 70	**Nephrotoxicity**

INTRAVENOUS ANESTHETICS

Drug Class	Agents	Unique Properties
Barbiturates	Thiopental, methohexital	**Redistribution** from brain terminates effects, but hepatic metabolism is required for elimination; used mainly for **induction** or short procedures; hyperalgesic; $\downarrow$ respiration, cardiac function, and cerebral blood flow
Benzodiazepines	Midazolam	Good amnesic; respiratory depression (can be reversed with **flumazenil**)
Dissociative	Ketamine	Patient remains conscious, but has amnesia, catatonia, and analgesia; related to phencyclidine (PCP)—causes **emergence reactions** (hallucinations, excitation, disorientation); **CV stimulant**
Opioids	Fentanyl, alfentanil, remifentanil, morphine	Chest wall rigidity, respiratory depression (can reverse with naloxone); **neuroleptanesthesia:** fentanyl + droperidol + nitrous oxide
Miscellaneous	Propofol, etomidate	Propofol—**rapid induction, antiemetic** Etomidate—**rapid induction; minimal CV or respiratory effects;** pain and myoclonus on injection; nausea

The Cardiovascular System

Embryology

Anatomy

Physiology

Pathology

Pharmacology

CARDIOVASCULAR EMBRYOLOGY

DEVELOPMENT OF THE HEART TUBE

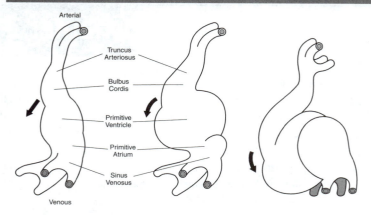

The primitive heart tube is formed from lateral plate mesoderm. The primitive heart tube undergoes dextral looping (bends to the right) and forms five dilatations. Four of the five dilatations become subdivided by a septum. Most of the common congenital cardiac anomalies result from defects in the formation of these septa.

ADULT STRUCTURES DERIVED FROM THE DILATATIONS OF THE PRIMITIVE HEART

Embryonic Dilatation	Adult Structure
Truncus arteriosus (neural crest)	Aorta Pulmonary trunk
Bulbus cordis	Smooth part of right ventricle (**conus arteriosus**) Smooth part of left ventricle (**aortic vestibule**)
Primitive ventricle	Trabeculated part of right ventricle Trabeculated part of left ventricle
Primitive atrium	Trabeculated part of right atrium Trabeculated part of left atrium
Sinus venosus (the only dilatation that does not become subdivided by a septum)	Right—smooth part of right atrium (**sinus venarum**) Left—coronary sinus Oblique vein of left atrium

ATRIAL SEPTUM

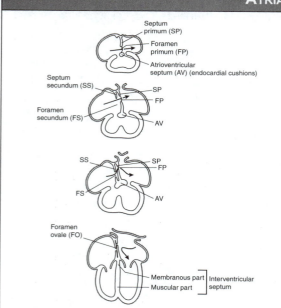

Atrial septal defects are called **ASDs**.

Secundum-type ASDs are caused by excessive resorption of the SP or reduced size of the SS or both. This results in an opening between the right and left atria. If the ASD is small, clinical symptoms may be delayed as late as age 30. This is the most clinically significant ASD.

The **foramen ovale** (FO) is the fetal communication between the right and left atria. It remains patent in up to 25% of normal individuals throughout life, although paradoxical emboli may pass through a large patent FO. **Premature closure of the FO** is the closure of the FO during prenatal life. This results in hypertrophy of the right side of the heart and underdevelopment of the left side.

VENTRICULAR SEPTUM

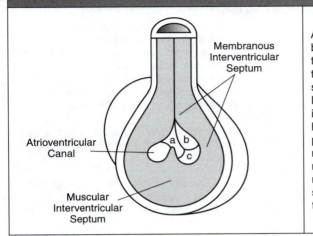

Membranous Interventricular Septum

Atrioventricular Canal

Muscular Interventricular Septum

A **membranous ventricular septal defect (VSD)** is caused by the failure of the membranous interventricular septum to develop, and it results in **left-to-right shunting** of blood through the interventricular foramen. Patients with left-to-right shunting complain of **excessive fatigue upon exertion**. Left-to-right shunting of blood is not cyanotic but causes increased blood flow and pressure to the lungs (pulmonary hypertension). Pulmonary hypertension causes marked proliferation of the tunica intima and media of pulmonary muscular arteries and arterioles. Ultimately, the pulmonary resistance becomes higher than systemic resistance and causes **right-to-left shunting** of blood and "late" **cyanosis**. At this stage, the condition is called **Eisenmenger complex**. VSD is the most common congenital cardiac anomaly.

Figure legend: a, right bulbar ridge; b, left bulbar ridge; c, AV cushions.

AORTICOPULMONARY SEPTUM

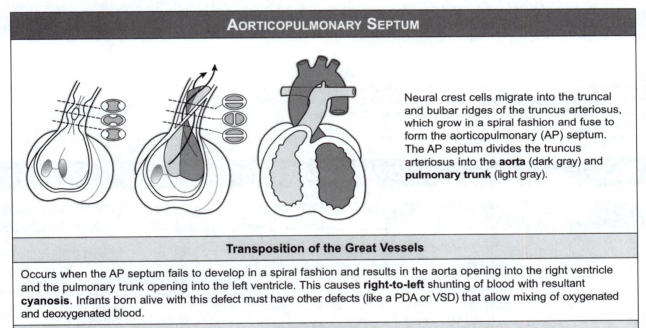

Neural crest cells migrate into the truncal and bulbar ridges of the truncus arteriosus, which grow in a spiral fashion and fuse to form the aorticopulmonary (AP) septum. The AP septum divides the truncus arteriosus into the **aorta** (dark gray) and **pulmonary trunk** (light gray).

Transposition of the Great Vessels

Occurs when the AP septum fails to develop in a spiral fashion and results in the aorta opening into the right ventricle and the pulmonary trunk opening into the left ventricle. This causes **right-to-left** shunting of blood with resultant **cyanosis**. Infants born alive with this defect must have other defects (like a PDA or VSD) that allow mixing of oxygenated and deoxygenated blood.

Tetralogy of Fallot

Occurs when the AP septum fails to align properly and results in (1) pulmonary stenosis, (2) overriding aorta, (3) interventricular septal defect, and (4) right ventricular hypertrophy. This causes **right-to-left** shunting of blood with resultant "early" **cyanosis**, which is usually present at birth. Tetralogy of Fallot is the most common congenital cyanotic cardiac anomaly.

Persistent Truncus Arteriosus

Occurs when there is only partial development of the AP septum. This results in a condition in which only one large vessel leaves the heart and receives blood from both the right and left ventricles. This causes **right-to-left** shunting of blood with resultant **cyanosis**. This defect is always accompanied by membranous ventricular septal defect.

Definition of abbreviation: PDA, patent ductus arteriosus.

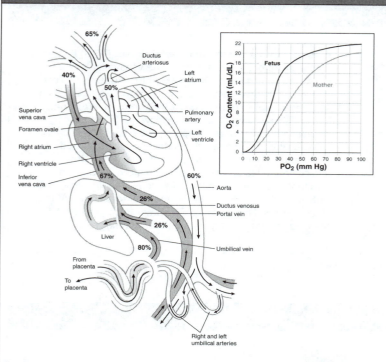

Clinical Correlation

Normally, the ductus arteriosus closes within a few hours after birth, via smooth muscle contraction, to form the ligamentum arteriosum. **Patent ductus arteriosus (PDA)** occurs when the ductus arteriosus (connection between the pulmonary trunk and aorta) fails to close after birth.

Prostaglandin E and intrauterine or neonatal asphyxia **sustain the patency** of the ductus arteriosus.

Prostaglandin inhibitors (e.g., indomethacin), acetylcholine, histamine, and catecholamines **promote closure** of the ductus arteriosus.

PDA is common in premature infants and cases of maternal rubella infection. It causes a left-to-right shunting of blood. (Note: During fetal development, the ductus arteriosus is a right-to-left shunt).

In the fetal circulation pathway, the ductus venosus allows fetal blood to bypass the liver, and the foramen ovale and the ductus arteriosus allow fetal blood to bypass the lungs. Note the sites where the oxygen saturation level of fetal blood is the highest (umbilical vein) and the lowest (ductus arteriosus).

CARDIOVASCULAR ANATOMY

STRUCTURES OF THE MEDIASTINUM

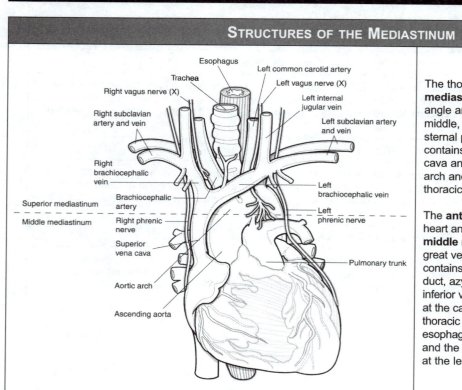

The thoracic cavity is divided into the **superior mediastinum** above the plane of the sternal angle and the **inferior mediastinum** (anterior, middle, and posterior mediastina) below that sternal plane. The superior mediastinum contains the thymic remnants, superior vena cava and its brachiocephalic tributaries, aortic arch and its branches, trachea, esophagus, thoracic duct, and the vagus and phrenic nerves.

The **anterior mediastinum** is anterior to the heart and contains remnants of the thymus. The **middle mediastinum** contains the heart and great vessels, and the **posterior mediastinum** contains the thoracic aorta, esophagus, thoracic duct, azygos veins, and the vagus nerves. The inferior vena cava passes through the diaphragm at the caval hiatus at the level of the eighth thoracic vertebra; the esophagus through the esophageal hiatus at the tenth thoracic vertebra; and the aorta courses through the aortic hiatus at the level of the twelfth thoracic vertebra.

ARTERIAL SUPPLY TO THE HEART

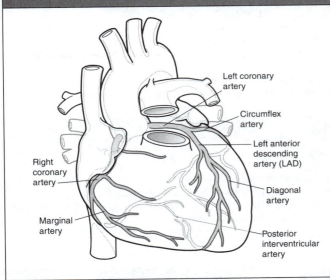

Left coronary artery

Circumflex artery

Left anterior descending artery (LAD)

Right coronary artery

Diagonal artery

Marginal artery

Posterior interventricular artery

Arterial supply to the heart muscle is provided by the **right and left coronary arteries**, which are branches of the ascending aorta. The **right coronary artery** supplies the right atrium, the right ventricle, the sinoatrial and atrioventricular nodes, and parts of the left atrium and left ventricle. The distal branch of the right coronary artery (in 70% of subjects) is the **posterior interventricular artery** that supplies, in part, the posterior aspect of the interventricular septum. The **left coronary artery** supplies most of the left ventricle, the left atrium, and the anterior part of the interventricular septum. The two main branches of the left coronary artery are the anterior interventricular artery (LAD) and the circumflex artery.

In a myocardial infarction, the LAD is obstructed in 50% of cases; the right coronary in 30%, and the circumflex artery in 20% of cases.

CHAMBERS AND VALVES OF THE HEART

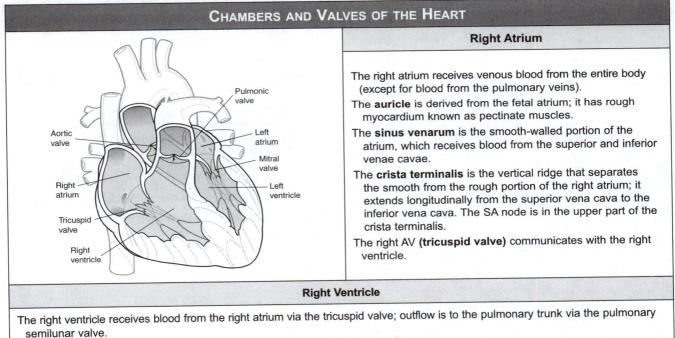

Pulmonic valve

Aortic valve

Left atrium

Mitral valve

Right atrium

Left ventricle

Tricuspid valve

Right ventricle

Right Atrium

- The right atrium receives venous blood from the entire body (except for blood from the pulmonary veins).
- The **auricle** is derived from the fetal atrium; it has rough myocardium known as pectinate muscles.
- The **sinus venarum** is the smooth-walled portion of the atrium, which receives blood from the superior and inferior venae cavae.
- The **crista terminalis** is the vertical ridge that separates the smooth from the rough portion of the right atrium; it extends longitudinally from the superior vena cava to the inferior vena cava. The SA node is in the upper part of the crista terminalis.
- The right AV (**tricuspid valve**) communicates with the right ventricle.

Right Ventricle

- The right ventricle receives blood from the right atrium via the tricuspid valve; outflow is to the pulmonary trunk via the pulmonary semilunar valve.
- The **trabeculae carneae** are the ridges of myocardium in the ventricular wall.
- The **papillary muscles** project into the cavity of the ventricle and attach to cusps of the AV valve by the strands of the chordae tendineae. Papillary muscles contract during ventricular contraction to keep the cusps of the AV valves closed.
- The **chordae tendineae** control closure of the valve during contraction of the ventricle.
- The **infundibulum** is the smooth area of the right ventricle leading to the pulmonary valve.

Left Atrium

- The left atrium receives oxygenated blood from the lungs via the pulmonary veins. There are four openings: the upper right and left and the lower right and left pulmonary veins.
- The left AV orifice is guarded by the **mitral (bicuspid) valve**; it allows oxygenated blood to pass from the left atrium to the left ventricle.

(Continued)

CHAMBERS AND VALVES OF THE HEART (CONT'D.)

Left Ventricle

Blood enters from the left atrium through the mitral valve and is pumped out to the aorta through the aortic valve.

Trabeculae carneae, the ridges of myocardium in the ventricular wall, are normally three times thicker than those of the right ventricle.

Papillary muscles (usually two large ones) are attached by the chordae tendineae to the cusps of the bicuspid valve.

The **aortic vestibule** leads to the aortic semilunar valve and ascending aorta; the right and left coronary arteries originate from the right and left aortic sinuses at the root of the ascending aorta.

Clinical Correlation

Murmurs

Murmurs in valvular heart disease result when there is valvular insufficiency or a stenotic valve. For most of **ventricular systole**, the mitral valve should be closed and the aortic valve should be open, so that "common systolic valvular defects" include mitral insufficiency and aortic stenosis. For most of **ventricular diastole**, the mitral valve should be open and the aortic valve should be closed, so that "common diastolic valvular defects" include mitral stenosis and aortic insufficiency.

BORDERS OF THE HEART

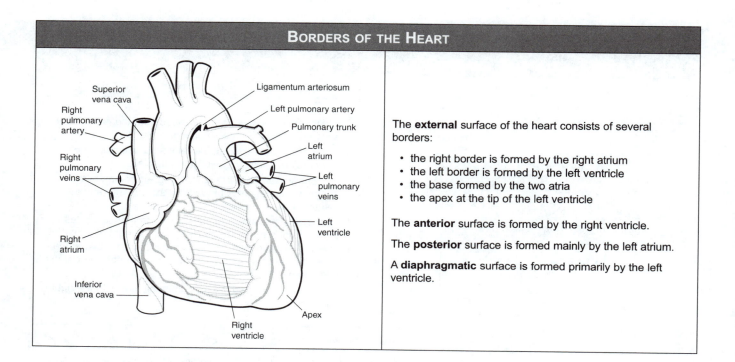

The **external** surface of the heart consists of several borders:

- the right border is formed by the right atrium
- the left border is formed by the left ventricle
- the base formed by the two atria
- the apex at the tip of the left ventricle

The **anterior** surface is formed by the right ventricle.

The **posterior** surface is formed mainly by the left atrium.

A **diaphragmatic** surface is formed primarily by the left ventricle.

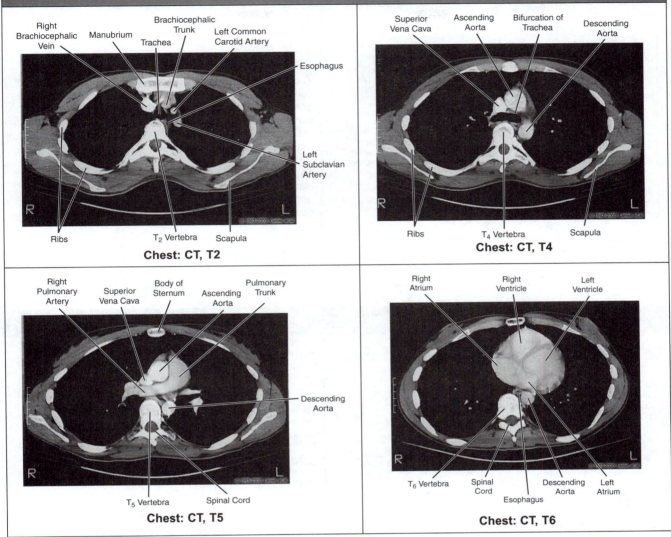

Chest: CT, T2

Right Brachiocephalic Vein — Manubrium — Trachea — Brachiocephalic Trunk — Left Common Carotid Artery — Esophagus — Left Subclavian Artery — Ribs — T2 Vertebra — Scapula

Chest: CT, T4

Superior Vena Cava — Ascending Aorta — Bifurcation of Trachea — Descending Aorta — Ribs — T4 Vertebra — Scapula

Chest: CT, T5

Right Pulmonary Artery — Superior Vena Cava — Body of Sternum — Ascending Aorta — Pulmonary Trunk — Descending Aorta — T5 Vertebra — Spinal Cord

Chest: CT, T6

Right Atrium — Right Ventricle — Left Ventricle — Descending Aorta — Left Atrium — Esophagus — Spinal Cord — T6 Vertebra

CONDUCTING SYSTEM OF THE HEART

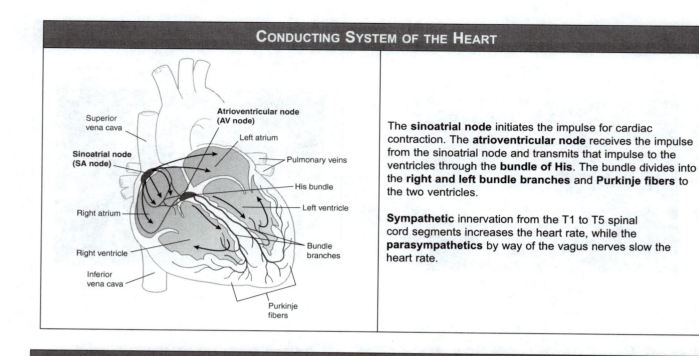

The **sinoatrial node** initiates the impulse for cardiac contraction. The **atrioventricular node** receives the impulse from the sinoatrial node and transmits that impulse to the ventricles through the **bundle of His**. The bundle divides into the **right and left bundle branches** and **Purkinje fibers** to the two ventricles.

Sympathetic innervation from the T1 to T5 spinal cord segments increases the heart rate, while the **parasympathetics** by way of the vagus nerves slow the heart rate.

ASSOCIATIONS OF COMMON TRAUMATIC INJURIES WITH VESSEL AND NERVE DAMAGE

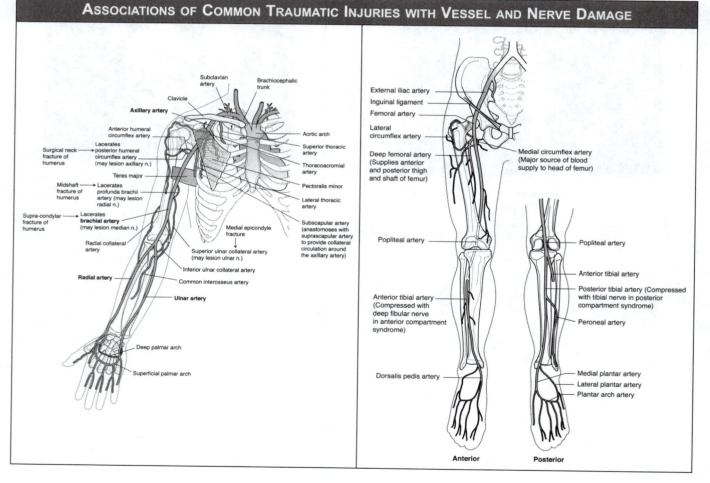

COMPARISON OF CARDIAC ACTION POTENTIALS

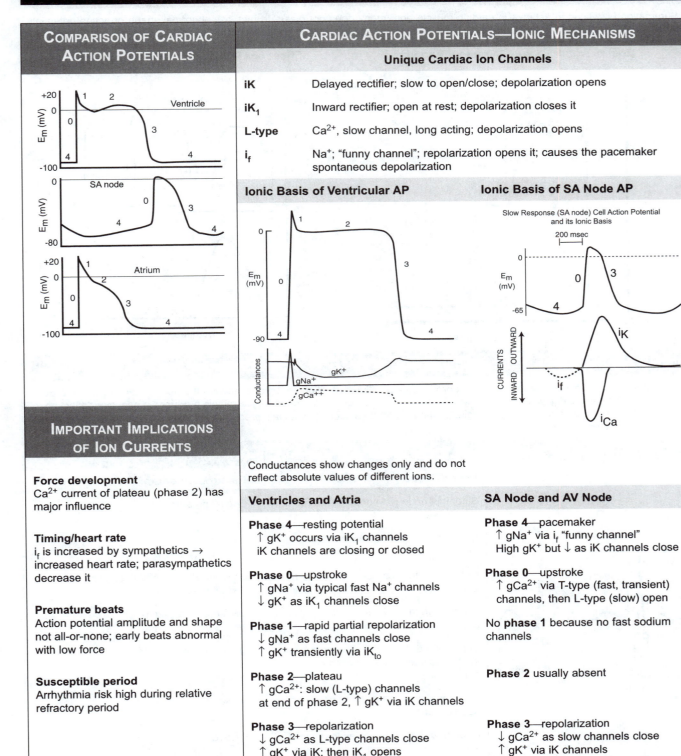

IMPORTANT IMPLICATIONS OF ION CURRENTS

Force development
Ca^{2+} current of plateau (phase 2) has major influence

Timing/heart rate
i_f is increased by sympathetics → increased heart rate; parasympathetics decrease it

Premature beats
Action potential amplitude and shape not all-or-none; early beats abnormal with low force

Susceptible period
Arrhythmia risk high during relative refractory period

CARDIAC ACTION POTENTIALS—IONIC MECHANISMS

Unique Cardiac Ion Channels

iK	Delayed rectifier; slow to open/close; depolarization opens
iK_1	Inward rectifier; open at rest; depolarization closes it
L-type	Ca^{2+}, slow channel, long acting; depolarization opens
i_f	Na^+; "funny channel"; repolarization opens it; causes the pacemaker spontaneous depolarization

Ionic Basis of Ventricular AP

Ionic Basis of SA Node AP

Conductances show changes only and do not reflect absolute values of different ions.

Ventricles and Atria

Phase 4—resting potential
↑ gK^+ occurs via iK_1 channels
iK channels are closing or closed

Phase 0—upstroke
↑ gNa^+ via typical fast Na^+ channels
↓ gK^+ as iK_1 channels close

Phase 1—rapid partial repolarization
↓ gNa^+ as fast channels close
↑ gK^+ transiently via iK_{to}

Phase 2—plateau
↑ gCa^{2+}: slow (L-type) channels
at end of phase 2, ↑ gK^+ via iK channels

Phase 3—repolarization
↓ gCa^{2+} as L-type channels close
↑ gK^+ via iK; then iK_1 opens

SA Node and AV Node

Phase 4—pacemaker
↑ gNa^+ via i_f "funny channel"
High gK^+ but ↓ as iK channels close

Phase 0—upstroke
↑ gCa^{2+} via T-type (fast, transient) channels, then L-type (slow) open

No **phase 1** because no fast sodium channels

Phase 2 usually absent

Phase 3—repolarization
↓ gCa^{2+} as slow channels close
↑ gK^+ via iK channels

REFRACTORY PERIODS

Summation is difficult to achieve in cardiac muscle and tetany does not occur. In fact, the abnormal shape of action potentials initiated during the relative refractory period reduces calcium influx and thus contractile force, as shown.

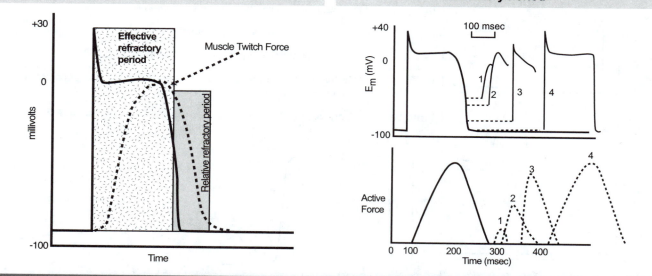

Muscle Twitch Versus Refractory Periods

Effect of AP Initiation During the Relative Refractory Period

BASIC PRINCIPLES OF THE ELECTROCARDIOGRAM

A moving wave of depolarization in the heart produces a positive deflection as it moves toward the positive terminals of the ECG electrodes. A depolarizing wave moving away from the positive (toward the negative) terminals produces a negative deflection. A wave of depolarization moving at right angles to the axis of the electrode terminals produces no deflection. Upon repolarization, the reverse occurs.

SEQUENCE OF MYOCARDIAL EXCITATION AND CONDUCTION

Event/Tissue	Electrocardiogram
Sinoatrial node (SA) depolarizes (primary pacemaker)	Beginning of P wave
Conduction of depolarization through atrial muscle	P wave
Conduction through atrioventricular node (AV)	Between P wave and QRS complex (PR interval)
Conduction through His-Purkinje system and ventricular septum	QRS complex begins
Ventricular depolarization apex to base; septum to lateral wall; endocardial to epicardial	QRS complex
Ventricles are in the plateau phase of depolarization	ST segment
Repolarization of ventricles in reverse sequence	T wave

Important ECG Values

PR interval	0.12–0.20 sec	Length measures AV conduction time
QRS duration	<0.12 sec	Measures ventricular conduction time
QT interval	0.35–0.45 sec	Total time of ventricular depolarization and repolarization Varies with heart rate, age
Heart rate, normal resting	60–100 beats/min	<60/min = bradycardia; >100/min = tachycardia

PRINCIPLES OF THE ELECTROCARDIOGRAM (EKG OR ECG)

Moving Electrical Charge		Creates Electrical Field Movement That Causes Ion Currents in Skin
Standard limb leads (frontal plane)	I	$\ominus$ right arm; $\oplus$ left arm; positive lead at 0°
	II	$\ominus$ right arm; $\oplus$ left leg; positive lead at +60°
	III	$\ominus$ left arm; $\oplus$ left leg; positive lead at +120°
Augmented limb leads (frontal plane)	aVR; aVL, aVF	aVR positive lead at –150°; aVL positive lead at –30°; aVF positive lead at +90°
Precordial	V_1–V_6 (chest)	Horizontal plane; positive leads front; negative leads back of chest
Chart speed	25 mm/sec	Each horizontal mm = 0.04 sec (40 msec)
Voltage	1 mV/10 mm	Measure ± voltages of QRS, add to get net voltage of each lead
Mean electrical axis	Vector sum of two leads	Measure of overall wave of ventricular depolarization: normal axis, left or right axis deviation

Four intervals = 75 beats/min
OR
Four beats in 3 sec = 4 X 20 = 80 beats/min

Estimation of Heart Rate

Triplet Method

How many dark lines are between R waves (5 mm apart)?
1 = 300/min; 2 = 150; 3 = 100; 4 = 75; 5 = 60; 6 = 50

Interval

Measure time interval (longer interval is better)
Count R waves
Multiply count to convert to 1 minute
   e.g., four R waves in 3 sec = 4 × 20 = 80 beats/min

IMPORTANT RHYTHMS TO RECOGNIZE

Rhythm	Characteristics

Sinus rhythm
    Normal   rate = 60–100
    Bradycardia   rate <60
    Tachycardia   rate >100
	Each beat originates in the SA node; therefore, the P wave precedes each QRS complex; PR interval is normal

AV conduction block	Abnormal conduction through AV node
First degree	PR interval (> 0.20 sec); 1:1 correspondence; P wave:R wave
Second degree Mobitz I (Wenckebach)	Progressively increased PR interval; then dropped (missing) QRS and then repeat of sequence
Second degree Mobitz II	Regular but prolonged PR interval; unexpected dropped QRS; may be a regular pattern, such as 2:1 = 2 P waves:1 QRS complex or 3:1, etc.
Third degree (complete)	No correlation of P waves and QRS complexes; usually high atrial rate and lower ventricular rate
Premature ventricular contraction (PVC)	Large, wide QRS complex originates in ectopic focus of irritability in ventricle; may indicate hypoxia
Ventricular tachycardia	Repeated large, wide QRS complexes like PVCs; Rate 150–250/min; acts like prolonged sequence of PVCs
Ventricular fibrillation	Total loss of rhythmic contraction; totally erratic shape

EVOLUTION OF AN INFARCTION: SIGNS ON THE EKG

Features to observe	QRS complex	Presence of prominent Q waves in leads where normally absent: infarct damage
	ST segment	Elevation or depression: acute injury
	T wave	Inversion; e.g., downward in lead where usually positive: acute ischemia
Acute myocardial infarction (MI)	Minutes to a few days	ST segment elevation or depression Inverted T waves Prominent Q waves
Resolving infarction (healing)	Weeks to months	Inverted T waves Prominent Q waves
Stable (old) MI	Months to years	Prominent Q waves as result of MI persist for the rest of life

Caution: Not all infarctions produce Q waves. Inverted T waves and/or ST abnormalities should always be investigated, even in absence of significant Q waves.

MEAN ELECTRICAL AXIS (MEA)

Definition	• Overall direction and force (vector) of the events of ventricular depolarization: obtained by vector sum of net voltage of two leads or by quadrant method using leads I and aVF • MEA tends to shift toward large mass and away from an MI
Normal axis	• Expected in the absence of cardiac disease • R wave: lead I, +; lead II, +; lead III, +
Left axis deviation	• May indicate left heart enlargement, as in hypertrophy or left dilated failure • Abnormally prolonged (slow) left ventricular conduction • Right heart MI, expiration, obesity, lying down • R wave: lead I, +; lead II, +; lead III, −
Right axis deviation	• Right ventricular hypertrophy or dilation • Prolonged right conduction • Left heart MI, inspiration, tall lanky people, standing up • R wave: lead I, −; lead II, +; lead III, +
Extreme right axis deviation	Difficult interpretation; one example: depolarization proceeding from abnormal focus in LV apex

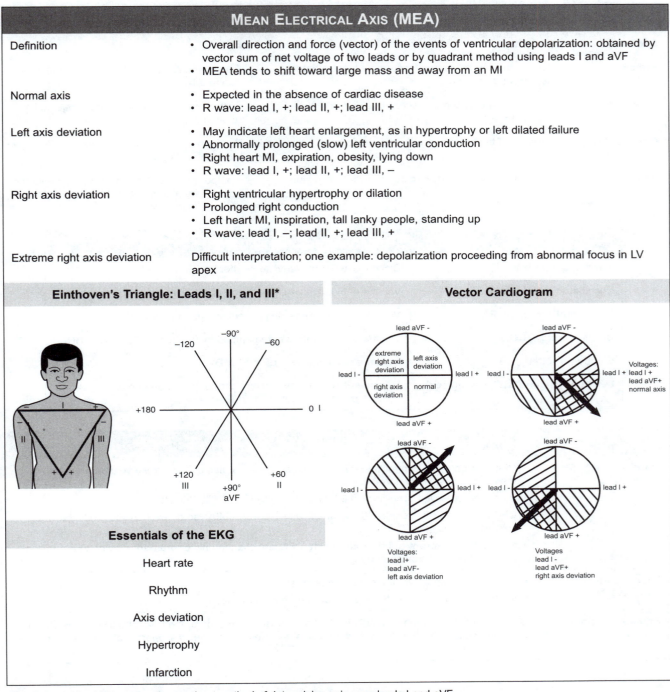

Einthoven's Triangle: Leads I, II, and III*

Vector Cardiogram

Essentials of the EKG

Heart rate

Rhythm

Axis deviation

Hypertrophy

Infarction

*The figure adds aVF because the quadrant method of determining axis uses leads I and aVF.

CARDIAC MECHANICAL PERFORMANCE

Factor	Definition	Effects
Preload	Cardiac muscle cell length (sarcomere length) **before contraction begins**	↑ preload causes ↑ active force development up to a limit
Afterload	Load on the heart during ejection of blood from the ventricle	↑ afterload ↓ the volume of blood ejected during a beat
Contractility	Capacity of the heart to produce active force at a specified preload	High contractility ↑ ability to work Low contractility ↓ ability to work
Rate	Heart rate (HR): number of cardiac cycles per minute	↑ output of blood per minute, but ↓ output per beat; very high rate (>≈150/min) ↓ output

CARDIAC PERFORMANCE: DEFINITIONS

Stroke volume (SV)	Blood ejected from ventricle per beat = EDV − ESV
End diastolic volume (EDV)	Volume of blood in ventricle at end of diastole; the preload
End systolic volume (ESV)	Volume of blood remaining in ventricle at end of systole
Cardiac output (CO)	Volume of blood per minute pumped by the heart; CO = SV × HR
Ejection fraction (EF)	Measure of contractility: EF = SV/EDV
Left ventricular dP/dT (mm Hg/sec)	Measure of contractility: maximum rate of change of pressure during isovolumic contraction

CARDIAC AND VASCULAR FUNCTION CURVES

Cardiac function curve (CFC)	• CFC generated by controlling preload and measuring cardiac output, stroke volume or other measure of systolic performance • ↑ preload improves actin-myosin interdigitation and thus ↑ SV, CO, etc. • CFC shifts **up** with ↑ **contractility; down** with ↓ **contractility**; so a new curve is produced when contractility changes • Moving to a **different point on the same CFC** is a change only of **preload**: moving to a **different CFC** is change of **contractility**
Vascular function curve (VFC)	• VFC relates venous return to right atrial pressure • ↑ **blood volume shifts VFC up,** ↓ **volume shifts VFC down**
Equilibrium point	Cardiac output is determined by both CFC and VFC. Intersection of the CFC and VFC is the stable operating point; if contractility or blood volume changes, the system will operate at the intersection of the two new curves.

CARDIAC AND VASCULAR FUNCTION CURVES: EXAMPLES

Stability of Typical CFC and VFC

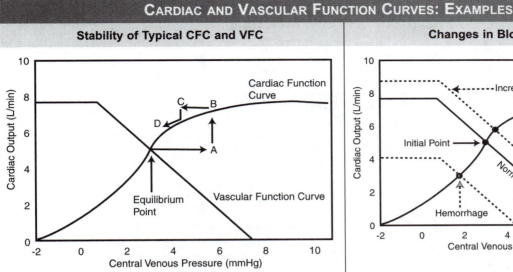

Diagram shows that cardiac output (CO, 5 L/min) changes only transiently when CFC and VFC are not changed. **Point A:** venous pressure is increased from 3 to 6 mm Hg because of sudden removal of blood from arterial system and injection into venous system. This causes **CO** to increase to **point B**. CO then returns to **equilibrium point** in steps (B → C, C → D) as blood is pumped from venous system back to arterial system.

Changes in Blood Volume

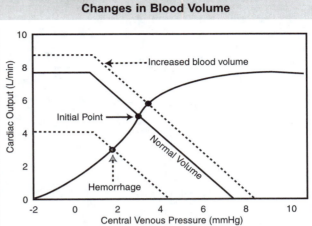

Increased blood volume (e.g., transfusion) shifts the VFC upward, which increases preload. Increased CO follows. Decreased blood volume (e.g., hemorrhage) shifts the VFC downward, which decreases preload. Decreased CO follows. Increases and decreases in preload produce increases and decreases in CO by the **Frank-Starling** mechanism.

Sympathetic Stimulation of Heart

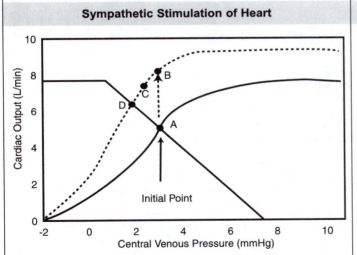

Increased contractility by cardiac sympathetic nerve stimulation shifts the CFC upward *(dashed line)*; however, this does not change the VFC. The initial large increase in CO *(point B)* returns to **point D** on the VFC as blood is transferred from the venous system to the arterial system.

Changes in CO After Heart Failure

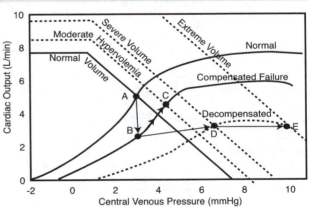

Reduced contractility shifts CO down **(point B)**, but preload immediately increases to intersect with the normal volume curve as shown. Within hours to days, blood volume increases, shifting VFC upward, and **point C** becomes the equilibrium point. With progressive failure, blood volume cannot increase enough to maintain CO at a normal level. **(point D)**. Blood volume continues to increase, which overstretches the heart **(point E)**.

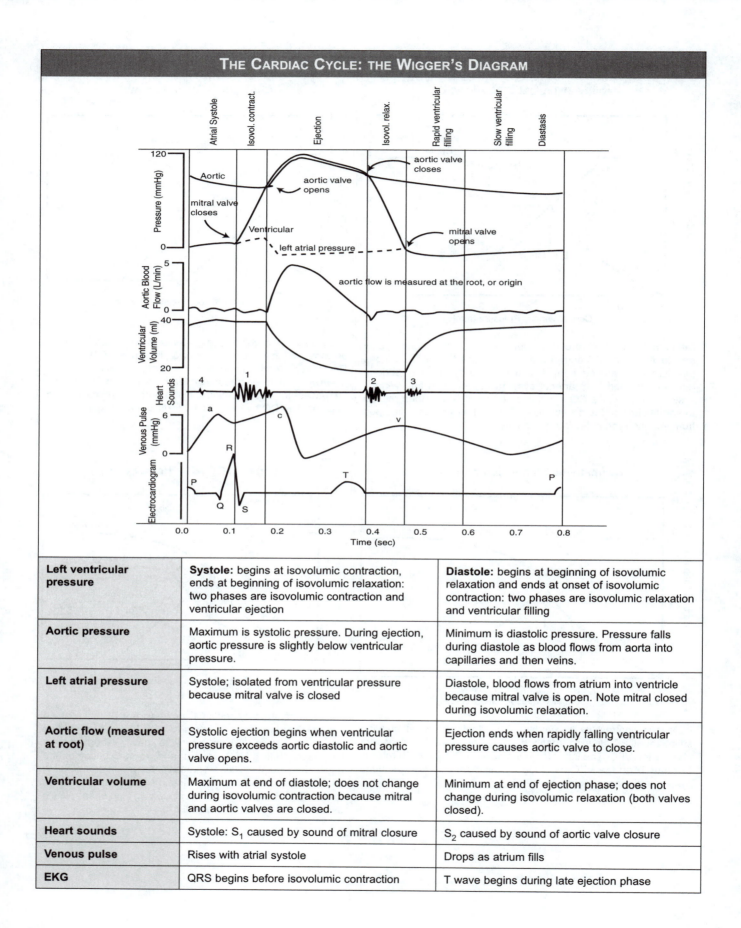

THE CARDIAC CYCLE: THE WIGGER'S DIAGRAM

Left ventricular pressure	**Systole:** begins at isovolumic contraction, ends at beginning of isovolumic relaxation: two phases are isovolumic contraction and ventricular ejection	**Diastole:** begins at beginning of isovolumic relaxation and ends at onset of isovolumic contraction: two phases are isovolumic relaxation and ventricular filling
Aortic pressure	Maximum is systolic pressure. During ejection, aortic pressure is slightly below ventricular pressure.	Minimum is diastolic pressure. Pressure falls during diastole as blood flows from aorta into capillaries and then veins.
Left atrial pressure	Systole; isolated from ventricular pressure because mitral valve is closed	Diastole, blood flows from atrium into ventricle because mitral valve is open. Note mitral closed during isovolumic relaxation.
Aortic flow (measured at root)	Systolic ejection begins when ventricular pressure exceeds aortic diastolic and aortic valve opens.	Ejection ends when rapidly falling ventricular pressure causes aortic valve to close.
Ventricular volume	Maximum at end of diastole; does not change during isovolumic contraction because mitral and aortic valves are closed.	Minimum at end of ejection phase; does not change during isovolumic relaxation (both valves closed).
Heart sounds	Systole: S_1 caused by sound of mitral closure	S_2 caused by sound of aortic valve closure
Venous pulse	Rises with atrial systole	Drops as atrium fills
EKG	QRS begins before isovolumic contraction	T wave begins during late ejection phase

CARDIAC PRESSURE–VOLUME LOOPS (PV LOOPS)

Phase	Pressure	Volume
Filling	Slightly ↑	Large ↑; point C = EDV
Isovolumic contraction	Rapid ↑; maximum dp/dt	No change, valves closed
Ejection	Continues to rise	↓ as ejection proceeds
Isovolumic relaxation	Rapid ↓	No change, valves closed

Applications

Area within loop = stroke work output	Increase work by ↑ stroke volume (volume work) or by ↑ LVP (pressure work)
Decreased blood volume (hemorrhage, dehydration, urination)	Line C–D shift left (↓ preload); ↓ stroke volume ↓ stroke work
Increase in contractility (sympathetics, or β-adrenergic drugs, digitalis)	Line F–A shifts left (↓ ESV) a major effect; slight ↓ EDV; overall ↑ stroke volume, ↑ stroke work
Decreased contractility, as in heart failure	Loop shifts to right and systolic pressure is lower: ↑↑ ESV, ↑ EDP, ↓ SV, ↓ stroke work
Volume expansion (normal heart)	Line C–D shifts right (↑ EDV); ↑ SV; ↑ stroke work

Normal PV Curve

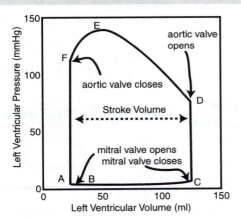

A–B: rapid filling
B–C: reduced or slower filling
C: end diastolic volume (EDV)
C–D: isovolumic contraction

D–F: ejection phase
F: end systolic volume (ESV)
F–A: isovolumic relaxation

- Area within loop = **stroke work**
- Increase work by ↑ stroke volume (volume work) or by ↑ LVP (pressure work)

Blood Volume Changes

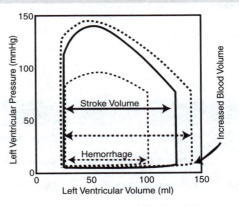

- **Decreased blood volume** (hemorrhage, dehydration): Line C–D shifts **left** (↓ preload); ↓ stroke volume, ↓ stroke work
- **Volume expansion** (normal heart): Line C–D shifts **right** (↑ EDV), ↑ SV, ↑ stroke work

(Continued)

CARDIAC PRESSURE–VOLUME LOOPS (PV LOOPS; CONT'D.)

Increased Afterload

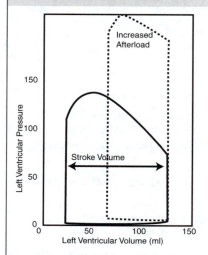

With increased afterload (e.g., ↑ aortic pressure), the velocity of shortening and the distance shortened are both decreased. Thus, ESV increases, causing SV to decrease.

Decreased Afterload

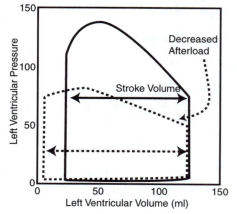

Decreased afterload produces the opposite changes as increased afterload. Thus, ESV decreases and SV increases.

Progressive Heart Failure

A: Normal

B: Acute loss of contractility without compensation

C: Compensated LV failure (SV partially restored because of moderate increase in preload)

D: Decompensated failure (SV remains low despite ↑↑↑ in preload)

Overall: Curves shift to the right and systolic pressures ↓.

Heart failure: ↑↑↑ ESV, ↑ EDV, ↓ SV, ↓ stroke work

THE CARDIAC VALVES

Mitral	Between LA and LV	Open during filling	Closed during ventricular systole and isovolumic relaxation
Aortic	Between LV and aorta	Open during ejection	Closed during diastole and isovolumic contraction
Tricuspid	Between RA and RV	Open during filling	Closed during ventricular systole and isovolumic relaxation
Pulmonic	Between RV and pulmonary artery	Open during ejection	Closed during diastole and isovolumic contraction

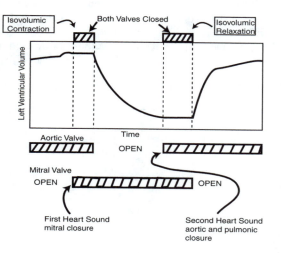

VALVULAR DISORDERS

Aortic Stenosis

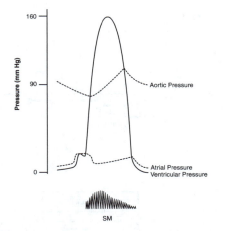

- Discrepancy of systolic LV and systolic aortic pressures
- Causes crescendo-decrescendo systolic murmur

Aortic Regurgitation

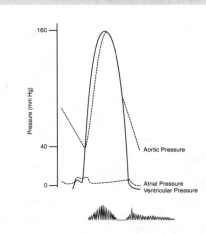

- Diastolic aortic decreases rapidly as blood flows back into ventricle; ventricular diastolic is elevated.
- Causes diastolic murmur

Mitral Valve Stenosis

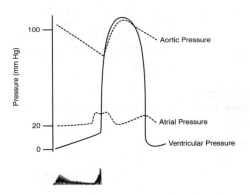

- Discrepancy of diastolic LVP and left atrial P during filling
- Causes diastolic murmur

Mitral Regurgitation

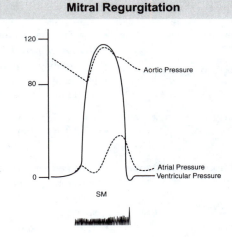

- Incompetent valve allows backflow into left atrium during ventricular systole
- Causes systolic murmur

Definition of abbreviation: SM, systolic murmur.

HEMODYNAMICS	
Poiseuille's equation: $Q = (P_1 - P_2)/R$	• Flow (Q); P_1 (input pressure); P_2 (output pressure); R (resistance); $(P_1 - P_2)$ = pressure gradient • $\uparrow$ pressure gradient $\rightarrow$ $\uparrow$ flow • $\uparrow$ resistance $\rightarrow$ $\downarrow$ flow
Series circuits: $R_T = R_1 + R_2 + R_3 \ldots R_n$	• R_T = total resistance • Flow is equal at all points in series circuit; pressure drops across each resistor • **Adding more resistors in series increases R_T.** Pressure drop increases along circuit with constant flow, and flow decreases with constant input pressure (P_1). • Various types of blood vessels lie in series.
Parallel circuits: $l/R_T = 1/R_1 + 1/R_2 + 1/R_3 \ldots 1/R_n$	• Flow divided between parallel resistors • R_T is always lower than the lowest resistor • **Adding more resistors in parallel decreases R_T.** • Produces low resistance circuit • Organs lie in parallel
Hydraulic Resistance Equation: $R = (P_1 - P_2)/Q = 8\eta l/\pi r^4$	• η = viscosity; l = length; r = radius • **Viscosity $\uparrow$ by $\uparrow$ hematocrit** • **Viscosity $\downarrow$ in anemia** • l is usually constant; r changes greatly for normal regulation and in disease. • 2× radius = 1/16 R $\rightarrow$ 16 × flow • ½ radius = 16 × R $\rightarrow$ 1/16 × flow • **Control of radius is the dominant mechanism to control resistance.**
Total peripheral resistance (TPR)	• Resistance of peripheral circuit: aorta $\rightarrow$ right atrium • **TPR $\uparrow$ by sympathetics, angiotensin II, and other vasoconstrictors** • Highest TPRs in **arterioles**; also main site of blood flow regulation
Total peripheral resistance equation **TPR = (MAP – RAP)/CO**	• Mean arterial pressure (MAP); right atrial pressure (RAP) • Pressure gradient is between aorta and right atrium. • TPR is calculated from MAP and cardiac output (CO). RAP is assumed to be 0 mm Hg, unless specified. • TPR is also known as SVR (systemic vascular resistance)
Compliance (C): $C = \Delta V / \Delta P$ **Pulse pressure (PP):** **PP = SP – DP**	• ΔV = volume change; ΔP = pressure change • High **compliance** means vessels easily distended by blood. • **Elasticity** is inverse of compliance; vessels are stiff when elasticity is high • SP = systolic pressure; DP = diastolic pressure $\downarrow$ compliance (e.g., arteriosclerosis) $\rightarrow$ $\uparrow$ SP and $\downarrow$ DP, so PP $\uparrow$ • **Compliance:** systemic veins > pulmonary circuit > systemic arteries (volume of blood is in same order) • **MAP = diastolic + 1/3 (pulse pressure)** • MAP = 80 + 1/3(120 – 80) = 80 = 13 = 93 mm Hg

(Continued)

HEMODYNAMICS (*CONT'D.*)

Cardiac output (Fick method)	$CO = \dot{V}O_2/(Ca - Cv)$ $\dot{V}O_2$ = oxygen consumption, Ca = arterial oxygen content, Cv = venous oxygen content	Used to measure cardiac output; most accurate if Ca is pulmonary venous and Cv is pulmonary arterial

AREA-VELOCITY RELATIONSHIP

- $V \propto 1/\text{cross sectional area}$
- $V \propto 1/r^2$,
- V = velocity; r = radius

- **Assuming total flow is equal in all vessel types, velocity increases as radius decreases.**

- **The aorta is a single large vessel, but its total area is small compared with numerous capillaries in parallel.**

- If low capillary velocity allows adequate time for diffusion, exchange is **perfusion limited**.

- If velocity is high, metabolic exchange may become **diffusion limited**.

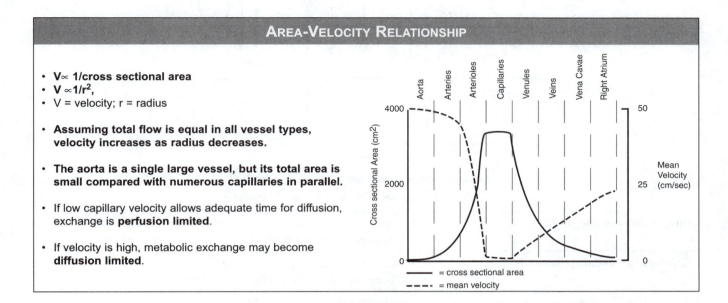

PRESSURES OF THE CARDIOVASCULAR SYSTEM

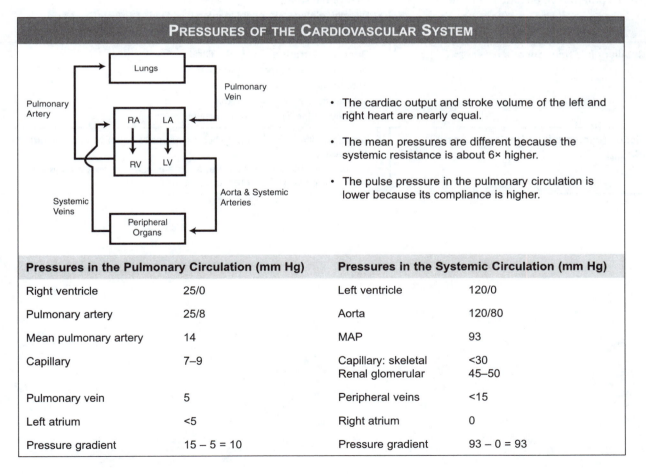

- The cardiac output and stroke volume of the left and right heart are nearly equal.

- The mean pressures are different because the systemic resistance is about 6× higher.

- The pulse pressure in the pulmonary circulation is lower because its compliance is higher.

Pressures in the Pulmonary Circulation (mm Hg)		Pressures in the Systemic Circulation (mm Hg)	
Right ventricle	25/0	Left ventricle	120/0
Pulmonary artery	25/8	Aorta	120/80
Mean pulmonary artery	14	MAP	93
Capillary	7–9	Capillary: skeletal Renal glomerular	<30 45–50
Pulmonary vein	5	Peripheral veins	<15
Left atrium	<5	Right atrium	0
Pressure gradient	15 – 5 = 10	Pressure gradient	93 – 0 = 93

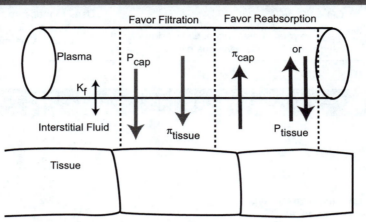

Filtration = K_f (forces favor − forces opposed)

Filtration = $K_f [(P_{capillary} + \pi_{tissue}) − (P_{tissue} + \pi_{capillary})]$

Ultrafiltration coefficient (K_f)	• Related to surface area, capillary porosity; different in each tissue/organ • Determines amount of ultrafiltration to given filtration pressure
Capillary hydrostatic pressure (P_{cap})	• **Favors filtration;** $\uparrow P_{cap} \rightarrow \uparrow$ filtration • Controlled by input pressure, arteriolar diameter, venous pressure
Tissue (interstitial) oncotic pressure (π_{tissue})	• **Favors filtration;** $\uparrow \pi_{tissue} \rightarrow \uparrow$ filtration • Directly related to [protein] in interstitial fluid • **Example:** $\uparrow$ permeability (e.g., sepsis) $\rightarrow \uparrow \pi_{tissue} \rightarrow \uparrow$ filtration

Capillary (plasma) oncotic pressure (π_{cap})	• **Opposes filtration;** $\uparrow \pi_{cap} \rightarrow \downarrow$ filtration
	• Directly related to [protein] in plasma
	• **Examples:**
	  – Liver failure $\downarrow \pi_{cap} \rightarrow$ edema
	  – Dehydration $\uparrow \pi_{cap} \rightarrow$ reabsorption

Tissue (interstitial) hydrostatic pressure (P_{tissue})	• Increases filtration when negative (is normally negative in many but not all tissues) • Opposes filtration when positive; edema causes positive pressure in interstitium, even when pressure is normally negative.

Factors That Alter Capillary Flow and Pressure

	Resistance	Capillary Flow	Capillary Pressure	Example
Arteriole dilation	↓	↑	↑	β-adrenergic agonist, α-adrenergic blocker, decreased sympathetic nervous system activity, metabolic dilation, ACE inhibitors
Arteriole constriction	↑	↓	↓	α-adrenergic agonist, β-adrenergic blocker, increased sympathetic nervous system activity, angiotensin II
Venous dilation	↓	↑	↓	Increased metabolism of tissue
Venous constriction	↑	↓	↑	Physical compression, increased sympathetic activity
Increased arterial pressure	N	↑	↑	Increased cardiac output, volume expansion
Decreased arterial pressure	N	↓	↓	Decreased cardiac output, hemorrhage, dehydration
Increased venous pressure	N	↓	↑	Congestive heart failure, physical compression
Decreased venous pressure	N	↑	↓	Hemorrhage, dehydration

Wall Tension: Law of Laplace

$T = P \times r$	• Tension (T) in wall • ↑ **pressure and** ↑ **radius** → ↑ **tension**	
Applications	**Arterial aneurysm:** • Weak wall balloons • Vessel radius ↑, causing ↑ wall tension. • ↑ tension causes ↑ radius (vicious cycle), increasing risk of rupture **Dilated heart failure:** • ↑ ventricular volume → ↑ ventricular radius, which in turn causes ↑ wall tension. • Thus, dilated ventricle must work harder than normal heart	Aortic Aneurysm Increased radius Pressure Increased Tension Risk of dissection and rupture!

Autonomic Control of Heart and Circulation

	Sympathetic	Parasympathetic
Heart		
Transmitter-receptor	Norepinephrine: β_1-adrenergic	Acetylcholine: muscarinic
Heart rate	↑ rate (i_f and Ca^{2+} currents): ⊕ chronotropic	↓ rate (↑ gK, ↓ i_f): ⊖ chronotropic
Contractility	↑ force (dp/dt, EF): ⊕ inotropic ↑ gCa^{2+}, ↑ cAMP, ↑ Ca^{2+} release from SR, ↓ duration: fast, strong, short duration	Modest effects: ⊖ inotropic ↓cAMP; ↓gCa^{2+} mainly at very high levels of activity only
Conduction	↑ atrial and ventricular conduction ↑ conduction AV node ↓ PR interval of EKG	↓ atrial and ventricular conduction ↓ conduction AV node ↑ PR interval of EKG
Arteries/arterioles	Norepinephrine: α_1 (mainly) constriction Epinephrine (adrenal): β_2 dilation High levels: α_1 constriction	No direct innervation of vascular smooth muscle
Veins	Norepinephrine: α_1 (mainly) constriction but not usually much ↑ resistance, rather, ↓ capacitance shifts blood toward heart	No direct innervation

Control of Organ Blood Flow

Organ/Tissue	Neural	Metabolic/Other
Skeletal muscle	**Resting:** α-adrenergic constriction **Exercising:** β-adrenergic dilation (epinephrine, adrenal medulla)	• **Metabolic vasodilation dominates in exercise** • Compression during static exercise blocks flow
Skin	• Thermoregulatory center • α-adrenergic constriction only	• Heat dilates, cold constricts, a direct effect
Heart	• α-adrenergic constriction • β-adrenergic dilation • Overridden by metabolism	• **Metabolic dilation is dominant** • ↑ Cardiac work → ↑ O_2 consumption →↑ coronary flow • Compression during systole, so most coronary flow is during diastole
Brain	Not generally under neural control: autoregulation	• **Metabolism dominates:** ↑ CO_2 → dilation

Autoregulation

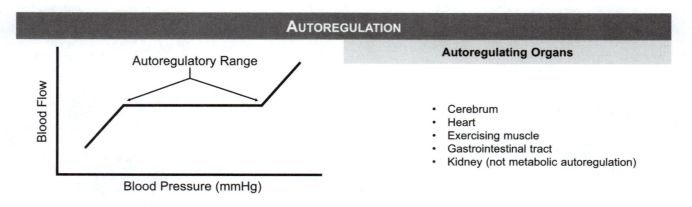

Autoregulating Organs

- Cerebrum
- Heart
- Exercising muscle
- Gastrointestinal tract
- Kidney (not metabolic autoregulation)

Basics of Integrated Control of Arterial Pressure and Cardiac Output

	Control	Major Actions
Baroreceptors: Carotid sinus (primary) Aortic arch (secondary)	↑ pressure →↑ activity ↓ pressure →↓ activity	↑ activity → ↑ PNS and ↓ SNS ↓ activity → ↓ PNS and ↑ SNS
Sympathetic (SNS)	↑ pressure → ↓ SNS ↓ pressure → ↑ SNS	• Vasoconstriction (↑ α-adrenergic) → ↑ TPR • ↑ Contractility heart (↑ β-adrenergic) → ↓ ESV → ↑ SV • ↑ Heart rate (β-adrenergic) • ↑ Cardiac output (CO)
Parasympathetic (PNS)	↑ pressure → ↑ PNS ↓ pressure → ↓ PNS	• ↓ heart rate (major); ↓ contractility (minor) • At rest, PNS dominant control of heart rate • ↓ cardiac output
Renal	↑ MAP → ↓ renin, angiotensin II (AII) ↑ MAP →↑ urination →↓ volume → ↓ preload	• AII vasoconstricts • **Renal control of blood volume and TPR dominant long-term control of blood pressure and CO**

Selected Applications of the Diagram

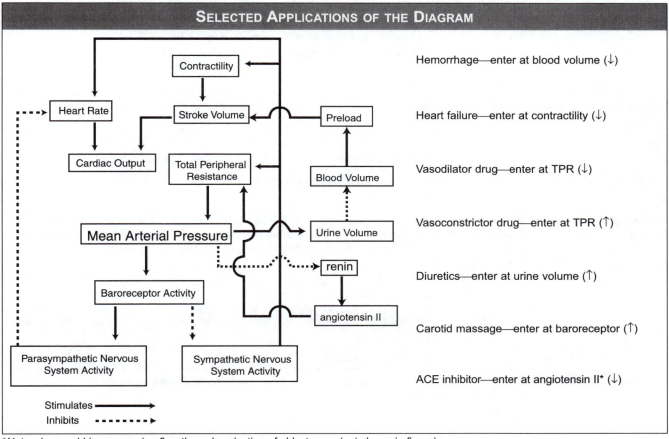

Hemorrhage—enter at blood volume (↓)

Heart failure—enter at contractility (↓)

Vasodilator drug—enter at TPR (↓)

Vasoconstrictor drug—enter at TPR (↑)

Diuretics—enter at urine volume (↑)

Carotid massage—enter at baroreceptor (↑)

ACE inhibitor—enter at angiotensin II* (↓)

Note: also would increase urine flow through reduction of aldosterone (not shown in figure)

CARDIOVASCULAR PATHOLOGY

CONGENITAL ABNORMALITIES OF THE HEART

- Congenital abnormalities occur before the end of week 16 (completion of heart development).
- Clinical significance depends on degree of shunt.
- Up to 90% of congenital heart disease is of unknown etiology.
- **Maternal rubella:** exposure at fifth to tenth week can lead to PDA, ASDs, and VSDs.
- **Fetal alcohol syndrome:** cardiovascular defects, including VSD

Acyanotic (Late Cyanosis) Congenital Heart Disease (Left-to-Right Shunts)

Initially a left-to-right shunt; causes chronic right heart failure and secondary pulmonary hypertension. Increased pressure causes **reversal of shunt flow** with late onset cyanosis: **Eisenmenger syndrome**

Ventricular septal defect (VSD)	• Usually of membranous interventricular septum • Often associated with other defects, including **trisomy 21**
Atrial septal defect (ASD)	**Ostium primum defect (5% of ASDs):** • Defect in lower atrial septum above the atrioventricular valves • Associated with anomaly of AV valves • Requires antibiotic prophylaxis for invasive procedures **Ostium secundum defects (90% of ASDs):** • Defect is in center of the atrial septum at the foramen ovale • Results from abnormalities of septum primum and/or septum secundum • AV valves normal • Antibiotic prophylaxis not needed
Complete endocardial cushion defect	Combination of ASD, VSD, and a common atrioventricular valve
Sinus venosus	• Defect in the upper part of the atrial septum • May cause anomalous pulmonary venous return into superior vena cava or right atrium
Patent foramen ovale	• Remnant of the foramen ovale, usually not of clinical significance • Risk of paradoxical emboli
Patent ductus arteriosus (PDA)	In the fetal circulation, the PDA shunts blood from the pulmonary artery into aorta. At birth, the pressure differential changes, and the flow is reversed (from aorta to pulmonary artery). This leads to pulmonary hypertension due to excess blood flowing through pulmonary artery. **Pharmacology:** • Indomethacin: closes PDA • Prostaglandin E: keeps PDA open

Cyanotic Congenital Heart Disease (Right-to-Left Shunts)

- Right-to-left shunt bypasses the lungs and hence produces cyanosis as early as birth.
- Paradoxical embolism (DVT causes systemic infarct) may occur.

Tetralogy of Fallot	• **Most common cyanotic congenital heart disease in older children and adults**
	• Associated with trisomy 21
	• Four lesions:
	   1) VSD
	   2) An overriding aorta that receives blood from both ventricles
	   3) Right ventricular hypertrophy
	   4) Pulmonic stenosis (right ventricular outflow obstruction)

(Continued)

Cyanotic Congenital Heart Disease (Right-To-Left Shunts; *Cont'd.*)	
Transposition of the great vessels	• Failure of the **truncoconal septum** to spiral • The aorta arises from the right ventricle, and the pulmonary artery arises from the left ventricle, producing two closed loops. This is fatal if a shunt (e.g., PDA, VSD, ASD, patent foramen ovale) is not present to mix the venous and systemic blood.
Persistent truncus arteriosus	• Failure of the aorta and pulmonary arteries to separate • Usually a membranous VSD • Truncus arteriosus receives blood from both ventricles, so cyanosis results.

Definition of abbreviation: DVT, deep venous thrombosis.

OBSTRUCTIVE CONGENITAL HEART DISEASE	
Does not usually cause cyanosis	
Coarctation of the aorta	**Preductal (infantile) type:** • Narrowing of the aorta proximal to the opening of the ductus arteriosus • Causes reversal of flow in intercostal arteries, leading to rib notching **Postductal (adult) type:** • Narrowing of the aorta distal to the opening of the ductus arteriosus • **Most common type**; allows survival into adulthood • **Disparity in pressure between the upper and lower extremities**
Pulmonic valve stenosis or atresia	• Unequal division of the truncus arteriosus so that the pulmonary trunk has no lumen or opening at the level of the pulmonary valve • May cause cyanosis if severe
Aortic valve stenosis or atresia	**Complete atresia:** incompatible with life **Bicuspid aortic valves:** asymptomatic, can lead to infective endocarditis, left ventricular overload, and sudden death • Calcify fifth to sixth decade (tricuspid aortic valves usually calcify 10 years later) • Most common cause of aortic stenosis (more than rheumatic fever)

Diseases Associated with Congenital Heart Defects
Marfan syndrome: 1/3 patients have aortic dilatation and incompetence, aortic dissection, and ASD **Down syndrome:** 20% of patients may have congenital cardiovascular disease **Turner syndrome:** Coarctation of the aorta and pulmonary stenosis

ISCHEMIC HEART DISEASE

- **Leading cause of death**
- Most angina pectoris caused by severe atherosclerotic narrowing of coronary arteries
- Result of decreased supply (anemia, carbon monoxide, pulmonary disease) and/or increased demand (exertion, hypertrophy)
- Sudden cardiac death the presenting symptom in 25% of patients with IHD

Angina pectoris	• Paroxysmal substernal or precordial chest pain • Transient **myocardial ischemia** without myocardial infarction
Stable angina pectoris	• Paroxysms are associated with a **fixed** amount of exertion, e.g., after walking three blocks • Typical attacks last less than 10 minutes and are **relieved with rest** or sublingual nitroglycerin • ECG may show **ST segment depression** (ischemia limited to subendocardium)
Prinzmetal angina	• Vasospasm causes decreased blood flow through atherosclerotic vessels • This form of attack frequently occurs at rest with **ST-segment elevation** on ECG • Treat with calcium channel blockers
Unstable angina	• Chest pain with progressively less exertion, then occurring at rest, **often precedes myocardial infarction** • May be unresponsive to nitroglycerin

MYOCARDIAL INFARCTION

- Ischemic necrosis of myocardium, most commonly transmural, but can be subendocardial
- Highest incidence of fatal MI: 55 to 64 years old
- Risk factors: male sex, hypertension, hypercholesterolemia, cigarette smoking, family history, diabetes mellitus, oral contraceptive use, sedentary lifestyle, type A personality, family history of MI in men under 45, women under 55 years of age

Clinical features	• Acute, severe, crushing chest pain, often radiating to the jaw or left arm; diaphoresis; little or no chest pain may be present in diabetic and elderly patients • ECG: **ST elevation and T-wave inversion** with or without Q-waves • **Elevated cardiac enzymes**
Prognosis	• Sudden cardiac death: secondary to a fatal arrhythmia, occurs in 25% • Mortality after myocardial infarction: 35% in the first year, 45% in second year, and 55% in third year • Complications: arrhythmias, CHF, cardiogenic shock, systemic emboli from mural thrombi, aneurysm • Wall/papillary muscle rupture (3–7 days after infarct), postinfarction pericarditis (Dressler syndrome; 2–10 weeks postinfarction)
Treatment and management	• **Coronary artery bypass:** saphenous vein or internal mammary artery grafts restore circulation; grafts last approximately 10 years before restenosis typically occurs • **Angioplasty** (balloon dilatation) also restores circulation, half re-stenose in 1 year

Appearance of Infarcted Myocardium

Time	Gross	Histologic
1 hour	No gross changes evident	Intracellular edema
6–12 hours		Wavy myocardial fibers, vacuolar degeneration, contraction band necrosis
12–24 hours	Pale, cyanotic, edematous	
24–48 hours	Well-demarcated, soft, pale	Neutrophilic infiltrate, increased cytoplasmic eosinophilia, and coagulation necrosis become evident
3–10 days	Infarct becomes soft, yellow, surrounded by hyperemic rim	Monocytic infiltrate predominates at 72 hours
2 weeks	Infarct area is surrounded by granulation tissue that is gradually replaced by scar tissue.	

Cardiac Enzymes

Troponin I peaks first (4 h): remains elevated

CK-MB peaks within 24 h: remains elevated

LDH peaks later (about 2 days): remains elevated

AST also rises and falls predictably in myocardial infarction, but may indicate liver damage instead

Definition of abbreviations: AST, aspartate aminotransferase; CK-MB, creatine kinase MB fraction; LDH, lactate dehydrogenase.

Rheumatic Fever and Rheumatic Heart Disease

Acute rheumatic fever	• Onset is typically 1–3 weeks after group A β-hemolytic streptococcal pharyngitis, otitis media • Children: 5–15 years old • Declining incidence secondary to penicillin use • Antistreptococcal antibodies cross-react with host connective tissue • Diagnosed using Jones criteria (two major or one major and two minor)

Jones Criteria	Major	Minor
	• **Migratory polyarthritis**—large joints that become red, swollen, and painful • **Erythema marginatum**—macular skin rash, often in "bathing suit" distribution • **Sydenham chorea**—involuntary, choreiform movements of the extremities • **Subcutaneous nodules** • **Carditis**—may affect the endocardium, myocardium, or pericardium; myocarditis causes most deaths during the acute stage	• Previous rheumatic fever • Fever • Arthralgias • Prolonged PR interval • Elevated ESR • Leukocytosis • Elevated C-reactive protein

Rheumatic heart disease	• Repeated bouts of endocarditis and inflammatory insult lead to scarring and thickening of the valve leaflets with nodules along lines of closure • **Mitral valve** most commonly (75–80%) affected; fibrosis and deformity lead to "fish mouth" or "buttonhole" stenosis. Next in frequency are the aortic and mitral valves together. Tricuspid and pulmonic valves are rarely affected. • **Aschoff bodies** are pathognomonic lesions; focal collections of perivascular fibrinoid necrosis surrounded by inflammatory cells including large histiocytes (**Anitschkow cells**) • Left atrial dilatation, mural thrombi, and right ventricular hypertrophy • Predisposes to infective endocarditis

CONGESTIVE HEART FAILURE (CHF)

Types	Etiology	Comments
Left-sided heart failure	• Ischemic heart disease • Aortic stenosis • Aortic insufficiency • Hypertension • Cardiomyopathies	• Increased back pressure produces pulmonary congestion and edema • Dyspnea, orthopnea, paroxysmal nocturnal dyspnea, and cough • Renal hypoperfusion stimulates renin-angiotensin-aldosterone axis • Retention of salt and water compounds the pulmonary edema
Right-sided heart failure	• Left-sided heart failure • Cor pulmonale • Pulmonary stenosis • Pulmonary insufficiency	• Chronic passive congestion of the liver (**nutmeg liver**), peripheral edema, ascites, jugular venous distension • Renal hypoperfusion with salt and water retention
Cor pulmonale	• Parenchymal disease (e.g., COPD, causing increased pulmonary vascular resistance) • Vascular disease (e.g., vasculitis, shunts, multiple emboli)	• Cor pulmonale is right ventricular failure, resulting specifically from pulmonary hypertension • May be acute (massive pulmonary embolus) or chronic.

SHOCK
Decreased Effective Circulatory Volume

Causes	• Decreased cardiac output (myocardial infarction, arrhythmia, tamponade) • Reduction of blood volume (hemorrhage, adrenal insufficiency, fluid loss) • Pooling in periphery: massive vasodilation caused by bacterial toxins and vasoactive substances
Complications	• Cellular hypoxia, lactic acidosis • Encephalopathy • Myocardial necrosis and infarcts • Pulmonary edema, adult respiratory distress syndrome • Acute tubular necrosis
Stages	**Compensated:** reflex tachycardia, peripheral vasoconstriction **Decompensated:** ↓ blood pressure, ↑ tachycardia, metabolic acidosis, respiratory distress, and ↓ renal output **Irreversible:** irreversible cellular damage, coma, and death

ENDOCARDITIS

Classic Signs

Janeway lesions—erythematous, nontender lesions on palms and soles
Roth spots—retinal hemorrhages
Osler nodes—erythematous, tender lesions on fingers and toes
(Also see anemia, **splinter hemorrhages**)

Acute	• Organism—high virulence; *Staphylococcus aureus* (50%) and streptococci (35%) • Affects **previously normal valves** • Often involves the **tricuspid valve in intravenous drug users** • Vegetations may form myocardial abscesses, septic emboli, or destroy the valve, causing insufficiency. • High fever with chills
Subacute bacterial endocarditis	• Organism—low virulence. ***Streptococcus viridans****, Staphylococcus epidermidis*, gram-negative bacilli • *Candida* is a rare cause (associated with indwelling vascular catheters) • Affects **previously abnormal valves** • More insidious onset, with positive blood cultures, fatigue, low-grade fever without chills, splinter hemorrhages
Nonbacterial thrombotic (marantic) endocarditis	• Associated with chronic illness • Mitral valve most commonly affected • Sterile, small vegetations, loosely adhering along lines of closure • May embolize and provide a nidus for infective endocarditis
Nonbacterial verrucous (Libman-Sacks) endocarditis	• Mitral and tricuspid valvulitis in patients with systemic lupus erythematosus (SLE) • Small, warty vegetations on **both sides** of their valve leaflets • Does not embolize and rarely provides a nidus for infection

MYOCARDITIS

• Dilatation and hypertrophy of all four chambers, diffuse, patchy hemorrhage, peripheral edema
• Inflammatory lesions with characteristic cellular infiltrate:
    Neutrophilic—bacterial myocarditis
    Mononuclear—viral myocarditis
    Eosinophilic—Fiedler myocarditis

Noninfectious myocarditis	Collagen vascular diseases, rheumatic fever, SLE, and drug allergies
Viral myocarditis	• **Most common form of myocarditis** • **Coxsackie B** (positive-sense RNA viruses, picornavirus family); also, polio, rubella, and influenza • Self-limited, but may be recurrent and lead to cardiomyopathy and death. • 1/3 of AIDS patients show focal myocarditis on autopsy
Bacterial myocarditis	Diphtheria (toxin-mediated), meningococci
Protozoal	• *Trypanosoma cruzi:* Chagas disease; myocardial pseudocysts can lead to CHF • Toxoplasmosis also causes pseudocysts • Myocardial involvement appears days to weeks after the primary infection • May be asymptomatic versus acute onset of dyspnea, tachycardia, weakness, or severe CHF • Most recover fully

VALVULAR HEART DISEASE

Mitral valve prolapse	• Mitral leaflets (usually posterior) project into left atrium during systole, leading to insufficiency • 7% of the United States population, most commonly in **young women** • Seen in most patients with **Marfan syndrome** • Characteristic **midsystolic click** and high-pitched murmur • Usually asymptomatic, but may have associated dyspnea, tachycardia, chest pain • *Complications:* atrial thrombosis, calcification, infective endocarditis, systemic embolization
Mitral stenosis	• Stenosis may be combined with mitral valve prolapse • Increased left atrial pressure and enlarged left atrium • Early diastolic **opening snap** • *Complications:* pulmonary edema, left atrial enlargement, chronic atrial fibrillation, atrial thrombosis and systemic emboli

Aortic valve insufficiency	• **Acute** (infective endocarditis)
	• Sudden left ventricular failure, increased left ventricular filling pressure, inadequate stroke volume.
	• **Chronic** (aortic root dilation):
	  – Volume overload, eccentric hypertrophy
	  – Wide pulse pressure (**bounding pulse**)
	  – Etiologies include congenitally bicuspid aortic valve, rheumatic heart disease, or syphilis

Aortic valve stenosis	• Rheumatic heart disease, bicuspid aortic valve • Thickening and fibrosis of valve cusps without fusion of valve commissures (fusion present in rheumatic heart disease) • Asymptomatic until late, presents with angina, syncope, and CHF • Systolic ejection click • *Complications:* sudden death, secondary to an arrhythmia or CHF

CARDIOMYOPATHIES
Diseases Not Related to Ischemic Injury

Dilated (congestive) cardiomyopathy	• Gradual dilatation of all four chambers, producing cardiomegaly, ↓ contractility, stasis, formation of mural thrombi. • Death from progressive CHF, thromboembolism, or arrhythmia • *Etiologies:* idiopathic, alcohol (reversible), doxorubicin (irreversible), thiamine deficiency, pregnancy, postviral
Hypertrophic cardiomyopathy (idiopathic hypertrophic subaortic stenosis)	• Marked **asymmetric hypertrophy** of the ventricular septum, **left ventricular outflow obstruction** • Decreased cardiac output may cause dyspnea, angina, atrial fibrillation, syncope, sudden death • Classic case: **young adult athletes** who die during strenuous activity • *Etiologies:* genetic (50%, autosomal dominant pattern)
Restrictive (infiltrative) cardiomyopathy	• Diastolic dysfunction (impaired filling) • Infiltration of extracellular material within myocardium • *Etiologies:* elderly—cardiac amyloidosis (may induce arrhythmias); young (<25 years old)—sarcoidosis associated with systemic sarcoidosis • Secondary cardiomyopathy: metabolic disorders, nutritional deficiencies

Pericardial Disease

- Usually secondary; local spread from adjacent mediastinal structures
- Primary pericarditis is usually due to systemic viral infection, uremia, and autoimmune diseases

Fibrinous pericarditis	• Exudate of fibrin • *Etiologies:* post myocardial infarction, trauma, rheumatic fever, radiation, SLE • Loud pericardial friction rub with chest pain, fever
Serous pericarditis	• Small exudative effusion with few inflammatory cells • *Etiologies:* nonbacterial, immunologic reaction (rheumatic fever, SLE), uremia, or viral • Usually asymptomatic
Suppurative pericarditis	• Purulent exudate; leads to constrictive pericarditis and cardiac insufficiency • *Etiologies:* bacterial, fungal, or parasitic infection • May have systemic signs of infection and a soft friction rub
Hemorrhagic pericarditis	• Exudate of blood with suppurative or fibrinous component • *Etiologies:* tuberculosis or a malignant neoplasm; organization • May lead to constrictive pericarditis
Caseous pericarditis	• Caseous exudate with fibrocalcific constrictive pericarditis • *Etiologies:* tuberculosis

Pericardial Effusion

Pericardial effusion is leakage of fluid (transudate or exudate) into the limited pericardial space. It may result in cardiac tamponade. Generally, the rate of filling rather than the absolute volume determines the degree of tamponade.

Serous effusion	• *Etiology:* hypoproteinemia or CHF • Develops slowly, rarely causing cardiac compromise
Serosanguineous effusion	• *Etiology:* history of trauma (e.g., cardiopulmonary resuscitation), tumor, or TB • Develops slowly, rarely causing cardiac compromise
Hemopericardium	• *Etiology:* penetrating trauma, ventricular rupture (after myocardial infarction), or aortic rupture • Develops quickly; **can cause cardiac tamponade** and death

Cardiac Neoplasms

Primary tumors (rare, majority benign)	**Myxoma: most common primary cardiac tumor in adults** • Most occur in the left atrium • May be any size; sessile or pedunculated • Complications include ball-valve obstructions of the mitral valve, embolization of tumor fragments **Rhabdomyoma: most common primary cardiac tumor in children** (especially those with **tuberous sclerosis**)
Metastases	Lung and lymphoma, involving the pericardium predominantly

VASCULITIDES				
Disease	**Involvement**	**Clinical**	**Comments**	**Treatment**
Buerger disease (thromboangiitis obliterans)	• Involves **small and medium-sized arteries** and veins in the **extremities** • **Microabscesses** and segmental **thrombosis** lead to vascular insufficiency, ulceration, **gangrene**	Causes severe pain (claudication) and Raynaud phenomenon in affected extremity	• Neutrophilic vasculitis that tends to involve the extremities of young men (usually under 40) who smoke heavily • Common in Israel, India, Japan, and South America	Smoking cessation
Churg-Strauss syndrome (allergic granulomatosis and angiitis)	Lung, spleen, kidney	Associated with bronchial **asthma**, **granulomas**, and **eosinophilia**	• Variant of polyarteritis nodosa • **P-ANCA** ⊕	Corticosteroids, occasionally immunosuppressants
Kawasaki disease (mucocutaneous lymph node syndrome)	• Segmental necrotizing vasculitis involves large, medium-sized, and small arteries • **Coronary arteries** commonly affected (70%)	• Fever • Conjunctivitis • Erythema and erosions of the oral mucosa • Generalized maculopapular skin rash • Lymphadenopathy • Mortality rate is 1–2% due to rupture of a **coronary aneurysm** or coronary thrombosis	Commonly affects infants and **young children** (age <4) in **Japan**, Hawaii, and U.S. mainland	IV immunoglobulin (IVIG), aspirin, sometimes anticoagulants
Polyarteritis nodosa	• Small and medium-sized arteries in skin, joints, peripheral nerves, kidney, heart, and GI tract • Lesions will be at different stages (acute, healing, healed)	• Affects young adults (male > female) • Low-grade fever, weight loss, malaise • Hematuria, renal failure, hypertension • Abdominal pain, diarrhea, GI bleeding • Myalgia and arthralgia	• Hepatitis B antigen (HBsAg) ⊕ in 30% of cases • P-ANCA (antimyeloperoxidase) found in many cases, but not diagnostic	Corticosteroids and cyclophosphamide (often fatal without treatment)
Takayasu arteritis (pulseless disease)	• Granulomatous vasculitis with massive intimal fibrosis that tends to involve **medium-sized to large arteries**, including the aortic arch and major branches • Produces characteristic narrowing of arterial orifices	• Fever, night sweats, muscle and joint aches, loss of pulse in upper extremities • May lead to visual loss and other neurologic abnormalities	Most common in **Asia, especially in young and middle-aged women** (ages 15–45)	Corticosteroids

(Continued)

Disease	Involvement	Clinical	Comments	Treatment
Temporal arteritis (giant cell arteritis)	• Usually segmental granulomatous involvement of small and medium-sized arteries, esp. the **cranial arteries** (temporal, facial, and ophthalmic arteries) • Multinucleated giant cells and **fragmentation of the internal elastic lamina** seen in affected segments.	• Headache, facial pain, tenderness over arteries, and visual disturbances (**can progress to blindness**) • Fever, malaise, weight loss, muscle aches, anemia • Patient usually middle-aged to elderly female • Elevated ESR	• Most common form of vasculitis • Associated with HLA-DR4 • **Polymyalgia rheumatica:** systemic flu-like symptoms; joint involvement also present	Corticosteroids (important to avoid blindness)
Wegener granulomatosis	• Necrotizing granulomatous vasculitis that affects small arteries and veins • Classically involves **nose, sinuses, lungs,** and **kidneys**	• Middle-aged adults, males > females • Bilateral pneumonitis with nodular and cavitary pulmonary infiltrates • Chronic sinusitis • Nasopharyngeal ulcerations • Renal disease (focal necrotizing glomerulonephritis)	Associated with **C-ANCA** (autoantibody against **proteinase 3**)	Corticosteroids, immunosuppressants

ADDITIONAL VASCULAR DISEASES

Arteriolosclerosis

• Refers to small artery and arteriolar changes, leading to luminal narrowing that are most often seen in patients with diabetes, hypertension, and aging
• Hyaline and hyperplastic (onion-skinning) types

Atherosclerosis

Characterized by lipid deposition and intimal thickening of large and medium-sized arteries. Abdominal aorta more likely involved than the thoracic aorta. Within the abdominal aorta, lesions tend to be more prominent around the ostia. After the abdominal aorta, others commonly affected are the coronary, popliteal, and internal carotid arteries.

Key process: intimal thickening and lipid accumulation produces atheromatous plaques

The earliest lesion is the **fatty streak**, which is seen almost universally in children and may represent reversible precursor. The progression of the disease is thought in part due to a response to injury from such agents as hypertension, hyperlipidemia, and tobacco smoke. This leads to inflammatory cell adherence, migration, and proliferation of smooth muscle cells from the media into the intima.

The **mature plaque** has a **fibrous cap**, a cellular zone composed of **smooth muscle cells, macrophages,** and lymphocytes and a **central core** composed of necrotic cells, **cholesterol clefts, and lipid-filled foam cells** (macrophages). **Complicated plaques** are seen in advanced disease. These plaques may rupture, form fissures or ulcerate, leading to myocardial infarcts, strokes, and mesenteric artery occlusion. Damage to the cell wall predisposes to aneurysm formation.

Major Risk Factors	Minor Risk Factors
Hyperlipidemia, hypertension, smoking, diabetes	Male sex, obesity, sedentary lifestyle, stress, elevated homocysteine, oral contraceptive use, increasing age, familial/genetic factors

(Continued)

ADDITIONAL VASCULAR DISEASES (CONT'D.)

Mönckeberg Medial Calcific Sclerosis

Asymptomatic medial calcification of medium-sized arteries

Raynaud Disease

An idiopathic small artery vasospasm that causes **blanching and cyanosis of the fingers and toes**; the term Raynaud phenomenon is used when similar changes are observed secondary to a systemic disease, such as scleroderma or systemic lupus erythematosus.

HYPERTENSION

Hypertension has been classically defined as a sustained diastolic pressure >85 mm Hg and/or systolic pressure >135 mm Hg. The classic 120/80 mm Hg is now defined as "prehypertensive"; 115/75 mm Hg is normal.

Most cases (90%) are idiopathic and termed essential hypertension. The majority of the remainder is secondary to intrinsic renal disease; less commonly, narrowing of the renal artery. Infrequent secondary causes include primary aldosteronism, Cushing disease, and pheochromocytoma.

Renal causes of hypertension can usually be attributed to increased renin release. This converts angiotensinogen to angiotensin I, which is converted to angiotensin II in the lung. Angiotensin II causes arteriolar constriction and stimulates aldosterone secretion and therefore sodium retention, which leads to an increased intravascular volume.

Benign hypertension	Common, initially silent disease that may eventually produce cardiac disease, accelerated atherosclerosis, aneurysm formation, and renal and CNS damage
Malignant hypertension	Much less common than benign hypertension and defined as markedly elevated pressures (e.g., diastolic >120 mm Hg), causing rapid end-organ damage. Often fatal within 2 years from renal failure, intracerebral hemorrhage, or chronic heart failure.

ANEURYSM

- A congenital or acquired weakness of the vessel wall media, resulting in a localized dilation or outpouching
- *Complications:* thrombus formation, compression of adjacent structures, and rupture with risk of sudden death

Type of Aneurysm	Associations	Anatomic Location	Comments
Atherosclerotic	Atherosclerosis, hypertension	Usually involve **abdominal aorta**, often below renal arteries	Half of aortic aneurysms >6 cm in diameter will rupture within 10 years
Syphilitic	Syphilitic obliterative endarteritis of vasa vasorum	**Ascending aorta** (aortic root)	May dilate the aortic valve ring, causing aortic insufficiency
Marfan syndrome	Lack of **fibrillin** leads to poor elastin function	Ascending aorta (aortic root)	May dilate the aortic valve ring, causing aortic insufficiency
Dissecting aneurysm (aortic dissection)	**Hypertension, cystic medial necrosis** (e.g., Marfan syndrome)	Blood enters intimal tear in aortic wall and spreads through media	Presents with severe tearing pain
Berry aneurysm	Congenital; some associated with **adult polycystic kidney disease**	Classic location: **Circle of Willis**	Rupture leads to **subarachnoid hemorrhage**

VENOUS DISEASE

Deep vein thrombosis	Involves deep leg veins	Major complication: **pulmonary embolus**
Varicose veins	Dilated, tortuous veins caused by increased intraluminal pressure	• Superficial veins of legs • Hemorrhoids • **Esophageal varices**

VASCULAR TUMORS

Angiosarcoma	• Malignant vascular tumor with a high mortality • Occurs most commonly in skin, breast, liver, soft tissues
Glomus tumor	• Small, painful tumors most often found under fingernails
Hemangioma	• Common, benign tumors that may involve skin, mucous membranes, or internal organs
Hemangioblastoma	• Associated with **von Hippel-Lindau disease** • Tends to involve the central nervous system and retina
Kaposi sarcoma	• Low-grade malignancy of endothelial cells • Viral etiology: **human herpesvirus 8** (HHV8) • Most often seen in AIDS patients in the U.S.

EDEMA AND SHOCK

Edema	• Fluid is maintained with vessels via balance between hydrostatic pressure ("pushing fluid out") and oncotic pressure ("pulling fluid in"). • Most causes of edema can be related to either increased hydrostatic pressure or reduced plasma osmotic pressure. Other causes included lymphatic obstruction, sodium retention. • Clinically, may see pitting edema in extremities (dependent) or massive generalized edema (anasarca).

Increased Hydrostatic Pressure	Reduced Plasma Osmotic Pressure
Local: deep vein thrombosis *Generalized:* congestive heart failure	Cirrhosis, nephrotic syndrome, protein losing enteropathy

Shock	Three major variants: cardiogenic, septic, and hypovolemic			
Type	**Comments**	**Heart Rate**	**Systemic Vascular Resistance**	**Cardiac Output**
Cardiogenic	Intrinsic pump failure. As the heart fails, stroke volume decreases, with compensatory increases in heart rate and systemic vascular resistance.	↑	↑	↓
Septic	Endotoxin mediated. Massive peripheral vasodilation with a decrease in systemic vascular resistance. There is peripheral pooling of blood (decreased effective circulatory volume). The heart compensates with an increase in heart rate.	↑	↓	↑
Hypovolemic	Blood loss. The effective circulatory volume decreases through actual loss. The heart is able to attempt to compensate with an increase in heart rate.	↑	↑	Unchanged

CARDIOVASCULAR PHARMACOLOGY

ANTIARRHYTHMIC DRUGS

Drugs	Mechanism of Action	Effect	Indications	Toxicities	Notes
Class I: Na⁺ Channel Blockers (Local Anesthetics)						

Class I: Na$^+$ Channel Blockers (Local Anesthetics)

These agents block the open or inactivated channel preferentially and therefore block frequently depolarized (e.g., abnormal) tissue better **(use dependence; state dependence)**. Class I drugs are subdivided into three groups based on their effect on AP duration.

Drugs	Mechanism of Action	Effect	Indications	Toxicities	Notes
Class IA quinidine procainamide disopyramide amiodarone	• ↓ Na$^+$ influx • **Slows phase 0 depolarization** in His-Purkinje fibers and cardiac muscle	• ↑ **AP duration** • ↑ ERP • Slows conduction	Atrial and ventricular arrhythmias	• *Quinidine:* **cinchonism** (headache, tinnitus, vertigo), ↑ QT interval, **torsades de pointes**, autoimmune reactions (e.g., thrombocytopenia) • *Procainamide:* reversible **SLE-like syndrome**	• Hyperkalemia enhances cardiotoxic effects • Quinidine enhances digoxin toxicity
Class IB lidocaine mexiletine tocainide	• ↓ Na$^+$ influx in ischemic or depolarized Purkinje and ventricular tissue (little effect on atrial or normal tissue) • **Shortens phase 3 repolarization**	• ↓ **AP duration**	Ventricular arrhythmias (e.g., post MI, digitalis toxicity)	CNS toxicity	Hyperkalemia enhances cardiotoxic effects
Class IC flecainide propafenone encainide	• ↓ Na$^+$ influx • **Markedly slows phase 0 depolarization** in His-Purkinje fibers and cardiac muscle	• **No effect on AP duration** • Slows conduction velocity • Increase QRS duration	Refractory ventricular arrhythmias (used as last resort)	**Proarrhythmic**	Can precipitate cardiac arrest and sudden death in patients with preexisting cardiac abnormalities
Class II: Beta Blockers						

Class II: Beta Blockers

These drugs slow AV conduction.

Drugs	Mechanism of Action	Effect	Indications	Toxicities	Notes

propranolol
metoprolol
esmolol
	• β-adrenoreceptor **blockade**
	  − ↓ cAMP
	  − ↓ Ca^{2+} current
	• ↓ **phase 0 depolarization in AV node**
	• ↓ **phase 4 depolarization in SA node**
		• ↓ AV node conduction
		
		• ↑ PR interval
			• SVT
			
			• Post-MI arrhythmia prophylaxis
				Impotence, bradycardia, depression, worsens asthma	• Used post MI; has a protective effect
					• May mask premonitory signs of hypoglycemia
					• **Esmolol**-very short acting

(Continued)

ANTIARRHYTHMIC DRUGS (*CONT'D.*)

Drugs	Mechanism of Action	Effect	Indications	Toxicities	Notes
Class III: K⁺ Channel Blockers These agents prolong the AP and increase the ERP.					
sotalol bretylium ibutilide dofetilide amiodarone	↓ **K⁺ current** (delayed rectifier current), **prolonging phase 3 repolarization** of AP	• ↑ **AP duration** • ↑ERP	Atrial fibrillation/ flutter, ventricular arrhythmias, refractory arrhythmias	• *General:* **torsade de pointes**, sinus bradycardia • *Amiodarone:* **pulmonary fibrosis**, **hepatotoxicity**, **cutaneous**, **photosensitivity**, corneal deposits, thyroid dysfunction • *Bretylium:* new arrhythmias, ↓ BP • *Sotalol:* excessive β blockade	• *Amiodarone:* also belongs to class IA • *Sotalol:* also class II
Class IV: Ca²⁺ Channel Blockers By blocking L-type Ca²⁺ channels, these agents slow AV node conduction.					
verapamil diltiazem	**Block L-type Ca²⁺ channels**	Decreased conductivity SA/AV nodes	• Atrial fibrillation/ flutter • Atrial automaticities • AV nodal reentry	Constipation, dizziness, flushing, AV block, negative inotropic effect, hypotension	—
Unclassified					

Adenosine: used for AV nodal arrhythmias; extremely short acting

Mg²⁺: used in digitalis-induced arrhythmias, torsade de pointes

K⁺: used in digitalis-induced arrhythmias; ↓ other ectopic pacemakers

Digitalis: used in rapid atrial flutter/fibrillation, AV nodal reentrant arrhythmias

ANTIANGINAL DRUGS

Angina pectoris, the primary symptom of ischemic heart disease, occurs in periods of inadequate oxygen delivery to the myocardium. Classically, this symptom is described as a crushing, pressure-like pain that occurs during periods of exertion. Strategies used to treat this condition include:

- increasing oxygen delivery through increased perfusion
- decreasing myocardial oxygen demands

	Drug Class		
	Nitrates (nitroglycerine, isosorbide dinitrate)	**Calcium Channel Blockers** (nifedipine, verapamil, diltiazem)	**Beta blockers** (propranolol, atenolol, others)
Molecular mechanism	Generation of endothelial NO activates GC → ↑ cGMP → dephosphorylates MLCK → relaxation of vascular smooth muscle	Inhibits voltage-gated "L-type" Ca^{2+} channels and ↓ Ca^{2+} influx in cardiac and vascular smooth muscle → ↓ muscle contractility	β-adrenergic antagonism
Physiologic mechanism	• **Venodilation** → ↓ **preload** → ↓ afterload • ↓ **myocardial O_2 demand**	• Arteriolar vasodilation → ↓ **afterload** • ↓ myocardial O_2 demand • ↓ AV node conduction velocity	↓ contractility, ↓ HR, ↓ BP (mild), ↓ myocardial O_2 demand, ↓ AV node conduction velocity
Indications	Angina (acute), pulmonary edema	Angina, HTN, SVT	Angina, HTN, arrhythmia
Adverse effects	Reflex tachycardia, orthostatic hypotension, headache, tachyphylaxis	Cardiac depression, peripheral edema, constipation	Impotence, depression, bradycardia
Notes	Contraindicated in patients taking sildenafil → hypotension and sudden death	Selectivity for vascular Ca^{2+} channels: **Nifedipine > diltiazem > verapamil** Verapamil primarily affects myocardium	Non-CV indications include migraine, familial tremor, stage fright, thyrotoxicosis, glaucoma

Definition of abbreviations: AV, atrioventricular; cGMP, cyclic guanosine monophosphate; GC, guanylate cyclase; HTN, hypertension; SVT, supraventricular tachycardia.

DRUGS USED IN HEART FAILURE

Heart failure results when tissue demands for circulation cannot be met by an ailing myocardium. Inadequate cardiac output secondary to decreased contractility leads to decreased exercise tolerance and muscle fatigue. Neurohumoral responses to this physiologic shortcoming play an integral role in the pathogenesis of heart failure; thus, drugs used to treat this condition may be aimed at these responses. Physiologically, these drugs may reduce afterload, reduce preload, or increase contractility.

Drug Class	Mechanism of Action	Effects	Indications	Toxicities	Notes
ACE inhibitors captopril enalapril lisinopril	Inhibits angiotensin-converting enzyme (ACE) → ↓ angiotensin II and ↑ bradykinin	• **Decreased aldosterone** → ↓ fluid retention • **Vasodilation** → ↓ preload and afterload	• CHF • Post-MI to prevent pathologic remodeling • Hypertension • Diabetic renal disease	**Cough,** hypotension, proteinuria, **fetal renal toxicity,** angioedema	• Cornerstone of CHF therapy • Prophylactic in post-MI because they oppose "remodeling" that leads to heart failure
Cardiac glycosides digoxin digitalis	Inhibits Na^+/K^+ ATPase → ↑ intracellular Na^+ → ↓ Na^+ gradient → ↓ Na^+-Ca^{2+} exchange → ↑ intracellular Ca^{2+}	• Increased myocardial Ca^{2+} → **increased contractility** • Delayed conduction at AV node. (parasympathomimetic effect)	• CHF (because ↑ contractility) • Atrial fibrillation (because ↓ AV conduction)	**Yellow vision,** nausea, vomiting, diarrhea, anorexia, hallucination, **life-threatening arrhythmias**	• **Hypokalemia** enhances toxicity • **Quinidine** → ↑ dig toxicity (↓ dig clearance) • **Digoxin antibodies** (Fab fragments) used in overdose • Digitalis does not improve survival following MI

(Continued)

DRUGS USED IN HEART FAILURE (*CONT'D.*)

Drug Class	Mechanism of Action	Effects	Indications	Toxicities	Notes
Angiotensin II–receptor blockers losartan candesartan	Block angiotensin II receptors	Same as ACE inhibitors	Same as ACE inhibitors	**Fetal renal toxicity**, no cough	Not as well studied as ACEIs, but seem to have same efficacy
Vasodilators nitroglycerin nitroprusside isosorbide dinitrate hydralazine	↑ nitric oxide → cGMP → vasodilation	*Nitroglycerin, isosorbide dinitrate:* predominantly venodilators *Nitroprusside:* dilation of arteries = veins	CHF, HTN, angina, pulmonary edema	Tachycardia, headache hypotension	• *Nitroprusside, nitroglycerin:* used in acute HF • *Hydralazine, isosorbide dinitrate:* used in chronic HF
Beta-receptor antagonists carvedilol labetalol metoprolol	These agents were once contraindicated in heart failure; now they are used to reduce the progression of mild to moderate heart failure. • *Carvedilol, labetalol:* nonselective β antagonist, α_1 antagonist • *Metoprolol:* β_1 antagonist • Contraindicated in patients with asthma or severe bradycardia				
Beta-1 agonists dobutamine dopamine	Used in **acute** heart failure *Dopamine:* ↓ dose → improves renal blood flow; moderate dose: stimulates myocardial contractility; ↑ doses → vasoconstrictor (alpha$_1$ receptors); used for cardiogenic shock *Dobutamine:* β_1 selective				
Diuretics	Used to reduce symptoms of fluid retention (pulmonary congestion, edema); loop diuretics most effective, thiazides can be effective in mild cases				

The Respiratory System

Embryology and Histology

Gross Anatomy

Physiology

Mechanics of Breathing

Gas Exchange

Pathology

RESPIRATORY EMBRYOLOGY AND HISTOLOGY

DEVELOPMENT OF THE RESPIRATORY SYSTEM

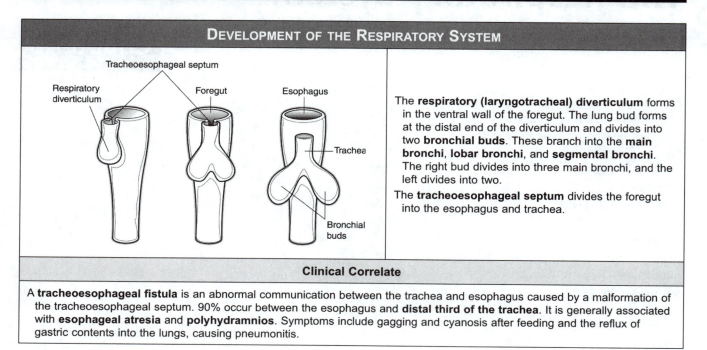

The **respiratory (laryngotracheal) diverticulum** forms in the ventral wall of the foregut. The lung bud forms at the distal end of the diverticulum and divides into two **bronchial buds**. These branch into the **main bronchi**, **lobar bronchi**, and **segmental bronchi**. The right bud divides into three main bronchi, and the left divides into two.

The **tracheoesophageal septum** divides the foregut into the esophagus and trachea.

Clinical Correlate

A **tracheoesophageal fistula** is an abnormal communication between the trachea and esophagus caused by a malformation of the tracheoesophageal septum. 90% occur between the esophagus and **distal third of the trachea**. It is generally associated with **esophageal atresia** and **polyhydramnios**. Symptoms include gagging and cyanosis after feeding and the reflux of gastric contents into the lungs, causing pneumonitis.

THE ALVEOLI AND BLOOD-GAS BARRIER

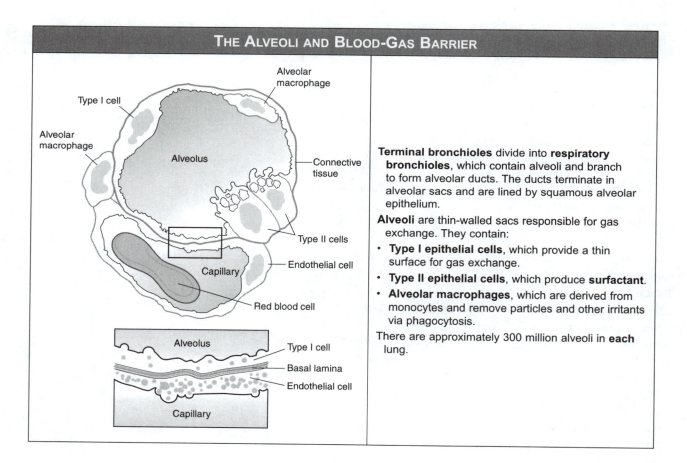

Terminal bronchioles divide into **respiratory bronchioles**, which contain alveoli and branch to form alveolar ducts. The ducts terminate in alveolar sacs and are lined by squamous alveolar epithelium.

Alveoli are thin-walled sacs responsible for gas exchange. They contain:

- **Type I epithelial cells**, which provide a thin surface for gas exchange.
- **Type II epithelial cells**, which produce **surfactant**.
- **Alveolar macrophages**, which are derived from monocytes and remove particles and other irritants via phagocytosis.

There are approximately 300 million alveoli in **each** lung.

GROSS ANATOMY

PHARYNX AND RELATED AREAS

The **pharynx** is a passageway shared by the digestive and respiratory systems. It has lateral, posterior, and medial walls throughout but is open anteriorly in its upper regions (**nasopharynx**, **oropharynx**), communicating with the nasal cavity and the oral cavity.

The **nasopharynx** is the region of the pharynx located directly posterior to the nasal cavity. It communicates with the nasal cavity through the **choanae** (i.e., posterior nasal apertures).

The **oropharynx** is the region of the pharynx located directly posterior to the oral cavity. It communicates with the oral cavity through a space called the **fauces**. The fauces are bounded by two folds, consisting of mucosa and muscle, known as the **anterior and posterior pillars**.

• The **anterior pillar of the fauces**, also known as the **palatoglossal fold**, contains the **palatoglossus muscle**.

• The **posterior pillar of the fauces**, also known as the **palatopharyngeal fold**, contains the **palatopharyngeus muscle**.

• The **tonsillar bed** is the space between the pillars that houses the **palatine tonsil**.

The **laryngopharynx** is the region of the pharynx that surrounds the larynx. It extends from the tip of the epiglottis to the cricoid cartilage. Its lateral extensions are known as the **piriform recesses**.

THE LARYNX

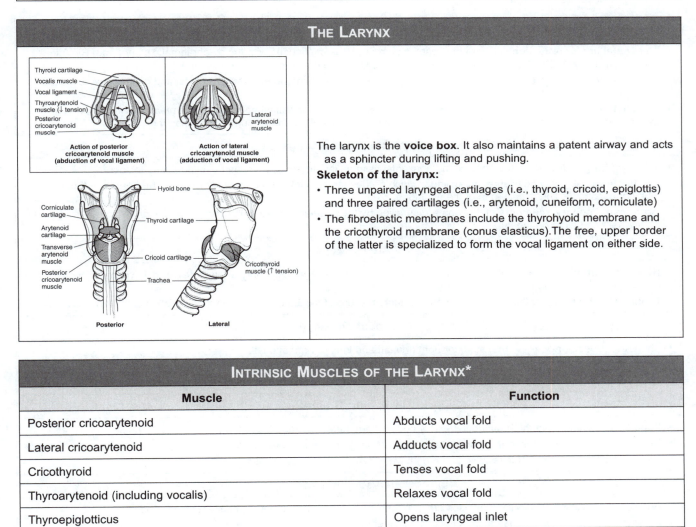

The larynx is the **voice box**. It also maintains a patent airway and acts as a sphincter during lifting and pushing.

Skeleton of the larynx:

• Three unpaired laryngeal cartilages (i.e., thyroid, cricoid, epiglottis) and three paired cartilages (i.e., arytenoid, cuneiform, corniculate)

• The fibroelastic membranes include the thyrohyoid membrane and the cricothyroid membrane (conus elasticus).The free, upper border of the latter is specialized to form the vocal ligament on either side.

INTRINSIC MUSCLES OF THE LARYNX*

Muscle	Function
Posterior cricoarytenoid	Abducts vocal fold
Lateral cricoarytenoid	Adducts vocal fold
Cricothyroid	Tenses vocal fold
Thyroarytenoid (including vocalis)	Relaxes vocal fold
Thyroepiglotticus	Opens laryngeal inlet
Aryepiglotticus	Closes laryngeal inlet
Oblique and transverse arytenoids	Close laryngeal inlet

*Note that the cricothyroid is innervated by the external laryngeal nerve, a branch of the superior laryngeal branch of the vagus nerve. All other intrinsic laryngeal muscles are supplied by the recurrent laryngeal branch of the vagus nerve.

PLEURA AND PLEURAL CAVITIES

Parietal pleura lines the inner surface of the thoracic cavity; **visceral pleura** follows the contours of the lung itself. Inflammation of the central part of the diaphragmatic pleura may produce pain referred to the shoulder (phrenic nerve; C3, C4, and C5).

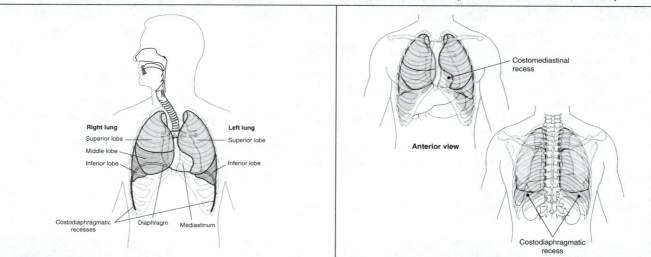

- The **costal line of reflection** is where the costal pleura becomes continuous with the diaphragmatic pleura from Rib 8 in the midclavicular line, to Rib 10 in the midaxillary line, and to Rib 12 lateral to the vertebral column.
- **Costodiaphragmatic recesses** are spaces below the inferior borders of the lungs where costal and diaphragmatic pleurae are in contact.
- The **costomediastinal recess** is a space where the left costal and mediastinal parietal pleurae meet, leaving a space due to the cardiac notch of the left lung. This space is occupied by the lingula of the left lung during inspiration.

Structure of the Lungs

- The **right lung** is divided by the oblique and horizontal fissures into three lobes: superior, middle, and inferior.
- The **left lung** has only one fissure, the oblique, which divides the lung into upper and lower lobes. The **lingula** of the upper lobe corresponds to the middle lobe of the right lung.
- **Bronchopulmonary segments** of the lung are supplied by the segmental (tertiary) bronchus, artery, and vein. There are 10 on the right and eight on the left.

Arterial Supply

- **Right and left pulmonary arteries** arise from the pulmonary trunk. The pulmonary arteries deliver deoxygenated blood to the lungs from the right side of the heart.
- **Bronchial arteries** supply the bronchi and nonrespiratory portions of the lung. They are usually branches of the thoracic aorta.

Venous Drainage

- There are **four pulmonary veins**: superior right and left and inferior right and left.
- Pulmonary veins carry oxygenated blood to the left atrium of the heart.
- The **bronchial veins** drain to the azygos system. They share drainage from the bronchi with the pulmonary veins.

Lymphatic Drainage

- Superficial drainage is to the bronchopulmonary nodes; from there, drainage is to the tracheobronchial nodes.
- Deep drainage is to the pulmonary nodes; from there, drainage is to the bronchopulmonary nodes.
- Bronchomediastinal lymph trunks drain to the right lymphatic and the thoracic ducts.

Innervation of Lungs

- Anterior and posterior pulmonary plexuses are formed by vagal (parasympathetic) and sympathetic fibers.
- Parasympathetic stimulation has a bronchoconstrictive effect.
- Sympathetic stimulation has a bronchodilator effect.

RESPIRATORY PHYSIOLOGY

LUNG VOLUMES AND CAPACITIES

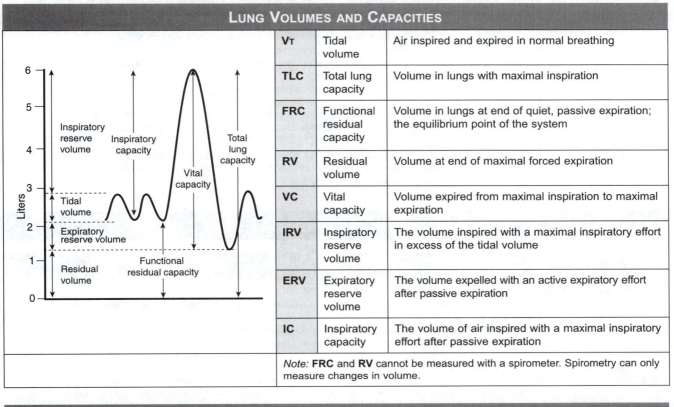

VT	Tidal volume	Air inspired and expired in normal breathing
TLC	Total lung capacity	Volume in lungs with maximal inspiration
FRC	Functional residual capacity	Volume in lungs at end of quiet, passive expiration; the equilibrium point of the system
RV	Residual volume	Volume at end of maximal forced expiration
VC	Vital capacity	Volume expired from maximal inspiration to maximal expiration
IRV	Inspiratory reserve volume	The volume inspired with a maximal inspiratory effort in excess of the tidal volume
ERV	Expiratory reserve volume	The volume expelled with an active expiratory effort after passive expiration
IC	Inspiratory capacity	The volume of air inspired with a maximal inspiratory effort after passive expiration

Note: **FRC** and **RV** cannot be measured with a spirometer. Spirometry can only measure changes in volume.

DEAD SPACE AND VENTILATION

V_D = dead space (no gas exchange)

Anatomic V_D = conducting airways

Alveolar V_D = alveoli with poor blood flow (ventilated but not perfused)

Physiologic V_D = anatomic + alveolar dead space

Standard Symbols

A = alveolar
a = arterial
V = volume
$\dot{V}$ = minute ventilation
P = pressure
P_{ACO_2} = alveolar pressure of CO_2
Pa_{CO_2} = arterial pressure of CO_2
P_{ECO_2} = P_{CO_2} in expired air

Abbreviation	Name	Definition	Normal Values
VD	Dead space	Volume that does not exchange gas with blood	150 mL
VA	Alveolar volume	Portion of tidal volume that reaches alveoli during inspiration	350 mL
VT	Tidal volume: $V_T = V_A + V_D$	Amount of gas inhaled and exhaled during normal breathing – the sum of dead space volume and alveolar volume	500 mL
n	Respiratory frequency	Breaths/minute	15/min
$\dot{V}_E$	Total ventilation: $V_Tn = V_An + V_Dn$ $\dot{V}_E = \dot{V}_A + \dot{V}_D$	Total ventilation per minute $V_Tn = (350\ mL \times 15/min) + (150\ mL \times 15/min) = 7,500\ mL/min$ $\dot{V}_E = 5,250\ mL/min + 2,250\ mL/min = 7,500\ mL/min$	7,500 mL/min

(Continued)

DEAD SPACE AND VENTILATION (CONT'D.)

$\dot{V}_A$	Alveolar ventilation $\dot{V}_A = (V_T - V_D) \times n$	Amount of inspired air that reaches the alveoli each minute. It is the effective part of ventilation.	5,250 mL/min
	$\dot{V}_A = \dfrac{\dot{V}_{CO_2}}{P_{CO_2}} \times K$	The adequacy of alveolar ventilation can be determined from the concentration of expired carbon dioxide. • $\dot{V}_{CO_2} = CO_2$ production (generally assume is normal and constant) • ↑ **alveolar ventilation → ↓ Pa$_{CO_2}$** • ↓ **alveolar ventilation → ↑ Pa$_{CO_2}$**	

Physiologic Dead Space

$\dfrac{V_D}{V_T} = \dfrac{Pa_{CO_2} - Pe_{CO_2}}{Pa_{CO_2}}$	All expired CO_2 comes from alveolar gas, not from dead space gas. Therefore, the fraction shows the dilution of CO_2 by the dead space. In the normal individual, anatomic dead space = physiologic dead space, and $V_D/V_T = 0.2$–0.35. In lung disease, this number can increase.

MECHANICS OF BREATHING

MUSCLES OF BREATHING

Muscles of inspiration	• **Diaphragm—most important** • Other muscles of inspiration are used primarily during exercise or in diseases that increase airway resistance (e.g., asthma): – **External intercostal muscles** (move ribs upward and outward) – **Accessory muscles** (elevate first two ribs and sternum)
Muscles of expiration	• Expiration is **passive** during quiet breathing. • Muscles of expiration are used during exercise or increased airway resistance (e.g., asthma): – **Abdominal muscles** (help push diaphragm up during exercise or increased airway resistance) – **Internal intercostal muscles** (pull ribs downward and inward)

ELASTIC PROPERTIES OF THE LUNG

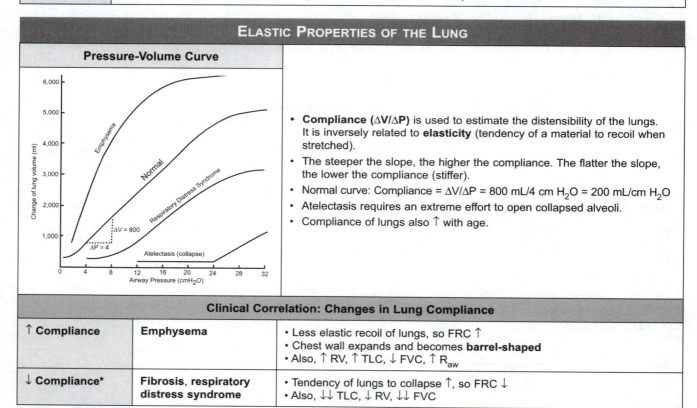

Pressure-Volume Curve

- **Compliance (ΔV/ΔP)** is used to estimate the distensibility of the lungs. It is inversely related to **elasticity** (tendency of a material to recoil when stretched).
- The steeper the slope, the higher the compliance. The flatter the slope, the lower the compliance (stiffer).
- Normal curve: Compliance = ΔV/ΔP = 800 mL/4 cm H_2O = 200 mL/cm H_2O
- Atelectasis requires an extreme effort to open collapsed alveoli.
- Compliance of lungs also ↑ with age.

Clinical Correlation: Changes in Lung Compliance

↑ Compliance	Emphysema	• Less elastic recoil of lungs, so FRC ↑ • Chest wall expands and becomes **barrel-shaped** • Also, ↑ RV, ↑ TLC, ↓ FVC, ↑ R$_{aw}$
↓ Compliance*	Fibrosis, respiratory distress syndrome	• Tendency of lungs to collapse ↑, so FRC ↓ • Also, ↓↓ TLC, ↓ RV, ↓↓ FVC

Definition of abbreviation: R$_{aw}$, airway resistance.
Restrictive lung disease: a condition that reduces the ability to inflate the lungs (e.g., ↓ compliance).

ELASTIC PROPERTIES OF THE LUNG AND CHEST WALL

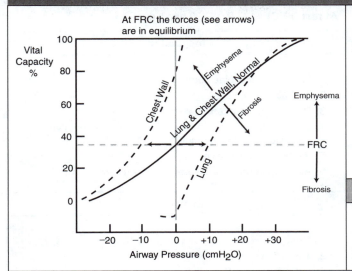

At FRC the forces (see arrows) are in equilibrium

Vital Capacity %

Airway Pressure (cmH₂O)

The figure to the left shows the pressure–volume relationships of the lung, the chest wall, and the lung and chest wall together.

- At FRC, the system is at equilibrium and the airway pressure = 0 cm H_2O. At FRC, the elastic recoil of the lungs tends to collapse the lungs. The tendency of the lungs to collapse is balanced exactly by the tendency of the chest wall to spring outward.
- The result of the opposing forces of the lungs and chest wall cause the intrapleural pressure (PIP) to be negative (a vacuum). The PIP is the pressure in the intrapleural space, which lies between the lungs and chest wall.

Clinical Correlation

If sufficient air is introduced into the intrapleural space, the PIP becomes atmospheric (0 mm Hg), and the lungs and chest wall follow their normal tendencies: the lungs collapse and the chest wall expands. This is a **pneumothorax**.

SURFACE TENSION

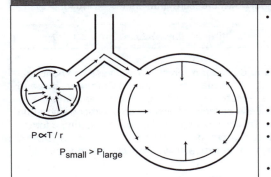

$P \propto T / r$

$P_{small} > P_{large}$

- The attractive forces between adjacent molecules of liquid are stronger than those between liquid and gas, creating a collapsing pressure.

- **Laplace's Law:** $P = \dfrac{2T}{r}$, where P = collapsing pressure
  T = surface tension
  r = radius of alveoli
- Large alveoli (↑r) have low collapsing pressures (easy to keep open).
- Small alveoli (↓r) have high collapsing pressures (difficult to keep open).
- **Surfactant** reduces surface tension (T). With ↓ surfactant (e.g., premature infants), smaller alveoli tend to collapse (**atelectasis**).
- **Surfactant**, produced by **type II alveolar cells**, ↑ **compliance.**

AIRWAY RESISTANCE

Airflow	$Q = \dfrac{\Delta P}{R}$	where Q = airflow ΔP = pressure gradient R = airway resistance
Airway resistance	$R = \dfrac{8\eta l}{\pi r^4}$	where R = resistance η = viscosity of inspired gas l = airway length r = airway radius **Medium-sized bronchi** are the major sites of airway resistance (not the smaller airways because there are so many of them).

Changes in airway resistance		• **Bronchial smooth muscle:**
		  – Parasympathetic nervous system → bronchoconstriction via M₃ muscarinic receptors (↑ resistance)
		  – Sympathetic nervous system → bronchodilation via β₂ receptors (↓ resistance)
		• **Lung volume:**
		  ↑ lung volume → ↓ resistance (greater radial traction on airways)
		  ↓ lung volume → ↑ resistance
		• **Viscosity or density of inspired gas:**
		  ↑ density → ↑ resistance (deep sea diving)
		  ↓ density → ↓ resistance (breathing helium)

THE BREATHING CYCLE

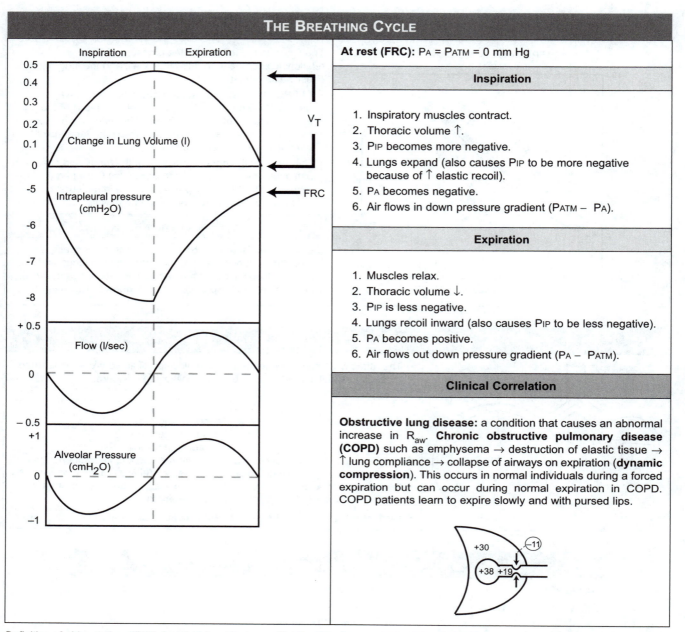

At rest (FRC): $P_A = P_{ATM} = 0$ mm Hg

Inspiration

1. Inspiratory muscles contract.
2. Thoracic volume ↑.
3. P_{IP} becomes more negative.
4. Lungs expand (also causes P_{IP} to be more negative because of ↑ elastic recoil).
5. P_A becomes negative.
6. Air flows in down pressure gradient ($P_{ATM} - P_A$).

Expiration

1. Muscles relax.
2. Thoracic volume ↓.
3. P_{IP} is less negative.
4. Lungs recoil inward (also causes P_{IP} to be less negative).
5. P_A becomes positive.
6. Air flows out down pressure gradient ($P_A - P_{ATM}$).

Clinical Correlation

Obstructive lung disease: a condition that causes an abnormal increase in R_{aw}. **Chronic obstructive pulmonary disease (COPD)** such as emphysema → destruction of elastic tissue → ↑ lung compliance → collapse of airways on expiration (**dynamic compression**). This occurs in normal individuals during a forced expiration but can occur during normal expiration in COPD. COPD patients learn to expire slowly and with pursed lips.

Definition of abbreviations: FRC, functional residual capacity; P_A, alveolar pressure; P_{ATM}, atmospheric pressure.

PULMONARY DISEASE

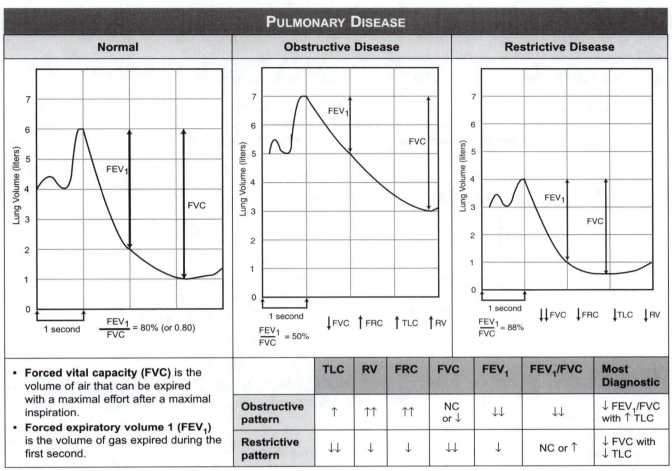

Normal	Obstructive Disease	Restrictive Disease
$\frac{FEV_1}{FVC} = 80\%$ (or 0.80)	$\frac{FEV_1}{FVC} = 50\%$ ↓FVC ↑FRC ↑TLC ↑RV	$\frac{FEV_1}{FVC} = 88\%$ ↓↓FVC ↓FRC ↓TLC ↓RV

- **Forced vital capacity (FVC)** is the volume of air that can be expired with a maximal effort after a maximal inspiration.
- **Forced expiratory volume 1 (FEV$_1$)** is the volume of gas expired during the first second.

	TLC	RV	FRC	FVC	FEV$_1$	FEV$_1$/FVC	Most Diagnostic
Obstructive pattern	↑	↑↑	↑↑	NC or ↓	↓↓	↓↓	↓ FEV$_1$/FVC with ↑ TLC
Restrictive pattern	↓↓	↓	↓	↓↓	↓	NC or ↑	↓ FVC with ↓ TLC

Definition of abbreviation: NC, no change.

SUMMARY OF CLASSIC LUNG DISEASES

Disease	Pattern	Characteristics
Asthma	Obstructive	R$_{aw}$ is ↑ and expiration is impaired. All measures of expiration are ↓ (FVC, FEV$_1$, FEV$_1$/FVC). Air is trapped →↑ FRC.
COPD	Obstructive	• Combination of **chronic bronchitis** and **emphysema** • There is ↑ **compliance**, and expiration is impaired. Air is trapped →↑ FRC. – **"Blue bloaters"** (mainly bronchitis): impaired alveolar ventilation → severe hypoxemia with cyanosis and ↑ Paco$_2$. They are blue and edematous from right heart failure. – **"Pink puffers"** (mainly emphysema): alveolar ventilation is maintained, so they have normal Paco$_2$ and only mild hypoxemia. They have a reddish complexion and breathe with pursed lips at an ↑ respiratory rate.
Fibrosis	Restrictive	• There is ↓ **compliance**, and inspiration is impaired. • **All lung volumes are decreased**, but because FEV$_1$ decreases less than FVC, FEV$_1$/FVC may be increased or normal.

GAS EXCHANGE

PARTIAL PRESSURES OF O_2 AND CO_2

Dalton's Law of Partial Pressures: Partial pressure (p_{gas}) = total pressure (P_T) × fractional gas concentration (F_{gas})

Alveolar gas equation: $P_{AO_2} = P_{IO_2} - P_{CO_2}/R$

Alveolar ventilation equation: $\dot{V}_{CO_2}K/R$; ($K = P_B - P_{H_2O} = 760 - 47 = 713$)

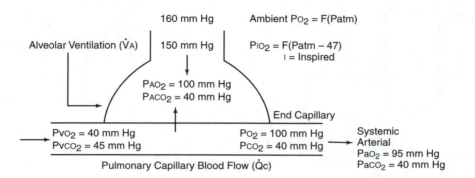

A = alveolar, a = systemic arterial

	Equation	O_2	CO_2
Dry inspired air (any altitude)	F_{gas}	0.21	0
Dry air at sea level	$P_{gas} = F_{gas} \times P_B$	0.21 (760) = 160	0
Inspired, humidified tracheal air	$P_{gas} = F_{gas} \times (P_B - P_{H_2O})$	0.21 (760 − 47) = **150**	0
Alveolar air ($P_{A_{gas}}$)	O_2: $P_{AO_2} = P_{IO_2} - P_{ACO_2}/R$ CO_2: $\dot{V}_{CO_2}K/R$	150 − 40/0.8 = **100**	(280 mL/min × 713)/5,000 mL/min = **40**
Systemic arterial blood ($P_{a_{gas}}$)	—	**100** (completely equilibrates with alveolar O_2 if no lung disease)	**40** (CO_2 is from pulmonary capillaries and equilibrates with alveolar gas)
Mixed venous blood ($P\bar{v}_{CO_2}$)	—	**40** (O_2 has diffused from arterial blood into tissues)	**45** (CO_2 has diffused from tissues to venous blood)

All pressures are expressed in mm Hg.

Definition of abbreviations: K, constant; P_{ACO_2}, partial pressure of alveolar carbon dioxide; P_{AO_2}, partial pressure of alveolar oxygen; P_B, barometric pressure; P_{H_2O}, water vapor pressure; P_{IO_2}, partial pressure of inspired oxygen; $\dot{V}_{CO_2}$, CO_2 production; R, respiratory exchange ratio.

DIFFUSION

Fick's Law of Diffusion	<ul><li>$V_{gas} \propto D(P_1 - P_2) \times A/T$ where V_{gas} = diffusion of gas, D = diffusion coefficient of a specific gas, A = surface area, T = thickness.</li><li>A and T are physical factors that change mainly in disease.</li><li>D of CO_2 >>> O_2</li></ul>
Time course in pulmonary capillary	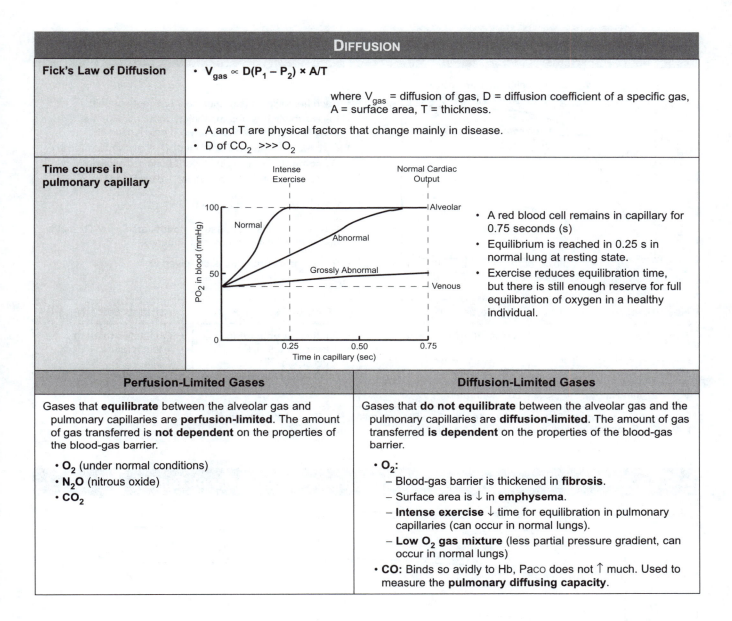 <ul><li>A red blood cell remains in capillary for 0.75 seconds (s)</li><li>Equilibrium is reached in 0.25 s in normal lung at resting state.</li><li>Exercise reduces equilibration time, but there is still enough reserve for full equilibration of oxygen in a healthy individual.</li></ul>

Perfusion-Limited Gases	Diffusion-Limited Gases
Gases that **equilibrate** between the alveolar gas and pulmonary capillaries are **perfusion-limited**. The amount of gas transferred is **not dependent** on the properties of the blood-gas barrier. <ul><li>**O_2** (under normal conditions)</li><li>**N_2O** (nitrous oxide)</li><li>**CO_2**</li></ul>	Gases that **do not equilibrate** between the alveolar gas and the pulmonary capillaries are **diffusion-limited**. The amount of gas transferred **is dependent** on the properties of the blood-gas barrier. <ul><li>**O_2:**<ul><li>Blood-gas barrier is thickened in **fibrosis**.</li><li>Surface area is ↓ in **emphysema**.</li><li>**Intense exercise** ↓ time for equilibration in pulmonary capillaries (can occur in normal lungs).</li><li>**Low O_2 gas mixture** (less partial pressure gradient, can occur in normal lungs)</li></ul></li><li>**CO:** Binds so avidly to Hb, Paco does not ↑ much. Used to measure the **pulmonary diffusing capacity**.</li></ul>

OXYGEN TRANSPORT AND THE HEMOGLOBIN–O$_2$ DISSOCIATION CURVE

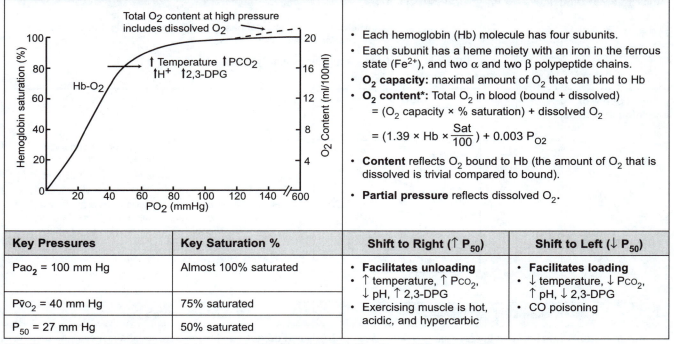

- Each hemoglobin (Hb) molecule has four subunits.
- Each subunit has a heme moiety with an iron in the ferrous state (Fe^{2+}), and two α and two β polypeptide chains.
- **O$_2$ capacity:** maximal amount of O_2 that can bind to Hb
- **O$_2$ content*:** Total O_2 in blood (bound + dissolved)

  = (O_2 capacity × % saturation) + dissolved O_2

  = $(1.39 \times Hb \times \dfrac{Sat}{100}) + 0.003\, P_{O2}$

- **Content** reflects O_2 bound to Hb (the amount of O_2 that is dissolved is trivial compared to bound).
- **Partial pressure** reflects dissolved O_2.

Key Pressures	Key Saturation %	Shift to Right (↑ P$_{50}$)	Shift to Left (↓ P$_{50}$)
Pao$_2$ = 100 mm Hg	Almost 100% saturated	• **Facilitates unloading** • ↑ temperature, ↑ Pco$_2$, ↓ pH, ↑ 2,3-DPG • Exercising muscle is hot, acidic, and hypercarbic	• **Facilitates loading** • ↓ temperature, ↓ Pco$_2$, ↑ pH, ↓ 2,3-DPG • CO poisoning
Pv̄o$_2$ = 40 mm Hg	75% saturated		
P$_{50}$ = 27 mm Hg	50% saturated		

Definition of abbreviations: Hb, hemoglobin concentration; Sat, saturation; P$_{50}$, Po$_2$ at 50% saturation.
*1.39 mL of O_2 binds 1 g of Hb (some texts use 1.34 or 1.36).

ADDITIONAL CHANGES IN THE HEMOGLOBIN–O$_2$ DISSOCIATION CURVE

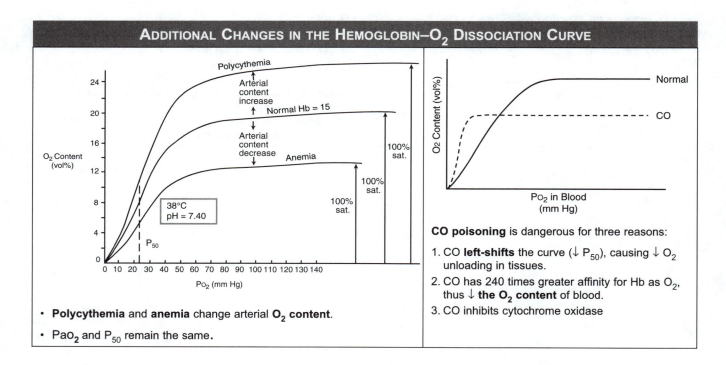

- **Polycythemia** and **anemia** change arterial **O$_2$ content**.
- Pao$_2$ and P$_{50}$ remain the same.

CO poisoning is dangerous for three reasons:

1. CO **left-shifts** the curve (↓ P$_{50}$), causing ↓ O_2 unloading in tissues.
2. CO has 240 times greater affinity for Hb as O_2, thus ↓ the **O$_2$ content** of blood.
3. CO inhibits cytochrome oxidase

CO₂ TRANSPORT

	Forms of CO_2
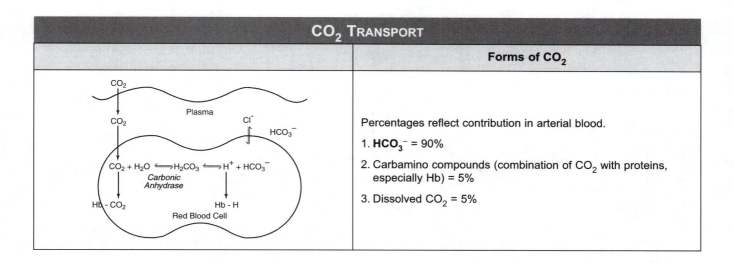	Percentages reflect contribution in arterial blood. 1. **HCO_3^- = 90%** 2. Carbamino compounds (combination of CO_2 with proteins, especially Hb) = 5% 3. Dissolved CO_2 = 5%

PULMONARY BLOOD FLOW

Resistance (R)	Very low
Compliance	Very high
Pressures	Very low compared with systemic circulation
Effect of P_{AO_2}	• **Alveolar hypoxia → vasoconstriction.** • This is a local effect and the opposite of other organs, where hypoxia → vasodilation. • This directs blood away from hypoxic alveoli to better ventilated areas • This is also why fetal pulmonary vascular resistance is so high. Pulmonary resistance ↓ when the first breath oxygenates the alveoli, causing pulmonary blood flow to rise.
Gravity	Upright posture: greatest flow in base; lowest in apex
Filter	Removes small clots from circulation
Vasoactive substances	Converts angiotensin I → AII; inactivates bradykinin; removes prostaglandin E_2 and $F_{2\alpha}$ and leukotrienes

VENTILATION–PERFUSION RELATIONSHIPS

$\dot{V}/\dot{Q}$: the ratio of alveolar ventilation ($\dot{V}$) to pulmonary blood flow ($\dot{Q}$).

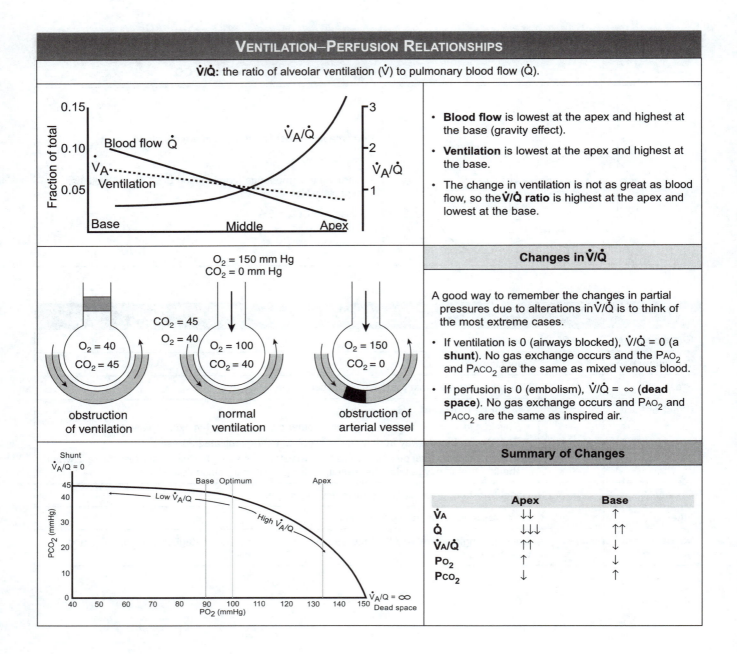

- **Blood flow** is lowest at the apex and highest at the base (gravity effect).
- **Ventilation** is lowest at the apex and highest at the base.
- The change in ventilation is not as great as blood flow, so the $\dot{V}/\dot{Q}$ **ratio** is highest at the apex and lowest at the base.

Changes in $\dot{V}/\dot{Q}$

A good way to remember the changes in partial pressures due to alterations in $\dot{V}/\dot{Q}$ is to think of the most extreme cases.

- If ventilation is 0 (airways blocked), $\dot{V}/\dot{Q} = 0$ (a **shunt**). No gas exchange occurs and the P_{AO_2} and P_{ACO_2} are the same as mixed venous blood.
- If perfusion is 0 (embolism), $\dot{V}/\dot{Q} = \infty$ (**dead space**). No gas exchange occurs and P_{AO_2} and P_{ACO_2} are the same as inspired air.

Summary of Changes

	Apex	Base
$\dot{V}_A$	↓↓	↑
$\dot{Q}$	↓↓↓	↑↑
$\dot{V}_A/\dot{Q}$	↑↑	↓
P_{O_2}	↑	↓
P_{CO_2}	↓	↑

DISORDERS THAT AFFECT ARTERIAL OXYGEN PRESSURE OR CONTENT

	Notes	Pa_{O_2}	Pa_{CO_2}	Ca_{O_2}	A-a*	Response to Supplemental O_2 ☠
Hypoventilation[1]	Drugs (e.g., opiates, barbiturates), head trauma, chest wall dysfunction	↓	↑	↓	NC	↑ Pa_{O_2}; ↑ Ca_{O_2}
↓ inspired pO_2	↑ altitude	↓	↓[2]	↓	NC	↑ Pa_{O_2}; ↑ Ca_{O_2}
Diffusion limitation[3]	PA_{O_2} and Pa_{O_2} do not fully equilibrate	↓	NC[2]	↓	↑	↑ Pa_{O_2}; ↑ Ca_{O_2}
Shunt[4]	Venous blood mixes with arterial system, bypassing ventilated areas of lung	↓	NC[2]	↓	↑	Poor
V̇/Q mismatch	Ventilation and perfusion are mismatched in the lung	↓	NC[2]	↓	↑	↑ Pa_{O_2}; ↑ Ca_{O_2}
CO poisoning	Exhaust fumes	NC	NC	↓	NC	↑ Pa_{O_2}; NC in Ca_{O_2}[5]
↓ [Hb]	Anemia	NC	NC	↓	NC	↑ Pa_{O_2}; NC in Ca_{O_2}[6]

Definition of abbreviation: NC, no change or minimal response.

*An increase in the A-a gradient indicates a problem with gas exchange.

☠ *Warning:* Supplemental O_2 in CNS depression and lung disease can shut off the hypoxic drive to ventilation and cause cessation of spontaneous breathing.

[1]Hypoventilation: ↓ V̇A, so ↑ PA_{CO_2} → ↓ PA_{O_2} → ↓ Pa_{O_2} (As ↑ CO_2 diffuses into alveoli from blood, it displaces O_2.)

[2]Result of hypoxia-induced increase of ventilation

[3]Diffusion limitation causes disease (blood gas barrier has less surface area or is thickened), ↓ transit time during intense exercise, exercise at high altitude

[4]Abnormal shunts (often congenital, e.g., Tetralogy of Fallot)

[5]Slow response of Ca_{O_2} due to extremely high affinity of Hb for carbon monoxide

[6]Can only increase dissolved O_2 because Hb is saturated at normal Pa_{O_2}.

CONTROL OF VENTILATION

Brainstem Respiratory Centers

Medulla	Rhythm generator	**Inspiratory center:** generates breathing rhythm **Expiratory center:** not active during normal, passive expiration; involved in active expiration (e.g., exercise)
Pons	Regulates medulla	**Apneustic center:** stimulates prolonged inspiration **Pneumotaxic center:** terminates inspiration
Cortex	Conscious and emotional response	Lesions above the pons eliminate voluntary control, but basic breathing pattern remains intact.

CHEMORECEPTORS

	Central (Medulla) Chemoreceptors (Respond to Changes in pH of CSF)	Peripheral Chemoreceptors (Carotid and Aortic Bodies)
O_2	No response	• ↓ PaO_2 (<60 mm Hg) → stimulates chemoreceptors → increased ventilation. • *Note:* stimulated by changes in pressure, not O_2 content; thus, not stimulated by anemia.
CO_2	↑ Pco_2 → stimulate chemoreceptors → ↑ **ventilation (via H⁺)**	• ↑ $Paco_2$ → stimulation →↑ ventilation. • Central chemoreceptor response is most important during normal breathing.
H⁺	↑ H⁺ → stimulation ↑ ventilation detects H⁺ in CSF; 80–95% of response to hypercapnia	• ↑ H⁺ → stimulation → ↑ ventilation. • *Note:* Most of the response to metabolic acidosis is peripheral because fixed acids penetrate blood/brain barrier poorly.

Clinical Correlation

Patients with severe lung disease can have chronic CO_2 retention, and the pH of their CSF can return to normal despite their hypercapnia. Having lost their CO_2 stimulus to ventilate, their hypoxic ventilatory drive becomes very important. If these patients are given enriched O_2 to breathe to correct their hypoxemia, their primary ventilatory drive will be removed, which can cause severe depression of ventilation.

Note: Other receptors such as pulmonary stretch receptors, irritant receptors, and joint and muscle receptors also have roles in the regulation of ventilation.

RESPONSE TO HIGH ALTITUDE

Parameter	Response
PAO_2	↓ (because PB is ↓)
PaO_2	↓ (hypoxemia because PAO_2 is ↓)
Respiratory rate	↑ (hypoxic stimulation of peripheral chemoreceptors)
$Paco_2$ and $PAco_2$	↓ (hyperventilation due to hypoxemia)
Arterial pH	↑ (because of respiratory alkalosis); later becomes normal (renal compensation)
[Hb]	↑ (polycythemia)
Hb % saturation	↓ (because ↓ Po_2)
Pulmonary vascular resistance	↑ (hypoxic vasoconstriction); this plus polycythemia lead to ↑ work and hypertrophy of right heart
[2,3-DPG]	↑
Hemoglobin-O_2 curve	Right-shift (because of ↑ 2,3-DPG)
Acute mountain sickness	Hypoxemia and alkalosis cause headache, fatigue, nausea, dizziness, palpitations, and insomnia. Treatment with acetazolamide can be therapeutic.
Chronic mountain sickness	Reduced exercise tolerance, fatigue, hypoxemia, polycythemia

RESPIRATORY PATHOLOGY

EAR, NOSE, THROAT, AND UPPER RESPIRATORY SYSTEM INFECTIONS

Type of Infection	Case Vignette/Key Clues	Common Causative Agents	Pathogenesis	Diagnosis	Treatment
Sinusitis	Sinus pain; low-grade fever	*Streptococcus pneumoniae*	Capsule, IgA protease	Gram ⊕ coccus, catalase ⊖	Penicillin
		Haemophilus influenzae	Capsule, IgA protease, endotoxin	Gram ⊖ rod, chocolate agar	Amoxicillin
		Moraxella catarrhalis	β-lactamase producer	Gram ⊖ coccus	Ceftriaxone
Oral cavitary disease	Sore mouth with thick, white coating that can be scraped off easily to reveal painful red base	*Candida albicans*	Overgrowth of normal flora, immunocompromised, overuse of antibiotics	Gram ⊕ yeast, germ tube test	Nystatin, miconazole
Sore throat	Inflamed tonsils/pharynx, abscesses; cervical lymphadenopathy, fever, ± stomach upset; ± sandpaper rash	*Streptococcus pyogenes*	Exotoxins A–C (superantigens)	Rapid antigen test; gram ⊕, catalase ⊖ coccus; β-hemolytic, bacitracin sensitive	Penicillin
	White papules with red base on posterior palate and pharynx, fever	Coxsackie A	Unknown	Virus culture or PCR	None
	Throat looks like *Streptococcus* with severe fatigue, lymphadenopathy, fever, ± rash	Epstein-Barr virus	Infects B lymphocytes by attachment to CD21, causes ↑ CTLs	Heterophile ⊕ (Monospot test); mononucleosis; 70% lymphocytosis (Downey type II cells = CTLs)	Supportive
	Low-grade fever with a 1–2 day gradual onset of membranous nasopharyngitis and/or obstructive laryngotracheitis; bull neck from lymphadenopathy; elevated BUN; abnormal ECG; little change in WBC; unvaccinated	*Corynebacterium diphtheriae*	Diphtheria toxin inactivates EF-2 in heart, nerves, epithelium; pseudomembrane → airway obstruction; released when exudate scraped off	Gram ⊕ nonmotile rod, Loeffler medium, ELEK test	Penicillin, antitoxin
Common cold	Rhinitis, sneezing, coughing; seasonal peaks	Rhinoviruses (summer–fall) Coronaviruses (winter–spring)	—	—	—
Acute otitis media	Red, bulging tympanic membrane, fever 102–103°F; pain goes away if drum ruptures or if ear tubes are patent	*Streptococcus pneumoniae*	Capsule, IgA protease	Gram ⊕ coccus, catalase ⊖	Penicillin
		H. influenzae (nontypeable)	Capsule, IgA protease, endotoxin	Gram ⊖ rod, chocolate agar	Amoxicillin
		Moraxella catarrhalis	β-lactamase producer	Gram ⊖ diplococcus	Ceftriaxone

(Continued)

EAR, NOSE, THROAT, AND UPPER RESPIRATORY SYSTEM INFECTIONS *(CONT'D.)*

Type of Infection	Case Vignette/Key Clues	Common Causative Agents	Pathogenesis	Diagnosis	Treatment
Otitis externa	Ear pain	*Staphylococcus aureus*	Normal flora enter abrasions	Gram ⊕, catalase ⊕, coagulase ⊕	β-lactamase-resistant penicillin
		Candida albicans	Normal flora enter abrasions	Gram ⊕ yeast, germ tube test	Nystatin, miconazole
		Proteus	From water source	Gram ⊖ rod, urease ⊕	Susceptibility testing*
		Pseudomonas	From water source	Gram ⊖ rod, oxidase ⊕, blue-green pigments	Susceptibility testing*
Malignant otitis externa	Severe ear pain in diabetic; life-threatening	*Pseudomonas aeruginosa*	Capsule	Gram ⊖ rod, oxidase ⊕, blue-green pigments	Susceptibility testing*

Definition of abbreviations: CTLs, cytotoxic T lymphocytes.

*Because there is so much drug resistance in these genera, susceptibility testing is necessary.

MIDDLE RESPIRATORY TRACT INFECTIONS

Disease	Case Vignette/Key Clues	Common Causative Agents	Pathogenesis	Diagnosis	Treatment
Epiglottitis	Inflamed epiglottis; patient often 2–3 years old and unvaccinated	*Haemophilus influenzae*	Capsule (polyribitol phosphate) inhibits phagocytosis; IgA protease	Gram ⊖ rod, chocolate agar requires hemin and NAD	Ceftriaxone
Croup	Infant with fever, sharp barking cough, inspiratory stridor, hoarse phonation	Parainfluenza virus (croup)	Viral cytolysis; multinucleated giant cells formed	Detect virus in respiratory washings	Ribavirin
Laryngotracheitis, laryngotracheobronchitis	Hoarseness, burning retrosternal pain	Parainfluenza virus	Viral cytolysis; multinucleated giant cells formed	Detect virus in respiratory washings	Ribavirin
Bronchitis	Wheezy; infant or child ≤5 years old	RSV	Fusion protein creates syncytia	Direct immunofluorescence for viral Ags	Ribavirin
	>5 years old	*Mycoplasma pneumoniae*, viruses	Release of O_2 radicals causes necrosis of epithelium	Slow growth on Eaton medium, cold agglutinins	Symptomatic

Definition of abbreviations: Ag, antigens; NAD, nicotinamide adenine dinucleotide; RSV, respiratory syncytial virus.

PNEUMONIA

Lobar pneumonia and bronchopneumonia—acute inflammation and consolidation (solidification) of the lung due to a bacterial agent. Lobar affects entire lobe (opacification = consolidation on x-ray); bronchopneumonia (patchy consolidation around bronchioles on x-ray).

Interstitial (atypical) pneumonia causes interstitial pneumonitis without consolidation and can be due to viral agents (influenza virus; parainfluenza; RSV, especially in young children; adenovirus; CMV, especially in immunocompromised; varicella, and *Mycoplasma pneumoniae*.

Clinical:
- Fever and chills
- Cough (may be productive)
- Tachypnea
- Pleuritic chest pain
- Decreased breath sounds, rales, and dullness to percussion
- Elevated WBC count with a left shift

Type of Infection	Case Vignette/ Key Clues	Most Common Causative Agents	Pathogenesis	Diagnosis	Treatment
Pneumonia—typical	Adults (including alcoholics), rusty sputum; Lobar pneumonia or less commonly, bronchopneumonia	*Streptococcus pneumoniae, Haemophilus influenzae*	Capsule antiphagocytic IgA protease	Gram ⊕ diplococcus, α hemolytic, catalase ⊖ lysed by bile, inhibited by Optochin	Third-generation cephalosporin, azithromycin
	Neutropenic patients, burn patients, CGD, CF	*Pseudomonas aeruginosa*	Opportunist	Gram ⊖ rod, oxidase ⊕, blue-green pigments	Sensitivity testing required
	Foul-smelling sputum, aspiration possible	Anaerobes, mixed infection (*Bacteroides, Fusobacterium, Peptococcus*)	Aspiration of vomitus → enzyme damage → anaerobic foci	Culture of sputum	Empiric antibiotic therapy (amoxicillin/ clavulanate, gentamicin)
	Alcoholic, abscess formation, aspiration, facultative anaerobic, gram ⊖ bacterium with huge capsule, currant jelly sputum	*Klebsiella pneumoniae*	Capsule protects against phagocytosis	Gram ⊖ rod, lactose fermenting, oxidase ⊖	Susceptibility testing necessary
Pneumonia—atypical	Poorly nourished, unvaccinated baby/child; giant cell pneumonia with hemorrhagic rash, Koplik spots	Measles: malnourishment ↑ risk of pneumonia and blindness	Cytolysis in lymph nodes, skin, mucosa	Serology	Supportive
	Pneumonia teens/ young adults; bad hacking, dry cough "walking pneumonia"	*Mycoplasma pneumoniae* (most common cause of pneumonia in school-age children)	Adhesin causes adhesion to mucus; oxygen radicals cause necrosis of epithelium	Serology, cold agglutinins	Tetracycline, erythromycin

(Continued)

PNEUMONIA (CONT'D.)

Type of Infection	Case Vignette/ Key Clues	Most Common Causative Agents	Pathogenesis	Diagnosis	Treatment
Pneumonia—atypical (*cont'd.*)	Air-conditioning exposure, common showers, especially >50 years, heavy smoker, drinker	*Legionella* spp.	Intracellular in macrophages	Direct fluorescent antibody	Erythromycin
	Bird exposure ± hepatitis	*Chlamydia psittaci*	Obligate intracellular	Direct fluorescent antibody, intracytoplasmic inclusions	Tetracycline, erythromycin
	AIDS patients with staccato cough; "ground glass" x-ray; biopsy: honeycomb exudate with silver staining cysts; premature infants	*Pneumocystis jiroveci (carinii)*	Attaches to type I pneumocytes, causes excess replication of type II pneumocytes	Silver-staining cysts in alveolar lavage	Trimethoprim sulfamethoxazole, pentamidine
	Primary influenza pneumonia Secondary (bacterial)	Influenza virus	Cytolysis in respiratory tract; cytokines contribute; secondary infections common	Virus culture	Amantadine, rimantadine
Acute pneumonia or chronic cough with weight loss, night sweats	Over 55 years, HIV ⊕, or immigrant from developing country	*Mycobacterium tuberculosis*	Facultative intracellular parasite → cell-mediated immunity and DTH	Auramine-rhodamine stain of sputum acid-fast bacilli	Multidrug therapy
	Dusty environment with bird or bat fecal contamination (Missouri chicken farmers, Ohio river)	*Histoplasma capsulatum*	Facultative intracellular	Yeast cells in sputum	Amphotericin B
	Desert sand S.W. United States	*Coccidioides immitis*	Acute, chronic lung infection, dissemination	Endospores in spherules in tissues	Amphotericin B
	Rotting, contaminated wood, same endemic focus as *Histoplasma* and east coast states	*Blastomyces dermatitidis*	Acute, chronic lung infection, dissemination	Yeast cells in sputum or skin	Ketoconazole
Sudden acute respiratory syndromes	Travel to Far East, Toronto, winter, early spring	SARS agent	Replication in cells of upper respiratory tree	Serology, virus, isolation	None
	"Four Corners" region (CO, UT, NM, AZ), spring, inhalation rodent urine	Hantavirus (Sin Nombre)	Virus disseminates to CNS, liver, kidneys, endothelium	Serology, virus, isolation	Ribavirin

Definition of abbreviations: CGD, chronic granulomatous disease; CMV, cytomegalovirus; CF, cystic fibrosis; DTH, delayed-type hypersensitivity; RSV, respiratory syncytial virus.

GRANULOMATOUS DISEASES

Tuberculosis

Causes **caseating granulomas** containing acid-fast mycobacteria; transmission is by inhalation of aerosolized bacilli; increasing incidence in the U.S., secondary to AIDS

- Primary tuberculosis (initial exposure) can produce a **Ghon complex**, characterized by a subpleural caseous granuloma above or below the lobar fissure, accompanied by hilar lymph node granulomas.
- Secondary tuberculosis (reactivation or reinfection) tends to involve the **lung apex**.
- Progressive pulmonary tuberculosis can take the forms of cavitary tuberculosis, miliary pulmonary tuberculosis, and tuberculous bronchopneumonia. Miliary tuberculosis can also spread to involve other body sites.

Clinical: fevers and night sweats, weight loss, cough, hemoptysis, positive skin test (PPD)

Sarcoidosis

Sarcoidosis is a granulomatous disease of unknown etiology; affects females > males, ages 20–60; most common in African American women. **Noncaseating granulomas** occur in any organ of the body; hilar and mediastinal adenopathy are typical.

Clinical: Cough, shortness of breath, fatigue, malaise, skin lesions, eye irritation or pain, fever/night sweats

Labs: ↑ serum **angiotensin-converting enzyme** (ACE)
Schaumann bodies: laminated calcifications
Asteroid bodies: stellate giant-cell cytoplasmic inclusions

OBSTRUCTIVE LUNG DISEASE

Increased resistance to airflow secondary to obstruction of airways

Chronic obstructive pulmonary disease (COPD) includes chronic bronchitis, emphysema, asthma, and bronchiectasis.

Disease	Characteristics	Clinical Findings
Chronic bronchitis	• Persistent cough and copious **sputum production for at least 3 months** each year in 2 consecutive years • Highly **associated with smoking** (90%)	• Cough, sputum production, dyspnea, frequent infections • Hypoxia, cyanosis, weight gain
Emphysema	• Associated with destruction of alveolar septa, resulting in enlarged air spaces and a loss of elastic recoil, and producing overinflated, enlarged lungs • Thought to be due to protease/antiprotease imbalance *Gross:* • **Overinflated, enlarged lungs** • Enlarged, grossly visible air spaces • Formation of apical blebs and bullae (centriacinar type)	• Progressive dyspnea • Pursing of lips and **use of accessory muscles** to breathe • **Barrel chest** • Weight loss
Centriacinar (centrilobular) emphysema	• **Proximal respiratory bronchioles** involved • Most common type (95%) • **Associated with smoking** • Worst in apical segments of upper lobes	
Panacinar (panlobular) emphysema	• **Entire acinus involved**; distal alveoli spared • Less common • **Alpha-1-antitrypsin deficiency** • *Distribution:* entire lung; worse in bases of lower lobes	
Asthma	• Due to hyperreactive airways, resulting in episodic **bronchospasm**, producing **wheezing**, severe **dyspnea**, and coughing. • Inflammation, edema, hypertrophy of mucous glands with **goblet cell hyperplasia** and **mucus plugs** are characteristic findings. • Hypertrophy of bronchial wall smooth muscle, thickened basement membranes	

(Continued)

OBSTRUCTIVE LUNG DISEASE (CONT'D.)

Extrinsic asthma	• **Type I hypersensitivit**y reaction • **Allergic (atopic)**—most common type • Childhood and young adults; ⊕ **family history** • Allergens: pollen, dust, food, molds, animal dander, etc. • Occupational exposure: fumes, gases, and chemicals
Intrinsic asthma	• Unknown mechanism • **Respiratory infections** (usually viral) • **Stress** • **Exercise** • **Cold** temperatures • Drug induced (**aspirin**)
Bronchiectasis	• An abnormal permanent airway dilatation due to **chronic necrotizing infection** • Most patients have underlying lung disease, such as bronchial obstruction, necrotizing pneumonias, **cystic fibrosis**, or **Kartagener syndrome**.

DRUGS FOR ASTHMA

Class	Agents	Mechanism	Comments
Bronchodilators			
β_2 agonists	Albuterol Terbutaline Metaproterenol Salmeterol Formoterol	Stimulate β_2 receptors → ↑ cAMP → smooth muscle relaxation	• Generally have the advantage of **minimal cardiac side effects** • Most often used as **inhalants** • Salmeterol and formoterol are **long-acting** agents, so are useful for prophylaxis • Cause skeletal muscle **tremors**; some **CV** side effects (tachycardia, arrhythmias) can still occur
Non-selective β agonists	Epinephrine ($\alpha_1, \alpha_2, \beta_1, \beta_2$) Isoproterenol ($\beta_1, \beta_2$)	Stimulate β_2 receptors → ↑ cAMP → smooth muscle relaxation	• Not used as much as the β_2 agonists • Epinephrine is used for **acute** asthma attacks and for **anaphylaxis**
Muscarinic antagonists	Ipratropium Tiotropium	Block muscarinic receptors, inhibiting vagally induced bronchoconstriction	• Used as an inhalant; there are minimal systemic side effects • Used in asthma and COPD • β_2 agonists are generally preferred for acute bronchospasm • These are useful in **COPD** because it decreases bronchial secretions and has fewer CV side effects • Tiotropium is longer-acting
Methylxanthines	Theophylline	Inhibit PDE; block adenosine receptors	• Available orally • Major use is for asthma (although β_2 agonists are first-line)
Leukotriene Antagonists			
Leukotriene antagonists	Zafirlukast Montelukast	Block LTD_4 (and LTE_4) leukotriene receptors	• Orally active; not used for acute asthma episodes • Prevents exercise-, antigen-, and aspirin-induced asthma
5-lipoxygenase inhibitors	Zileuton	Block leukotriene synthesis	
Anti-inflammatory Agents			
Corticosteroids	Beclomethasone Prednisone, prednisolone Others	Inhibit phospholipase A_2 → ↓ arachidonic acid synthesis	• ↓ inflammation and edema • Used orally and inhaled • IV use in status asthmaticus
Release inhibitors	Cromolyn Nedocromil	Inhibit mast cell degranulation	• Can prevent allergy-induced bronchoconstriction • Available as nasal spray, oral, eye drops

RESTRICTIVE LUNG DISEASE
(Decreased Lung Volumes and Capacities)

Examples

Chest wall disorders: obesity, kyphoscoliosis, polio, etc.

Intrinsic lung disease:

Adult respiratory distress syndrome (ARDS)

Neonatal respiratory distress syndrome (NRDS)

Pneumoconioses (silicosis, asbestosis, "black lung" disease from coal dust)

Sarcoidosis

Idiopathic pulmonary fibrosis (Hamman-Rich syndrome)

Goodpasture syndrome

Wegener granulomatosis

Eosinophilic granuloma

Collagen-vascular diseases

Hypersensitivity pneumonitis

Drug exposure

RESPIRATORY DISTRESS SYNDROMES

Adult Respiratory Distress Syndrome (ARDS)

- Diffuse damage to the alveolar epithelium and capillaries, resulting in progressive respiratory failure unresponsive to oxygen therapy
- **Causes:** shock, sepsis, trauma, gastric aspiration, radiation, oxygen toxicity, drugs, pulmonary infections, and many others
- **Clinical presentation:** dyspnea, tachypnea, hypoxemia, cyanosis, and use of accessory respiratory muscles
  - X-ray: **bilateral lung opacity** ("white out")
  - Gross: heavy, **stiff, noncompliant lungs**
  - Micro:

    Interstitial and intra-alveolar edema

    Interstitial inflammation

    Loss of type I pneumocytes

    Hyaline membrane formation
  - Overall mortality 50%

Neonatal Respiratory Distress Syndrome (NRDS)

Also known as **hyaline membrane disease of newborns**. Causes respiratory distress within hours of birth and is seen in infants with **deficiency of surfactant** secondary to prematurity (gestational age of <28 weeks has a 60% incidence), maternal diabetes, multiple births, or C-section delivery

- Clinical presentation: often normal at birth, but within a few hours develop increasing respiratory effort, tachypnea, nasal flaring, use of accessory muscle of respiration, an expiratory grunt, cyanosis
- X-ray: "**ground-glass**" reticulogranular densities
- Labs: lecithin: sphingomyelin ratio <2
- Micro: atelectasis and **hyaline membrane formation**
- Treatment: surfactant replacement and oxygen
- Complications of oxygen treatment in newborns:
  - **Bronchopulmonary dysplasia**
  - **Retrolental fibroplasia** (retinopathy of prematurity)
- **Prevention:** delay labor and corticosteroids to mature the lung

TUMORS OF LUNG AND PLEURA

Bronchogenic carcinoma is the leading cause of cancer deaths among both men and women.

Major Risk Factors

- **Cigarette smoking**
- Occupational exposures (asbestosis, uranium mining, radiation)
- Air pollution

Histologic Types

Adenocarcinoma, bronchioloalveolar carcinoma, squamous cell carcinoma, small cell carcinoma, and large cell carcinoma

- Oncogenes
    - **L-*myc:*** small cell carcinomas
    - **K-*ras:*** adenocarcinomas
- Tumor suppressor genes
    - **p53** and the retinoblastoma gene

Complications

- **Spread to hilar, bronchial, tracheal, or mediastinal nodes** in 50% of cases
- **Superior vena cava syndrome** (obstruction of SVC by tumor)
- **Esophageal obstruction**
- **Recurrent laryngeal nerve** involvement (hoarseness)
- **Phrenic nerve** damage, causing diaphragmatic paralysis
- Extrathoracic metastasis to adrenal, liver, brain, and bone
- **Pancoast tumor:** compression of cervical sympathetic plexus, leading to ipsilateral **Horner syndrome** (miosis, ptosis, anhidrosis)

Type of Cancer/(Percentage of Total)	Association with Smoking; Sex Preference	Location	Pathology
Adenocarcinoma/35% **Bronchioloalveolar carcinoma** (5%)—subset of adenocarcinoma	**Less strongly related**; female > male; most common lung cancer in nonsmokers	**Peripheral**, may occur in scars; can have associated pleural involvement	Forms glands and may produce mucin
Squamous cell/30%	**Strongly related;** male > female	**Central**	• Invasive nests of squamous cells, intercellular bridges (desmosomes); keratin production ("**squamous pearls**") • Hyperparathyroidism secondary to increased secretion of parathyroid related peptide
Small cell (oat cell) carcinoma/20%	**Strongly related;** male > female	**Central**	• Very aggressive; micro: small round cells • Frequently associated with paraneoplastic syndromes, including production of ACTH (Cushing syndrome), ADH, and parathyroid related peptide
Large cell/10%	—	—	Large anaplastic cells without evidence of differentiation
Carcinoid/<5%	—	Bronchial	May produce carcinoid syndrome

DISEASES OF THE PLEURA	
Pleural effusion	• Accumulation of **fluid in the pleural cavity**; may be a transudate or exudate • Chylous fluid in pleural space secondary to obstruction of thoracic duct (usually by tumor) = chylothorax
Pneumothorax	• **Air in the pleural cavity**, often due to penetrating chest wall injuries • *Spontaneous pneumothorax:* young adults with rupture of emphysematous blebs • *Tension pneumothorax:* life-threatening shift of thoracic organs across midline • Clinical: ↓ breath sounds, hyperresonance, tracheal shift to opposite side
Mesothelioma	• Highly malignant tumor of pleura (and peritoneum) • Pleural mesothelioma is associated with **asbestos exposure** in 90% of cases (**bronchogenic carcinoma** also strongly associated with asbestos exposure)

PULMONARY VASCULAR DISORDERS	
Pulmonary edema	Fluid accumulation within the lungs that can be due to many causes, including left-sided heart failure, mitral valve stenosis, fluid overload, nephrotic syndrome, liver disease, infections, drugs, shock, and radiation
Pulmonary emboli	Mostly arise from **deep vein thrombosis** in the leg (also arise from pelvic veins) and may be asymptomatic, cause pulmonary infarction, or cause sudden death; severity related to size of embolus and other comorbid conditions
Pulmonary hypertension	Pulmonary hypertension is increased artery pressure, usually due to increased vascular resistance or blood flow; can be idiopathic or related to underlying COPD, interstitial disease, pulmonary emboli, mitral stenosis, left heart failure, and congenital heart disease with left-to-right shunt

The Renal and Urinary System

DEVELOPMENT OF THE KIDNEY AND URETER (MESODERM)

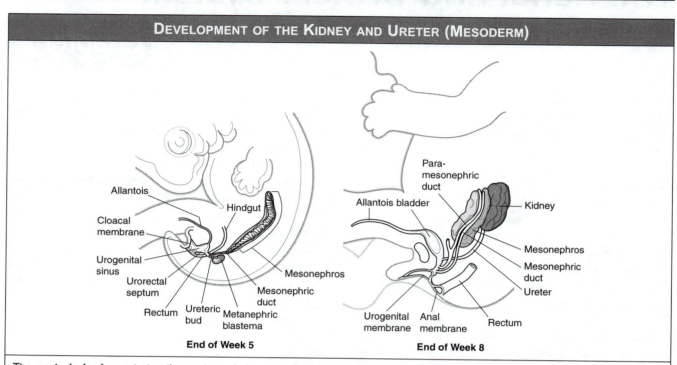

End of Week 5

End of Week 8

The **ureteric bud** penetrates the **metanephric mass**, which condenses around the diverticulum to form the metanephrogenic blastema. The **bud** dilates to form the **renal pelvis**, which subsequently splits into the cranial and caudal **major calyces**, which form the **minor calyces**. One to 3 million collecting tubules develop from the minor calyces, forming the renal pyramids.

Penetration of collecting tubules into the metanephric mass induces cells of the tissue cap to form nephrons, or excretory units.

- The **proximal nephron forms Bowman capsule**, whereas the **distal nephron connects to a collecting tubule**.
- Lengthening of the excretory tubule gives rise to the **proximal convoluted tubule**, the **loop of Henle**, and the **distal convoluted tubule**.

The kidneys develop in the pelvis but appear to ascend into the abdomen as a result of fetal growth of the lumbar and sacral regions. With their ascent, the ureters elongate, and the kidneys become vascularized by lateral splanchnic arteries, which arise from the abdominal aorta.

DEVELOPMENT OF THE BLADDER AND URETHRA (ENDODERM)

Bladder

- The **urorectal septum** divides the cloaca into the **anorectal canal** and the **urogenital sinus** by Week 7. The upper and largest part of the urogenital sinus becomes the **urinary bladder**, which is initially continuous with the **allantois**. As the lumen of the allantois becomes obliterated, a fibrous cord, the **urachus**, connects the apex of the bladder to the umbilicus. In the adult, this structure becomes the **median umbilical ligament**.

- The **mucosa** of the trigone of the bladder is initially formed from mesodermal tissue, which is replaced by **endodermal epithelium**. The smooth muscle of the bladder is derived from splanchnic mesoderm.

Urethra

- The **male urethra** is anatomically divided into three portions: **prostatic**, **membranous**, and **spongy** (penile). The **prostatic urethra, membranous urethra, and proximal penile urethra** develop from the narrow portion of the **urogenital sinus** below the urinary bladder. The **distal spongy urethra** is derived from the **ectodermal cells** of the glans penis.

- The **female urethra** is derived entirely from the **urogenital sinus** (endoderm).

CONGENITAL ABNORMALITIES

Renal agenesis	Failure of one or both kidneys to develop because of early degeneration of the ureteric bud. Unilateral genesis is fairly common; bilateral agenesis is fatal (associated with oligohydramnios, and the fetus may have **Potter sequence**: clubbed feet, pulmonary hypoplasia, and craniofacial anomalies).
Pelvic and horseshoe kidney	Pelvic kidney is caused by a failure of one kidney to ascend. **Horseshoe kidney** (usually **normal renal function**, predisposition to calculi) is a fusion of both kidneys at their ends and failure of the fused kidney to ascend.
Double ureter	Caused by the early splitting of the ureteric bud or the development of two separate buds.
Patent urachus	**Failure of the allantois to be obliterated**. It causes urachal fistulas or sinuses. In male children with congenital valvular obstruction of the prostatic urethra or in older men with enlarged prostates, a patent urachus **may cause drainage of urine through the umbilicus**.

GROSS ANATOMY OF THE KIDNEY

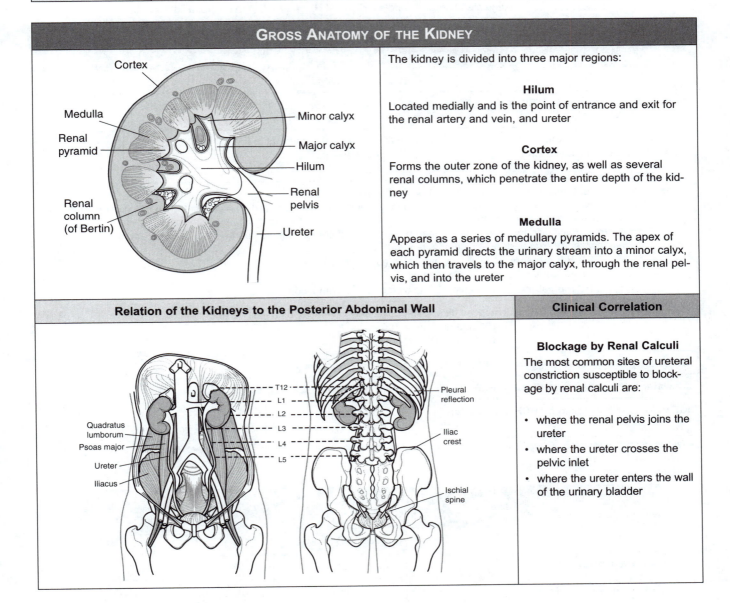

The kidney is divided into three major regions:

Hilum
Located medially and is the point of entrance and exit for the renal artery and vein, and ureter

Cortex
Forms the outer zone of the kidney, as well as several renal columns, which penetrate the entire depth of the kidney

Medulla
Appears as a series of medullary pyramids. The apex of each pyramid directs the urinary stream into a minor calyx, which then travels to the major calyx, through the renal pelvis, and into the ureter

Relation of the Kidneys to the Posterior Abdominal Wall

Clinical Correlation

Blockage by Renal Calculi
The most common sites of ureteral constriction susceptible to blockage by renal calculi are:

- where the renal pelvis joins the ureter
- where the ureter crosses the pelvic inlet
- where the ureter enters the wall of the urinary bladder

BASIC FUNCTIONS OF THE KIDNEYS

Fluid balance	Maintain normal extracellular (ECF) and intracellular (ICF) fluid volumes
Electrolytes	Balance excretion with intake to maintain normal plasma concentrations
Wastes	Excrete metabolic wastes (nitrogenous products, acids, toxins, etc.)
Fuels	Reabsorb metabolic fuels (glucose, lactate, amino acids, etc.)
Blood pressure	Regulate ECF volume for the long-term control of blood pressure
Acid–base	Regulate absorption and excretion of H^+ and HCO_3^- to control acid–base balance

FLUID BALANCE: ESTIMATION OF FLUID VOLUMES

Basic Concepts

Body fluid compartments: TBW = ICF + ECF   ECF = plasma + ISF   TBW = ICF + (plasma + ISF)

Estimating body fluid volumes:
(must assume normal hydration)

TBW in Liters = 0.6 × weight in kg
ICF = 0.4 × weight
ECF = 0.2 × weight

Measuring body fluid volumes (indicator dilution principle):

$V = Q/C$, where V = body fluid volume, Q = quantity of indicator administered, C = concentration of indicator after dilution in body fluid compartment

Indicators: must disperse evenly in compartment, must disperse only in compartment of interest, and cannot be metabolized or excreted (no indicator is perfect)

TBW indicators: D_2O, ^3H_2O, antipyrine ($C_{11}H_{12}N_2O$)
ECF indicators: ^{22}Na, inulin, mannitol
PV indicators: ^{125}I-albumin, Evans blue dye, ^{51}Cr-red blood cells

Osmolarity vs. molarity: Ionic substances dissociate, covalently bonded substances do not, therefore:
- 100 mM glucose = 100 mOsm/L
- 100 mM NaCl = 200 mOsm/L

Osmolarity of ECF always = osmolarity of ICF: Estimate by 2× plasma [Na^+]

All water and solutes pass through ECF: Evaluate changes in ECF first, then ICF

ICF volume is controlled by ECF osmolarity:
- ECF volume does not control ICF volume
- Water enters/leaves ICF to keep osmolarity of ICF = ECF

Definition of abbreviations: ECF, extracellular fluid; ICF, intracellular fluid; ISF, interstitial fluid; PV, plasma volume; TBW, total body water.

NORMAL VALUES
(Body weight = 100 kg, 300 mOsm/L)

	ECF	ICF	TBW
Volume (liters)	20	40	60
Osmolarity (mOsm /L)	300	300	300
Solute mass in compartment (mOsm)	6,000	12,000	18,000

FLUID AND ELECTROLYTE ABNORMALITIES

Diarrhea

- Weight loss = 4 kg (assume all weight loss is fluid loss)
- Solutes lost from ECF
- Isoosmotic loss: osmolarity remains at 300 mOsm/L; calculate TBW, ECF, ICF

	ECF	ICF	TBW
Volume (liters)	V = 4,800/300 = 16	ICF = TBW − ECF 56 − 16 = 40	60 − 4 = 56
Osmolarity (mOsm/L)	300	300	300
Solute mass in compartment (mOsm)	6,000 − (300 × 4) = 4,800	12,000	56 × 300 = 16,800

Conclusion: Isoosmotic volume gain or loss only changes ECF volume; ICF volume is unchanged.

Sweating

- Weight loss = 8 kg (assume all weight loss is fluid loss)
- Solutes lost from ECF
- Loss of hypoosmotic fluid, osmolarity = 330 mOsm/L; calculate TBW, ECF, ICF

	ECF	ICF	TBW
Volume (liters)	V = 5,160/330 = 15.6	ICF = TBW − ECF 52 − 15.6 = 36.4	60 − 8 = 52
Osmolarity (mOsm/L)	330	330	330
Solute mass in compartment (mOsm)	6,000 − 840 = 5,160	12,000	52 × 330 = 17,160 = loss of 840 from ECF

Conclusion: ECF loss of water and solutes, but ↑ osmolarity → ↓ ICF volume due to water shift.

Drink 3 L Pure Water

- Weight gain = 3 kg
- No solutes lost or gained
- Gain of hypoosmotic fluid; calculate new osmolarity, TBW, ECF, ICF

	ECF	ICF	TBW
Volume (liters)	V = 6,000/285.7 = 21	V = 12,000/285.7 = 42	60 + 3 = 63
Osmolarity (mOsm/L)	285.7	285.7	18,000/63 = 285.7
Solute mass in compartment (mOsm)	21 × 285.7 = 6,000	42 × 285.7 = 12,000	63 × 285.7 = 18,000

Conclusion: Addition of pure water ↓ osmolarity, causing proportionate increases in ICF and ECF volumes.

PROCESSES IN THE FORMATION OF URINE

Filtration	• Glomerular capillaries—same forces as described in cardiovascular section • Glomerular filtration rate **(GFR)**
Secretion (S)	Active transport of solutes from plasma (via interstitial fluid) into tubular fluid
Reabsorption (R)	Passive or active movement of solutes and water from tubular fluid back into capillaries
Excretion of X (E_x)	• Result of the balance of filtration, secretion, and reabsorption • $E_x = \dot{V} \times [X]_{urine}$; $\dot{V}$ = urine flow; $[X]_{urine}$ = urinary concentration of X
Filtered load (F)	• $F = GFR \times [solute]_{plasma}$ • Solute fraction bound to plasma protein does not filter
Mass balance	$E = F + S - R$

EXAMPLES USING MASS BALANCE TO EVALUATE RENAL PROCESSING OF A SOLUTE

Data	Calculations	Conclusions
• GFR = 100 mL/min • $[Subst.]_{plasma}$ = 1 µg/mL • $\dot{V}$ = 2 mL/min • $[Subst.]_{urine}$ = 75 µg/mL	F = 100 × 1 = 100 µg/min E = 2 × 75 = 150 µg/min	Subst. must be secreted because the amount excreted is > the amount filtered. S ≈ 50 µg/min*
• GFR = 100 mL/min • $[Subst.]_{plasma}$ = 3 µg/mL • $\dot{V}$ = 1 mL/min • $[Subst.]_{urine}$ = 100 µg/mL	F = 100 × 3 = 300 µg/min E = 1 × 100 = 100 µg/min	Subst. must be reabsorbed because the amount filtered is > the amount excreted. R ≈ 200 µg/min†
• GFR = 100 mL/min • $[Subst.]_{plasma}$ = 2 µg/mL • $\dot{V}$ = 4 mL/min • $[Subst.]_{urine}$ = 50 µg/mL	F = 100 × 2 = 200 µg/min E = 4 × 50 = 200 µg/min	Subst. is neither secreted nor reabsorbed because the amount excreted = the amount filtered.¶

Definition of abbreviation: Subst., substance.

*Assumes no reabsorption

†Assumes no secretion

¶Still possible that S = R, but this is unlikely.

CLEARANCE AND ITS APPLICATIONS

Definition	Volume of plasma from which a substance is removed (cleared) per unit time
Concept	Relates the excretion of a substance to its concentration in plasma
Calculation	$C_s = (U_s \times \dot{V})/P_s$ where, C_s = clearance of substance, U_s = urine concentration of substance, $\dot{V}$ = urine flow, P_s = plasma concentration of substance
Application: GFR	• **Inulin clearance** can be used to calculate **GFR**. • Rationale: inulin is filtered, but is neither secreted nor reabsorbed. Therefore, $$\text{Clearance of inulin} = (U_{[inulin]} \times \dot{V})/P_{[inulin]} = GFR$$ • **Creatinine clearance** is the best clinical measure of GFR because it is produced continually by the body and is freely filtered but not reabsorbed. Creatinine is partially secreted, but its clearance is still a reasonable clinical estimate of GFR.
Application: Renal plasma flow (RPF) Renal blood flow (RBF)	**Para-aminohippuric acid (PAH)** is filtered and secreted; at low doses it is almost completely cleared from blood flowing through the kidneys during a single pass. Therefore, PAH clearance = RPF. However, PAH clearance is a measure of *plasma* flow rather than *blood* flow. Renal blood flow (RBF) can be calculated as follows: **RBF = RPF / (1 – hematocrit)**, using hematocrit as decimal proportion, e.g., 0.40
Application: Free water clearance (C_{H_2O})	• C_{H_2O} is not a true clearance. It is the volume of water that would have to be added to or removed from urine to make the urine isoosmotic to plasma. • C_{H_2O} is the difference between water excretion (urine flow) and osmolar clearance. Thus: $$C_{H_2O} = \dot{V} - C_{osm} = \dot{V} - (U_{osm} \times \dot{V})/P_{osm}$$ • **Positive C_{H_2O}:** Urine is hypotonic, ADH is low, "free water" has been removed from body, and plasma osmolarity is being increased. • **Negative C_{H_2O}:** Urine is hypertonic, ADH is high, water is being conserved, and plasma osmolarity is being decreased.

Definition of abbreviation: ADH, antidiuretic hormone.

STRUCTURE OF THE NEPHRON
(Approximately 1 million nephrons/kidney)

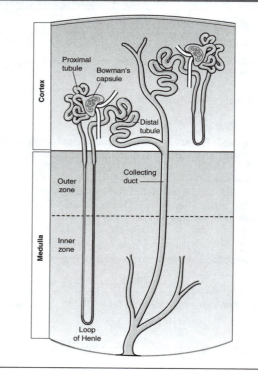

Sequence of Fluid Flow in a Nephron

Structure	Basic Function
Bowman capsule	Formation of filtrate
Proximal tubule (PT)	Reabsorption of H_2O, solutes; some secretion
Descending thin loop of Henle (DTL)	Reabsorption of H_2O, no solute transport
Ascending thin loop of Henle (ATL)	Reabsorption of solutes, not water
Thick ascending loop of Henle (TAL)	Reabsorption of solutes, not water
Early distal tubule (EDT)	Reabsorption of solutes; special sensory region
Late distal tubule (LDT); cortical collecting duct (CCD)	Reabsorption of solutes and water; regulation of acid–base status
Medullary collecting duct (MCD)	Reabsorption of H_2O; final control of urine volume and osmolarity

ASSOCIATION OF BLOOD VESSELS WITH THE NEPHRON

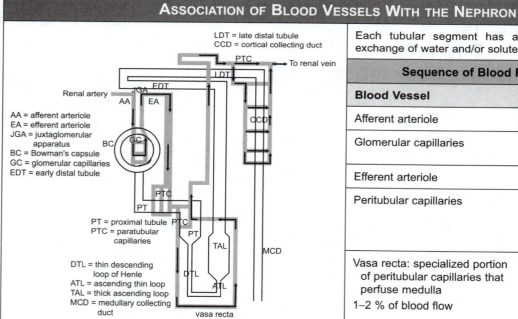

LDT = late distal tubule
CCD = cortical collecting duct

AA = afferent arteriole
EA = efferent arteriole
JGA = juxtaglomerular apparatus
BC = Bowman's capsule
GC = glomerular capillaries
EDT = early distal tubule

PT = proximal tubule
PTC = paratubular capillaries

DTL = thin descending loop of Henle
ATL = ascending thin loop
TAL = thick ascending loop
MCD = medullary collecting duct

Each tubular segment has a blood supply that allows exchange of water and/or solute.

Sequence of Blood Flow in Nephrons

Blood Vessel	Tubular Segment
Afferent arteriole	No exchange
Glomerular capillaries	Bowman capsule
Efferent arteriole	No exchange
Peritubular capillaries	Sequence: proximal tubule → loop of Henle → distal tubule → collecting duct
Vasa recta: specialized portion of peritubular capillaries that perfuse medulla 1–2 % of blood flow	Loop of Henle, collecting duct

THE JUXTAGLOMERULAR APPARATUS (JGA)

The **juxtaglomerular apparatus** includes the site of **filtration** (Bowman capsule [BC] and glomerular capillaries), as well as the arterioles and macula densa tubule cells found at the end of the thick ascending limb. Macula densa cells sense tubular fluid NaCl and contribute to **autoregulation** and regulation of **renin secretion**.

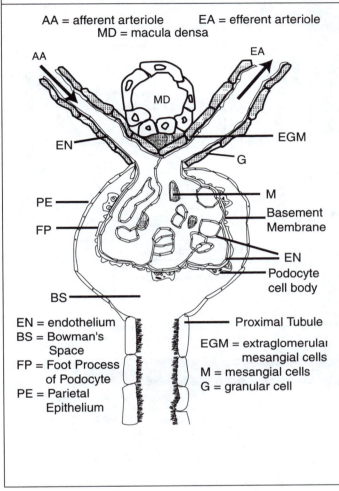

AA = afferent arteriole   EA = efferent arteriole
MD = macula densa

EN = endothelium
BS = Bowman's Space
FP = Foot Process of Podocyte
PE = Parietal Epithelium

EGM = extraglomerular mesangial cells
M = mesangial cells
G = granular cell

Filtration	
Bowman capsule	A pouch wrapped around capillaries
Podocytes	Specialized cells of BC, which help prevent protein filtration
Glomerular capillaries (GC)	Fenestrated, which allows rapid filtration of water and small solutes, but prevents protein filtration

$$\text{Filtration} = \text{GFR} = K_f[(P_{GC} - P_{BC}) - (\varpi_{GC} - \varpi_{BC})]$$
(same forces as discussed in CV)

K_f	Filtration coefficient is high for H_2O, electrolytes, small solutes
P_{GC}	Remains high along GC due to very low GC resistance, favoring filtration
P_{BC}	Remains low unless urinary tract obstruction is present
π_{GC}	Rises along GC due to high filtration, until filtration ceases in distal capillary; reduced with low plasma protein
π_{BC}	≈ zero normally, proteinuria increases it

Filtration Fraction = GFR/RPF

Ranges from 15–30%, usually ≈20%
- Nonrenal capillary filtration fraction ≈1–2%
- Nonrenal P_{cap} falls along capillary due to capillary resistance, so filtration only occurs at proximal end and reabsorption occurs distally.

AUTOREGULATION OF GFR AND RBF

An isolated change in renal perfusion pressure between 75 and 175 mm Hg will not change RBF or GFR significantly because **autoregulation** maintains RBF at a constant level by adjusting afferent and efferent arteriolar resistances. Autoregulation occurs via a **myogenic response** and **tubuloglomerular feedback**.

Mechanisms of Autoregulation		
Myogenic	↑ arterial pressure stretches vessel wall, which ↑ calcium movement into smooth muscle cells, causing them to contract.	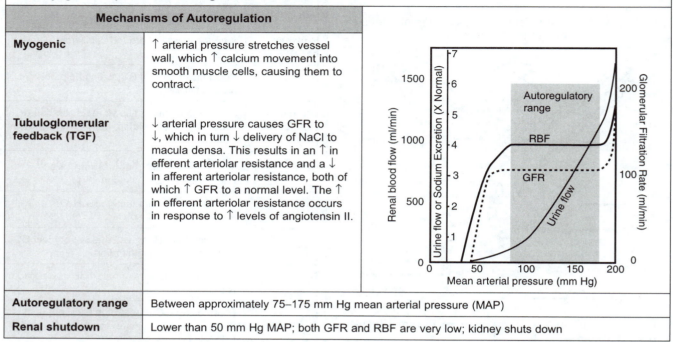
Tubuloglomerular feedback (TGF)	↓ arterial pressure causes GFR to ↓, which in turn ↓ delivery of NaCl to macula densa. This results in an ↑ in efferent arteriolar resistance and a ↓ in afferent arteriolar resistance, both of which ↑ GFR to a normal level. The ↑ in efferent arteriolar resistance occurs in response to ↑ levels of angiotensin II.	
Autoregulatory range	Between approximately 75–175 mm Hg mean arterial pressure (MAP)	
Renal shutdown	Lower than 50 mm Hg MAP; both GFR and RBF are very low; kidney shuts down	

REGULATION OF FILTRATION (GFR AND RBF)

Vessel	Constriction			Dilation		
	P_{cap}	GFR	RBF	P_{cap}	GFR	RBF
Afferent arteriole	↓	↓	↓	↑	↑	↑
Efferent arteriole	↑	↑	↓	↓	↓	↑

TUBULAR FUNCTION: REABSORPTION AND SECRETION

Active Facilitated Transporters Display Maximum Transport (T_{max}) Rates	
Transport maximum	T_{max} = mass of solute per time transported *when carriers saturated*
Limited carrier population	Transport mediated by these carriers is saturable under pathophysiologic conditions, e.g., glucose transporters
Reabsorption < T_{max}	None of solute in urine until filtered load > T_{max}
Secretion < T_{max}	All of solute delivered in plasma appears in urine until delivery > T_{max}
Interpretation	Reduced T_{max} for glucose indicates reduced number of functioning nephrons

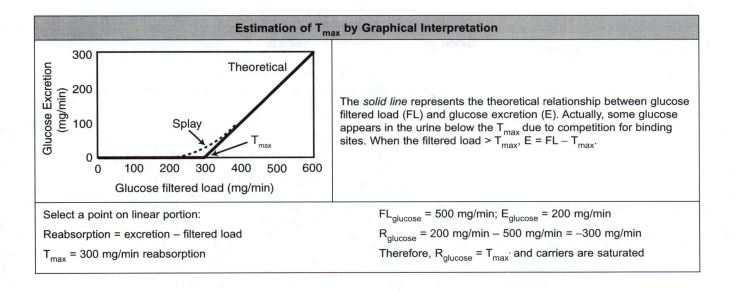

Estimation of T_{max} by Graphical Interpretation

The *solid line* represents the theoretical relationship between glucose filtered load (FL) and glucose excretion (E). Actually, some glucose appears in the urine below the T_{max} due to competition for binding sites. When the filtered load > T_{max}, $E = FL - T_{max}$.

Select a point on linear portion:

Reabsorption = excretion − filtered load

T_{max} = 300 mg/min reabsorption

$FL_{glucose}$ = 500 mg/min; $E_{glucose}$ = 200 mg/min

$R_{glucose}$ = 200 mg/min − 500 mg/min = −300 mg/min

Therefore, $R_{glucose} = T_{max}$, and carriers are saturated

Proximal Tubule

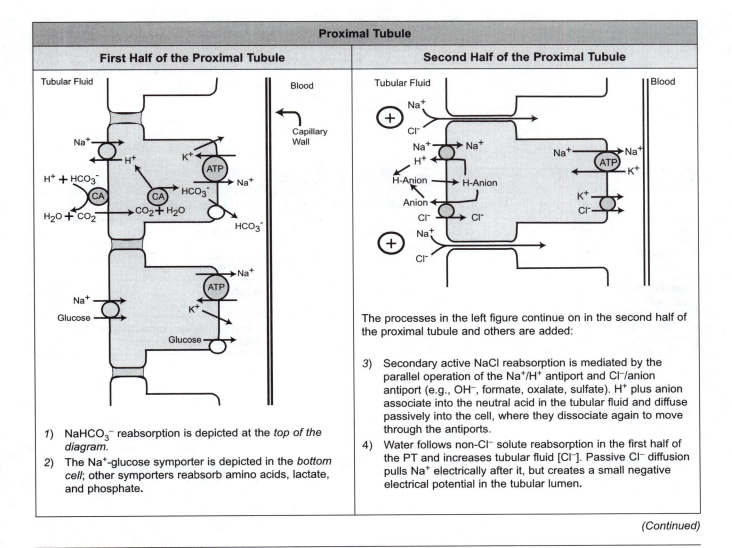

First Half of the Proximal Tubule

1) $NaHCO_3^-$ reabsorption is depicted at the *top of the diagram.*
2) The Na^+-glucose symporter is depicted in the *bottom cell*; other symporters reabsorb amino acids, lactate, and phosphate.

Second Half of the Proximal Tubule

The processes in the left figure continue on in the second half of the proximal tubule and others are added:

3) Secondary active NaCl reabsorption is mediated by the parallel operation of the Na^+/H^+ antiport and Cl^-/anion antiport (e.g., OH^-, formate, oxalate, sulfate). H^+ plus anion associate into the neutral acid in the tubular fluid and diffuse passively into the cell, where they dissociate again to move through the antiports.
4) Water follows non-Cl^- solute reabsorption in the first half of the PT and increases tubular fluid $[Cl^-]$. Passive Cl^- diffusion pulls Na^+ electrically after it, but creates a small negative electrical potential in the tubular lumen.

(Continued)

Proximal Tubule (Cont'd.)		
Substance	**Action**	**Mechanism**
Water	67% reabsorbed	• Simple diffusion; filtration forces favor reabsorption • Solute reabsorption creates osmotic gradient, water follows it; paracellular and transcellular • Cell membranes permeable to water
Na^+	67% reabsorbed	• Na^+/K^+-ATPase in the basolateral membrane creates an electrochemical gradient; secondary active transport, luminal (apical) surface; co- and countertransport • Simple diffusion, paracellular
Glucose, lactate, amino acids, phosphate	≈100% reabsorbed	• Secondary active transport at the luminal (apical) surface; cotransport with Na^+; Na^+ electrochemical gradient provides the power • Transport maximum processes (*see* below)
H^+	Secreted	Primary ATPase and secondary active antiport with Na^+
HCO_3^-	≈100% reabsorbed	Reabsorbed as CO_2 at the apical surface; facilitated diffusion and exchange with Cl^- on basolateral surface; carbonic anhydrase located at the apical surface and intracellularly
Cl^-	≈67% reabsorbed	• Transcellular: at the apical surface, exchange with anions; at the basolateral surface, facilitated diffusion and symport with K^+ • Paracellular, simple diffusion
Ca^{2+}	≈70% reabsorbed	80% of proximal tubule reabsorption paracellular; 20% transcellular
Organic cations, anions	Mainly secreted	Various mechanisms

Loop of Henle: Overview			
	Descending Thin Limb (DTL)	**Ascending Thin Limb (ATL)**	**Thick Ascending Limb (TAL)**
H_2O	Reabsorbs 15% of GFR	Impermeable	Impermeable
Solutes	Diffuse into tubule	Slight active reabsorption	Reabsorbs 25% FL of NaCl, K^+; 20% FL of Ca^{2+}; 50–60% FL of Mg^{2+}
Tubular fluid volume	Decreases	No change	No change
Tubular fluid osmolarity	Increases; DTL is called the "concentrating segment"	Decreases	Decreases below normal plasma; TAL is called the "diluting segment"

Definition of abbreviation: FL, filtered load.

Thick Ascending Loop of Henle

Tubular Fluid

$+$

Na$^+$
2Cl$^-$
K$^+$

K$^+$

Na$^+$

H$^+$

CA

CO$_2$ + H$_2$O

$+$

Na$^+$
K$^+$
Ca^{2+}
Mg^{2+}

Ca^{++}

H$_2$O

$+$

Cl$^-$ K$^+$

ATP

Na$^+$

HCO$_3^-$

HCO$_3^-$

Ca^{++}

ATP

Ca^{++}

Ca^{++}

3Na$^+$

2H$^+$

Blood

Capillary
Wall

Mechanisms of Solute Transport, Thick Ascending Loop of Henle

Na$^+$	**Reabsorption:** • Symport with Cl$^-$ and K$^+$ • Antiport with H$^+$ • Paracellular due to electrical force
K$^+$	**Reabsorption:** • Paracellular reabsorption (electrical force) • Symport with Na$^+$ and Cl$^-$
Ca^{2+}	**Reabsorption:** • Paracellular (electrical force) • Transcellular, apical surface, simple diffusion • Basolateral Ca^{2+}-ATPase, Na$^+$-Ca^{2+} exchange • 2H$^+$/Ca^{2+} ATPase antiport; parathyroid hormone stimulates
Mg^{2+}	**Reabsorption:** • Paracellular (electrical force) • Transcellular, active transport
H$^+$	**Secretion:** • Na$^+$/H$^+$ exchange, NH$_4^+$

"Diluting segment": reabsorption of solutes without reabsorption of water produces hyperosmotic interstitium of medulla; needed for descending loop water reabsorption and collecting duct ability to regulate water reabsorption

Distal Tubule and Collecting Duct Overview

	Tubular Fluid Volume	Tubular Fluid Osmolarity	Tubular Fluid Solutes
Delivered from TAL	≈15% of GFR	Hypotonic at ≈1/2 P$_{OSM}$	• ≈10% FL of NaCl, K$^+$, and Ca^{2+} • ≈5% FL of HCO$_3^-$
Early distal convoluted tubule (EDT)	No H$_2$O reabsorbed	Hypotonic at ≈1/3 P$_{OSM}$	• Reabsorb ≈5% FL of NaCl via **apical Na$^+$-Cl$^-$ symporter** (NCC) in secondary active transport inhibited by **thiazide** diuretics • Reabsorb ≈10% FL of Ca^{2+} via secondary active transport stimulated by **parathyroid hormone (PTH)** and indirectly by **thiazide** diuretics
Late distal tubule (LTD) and cortical collecting duct (CCD)	H$_2$O reabsorption regulated by **antidiuretic hormone (ADH)**	Varies primarily with H$_2$O reabsorption	• Reabsorb ≈4% of FL of NaCl via active transport regulated by **aldosterone** • Reabsorb ≈5% FL of HCO$_3^-$ via active transport regulated by **aldosterone** • Secretion of K$^+$ determines total excretion; active secretion regulated by **aldosterone**
Medullary collecting duct (MCD)	H$_2$O reabsorption regulated by **ADH**	Varies primarily with H$_2$O reabsorption	Reabsorb ≈60% of FL of urea passively via transporter regulated by **ADH**; urea reabsorption is needed for medullary osmolarity

Definition of abbreviation: FL, filtered load.
*Some refer to the LDT as the connecting tubule.

	Overview			
	Steady-State Balance (maintained by renal regulation of excretion)	**Fractional E =** **(Excreted)/(Filtered)**		**Major Regulators of Renal Excretion**
		Range	**Typical**	
Water	Volume liquid drunk/day = E_{H_2O}	0.5–14%	≈1%	**Antidiuretic hormone (ADH)** acting on LDT and **collecting duct**
Solute	Osmols generated as water soluble wastes = E_{osmols}		≈1.5%	Major osmoles excreted are salts, acids, and nitrogenous wastes; excrete ≈600–900 mOsm/day
NaCl	Amount NaCl eaten/day = E_{NaCl}	0.1–5%	≈0.5–1%	• **Aldosterone** acting on LDT and **CCD**; renal **SNS** tone acting on **PT** • **Angiotensin II** on multiple segments • Atrial natriuretic peptide, etc.
K^+	Amount K^+ eaten/day ≈E_{K^+}	1–80%	≈15%	• **Aldosterone** acting on LDT and **CCD**; other factors described later
Ca^{2+}	Amount Ca^{2+} absorbed from GI/day = $E_{Ca^{2+}}$	0.1–3%	≈1%	**Parathyroid hormone** (PTH) acting on **DCT**
HCO_3^-	• *New* HCO_3^- added to blood/day = net acid excretion (NAE) = $(E_{ammonium}) + (E_{H_2PO_4^-}) - (E_{bicarbonate})$ • NAE determines $[HCO_3^-]_{plasma}$	HCO_3^- ≈0% $H_2PO_4^-$ ≈20%		**Aldosterone** acting on LDT and **CCD**; plasma pH and other factors described later
Urea	Amount generated/day = E_{urea}	20% – 80%	≈40%	Synthesis depends on protein metabolism; regulated by **ADH** acting on medullary **collecting duct**

Definition of abbreviations: CCD, cortical collecting duct.

Regulation Of Urine Osmolarity and Urine Flow—Antidiuretic Hormone (ADH)

Collecting Duct

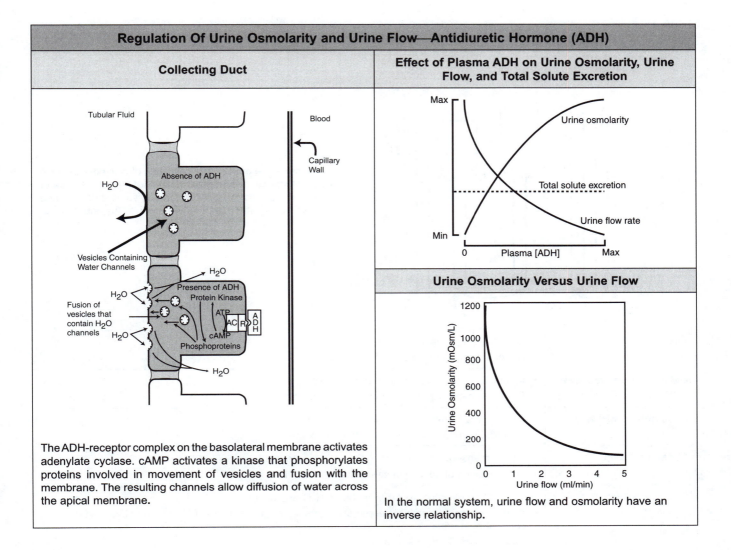

The ADH-receptor complex on the basolateral membrane activates adenylate cyclase. cAMP activates a kinase that phosphorylates proteins involved in movement of vesicles and fusion with the membrane. The resulting channels allow diffusion of water across the apical membrane.

Effect of Plasma ADH on Urine Osmolarity, Urine Flow, and Total Solute Excretion

Urine Osmolarity Versus Urine Flow

In the normal system, urine flow and osmolarity have an inverse relationship.

Loop of Henle and the Countercurrent Mechanism Antidiuresis (Presence of ADH)

In the presence of ADH, the collecting duct is permeable to water. Because of the high osmolarity of the medulla, water is reabsorbed, so the urine volume is small and the urine concentration is the same as the medulla (hyperosmotic).

Vasa recta	• Only 1–2% of renal blood flow
	• Reabsorbed solutes "trapped" in medulla
Balance of solutes and water	• In total loop, more solute than H_2O reabsorbed
	• Produces hyperosmotic interstitium of medulla
Descending thin loop	• Fluid enters isoosmotic with normal plasma
	• H_2O reabsorption $\rightarrow$ ↓volume with ↑ osmolarity
Ascending loop	• Solute reabsorption only, not $H_2O \rightarrow$ hypoosmotic tubular fluid
	• Accumulation of solutes in interstitium of medulla
Collecting duct	• With ADH, collecting duct permeable to H_2O and urea
	• As duct passes through hyperosmotic interstitium, reabsorption of $H_2O \rightarrow$ small volume of concentrated urine
	• Negative CH_2O; dilutes plasma

Loop of Henle and the Countercurrent Mechanism
Water-Induced Diuresis (Absence of ADH)

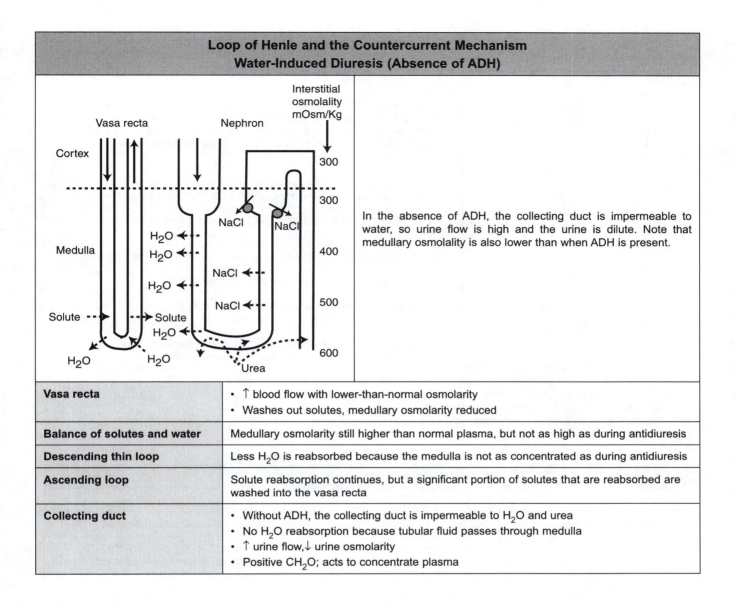

In the absence of ADH, the collecting duct is impermeable to water, so urine flow is high and the urine is dilute. Note that medullary osmolality is also lower than when ADH is present.

Vasa recta	• ↑ blood flow with lower-than-normal osmolarity • Washes out solutes, medullary osmolarity reduced
Balance of solutes and water	Medullary osmolarity still higher than normal plasma, but not as high as during antidiuresis
Descending thin loop	Less H_2O is reabsorbed because the medulla is not as concentrated as during antidiuresis
Ascending loop	Solute reabsorption continues, but a significant portion of solutes that are reabsorbed are washed into the vasa recta
Collecting duct	• Without ADH, the collecting duct is impermeable to H_2O and urea • No H_2O reabsorption because tubular fluid passes through medulla • ↑ urine flow, ↓ urine osmolarity • Positive CH_2O; acts to concentrate plasma

Regulation of Plasma Osmolarity by ADH

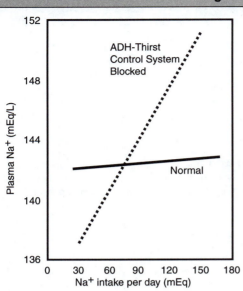

ADH secretion is increased by elevated plasma sodium or osmolarity and decreased by high blood volume or high pressure. This acts as a negative feedback system to control plasma osmolarity. (See **Antidiuretic Hormone and Control of Osmolarity and Volume** in the Endocrine section.)

Calculation of Plasma Osmolality (mOsm/kg solution)
Plasma osmolality = 2 (plasma [Na$^+$]) + [glucose mg/dL]/18 + [urea mg/dL]/2.8
Example: sodium = 145 mEq/L, glucose = 180 mg/dL, urea = 28 mg/dL Plasma osmolality = 290 + 10 + 10 = 310 mOsm/kg
However: plasma Na$^+$ dominates control of ADH because of its osmotic effect; urea and glucose usually irrelevant.
Note: glucose may be important part of **urine** osmolality (especially in diabetes); when present, it causes osmotic diuresis.

Normal function of the control system for ADH secretion and water consumption prevents large changes of plasma sodium concentration. Loss of this system causes plasma sodium concentration to increase in proportion to sodium intake.

Control Signals for Na$^+$ and H$_2$O Excretion		
System	**Action**	**Segment/Site**
Renal sympathetic nerves	↓ GFR	Afferent arteriole constriction
	↑ NaCl reabsorption	Proximal, TAL, DT, CD → ↑ H$_2$O reabsorption (except TAL, due to impermeability of water)
Renin–angiotensin II–aldosterone	Angio II → ↑ NaCl reabsorption	Proximal → ↑ H$_2$O reabsorption
	Aldosterone →↑ NaCl reabsorption	TAL, DT, CD →↑ H$_2$O reabsorption (except TAL, due to impermeability of water)
Atrial natriuretic peptide (ANP)	↑ GFR	Glomerulus
	↓ renin, angio II, aldosterone	JGA and adrenal cortex
	↓ NaCl and H$_2$O reabsorption	CD (urodilatin* assists)
	↓ ADH secretion and actions	Posterior pituitary and CD
ADH	↑ permeability to H$_2$O	CD → ↑ H$_2$O reabsorption → ↓ urine flow and ↑ urine osmolarity

*Urodilatin is a peptide produced by DT and CD when blood pressure/volume increase. Very potent inhibition of NaCl and water reabsorption, but only local action; it does not circulate.

Disorders of Solute and Water Regulation

Disorder	ECF Volume	$[Na^+]_{plasma}$	Blood Pressure	Urine Volume and Osmolarity	Arterial pH	$[K^+]_{plasma}$
Diabetes insipidus*	↓	↑	– or ↓	↑ volume ↓ osmolarity	↑	↓ (↑ aldosterone and alkalosis)
SIADH	↑	↓	↑ or –	↓ volume ↑ osmolarity	↓	↑ (but negative balance)
Aldosterone deficiency (primary)	↓	↓	↓	↑ volume ↑ osmolarity	↓	↑ positive balance
Aldosterone excess (primary)	↑	↑	↑	↓ volume ↓ osmolarity	↑	↓ negative balance
Polydipsia	↑	↓	–	↑ volume ↓ osmolarity	↓	↑ balance variable
Water deprivation (dehydration)	↓	↑	↓	↓ volume ↑ osmolarity	↑	↑, ↓, – depends on multiple factors

Definition of abbreviation: SIADH, syndrome of inappropriate (excessive) ADH secretion.

*ADH deficiency is called primary, central, or neurogenic; ↓ renal response to ADH is nephrogenic. Distinguish by response to administration of ADH; ↑ urine osmolarity in response to ADH injection indicates primary.

Osmotic Diuresis

Cause	Effect
Excessive solute in tubular fluid	Decrease reabsorption of H_2O
Diabetic ketoacidosis	• Glucose and ketones in urine → polyuria, K^+ wasting • Na^+ loss → hyponatremia
Starvation and alcoholic ketoacidosis	Ketonuria → polyuria, K^+ wasting, hyponatremia
Osmotic diuretics (mannitol, carbonic anhydrase inhibitors)	Inhibit proximal tubule H_2O reabsorption → diuresis, K^+ wasting (due to ↑ flow)
Loop diuretics (furosemide) and distal tubule diuretics (thiazides)	Inhibit NaCl reabsorption → ↑ tubular solutes → diuresis and K^+ wasting

Causes of Increased Potassium Excretion

Tubular Flow and K⁺ Secretion	Factor	Mechanism
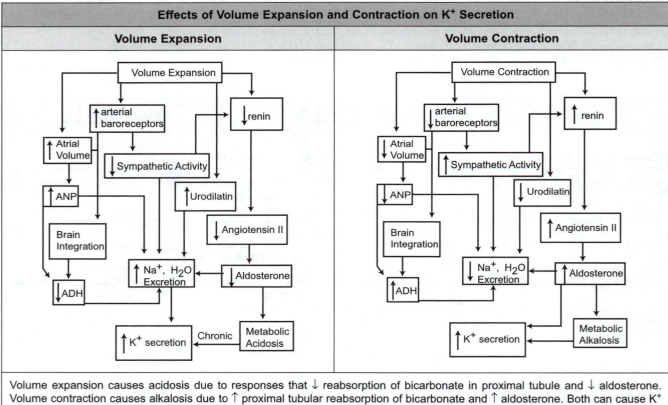	↑ Tubular flow	Washes K⁺ out of tubular cells
	↑ Tubular load of Na⁺	Stimulates DT Na⁺ pump →↑ tubular cells K⁺
	↑ Plasma K⁺	↑ FL and →↑ aldosterone →↑ K⁺ secretion
	Aldosterone on DT	↑ Apical permeability K⁺ ↑ Na⁺ pump →↑ DT cell K⁺ →↑ K⁺ secretion
	Metabolic alkalosis	↑ Tubular cell K⁺ →↑ secretion of K⁺
	Chronic metabolic acidosis	Osmotic diuresis and ↑ aldosterone

- *Shaded bar*: normal flow range
- High flow → high secretion
- Flow is not a normal control mechanism; changes are pathologic.

Effects of Volume Expansion and Contraction on K⁺ Secretion

Volume Expansion	Volume Contraction

Volume expansion causes acidosis due to responses that ↓ reabsorption of bicarbonate in proximal tubule and ↓ aldosterone. Volume contraction causes alkalosis due to ↑ proximal tubular reabsorption of bicarbonate and ↑ aldosterone. Both can cause K⁺ wasting because metabolic alkalosis and chronic metabolic acidosis both ↑ K⁺ secretion in distal tubule and collecting duct.

Effects of Metabolic Alkalosis and Acidosis on K⁺ Excretion

Metabolic Alkalosis	Metabolic Acidosis

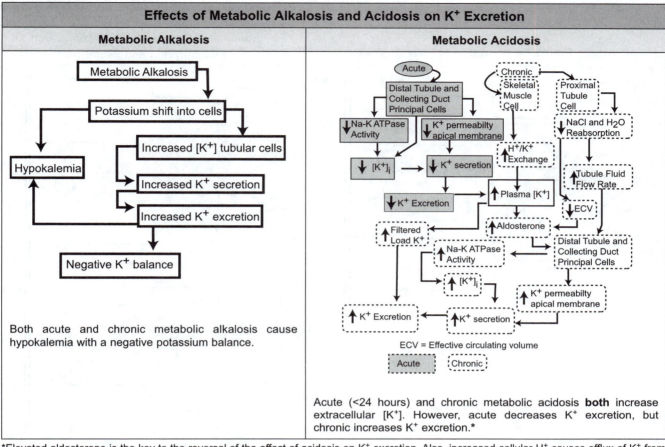

Both acute and chronic metabolic alkalosis cause hypokalemia with a negative potassium balance.

ECV = Effective circulating volume

Acute (<24 hours) and chronic metabolic acidosis **both** increase extracellular [K⁺]. However, acute decreases K⁺ excretion, but chronic increases K⁺ excretion.*

*Elevated aldosterone is the key to the reversal of the effect of acidosis on K⁺ excretion. Also, increased cellular H⁺ causes efflux of K⁺ from cells; low cellular H⁺ causes influx. Acidosis impairs metabolism; thus, ↓ solute reabsorption causes osmotic diuresis.

RENAL MECHANISMS FOR ACID/BASE REGULATION

Fundamental Principles

Tubular cell pH	• If a cell is acidotic, it will secrete acid. • If a cell is alkalotic, it will ↓ reabsorption of bicarbonate or secrete it.
Fluid volume	If ECV is decreased, ↑ Na⁺ reabsorption will be accompanied by ↑ bicarbonate reabsorption.
Overall role of kidneys	This is the only significant mechanism for excretion of nonvolatile, metabolic acids.
Response time	Requires 24–72 hours for maximal compensatory response
Net acid excretion (NAE)	There is no net excretion of newly formed acid unless all bicarbonate is reabsorbed. $$NAE = \dot{V} \times [NH_4{}^+] + \dot{V} \times [H_2PO_4{}^-] - \dot{V} \times [HCO_3{}^-]$$
Free H⁺ excretion	Trivial amount even at most acidic urine pH $\cong 4.4$
NH₄⁺ excretion	Largest quantity of excreted acid; metabolized from glutamine; "nontitratable acid"
H₂PO₄⁻ excretion	Second largest quantity; "titratable acid"
NH₄⁺ secretion	NH₄⁺ secreted in the proximal tubule is reabsorbed in TAL and added to interstitium; it is then taken up by DT and CD cells and secreted.

Tubular Handling of Bicarbonate

Proximal Tubule Reabsorption of Bicarbonate Ion

Intercalated Cells of the Collecting Duct: Reabsorption and Secretion

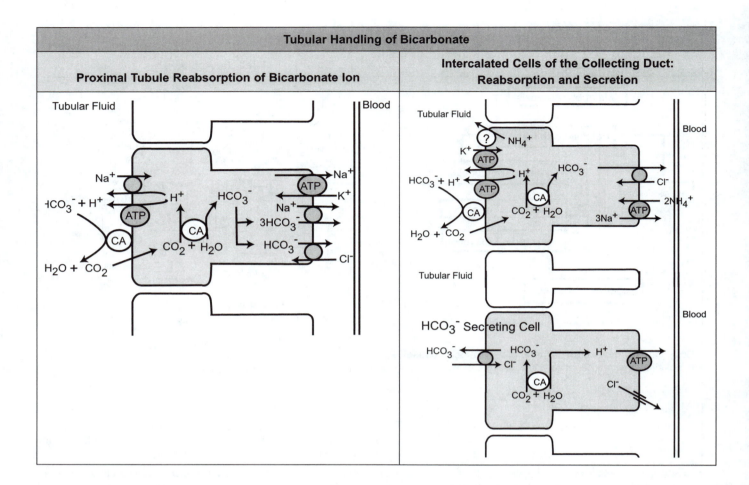

Tubular Handling of Ammonia

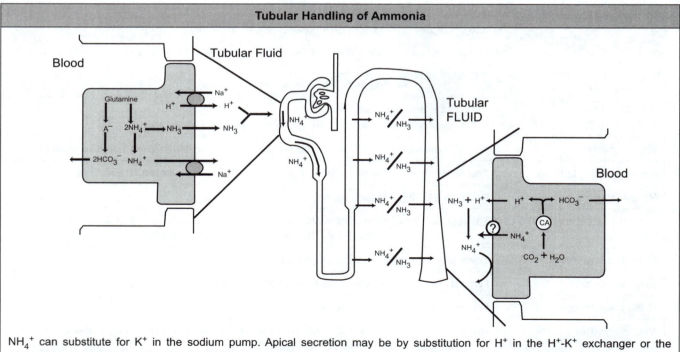

NH_4^+ can substitute for K^+ in the sodium pump. Apical secretion may be by substitution for H^+ in the H^+-K^+ exchanger or the H^+-ATPase. Production of NH_4^+ adds HCO_3^- to blood.

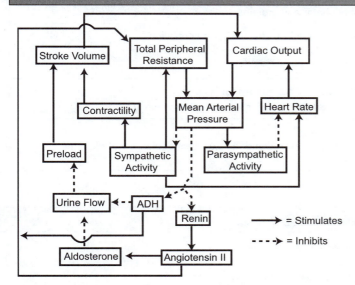

Notes on Use of Feedback Diagram

- Many intermediate steps omitted.
- ADH (vasopressin) also vasoconstricts.
- Diagram merges elements of cardiovascular and endocrine physiology.
- For applications, make the most direct connection; e.g., hemorrhage: begin at reduced preload →↓ stroke volume, and so on. For an understanding of ACE inhibition, begin at ↓ angiotensin II.

→ = Stimulates

----→ = Inhibits

ACID/BASE AND ITS REGULATION

Fundamental Principles	
Carbonic anhydrase reaction	Produces strong acid and weak base → acidic solution
Respiratory contribution	Determined by arterial P_{CO_2}: ↑ P_{CO_2} → acidosis; ↓ P_{CO_2} → alkalosis
Metabolic contribution	Determined by arterial HCO_3^-: ↑ HCO_3^- → alkalosis ; ↓ HCO_3^- → acidosis
Simple disorder	One disorder with or without compensation
Mixed or combined disorder	Two simultaneous disorders
Compensation	• A response that tends to correct pH: compensation is never perfect. • Fully compensated means that the mechanism has come as close as possible to restoring normal pH.
Normal arterial blood gas	pH = 7.40; P_{CO_2} = 40 mm Hg; P_{O_2} = 83 – 100 mm Hg; HCO_3^- = 24 mEq/L
Henderson-Hasselbalch Eq.	Several forms; they show relationship between pH, P_{CO_2}, and HCO_3^-.

The Carbonic Anhydrase Reaction	Henderson-Hasselbalch Equation
$$CO_2 + H_2O \underset{CA}{\rightleftharpoons} H_2CO_3 \rightleftharpoons H^+ + HCO_3^-$$ CA, carbonic anhydrase	$$pH = 6.1 \log \frac{[HCO_3^-]}{0.03\ PCO_2}$$ • ↑ P_{CO_2} → ↓ pH • ↑ HCO_3^- → ↑ pH

Examples of Calculations	
P_{CO_2} = 60 mm Hg; HCO_3^- = 18 mEq/L	pH = 6.1 + log (18/1.8) = 6.1 + log 10 = 6.1 + 1 = 7.1
P_{CO_2} = 40 mm Hg; HCO_3^- = 24 mEq/L	pH = 6.1 + log (24/1.2) = 6.1 + log 20 = 6.1 + 1.3 = 7.4
P_{CO_2} = 20 mm Hg; HCO_3^- = 24 mEq/L	pH = 6.1 + log (24/0.6) = 6.1 + log 40 = 6.10 + 1.60 = 7.70
P_{CO_2} = 60 mm Hg; HCO_3^- = 36 mEq/L	pH = 6.1 + log (36/1.8) = 6.1 + log 20 = 6.1 + 1.3 = 7.4
Note: pH is normal, but this is not normal acid/base status; both PCO_2 and HCO_3^- are abnormal.	

Fundamental Mechanisms to Control pH

Buffers	Fast, seconds: ECF bicarbonate (largest), phosphate, and proteins
Respiratory	Ventilation response fast, within a few minutes: change P_{CO_2} by changing ventilation. • ↑ ventilation →↓ P_{CO_2} → alkalosis • ↓ ventilation →↑ P_{CO_2} → acidosis
Renal	• Slow; 24–72 hours; powerful: major mechanism to excrete nonvolatile acids. • Change in renal acid excretion and HCO_3^- production is called a metabolic response.
Primary disorders	• Primary disorder ventilation = respiratory acid/base disorder • Primary disorder excess production of acid, ↓ renal excretion of acid, or loss of bicarbonate in urine or feces = metabolic disorder

The Davenport Diagram

- Above the base buffer line, there is excess metabolic base (a positive base excess).
- Below it, there is excess metabolic acid (negative base excess).
- Read pH perpendicular to the *x*-axis; HCO_3^- perpendicular to the *y*-axis, but P_{CO_2} along the curves.

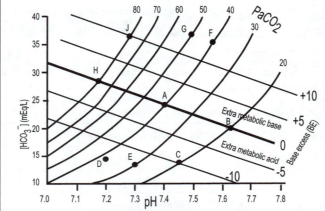

Point	Interpretation
A	Normal acid/base status
B	Uncompensated respiratory alkalosis
C	Respiratory alkalosis with compensatory metabolic acidosis
D	Uncompensated metabolic acidosis
E	Metabolic acidosis with compensatory respiratory alkalosis
F	Uncompensated metabolic alkalosis
G	Metabolic alkalosis with compensatory respiratory acidosis
H	Uncompensated respiratory acidosis
J	Respiratory acidosis with compensatory metabolic alkalosis

Patient Examples

Predicted bicarbonate concentration with changes of PCO_2

PCO_2 (mm Hg)	80	60	40	20
HCO_3^- (mEq/L)	29	27	24	21

Draw a vertical line through the PCO_2 to get the predicted HCO_3^-

PCO_2 (mm Hg)	80	60	40	20
HCO_3^- (mEq/L)	29	27	24	21

A patient has PCO_2 = 60 mm Hg and $[HCO_3^-]$ = 28 mEq/L
Has metabolism changed?
No: the bicarbonate is almost exactly as expected from the PCO_2

PCO_2 (mm Hg)	80	60	40	20
HCO_3^- (mEq/L)	29	27	24	21

A patient has PCO_2 = 80 mm Hg and $[HCO_3^-]$ = 35 mEq/L

What is the predicted bicarbonate? 29 mEq/L
Is there more or less bicarbonate than predicted? More
Has metabolism changed? Yes, there is excess bicarbonate.
What is the metabolic contribution? Alkalosis

Simple Acid–Base Disorders			
Type of Disorder	pH	Paco₂	HCO₃⁻
Metabolic acidosis	↓	↓*	↓
Metabolic alkalosis	↑	↑*	↑
Respiratory acidosis	↓	↑	↑*
Respiratory alkalosis	↑	↓	↓*

*Change due to compensation

A Step-by-Step Approach to Diagnosis of Simple Disorders

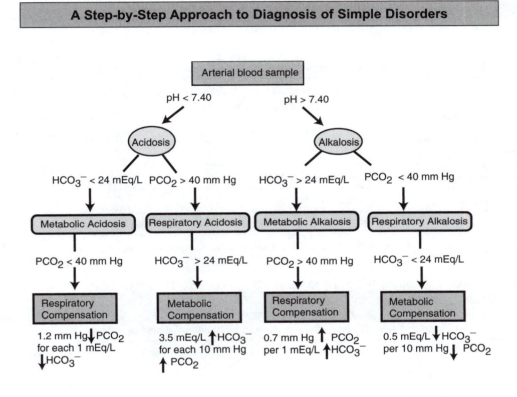

1. What is the pH? Acidotic or alkalotic?
2. What is the respiratory contribution? Acidosis, alkalosis, or no change?
3. What is the metabolic contribution? Acidosis, alkalosis, or no change?
4. What causes the acid–base disorder? *Ans:* the factor (respiratory or metabolic) that would produce the abnormal pH.
5. Is there compensation? Did the other factor change in the direction that would help offset the disorder?

Use of the Plasma Anion Gap (PAG)

Use	To determine whether the cause of a metabolic acidosis is due to $\uparrow$ concentration of nonvolatile acid
Discriminates	Whether the primary disorder is loss of bicarbonate in urine or feces
Principle	Cations = anions in plasma, if all were measured; commonly measure Na^+, Cl^-, and HCO_3^-; metabolic acids are not measured. So there is a gap between cations and anions as measured.
Calculation	$PAG = [Na^+] - ([Cl^-] + [HCO_3^-])$; normal = 12 ± 2
Interpretation $\uparrow$ PAG	Excess molecules of acid, e.g., diabetic ketoacidosis, aspirin, lactic acidosis, etc.
Non-anion gap acidosis (normal PAG)	Acidosis due to loss of bicarbonate in urine or diarrhea results in hyperchloremic acidosis; kidneys reabsorb excess Cl^- in replacement for bicarbonate

Urinary Anion Gap (UAG)

Principle	Hard to measure NH_4^+ in urine, but it is the major form of acid excreted Cations = anions in urine, if all are measured
Ions measured	Na^+, K^+, Cl^-: anions > cations because did not measure NH_4^+
UAG calculation	$UAG = [Na^+] + [K^+] - [Cl^-]$
Interpretation of negative	Kidneys are excreting acid
Interpretation of positive	Kidneys are excreting base
In acidosis	UAG should be negative if kidneys are compensating appropriately
In alkalosis	UAG should be positive if kidneys are compensating appropriately

Sample case:

Arterial: pH = 7.15, Pa_{CO_2} = 30 mm Hg, $[HCO_3^-]$ = 10 mEq/L, Cl^- = 100 mEq/L, Na^+ = 145 mEq/L

Urine: Na^+ = 100 mEq/L, K^+ = 90 mEq/L, Cl^- = 140 mEq/L

Diagnosis: metabolic acidosis with respiratory compensation; PAG = 35; therefore, grossly excessive acid in the body. UAG is positive, so kidneys are not excreting acid. Primary cause is likely to be retention of acid by kidneys.

DIURETICS: MECHANISMS

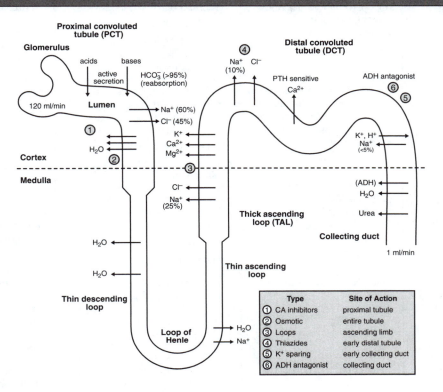

	Type	Site of Action
①	CA inhibitors	proximal tubule
②	Osmotic	entire tubule
③	Loops	ascending limb
④	Thiazides	early distal tubule
⑤	K+ sparing	early collecting duct
⑥	ADH antagonist	collecting duct

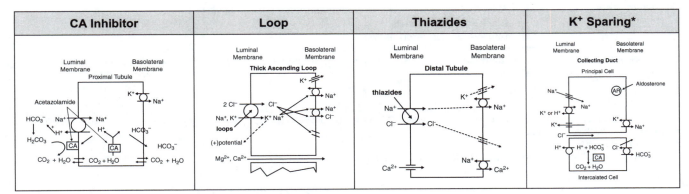

*Note: K+ sparing includes aldosterone blockers and Na+ channel blockers.

DIURETICS

Diuretics	Mechanism	Clinical Uses	Side Effects
1. **CA inhibitors** (acetazolamide, dorzolamide*)	Inhibits carbonic anhydrase in PCT (brush border and intracellular) and other tissues	• **Glaucoma** ($\downarrow$ aqueous humor secretion) • Acute mountain sickness • Metabolic alkalosis • Urinary alkalinization (eliminates acidic drugs)	Acidosis, hypokalemia, hyperchloremia, renal stones, sulfa allergy, paresthesias, possible ammonia toxicity in patients with hepatic failure
2. **Osmotic** (mannitol)	Is freely filtered and poorly reabsorbed, so $\uparrow$ tubular fluid osmolarity, preventing H_2O reabsorption in PCT† via an osmotic effect	• $\uparrow$ urine flow in solute overload (hemolysis, rhabdomyolysis) and if renal blood flow is $\downarrow$ (e.g., shock) • $\downarrow$ intracranial pressure • $\downarrow$ intraocular pressure (acute glaucoma)	Pulmonary edema, hypovolemia, hypernatremia, nausea/vomiting
3. **Loop** (furosemide, ethacrynic acid)	Inhibit $Na^+/K^+/2Cl^-$ cotransporter in TAL	• Edematous states (e.g., heart failure, ascites) • Pulmonary edema • Hypertension • Hypercalcemia	Hypokalemic metabolic alkalosis, hypovolemia, ototoxicity, sulfa allergy (furosemide)
4. **Thiazides** (hydrochlorothiazide, metolazone)	Inhibit Na^+/Cl^- cotransporter in DCT	• Hypertension • Edematous states (e.g., CHF)	Hyponatremia, hypokalemic metabolic alkalosis, hyperglycemia (esp. diabetics), hyperuricemia, hypercalcemia, hyperlipidemia
5. **K$^+$ sparing** (spironolactone, eplerenone, amiloride, triamterene)	• Act in cortical collecting tubules • Block aldosterone receptor (spironolactone, eplerenone) • Block sodium channels (amiloride, triamterene)	• Adjunct with other diuretics to prevent K$^+$ loss (HTN, CHF) • Hyperaldosteronism (spironolactone) • Antiandrogen (spironolactone)	Hyperkalemia, endocrine effects, such as gynecomastia, antiandrogen effects (spironolactone)
6. **ADH antagonists** (demeclocycline, lithium)	V_2 antagonists	• SIADH (demeclocycline)	Bone/teeth abnormalities (demeclocycline); nephrogenic diabetes insipidus (lithium)

Definition of abbreviations: DCT, distal convoluting tubule; PCT, proximal convoluting tubule; SIADH, syndrome of inappropriate antidiuretic hormone; TAL, thick ascending limb.
*Topical for eye
†More minor effects in descending loop of Henle, collecting tubule

ELECTROLYTE CHANGES BY DIURETICS

	Urinary NaCl	Urinary NaHCO$_3$	Urinary K$^+$	Urinary Ca^{2+}	Body pH
CA inhibitors	$\uparrow$	$\uparrow\uparrow$	$\uparrow$	$\uparrow$	$\downarrow$
Loop	$\uparrow\uparrow\uparrow$	$\downarrow, -$	$\uparrow$	$\uparrow$	$\uparrow$
Thiazides	$\uparrow\uparrow$	$-$	$\uparrow$	$\downarrow$	$\uparrow$
K$^+$ sparing	$\uparrow$	$-$	$\downarrow$	$-$	$\downarrow$

RENAL PATHOLOGY

CYSTIC DISEASE OF THE KIDNEY

Childhood polycystic disease	• Rare **autosomal recessive** disease, presenting in infancy with renal (and often hepatic) cysts and progressive renal failure • *Gross:* bilaterally enlarged kidneys with smooth surfaces. *Cut section:* sponge-like appearance with multiple small cysts in the cortex and medulla
Adult polycystic disease	• **Autosomal dominant**, usually have normal renal function until middle age • Present with renal insufficiency, hematuria, flank pain, and hypertension • *Extrarenal manifestations:* liver cysts, **circle of Willis berry aneurysms**, mitral valve prolapse • *Gross:* marked bilateral enlargement with large cysts bulging through the surface • *Micro:* cysts involve <10% of nephrons
Simple cysts	Common, can be single or multiple; have little clinical significance
Medullary sponge kidney	• Multiple **cystic dilatations of collecting ducts in medulla** • Most are asymptomatic
Acquired cystic disease	• Multiple cortical and medullary cysts may result from **prolonged renal dialysis** • Unclear whether ↑ risk for development into renal cell carcinoma

GLOMERULAR DISEASES

Type	Clinical Presentation	Mechanism	Prognosis	Light Microscopy	Electron Microscopy	Immuno-fluorescence
Poststreptococcal glomerulonephritis	Nephritis; **elevated ASLO;** low complement; children > adults	Immunologic (type III hyper-sensitivity)	Most completely recover; occasionally progress to RPGN	Polymorphonuclear neutrophil leukocyte infiltration; proliferation	**Subepithelial humps**	**Granular pattern;** GBM and mesangium contain IgG and C3
Lipoid nephrosis (minimal change)	**Nephrotic syndrome; children > adults**	Unknown	Renal function usually preserved; may respond to steroids	Normal	No deposits; **loss of epithelial foot processes**	Negative
Membranous glomerulonephritis	**Nephrotic syndrome; adults > children**	Immunologic	Less than 50% progress; may respond to steroids	Capillary wall thickening	**Subepithelial spikes;** loss of epithelial foot processes	Granular pattern of IgG and C3
Membranoproliferative glomerulonephritis	Variable: mild proteinuria, mixed nephritic/ nephrotic, or frank nephrotic syndrome	*Type I:* immune complex and both classic and alternate complement pathways *Type II:* immune complex and alternate complement pathway	Poor response to steroids	Basement membrane thick and split; mesangial proliferation	*Type I:* **sub-endothelial deposits** *Type II:* **dense deposit disease**	*Type I:* IgG and C3, C1q, and C4 *Type II:* C3 (IgG, C1q, and C4 usually absent) "C3 nephritic factor"

(Continued)

Type	Clinical Presentation	Mechanism	Prognosis	Light Microscopy	Electron Microscopy	Immuno-fluorescence
Focal segmental glomerulosclerosis	Nephrotic syndrome	Immunologic; aggressive variant of lipoid nephrosis; **IV drug use; HIV nephropathy**	Poor, rare steroid response	Focal and segmental sclerosis and hyalinization	Epithelial damage; loss of foot processes	IgM and C3 focal deposits
Goodpasture syndrome	RPGN + pulmonary hemorrhage	**Anti-GBM antibodies** (type II hypersensitivity)	Often poor, but some response to steroids, plasmapheresis, and cytotoxic drugs	**Crescents**; mesangial proliferation in early cases	GBM disruption; no deposits	**Linear IgG and C3**
Idiopathic RPGN	RPGN; may follow flu-like syndrome	Immunologic	Extremely poor	**Crescents**	Variable, ± deposits; all have GBM ruptures	Granular or linear
Focal proliferative glomerulonephritis	Primary focal glomerulonephritis or part of multisystem disease; may be subclinical or present with hematuria, proteinuria, nephrotic syndrome	Immunologic	Variable	Proliferation limited to certain segments of particular glomeruli	Variable; may show mesangial deposits	Variable; may show mesangial deposits
IgA nephropathy (Berger disease)	Variable: recurrent hematuria, mild proteinuria, nephrotic syndrome; children and young adults	Unknown	Usually slowly progressive	Variable: normal or segmental/ mesangial proliferation or crescentic	Mesangial deposits	**Mesangial IgA deposition**
Chronic glomerulonephritis	Chronic renal failure; may follow a variety of acute glomerulopathies	Variable	Poor	**Hyalinized glomeruli**	Negative	Negative or granular
Alport syndrome	Hematuria, proteinuria, which slowly progress to renal failure; **deafness**; ocular disorders	**X-linked** disorder of collagen	Renal failure often by age 50; deafness may be permanent	Segmental and focal glomerulosclerosis, tubular atrophy, interstitial fibrosis, chronic inflammation	**Thickening** (sometimes thinning) and **splitting the basement membrane**	**Immunofluorescence for individual chains of type IV collagen** can be diagnostic

Definition of abbreviations: ASLO, antistreptolysin O; GBM, glomerular basement membrane; RPGN, rapidly progressive glomerulonephritis.

TUBULAR DISEASES OF THE KIDNEY

Acute Tubular Necrosis (ATN)	**Most common cause of acute renal failure**; associated with reversible injury to the tubular epithelium; excellent prognosis if patient survives disease responsible for the ATN
Ischemic ATN	• Most common cause of ATN • ↓ blood flow caused by severe renal vasoconstriction, hypotension, or shock
Nephrotoxic ATN	Caused by heavy metals such as mercury, drugs, and myoglobin
Four Phases of ATN	
Initial phase	*36 hours*: after precipitating event occurs
Oliguric phase	*10 days:* ↓ urine output; uremia, fluid overload, and hyperkalemia may occur
Diuretic phase	*2–3 weeks:* gradual ↑ in urine volume (up to 3 L/day); hypokalemia, electrolyte imbalances, and infection may occur
Recovery phase	*3 weeks:* improved concentrating ability, restoration of tubular function; normalization of BUN and creatinine

TUBULOINTERSTITIAL DISEASES OF THE KIDNEY

Pyelonephritis	• Infection of the renal pelvis, tubules, and interstitium • **Ascending infection is the most common route** with organisms from the patient's fecal flora; hematogenous infection is much less common. • Etiologic agents usually gram-negative bacilli (e.g., *E. coli, Proteus,* and *Klebsiella*). *E. coli* pili mediate adherence, motility aids movement against flow of urine. *Proteus* (urease, alkaline urine, struvite stones), *Klebsiella* (large capsule)
Acute pyelonephritis	• Risk factors: urinary obstruction, vesicoureteral reflux, pregnancy, instrumentation, diabetes mellitus • Under 40 more common in women (shorter urethra); over 40, ↑ incidence in men due to benign prostatic hypertrophy • **Symptoms:** fever, malaise, dysuria, frequency, urgency, and costovertebral angle (CVA) tenderness. **Fever, CVA tenderness,** and **WBC casts** distinguish pyelonephritis from cystitis. • **Urine:** many WBCs and WBC casts • **Gross:** scattered yellow microabscesses on the renal surface • **Micro:** foci of interstitial suppurative necrosis and tubular necrosis • Blunting of the calyces may be seen on intravenous pyelogram
Chronic pyelonephritis	• **Reflux nephropathy** most common cause • Interstitial parenchymal scarring deforms the calyces and pelvis • **Symptoms:** onset can be insidious or acute; present with renal failure and hypertension • **Gross:** irregular scarring and deformed calyces with overlying corticomedullary scarring • **Micro:** chronic inflammation with tubular atrophy • Pyelogram diagnostic
Acute allergic interstitial nephritis	• **Hypersensitivity reaction** to infection or drugs (e.g., NSAIDs, penicillin) • Leads to interstitial edema with a mononuclear infiltrate • Presents 2 weeks after exposure with hematuria, pyuria, eosinophilia, and azotemia
Analgesic nephritis	Interstitial nephritis and renal papillary necrosis, induced by large doses of analgesics
Gouty nephropathy	• **Urate crystals** in tubules, inducing tophus formation and a chronic inflammatory reaction • *Note:* Urate crystals appear as **birefringent, needle-shaped crystals** on light microscopy.
Acute urate nephropathy	• Precipitation of crystals in the collecting ducts, causing obstruction • Seen in **lymphoma and leukemia**, especially after chemotherapy
Multiple myeloma	**Bence-Jones proteins** are directly toxic to tubular epithelium

Vascular Diseases of the Kidney

Ischemia	• Caused by embolization of mural thrombi usually left side of heart or aorta • **Gross:** sharply demarcated, wedge-shaped pale regions, which undergo necrosis with subsequent scarring • **Symptoms:** infarcts may be asymptomatic or may cause pain, hematuria, and hypertension
Renal vein thrombosis	• Thrombosis of one or both renal veins may occur • Associated with the nephrotic syndrome, particularly membranous glomerulonephritis • Renal cell carcinoma may also provoke renal vein thrombosis as a result of direct invasion by tumor • Presents with hematuria, flank pain, and renal failure • **Gross:** kidney enlarged • **Micro:** hemorrhagic infarction of renal tissue

Urolithiasis

• Affects 6% of the population; men > women
• Renal colic may occur if small stones pass into the ureter, where they may also cause hematuria and urinary obstruction and predispose to infection

Calcium stones	• **75% of stones**; most patients have hypercalciuria without hypercalcemia • Calcium stones are **radiopaque**; they are the only ones that can be seen on x-ray
Magnesium-ammonium phosphate stones	• 15% of stones; occur after infection by urease-producing bacteria, such as *Proteus* • Urine becomes alkaline, resulting in precipitation of **magnesium-ammonium phosphate salts**; may form large stones (e.g., **staghorn calculi**)
Uric acid stones	Seen in **gout**, **leukemia**, and in patients with acidic urine
Cystine stones	• Very rare • Associated with an autosomal recessive amino acid transport disorder, leading to **cystinuria** • Most stones are unilateral and formed in calyx, pelvis, bladder

Obstructive Uropathy And Hydronephrosis

Hydronephrosis	• Multiple etiologies, including stones, benign prostatic hypertrophy, pregnancy, neurogenic bladder, tumor, inflammation, and posterior urethral valves
	• Persistence of glomerular filtration despite urinary obstruction, causing dilation of calyces and pelvis. High pressure in the collecting system causes atrophy and ischemia.
	• **Gross:** dilatation of the pelvis and calyces with blunting of renal pyramids
	• **Symptoms:**
	  – *Unilateral:* may remain asymptomatic as the kidney atrophies
	  – *Bilateral incomplete:* loses concentrating ability, causing urinary frequency, polyuria and nocturia
	  – *Bilateral complete:* causes anuria, uremia, and death if untreated

TUMORS OF THE KIDNEY

Benign

Cortical adenomas	• Common finding at autopsy • **Gross:** yellow, encapsulated cortical nodules • **Micro:** may be identical to renal cell carcinoma, distinguished by size
Angiomyolipomas	• Hamartomas, composed of fat, smooth muscle, and blood vessels • Particularly common in patients with tuberous sclerosis

Malignant

Renal cell carcinomas	• 90% of all renal cancers in adults; seen in ages 50–70 with no sex predilection • Moderate association with smoking and a familial predisposition • Occurs in 2/3 of patients with von Hippel-Lindau disease • **Symptoms:** "classic" triad of hematuria, palpable mass, and costovertebral pain (10% of cases); hematuria in middle-aged patient should raise concern • **Gross:** most common in the upper pole; usually solitary, with areas of necrosis and hemorrhage; often invades the renal vein and extends into the vena cava and heart • **Micro:** polygonal clear cells with abundant clear cytoplasm • Paraneoplastic syndrome: polycythemia • High incidence of metastasis on initial presentation • 5-year survival depends on stage, especially poor (25–50%) if tumor extends into the renal vein
Wilms tumor (nephroblastoma)	• Common childhood malignancy with peak incidence at age 2 • **Symptoms**: abdominal mass and hypertension, nausea, hematuria, intestinal obstruction • May be associated with other congenital anomalies • **Gross**: very large, demarcated masses; most are unilateral, but may be bilateral if familial • **Micro**: embryonic glomerular and tubular structures surrounded by mesenchymal spindle cells • 90% survival rate when patients are treated with surgery, chemotherapy, radiotherapy

ANOMALIES OF THE URETERS

Double ureters	• Form when two same-sided ureters join at some point before the junction to the bladder or enter the bladder separately • Associated with double renal pelvises or an abnormally large kidney

Ureteral Obstruction in Hydroureter and Hydronephrosis

Internal obstruction	• **Renal calculi** are most common cause; usually impact at the ureteropelvic junction, entrance to the bladder, and where they cross iliac vessels • Other causes: strictures, tumors
External obstruction	• Pelvic tumors may compress or invade the ureteral wall; sclerosing retroperitonitis, a fibrosis of retroperitoneal structures, can cause obstruction. • Pregnancy does not cause obstruction, but does cause dilation (secondary to progesterone).

PATHOLOGY OF THE BLADDER	
Diverticula	• **Pouch-like evaginations** of the bladder wall • Occur in older men and women and may lead to urinary stasis and therefore infection
Exstrophy of bladder	• Caused by **absence of the anterior musculature** of the bladder and abdominal wall; developmental failure of downgrowth of mesoderm over the anterior bladder • Site of severe chronic infections, with ↑ incidence of adenocarcinoma
Patent urachus	• Fistula that **connects the bladder with the umbilicus**; isolated persistence of the central urachus termed a urachal cyst • Carcinomas may develop in these cysts
Infectious cystitis	• Cystitis causes frequency, urgency, dysuria, and suprapubic pain • **Causative organisms:** *E. coli, Staphylococcus saprophyticus* (associated with intercourse), *Proteus, Klebsiella* (esp. in diabetics), *Pseudomonas* (capsule is antiphagocytic, exotoxin A inhibits EF-2, esp. in patients with structural abnormalities and antibiotic usage), *Enterococcus* (esp. in males with prostate problems) • No WBC casts in urine (as compared with pyelonephritis) • Systemic signs, such as fever and chills, are also uncommon with lower urinary tract infections; CVA tenderness usually absent
Hemorrhagic cystitis	Marked mucosal hemorrhage secondary to viruses, radiation, or chemotherapy (**cyclophosphamide**)
Cystitis emphysematosa	• Submucosal gas bubbles • Occurs mostly in diabetics
Bladder obstruction	• **Men:** benign prostatic hyperplasia or carcinoma most common cause • **Women:** cystocele of the bladder most common cause • **Gross:** thickening, hypertrophy, and trabeculation of the smooth muscle bladder wall
Carcinoma of the bladder	• **Transitional cell carcinoma:** 90% of primary bladder neoplasms • **Risk factors: Smoking,** occupational exposure **(e.g., naphthylamine),** infection with *Schistosoma haematobium* **(more commonly associated with squamous cell carcinoma)** • 3% of all cancer deaths in the United States - peak incidence between 40 and 60 years of age. • Usually presents with painless hematuria, may also cause dysuria, urgency, frequency, hydronephrosis, and pyelonephritis. • Prognosis. High incidence of recurrence at multiple locations.

The Gastrointestinal System

EMBRYOLOGY OF THE GASTROINTESTINAL SYSTEM

DEVELOPMENT OF THE GASTROINTESTINAL TRACT

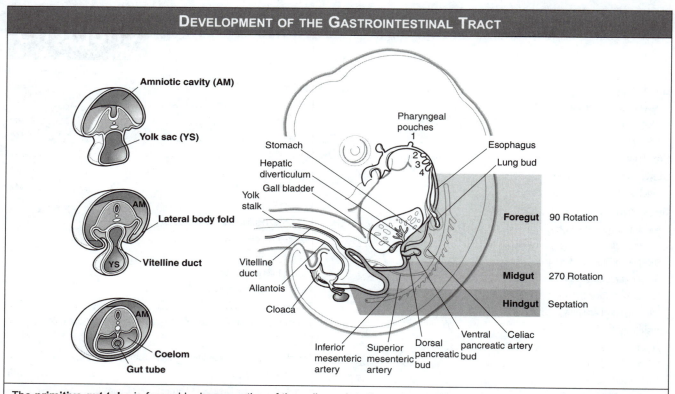

The **primitive gut tube** is formed by incorporation of the yolk sac into the embryo during cranial–caudal and lateral folding.

- The epithelial lining and glands of the mucosa are derived from **endoderm**. The epithelial lining of the gut tube proliferates rapidly and obliterates the lumen, followed by recanalization.
- The lamina propria, muscularis mucosa, submucosa, muscularis externa, and adventitia/serosa are derived from **mesoderm**.

The primitive gut tube is divided into the **foregut**, **midgut**, and **hindgut**, each supplied by a specific artery, each receiving a slightly different autonomic innervation, and each having slightly different relationships to a mesentery.

ADULT STRUCTURES DERIVED FROM EACH OF THE THREE DIVISIONS OF THE PRIMITIVE GUT TUBE		
Foregut	**Midgut**	**Hindgut**
Artery: celiac	**Artery:** superior mesenteric	**Artery:** inferior mesenteric
Parasympathetic innervation: vagus nerves	**Parasympathetic innervation:** vagus nerves	**Parasympathetic innervation:** pelvic splanchnic nerves
Sympathetic innervation: greater splanchnic nerves, T5–T9*	**Sympathetic innervation:** lesser and lowest splanchnic nerves, T9–T12*	**Sympathetic innervation:** lumbar splanchnic nerves L1–L2*
Foregut Derivatives	**Midgut Derivatives**	**Hindgut Derivatives**
Esophagus Stomach Duodenum (first and second parts) Liver Pancreas Biliary apparatus Gall bladder Pharyngeal pouches† Lungs† Thyroid† Spleen‡	Duodenum (second, third, and fourth parts) Jejunum Ileum Cecum Appendix Ascending colon Transverse colon (proximal two thirds)	Transverse colon (distal third) Descending colon Sigmoid colon Rectum Anal canal (above pectinate line)

*Referred pain—stimulation of visceral pain fibers that innervate a gastrointestinal structure results in a dull, aching, poorly localized pain that is referred over the T5 through L1 dermatomes. The **sites of referred pain** generally correspond to the spinal cord segments that provide the sympathetic innervation to the affected gastrointestinal structure.

†Derivatives of endoderm, but not supplied by the celiac artery or innervated as above.

‡Spleen is not a foregut derivative, but is supplied by the celiac artery.

GASTROINTESTINAL HISTOLOGY

LAYERS OF THE DIGESTIVE TRACT

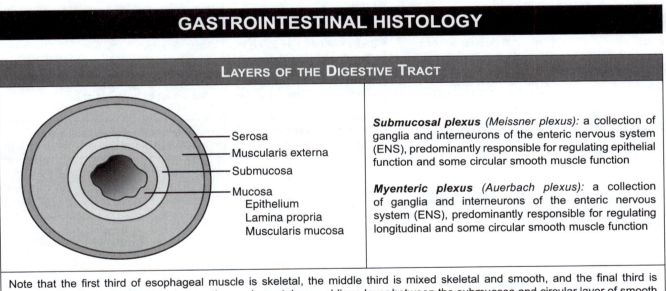

Serosa
Muscularis externa
Submucosa
Mucosa
  Epithelium
  Lamina propria
  Muscularis mucosa

Submucosal plexus (Meissner plexus): a collection of ganglia and interneurons of the enteric nervous system (ENS), predominantly responsible for regulating epithelial function and some circular smooth muscle function

Myenteric plexus (Auerbach plexus): a collection of ganglia and interneurons of the enteric nervous system (ENS), predominantly responsible for regulating longitudinal and some circular smooth muscle function

Note that the first third of esophageal muscle is skeletal, the middle third is mixed skeletal and smooth, and the final third is smooth muscle. Also, the stomach smooth muscle contains an oblique layer between the submucosa and circular layer of smooth muscle.

	HISTOLOGY OF SPECIFIC REGIONS		
Region	**Major Characteristics**	**Mucosal Cell Types at Surface**	**Function of Surface Mucosal Cells**
Esophagus	• Nonkeratinized stratified squamous epithelium • Skeletal muscle in muscularis externa (upper 1/3) • Smooth muscle (lower 1/3)	—	—
Stomach (body and fundus)	*Rugae:* shallow pits; deep glands	Mucous cells Chief cells Parietal cells Enteroendocrine (EE) cells	Secrete mucus; form protective layer against acid; tight junctions between these cells probably contribute to the acid barrier of the epithelium. Secrete pepsinogen and lipase precursor Secrete HCl and intrinsic factor Secrete a variety of peptide hormones
Pylorus	Deep pits; shallow branched glands	Mucous cells Parietal cells EE cells	Same as above Same as above High concentration of gastrin
Small intestine	Villi, plicae, and crypts	Columnar absorptive cells	Contain numerous microvilli that greatly increase the luminal surface area, facilitating absorption
Duodenum	Brunner glands, which discharge alkaline secretion	Goblet cells Paneth cells EE cells	Secrete acid glycoproteins that protect mucosal linings Contains granules that contain lysozyme. May play a role in regulating intestinal flora High concentration of cells that secrete cholecystokinin and secretin
Jejunum	Villi, well developed plica, crypts	Same cell types as found in the duodenal epithelium	Same as above
Ileum	Aggregations of lymph nodules called Peyer patches	M cells found over lymphatic nodules and Peyer patches	Endocytose and transport antigen from the lumen to lymphoid cells
Large intestine	Lacks villi, crypts	Mainly mucus-secreting and absorptive cells	Transports Na^+ (actively) and water (passively) out of lumen

ABDOMINAL VISCERA

Common bile duct · Portal vein · Proper hepatic artery · Epiploic foramen · Liver · Omental bursa (lesser peritoneal sac) · IVC · A · Kidney · Spl · Stomach · Greater peritoneal sac · Lesser omentum · Gastrosplenic ligament · Splenorenal ligament

Viscera are classified as:

- **Peritoneal organs**—have a mesentery and are almost completely enclosed in peritoneum. These organs are mobile.

- **Retroperitoneal organs**—are partially covered with peritoneum and are immobile or fixed organs.

This figure is a cross-section of the abdomen that shows the greater and lesser peritoneal sacs and associated abdominal viscera.

Major Peritoneal Organs (suspended by a mesentery)	**Major Secondary Retroperitoneal Organs** (lost a mesentery during development)	**Major Primary Retroperitoneal Organs** (never had a mesentery)
Stomach	Midgut duodenum	Kidneys
Liver and gallbladder	Head, neck, and body of pancreas	Adrenal glands
Spleen	Ascending colon	Ureter
Foregut duodenum	Descending colon	Aorta
Tail of pancreas	Upper rectum	Inferior vena cava
Jejunum		Lower rectum
Ileum		Anal canal
Appendix		
Transverse colon		

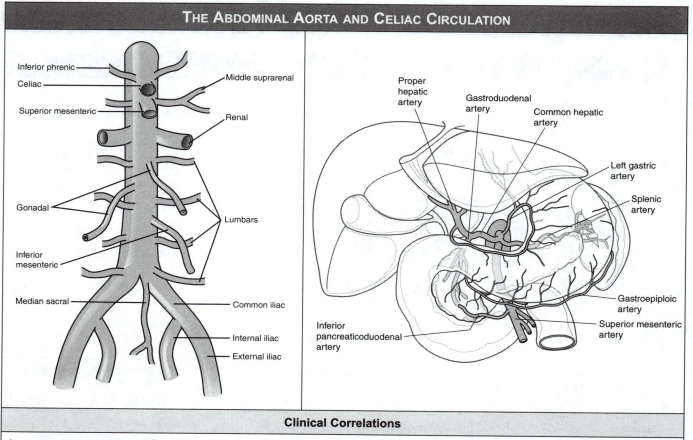

Clinical Correlations

In an **occlusion of the celiac artery** at its origin from the abdominal aorta, collateral circulation may develop in the **head of the pancreas** by way of anastomoses between the **pancreaticoduodenal branches of both the superior mesenteric** and the gastroduodenal arteries.

Branches of the **celiac circulation** may be subject to **erosion** if an ulcer penetrates the posterior wall of the stomach or the posterior wall of the duodenum.

- The **splenic artery** may be subject to erosion by a penetrating ulcer of the **posterior wall** of the stomach.
- The **left gastric artery** may be subject to erosion by a penetrating ulcer of the **lesser curvature** of the stomach.
- The **gastroduodenal artery** may be subject to erosion by a penetrating ulcer of the **posterior wall** of the first part of the duodenum.

Patients with a penetrating ulcer may have **pain referred to the shoulder**, which occurs when air escapes through the ulcer and stimulates the peritoneum covering the inferior aspect of the diaphragm. The contents of a **penetrating ulcer** of the posterior wall of the stomach or the duodenum may enter the **omental bursa**.

Hematemesis may result from bleeding into the lumen of the esophagus, stomach, or duodenum proximal to the ligament of Treitz. Hematemesis is commonly caused by a duodenal ulcer, a gastric ulcer, or esophageal varices.

SUPERIOR AND INFERIOR MESENTERIC ARTERIES

Superior Mesenteric Artery Distribution	Inferior Mesenteric Artery Distribution

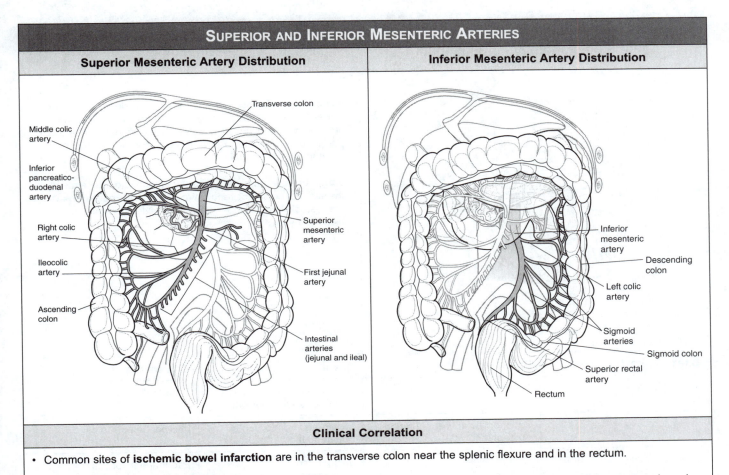

Clinical Correlation

- Common sites of **ischemic bowel infarction** are in the transverse colon near the splenic flexure and in the rectum.

- **Infarction of the transverse colon** occurs between the distal parts of the middle colic branches of the superior mesenteric and left colic branches of the inferior mesenteric arteries.

- **Infarction of the rectum** occurs between the distal parts of the superior rectal branches of the inferior mesenteric artery and the middle rectal branches of the internal iliac artery.

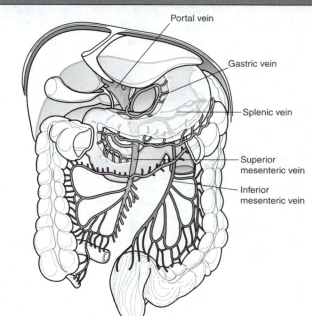

Clinical Correlation

Patients with cirrhosis of the liver may develop **portal hypertension**, in which venous blood from gastrointestinal structures, which normally enters the liver by way of the portal vein, is forced to flow in the retrograde direction in tributaries of the portal vein.

Retrograde flow forces portal venous blood into tributaries of the superior or inferior vena cava; **portacaval anastomoses** are established at these sites, permitting portal venous blood to bypass the liver.

Sites of Anastomoses	Portal	Caval	Clinical Signs
1. Umbilicus	Paraumbilical veins	Superficial veins of the anterior abdominal wall	Caput medusa
2. Rectum	Superior rectal veins (inferior mesenteric vein)	Middle and inferior rectal veins (internal iliac vein)	Internal hemorrhoids
3. Esophagus	Gastric veins	Veins of the lower esophagus, which drain into the azygos system	Esophageal varices
4. Retroperitoneal organs	Tributaries of the superior and inferior mesenteric veins	Veins of the posterior abdominal wall	Not clinically relevant

INFERIOR VENA CAVA (IVC) AND TRIBUTARIES

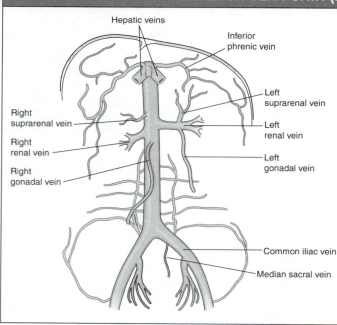

The **inferior vena cava** is formed at about the level of the L5 vertebra by the union of the common iliac veins. It ascends just to the right of the midline.

On the right, the renal, adrenal, and gonadal veins drain directly into the inferior vena cava.

On the left, only the **left renal vein** drains directly into the inferior vena cava; the left gonadal and the left adrenal veins drain into the left renal vein. The left renal vein crosses the anterior aspect of the aorta just inferior to the origin of the superior mesenteric artery.

Clinical Correlation

The **left renal vein may be compressed** by an **aneurysm of the superior mesenteric artery** as the vein crosses anterior to the aorta. Patients with compression of the left renal vein may have renal and adrenal hypertension on the left, and, in males, a varicocele on the left.

CROSS-SECTIONAL ANATOMY

Abdomen: CT, T$_{11}$

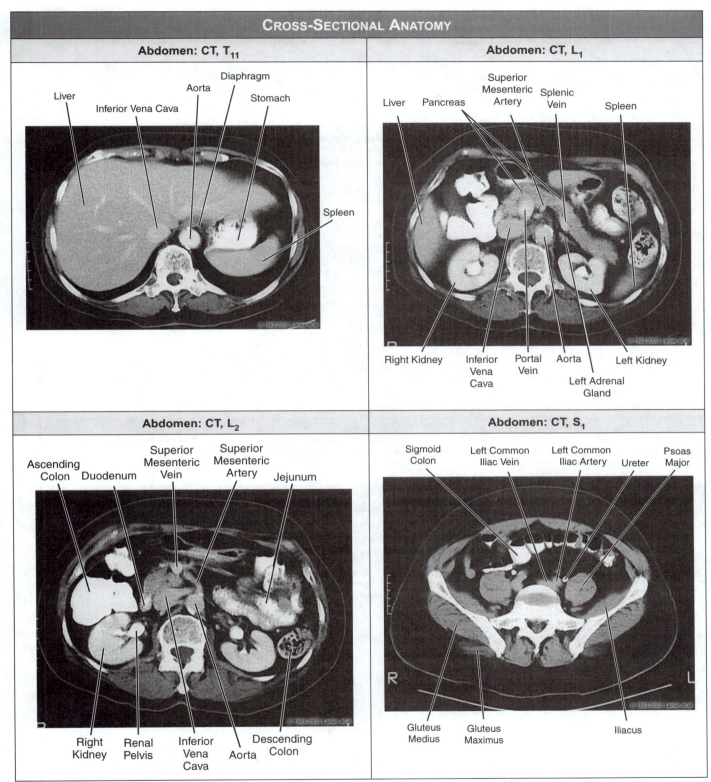

Liver
Inferior Vena Cava
Aorta
Diaphragm
Stomach
Spleen

Abdomen: CT, L$_1$

Liver
Pancreas
Superior Mesenteric Artery
Splenic Vein
Spleen

Right Kidney
Inferior Vena Cava
Portal Vein
Aorta
Left Adrenal Gland
Left Kidney

Abdomen: CT, L$_2$

Ascending Colon
Duodenum
Superior Mesenteric Vein
Superior Mesenteric Artery
Jejunum

Right Kidney
Renal Pelvis
Inferior Vena Cava
Aorta
Descending Colon

Abdomen: CT, S$_1$

Sigmoid Colon
Left Common Iliac Vein
Left Common Iliac Artery
Ureter
Psoas Major

Gluteus Medius
Gluteus Maximus
Iliacus

Images copyright 2005 DxR Development Group Inc. All rights reserved.

GASTROINTESTINAL PHYSIOLOGY

APPETITE

Appetite is primarily regulated by two regions of the hypothalamus: a feeding center and a satiety center. Normally, the feeding center is active, but is transiently inhibited by the satiety center.

Hypothalamus

	Location	Stimulation	Destruction
Feeding center	Lateral hypothalamic area	Feeding	Anorexia
Satiety center	Ventromedial nucleus of hypothalamus	Cessation of feeding	Hypothalamic obesity syndrome

Hormones That May Affect Appetite

Cholecystokinin (CCK)	• Released from I-cells in the mucosa of the small intestine • CCK-A receptors are in the periphery • CCK-B receptors are in the brain—both reduce appetite when stimulated
Calcitonin	• Released mainly from the thyroid gland • Has also been reported to decrease appetite by an unknown mechanism

Mechanical Distention

• Distention of the alimentary tract inhibits appetite, whereas the contractions of an empty stomach stimulate it.
• Some satiety is derived from mastication and swallowing alone.

Miscellaneous

Other factors that help to determine appetite and body weight include body levels of fat and genetic factors.

SALIVA

Salivary glands Submandibular Parotid Sublingual	• Produce approximately 1.5 L/day of saliva • The presence of food in the mouth, the taste, smell, sight, or thought of food, or the stimulation of vagal afferents at the distal end of the esophagus increase the production of saliva.
Functions	• Initial triglyceride digestion (lingual lipase) • Initial starch digestion (α-amylase) • Lubrication
Composition	**Ions:** HCO_3^- 3× [plasma]; K^+ 7 × [plasma]; Na^+ 0.1 × [plasma]; Cl^- 0.15 × [plasma] **Enzymes:** α-amylase, lingual lipase **Hypotonic** **pH:** 7–8 **Flow rate:** alters the composition **Antibacterial:** lysozyme, lactoferrin, defensins, IgA
Regulation	**Parasympathetic** — $\uparrow$ synthesis and secretion of **watery** saliva via muscarinic receptor stimulation; (anticholinergics → dry mouth)
	Sympathetic — $\uparrow$ synthesis and secretion of **viscous** saliva via β-adrenergic receptor stimulation

SWALLOWING

Swallowing is a reflex action coordinated in the **swallowing center** in the medulla. Afferents are carried by the glossopharyngeal (CN IX) and vagus (CN X) nerves. Food is moved to the esophagus by the movement of tongue (hypoglossal nerve, CN XII) and the palatal and pharyngeal muscles (CNs IX and X).

1. **Initiation of swallowing** occurs voluntarily when the mouth is closed on a bolus of food and the tongue propels it from the oral cavity into the pharynx.
2. **Involuntary contraction** of the **pharynx** advances the bolus into the esophagus.
3. Automatic **closure of the glottis** during swallowing inhibits breathing and prevents aspiration.
4. Relaxation of the **upper esophageal sphincter (UES)** allows food to enter the esophagus.
5. **Peristaltic contraction of the esophagus** propels food toward the **lower esophageal sphincter (LES)**, the muscle at the gastroesophageal junction.
6. The LES is tonically contracted, relaxing on swallowing. **Relaxation of the LES** is mediated via the vagus nerve; **VIP** (vasoactive inhibitory peptide) is the major neurotransmitter causing LES relaxation.

Clinical Correlation

Achalasia	**Pathologic inability of the LES to relax** during swallowing. Food accumulates in the esophagus, sometimes causing **megaesophagus**.
Gastric reflux	**LES tone** is low, allowing acid reflux into the esophagus; can lead to gastroesophageal reflux disease (**GERD**).

THE STOMACH

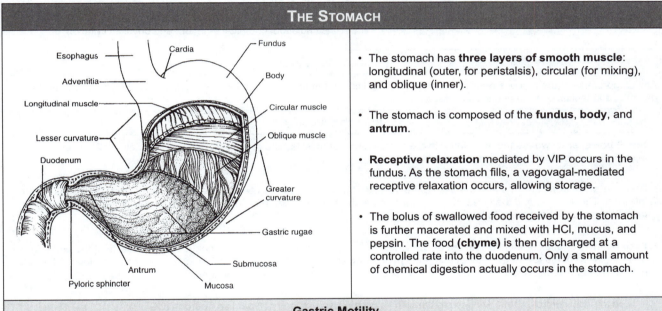

- The stomach has **three layers of smooth muscle**: longitudinal (outer, for peristalsis), circular (for mixing), and oblique (inner).

- The stomach is composed of the **fundus**, **body**, and **antrum**.

- **Receptive relaxation** mediated by VIP occurs in the fundus. As the stomach fills, a vagovagal-mediated receptive relaxation occurs, allowing storage.

- The bolus of swallowed food received by the stomach is further macerated and mixed with HCl, mucus, and pepsin. The food **(chyme)** is then discharged at a controlled rate into the duodenum. Only a small amount of chemical digestion actually occurs in the stomach.

Gastric Motility

- A pacemaker within the greater curvature produces a **basal electric rhythm (BER)** of 3 to 5 waves/min.
- The **magnitude** of the gastric contractions are **increased by parasympathetic** and **decreased by sympathetic stimulation**.
- **Migrating motor complexes (MMC)** are propulsive contractions initiated during fasting that begin in the stomach and move undigested material from the stomach and small intestine into the colon. They repeat every 90 to 120 minutes and are mediated by **motilin**. This housekeeping function lowers the bacterial count in the gut.

Gastric Emptying

- The **pylorus** is continuous with the circular muscle layer and acts as a "valve" to control gastric emptying.
- The contractions of the stomach (peristalsis) propel chyme through the pylorus at a regulated rate.
- Pyloric sphincter contraction at the time of antral contraction limits the movement of chyme into the duodenum and promotes mixing by forceful regurgitation of antral contents back into the fundus (**retropulsion**).
- **Gastric emptying is delayed by:**
  - **Fat/protein in the duodenum stimulating CCK release**, which increases gastric distensibility
  - **H$^+$ in the duodenum** via neural reflexes
  - Stomach contents that are hypertonic or hypotonic

Definition of abbreviation: VIP, vasoactive intestinal peptide.

THE SMALL INTESTINE

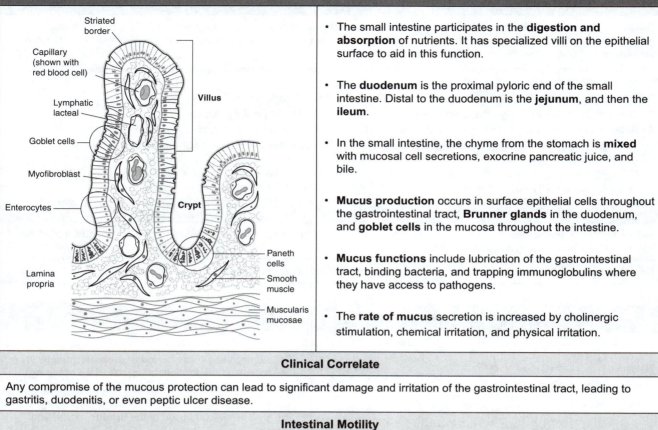

- The small intestine participates in the **digestion and absorption** of nutrients. It has specialized villi on the epithelial surface to aid in this function.

- The **duodenum** is the proximal pyloric end of the small intestine. Distal to the duodenum is the **jejunum**, and then the **ileum**.

- In the small intestine, the chyme from the stomach is **mixed** with mucosal cell secretions, exocrine pancreatic juice, and bile.

- **Mucus production** occurs in surface epithelial cells throughout the gastrointestinal tract, **Brunner glands** in the duodenum, and **goblet cells** in the mucosa throughout the intestine.

- **Mucus functions** include lubrication of the gastrointestinal tract, binding bacteria, and trapping immunoglobulins where they have access to pathogens.

- The **rate of mucus** secretion is increased by cholinergic stimulation, chemical irritation, and physical irritation.

Clinical Correlate

Any compromise of the mucous protection can lead to significant damage and irritation of the gastrointestinal tract, leading to gastritis, duodenitis, or even peptic ulcer disease.

Intestinal Motility

- **Small bowel slow waves** move caudally in the circular smooth muscle. The rate slows from approximately 12/min in the jejunum to approximately 9/min in the ileum.

- **Segmentation contractions** are ring-like contractions that **mix intestinal contents**. They occur at random "nodes" along the intestine. These relax, and then new nodes are formed at the former internodes. This action moves the chyme back and forth, increasing mucosal exposure to the chyme.

- **Peristalsis** is a reflex response initiated by stretching of the lumen of the gut. There is contraction of muscle at the oral end and relaxation of muscle at the caudal end, thus **propelling the contents caudally**. Although peristalsis is modulated by autonomic input, it can occur even in isolated loops of small bowel with no extrinsic innervation.

  - The intrinsic control system senses stretch with calcitonin gene-related polypeptide neurons (CGRP).
  - The contractile wave is initiated by acetylcholine (ACh) and substance P.
  - The relaxation caudal to the stimulus is initiated by nitric oxide (NO) and VIP.

- **Parasympathetic stimulation** ↑ **contractions** and **sympathetic stimulation** ↓ **contractions.**

- The **gastroileal reflex** is caused by food in the stomach, which stimulates peristalsis in the ileum and relaxes the ileocecal valve. This delivers intestinal contents to the large intestine.

- Small intestinal **secretions** are generally **alkaline**, serving to neutralize the acidic nature of the chyme entering from the pylorus.

Clinical Correlation

Peristalsis is activated by the **parasympathetic system**. For those suffering from decreased intestinal motility manifesting as constipation (paralytic ileus, diabetic gastroparesis), dopaminergic and cholinergic agents are often used (e.g., metoclopramide).

LARGE INTESTINE (COLON)

General Features

- The colon is larger in diameter and shorter in length than is the small intestine. Fecal material moves from the **cecum**, through the colon (**ascending**, **transverse**, **descending**, and **sigmoid colons**), rectum, and anal canal.
- Three longitudinal bands of muscle, the **teniae coli**, constitute the outer layer. Because the colon is longer than these bands, pouching occurs, creating **haustra** between the teniae and giving the colon its characteristic "caterpillar" appearance.
- The mucosa has **no villi**, and mucus is secreted by short, inward-projecting colonic glands.
- Abundant lymphoid follicles are found in the cecum and appendix and more sparsely elsewhere.
- The major functions of the colon are **reabsorption of fluid and electrolytes** and **temporary storage of feces**.

Colonic Motility

- **Peristaltic waves** briefly open the normally closed ileocecal valve, passing a small amount of chyme into the cecum. Peristalsis also advances the chyme in the colon. Slow waves, approximately 2/min, are initiated at the ileocecal valve and increase to approximately 6/min at the sigmoid colon.
- **Segmentation contractions** mix the contents of the colon back and forth.
- **Mass movement contractions** are found only in the colon. Constriction of long lengths of colon propels large amounts of chyme distally toward the anus. Mass movements propel feces into the rectum. Distention of the rectum with feces initiates the **defecation reflex**.

Absorption

The mucosa of the colon has great absorptive capability. **Na^+ is actively transported with water following, and K^+ and HCO_3^- are secreted into the colon.**

Defecation

Feces	Contains undigested plant fibers, bacteria, inorganic matter, and water. Nondietary material (e.g., sloughed-off mucosa) constitutes a large portion of the feces. In normal feces, 30% of the solids may be bacteria. Bacteria synthesize **vitamin K**, B-complex vitamins, and folic acid, split urea to NH_3, and produce small organic acids from unabsorbed fat and carbohydrate.
Defecation	Rectal distention with feces activates intrinsic and cord reflexes that cause relaxation of the internal anal sphincter (smooth muscle) and produce the urge to defecate. If the external anal sphincter (skeletal muscle innervated by the **pudendal nerve**) is then voluntarily relaxed, and intra-abdominal pressure is increased via the **Valsalva maneuver**, defecation occurs. If the external sphincter is held contracted, the urge to defecate temporarily diminishes.
Gastrocolic reflex	Distention of the stomach by food **increases the frequency of mass movements** and produces the urge to defecate. This reflex is mediated by **parasympathetic** nerves.

VOMITING

Vomiting occurs in three phases: **nausea**, **retching**, and **vomiting**.

- **Nausea**—hypersalivation, decreased gastric tone, increased duodenal and proximal jejunal tone → reflux of contents into stomach
- **Retching**—Gastric contents travel to the esophagus. Retching occurs if upper esophageal sphincter (UES) remains closed.
- **Vomiting**—If pressure increases enough to open the UES, vomiting occurs; vomiting can be triggered by oropharyngeal stimulation, gastric overdistention and gastroparesis, vestibular stimulation, or input from the **chemoreceptor trigger zone**, located in the **area postrema** in the floor of the fourth ventricle, which stimulates the medullary vomiting center.

ANTIEMETICS		
Drug Class	**Agents**	**Comments**
5HT$_3$ antagonists	**Ondansetron** Granisetron, dolasetron	May act in chemoreceptor trigger zone and in peripheral sites
DA antagonists	**Phenothiazine**, metoclopramide*	Block D$_2$ receptors in chemoreceptor trigger zone
Cannabinoids	**Dronabinol**	Active ingredient in marijuana

EMETICS	
Ipecac	• Locally irritates the GI tract and stimulates the chemoreceptor trigger zone • If emesis does not occur in 15-20 min, lavage must be used to remove ipecac
Apomorphine	• Dopamine-receptor agonist that stimulates the chemoreceptor trigger zone • Vomiting should occur within 5 min

*Also a prokinetic agent

GASTROINTESTINAL HORMONES

Gastrointestinal hormones are released into the systemic circulation after physiologic stimulation (e.g., by food in gut), can exert their effects independent of the nervous system when administered exogenously, and have been chemically identified and synthesized. The five gastrointestinal hormones include **secretin**, **gastrin**, **cholecystokinin (CCK)**, **gastric inhibitory peptide (GIP)**, and **motilin**.

Hormone	Source	Stimulus	Actions
Gastrin*, ‡	**G cells** of gastric antrum	• **Small peptides, amino acids, Ca^{2+} in lumen of stomach** • Vagus (via **GRP**) • **Stomach distension** • **Inhibited by: H$^+$ in lumen of antrum**	• ↑ **HCl secretion by parietal cells** • **Trophic effects on GI mucosa** • ↑ pepsinogen secretion by chief cells • ↑ histamine secretion by ECL cells
CCK*	**I cells** of duodenum and jejunum	• **Fatty acids, monoglycerides** • **Small peptides and amino acids**	• **Stimulates gallbladder contraction** and **relaxes sphincter of Oddi** • ↑ **pancreatic enzyme secretion** • Augments secretin-induced stimulation of pancreatic HCO$_3^-$ • **Inhibits gastric emptying** • Trophic effect on exocrine pancreas/gallbladder
Secretin†	**S cells** of duodenum	• ↓ **pH** in duodenal lumen • **Fatty acids** in duodenal lumen	• ↑ **pancreatic HCO$_3^-$ secretion** (neutralizes H$^+$) • Trophic effect on exocrine pancreas • ↑ **bile production** • ↓ **gastric H$^+$ secretion**
GIP†	K cells of duodenum and jejunum	**Glucose, fatty acids, amino acids**	• ↑ **insulin release** • ↓ **gastric H$^+$ secretion**
Motilin	Enterochromaffin cells in duodenum and jejunum	Absence of food for >2 hours	Initiates MMC motility pattern in stomach and small intestine

(Continued)

GASTROINTESTINAL HORMONES (CONT'D.)

Paracrines/ Neurocrines	Source	Stimulus	Actions
Somatostatin	D cells throughout GI tract	$\downarrow$ pH in lumen	• $\downarrow$ gallbladder contraction, pancreatic secretion • $\downarrow$ gastric acid and pepsinogen secretion • $\downarrow$ small intestinal fluid secretion • $\downarrow$ ACh release from the myenteric plexus and decreases motility • $\downarrow$ α-cell release of glucagon, and β-cell release of insulin in pancreatic islet cells
Histamine	Enterochromaffin cells	• Gastrin • ACh	$\uparrow$ **gastric acid secretion** (directly, and potentiates gastrin and vagal stimulation)
VIP†, ¶	Neurons in GI tract	• Vagal stimulation • Intestinal distention	• **Relaxation of intestinal smooth muscle, including sphincters** • $\uparrow$ **Pancreatic HCO$_3^-$ secretion** • **Stimulates intestinal secretion of electrolytes and H$_2$O**
GRP	Vagal nerve endings	Cephalic stimulation, gastric distension	**Stimulates gastrin release** from G cells
Pancreatic polypeptide	F cells of pancreas, small intestine	Protein, fat, glucose in lumen	$\downarrow$ pancreatic secretion
Enteroglucagon	L cells of intestine	—	• $\downarrow$ gastric, pancreatic secretions • $\uparrow$ insulin release

Definition of abbreviations: ECL, enterochromaffin-like cells; GIP, gastric inhibitory peptide; GRP, gastrin-releasing peptide.

*Member of gastrin-CCK family

†Member of secretin-glucagon family

Clinical Correlates:

‡**Zollinger-Ellison syndrome (gastrinoma)**—non-β islet-cell pancreatic tumor that produces gastrin, leading to $\uparrow$ in gastric acid secretion and development of peptic ulcer disease

¶**VIPoma**—tumor of non-α, non-β islet cells of the pancreas that secretes VIP, causing watery diarrhea

GASTRIC SECRETIONS

Secretion Product	Cell Type	Region of Stomach	Stimulus for Secretion	Inhibitors of Secretion	Action of Secretory Product
HCl	Parietal (oxyntic) cells	Body/fundus	• Gastrin • ACh (from vagus) • Histamine	• **Low pH** inhibits (by inhibiting gastrin) • Prostaglandins • Chyme in duodenum (via GIP and secretin)	• Kills pathogens • Activates pepsinogen to pepsin
Intrinsic factor					Necessary for **vitamin B$_{12}$** absorption by the ileum; forms complex with vitamin B$_{12}$
Pepsinogen (zymogen, precursor of **pepsin**)	Chief cells	Body/fundus	• ACh (from vagus) • Gastrin • HCl	H$^+$ (via somatostatin)	• Converted to pepsin by ↓ pH and pepsin (autocatalytic) • **Digests up to 20% of proteins**
Gastrin	G cells	Antrum	• Small peptides/aa • Vagus (via GRP) • Stomach distention	H$^+$ (via somatostatin)	• ↑ **HCl secretion (parietal cells)** • ↑ pepsinogen secretion (chief cells) • ↑ histamine secretion by ECL cells
Mucus	Mucous cells	Entire stomach	ACh (from vagus)		Forms gel on mucosa to protect mucosa from HCl and pepsin; traps HCO$_3^-$ to help neutralize acid

Definition of abbreviations: aa, amino acids; ECL, enterochromaffin-like cells.

MECHANISM OF GASTRIC H$^+$ SECRETION

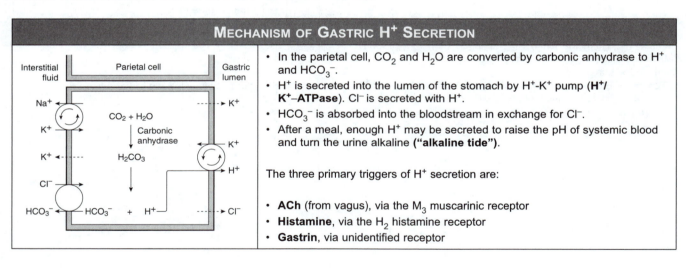

- In the parietal cell, CO$_2$ and H$_2$O are converted by carbonic anhydrase to H$^+$ and HCO$_3^-$.
- H$^+$ is secreted into the lumen of the stomach by H$^+$-K$^+$ pump (**H$^+$/K$^+$–ATPase**). Cl$^-$ is secreted with H$^+$.
- HCO$_3^-$ is absorbed into the bloodstream in exchange for Cl$^-$.
- After a meal, enough H$^+$ may be secreted to raise the pH of systemic blood and turn the urine alkaline (**"alkaline tide"**).

The three primary triggers of H$^+$ secretion are:

- **ACh** (from vagus), via the M$_3$ muscarinic receptor
- **Histamine**, via the H$_2$ histamine receptor
- **Gastrin**, via unidentified receptor

DRUGS FOR PEPTIC ULCER DISEASE

Drug Class	Agents	Comments
Antacids	Magnesium hydroxide, aluminum hydroxide, calcium carbonate	*Magnesium:* **laxative** effect *Aluminum hydroxide:* **constipating** effect
H$_2$ antagonists	**Cimetidine**, ranitidine, famotidine, nizatidine	• Useful in PUD, GERD, Zollinger-Ellison syndrome, but not as effective as proton pump inhibitors • **Cimetidine inhibits hepatic drug metabolizing enzymes** and has **antiandrogen effects**
Proton pump inhibitors	**Omeprazole**, lansoprazole, esomeprazole, pantoprazole, rabeprazole	• Irreversibly **inactivate H$^+$/K$^+$-ATPase**, thus blocking H$^+$ secretion. • Work very well—useful in PUD, Zollinger-Ellison syndrome, and GERD
Mucosal protective agents	**Sucralfate**	Polymerizes in the stomach and forms protective coating over ulcer beds.
	Misoprostol	PGE$_1$ derivative used for peptic ulcers caused by NSAIDs
Antibiotics	Macrolides, metronidazole, tetracyclines (various combinations)	To treat *H. pylori*

Definition of abbreviations: GERD, gastroesophageal reflux disorder; PGE$_1$, prostaglandin E$_1$; NSAIDs, nonsteroidal antiinflammatory drugs; PUD, peptic ulcer disease.

PHASES OF GASTRIC SECRETION

Cephalic phase	The smell, sight, thought, or chewing of food can increase gastric secretion via parasympathetic (vagal) pathways. Responsible for approximately 30% of acid secreted.
Gastric phase	Food in the stomach ↑ secretion. The greatest effects occur with proteins and peptides, leading to **gastrin** release (alcohol and caffeine also exert a strong effect). Gastric distention initiates vagovagal reflexes. Accounts for approximately 60% of acid secreted.
Intestinal phase	Protein digestion products in the duodenum stimulate duodenal gastrin secretion. In addition, absorbed amino acids act to stimulate H$^+$ secretion by parietal cells. The intestinal phase accounts for less than 10% of the gastric secretory response to a meal.

PANCREATIC SECRETIONS

The exocrine secretions of the pancreas are produced by the **acinar cells**, which contain numerous enzyme-containing granules in their cytoplasm, and by the **ductal cells**, which secrete HCO_3^-. The secretions reach the duodenum via the **pancreatic duct**.

Bicarbonate (HCO_3^-)	• HCO_3^- in the duodenum **neutralizes HCl in chyme** entering from the stomach. This also deactivates pepsin. • When H^+ enters the duodenum, S cells secrete **secretin**, which acts on pancreatic ductal cells to increase HCO_3^- production. • HCO_3^- is produced by the action of **carbonic anhydrase** on CO_2 and H_2O in the pancreatic ductal cells. HCO_3^- is secreted into the lumen of the duct in exchange for Cl^-.

Pancreatic enzymes	• Approximately 15 enzymes are produced by the pancreas, which are responsible for **digesting proteins, carbohydrates, lipids, and nucleic acids**.
	• When small peptides, amino acids, and fatty acids enter the duodenum, **CCK** is released by I cells, stimulating pancreatic enzyme secretion.
	• **ACh** (via vagovagal reflexes) also stimulates enzyme secretion and potentiates the action of secretin.
	• **Protection of pancreatic acinar cells against self-digestion:**
	  – **Proteolytic enzymes are secreted as inactive precursors**, which are activated in the gut lumen. For example, the duodenal brush border enzyme, **enterokinase**, converts trypsinogen to the active enzyme, trypsin. Trypsin then catalyzes the formation of more trypsin and activates chymotrypsinogen, procarboxypeptidase, and prophospholipases A and B. Ribonucleases, amylase, and lipase do not exist as proenzymes.
	  – Produce **enzyme inhibitors** to inactivate trace amounts of active enzyme formed within.

Enzyme	Reaction Catalyzed
Proteases:	
Trypsin	Proteins → peptides
Chymotrypsin	Proteins → peptides
Carboxypeptidase	Peptides → amino acids
Polysaccharidase:	
Amylase	Starch and glycogen → maltose, maltotriose, and α-limit dextrins
Lipases:	
Phospholipases A and B	Phospholipids → phosphate, fatty acids, and glycerol
Esterases	Cholesterol esters → free cholesterol and fatty acids
Triacylglycerol lipases	Triglycerides → fatty acids and monoglycerides
Nucleases:	
Ribonuclease	RNA → ribonucleotides
Deoxyribonuclease	DNA → deoxyribonucleotides

HEPATIC EXCRETION	
Physiologic roles	• Excretion of **bilirubin**, **cholesterol**, drugs, and **toxins** • Promotion of **intestinal lipid absorption** • Delivery of **IgA** to small intestine
Components of bile	• Bile—composed of **bile salts, phospholipids, cholesterol, bilirubin (bile pigments), water, and electrolytes**

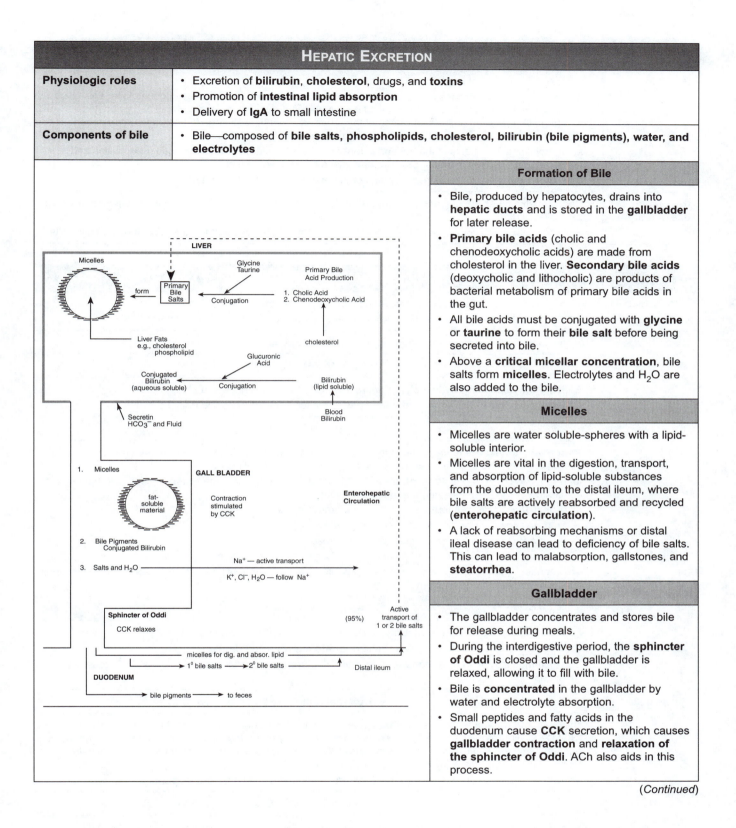

Formation of Bile

- Bile, produced by hepatocytes, drains into **hepatic ducts** and is stored in the **gallbladder** for later release.
- **Primary bile acids** (cholic and chenodeoxycholic acids) are made from cholesterol in the liver. **Secondary bile acids** (deoxycholic and lithocholic) are products of bacterial metabolism of primary bile acids in the gut.
- All bile acids must be conjugated with **glycine** or **taurine** to form their **bile salt** before being secreted into bile.
- Above a **critical micellar concentration**, bile salts form **micelles**. Electrolytes and H_2O are also added to the bile.

Micelles

- Micelles are water soluble-spheres with a lipid-soluble interior.
- Micelles are vital in the digestion, transport, and absorption of lipid-soluble substances from the duodenum to the distal ileum, where bile salts are actively reabsorbed and recycled (**enterohepatic circulation**).
- A lack of reabsorbing mechanisms or distal ileal disease can lead to deficiency of bile salts. This can lead to malabsorption, gallstones, and **steatorrhea**.

Gallbladder

- The gallbladder concentrates and stores bile for release during meals.
- During the interdigestive period, the **sphincter of Oddi** is closed and the gallbladder is relaxed, allowing it to fill with bile.
- Bile is **concentrated** in the gallbladder by water and electrolyte absorption.
- Small peptides and fatty acids in the duodenum cause **CCK** secretion, which causes **gallbladder contraction** and **relaxation of the sphincter of Oddi**. ACh also aids in this process.

(Continued)

HEPATIC EXCRETION *(CONT'D.)*	
Bilirubin	• Bilirubin is a product of **heme metabolism**. • It is taken up by hepatocytes and **conjugated with glucuronic acid** prior to secretion into bile. This gives bile a golden yellow color. In the large intestine, bilirubin is deconjugated and metabolized by bacteria to form **urobilinogens** (colorless). Some of the urobilinogens are reabsorbed; most of the reabsorbed urobilinogens are secreted into bile, with the remainder excreted in the urine. • Most urobilinogen remains in the gut and is further reduced to pigmented compounds (stercobilins and urobilins) and excreted in feces. **Stercobilins** give a brown color to feces. • **Jaundice** (yellowing of the skin and whites of the eyes) is a result of **elevated bilirubin**.
Regulation of bile secretion	• **Secretin** stimulates the secretion of bile **high in HCO_3^- content** from the biliary ductules, but does not alter bile salt output. • Secretion of bile salts by hepatocytes is directly proportional to hepatic portal vein concentration of bile salts.

DIGESTION AND ABSORPTION

- Carbohydrates, lipids, and proteins are digested and absorbed in the small intestine.
- The brush border of the small intestine increases surface area, greatly facilitating absorption of nutrients.

Carbohydrate digestion	Must be converted to **monosaccharides** in order to be absorbed
	Mouth
	• **Salivary amylase** normally hydrolyzes approximately 10 to 20% of ingested starch. • It **hydrolyzes** only α-(1:4)-**glycosidic linkages** to maltose, maltotriose, and α-limit dextrins.
	Intestine

	• **Pancreatic amylase** is found in the highest concentration in the duodenal lumen, where it rapidly hydrolyzes starch to oligosaccharides, maltose, maltotriose, and α-limit dextrins.
	• **Maltase, α-dextrinase, lactase, sucrase,** and **isomaltase** are found in the **brush border**, with the highest concentrations in the mid-jejunum and proximal ileum.
	  – **α-dextrinase:** cleaves terminal α-1,4 bonds, producing free glucose
	  – **Lactase:** converts lactose to glucose and galactose
	  – **Sucrase:** converts sucrose to glucose and sucrose
	  – **Maltase:** converts maltose and maltotriose to 2 and 3 glucose units, respectively.
	• The monosaccharide end products (**glucose, galactose,** and **fructose**) are readily absorbed from the small intestine, primarily in the jejunum.

	Clinical Correlation
	• **Lactase deficiency** causes an inability to digest lactose into glucose and galactose. • *Consequence:* ↑ osmotic load, giving rise to **osmotic diarrhea** and **flatulence**. • Very common in African Americans, Asians, and Mediterraneans, and to a lesser degree, in Europeans/Americans.
Carbohydrate absorption	**Luminal Membrane**
	• **Glucose and galactose** compete for transport across the brush border by a **Na⁺-dependent coporter (SGLUT 1)**. Na⁺ moves down its gradient out of the enterocyte and the sugars move up their concentration gradients into the enterocyte (secondarily active). A Na⁺-K⁺ ATPase in the basolateral membrane helps maintain the Na⁺ gradient (by keeping intracellular Na⁺ low). • **Fructose:** facilitated diffusion (down its concentration gradient) via GLUT-5 transporter
	Basolateral Membrane
	Glucose, galactose, and **fructose** are transported across the basolateral membrane via facilitated diffusion (GLUT-2 transporter).

(Continued)

DIGESTION AND ABSORPTION (CONT'D.)

Lipid digestion	**Stomach**
	• Fatty materials are **pulverized** to decrease particle size and increase surface area. • **CCK** slows gastric emptying to allow enough time for digestion and absorption in the small intestine.
	Small Intestine
	• **Bile acid micelles** emulsify fat. • **Pancreatic lipases** digest fat. • Fats are hydrolyzed by pancreatic lipases to **free fatty acids**, **monoacylglycerols**, and other lipids (e.g., **cholesterol**, and **fat-soluble vitamins A, D, E, K**), which collect in micelles.
Lipid absorption	• **Micelles** carry products of fat digestion in the aqueous fluid of the gut lumen to the brush border, where they can diffuse into the enterocyte. • Enterocytes **re-esterify the fatty acids** to form triacylglycerols, phospholipids, and cholesteryl esters, which are incorporated with **apoproteins** into **chylomicrons**. • Chylomicrons are **released by exocytosis** into the intercellular spaces, where they **enter the lacteals** of the lymphatic system. They then enter the venous circulation via the **thoracic duct**. • Glycerol diffuses into portal blood and is either oxidized for energy or stored as glycogen. • **Triacylglycerols** with **medium- and short-chain fatty acids** are hydrolyzed quickly and do not require micelle formation for absorption. They undergo little re-esterification and are absorbed directly into the portal venous system.
	Clinical Correlation
	Abetalipoproteinemia results from a deficiency of apoprotein B, causing an inability to transport chylomicrons out of intestinal cells.
Protein digestion	**Stomach**
	Pepsin begins protein digestion in the stomach. It functions best at pH 2 and is irreversibly deactivated above pH 5; therefore, it will be inactivated in the duodenum. Pepsin is not an essential enzyme.
	Small Intestine
	Protein digestion continues with **pancreatic proteases** (trypsin, chymotrypsin, elastase, carboxypeptidases A and B) activated by brush border peptidases. These are essential enzymes.
Protein absorption	**Luminal Membrane**
	• Protein products can be absorbed as **amino acids**, **dipeptides**, and **tripeptides**. • Amino acids are absorbed via **Na$^+$-dependent amino acid cotransport**. Many different transport systems have been identified, e.g., carriers for neutral, basic, acidic, and imino amino acids. • Dipeptides and tripeptides are absorbed via an **H$^+$-dependent cotransport** mechanism.
	Basal Membrane
	• Dipeptides and tripeptides are hydrolyzed to amino acids intracellularly. • Amino acids are transported to the blood by facilitated diffusion.
	Clinical Correlation
	Hartnup disease is a disorder in which neutral amino acids cannot be absorbed.
Water and electrolyte absorption	The absorption of water and electrolytes occurs mainly in the **small intestine**. Approximately 5–10 liters of fluid must be absorbed daily (intake and secretion), with 80–90% being absorbed in the small intestine at a maximal rate of 700 mL/h.

(Continued)

DIGESTION AND ABSORPTION *(CONT'D.)*	
NaCl	• In the **proximal intestine**, there is **Na^+-H^+ exchange, Na^+-glucose or Na^+-amino acid cotransport, Na^+-Cl^- cotransport,** and **passive diffusion** through Na^+ channels. • In the colon, passive diffusion through Na^+ channels is more important and is stimulated by **aldosterone**. • Cl^- is absorbed via Na^+-Cl^- cotransport, Cl^--HCO_3^- exchange, and passive diffusion.
K^+	• K^+ absorption occurs in the small intestine by passive diffusion. • K^+ is secreted in the colon (stimulated by aldosterone).
Ca^{2+}	• Absorption in the small intestine is via a vitamin D-dependent carrier. • Vitamin D deficiency $\rightarrow$ $\downarrow$ Ca^{2+} absorption $\rightarrow$ **osteomalacia** (adults) and **rickets** (children).
H_2O	• Secondary to solute absorption • Isoosmotic absorption in gallbladder and small intestine; permeability is lower in colon.
Iron	• Absorbed as **free Fe^{2+}** or as **heme** iron, primarily in the duodenum • Fe^{2+} is bound to transferrin in the blood.
Vitamins	• **Fat-soluble (A, D, E, K)**—incorporated into micelles and absorbed • **Water soluble**—usually via Na^+-dependent cotransporters • **Vitamin B_{12}**—absorption occurs in ileum and is transported while bound to intrinsic factor; $\downarrow$ intrinsic factor (gastrectomy) $\rightarrow$ **pernicious anemia**
H_2O, electrolyte secretion	Secretion occurs in **crypts**. Cl^- is the main ion secreted, via cAMP-regulated channels in the luminal membrane.
	Clinical Correlation
	Cholera toxin stimulates adenylate cyclase $\rightarrow$ $\uparrow$ cAMP $\rightarrow$ open Cl^- channels; Na^+ and H_2O follow $\rightarrow$ secretory diarrhea.

GASTROINTESTINAL PATHOLOGY

LESIONS OF THE ORAL CAVITY

Leukoplakia	• White plaques on oral mucosa, produced by hyperkeratosis of the epithelium • 10% have epithelial dysplasia, a precancerous lesion • *Predisposing factors:* smoking, smokeless tobacco, alcohol abuse, chronic friction, and irritants
Erythroplakia	• Flat, smooth, and red. • Significant numbers of atypical epithelial cells • High risk of malignant transformation
Hairy leukoplakia	• Wrinkled surface • Patches on the side rather than the middle of tongue • No malignant transformation
Lichen planus	White reticulate lesions on the buccal mucosa and tongue
Tumors of the Oral Cavity	
Benign tumors	Hemangiomas, hamartomas, fibromas, lipomas, adenomas, papillomas, neurofibromas, and nevi
Malignant tumors	• **Squamous carcinoma** most common. Peak incidence from ages 40–70 years. • Associated with tobacco and alcohol use, particularly when used together • **Lower lip** most common site, but may affect floor of mouth and tongue

ESOPHAGEAL PATHOLOGY

Achalasia	• **Lack of relaxation of the LES** secondary to loss of myenteric plexus • *Most common ages:* 30–50. • *Symptoms:* dysphagia, regurgitation, aspiration, chest pain • Can be idiopathic, secondary to Chagas disease (*Trypanosoma cruzi*), or malignancy	
Barrett esophagus	• Gastric or intestinal **columnar epithelium** replaces normal squamous epithelium • Occurs with chronic insult, usually reflux (**increases risk of adenocarcinoma** 30–40 times)	

Diverticula	• Sac-like protrusions of one or more layers of the pharyngeal or esophageal wall
	• **Zenker diverticula:**
	  – Occur at the junction of the pharynx and esophagus in elderly men
	  – *Symptoms:* dysphagia and regurgitation of undigested food soon after ingestion
	• **Traction diverticula:** true diverticula in mid-esophagus; usually asymptomatic	

Esophageal carcinoma	• Most are **adenocarcinomas** occurring after 50 and have male:female ratio of 4:1 • Incidence higher in northern Iran, Central Asia • Associated with smoking, alcohol, nitrosamines, achalasia, Barrett esophagus, and vitamin A deficiency • Presents with dysphagia (first to solids) • Liver and lung most common sites of metastasis; poor prognosis	
Esophageal varices	• Dilated tortuous vessels of the esophageal venous plexus resulting from **portal hypertension** • Esophageal varices are prone to **bleeding**; may be life-threatening	
Hernia	**Sliding**	90% of cases, gastroesophageal junction above diaphragm, associated with **reflux**
	Paraesophageal	Gastric cardia above diaphragm, gastroesophageal junction remains in the abdomen; herniated organ at risk for strangulation and infarction

(Continued)

ESOPHAGEAL PATHOLOGY *(CONT'D.)*	
Mallory-Weiss tears	Occur at gastroesophageal junction secondary to recurrent **forceful vomiting**, usually seen in **alcoholics**
Schatzki rings	Mucosal rings at the squamocolumnar junction below the aortic arch
Tracheoesophageal fistula	• Usually esophageal blind pouch with a fistula between the lower segment of the esophagus and trachea • Associated with congenital heart disease and other gastrointestinal malformations
Webs	• Mucosal folds in the upper esophagus above the aortic arch • **Plummer-Vinson syndrome:** dysphagia, glossitis, iron-deficiency anemia, and esophageal webs

Definition of abbreviation: LES, lower esophageal sphincter.

STOMACH	
Acute gastritis (erosive)	Can be caused by alcohol, aspirin, smoking, shock, steroids, and uremia Patients experience heartburn, epigastric pain, nausea, vomiting and hematemesis

Chronic gastritis
   Fundal (type A)
   Antral (type B)
	Autoimmune; associated with **pernicious anemia**, achlorhydria, and intrinsic factor deficiency
	Caused by *Helicobacter pylori* and is most common form of chronic gastritis in U.S.

Carcinoma	• *Risk factors:* genetic predisposition, diet, hypochlorhydria, pernicious anemia, and nitrosamines • Usually asymptomatic until late, then presents with anorexia, weight loss, anemia, epigastric pain. Virchow node (left supraclavicular lymph node) common site of metastasis • *Pathology:* 50% arise in the antrum and pylorus • *Linitis plastica:* infiltrating gastric carcinoma with a diffuse fibrous response • *Histology:* signet ring cells characteristic of gastric carcinoma
Peptic ulcers	• *Common locations:* proximal duodenum, stomach, and esophagus • *H. pylori* infection important etiologic factor. Modification of acid secretion coupled with antibiotic therapy that eradicates *H. pylori* is apparently curative in most patients. • *Symptoms:* episodic epigastric pain; *complications:* hemorrhage, perforation • Duodenal ulcers do not become malignant. Gastric ulcers only rarely • *Stress ulcers:* burns → Curling ulcers; CNS trauma → Cushing ulcers
Pyloric stenosis	• Congenital hypertrophy of pyloric muscle • *Classic case:* firstborn boy, presenting with **projectile vomiting** 3–4 weeks after birth; associated with a palpable **"olive" mass** in epigastric region • *Treatment:* surgical

SMALL INTESTINE	
Celiac sprue	• Allergic reaction to the **gliadin** component of gluten; genetic predisposition • Predisposes to neoplasm, especially lymphoma • *Pathology:* atrophy of villi in the jejunum; affects only **proximal** small bowel
Congenital anomalies	• **Meckel diverticulum:** persistent omphalomesenteric vitelline duct. Located near ileocecal valve. May contain ectopic gastric, pancreatic, or endometrial tissue, which may produce ulceration • **Vitelline fistula:** direct connection between the intestinal lumen and the outside of the body at the umbilicus due to persistence of the vitelline duct. Associated with drainage of meconium from the umbilicus • Atresia: congenital absence of a region of bowel (e.g., **duodenal atresia**); polyhydramnios, obstruction, and bile-stained vomiting in neonate • Stenosis: narrowing that may cause obstruction • **Omphalocele:** when the midgut loop fails to return to the abdominal cavity, forming a light gray shiny sac at the base of the umbilical cord filled with loops of small intestine
Hernias	Cause 15% of small intestinal obstruction most commonly at inguinal and femoral (women) canals
Ischemic bowel disease	• Thrombosis or embolism of the **superior mesenteric artery** accounts for approximately 50% of cases; venous thrombosis for 25% of cases • Internal hernias can strangulate entrapped loops of bowel • Usually after age 60 and presents with abdominal pain, nausea, and vomiting
Intussusception	• Telescoping of one segment of bowel into another; lead point usually an intraluminal mass • More common in infants and children; may be reduced with a diagnostic barium enema
Lymphoma	• Usually non-Hodgkin, large cell, diffuse type • In immunosuppressed patients, the incidence of primary lymphomas of small intestine is increasing. • **MALToma:** often follicular and follow a more benign course; associated with *H. pylori* infection; may regress after antibiotic therapy.
Tropical sprue	• Unknown etiology; high incidence in the tropics; especially Vietnam, Puerto Rico • *Pathology:* similar to changes in celiac disease, but affects **entire** length of small bowel
Volvulus	• Twisting of the bowel about its mesenteric base; may cause obstruction and infarction • May be associated with malrotation of the midgut
Whipple disease	• Rare, periodic acid-Schiff (PAS)–positive **macrophages in the lamina propria** of intestines • Caused by small bacilli *(Tropheryma whippelii)*; more common in men (10:1)

APPENDIX	
Appendicitis	• The vermiform appendix may become inflamed as a result of either an obstruction by stool, which forms a **fecalith** (common in adults), or **hyperplasia** of its lymphatic tissue (common in children). • An inflamed appendix may stimulate visceral pain fibers, which course back in the lesser splanchnic nerves and result in colicky pain referred over the umbilical region.

LARGE INTESTINE

Angiodysplasia	• Dilated tortuous vessels of the right colon → lower gastrointestinal bleeding in elderly • Highest incidence in the cecum
Diverticular disease	• Multiple outpouchings of colon present in 30–50% of adults; higher incidence with ↑ age • Presents with pain and fever
Hirschsprung disease	• **Absence of ganglion cells** of Meissner and Auerbach plexus in distal colon • Produces markedly distended colon, proximal to aganglionic portion • **Failure to pass meconium**, with constipation, vomiting, and abdominal distention
Imperforate anus	Failure of perforation of the membrane that separates endodermal hindgut from ectodermal anal dimple
Polyps	
Tubular adenomas	• Pedunculated polyps; 75% of adenomatous polyps • Sporadic or familial; average age of onset is 60; most occur in left colon • Cancer occurs in approximately 4% of patients
Villous adenomas	• Largest, least common polyps; usually sessile • **1/3 cancerous**
Tubulovillous adenomas	• Combined tubular and villous elements • **Increased villous elements →↑ likelihood of malignant transformation**
Polyposis Syndromes	
Peutz-Jeghers syndrome	• **Autosomal dominant**; involves entire gastrointestinal tract; **melanin pigmentation** of the buccal mucosa • Polyps—**hamartomas**; not premalignant
Turcot syndrome	Colonic polyps associated with brain tumors
Familial multiple polyposis	• **Autosomal dominant**; appearance of polyps during adolescence • Start in rectosigmoid area and spread to cover entire colon • **Virtually all patients develop cancers**; prophylactic total colectomy recommended
Gardner syndrome	• Colonic polyps associated with **desmoid tumors** • **Risk of colon cancer nearly 100%**
Malignant Tumors	
Adenocarcinoma	• **98% of all colonic cancers**; third most common tumor in both women and men; peak incidence in 60s • *Symptoms:* rectal bleeding, change in bowel habits, weakness, malaise, and weight loss • Tumor spreads by direct extension and **metastasis to nodes, liver, lungs, bones** • **Carcinoembryonic antigen (CEA) tumor marker** helps to monitor tumor recurrence after surgery • 75% of tumors in rectum, sigmoid colon • **Left-sided lesions:** annular constriction, infiltration of the wall, **obstruction** • **Right-sided lesions:** often bulky, polypoid, protuberant masses; **rarely obstruct** because fecal stream is liquid on right side
Squamous cell carcinoma	• Occur in anal region, associated with **papilloma viruses** • Incidence rising in homosexual men with AIDS

Exocrine Pancreas

Acute hemorrhagic pancreatitis	• Diffuse necrosis of the pancreas by release of activated enzymes • Most often associated with **alcoholism** and **biliary tract disease** • *Symptoms:* sudden onset of acute, continuous, and intense abdominal pain, often radiating to back; accompanied by nausea, vomiting, and fever → frequently results in shock • *Lab values:* **high amylase**, **high lipase** (elevated after 3–4 days), leukocytosis • *Gross:* gray areas of enzymatic destruction, white areas of fat necrosis, red areas of hemorrhage
Chronic pancreatitis	• Remitting and relapsing episodes of mild pancreatitis → progressive pancreatic damage • X-rays reveal **calcifications** in pancreas • Chronic pancreatitis may result in **pseudocyst formation**, **diabetes**, steatorrhea
Pseudocysts	• Possible sequelae of pancreatitis or trauma • Up to 10 cm in diameter with a fibrous capsule; no epithelial lining or direct communication with ducts
Carcinoma	• *Risk factors:* smoking, high-fat diet, chemical exposure • Commonly develop in **head of the pancreas**, may result in compression of bile duct and main pancreatic duct → obstructive jaundice • **Asymptomatic until late** in course, then weight loss, abdominal pain (classically, epigastric pain radiating to back), jaundice, weakness, anorexia; **Trousseau syndrome** (**migratory thrombophlebitis**) often seen • Very poor prognosis
Cystic fibrosis	• Autosomal recessive; *CFTR* (cystic fibrosis transmembrane conductance regulator protein) gene located on chromosome 7 • **Defective chloride channel**: secretion of very thick mucus and **high sodium and chloride levels in sweat** • 15% present with **meconium ileus** (most present during first year with steatorrhea, **pulmonary infections**, and obstructive pulmonary disease) • *Pseudomonas aeruginosa* is most common etiologic agent • Mean survival age 20; mortality most often due to pulmonary infections
Annular pancreas	Occurs when the ventral and dorsal pancreatic buds form a ring around the duodenum → obstruction of the duodenum

Congenital Hepatic Malformations

Extrahepatic biliary atresia	• Incomplete recanalization → cholestasis, cirrhosis, portal hypertension • **Within first weeks of life:** jaundice, dark urine, light stools, hepatosplenomegaly
Intrahepatic biliary atresia	• Diminished number of bile ducts; sometimes associated with α-**1-antitrypsin deficiency** • **Presents in infancy** with cholestasis, pruritus, growth retardation, ↑ serum lipids • Icterus visible when serum bilirubin exceeds 2 mg/dL (true in any case of jaundice)
Conjugated hyperbilirubinemia	• **Dubin-Johnson syndrome:** benign conjugated hyperbilirubinemia due to impaired transport; liver grossly **black** • **Rotor syndrome:** asymptomatic, similar to Dubin-Johnson, but the liver **not pigmented**

Unconjugated hyperbilirubinemia	• Can be due to hemolysis, diffuse hepatocellular damage, enzymatic defect
	• **Gilbert syndrome:** autosomal recessive disease; deficiency of glucuronyl transferase; benign
	• **Crigler-Najjar syndrome:**
	  – *Type 1:* autosomal recessive with **complete absence of glucuronyl transferase**, marked unconjugated hyperbilirubinemia, severe kernicterus, death
	  – *Type 2:* autosomal dominant with **mild deficiency of glucuronyl transferase**; no kernicterus

Cholestasis	• Impaired excretion of conjugated bilirubin; can have chalky stool • *Intrahepatic:* viral hepatitis, cirrhosis, drug toxicity • *Extrahepatic:* gallstones, carcinoma of bile ducts, ampulla of Vater or head of pancreas
Hepatic failure	Causes jaundice, encephalopathy, renal failure, palmar erythema, spider angiomas, gynecomastia, testicular atrophy, prolonged prothrombin time, hypoalbuminemia
Chronic passive congestion	• Associated with **right heart failure** • *Pathology:* congestion of central veins and centrilobular hepatic sinusoids (known as **"nutmeg liver"**)

ACQUIRED HEPATIC DISEASES

Alcoholic liver disease	• Three major stages: 1) **fatty liver**, 2) **alcoholic hepatitis**, 3) **alcoholic cirrhosis** • Alcoholic hepatitis usually associated with fatty change; occasionally seen with cirrhosis • Results from prolonged alcoholic abuse • *Note:* **Mallory bodies** may be seen, but may also be seen in Wilson disease, hepatocellular carcinoma, and primary biliary cirrhosis
Alpha-1-antitrypsin deficiency	• Autosomal recessive; characterized by deficiency of a protease inhibitor • Results in **pulmonary emphysema** and **hepatic damage (cirrhosis)**
Cirrhosis	• Third leading cause of death in the 25- to 65-year-old age group • *Leading etiologies:* **alcoholism** and **hepatitis C**
Hemochromatosis	• **Primary** form **autosomal recessive** inheritance; **secondary** form usually **related to multiple blood transfusions** • Deposits of iron in the liver, pancreas, heart, adrenal, skin **"bronze diabetes"** • *Also seen:* cardiac arrhythmias, gonadal insufficiency, arthropathy • High incidence of hepatocellular carcinoma
Portal hypertension	• **Intrahepatic:** most common cause and usually secondary to cirrhosis of the liver; *other causes:* schistosomiasis, sarcoid • **Posthepatic:** right-sided heart failure, Budd-Chiari syndrome • **Prehepatic:** portal vein obstruction • *Clinical:* ascites, portosystemic shunts that form hemorrhoids, **esophageal varices**, periumbilical varices (**caput medusae**), **encephalopathy**, splenomegaly • *Additionally,* impaired estrogen metabolism: **gynecomastia**, gonadal atrophy, amenorrhea in females, **spider angiomata**, palmar erythema
Primary biliary cirrhosis	• Autoimmune etiology; causes sclerosing cholangitis, cholangiolitis • Associated with other autoimmune diseases; **primarily affects middle-aged women** • Presents with fatigue and pruritus; elevated alkaline phosphatase • **Antimitochondrial antibody** in over 90% of patients
Secondary biliary cirrhosis	• Longstanding large bile duct obstruction, stasis of bile, inflammation, secondary infection, and scarring • Usually presents with jaundice
Reye syndrome	• Usually affects children between 6 months and 15 years of age • Characterized by **fatty change in the liver, edematous encephalopathy** • *Etiology:* unclear; **frequently preceded by a mild upper respiratory infection, varicella, influenza** A or B infection • Also associated with **aspirin** administration at levels not ordinarily toxic
Sclerosing cholangitis	• Chronic fibrosing inflammatory disease of the extrahepatic and larger intrahepatic bile ducts • Associated with inflammatory bowel disease; predisposition for cholangiocarcinoma
Wilson disease (hepatolenticular degeneration)	• **Autosomal recessive—inadequate excretion of copper** • *Clinical:* rarely manifests before age 6, then presents with weakness, **jaundice**, fever, angiomas, and eventually **portal hypertension**; *CNS* manifestations: **tremor, rigidity**, disorders of affect and thought • *Labs:* **low serum ceruloplasmin**; ↑ urinary copper excretion • *Pathology:* macronodular cirrhosis, degenerative changes in the lenticular nuclei of brain, pathognomonic **Kayser-Fleischer rings**, a deposition of copper in Descemet membrane of the corneal limbus

HEPATIC TUMORS

Liver cell adenoma (benign)	• ↑ incidence with **anabolic steroid** and **oral contraceptive use** • Forms a mass, which may be mistaken for carcinoma, or may rupture (especially during pregnancy)
Nodular hyperplasia (benign)	• Appears as solitary nodule that often has a fibrous capsule and bile ductules • Stellate fibrous core usually present • Nodular regenerative hyperplasia—multiple nodules composed of normal hepatocytes with loss of normal architecture
Cholangiocarcinomas	• 10% of primary liver neoplasms; **associated with primary sclerosing cholangitis** • In developing countries, also associated with **infection with *Clonorchis sinensis*** (liver fluke) • *Clinical:* weight loss, jaundice, pruritus • 50% metastasize to lungs, bones, adrenals, and brain, exhibiting both hematogenous and lymphatic spread
Hepatoblastoma	• Rare, malignant neoplasm of children • Hepatomegaly, vomiting, diarrhea, weight loss, elevated serum levels of AFP
Hepatocellular carcinoma	• **90% of primary liver neoplasms; strongly associated with cirrhosis, HCV and HBV** infections • *Clinical:* tender hepatomegaly, ascites, weight loss, fever, polycythemia, hypoglycemia • **Alpha-fetoprotein is present in 50–90%** of patients' serum (AFP also found with other forms of liver disease, pregnancy, fetal neural tube defects, germ-cell carcinomas of the ovaries and testes) • Death due to gastrointestinal bleed and liver failure; generally, metastases first occur in lungs

HEPATIC INFECTIONS

Acute viral hepatitis	• Can be icteric or anicteric • *Symptoms:* malaise, anorexia, fever, nausea, upper abdominal pain, hepatomegaly • *Labs:* elevated liver enzymes
Chronic hepatitis	• 5–10% of HBV infections and **well over 50% of HCV**; *other etiologies:* drug toxicity, Wilson disease, alcohol, α-1-antitrypsin deficiency, autoimmune hepatitis • *Histology:* chronic inflammation with hepatocyte destruction, cirrhosis, liver failure
Fulminant hepatitis	• **Massive hepatic necrosis** and progressive hepatic dysfunction; mortality of 25–90% • *Etiologies:* HBV, HCV, delta virus (HDV) superinfection, HEV, chloroform, carbon tetrachloride, certain mushrooms, acetaminophen overdose • *Pathology:* progressive shrinkage of liver as parenchyma is destroyed
Liver abscesses	Pyogenic: • *E. coli, Klebsiella, Streptococcus, Staphylococcus*; ascending cholangitis most common cause • Seeding of liver due to bacteremia another potential cause Parasitic: • *Entamoeba histolytica:* especially in men over age 40 following intestinal disease; thick, brown abscess fluid • *Ascaris lumbricoides:* can cause blockage of bile ducts, eosinophilia, verminous abscesses
Parasitic infections	• **Schistosomiasis:** splenomegaly, portal hypertension, ascites • **Amebiasis:** *Entamoeba histolytica*, bloody diarrhea, pain, fever, jaundice, hepatomegaly

Definition of abbreviations: HBV, hepatitis B virus; HCV, hepatitis C virus.

CHARACTERISTICS OF VIRAL HEPATITIDES

	Hepatitis A	Hepatitis B	Hepatitis C	Hepatitis D	Hepatitis E
Nucleic acid	RNA (Picornavirus)	DNA (Hepadna)	RNA (Flavivirus)	RNA	RNA (Calcivirus)
Characteristics	• 50% seropositivity in people >50 • *Clinical disease:* mild or asymptomatic; rare after childhood	• Worldwide carrier rate 300 million • 300,000 new infections/year in U.S.	• 150,000 new cases/year in U.S. • **Most important cause of transfusion-related hepatitis**	• Replication defective • **Dependent on HBV coinfection** for multiplication	**Fulminant hepatitis 0.3–3%; 20% in pregnant women**
Transmission	• **Fecal-oral**, raw shellfish (concentrate virus) • Not shed in semen, saliva, urine • Shed in stool 2 weeks before onset of jaundice and 1 week after	• **Parenteral**, close personal contact • Transfusion • Dialysis • Needle-sticks • IV drug use • Male homosexual activity	• **Parenteral**, close personal contact • **Route of transmission undetermined in 40–50%** of cases	**Parenteral**, close personal contact	• **Waterborne** • Young adults
Incubation	2–6 weeks	4–26 weeks	2–26 weeks	4–7 weeks in superinfection	2–8 weeks
Carrier state	**None**	1% blood donors	1%	1–10% in drug addicts	Unknown
Progression to chronic hepatitis	None	5–10% acute infections	**>50%**	• <5% in coinfection* • 80% superinfection†	None
Increased risk of hepatocellular carcinoma	No	**Yes**	**Yes**	**Yes**, same as for B	Unknown, although not likely
Viral antigen markers	—	• **HBsAg indicates current infection** • **HBeAg indicates infectivity**	—	—	—

*Coinfection: hepatitis B and delta agent acquired at the same time
†Superinfection: delta agent acquired during chronic hepatitis B infection

BILIARY DISEASE

Cholelithiasis (gallstones)	• 20% of women and 8% of men in U.S.; rare before age 20, but seen in 25% of persons >60 years • Most stones remain in gallbladder and are asymptomatic • Famous **"4 Fs": fat, female, fertile (multiparous), older than 40 years**

Three Types of Stones

Cholesterol Stones

Pure cholesterol stones are radiolucent, solitary, 1–5 cm (diameter), yellow, more common in Northern Europeans

Pigment Stones

• Small, black, multiple, and radiolucent; high incidence in Asians
• Associated with **hemolytic disease**, e.g., hereditary spherocytosis
• Cholelithiasis occurs in the young; think of hereditary spherocytosis, sickle cell disease, or other chronic hemolytic process

Mixed Stones

• 80% of all stones and **associated with chronic cholecystitis**
• Composed of cholesterol and calcium bilirubinate

Carcinoma of gallbladder	• Disease asymptomatic until late • *Symptoms:* dull abdominal pain, mass, weight loss, anorexia • *Pathology:* typically involves fundus and neck; 90% differentiated or undifferentiated adenocarcinomas • Poor prognosis, with 3% 5-year survival rate • *Risk factors:* cholelithiasis and cholecystitis (in up to 90% of patients), porcelain gallbladder (due to calcium deposition in gallbladder wall); occurs predominantly in elderly
Carcinoma of bile ducts (cholangiocarcinoma)	• Not associated with gallstones • Men are affected more frequently; usually elderly • *Symptoms:* obstructive jaundice • *Risk factors:* chronic inflammation, infections, (e.g., liver flukes), ulcerative colitis

INFLAMMATORY BOWEL DISEASE: CROHN DISEASE VERSUS ULCERATIVE COLITIS

	Crohn Disease	Ulcerative Colitis
Most common site	Terminal ileum	Rectum
Distribution	Mouth to anus	Rectum → colon; "backwash" ileitis
Spread	Discontinuous/"skip"	Continuous
Gross features	Focal ulceration with intervening normal mucosa, linear fissures, cobblestone appearance, thickened bowel wall, "creeping fat"	Extensive ulceration, pseudopolyps
Micro	Noncaseating granulomas	Crypt abscesses
Inflammation	Transmural	Limited to mucosa and submucosa
Complications	Strictures, "string sign" on barium studies, obstruction, abscesses, fistulas, sinus tracts	Toxic megacolon
Genetic association	Family history of any type of inflammatory bowel disease is associated with increased risk.	
Extraintestinal manifestations	Less common	Common (e.g., arthritis, spondylitis [HLA B27 positive], primary sclerosing cholangitis, erythema nodosum, pyoderma gangrenosum)
Cancer risk	Slight 1–3%	5–25%

GASTROINTESTINAL MICROBIOLOGY

MICROBIAL DIARRHEA: ORGANISMS CAUSING INFLAMMATORY DIARRHEA/DYSENTERY
(Invasive Organisms Eliciting Blood, Pus In Stool, Fever)

Most Common Sources	Common Age Group Infected	Incubation Period	Pathogenesis/ Vignette Clues	Organism	Diagnosis	Treatment
Poultry, domestic animals, water	All	3–5 days	**Invades epithelium**, RBC and WBC in stools (most common bacterial diarrhea in U.S.)	*Campylobacter jejuni*	Oxidase ⊕, gram ⊖, curved rod, seagull-wings shape; grows at 42°C; microaerophile	• Treatment for severe cases only • Erythromycin for invasive disease
Poultry, domestic animals, water	All	8–48 hours	Penetrates to lamina propria of ileocecal region → **PMN response and prostaglandin synthesis, which stimulates** cAMP	*Salmonella* spp.	Gram ⊖, motile rods; nonencapsulated, oxidase ⊖	• Severe cases only • Sensitivity testing required
Water, no animal reservoirs, fecal-oral transmission	All	1–7 days	**Shallow mucosal ulcerations and dysentery; septicemia rare**	*Shigella* spp.	Gram ⊖ rod; nonlactose fermenting; nonmotile	• Severe cases only • Fluoroquinolones, trimethoprim-sulfamethoxazole
Milk, wild and **domestic animals**, fecal-oral	All	2–7 days	Cold-climate pseudoappendicitis; heat-stable enterotoxin; arthritis may occur	*Yersinia enterocolitica*	Gram ⊖, motile rod; nonencapsulated, oxidase ⊖; urease ⊕; bipolar staining; best growth at 25°C	• Severe cases only • Aminoglycosides, trimethoprim-sulfamethoxazole
Associated with **antibiotic use**	Pt. on antibiotics	NA	Pt. on antibiotic (clindamycin)	*Clostridium difficile*	Gram ⊕ rod; anaerobic spore former	Switch antibiotic; metronidazole
Food, water, fecal-oral	Adults	2–3 days	Similar to *Shigella*	**Enteroinvasive E. coli**	Gram ⊖ rod; motile, lactose fermenter; serotyping compares O, H, K antigens	Sensitivity testing required
Food, water, fecal-oral	All	2–4 weeks	Trophozoites invade colon; **flask-like lesions, extraintestinal abscesses (liver)**; travelers to Mexico	*Entamoeba histolytica*	Motile trophozoites or quadrinucleate cysts	Metronidazole

Definition of abbreviation: Pt., patient.

MICROBIAL DIARRHEA: ORGANISMS CAUSING NONINFLAMMATORY DIARRHEA
(Noninvasive Organisms: No Blood, Pus In Stool)

Most Common Sources	Common Age Group Infected	Incubation Period	Pathogenesis/ Vignette Clues	Organism	Diagnosis	Treatment
Day care, water, fecal-oral	**Infants** and toddlers	1–3 days	Microvilli of small intestine blunted; dehydration	**Rotaviruses**	Diagnosis by exclusion: dsRNA naked, double-shelled, icosa-hedral (Reovirus family)	Supportive
Water, food, fecal-oral	**Older kids and adults**	18–48 hours	Blunting of micro-villi; "cruise ship" diarrhea	**Norwalk virus** Norovirus (Norwalk-like)	Diagnosis by exclusion: ⊕ ssRNA, naked, icosahedral (Calicivirus family)	Supportive
Nosocomial	Young kids, immunocom-promised	7–8 days	Death of enteric cells causes diarrhea	**Adenovirus 40/41**	Diagnosis by exclusion: naked, dsDNA, icosa-hedral	No specific therapy
Beef, poultry, gravies, Mexican food	All	8–24 hours	**Enterotoxin**	***Clostridium perfringens***	Anaerobic, gram ⊕ rods, spore-forming, Nagler reaction	Not indicated
Water, food, fecal-oral	All ages	9–72 hours	• Toxin stimulates adenylate cyclase • Rice water stools	***Vibrio cholerae***	Curved, gram ⊖ rod; oxidase ⊕; "shooting-star" motility	Oral rehydration therapy; tetra-cycline shortens symptoms
Raw or **undercooked shellfish**	Anyone eating raw shellfish	5–92 hours	Self-limited gastro-enteritis mimicking cholera	***Vibrio parahaemo-lyticus***	Curved, gram ⊖ rod; oxidase ⊕; "shooting-star" mobility	Not indicated
Water, uncooked fruits and veg-etables	All ages	12–72 hours	**Heat labile toxin (LT) stimulates adenylate cyclase; stable toxin stimu-lates guanylate cyclase**	**Enterotoxigenic *E. coli* (ETEC)**	Gram ⊖ rod; motile; lactose fermenter; sero-typing compares O, H, K antigens	Sensitivity test-ing required
Food, water, fecal-oral	Infants in developing countries	2–6 days	**Adherence to enterocytes through pili → damage to** adjoin-ing microvilli	**Enteropathogenic *E. coli* (EPEC)**	Gram ⊖ rod; motile; lactose fermenter; sero-typing compares O, H, K antigens	Sensitivity test-ing required
Food, fecal-oral (**ham-burger**)	50% <10 years, all	3–5 days	**Verotoxin (a cyto-toxin) causes bloody diarrhea**	**Enterohemorrhagic *E. coli* (EHEC)**	• Gram ⊖ rod; motile; lactose fermenter; serotyping compares O, H, K antigens • O157H7 most common	Antibiotics may increase risk of hemolytic-uremic syndrome

(Continued)

(Noninvasive Organisms: No Blood, Pus In Stool)

Most Common Sources	Common Age Group Infected	Incubation Period	Pathogenesis/ Vignette Clues	Organism	Diagnosis	Treatment
Water, day care, camping, beavers, dogs, etc.	All, children	5–25 days	Cysts ingested; trophozoites; **multiply and attach to small intestinal villi by sucking disk**	*Giardia lamblia*	Flagellated binucleate trophozoites; "falling-leaf" motility; quadrinucleate cysts	Metronidazole
Day care, fecal-oral, animals, homosexuals	Children, AIDS patients	2–4 weeks	Parasites intracellular in brush border	*Cryptosporidium parvum*	Acid-fast oocytes in stool	• Spiramycin in immunocompromised • Unrelenting in AIDS patients even with treatment

DIARRHEA BY INTOXICATION

Most Common Sources	Common Age Group Infected	Incubation Period	Pathogenesis	Symptoms	Organism	Diagnosis	Treatment
Ham, potato salad, cream pastries	All	**1–6 hours**	Heat-stable enterotoxin is produced in food (contamination by food handler with skin lesions); food sits at room temperature	Abdominal cramps, vomiting, diarrhea; sweating and headache my occur; no fever	*Staphylococcus aureus*	Symptoms, time of onset, food source	Recovery without treatment
Fried rice	All	**<6 hours**	Heat-stable toxin causes vomiting	Vomiting 1–6 hours; diarrhea 18 hours	*Bacillus cereus:* **emetic form**	Symptoms, time of onset, food source	Recovery without treatment
Meat, vegetables	All	>6 hours	Heat-labile toxin causes diarrhea (similar to *E. coli* LT)	Nausea, abdominal cramps, diarrhea	*Bacillus cereus:* diarrheal form	Symptoms, time of onset, food source	Recovery without treatment
Meat, vegetables	All	18–24 hours	Enterotoxin	Nausea, abdominal cramps, diarrhea	*Clostridium perfringens*	Symptoms, time of onset, food source	Recovery without treatment

Definition of abbreviation: LT, labile toxin.

ADDITIONAL PHARMACOLOGY

ANTIDIARRHEALS

Drug Class	Agents	Mechanism
Opioid derivatives	Diphenoxylate Loperamide	*Diphenoxylate:* in combination with atropine to prevent abuse *Loperamide:* available over-the-counter

LAXATIVES

Drug Class	Agents	Mechanism
Stimulant	Castor oil, phenolphthalein, senna	Have stimulant or irritant actions on bowel
Bulk-forming	Psyllium, methylcellulose	Indigestible and hydrophilic; absorb H_2O to form bulky stools → reflex bowel contraction
Osmotic	$Mg[OH]_2$ (milk of magnesia), lactulose	↑ fecal liquidity
Stool-softener/ lubricant	Docusate, glycerin, mineral oil	Softens stool, enabling easier passage; glycerin and mineral oil lubricate

DRUGS THAT STIMULATE GASTROINTESTINAL MOTILITY

Agent	Mechanism	Notes
Metoclopramide, cisapride*	Cause cholinergic stimulation; metoclopramide—also a DA antagonist, cisapride—also a $5HT_4$ agonist	Used for gastroparesis (e.g., from diabetes), GERD

*Cisapride has been taken off the market due to fatal arrhythmias; it is now available only on a limited basis.

MISCELLANEOUS GASTROINTESTINAL AGENTS

Ursodiol, chenodiol	Used for dissolution of small gallstones
Pancrelipase	Used for steatorrhea, which is caused by pancreatic enzyme insufficiency

The Endocrine System

ENDOCRINE SYSTEM

GENERAL CHARACTERISTICS OF HORMONES

	Peptides and Proteins (Water Soluble)	Steroids and Thyroid Hormones (Lipid Soluble)
Receptors	Membrane surface	Cytoplasm and/or nucleus
Mechanism	Second messenger	mRNA transcription
Storage	Yes	No (except thyroid as thyroglobulin)
Plasma protein binding	No (except somatomedins)	Yes; acts as pool and prolongs effective half-life
Synthesis	Rough endoplasmic reticulum	Smooth endoplasmic reticulum

HYPOTHALAMUS AND PITUITARY OVERVIEW

HYPOTHALAMUS-ANTERIOR PITUITARY SYSTEM

Hypothalamus and Anterior Pituitary Vascular System

General Characteristics of the Pituitary

	Anterior Pituitary	Posterior Pituitary
Tissue	Glandular	Neuronal
Vascular	Indirect (portal via hypothalamus)	Direct
Control	Neurohormones	Neural
Hormones secreted	TSH, ACTH, LH FSH, GH, prolactin	ADH Oxytocin

Occlusion or lesion of pituitary stalk reduces secretion of all anterior and posterior pituitary hormones, *except* prolactin, which is controlled by inhibitory effects of dopamine.

Hypothalamus	Anterior Pituitary	Peripheral Target
Thyrotropin-releasing hormone (TRH)	Increases secretion of **thyroid-stimulating hormone (TSH)**	TSH stimulates synthesis and secretion of thyroid hormones; hypertrophy of thyroid gland
Corticotropin-releasing hormone (CRH)	Increases secretion of **adrenocorticotropic hormone (ACTH)**	ACTH stimulates synthesis and secretion of cortisol; hypertrophy of adrenal cortex
Gonadotropin-releasing hormone (GnRH)	Increases secretion of **luteinizing hormone (LH)** and **follicle-stimulating hormone (FSH)**	• LH stimulates gonadal steroids • FSH stimulates follicular development (females) and spermatogenesis (males)
Growth hormone–releasing hormone (GHRH) (the dominant control of GH)	Increases secretion of **growth hormone (GH)**	GH actions: causes liver to produce somatomedins; metabolic and growth effects other tissues
Somatostatin (also known as growth hormone–inhibiting hormone [GHIH])	Inhibits secretion of **GH**	—
Prolactin-inhibiting factor (dopamine [PIH])	Inhibits secretion of **prolactin**	Prolactin stimulates lactation and inhibits GnRH, LH, and FSH

ANTERIOR PITUITARY HYPERFUNCTION		
Hyperprolactinemia	• Elevated serum prolactin associated with prolactinoma (chromophobic); **most common pituitary tumor** • Women: amenorrhea and galactorrhea; men: galactorrhea and infertility • **Treatment:** dopamine agonists (e.g., pergolide, bromocriptine)	
Excess GH	**Gigantism**	• Results from excess GH secretion before fusion of growth plates • Excessive skeletal growth may result in heights close to 9 feet • Eosinophilic granuloma
	Acromegaly	• Results from excess GH secretion after fusion of growth plates • Circumferential deposition of bones—enlargement of the hands and feet with frontal bossing • Classic case—hat does not fit any more
Cushing disease	• ACTH-secreting tumors in the anterior pituitary (compare with Cushing syndrome); rarely cause mass effect	
Pathology	• May be micro- or macroadenomas; generally, if active compound is released, lesion is noticed when small • Large lesions can cause mass affect on the optic chiasm; very large masses (10 cm) may invade surrounding structures	

PITUITARY HYPOFUNCTION		
Anterior pituitary hypofunction	• **Sheehan syndrome:** postpartum hemorrhagic infarction of pituitary associated with excessive bleeding; presents as failure to lactate • **Empty sella syndrome:** atrophy of the pituitary; sella is enlarged on skull x-ray and may mimic neoplasm	
Posterior pituitary hypofunction	**Diabetes insipidus (DI)**	• Insufficient or absent antidiuretic hormone • *Clinical:* polydipsia, polyuria, **hypotonic urine, high serum osmolality, hypernatremia** • Central DI responds to exogenous ADH therapy; nephrogenic DI does not
Posterior pituitary hyperfunction	• **Syndrome of inappropriate ADH secretion (SIADH):** as name suggests, inappropriate, excessive ADH secretion unrelated to serum osmolality • *Causes:* May be paraneoplastic (**small cell lung cancer**), CNS damage, drugs, or infections (TB) • *Clinical:* fluid retention, weight gain, and lethargy, **low serum osmolality, hypertonic urine, hyponatremia**	

Definition of abbreviation: GH, growth hormone.

ADRENAL GLAND

ADRENAL HORMONES

Adrenal Gland: Cortex and Medulla

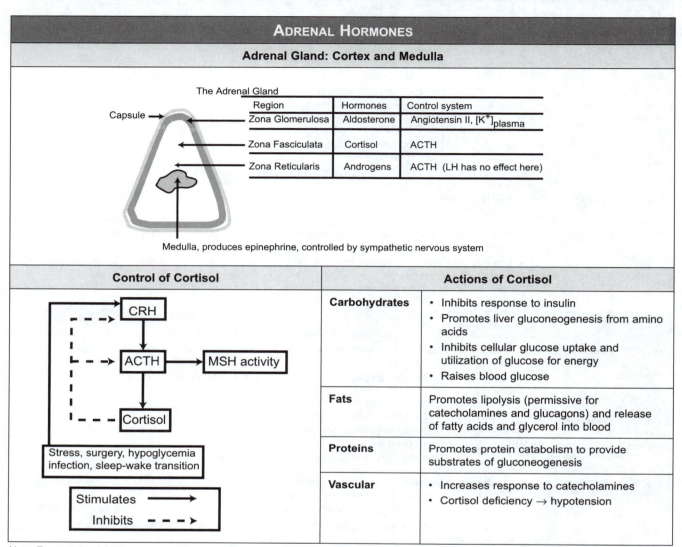

The Adrenal Gland

Region	Hormones	Control system
Zona Glomerulosa	Aldosterone	Angiotensin II, $[K^+]_{plasma}$
Zona Fasciculata	Cortisol	ACTH
Zona Reticularis	Androgens	ACTH (LH has no effect here)

Capsule →

Medulla, produces epinephrine, controlled by sympathetic nervous system

Control of Cortisol	Actions of Cortisol	
CRH → ACTH → MSH activity; ACTH → Cortisol; Stress, surgery, hypoglycemia infection, sleep-wake transition; Stimulates ——→ Inhibits - - - →	**Carbohydrates**	• Inhibits response to insulin • Promotes liver gluconeogenesis from amino acids • Inhibits cellular glucose uptake and utilization of glucose for energy • Raises blood glucose
	Fats	Promotes lipolysis (permissive for catecholamines and glucagons) and release of fatty acids and glycerol into blood
	Proteins	Promotes protein catabolism to provide substrates of gluconeogenesis
	Vascular	• Increases response to catecholamines • Cortisol deficiency → hypotension

Note: Fragments of ACTH precursor proopiomelanocortin (POMC) are also released and have biologic effects, notably melanocyte-stimulating hormone (MSH) activity.

CUSHING SYNDROME

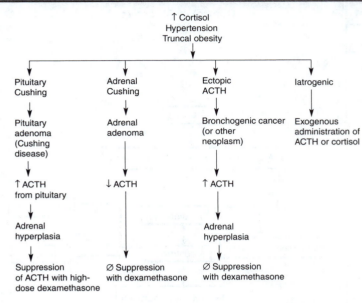

↑ Cortisol
Hypertension
Truncal obesity

Pituitary Cushing → Pituitary adenoma (Cushing disease) → ↑ACTH from pituitary → Adrenal hyperplasia → Suppression of ACTH with high-dose dexamethasone

Adrenal Cushing → Adrenal adenoma → ↓ ACTH → Ø Suppression with dexamethasone

Ectopic ACTH → Bronchogenic cancer (or other neoplasm) → ↑ ACTH → Adrenal hyperplasia → Ø Suppression with dexamethasone

Iatrogenic → Exogenous administration of ACTH or cortisol

Cushing (pituitary)	↑ cortisol ↑ ACTH
Cushing (adrenal)	↑ cortisol ↓ ACTH ↑ aldosterone (often)
Clinical	
Truncal obesity, buffalo hump, moon facies, facial plethora, hirsutism, menstrual disorders, hypertension, muscle weakness, back pain (osteoporosis), striae, acne, psychological disorders, bruising	

DIFFERENTIAL DIAGNOSIS OF CORTISOL EXCESS AND DEFICIENCY BASED ON FEEDBACK CONTROL

Disorder	Plasma Cortisol	Plasma CRH	Plasma ACTH	Hyperpigmentation
Primary (adrenal) excess	↑	↓	↓	No
Primary deficiency	↓	↑	↑	Yes
Secondary (pituitary) excess	↑	↓	↑	Yes
Secondary deficiency	↓	↑	↓	No
Steroid administration (synthetics other than cortisol)	↓ (but symptoms of excess)	↓	↓	No

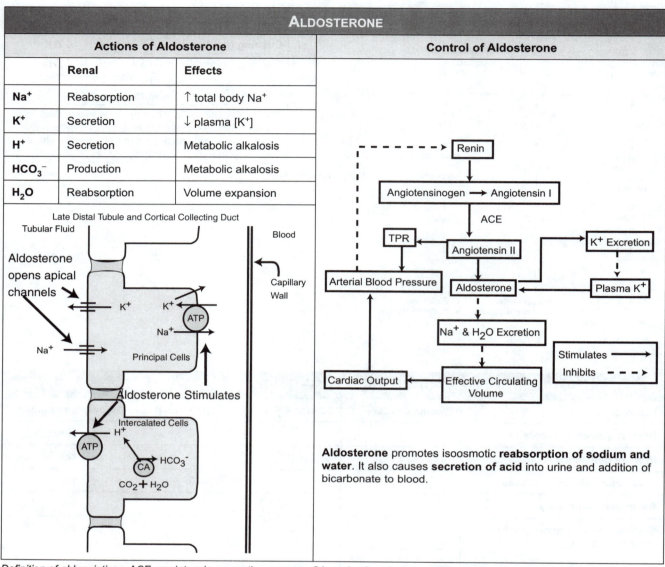

ALDOSTERONE

Actions of Aldosterone

	Renal	Effects
Na⁺	Reabsorption	↑ total body Na⁺
K⁺	Secretion	↓ plasma [K⁺]
H⁺	Secretion	Metabolic alkalosis
HCO₃⁻	Production	Metabolic alkalosis
H₂O	Reabsorption	Volume expansion

Late Distal Tubule and Cortical Collecting Duct

Tubular Fluid — Blood

Aldosterone opens apical channels

Capillary Wall

K⁺   K⁺

ATP

Na⁺

Principal Cells

Na⁺

Aldosterone Stimulates

Intercalated Cells

H⁺

ATP

CA   HCO₃⁻

CO₂ + H₂O

Control of Aldosterone

Renin

Angiotensinogen → Angiotensin I

ACE

TPR ← Angiotensin II → K⁺ Excretion

Arterial Blood Pressure ← Aldosterone ← Plasma K⁺

Na⁺ & H₂O Excretion

Stimulates →
Inhibits ⇢

Cardiac Output ← Effective Circulating Volume

Aldosterone promotes isoosmotic **reabsorption of sodium and water**. It also causes **secretion of acid** into urine and addition of bicarbonate to blood.

Definition of abbreviations: ACE, angiotensin-converting enzyme; CA, carbonic anhydrase; TPR, total peripheral resistance.

LONG-TERM CONTROL OF BLOOD PRESSURE BY RENIN-ANGIOTENSIN-ALDOSTERONE

Event	Effects	Compensation
Volume expansion Saline infusion Polydipsia	↑ preload, cardiac output, and BP	• ↓ renin →↓ AII and ALD • ↓ AII, ↓ ALD →↓ Na⁺ and H₂O reabsorption →↑ urine flow →↓ EFV →↓ preload and cardiac output →↓ BP to normal
Volume loss Hemorrhage Dehydration	↓ preload, cardiac output, and BP	↑ renin →↑ AII and ALD →↑ Na⁺ and H₂O reabsorption → ↓ urine flow →↑ EFV →↑ preload and cardiac output toward normal →↑ BP to normal
Heart failure	↓ cardiac output and BP	↑ renin →↑ AII and ALD → ↑ Na⁺ and H₂O reabsorption →↓ urine flow →↑ EFV →↑ preload and cardiac output toward normal

Definition of abbreviations: AII, angiotensin II; ALD, aldosterone; BP, blood pressure; EFV, extracellular fluid volume.

HYPERALDOSTERONISM	
Primary hyperaldosteronism (Conn syndrome)	• ↑ aldosterone secretion • Adrenal adenoma most common cause • **Clinical:** diastolic hypertension, weakness, fatigue, polyuria, polydipsia, headache, no edema • **Lab values: hypokalemia, low renin levels, metabolic alkalosis, hypernatremia,** failure to suppress aldosterone with salt loading • **Pathology:** single well-circumscribed adenoma with lipid-laden clear cells
Secondary hyperaldosteronism	• Etiologies: congestive heart failure, decreased renal blood flow (increased renin), renin-producing neoplasms, and Bartter syndrome (juxtaglomerular cell hyperplasia, hyperreninemia, hyperaldosteronism) • **Clinical:** Same as for primary, but edema may be present • **Lab values: high renin levels, hypernatremia, hypokalemia**

STEROID SYNTHETIC PATHWAYS MOST COMMONLY INVOLVED IN PATHOLOGY

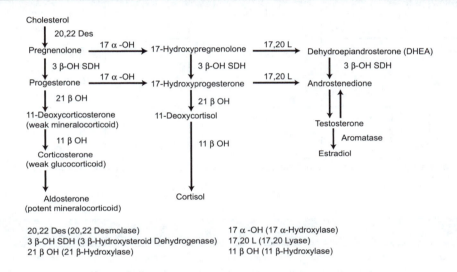

Simplified scheme for understanding enzyme deficiencies; a vertical cut (e.g. 17 α -OH deficiency) all products to the right are deficient (cortisol, androgens) and products to the left are in excess (mineralocorticoids); a horizontal cut (e.g. 11 β OH) all products above are excess (11-Deoxycorticosterone, 11-Deoxycortisol, androgens) and below are deficient (Aldosterone, Cortisol).

| **Congenital Adrenal Hyperplasia** | • Usually due to a congenital enzyme deficiency characterized by **cortisol deficiency and enlargement of adrenal glands**
• The 3 most common forms **all cause virilism** and are called **adrenogenital syndromes:**
  – **Partial 21-hydroxylase deficiency:** normal aldosterone function and impaired cortisol production.
  – **Salt-losing syndrome: near total 21-hydroxylase deficiency** and aldosterone deficiency; infants present with vomiting, dehydration, hyponatremia, hyperkalemia
  – **11-hydroxylase deficiency:** leads to excessive androgen production and buildup of 11-deoxycorticosterone (strong mineralocorticoid), causing virilization, hypertension, hypokalemia |

Congenital Enzyme Deficiency Syndromes

Enzyme Deficiency	Glucocorticoids	Mineralocorticoids	Androgens	Other Effects
20,22 desmolase	↓	↓	↓	Lethal if complete
3 β-OH SDH	↓	↓	↑ DHEA	• Masculinization of females in utero • Incomplete precocious puberty (males) • Adrenal hyperplasia • Hyponatremia and hypovolemia
21 β-OH	↓	↓	↑	• Masculinization of females in utero • Incomplete precocious puberty (males) • Adrenal hyperplasia • Hyponatremia and hypovolemia
11 β-OH	↓	↓ aldosterone ↑↑↑ DOC*	↑	• Mineralocorticoid excess (DOC) • Hypervolemia and hypernatremia • Sexual effects as above
17 α-OH	↓	↓ aldosterone ↑↑↑ DOC*	↓↓	• DOC excess • Absent secondary sexual aspects both sexes • Amenorrhea
17, 20 L	Normal	Normal	↓↓	• Absent secondary sexual aspects both sexes • Amenorrhea

*11-deoxycorticosterone, a weak mineralocorticoid that causes symptoms of mineralocorticoid overload when excessive amounts are secreted

Adrenal Cortical Hypofunction

Acute adrenocortical insufficiency	• Rapid withdrawal of exogenous steroids in patients with chronic adrenal suppression • Adrenal apoplexy seen in **Waterhouse-Friderichsen syndrome** (adrenal hemorrhage associated with meningococcal septicemia)
Primary adrenocortical insufficiency (Addison disease)	• Etiology: most common idiopathic; other causes: tuberculosis, other infections, iatrogenic, metastases, adrenal hemorrhage, pituitary insufficiency • For clinically apparent insufficiency, 90% of the adrenal gland must be nonfunctional • **Clinical:** weakness, weight loss, anorexia, nausea, vomiting, hypotension, skin pigmentation, hypoglycemia with prolonged fasting, inability to tolerate stress, abdominal pain • **Lab values:** hyponatremia, hypochloremia, hyperkalemia, metabolic acidosis; ACTH levels high, cortisol and ALD levels low • **Pathology:** bilateral atrophied adrenal glands • ACTH and MSH share amino acid sequences; in cases of high ACTH → skin pigmentation
Secondary (pituitary) adrenocortical insufficiency	• **Etiology:** metastases, irradiation, infection, infarction, affecting the hypophysial-pituitary axis • Results in decreased ACTH (less skin pigmentation)
Hypoaldosteronism **Primary** **Secondary**	Hyponatremia, hypovolemia, hypotension, metabolic acidosis, hyperkalemia • ↓ aldosterone, ↑ renin and AII • ↓ aldosterone, ↓ renin and AII, ↓ total peripheral resistance

Definition of abbreviations: AII, angiotensin II; ACTH, adrenocorticotropic hormone; ALD, aldosterone; MSH, melanocyte-stimulating hormone.

ADRENAL CORTICAL NEOPLASMS

Adrenal adenomas	• Mostly asymptomatic and not steroid-producing • Steroid-producing adenomas may produce Conn syndrome, Cushing syndrome, or virilization in women • **Pathology:** small and unilateral nodule, yellow-orange on cut section, poorly encapsulated
Adrenal carcinomas	• Relatively rare and usually very malignant • Greater than 90% are steroid-producing • Pathology: tumors often large and yellow with areas of hemorrhage and necrosis

ADRENAL MEDULLA

Tissue	Hormones	Control	Actions
Neural, chromaffin	Epinephrine (80%) Norepinephrine (20%)	Sympathetic nervous system	Glycogenolysis, lipolysis, ↑ blood glucose, ↑ metabolic rate (requires cortisol and thyroid)

Disorders of Adrenal Medulla

Pheochromocytoma	• Neoplasm of **neural crest-derived chromaffin cells** that secrete catecholamines (usually norepinephrine) → hypertension
	• Highest incidence in children and adults age 30–50
	• **Clinical:** paroxysmal or constant hypertension is most classic symptom; also, sweating, headache, arrhythmias, palpitations
	• **Lab values:** elevated urinary homovanillic acid (HVA) and vanillylmandelic acid (VMA)
	• **The Rule of 10s for pheochromocytoma:**
	  – 10% extra-adrenal
	  – 10% bilateral
	  – 10% malignant
	  – 10% affect children
	  – 10% familial

Neuroblastoma	• **Most common malignant extracranial solid tumor of childhood** • Occurs most frequently in the adrenal medulla, but may arise in sympathetic chain • Amplification of the **N-*myc*** oncogene—more copies = more aggressive • **Clinical:** tumors grow rapidly, metastasize widely (especially to bone); prognosis in younger patients (less than 1 year old) better than for older children • **Pathology:** lobulated with areas of necrosis, hemorrhage, calcification • **Microscopic appearance:** rosette pattern of small cells

TREATMENT FOR ADRENOCORTICAL DISEASE

Class	Mechanism	Indications
Glucocorticoids (hydrocortisone)	Replacement therapy	For adrenocortical insufficiency (Addison disease, acute adrenal insufficiency from other causes)
Mineralocorticoids (fludrocortisone)	Replacement therapy	For chronic treatment of Addison disease in patients requiring mineralocorticoids
Glucocorticoid synthesis inhibitors (aminoglutethimide metyrapone ketoconazole)	Inhibits glucocorticoid synthesis via different mechanisms	To suppress adrenocortical steroid production in variety of disorders, e.g., Cushing disease, Cushingoid states, congenital adrenal hyperplasia

ANTIDIURETIC HORMONE AND CONTROL OF OSMOLARITY AND VOLUME

Normal function of antidiuretic hormone (ADH, vasopressin): prevents changes of plasma osmolarity, restores normal blood volume and blood pressure, ↑ **permeability of renal collecting duct to water,** ↑ **reabsorption of water, causes** ↓ **urine flow, and** ↑ **urine osmolarity**

ADH Control of Plasma Osmolarity and ECF Volume	Release of ADH from the Pituitary

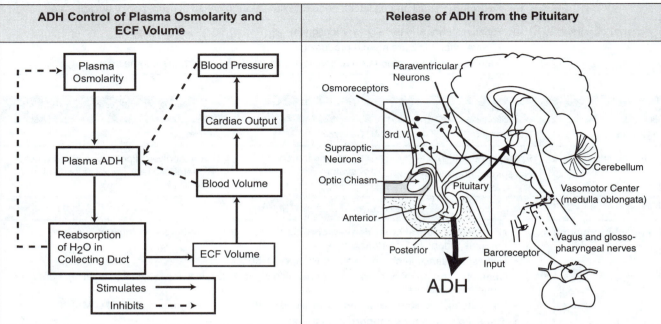

Secretion of ADH by neurons with cell bodies located in the **supraoptic and paraventricular nuclei** of the hypothalamus is **under the control of osmoreceptors and baroreceptors.** The osmoreceptors are in the AV3V region and are influenced by blood osmolarity. Atrial stretch receptors (detecting blood volume) are the largest cardiovascular influence, and arterial baroreceptors, including the carotid sinus (moderate effect) and the aortic arch (minor effect), are processed in medullary centers that regulate cardiovascular function, such as the nucleus tractus solitarius (NTS). The NTS sends efferents to the ADH-secreting neurons. The axon terminals of these neurons are in the posterior pituitary and release the hormone into the blood. Normally, osmolarity dominates control of ADH secretion; extreme changes of blood volume or cardiac output can overrride osmolarity.

DISORDERS OF ANTIDIURETIC HORMONE (VASOPRESSIN)

Diabetes insipidus ↓ ADH (central, neurogenic) ↓ response (nephrogenic)	• Hypovolemia, hypernatremia, metabolic alkalosis, tendency toward hypotension, large volume of dilute urine (distinguishes from dehydration) • Distinguish central versus nephrogenic by testing response to ADH injection (nephrogenic → no response; central → response = concentration of urine)
Dehydration (water deprived) ↑ ADH to compensate	Hypovolemia, hypernatremia, metabolic alkalosis, tendency toward hypotension, small volume of concentrated urine (distinguishes from diabetes insipidus)
Syndrome of inappropriate ADH (SIADH; ↑ ADH)	Hypervolemia, hyponatremia, metabolic acidosis, small volume of concentrated urine (distinguishes from polydipsia)
Primary polydipsia	Hypervolemia, hyponatremia, large volume of dilute urine

ATRIAL NATRIURETIC PEPTIDE

Secretion	• Secreted by **heart (right atrium)** • Stimulated by **stretch (blood volume)**
Actions	• ↑ renal sodium excretion due to ↑ GFR and ↓ reabsorption of sodium (late distal tubule and collecting duct) • ↓ reabsorption of water due to ↓ reabsorption of sodium • Inhibits response to ADH
Clinical	• No known disorder caused by deficiency • Elevated levels have clinical use as index of the severity of congestive heart failure

PANCREAS

ENDOCRINE PANCREAS
Hormones of the Islets of Langerhans

Hormone	Control of Secretion	Target Tissues	Actions
Insulin (β cells)	• Glucose, amino acids • Effect of glucose via ↑ ATP, closes ATP-dependent K$^+$ channels, producing depolarization and exocytosis of insulin • Gastric inhibitory peptide (GIP) stimulates release	Liver	↑ glucose uptake (enzymatic effect) ↑ glucose utilization ↑ triglyceride synthesis ↑ protein synthesis ↑ glycogen synthesis ↓ gluconeogenesis ↓ glycogenolysis ↓ lipolysis ↓ protein catabolism ↓ ureagenesis, ketogenesis ↓ **blood glucose concentration**
		Muscle	↑ glucose uptake (GLUT4 transport) ↑ glucose utilization ↑ protein synthesis ↓ glycogenolysis ↓ protein catabolism ↓ **blood glucose concentration**
		Adipose	↑ glucose uptake (GLUT4 transport) ↑ triglyceride synthesis (↑ lipoprotein lipase to ↑ uptake of fatty acids) ↓ lipolysis (↓ hormone-sensitive lipase) ↓ **blood glucose concentration**
Glucagon (α cells)	• Glucose inhibits • Hypoglycemia stimulates • Amino acids stimulate	Liver	↑ gluconeogenesis ↑ glycogenolysis ↑ lipolysis ↑ protein catabolism ↑ ureagenesis, ketogenesis ↑ **blood glucose concentration**
Somatostatin (δ cells)	Stimulated by glucose, amino acids, fatty acids	Pancreas, GI tract	Inhibits secretion of insulin and glucagon; role is disputed

Use the fact that a carbohydrate meal increases plasma glucose as a sample application. Tracking through the feedback diagram predicts effects on carbohydrate, fat, and protein metabolism.

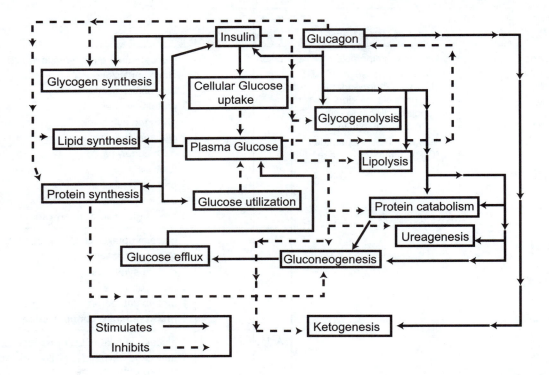

SUMMARY OF GLUCOSE COUNTER-REGULATION

Hormone	Stimulus	Actions
Glucagon	• Fasting, hypoglycemia, stress • **Insulin/glucagon ratio is key to metabolism balance**	• Inhibits response to insulin (mainly in liver) • Promotes catabolism, gluconeogenesis, glycogenolysis
Cortisol	Stress, fasting, hypoglycemia	• Inhibits response to insulin • Reduces cellular glucose uptake • Permissive for lipolysis • Increases gluconeogenesis and protein catabolism • Inhibits cellular glucose uptake
Epinephrine	Stress, severe hypoglycemia	• Increases glycogenolysis and lipolysis
Growth hormone	Fasting, sleep, stress	• Inhibits cellular uptake of glucose • Stimulates lipolysis
Thyroid hormone	Cold, stress	• Permissive for epinephrine's effects • Required for production of GH

INSULIN-RELATED PATHOPHYSIOLOGY

	Glucose	Insulin	C-peptide	Ketoacidosis	Other Features
Diabetes type 2	↑	↑ or ↔	↑ or ↔	Uncommon	Familial, often obese
Diabetes type 1	↑	↓	↓	Yes	Often islet antibodies
Insulinoma	↓	↑	↑	No	Tachycardia (epinephrine)
Insulin overdose	↓	↑	↓	No	Tachycardia (epinephrine)
Fasting hypoglycemia	↓	↑	↑	No	Insulin remains at postprandial level in fasting
Reactive hypoglycemia	↓	↑	↑	No	Excessive secretion with oral glucose tolerance test

DISORDERS OF THE ENDOCRINE PANCREAS

Diabetes mellitus (DM) 　**Type 1** 　**Type 2**	• Often, abrupt onset with **ketoacidosis** • Marked, absolute insulin deficiency, resulting from **diminished β-cell mass** • Characterized by **low serum insulin** levels • Constitutes most cases of idiopathic diabetics, characterized by **peripheral insulin resistance** • Most patients have **central obesity**; onset of disease usually after age 40 • These patients are **not prone to ketoacidosis**
Acute metabolic complications of diabetes	• **Diabetic ketoacidosis** (DKA) may occur in type 1 diabetics, rarely in type 2 • Metabolic acidosis results from accumulation of ketones • High blood glucose → dehydration via an **osmotic diuresis** • Treatment with insulin normalizes the metabolism of carbohydrate, protein, fat • Fluids given to correct the dehydration • **Hyperosmolar nonketotic coma** in patients with mild type 2; blood glucose can be elevated; treatment similar to treatment of DKA
Late complications of diabetes	• Series of long-term complications, including **atherosclerosis** (leading to strokes, myocardial infarcts, gangrene), **nephropathy, neuropathy** (distal, symmetric polyneuropathy with "stocking-glove" distribution), **retinopathy** that may lead to blindness • Patients with DM are also at high-risk for: 　– *Klebsiella pneumoniae* 　– **Sinus mucormycosis** 　– **Malignant otitis externa (*Pseudomonas aeruginosa*)**
ß-cell tumors	• Insulinomas most commonly occur between ages of 30 and 60 • **Pathogenesis:** β-cell tumors produce hyperinsulinemia → hypoglycemia • **Clinical features:** patients experience episodes of altered sensorium (i.e., disorientation, dizziness, diaphoresis, nausea, tremulousness, coma), which are relieved by glucose intake • **Pathology:** most tumors solitary, well-encapsulated, well-differentiated adenomas of various sizes.; 10% are malignant carcinomas
Zollinger-Ellison syndrome	• Due to gastrinoma and often associated with **MEN type I** • **Pathogenesis:** tumors of pancreatic islet cells secrete gastrin → gastric hypersecretion of acid • **Clinical:** includes intractable peptic ulcer disease and severe diarrhea • **Pathology:** 60% malignant; most tumors located in pancreas (10% in duodenum)
MEN I	• Tumors of parathyroids, adrenal cortex, pituitary gland, pancreas • Associated with peptic ulcers and Zollinger-Ellison syndrome
MEN IIa	Tumors of adrenal medulla (pheochromocytoma), medullary carcinoma of thyroid, parathyroid hyperplasia or adenoma
MEN IIb/III	Medullary carcinoma of the thyroid, pheochromocytoma, and mucosal neuromas.

TREATMENT OF DIABETES

Insulin

Classes	Peak (hours)	Duration (hours)	Insulin Types
Ultra rapid-acting	0.25–0.5	3–4	Lispro
Rapid-acting	0.5–3	5–7	Regular
Intermediate-acting	8–12	18–24	NPH, Lente
Long-acting	8–16	18–28	Ultralente
Ultra long-acting	No peak	>24	Glargine

Oral Hyperglycemic Agents

Drug	Mechanism	Notes
Insulin secretogogues • **Sulfonylureas (glyburide, glipizide)** • **Meglitinides (repaglinide, nateglinide)**	• Lower blood glucose by stimulating the pancreatic beta-cells to release insulin • May improve binding between insulin and insulin receptors and/or ↑ number of insulin receptors	• Requires functional beta cells • Repaglinide: faster onset and duration than sulfonylureas; taken before meals to control postprandial glucose levels • Side effects: hypoglycemia, weight gain
Biguanides (metformin)	May ↑ tissue sensitivity to insulin and/or ↓ hepatic gluconeogenesis	• Does not require functional beta cells • Will not cause hypoglycemia • Most serious side effect: lactic acidosis
Thiazolidinediones (rosiglitazone, pioglitazone)	• Bind peroxisome proliferator-activated receptor-γ (PPAR-γ receptor) • ↑ target tissue sensitivity to insulin, inhibits hepatic glucose output, ↑ glucose uptake	• Hypoglycemia rare
α-Glucosidase inhibitors (acarbose, miglitol)	Inhibits intestinal α-glucosidase →↓ glucose absorption →↓ postprandial glucose →↓ demand for insulin	• GI distress, flatulence, diarrhea

Hyperglycemic Drugs

Glucagon	↑ hepatic glycogenolysis and gluconeogenesis, ↑ heart rate and force of contraction, relaxes smooth muscle	• Administered via intramuscular injection • Major side effect: hyperglycemia • Glucagon receptors stimulate adenylate cyclase and ↑ cAMP; this is basis for its use in beta-blocker overdose

ENDOCRINE REGULATION OF CALCIUM AND PHOSPHATE

OVERVIEW OF HORMONAL REGULATION OF CALCIUM AND PHOSPHATE

Hormone	Site Produced	Stimuli to Secretion or Production	Effect on Plasma Free Ca^{2+}	Effect on Plasma Phosphate
Parathyroid Hormone (PTH)	Parathyroid gland	Low plasma Ca^{2+}	↑	↓
1,25-(OH)$_2$-vitamin D$_3$	Skin → liver → kidney	Sunlight, PTH, dietary intake	↑	↑
Calcitonin (not essential for control)	Parafollicular cells of thyroid	High plasma Ca^{2+}	↓	Little net effect

PARATHYROID HORMONE

Effects on kidneys	• Calcium ↑ reabsorption • Phosphate ↓ reabsorption • Vitamin D ↑ production of active form 1,25 (OH)$_2$ vitamin D$_3$ from precursor 25-OH D$_3$ formed in liver
Effects on bone	• Receptors on osteo*blasts*, not on osteo*clasts* • Rapid mobilization of Ca^{2+} and phosphate from bone fluid • ↑ osteoclast activity via mediators released from osteoblasts • Causes bone resorption, release of Ca^{2+}, phosphate into plasma
Effects on GI tract	Indirectly stimulates Ca^{2+} and phosphate absorption in small intestine through its effect to produce active form of vitamin D$_3$

VITAMIN D (CALCITRIOL)

Effects on kidneys	↓ Ca^{2+} and phosphate excretion (by ↑ reabsorption of both)
Effects on bone	↑ resorption (with PTH); releases Ca^{2+} and phosphate into plasma (but normal growth and maintenance also requires both vitamin D and PTH)
Effects on GI tract	↑ Ca^{2+} and phosphate absorption in intestine, ↑ both in plasma

CALCITONIN

Effects on kidneys	↑ phosphate excretion; ↓ Ca^{2+} excretion (minor effect)
Effects on bone	↓ resorption; ↑ deposition; ↓ plasma Ca^{2+} (major effect)
Effects on GI tract	↑ Ca^{2+} and phosphate absorption in intestine (minor effect)

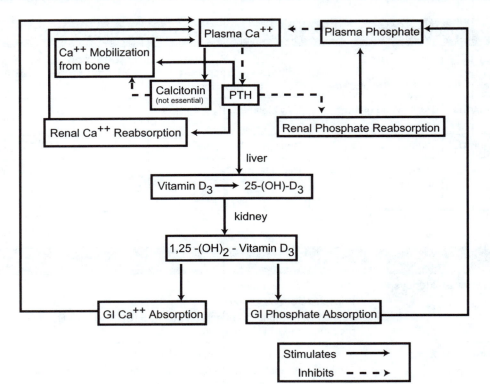

DISORDERS OF CALCIUM AND PHOSPHATE REGULATION

	Plasma (Ca^{2+})	Plasma (Phosphate)	Effects on Bone
Primary hyperparathyroidism	↑	↓	Demineralization and osteopenia
Primary hypoparathyroidism	↓	↑	Malformation
Deficient vitamin D (secondary hyperparathyroidism)	↓	↓	• Osteomalacia in adults • Rickets in children
Excess vitamin D (secondary hypoparathyroidism)	↑	↑	Osteoporosis
Renal failure with high plasma phosphate (secondary hyperparathyroidism)	↓ (precipitation)	↑	Osteomalacia and osteosclerosis

Note: Clinical presentation of hypocalcemia often includes muscle spasms and tetany; hypercalcemia presents with weakness and flaccid paralysis.

Pathophysiology of Calcium Homeostasis

Primary hyperparathyroidism	• Parathyroid adenoma is the most common cause; can see in MEN I and MEN IIa • **Clinical:** elevated serum calcium often asymptomatic • **Lab values:** ↑ **PTH and alkaline phosphatase, hypercalcemia, hypophosphatemia**
Osteitis fibrosa cystica (von Recklinghausen disease of bone)	• Occurs in **chronic primary hyperparathyroidism** • Cystic changes in bone occur due to osteoclastic resorption • Fibrous replacement of resorbed bone may lead to a non-neoplastic "brown tumor"
Secondary hyperparathyroidism	• Usually caused by **chronic renal failure** and decreased Ca^{2+} absorption, stimulating PTH • Vitamin D deficiency and malabsorption less common causes • May show soft tissue calcification and osteosclerosis • **Lab values:** ↑ **PTH and alkaline phosphatase, hypocalcemia, hyperphosphatemia**
Hypoparathyroidism	• Common causes are accidental removal during thyroidectomy, idiopathic, and DiGeorge syndrome • **Clinical:** irritability, anxiety, tetany, intracranial and lens calcifications • **Lab values: hypocalcemia, hyperphosphatemia**
Pseudohypoparathyroidism	• Autosomal recessive disorder, resulting in kidney unresponsive to circulating PTH • Skeletal abnormalities: short stature, shortened fourth and fifth carpals and metacarpals
Hypercalcemia	• Mnemonic "MISHAP": Malignancy, Intoxication (vitamin D), Sarcoidosis, Hyperparathyroidism, Alkali syndrome (Milk-Alkali), and Paget disease • **Clinical:** renal stones, abdominal pain, drowsiness, metastatic calcification

Drugs in Bone and Mineral Disorders

Drug	Mechanism	Notes
Bisphosphonates (alendronate, etidronate, pamidronate, risedronate)	↓ bone resorption	• Osteoporosis • Paget disease • Esophageal ulceration may occur

THYROID

PHYSIOLOGIC ACTIONS OF THYROID HORMONE

Metabolic rate	↑ metabolic rate: high O_2 consumption, mitochondrial growth, ↑ Na^+/K^+-ATPase activity, ↑ food intake, thermogenesis, sweating, ↑ ventilation
Energy substrates	Mobilization of carbohydrates, fat and protein; ↑ ureagenesis; ↓ muscle and adipose mass
Growth	Required after birth for normal brain development and bodily growth (protein anabolic)
Circulation	↑ cardiac output (linked to metabolism), ↑ β-adrenergic receptors on heart

CONTROL OF THYROID HORMONE

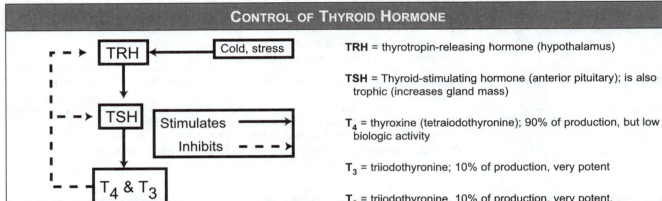

TRH = thyrotropin-releasing hormone (hypothalamus)

TSH = Thyroid-stimulating hormone (anterior pituitary); is also trophic (increases gland mass)

T_4 = thyroxine (tetraiodothyronine); 90% of production, but low biologic activity

T_3 = triiodothyronine; 10% of production, very potent

T_3 = triiodothyronine, 10% of production, very potent.

SYNTHESIS AND STORAGE

Process	Mechanism	Result
Uptake of I⁻	Active transport	↑ follicular cell iodide
Oxidation	Peroxidase	Produce oxidized iodine
Iodination	Peroxidase	Produces MIT and DIT within thyroglobulin
Coupling	Peroxidase	Links MITs and DITs to form T_4 and T_3
Exocytosis	Exocytosis into lumen	Storage of thyroglobulin

Definition of abbreviations: DIT, diiodotyrosine; MIT, monoiodotyrosine.

SECRETION

Process	Mechanism	Result
Transport	Endocytosis	Colloid taken up by follicular cells
Fusion	Lysosomes and colloid fuse	Incorporation in lysosomes
Proteolysis	Lysosomal enzymes	Cleave thyroglobulin into T_3, T_4, MITs, and DITs
Secretion	Simple diffusion	Lipid-soluble T_3 and T_4 diffuse into extracellular fluid to plasma
Deiodination	Deiodinase	Removes iodide from MITs and DITs to recycle it

REGULATION OF THYROID ACTIVITY

Transport	99% bound to thyroid binding globulin, 1% free; represents a pool to prevent rapid change of thyroid level
Peripheral Conversion	T_4 converted to more active T_3 by 5′-monodeiodinase or to inactive reverse T_3 by 5-monodeiodinase; occurs in most tissues giving local control of hormone action
Mechanism of action	Binding to nuclear receptors: T_4 has low affinity, T_3 has high affinity, so is responsible for most thyroid hormone effects
Degradation	Successive deiodination steps to thyronine, also sulfates and glucuronides

THYROID DISORDERS

Disorder	T_4	TSH	TRH	Gland Mass
Primary hypothyroidism	↓	↑	↑	↑, goiter possible
Pituitary hypothyroidism	↓	↓	↑	↓, due to low TSH
Hypothalamic hypothyroidism	↓	↓	↓	↓, due to low TSH
Iodine deficiency (prolonged, severe)	↓	↑	↑	↑, goiter likely
Pituitary hyperthyroidism	↑	↑	↓	↑, goiter possible
Primary hyperthyroidism (tumor)	↑	↓	↓	↓, due to low TSH
Graves disease (autoimmune production of thyroid-stimulating immunoglobulins [TSIs])	↑	↓	↓	↑, goiter possible

DISORDERS OF THE THYROID GLAND

Hyperthyroidism	• Seen most often in Graves disease, toxic multinodular goiter, toxic adenoma • Clinical: tachycardia, cardiac palpitations (β-adrenergic effect), skin warm and flushed, ↑ body temperature, heat intolerance, hyperactivity, tremor, weight loss, osteoporosis, diarrhea and oligomenorrhea, eyes show a wide stare with lid lag; **exophthalmos** seen **only in Graves disease** • Thyrotoxic storm: severe hypermetabolic state with 25% fatality • **Lab values:** low TSH and elevated T_4; low TSH is most important • Note: in pregnancy, ↑ in TBG secondary to high estrogen levels elevates total serum T_4, but not free serum T_4
Graves disease	• Peaks in the third and fourth decades; more common in women; associated with other autoimmune diseases (including Hashimoto thyroiditis) • Production of TSI and TGI bind and activate TSH receptors • **Pathology:** diffuse, moderate, symmetric enlargement of gland • **Microscopic appearance:** hypercellular with small follicles and little colloid
Hypothyroidism	• Clinical features depend on age group • Lab values: elevated TSH and low T_4
Infants	• Develop **cretinism**; major effects are on skeletal and CNS development; once apparent, syndrome is irreversible; neonatal screening for elevated TSH for early detection • **Clinical:** protuberant abdomens, wide-set eyes, dry rough skin, broad nose, delayed epiphyseal closure
Older children	Short stature, retarded linear growth (GH deficiency caused by thyroid hormone deficiency), delayed onset of puberty
Adults	• Lethargy, weakness, fatigue, decreased appetite, weight gain, cold intolerance, constipation • Myxedema: associated with severe hypothyroidism; periorbital puffiness, sparse hair, cardiac enlargement, pleural effusions, anemia
Hashimoto thyroiditis	• Chronic lymphocytic thyroiditis featuring goitrous thyroid gland enlargement • Autoimmune; may be autoantibodies to the TSH receptors, T_3 and T_4; **antimicrosomal antibodies** also seen • **Most common type of thyroiditis;** highest incidence in **middle aged females** • **Pathology:** painless goiter, gland enlarged and firm • **Microscopic appearance:** lymphocytic and plasma cell infiltrate with **Hürthle cells** (follicular cells with eosinophilic granular cytoplasm)
Diffuse nontoxic goiter	Diffuse enlargement of gland in euthyroid patients; high incidence in certain geographic areas with iodine-deficient diets
de Quervain granulomatous subacute thyroiditis	• Self-limited disease; seen more often in females in the second to fifth decades • Follows **viral** syndrome, lasts several weeks with a **tender** gland • May initially have mild hyperthyroidism later, usually euthyroid
Thyroglossal duct cyst	• May communicate with skin or base of tongue • Remnant of incompletely descended midline thyroid tissue
Ectopic thyroid nests	Usually at the base of tongue; prior to removal, it must be documented that patient has other functioning thyroid tissue

Definition of abbreviations: GH, growth hormone; TBG, thyroid-binding globulin; TGI, thyroid growth immunoglobulin; TSI, thyroid-stimulating immunoglobulin; TSH, thyroid-stimulating hormone.

DRUGS FOR THYROID GLAND DISORDERS

Class	Mechanism	Comments/Agents
Hyperthyroidism Agents	These agents are used for short-term or long-term treatment of hyperthyroid states. The most common adverse effects are related to signs and symptoms of hypothyroidism.	
Thioamides	• Inhibit synthesis of thyroid hormones • They do *not* inactivate existing T_4 and T_3 • Propylthiouracil is able to inhibit peripheral conversion of T_4 to T_3	• **Examples:** PTU, methimazole • **Indications:** long-term hyperthyroid therapy, which may lead to disease remission and short-term treatment before thyroidectomy or radioactive iodine therapy • **Side effects:** skin rash (common), hematologic effects (rare)
Iodides	• Inhibit the release of T_4 and T_3 (primary) • Inhibit the biosynthesis of T_4 and T_3 and ↓ the size and vascularity of thyroid gland	• **Examples:** Lugol's solution (iodine and potassium iodide) and potassium iodide alone • **Indications:** preparation for thyroid surgery; treatment of thyrotoxic crisis and thyroid blocking in radiation emergency • **Note:** therapeutic effects can be seen for as long as 6 weeks
Beta-Blockers	Nonselective β-receptor blockers used for palpitations, anxiety, tremor, heat intolerance; partially inhibit peripheral conversion of T_4 to T_3	• **Examples: nadolol, propranolol** • Used to treat the signs and symptoms of hyperthyroidism
Radioactive Iodine [^{131}I]	Ablation of thyroid gland	• **Indications:** first-line therapy for Graves disease; treatment of choice for recurrent thyrotoxicosis in adults and elderly
Hypothyroidism Agents	These agents are used as thyroid replacement therapy. The most common adverse effects are related to signs and symptoms of hyperthyroidism.	
Thyroid Hormones	Acts by controlling DNA transcription and protein synthesis	**Examples:** synthetic T_4, synthetic T_3, or combination of synthetic T_4:T_3 in 4:1 ratio

Definition of abbreviation: PTU, propylthiouracil.

THYROID NEOPLASMS

Adenomas	• Follicular adenoma is most common; may cause pressure symptoms, pain, and rarely thyrotoxicosis • **Pathology:** usually small, well-encapsulated solitary lesions
Papillary carcinoma	• Most common thyroid carcinoma • Incidence higher in women • **Pathology:** papillary branching pattern; 40% have tumors containing psammoma bodies • Spread to local nodes is common; **hematogenous spread rare** • Resection curative in most cases
Follicular carcinoma	• More malignant than papillary cancer • **Pathology:** may be encapsulated, with penetration through the capsule; colloid sparse • Local invasion and pressure → dysphagia, dyspnea, hoarseness, cough • **Hematogenous metastasis to lungs or bones common**
Anaplastic carcinoma	• Rapid growing, aggressive with poor prognosis; affects older patients • **Pathology:** tumors usually bulky and invasive with undifferentiated anaplastic cells • **Clinical:** early, widespread metastasis and death within 2 years

GROWTH HORMONE

CONTROL OF GROWTH HORMONE

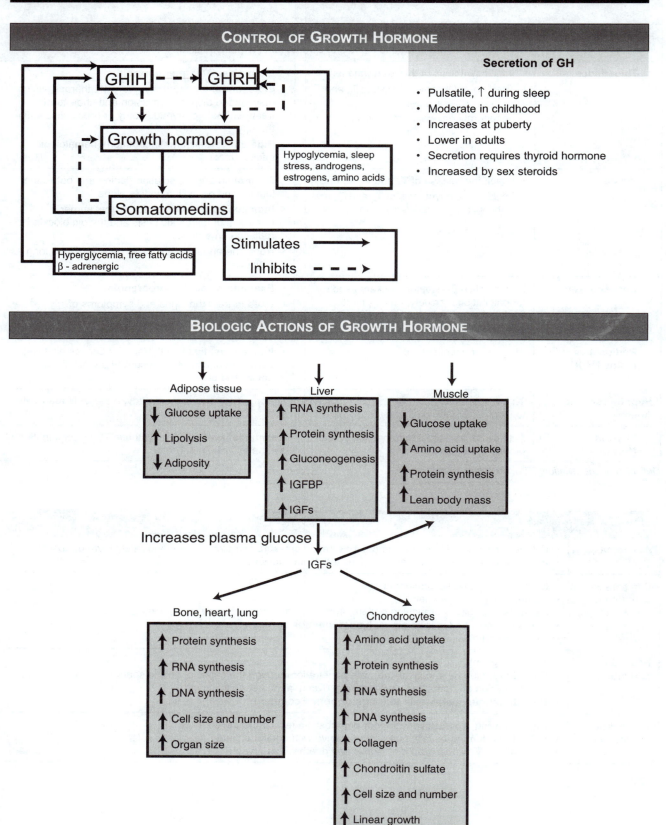

Secretion of GH

- Pulsatile, ↑ during sleep
- Moderate in childhood
- Increases at puberty
- Lower in adults
- Secretion requires thyroid hormone
- Increased by sex steroids

GHIH - - - GHRH

Growth hormone

Somatomedins

Hypoglycemia, sleep stress, androgens, estrogens, amino acids

Hyperglycemia, free fatty acids β - adrenergic

Stimulates ⟶
Inhibits - - - ➤

BIOLOGIC ACTIONS OF GROWTH HORMONE

Adipose tissue
- ↓ Glucose uptake
- ↑ Lipolysis
- ↓ Adiposity

Liver
- ↑ RNA synthesis
- ↑ Protein synthesis
- ↑ Gluconeogenesis
- ↑ IGFBP
- ↑ IGFs

Muscle
- ↓ Glucose uptake
- ↑ Amino acid uptake
- ↑ Protein synthesis
- ↑ Lean body mass

Increases plasma glucose

IGFs

Bone, heart, lung
- ↑ Protein synthesis
- ↑ RNA synthesis
- ↑ DNA synthesis
- ↑ Cell size and number
- ↑ Organ size

Chondrocytes
- ↑ Amino acid uptake
- ↑ Protein synthesis
- ↑ RNA synthesis
- ↑ DNA synthesis
- ↑ Collagen
- ↑ Chondroitin sulfate
- ↑ Cell size and number
- ↑ Linear growth

CHILDHOOD DISORDERS	

Dwarfism	• Caused by:
	  – ↓ GH or ↓ liver production of IGF (Laron syndrome)
	  – Defective GH receptors
	• Mental development normal
	• Reversible with GH treatment

Gigantism	• Caused by ↑ GH prior to epiphyseal closure • Increased height, increased body mass

Definition of abbreviation: GH, growth hormone; IGF, insulin-like growth factor.

ADULT DISORDERS OF GROWTH HORMONE		
Acromegaly	↑ GH	• Enlargement of hands and feet • Protrusion of lower jaw, coarse facial features • ↑ lean body mass • ↓ body fat • ↑ size of visceral organs • Impaired cardiac function (related to mass) • Abnormal glucose tolerance with tendency to hyperglycemia
Deficiency	↓ GH	• Tendency to hypoglycemia when fasting • Susceptible to insulin-induced hypoglycemia • Significance of other effects disputed

Definition of abbreviation: GH, growth hormone.

TREATMENT OF GROWTH HORMONE DISORDERS		
Class	**Mechanism**	**Comments/Agents**
GH	Stimulation of linear/skeletal growth (pediatric patients only); potentiation of cell and organ growth; enhanced protein, carbohydrate and lipid metabolism	• **Somatropin** and **somatrem** (recombinant forms of human GH) • **Indications:** growth failure, Turner syndrome, cachexia, somatotropin deficiency
Octreotide	• Long-acting octapeptide that mimics somatostatin • Inhibits release of GH, glucagon, gastrin, thyrotropin, insulin	• **Indications:** acromegaly, carcinoid, glucagonoma, gastrinoma, other endocrine tumors

Definition of abbreviation: GH, growth hormone.

The Reproductive System

Chapter 7

REPRODUCTIVE SYSTEM

MALE AND FEMALE DEVELOPMENT

Adult Female and Male Reproductive Structures Derived From Precursors of the Indifferent Embryo

Adult Female	Indifferent Embryo	Adult Male
Ovary, follicles, rete ovarii	Gonads	Testes, seminiferous tubules, rete testes
Uterine tubes, uterus, cervix, and upper part of vagina	Paramesonephric ducts	Appendix of testes
Duct of Gartner	Mesonephric ducts	Epididymis, ductus deferens, seminal vesicle, ejaculatory duct
Clitoris	Phallus	Glans and body of penis
Labia minora	Urogenital folds	Ventral aspect of penis
Labia majora	Labioscrotal swellings	Scrotum

Congenital Reproductive Anomalies

Female Pseudointersexuality

- 46,XX genotype
- Have ovarian (but no testicular) tissue and masculinization of the female external genitalia
- Most common cause is **congenital adrenal hyperplasia**, a condition in which the fetus produces excess androgens

Male Pseudointersexuality

- 46,XY genotype
- Testicular (but no ovarian) tissue and stunted development of male external genitalia
- Most common cause is inadequate production of testosterone and müllerian-inhibiting factor (MIF) by the fetal testes; due to a 5α-reductase deficiency

5α-reductase 2 deficiency	• Caused by a mutation in the **5α-reductase 2 gene** that renders 5α-reductase 2 enzyme underactive in catalyzing the conversion of testosterone to dihydrotestosterone • *Clinical findings:* underdevelopment of the penis and scrotum (microphallus, hypospadias, and bifid scrotum) and prostate gland; epididymis, ductus deferens, seminal vesicle, and ejaculatory duct are normal • At puberty, they undergo virilization due to an increased **T:DHT ratio**
Complete androgen insensitivity (CAIS, or testicular feminization syndrome)	• Occurs when a fetus with a 46,XY genotype develops testes and female external genitalia with a rudimentary vagina; the uterus and uterine tubes are generally absent • Testes may be found in the labia majora and are surgically removed to circumvent malignant tumor formation • Individuals present as normal-appearing females, and their psychosocial orientation is female despite their genotype • Most common cause is a mutation in the **androgen receptor (AR) gene** that renders the AR inactive

MALE AND FEMALE REPRODUCTIVE ANATOMY

Male

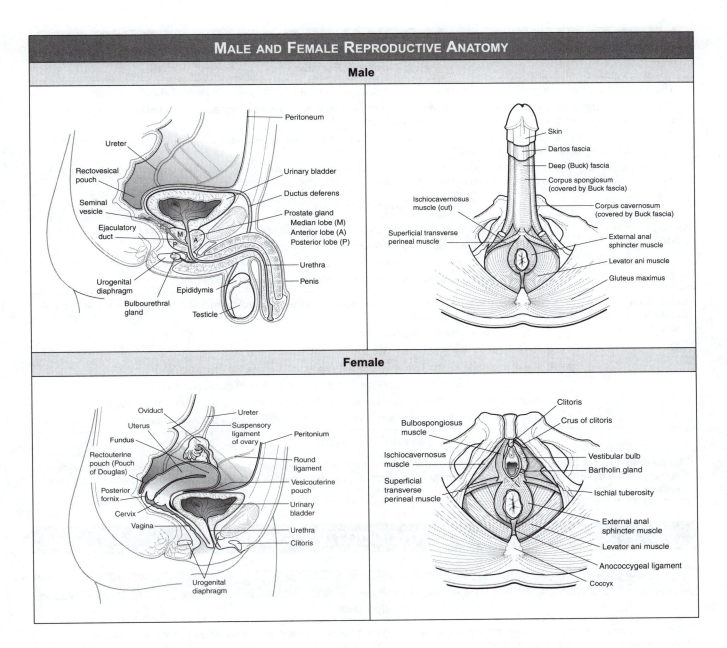

Female

Pelvic Floor and Perineum

- The floor of the pelvis is formed by the **pelvic diaphragm** (two layers of fascia with a middle layer of skeletal muscle).
- The muscles forming the middle layer are the **levator ani** and **coccygeus**. The levator ani acts as a muscular sling for the rectum and marks the boundary between the rectum and anal canal.
- The region below the pelvic diaphragm is the **perineum**, which contains the **ischioanal fossa**, the fat-filled region below the pelvic diaphragm surrounding the anal canal.
- The **urogenital diaphragm** is in the perineum and extends between the two ischiopubic rami. The urogenital diaphragm (like the pelvic diaphragm) is composed of two layers of fascia with a middle layer of skeletal muscle.

Perineal Pouches

Deep perineal pouch (space)	The deep perineal pouch is the middle (muscle) layer of the urogenital diaphragm. It contains: • Sphincter urethrae muscle—serves as external sphincter of the urethra • Deep transverse perineal muscle • Bulbourethral (Cowper) gland (in the male only)—duct enters bulbar urethra
Superficial perineal pouch (space)	The superficial perineal pouch is the region below the urogenital diaphragm and is enclosed by the superficial perineal (Colles) fascia. It contains: • Crura of penis or clitoris—erectile tissue • Bulb of penis (in the male)—erectile tissue; contains urethra • Bulbs of vestibule (in the female)—erectile tissue; in lateral walls of vestibule • Ischiocavernosus muscle—skeletal muscle that covers crura of penis or clitoris • Bulbospongiosus muscle—skeletal muscle that covers bulb of penis or bulbs of vestibule • Greater vestibular (Bartholin) gland (in female only)—homologous to Cowper gland

Pelvic Innervation

The **pudendal nerve (S2, S3, S4 ventral rami) and its branches** innervate the skeletal muscles in the pelvic and urogenital diaphragms, the external anal sphincter and the sphincter urethrae, skeletal muscles in both perineal pouches, and the skin that overlies the perineum.

MALE REPRODUCTIVE SYSTEM

MALE REPRODUCTIVE PHYSIOLOGY

Penile Erection

Erection occurs in response to **parasympathetic** stimulation (pelvic splanchnic nerves). **Nitric oxide** is released, causing relaxation of the corpus cavernosum and corpus spongiosum, which allows blood to accumulate in the trabeculae of erectile tissue.

Ejaculation

- **Sympathetic** nervous system stimulation (lumbar splanchnic nerves) mediates movement of mature spermatozoa from the epididymis and vas deferens into the ejaculatory duct.
- Accessory glands, such as the bulbourethral (Cowper) glands, prostate, and seminal vesicles, secrete fluids that aid in sperm survival and fertility.
- **Somatic motor efferents** (pudendal nerve) that innervate the bulbospongiosus and ischiocavernous muscles at the base of the penis stimulate the rapid ejection of semen out the urethra during ejaculation. Peristaltic waves in the vas deferens aid in a more complete ejection of semen through the urethra.

Clinical Correlation

- Injury to the bulb of the penis may result in extravasation of urine from the urethra into the superficial perineal space. From this space, urine may pass into the scrotum, into the penis, and onto the anterior abdominal wall.
- Accumulation of fluid in the scrotum, penis, and anterolateral abdominal wall is indicative of a laceration of either the membranous or penile urethra (deep to Scarpa fascia). This can be caused by trauma to the perineal region (saddle injury) or laceration of the urethra during catheterization.

AGENTS FOR ERECTILE DYSFUNCTION

Drug	Mechanism	Comments
Selective phosphodiesterase (PDE) 5 inhibitors **(sildenafil, vardenafil, tadalafil)**	Inhibits the enzyme phosphodiesterase (PDE) 5, which inactivates cGMP, leading to ↑ cGMP → vasodilation, more inflow of blood → better erection	PDE 5 inhibitors + **nitrates** (which ↑ cGMP production) → **severe hypotension**
Synthetic prostaglandin E$_1$ (PGE$_1$) agents **(alprostadil)**	↑ cAMP (via adenylate cyclase) → smooth muscle relaxation	Administered via transurethral or intracavernosal injection *Contraindications:* intercourse with pregnant women (can stimulate uterine contractions unless used with a condom); conditions that might predispose a patient to priapism (e.g., sickle cell anemia, multiple myeloma, leukemia)
Testosterone	Replacement/supplementation for males whose serum androgen concentrations are below normal	Used if diminished libido is a significant patient complaint

DISEASES OF THE PENIS AND PROSTATE

Noninfectious Disorders of the Penis

Hypospadias and epispadias	With hypospadias, urethra opens onto the ventral surface of penis Often associated with a poorly developed penis that curves ventrally, known as **chordee** With epispadias, urethra opens onto dorsal surface; often associated with exstrophy of bladder Either of these malformations may cause infertility
Phimosis	Prepuce orifice too small to be retracted normally Interferes with hygiene; can also predispose to bacterial infections; if foreskin retracted over the glans, it may lead to urethral constriction → paraphimosis *Treatment:* circumcision
Penile carcinoma **Bowen disease**	Carcinoma in situ; can be associated with visceral malignancy Men >35 years; tends to involve shaft of the penis and scrotum *Gross:* thick, ulcerated plaque *Micro:* squamous cell carcinoma in situ
Squamous cell carcinoma	1% of cancers in men in the United States, usually age 40–70. Usually slow growing and non-painful; patients often delay seeking medical attention. Circumcision decreases the incidence. Human Papilloma virus (types 16 and 18) infection is closely associated. Gross: Plaque progressing to an ulcerated papule or fungating growth. Metastases can go to local lymph nodes.

(Continued)

DISEASES OF THE PENIS AND PROSTATE (CONT'D.)

Diseases of the Prostate

Prostatic carcinoma	• Most common cancer in men; usually occurs after age 50, and the incidence increases with age • Associated with race (more common in African Americans than in Caucasians, relatively rare in Asians) • May present with urinary problems or a palpable mass on rectal examination • Prostate cancer more common than lung cancer, but lung cancer is bigger killer • Metastases may occur via the lymphatic or hematogenous route • Bone commonly involved with osteoblastic metastases, typically in the pelvis and lower vertebrae • Elevated PSA, together with an enlarged prostate on digital rectal exam, highly suggestive of carcinoma • Most patients present with advanced disease and have a 10-year survival rate of <30% • *Treatment:* surgery, radiation, and hormonal modalities (orchiectomy and androgen blockade).
Benign prostatic hyperplasia	• Formation of large nodules in the periurethral region (median lobe) of the prostate • May narrow the urethral canal to produce varying degrees of urinary obstruction and difficulty urinating • It is increasingly common after age 45; incidence increases steadily with age • Can follow an asymptomatic pattern, or can result in urinary symptoms and urinary retention
Prostatitis Acute	• Results from a bacterial infection of the prostate • Pathogens are often organisms that cause urinary tract infection • *Escherichia coli* most common • Bacteria spread by direct extension from the posterior urethra or the bladder; lymphatic or hematogenous spread can also occur
Chronic	• Common cause of recurrent urinary tract infections in men • Two types: bacterial and nonbacterial • Both forms may be asymptomatic or may present with lower back pain and urinary symptoms

ANTIANDROGENS

Drug	Mechanism	Clinical Uses
Flutamide	Androgen receptor antagonist	Prostate cancer
Spironolactone	Androgen receptor antagonist (also a potassium-sparing diuretic)	Hirsutism
Leuprolide	GnRH analog	Depot form is used for prostate cancer
Finasteride	5α-reductase inhibitor (prevents conversion of testosterone to DHT)	Benign prostatic hypertrophy (BPH), male pattern baldness
Ketoconazole	Inhibits steroid synthesis (also an antifungal agent)	Androgen receptor–positive prostate cancer

Definition of abbreviation: DHT, dihydrotestosterone.

THE TESTES

Descent of the Testes

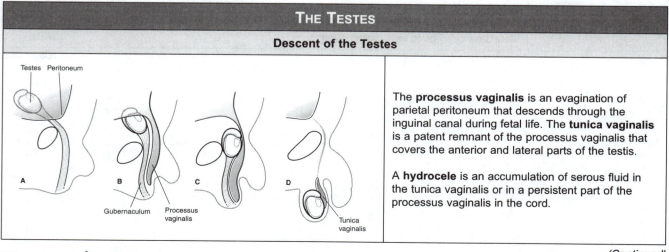

The **processus vaginalis** is an evagination of parietal peritoneum that descends through the inguinal canal during fetal life. The **tunica vaginalis** is a patent remnant of the processus vaginalis that covers the anterior and lateral parts of the testis.

A **hydrocele** is an accumulation of serous fluid in the tunica vaginalis or in a persistent part of the processus vaginalis in the cord.

(Continued)

THE TESTES (CONT'D.)

Normal Anatomy and Anatomic Abnormalities

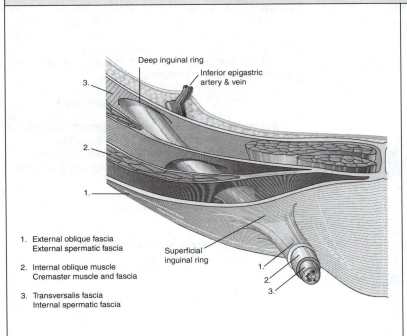

Deep inguinal ring

Inferior epigastric artery & vein

3.

2.

1.

1. External oblique fascia
   External spermatic fascia

2. Internal oblique muscle
   Cremaster muscle and fascia

3. Transversalis fascia
   Internal spermatic fascia

Superficial inguinal ring

1.
2.
3.

The **inguinal canal** is formed by four of the eight tissue layers of the anterior abdominal wall; outpocketings of three of these layers give rise to **spermatic fasciae**, which cover the testis and structures in the **spermatic cord**.

The spermatic cord contains the:

- **Ductus deferens**, which conveys sperm from the epididymis to the ejaculatory duct in the male pelvis
- **Testicular artery**, which arises from the abdominal aorta between the L2 and the L3 vertebrae
- **Artery to the ductus deferens**, which arises from a branch of the internal iliac artery
- **Pampiniform plexus of the testicular vein**
- **Right testicular vein**, which drains into the inferior vena cava
- **Left testicular vein**, which drains into the left renal vein.
- **Lymphatic vessels** that drain the testis. Testicular lymphatic vessels pass through the inguinal canal and drain directly to **lumbar nodes** in the posterior abdominal wall.

Cremasteric Reflex

The **cremasteric reflex** utilizes sensory and motor fibers in the ventral ramus of the L1 spinal nerve. Stroking the skin of the superior and medial thigh stimulates sensory fibers of the **ilioinguinal nerve**. **Motor fibers** from the genital branch of the **genitofemoral nerve** cause the cremaster muscle to contract, elevating the testis.

Abnormalities

Cryptorchidism	<ul><li>Failure of normal descent of intra-abdominal testes into the scrotum</li><li>Most common location of a cryptorchid testis is in the inguinal canal</li><li>Unilateral or bilateral, more often on right side</li><li>Bilateral cryptorchidism can cause infertility</li><li>Maldescended testes are associated with a greatly increased incidence of testicular cancer, even once repositioned within scrotum</li></ul>
Torsion	<ul><li>Precipitated by sudden movement, trauma, and congenital anomalies</li><li>Twisting of spermatic cord may compromise both arterial supply and venous drainage</li><li>Sudden onset of testicular pain and a loss of the cremasteric reflex are characteristic</li><li>If not surgically corrected early, may result in testicular infarction</li></ul>
Hydrocele	<ul><li>Congenital hydrocele occurs when a small patency of the processus vaginalis remains so that peritoneal fluid can flow into the processus vaginalis; may occur later in life, often inflammatory causes (e.g., epididymitis)</li><li>Results in fluid-filled cyst near testes</li></ul>
Varicocele	<ul><li>Results from dilatations of tributaries of the testicular vein in the pampiniform plexus</li><li>Varicosities of the pampiniform plexus are observed when the patient is standing and disappear when the patient is lying down</li></ul>

SPERMATOGENESIS

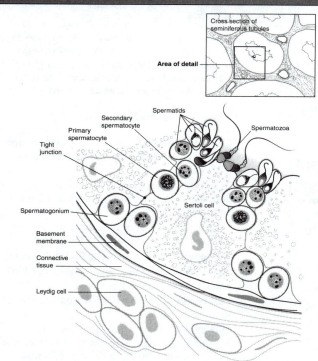

Cross-section of seminiferous tubules

Area of detail

Spermatids
Secondary spermatocyte
Spermatozoa
Primary spermatocyte
Tight junction
Sertoli cell
Spermatogonium
Basement membrane
Connective tissue
Leydig cell

Spermatogenesis occurs in the seminiferous tubules between the **Sertoli cells**, which extend from the seminiferous tubule basement membrane to the lumen and are separated by tight junctions (blood–testis barrier) and germ cells in varying stages of spermatogenesis. The **blood–testis barrier** protects the spermatocytes and spermatids from the immune system

Three Stages of Spermatogenesis

1. **Spermatocytogenesis** begins at puberty adjacent to the basement membrane of the Sertoli cell. Spermatogonia first undergo spermatocytogenesis, during which mitosis divides the spermatogonia into spermatocytes.

2. **Meiosis** reduces the diploid spermatocytes into haploid spermatids.

3. **Spermiogenesis** is the maturation of spermatids into mature spermatozoa.

Spermiogenesis

During **spermiogenesis**, the spermatids undergo chromatin condensation and nuclear elongation, which forms the head of the spermatozoa.

The **acrosome**, a hydrolytic enzyme-containing region on the sperm cell head, also forms during this time.

The midpiece of the sperm has as a mitochondrial sheath that contains much of the ATP necessary for sperm movement. The **flagellum** contains an array of **9 + 2 microtubular pairs** linked by **dynein** for sperm motility. Patients with defective or absent dynein in **Kartagener syndrome** have reduced sperm motility, as well as reduced mucus clearance in the respiratory pathways, leading to bronchiectasis.

Once formed, spermatozoa detach from the Sertoli cells and combine with a fluid that aids in the movement of spermatozoa into the epididymis. In the epididymis, the fluid is reabsorbed, thereby concentrating sperm, and sperm interact with **forward motility factor**, a protein that aids in sperm motility. Ejaculated sperm must undergo **capacitation** in the uterus before fertilization can occur.

Fertilization

Fertilization is a three-step process:

1. **Acrosome reaction:** Sperm close to the corona radiata release hyaluronidase, which dissolves material between corona radiata cells, allowing sperm to reach the zona pellucida.
2. **Zonal reaction:** Sperm bind to a glycoprotein of the zona and release acrosin, which facilitates penetration of the zona by the sperm head.
3. **Cortical reaction:** The first sperm to penetrate the zona fuses with the plasma membrane of the ovum and induces a calcium-dependent release of cortical granules that prevents polyspermy.

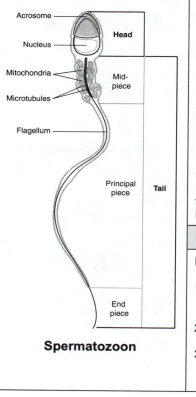

Acrosome
Nucleus
Head
Mitochondria
Microtubules
Mid-piece
Flagellum
Principal piece
Tail
End piece

Spermatozoon

HORMONAL CONTROL OF STEROIDOGENESIS AND SPERMATOGENESIS

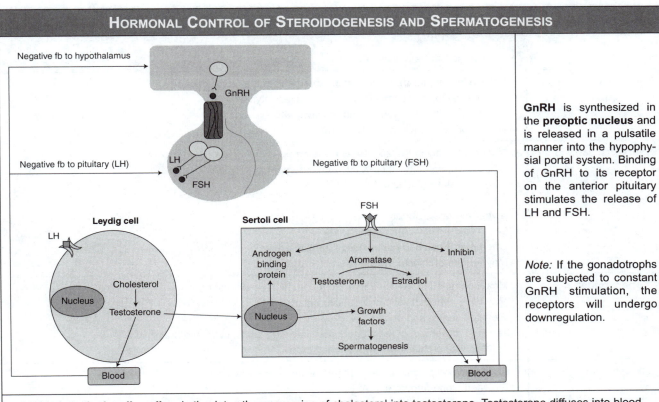

GnRH is synthesized in the **preoptic nucleus** and is released in a pulsatile manner into the hypophysial portal system. Binding of GnRH to its receptor on the anterior pituitary stimulates the release of LH and FSH.

Note: If the gonadotrophs are subjected to constant GnRH stimulation, the receptors will undergo downregulation.

- **LH** binds to the **Leydig cell** and stimulates the conversion of cholesterol into testosterone. Testosterone diffuses into blood and feeds back to inhibit hypothalamic GnRH and pituitary LH. Testosterone diffuses into the Sertoli cell and increases transcription of androgen-binding protein and growth factors that mediate spermatogenesis.

- **FSH** binds to the **Sertoli cell** and stimulates transcription of androgen-binding protein, the conversion of testosterone to estradiol, and the secretion of inhibin. Inhibin feeds back to inhibit further production of pituitary FSH.

- Sertoli cell-derived **androgen binding protein** provides an important reserve of testosterone in the testes. Because spermatogenesis is dependent on intratesticular testosterone rather than systemic testosterone, these reserves are important to normal spermatogenesis.

INFLAMMATORY LESIONS

Mumps	• Orchitis develops in approximately 25% of patients over age 10, but is less common in patients under 10 • Rarely leads to sterility
Gonorrhea	• Neglected urethral gonococcal infection may spread to prostate, seminal vesicles, and epididymis, but rarely to testes
Syphilis	• Acquired or congenital syphilis may involve the testes • Two forms: gummas or a diffuse interstitial/lymphocytic plasma cell infiltrate • Can lead to sterility
Tuberculosis	• TB usually spreads from epididymis; this is almost always associated with foci of TB elsewhere

TESTICULAR NEOPLASMS

Germ Cell Tumors
Most common malignancy in men 15 to 34 years of age

Seminoma	• Rare in infants, incidence increases to a peak in the fourth decade • 10% are anaplastic seminomas; show nuclear atypia • *Prognosis:* with treatment; 5-year survival rate exceeds 90% • Highly radiosensitive; metastases rare
Embryonal carcinoma	• Most commonly in the 20–30-year-age group • Aggressive, present with testicular enlargement • 30% metastatic disease at time of diagnosis • Serum AFP: elevated • 5-year mortality rate 65% • Less radiosensitive than seminomas • Often metastasize to nodes, lungs, and liver • May require orchiectomy and chemotherapy
Choriocarcinoma	• Most common in men 15–25 years of age, highly malignant • May have gynecomastia or testicular enlargement • Elevated serum and urine hCG levels • Tends to disseminate hematogenously, invading lungs, liver, and brain • Treated with orchiectomy and chemotherapy
Yolk sac tumor	• Most common in children and infants, although rare overall • Elevated alpha fetoprotein (AFP) • Very aggressive; exhibiting a 50% 5-year mortality rate • May be considered a variant form of embryonal carcinoma
Teratoma	• Can occur at any age, but are most common in infants and children • Appears as a testicular mass • Exhibit a variety of tissues, such as nerve, muscle, cartilage, and hair • Benign behavior during childhood, variable in adults • 2-year mortality is 30% • *Treatment:* orchiectomy, followed by chemotherapy and radiation

Non–Germ Cell Tumors

Leydig cell tumor	• Usually unilateral • Can produce androgens or estrogens • *Children:* present with masculinization or feminization; *adults:* gynecomastia • Usually benign and only 10% are invasive; surgery may be curative
Sertoli cell	• Usually unilateral • Can produce small amounts of androgens or estrogens, usually not enough to cause endocrinologic changes • Present with testicular enlargement • Over 90% are benign
Lymphoma	• Lymphomas are the most common testicular cancer in elderly men • The tumors are rarely confined to the testes (often disseminated)

Note: Testicular neoplasms tend to metastasize to the **lumbar nodes**, whereas scrotal disease affects **superficial inguinal nodes**.

HORMONAL CONTROL OF STEROIDOGENESIS

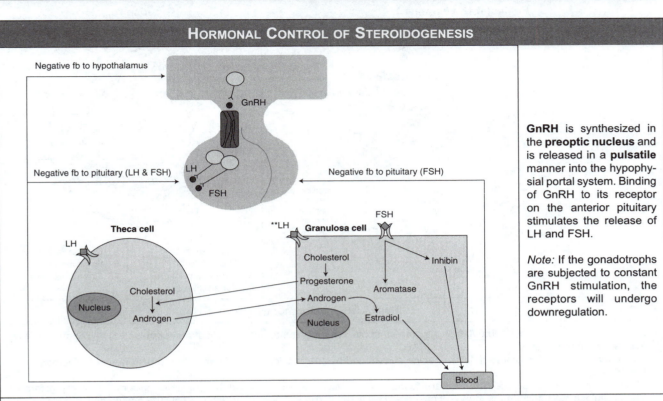

GnRH is synthesized in the **preoptic nucleus** and is released in a **pulsatile** manner into the hypophysial portal system. Binding of GnRH to its receptor on the anterior pituitary stimulates the release of LH and FSH.

Note: If the gonadotrophs are subjected to constant GnRH stimulation, the receptors will undergo downregulation.

- **LH** binds receptors on **theca cells**, resulting in production of androstenedione or testosterone. Androgens produced by the theca cells enter the granulosa cells to be converted into estrogens.

- **LH** also binds receptors on **granulosa cells** during the luteal phase and stimulates production of progesterone, which enters the theca cells. During the luteal phase, progesterone is required to maintain pregnancy if fertilization/implantation occur.

- **FSH** binds receptors on **granulosa cells**, resulting in aromatization of androgens to estradiol and synthesis of new LH receptors on the granulosa cells. Estradiol can be released into the blood or can act locally to increase granulosa cell proliferation and sensitivity to FSH.

- **FSH** also stimulates the production of **inhibin**, which negatively feeds back to inhibit further FSH secretion.

- **Estradiol** secreted into the blood negatively feeds back to inhibit hypothalamic and pituitary secretion of GnRH, and LH and FSH, respectively. This action does not occur near the ovulatory period.

Definition of abbreviations: LH, luteinizing hormone; FSH, follicle-stimulating hormone; GnRH, gonadotropin-releasing hormone.

FOLLICULOGENESIS AND OVULATION

Follicular Development	Graafian follicle

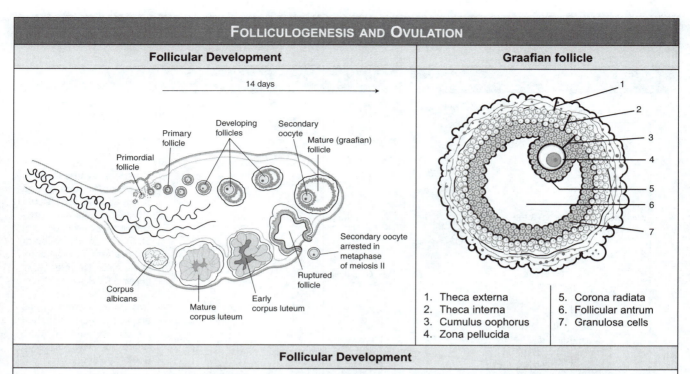

1. Theca externa
2. Theca interna
3. Cumulus oophorus
4. Zona pellucida
5. Corona radiata
6. Follicular antrum
7. Granulosa cells

Follicular Development

- At puberty, there are about 400,000 follicles present in the ovarian stroma, but only about 450 of these will develop (remaining follicles undergo atresia).
- The immature or **primordial follicle** (an oocyte surrounded by pregranulosa cells) is **arrested in prophase I of meiosis** until maturation.
- The primordial follicle becomes the **primary follicle** when the oocyte enlarges and the granulosa cells mature and proliferate. The granulosa cells secrete mucopolysaccharides, creating the **zona pellucida**, which protects the oocyte and provides an avenue for the oocyte to receive nutrients and chemical signals from the granulosa cells.
- As the follicle matures, additional granulosa cell layers are added and a layer of androgen-producing theca cells known as the **theca interna** surround the now **secondary follicle**. The secondary follicle continues to grow, and a fibrous theca externa surrounds the follicle. A follicular cavity (**antrum**) forms from granulosa cell secretions.
- The mature follicle, the **graafian follicle**, is now ready for ovulation. At the time of the LH surge, the oocyte resumes meiosis and **completes the first meiotic division prior to ovulation**. Meiosis produces a nonfunctional first polar body, which degenerates, and a larger secondary haploid oocyte.

Ovulation

- As the antral fluid increases, the pressure becomes greater until the follicle ruptures and the oocyte is extruded.
- Following ovulation, the theca cells enlarge and begin secreting estrogen and the granulosa cells enlarge and secrete progesterone. This new endocrine organ is called the **corpus luteum** and reaches maximal development about 7 days after ovulation.
- If fertilization does not occur, the corpus luteum degenerates.
- If fertilization does occur, the corpus luteum continues to grow for about 3 months and is maintained by **human chorionic gonadotropin (hCG)** from the embryo. Once the placenta is functional, the corpus luteum is no longer necessary to maintain pregnancy.

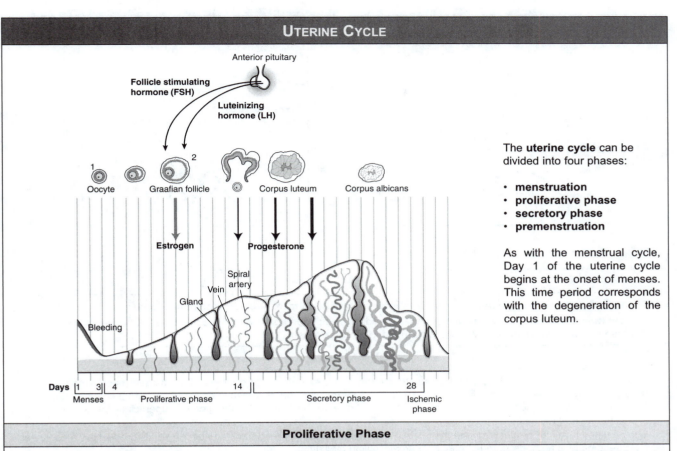

The **uterine cycle** can be divided into four phases:

- **menstruation**
- **proliferative phase**
- **secretory phase**
- **premenstruation**

As with the menstrual cycle, Day 1 of the uterine cycle begins at the onset of menses. This time period corresponds with the degeneration of the corpus luteum.

Proliferative Phase

- The **proliferative phase** follows menses, corresponding to the latter portion of the follicular phase of the menstrual cycle and ending near ovulation.
- During this time, elevated estrogen levels stimulate the **proliferation of endometrial cells**, an **increase in length and number of endometrial glands**, and **increased blood flow** to the uterus.
- The endometrium increases in thickness sixfold and becomes contractile. Estrogen also stimulates a marked increase in progesterone receptors in the endometrium to prepare it for fertilization. **Edema** develops in the uterus toward the end of the proliferative phase and continues to develop during the secretory phase.

Secretory Phase

- The **secretory phase** corresponds with the luteal phase of the menstrual cycle and is characterized by **endometrial cell hypertrophy, increased vascularity, and edema**.
- **Progesterone levels are elevated** during this phase and lead to a thick secretion consisting of glycoprotein, sugars, and amino acids. Like estrogen, progesterone increases cell proliferation and vascularization, but unlike estrogen, progesterone depresses uterine contractility.

Premenstrual Phase

- The **premenstrual phase** consists of constriction of arteries, causing ischemia and anoxia. The **superficial layer of the endometrium degenerates**, and blood and tissue appear in the uterine lumen.

MENSTRUAL CYCLE

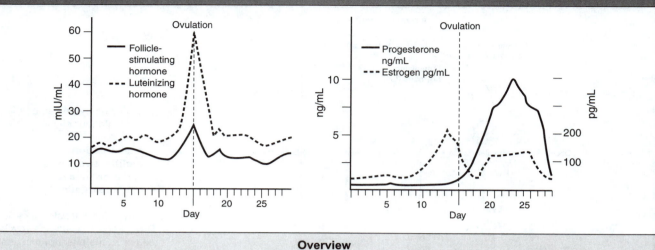

Overview

- There are **four phases** in the menstrual cycle: **menses**, **follicular phase**, **ovulation**, and **luteal phase**.
- The **average cycle length** is **28 days**, but can vary widely. The period from ovulation to the onset of menses is always 14 days, so any variation from 28 days occurs during the **follicular** phase.

Menses

- The onset of menses marks **Day 1** of the menstrual cycle and is triggered by a **decrease in estrogen** (decreased estrogen synthesis by granulosa cells and decreased LH) and **progesterone**. The decrease in estrogen and progesterone support for the endometrium results in tissue necrosis and arterial rupture, leading to sloughing of the superficial layer of the endometrium and bleeding.
- The elevated levels of progesterone in the luteal phase act to negatively feed back and decrease LH production. Also, luteal cells become less responsive to LH about 1 week following ovulation.

Follicular Phase

- The **follicular phase** begins on about **Day 5** of the menstrual cycle and lasts an average of 9 days.
- When progesterone and estrogen levels decrease, the negative feedback on the hypothalamus and pituitary is removed, allowing an **increase in the frequency of GnRH pulses**. This, in turn, **stimulates FSH secretion**, thereby stimulating follicular growth (and estrogen production from proliferating granulosa cells).
- One follicle will secrete more estradiol than the others and will become the **dominant follicle** while the others undergo atresia. **Estrogen** levels continue to increase until they reach a critical point, at which estrogen changes from **negative to positive feedback** to increase GnRH pulse frequency and LH and FSH secretion. This rapid rise in GnRH pulse frequency results in a surge of both LH and FSH.

Ovulation

- The **LH surge** and **high estrogen levels trigger ovulation** on about **Day 14** of the cycle.
- The **follicle ruptures about 24 to 36 hours after the LH surge**, during which the oocyte resumes meiosis and the first polar body is extruded.

Luteal Phase

- The **luteal phase** begins after ovulation around Day 14 and extends to about Day 28.
- During this time the follicular cells form the **corpus luteum** and secrete **high levels of progesterone** and a lower level of estrogen (even without LH stimulation). Progesterone negatively feeds back to slow the frequency of GnRH pulses, so LH and FSH levels remain low.
- In the absence of fertilization, the corpus luteum undergoes luteolysis, causing progesterone and estrogen levels to decrease until the hormonal support for the endometrial lining declines and the cells undergo apoptosis. Menses occurs and the cycle is back at the beginning.

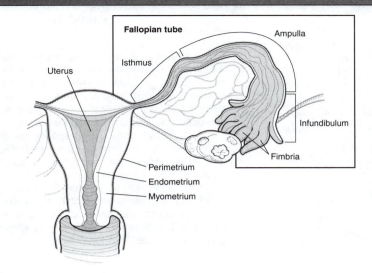

The ovulated oocyte is picked up from the intraperitoneal cavity by fimbria of the fallopian tube. Peristaltic contractions of the fallopian tube move the oocyte into the ampulla, where fertilization usually occurs 8 to 25 hours after ovulation.

- Semen ejaculated into the vagina quickly coagulates and **neutralizes** the **acidic vaginal fluids** to permit sperm survival. About 100,000 of the approximately 60 million sperm that enter the vagina will make it through the cervix. **Elevated estrogen** before ovulation **thins the cervical mucus**, allowing for easier transit of sperm to the uterus.
- Uterine fluid solubilizes the glycoproteins coating the sperm in a process called **capacitation**. Capacitation aids in fertilization by increasing energy metabolism, enhancing motility, and allowing the **acrosome reaction** that occurs at the zona pellucida. Sperm movement through the uterus is primarily accomplished by contraction of the female reproductive tract, primarily the uterus.

- Sperm are capable of fertilizing for as long as 72 hours after ejaculation. Once sperm reach the oocyte, they **bind to the zona pellucida** and **undergo the acrosome reaction**. This reaction releases hydrolytic enzymes stored in the acrosome cap, which dissolve the zona pellucida. Sperm motility is important to push the sperm head toward the oocyte. When the sperm reach the oocyte, the two membranes fuse and the contents of the sperm cell enter the oocyte. At this point, a **cortical reaction** occurs, during which the zona pellucida hardens and prevents additional sperm from entering the oocyte.
- Prior to fusing of the male and female pronucleus, the oocyte undergoes a second meiotic division, producing the second polar body and the female pronucleus. **The contents of the sperm form the male pronucleus, which fuses with the female pronucleus, forming the embryo**.

- The embryo remains in the ampulla several days, during which time rising levels of progesterone relax the uterine and fallopian tube musculature, making it easier for the embryo to pass into the uterus.
- The **embryo** usually **arrives in the uterus** by about the **third day following fertilization**, but **does not implant in the uterus for about 3 more days**. During the latter 3 days, the embryo develops a vascular system that aids in taking up nutrients it receives from uterine secretions.

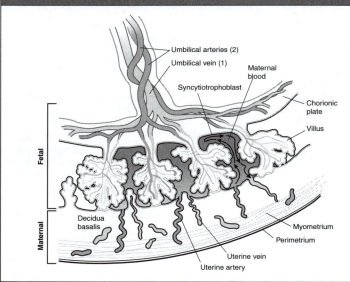

Implantation

At the time of implantation, the trophectoderm cells of the embryo contact the maternal epithelium, resulting in increased vascular permeability in the embryo, edema in the intracellular matrix, swelling of the stromal cells with addition of glycogen granules, and sprouting and ingrowth of capillaries. This reaction is called **decidualization** and prepares the decidua for the embryo. Within about 12 days after fertilization, the embryo is completely embedded in the decidua.

Between 8 to 12 days after fertilization, **human chorionic gonadotropin (hCG) is synthesized by the blastocyst** and is structurally and functionally similar to LH. It acts on the ovary to stimulate luteal growth and to suppress luteolysis.

Placenta

- The **placenta** allows for the exchange of nutrients and waste products between the maternal and fetal circulations. By about 5 weeks postfertilization, the placenta is developed and functional, although not fully mature.
- The placenta consists of **villi** from cell columns of chorionic **syncytiotrophoblast**, which have fetal blood vessels throughout. The villi branch and penetrate the maternal stroma, forming a mass of terminal villi that is separated from fetal capillaries by the thin layer of the villi.

Lactation

- During pregnancy, **estrogen and progesterone** stimulate the development of the mammary glands for **lactation** while preventing milk production.
- Following delivery, estrogen and progesterone levels decline and milk production is permitted.
- The production of milk requires **prolactin**, a hormone produced by the anterior pituitary. Prolactin is normally inhibited by hypothalamic dopamine, but suckling decreases dopamine release.
- The ejection of milk requires **oxytocin**, a hormone produced in the hypothalamus and released from the posterior pituitary. **Oxytocin is released in response to suckling or baby crying** and acts on the myoepithelial cells to stimulate contraction (milk let-down). Milk is then ejected from the nipple.

FEMALE REPRODUCTIVE PHARMACOLOGY

Class	Mechanism	Comments/Agents
Contraception		
The most common methods of reversible contraception include oral contraceptives, long-acting injectable or implantable progestins, condoms, spermicides, withdrawal, diaphragm and intrauterine devices, and timely abstinence.		
Estrogens and progestins	Suppresses production of FSH and LH, which leads to inhibition of ovulation and alteration of cervical mucus and the endometrium.	• Commonly used estrogens: ethinyl estradiol and mestranol • Commonly used progestins: norgestrel, norethindrone, and medroxyprogesterone • Are available orally as monophasic, biphasic, and triphasic combinations; also available as progestin-only preparations • Are available in many other forms, including transdermal patches, vaginal rings, IUDs, and long-acting injections • Can cause nausea, breast tenderness, headache, depression, thromboembolism, and weight gain • Absolute contraindications include thrombophlebitis, thromboembolic disorders, cerebral vascular disease, coronary occlusion, known or suspected pregnancy, smokers over the age of 35; dramatically impaired liver function, and suspected breast cancer • Other uses: female hypogonadism, HRT, dysmenorrhea, uterine bleeding, and acne
Postcoital contraceptives	Prevents pregnancy if used within 72 hours of unprotected intercourse	Different types include estrogens alone, progestins alone, combination pills, mifepristone (RU486)
Intrauterine devices (IUD)	"Devices" that create a hostile environment in the endometrium through low-grade intrauterine inflammation and increased prostaglandin formation; therefore interfere with the implantation of the fertilized ovum	Examples: Copper-T 380 (IUD) and Progesterone T (IUD)
Hormone Replacement Therapy (HRT)		
• Used in the treatment of menopause, which is defined as a permanent cessation of menstruation secondary to a loss of ovarian follicular activity. HRT is used to prevent hot flashes, atrophic changes in the urogenital tract, and osteoporosis. • When ERT is administered alone, it may induce endometrial growth and cancer; concomitant progesterone use prevents this. HRT has been associated with an increased breast cancer and stroke risk and is no longer as widely used.		

(Continued)

FEMALE REPRODUCTIVE PHARMACOLOGY *(CONT'D.)*

Class	Mechanism	Comments/Agents
Selective Estrogen Receptor Modulator (SERM) These drugs act as estrogen agonists, partial agonists, or antagonists, depending on the target tissue.		
Tamoxifen	• Estrogen antagonist in breast • Estrogen agonist in endometrium • Estrogen agonist in bone	• Used in hormone-responsive breast CA; reduces risk of breast CA in very high risk women • Increases risk of endometrial CA • Prevents osteoporosis in woman using it for breast CA • Causes hot flashes and increases risk of venous thrombosis
Raloxifene	• Partial estrogen agonist in bone • Estrogen antagonist in breast • Estrogen antagonist in uterus	• Prevents osteoporosis in postmenopausal women • Reduces risk of breast CA in very high risk women • No increased endometrial CA risk • Causes hot flashes and increases risk of venous thrombosis
Miscellaneous Agents		
Clomiphene	Fertility agent; nonsteroidal agent that selectively blocks estrogen receptors in the pituitary, reducing negative feedback mechanism and thereby increasing FSH and LH and stimulation of ovulation	Most common side effect: multiple birth pregnancy
Danazol	Inhibits ovarian steroid synthesis	Used in endometriosis and fibrocystic breast disease
Anastrozole	Aromatase inhibitor (decrease in estrogen synthesis)	Used in breast CA
Mifepristone (RU 486)	Progesterone and glucocorticoid antagonist	Used as postcoital contraceptive and abortifacient

Definition of abbreviations: CA, cancer; ERT, estrogen replacement therapy; FSH, follicle-stimulating hormone; HRT, hormone-replacement therapy; LH, luteinizing hormone.

FEMALE REPRODUCTIVE SYSTEM PATHOLOGY

DISEASES OF THE VULVA

Disease	Description	Distribution	Etiology/Comments
Condyloma acuminatum	Verrucous, wartlike lesions Koilocytosis, acanthosis, hyperkeratosis, and parakeratosis	Vulva, perineum, vagina, and cervix	Associated with human papillomavirus (HPV) serotypes 6 and 11 Greatly increased risk of cervical carcinoma
Papillary hidradenoma	Benign tumor similar to an intraductal papilloma of the breast	Occur along the milk line	
Extramammary Paget disease of the vulva	Erythematous, crusted rash Intraepidermal malignant cells with pagetoid spread	Labia majora	Not associated with underlying tumor
Candida vulvovaginitis	Erythema, thick white discharge	Vulva and vagina	Extremely common, especially in diabetics and after antibiotic use

Note: See also Sexually Transmitted Diseases, pages 402–403.

DISEASES OF THE VAGINA

Vaginal Adenosis and Clear Cell Adenocarcinoma

- Rare in the general population, but greatly increased risk in females exposed to diethylstilbestrol (DES) in utero (1940–1970)
- Vaginal adenosis—benign condition thought to be a precursor of clear cell carcinoma

Embryonal Rhabdomyosarcoma (Sarcoma Botryoides)

- Rare tumor affecting female infants and young children (age <4)
- Polypoid, "grapelike," soft tissue mass protruding from the vagina
- Spindle-cell tumor, may show cross-striations, positive for desmin, indicating skeletal muscle origin

DISEASES OF THE CERVIX/FALLOPIAN TUBES

Disease	Description	Etiologies	Disease Manifestations	Clinical
Pelvic inflammatory disease	Ascending infection from cervix to endometrium, fallopian tubes, and pelvic cavity	**Neisseria gonorrhoeae** **Chlamydia trachomatis**	Cervicitis, endometritis, salpingitis, peritonitis, pelvic abscess, perihepatitis (Fitz-Hugh-Curtis syndrome). *Complications:* tubo-ovarian abscess, tubal scarring, infertility, ectopic pregnancy, intestinal obstruction	• Vaginal discharge/bleeding • Midline abdominal pain, bilateral lower abdominal and pelvic pain • Abdominal tenderness and peritoneal signs • Fever
Cervical carcinoma	Third most common malignant tumor of the female genital tract in United States; peak incidence in the 40s	Associated with early first intercourse, multiple sexual partners, infection by **HPV types 16, 18**, 31 and 33, smoking, and immunosuppression	**Begins as cervical intraepithelial neoplasia (CIN)** → carcinoma in situ → invasive squamous cell cancer	May be asymptomatic, or may have postcoital bleeding, dyspareunia, discharge Early detection possible with **Papanicolaou (Pap) smear**

DISEASES OF THE UTERUS

Disease	Description	Location	Pathology	Clinical
Endometritis	Ascending infection from the cervix	Endometrium and decidua	*Ureaplasma, Peptostreptococcus, Gardnerella, Bacteroides,* Group B *Streptococcus, Chlamydia trachomatis*	Associated with pregnancy or abortions (acute) Associated with PID and intrauterine devices (IUDs) (chronic)
Endometriosis	• Presence of endometrial glands and stroma outside the uterus • Most commonly affects women of reproductive age	Ovary Ovarian and uterine ligaments Pouch of Douglas Serosa of bowel and bladder Peritoneal cavity	Red-brown serosal nodules (**"powder burns"**) Endometrioma: ovarian **"chocolate" cyst** Adenomyosis = endometrial glands in the myometrium	Chronic pelvic pain linked to menses Dysmenorrhea and dyspareunia Rectal pain and constipation Infertility
Leiomyoma	• **Benign smooth muscle tumor that grows in response to estrogen.** • Higher incidence in African Americans Malignant variant: leiomyosarcoma	May occur in subserosal, intramural, or submucosal locations in the myometrium	Well circumscribed, rubbery, white-tan "whorled" masses Often multiple	Menorrhagia Abdominal mass Pelvic pain, back pain, or suprapubic discomfort Infertility
Endometrial adenocarcinoma	Most common malignant tumor of the female genital tract Most commonly affects postmenopausal women	Begins in endometrium and may invade myometrium	**Gross:** Tan polypoid endometrial mass Invasion of myometrium is prognostically important **Micro:** endometrioid adenocarcinoma (most common type)	Postmenopausal vaginal bleeding **RISK FACTORS:** **Early menarche and late menopause** **Nulliparity** Hypertension and diabetes Obesity **Chronic anovulation** **Estrogen-producing ovarian tumors, estrogen replacement therapy and tamoxifen** Endometrial hyperplasia Lynch syndrome (colon, endometrial, and ovarian cancers = HNPCC)

Definition of abbreviations: HNPCC, hereditary nonpolyposis colorectal cancer.

DISEASES OF THE OVARY

Disease	Presentation	Laboratory/Pathology	Etiology	Treatment
Polycystic ovary disease (Stein-Leventhal syndrome)	• Young, **obese, hirsute** females of reproductive age • Oligomenorrhea or secondary amenorrhea • **Infertility**	• **Elevated luteinizing hormone (LH)** • Low follicle stimulating hormone (FSH) • **Elevated testosterone** Bilaterally enlarged ovaries with multiple follicular cysts	Increased LH stimulation leads to increased androgen synthesis and anovulatory cycles	Oral contraceptives or medroxyprogesterone, surgical wedge resection
Epithelial Tumors				
Cystadenoma	Most common benign ovarian tumor Pathology: Unilocular cyst with simple serous or mucinous lining			
Cystadeno-carcinoma	Most common malignant ovarian tumor. Often asymptomatic until far advanced (presenting symptoms may be increased abdominal girth due to ascites, bowel or bladder problems) Can produce **pseudomyxoma peritonei**	CA-125- marker for cystadenocarcinoma of ovary. Used to monitor recurrence, measure response to therapy. Complex multiloculated cyst with solid areas • Serous (serous cystadenocarcinoma) or mucinous (mucinous cystadenocarcinoma) lining with tufting, papillary structures with **psammoma bodies** • Spreads by seeding pelvic cavity	**Genetic risk factors:** • BRCA-1: breast and ovarian cancers • Lynch syndrome	Surgery, antineoplastic drugs
Borderline tumor	Tumors of low malignant potential			
Germ Cell Tumors				
Teratoma	• Most are benign • Occur in younger women • Contain elements from **all three germ layers (ectoderm, mesoderm, endoderm)** • **Immature teratoma-** contains primitive cells – **higher malignant potential**	Ovarian cyst containing hair, teeth, and sebaceous material	May be due to abnormal differentiation of fetal germ cells that arise from the fetal yolk sac	Surgical
Dysgerminoma	• Malignant • Affects mainly young adults	Similar to seminoma in appearance	**Risk factors:** Turner syndrome, pseudohermaphroditism	Radiosensitive, so good prognosis

(Continued)

DISEASES OF THE OVARY (CONT'D.)

Sex Cord-Stromal Tumors

Ovarian fibroma	Common tumor. Associated with Meigs syndrome = fibroma + ascites + pleural effusion
Granulosa cell tumor	Potentially malignant, **produces estrogen** and can produce precocious puberty, irregular menses, or dysfunctional uterine bleeding. Microscopic: made of polygonal tumor cells with formation of follicle-like structures **(Call-Exner bodies)** Complications: endometrial hyperplasia and cancer
Sertoli-Leydig cell tumor (androblastoma)	• Androgen producing tumor, presents with virilization

GESTATIONAL TROPHOBLASTIC DISEASE

Hydatidiform Mole (Molar Pregnancy)—tumor of placental trophoblast

Incidence	1:1,000 pregnancies
Clinical	"Size greater than dates," vaginal bleeding, passage of edematous, grape-like tissue, elevated β-hCG, invasive moles invade myometrium
Treatment	Curettage, follow β-hCG levels

Types

Complete mole	Results from fertilization of an ovum that lost all its chromosomal material; all chromosomal material is derived from sperm	90% 46,XX; 10% contain a Y chromosome
Partial mole	Results from fertilization of an ovum by two sperm, one 23,X and one 23,Y	Partial moles are triploid = 69, XXY (23,X [maternal] + 23X [one sperm] +23Y [the other sperm])
Choriocarcinoma	• **Malignant** germ cell tumor derived from trophoblast • Gross: necrotic and hemorrhagic mass • Micro: proliferation of cytotrophoblasts, intermediate trophoblasts, and syncytiotrophoblasts • Hematogenous spread to lungs, brain, liver, etc. • Responsive to chemotherapy	

PARTIAL MOLES VERSUS COMPLETE MOLES

Properties	Partial Mole	Complete Mole
Ploidy	Triploid	Diploid
Number of chromosomes	69	46 (All paternal)
β-hCG	Elevated (+)	Elevated (+++)
Chorionic villi	Some are hydropic	All are hydropic
Trophoblast proliferation	Focal	Marked
Fetal tissue	Present	Absent
Invasive mole	10%	10%
Choriocarcinoma	Rare	2%

BREAST PATHOLOGY

FIBROCYSTIC DISEASE

- Most common breast disorder, affecting approximately 10% of women; may be mistaken for CA
- Develops during reproductive life, distortion of the normal breast changes associated with the menstrual cycle
- Patients often have lumpy, tender breasts
- *Pathogenesis:* possibly due to high estrogen levels, coupled with progesterone deficiency
- *Pathology:* several morphologic patterns recognized

Fibrosis	• Women 35 to 49 years of age; not premalignant
	• *Gross:* dense, rubbery mass; usually unilateral, most often in the upper outer quadrant
	• *Histology:* increase in stromal connective tissue; cysts are rare
Cystic disease	• Women 45 to 55 years of age; may predispose to malignancy
	• *Gross:* serous cysts, firm to palpation, may be hemorrhagic; usually multifocal, often bilateral
	• *Histology:* cysts lined by cuboidal epithelium, may have papillary projections
	• May be an accompanying stromal lymphocytic infiltrate (chronic cystic mastitis)
Sclerosing adenosis	• Women 35 to 45 years of age; probably does not predispose to CA
	• *Gross:* palpable, ill-defined, firm area most often in upper outer quadrant; usually unilateral.
	• *Histology:* glandular patterns of cells in a fibrous stroma; may be difficult to distinguish from cancer
Epithelial hyperplasia	• Women over 30 years of age, increased CA risk
	• *Gross:* variable with ill-defined masses
	• Histology: ductal epithelium is multilayered and produces glandular or papillary configurations

TUMORS

Fibroadenoma	• Most common benign breast tumor
	• Single movable breast nodule, often in the upper outer quadrant; not fixed to skin
	• Occurs in reproductive years, generally before age 30, possibly related to increased estrogen sensitivity
	• May show menstrual variation and increased growth during pregnancy; postmenopausal regression usual
	• *Gross:* round and encapsulated with a gray-white cut surface
	• *Histology:* glandular epithelial-lined spaces with a fibroblastic stroma
	• Surgery required for definitive diagnosis
Cystosarcoma phyllodes	• Fibroadenoma-like tumors that have become large, cystic, and lobulated
	• Distinguished by the nature of the stromal component
	• Malignant fibrous, cartilaginous; bony elements may be present
	• *Gross:* irregular mass; often fungating or ulcerated
	• *Histology:* myxoid stroma with increased cellularity, anaplasia, and increased mitoses
	• Tumor initially localized but may spread later, usually to distant sites but not to local lymph nodes
Intraductal papilloma	• Most common in women 20–50 years of age; solitary lesion within a duct
	• May present with nipple discharge (serous or bloody), nipple retraction, or small subareolar mass
	• *Gross:* small, sessile or pedunculated, usually close to the nipple in major ducts
	• *Histology:* multiple papillae
	• Single intraductal papillomas may be benign, but multiple papillomas associated with an increased risk of CA

CARCINOMA OF THE BREAST

General features	• Most common cause of CA in women • Lung CA causes more deaths • Rare in women under age 25 • Lifetime risk of breast CA for the average woman with no family history: 8 to 10%
Risk factors	• Increasing age (40+ years) • Fibrocystic disease • Nulliparity • Previous history of breast cancer • Family history • Obesity • Early menarche • High-fat diet • Late menopause
Clinical features	• 50% in the upper outer quadrant • Ninety percent arise in ductal epithelium • Slightly more common in the left breast; bilateral or sequential in 4% of cases • Breast mass usually discovered after self-examination or on routine physical

Tumor suppressor genes: *BRCA1* and *BRCA2*	Mutated *BRCA1*—
	  • Almost 100% lifetime risk for breast CA, often in the third and fourth decades of life
	  • Also at increased risk for ovarian CA (men may be at increased risk for prostate CA)
	Mutated *BRCA2*—
	  • Increased incidence of breast CA in both women and men
	  • Does not increase the incidence of ovarian CA in women

Invasion	• May grow into the thoracic fascia to become fixed to the chest wall • May extend into the skin, causing dimpling and retraction • May cause obstruction of subcutaneous lymphatics, causing an orange-peel consistency to skin called "peau d'orange" • May invade Cooper ligaments within ducts to cause nipple retraction
Metastases	• Most breast CAs disseminate via lymphatic or hematogenous routes • Involve axillary, supraclavicular, and internal thoracic nodes • Can also involve nodes of the contralateral breast

BREAST CARCINOMA TYPES

Infiltrating ductal carcinoma	• Most common breast CA • *Gross:* rock hard, cartilaginous consistency, usually 2 to 5 cm in diameter, foci of necrosis and calcification common (may be seen on mammography) • *Histology:* anaplastic duct epithelial cells appear in masses, invading the stroma. • Fibrous reaction responsible for the hard, palpable mass
Paget disease of the breast	• Older women; poor prognosis • Form of intraductal carcinoma involving areolar skin and nipple • *Gross:* skin of the nipple and areola ulcerated and oozing • *Histology:* ductal carcinoma, as well as large, anaplastic, hyperchromatic "Paget cells"
Noninfiltrating intraductal carcinoma	• *Gross:* focus of increased consistency in breast tissue • *Histology:* typical duct epithelial cells proliferate and fill ducts, leading to ductal dilatation • Often called "comedocarcinomas" because cheesy, necrotic tumor tissue may be expressed from ducts. • Rarely have a papillary pattern
Medullary carcinoma with lymphoid infiltration	• Better prognosis than infiltrating ductal carcinoma • *Gross:* fleshy masses, often 5 to 10 cm in diameter, little fibrous tissue, although foci of hemorrhage and necrosis common • *Histology:* sheets of large, pleomorphic cells with increased mitotic activity and a lymphocytic infiltrate
Colloid (mucinous) carcinoma	• Older women, slow growing, has a better prognosis than infiltrating ductal carcinoma • *Gross:* soft, large, gelatinous tumors • *Histology:* islands of tumor cells with copious mucin
Lobular carcinoma	• Multicentric; usually have estrogen receptors, arise from terminal ductules • *Gross:* rubbery and ill-defined (result of their multicentric nature) • *Histology:* tumor cells small and may be arranged in rings

FIBROCYSTIC DISEASE VERSUS BREAST CANCER

Fibrocystic Disease	Breast Cancer
• Often bilateral • May have multiple nodules • Menstrual variation • Cyclic pain and engorgement • May regress during pregnancy	• Often unilateral • Usually single nodule • No menstrual variation • No cyclic pain and engorgement • Does not regress during pregnancy

MISCELLANEOUS BREAST CONDITIONS

Acute mastitis	• Fissures in nipples during early nursing predispose to bacterial infection; usually unilateral with pus in ducts; necrosis may occur • Usual pathogens: *Staphylococcus aureus* and *Streptococcus* • Antibiotics and surgical drainage may be adequate therapy
Mammary duct ectasia (plasma cell mastitis)	• Occurs in fifth decade in multiparous women • Presents with pain, redness, and induration around the areola with thick secretions; usually unilateral • Skin fixation, nipple retraction, and axillary lymphadenopathy may occur—must be distinguished from malignancy
Gynecomastia	• Enlargement of the male breasts; most often unilateral, but may be bilateral • Secondary to Klinefelter syndrome, testicular tumors, puberty, or old age • Associated with hepatic cirrhosis (cirrhotic liver cannot degrade estrogens) • May be important signal that patient has high-estrogen state

GENITOURINARY SYSTEM DISEASE

	SEXUALLY TRANSMITTED DISEASES (STDs)				
Type Infection	Case Vignette/Key Clues	Most Common Causative Agent(s)	Pathogenesis	Diagnosis	Treatment
Urethritis	Gram ⊖ diplococci in PMNs in urethral exudate	*Neisseria gonorrhoeae*	Invasive; pili assist adherence; have antigenic variation; are antiphagocytic; IgA protease	Gram ⊖ diplococci in PMNs, growth on Thayer-Martin agar, DNA probes	Ceftriaxone
	Culture ⊖, inclusion bodies	*Chlamydia trachomatis*	Obligate intracellular in epithelial cells; CMI and DTH cause scarring	Tissue culture; glycogen-containing inclusion bodies in cytoplasm	Tetracyclines, erythromycin
	Urease ⊕, no cell wall	*Ureaplasma urealyticum*	Urease raises pH of urine → struvite stones	Not gram staining; diagnosed by exclusion, urinary pH	Tetracycline, erythromycin
	Flagellated protozoan with corkscrew motility	*Trichomonas vaginalis*	Unknown, PMN filtrate	Flagellated protozoan, corkscrew motility	Metronidazole
Cervicitis	Friable, inflamed cervix with mucopurulent discharge	*Neisseria gonorrhoeae*	Invades mucosa, PMN infiltration, pili, IgA protease	Gram ⊖ diplococci, Thayer-Martin agar	Ceftriaxone
		Chlamydia trachomatis	Obligate intracellular, CMI and DTH → scarring	Tissue culture, cytoplasmic inclusions	Tetracycline, erythromycin
		Herpes simplex virus	Vesicular lesions, painful	dsDNA, nuclear envelope, icosahedral; Tzanck smear, intranuclear inclusions	Acyclovir
Vulvovaginitis	Adherent yellowish discharge, pH >5, fishy amine odor in KOH, clue cells, gram ⊖ cells dominate	Bacterial vaginosis	Overgrowth of *Gardnerella vaginalis*, anaerobes	Clue cells, gram ⊖ rods	Metronidazole
	Vulvovaginitis, pruritus, erythema, discharge with consistency of cottage cheese	*Candida* spp.	Antibiotic use → overgrowth, immunocompromised	Germ tube test, gram ⊕ yeasts in vaginal fluids	Nystatin, miconazole
	"Strawberry cervix," foamy, purulent discharge; many PMNs and motile trophozoites microscopically (corkscrew motility)	*Trichomonas vaginalis*	Vaginitis with discharge	Pear-shaped trophozoites with corkscrew motility	Metronidazole

(Continued)

Type Infection	Case Vignette/Key Clues	Most Common Causative Agent(s)	Pathogenesis	Diagnosis	Treatment
Condyloma acuminatum (genital warts)	Lesions are papillary/wart-like, may be sessile or pedunculated, koilocytotic atypia is present, anogenital	Human papilloma virus (HPV; most common U.S. STD)	HPV proteins E6 and E7 inactivate cellular antioncogene Associated with cervical CA	dsDNA, naked, icosahedral, intranuclear inclusion bodies	None
Genital herpes	Multiple, painful, vesicular, coalescing, recurring	Herpes simplex	Latent virus in sensory ganglia reactivates	Virus culture, intranuclear inclusions, syncytia (Tzanck smear), dsDNA enveloped (nuclear), icosahedral	Acyclovir
Syphilis Primary	Painless chancre forms on glans, penis (or vulva/cervix) and heals within 1 to 3 months.	Treponema pallidum	3-week incubation during which spirochetes spread throughout the body	Serology—VDRL ⊕ (nonspecific); FTA-ABS (specific)	Penicillin
Secondary	Local or generalized rash lasting 1 to 3 months, can involve the palms and soles		Develops 1 to 2 months after primary stage		
Tertiary	Affects central nervous system, heart, and skin; characteristic lesion is gumma, may be single or multiple; most common in the liver, testes, and bone		Develops in one-third of untreated patients; neurosyphilis: including meningovascular, tabes dorsalis, and general paresis; obliterative endarteritis of vasa vasorum of the aorta can lead thoracic aneurysm		
Chancroid	Nonindurated, painful ulcer, suppurative with adenopathy; slow to heal	Haemophilus ducreyi	Unknown	Gram ⊖ rods, chocolate agar (requires NAD and hemin)	Cefotaxime, ceftriaxone
Lymphogranuloma venereum	Initial papule heals, lymph nodes enlarge and develop fistulas, genital elephantiasis may develop	Chlamydia trachomatis serotypes L1–3	Obligate intracellular	Cell culture, glycogen-containing inclusions	Tetracyclines, erythromycin

SEXUALLY TRANSMITTED DISEASES (STDs; *CONT'D.*)

Definition of abbreviations: CA, cancer; CMI, cell-mediated immunity; ds, double-stranded; DTH, delayed type hypersensitivity; PMNs, polymorphonuclear leukocytes.

The Musculoskeletal System, Skin, and Connective Tissue

Chapter 8

FEATURES OF SKELETAL, CARDIAC, AND SMOOTH MUSCLE			
Characteristics	Skeletal	Cardiac	Smooth
Appearance	Striated, unbranched fibers	Striated, branched fibers	Nonstriated, fusiform fibers
	Z lines	Z lines	No Z lines; have dense bodies
	Multinucleated	Single nucleus	Single nucleus
T tubules	Form triadic contacts with SR at A-I junction	Form dyadic contacts with SR near Z line	Absent; have limited SR
Cell junctions	Absent	Junctional complexes between fibers (intercalated discs), including gap junctions	Gap junctions
Innervation	Each fiber innervated	Electrical syncytium	Electrical syncytium
Action potential Upstroke	Inward Na^+ current	• Inward Ca^{2+} current (SA node) • Inward Na^+ current (atria, ventricles, Purkinje fibers)	Inward Na^+ current
Plateau	No plateau	• No plateau (SA node) • Plateau present (atria, ventricles, Purkinje fibers)	No plateau
Excitation-contraction coupling	AP → T tubules → Ca^{2+} released from SR	Inward Ca^{2+} current during plateau → Ca^{2+} release from SR	AP → opens voltage-gated Ca^{2+} channels in sarcolemma; hormones and neurotransmitters → open IP_3-gated Ca^{2+} channels in SR
Calcium binding	Troponin	Troponin	Calmodulin

Definition of abbreviations: AP, action potential; IP_3, inositol triphosphate; SR, sarcoplasmic reticulum.

SKELETAL MUSCLE FIBER MORPHOLOGY AND FUNCTION

Skeletal muscle connective tissue (*see* right):

Epimysium: dense connective tissue that surrounds the entire muscles

Perimysium: thin septa of connective tissue that extends inward from the epimysium and surrounds a bundle (fascicle) of muscle fibers

Endomysium: delicate connective tissue that surrounds each muscle fiber

Subcellular components (*see* below):

Myofibrils: long, cylindrical bundles that fill the sarcoplasm of each fiber

Myofilaments: actin and **myosin**; are within the each myofibril and organize into units called **sarcomeres**

During contraction:

A band: no change   **I band:** shortens
H band: shortens   **Z lines:** move closer together

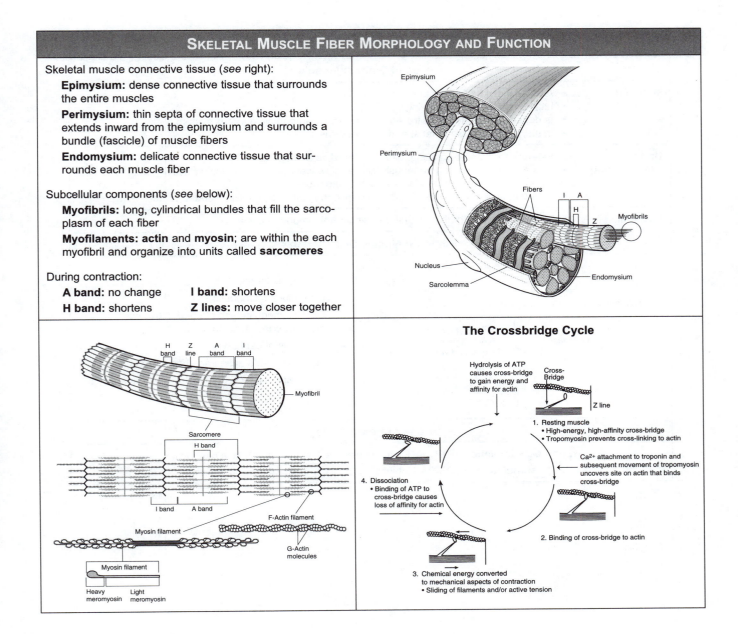

The Crossbridge Cycle

Hydrolysis of ATP causes cross-bridge to gain energy and affinity for actin

1. Resting muscle
 • High-energy, high-affinity cross-bridge
 • Tropomyosin prevents cross-linking to actin

Ca2+ attachment to troponin and subsequent movement of tropomyosin uncovers site on actin that binds cross-bridge

2. Binding of cross-bridge to actin

3. Chemical energy converted to mechanical aspects of contraction
 • Sliding of filaments and/or active tension

4. Dissociation
 • Binding of ATP to cross-bridge causes loss of affinity for actin

RED VERSUS WHITE SKELETAL MUSCLE FIBERS

Red Fibers (Type I)	White Fibers (Type II)
Slow contraction	Fast contraction
↓ ATPase activity	↑ ATPase activity
↑ Capacity for aerobic metabolism	↑ Capacity for anaerobic glycolysis
↑ Mitochondrial content	↓ Mitochondrial content
↑ Myoglobin (imparts red color)	↓ Myoglobin
Best for slow, posture-maintaining muscles, e.g., back (think chicken drumstick/thigh)	Best for fast, short-termed, skilled motions, e.g., extraocular muscles of eye, sprinter's legs, hands (think chicken breast meat and wings)

SMOOTH MUSCLE FUNCTION

Types of Smooth Muscle

Multiunit	• Acts as individual motor unit • Little or no electrical coupling • Is densely innervated; contraction controlled by autonomic nervous system • In iris, ciliary muscle of lens, and vas deferens
Unitary (single unit)	• Extensive electrical coupling, allowing coordinated contraction • Has a resting tone; spontaneously active (slow waves), has pacemaker activity; activity is modulated by neurotransmitters and neurohormones • Found mainly in the walls of hollow viscera, e.g., GI tract, uterus, bladder, ureters
Vascular	• Has properties of both multiunit and single-unit smooth muscle

Smooth Muscle Contraction

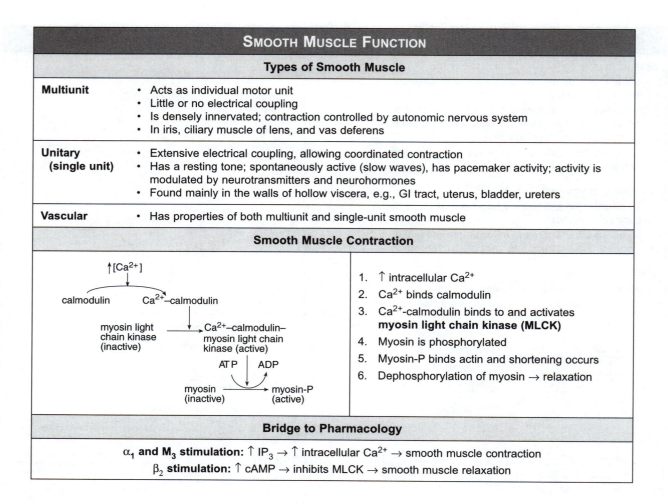

1. $\uparrow$ intracellular Ca^{2+}
2. Ca^{2+} binds calmodulin
3. Ca^{2+}-calmodulin binds to and activates **myosin light chain kinase (MLCK)**
4. Myosin is phosphorylated
5. Myosin-P binds actin and shortening occurs
6. Dephosphorylation of myosin $\rightarrow$ relaxation

Bridge to Pharmacology

α_1 **and M$_3$ stimulation:** $\uparrow$ IP$_3$ $\rightarrow$ $\uparrow$ intracellular Ca^{2+} $\rightarrow$ smooth muscle contraction

β_2 **stimulation:** $\uparrow$ cAMP $\rightarrow$ inhibits MLCK $\rightarrow$ smooth muscle relaxation

SKELETAL MUSCLE RELAXANTS

There are two general classes of skeletal muscle relaxants: **neuromuscular blockers** and **spasmolytics**. Neuromuscular blockers are used during surgical procedures and act on **skeletal muscle nicotinic cholinergic receptors**. There are two classes of neuromuscular blockers: **nondepolarizing (competitive)** and **depolarizing**. **Spasmolytics** are used for CNS disorders and acute muscle spasm and have varying mechanisms of action.

Neuromuscular Blockers

Nondepolarizing Blockers

These agents are competitive antagonists at the nAChR on skeletal muscle and can be therefore be reversed by acetylcholinesterase inhibitors (e.g., neostigmine, pyridostigmine).

Drug	Duration	Elimination	Notes
Atracurium	Intermediate	Spontaneous	Safer in renal and hepatic disease
d-Tubocurarine	Long	Renal	Also blocks autonomic ganglia and causes histamine release
Mivacurium	Short	Plasma ChE	—
Pancuronium	Long	Renal	Blocks muscarinic receptors
Rocuronium	Intermediate	Hepatic	—
Vecuronium	Intermediate	Hepatic	—

Depolarizing Blockers:

These agents act as nicotinic agonists and **depolarize** skeletal muscle. Patients often initially have **fasciculations**. Continuous depolarization of the motor end-plate leads to flaccid paralysis. When given continuously, two phases occur:

Phase I block (depolarizing)—fasciculations, flaccid paralysis; this phase is **augmented by AChE inhibitors**

Phase II block (desensitizing)—the end-plate repolarizes, but is unresponsive to ACh; **reversed by AChE inhibitors**

Drug	Duration	Elimination	Notes
Succinylcholine	Ultrashort	Plasma ChE	Stimulates autonomic ganglia and muscarinic receptors; can → hyperkalemia; postoperative muscle pain

Spasmolytics

The spasmolytics reduce excessive muscle tone in CNS disorders (e.g., cerebral palsy, multiple sclerosis, stroke) or in acute muscle injury.

Drug	Mechanism of Action	Location of Action	Clinical Uses
Baclofen	GABA$_B$ receptor agonist	CNS	CNS dysfunction
Diazepam	Benzodiazepine, potentiates GABA$_A$ receptors	CNS	CNS dysfunction
Tizanidine	α_2-receptor agonist	CNS	CNS dysfunction
Botulinum toxin	Blocks ACh release	Muscle	CNS dysfunction; injected into muscle
Dantrolene	Blocks ryanodine receptors on SR to prevent Ca^{2+} release	Muscle	Malignant hyperthermia; neuroleptic malignant syndrome
Cyclobenzaprine	—	CNS	Acute muscle spasm

Definition of abbreviation: SR, sarcoplasmic reticulum.

SKELETAL MUSCLES INNERVATED BY CRANIAL NERVES			
Muscles Derived from a Pharyngeal Arch	**Cranial Nerve**	**Muscles**	**Skeletal Elements (from neural crest)**
First arch—mandibular (Mandibular hyperplasia is seen in **Treacher Collins syndrome** and in the **Robin sequence**. Both involve neural crest cells.)	**Trigeminal mandibular nerve (V3)**	Four muscles of mastication: • Masseter • Temporalis • Lateral pterygoid • Medial pterygoid Plus: • Digastric (anterior belly) • Mylohyoid • Tensor tympani • Tensor veli palatini	Mandibular process Maxillary process Malleus Incus
Second arch—hyoid	**Facial (VII)**	Muscles of facial expression: • Orbicularis oculi • Orbicularis oris • Buccinator and others Plus: • Digastric (posterior belly) • Stylohyoid • Stapedius	Hyoid (superior part) Styloid process Stapes
Third arch	**Glossopharyngeal (IX)**	Stylopharyngeus	Hyoid (inferior part)
Fourth arch	**Vagus (X) superior laryngeal (external branch)** **Vagus (X) pharyngeal branches**	Cricothyroid Levator veli palatini Uvular muscle Pharyngeal constrictors Salpingopharyngeus Palatoglossus Palatopharyngeus	Thyroid cartilage
Fifth arch	**Lost**	—	—
Sixth arch **Muscles of myotome origin**	**Vagus (X) recurrent laryngeal** **Accessory (XI)** **Hypoglossal (XII)** **Oculomotor (III)** **Trochlear (IV)** **Abducens (VI)**	Lateral cricoarytenoid Posterior cricoarytenoid Transverse arytenoid Oblique arytenoid Thyroarytenoid (vocalis) Trapezius Sternocleidomastoid Genioglossus Hyoglossus Styloglossus Superior, inferior, and medial rectus; inferior oblique, levator palpebrae superioris Superior oblique Lateral rectus	Cricoid, arytenoid, corniculate, cuneiform cartilages

PHARYNGEAL POUCHES

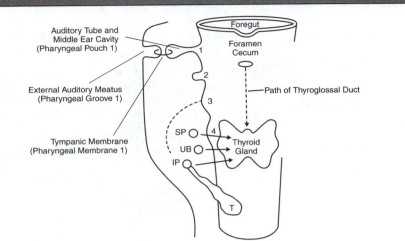

Adult Structures Derived from the Fetal Pharyngeal Pouches

Pouch	Adult Derivatives	Clinical Correlate
1	Epithelial lining of auditory tube and middle ear cavity	The **DiGeorge sequence** occurs when pharyngeal pouches 3 and 4 fail to differentiate into the parathyroid glands and thymus. Patients have immunologic problems, hypocalcemia, and may have cardiovascular defects (persistent truncus arteriosus), abnormal ears, and micrognathia.
2	Epithelial lining of crypts of palatine tonsil	
3	Inferior parathyroid gland (IP)	
	Thymus (T)	
4	Superior parathyroid gland (SP)	
	Ultimobranchial body (UB)	

The thyroid gland does not develop in a pharyngeal pouch; it develops from midline endoderm of the oropharynx and migrates inferiorly along the path of thyroglossal duct. Neural crest cells migrate into the UB to form parafollicular C cells of the thyroid.

The external auditory meatus is the only postnatal remnant of a pharyngeal groove or cleft.

PALATE AND FACE DEVELOPMENT

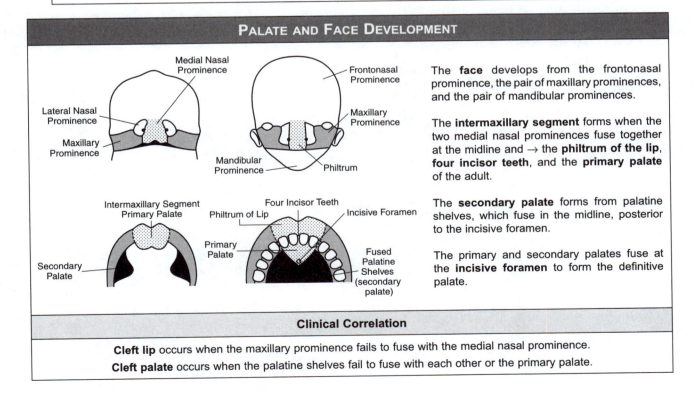

The **face** develops from the frontonasal prominence, the pair of maxillary prominences, and the pair of mandibular prominences.

The **intermaxillary segment** forms when the two medial nasal prominences fuse together at the midline and → the **philtrum of the lip**, **four incisor teeth**, and the **primary palate** of the adult.

The **secondary palate** forms from palatine shelves, which fuse in the midline, posterior to the incisive foramen.

The primary and secondary palates fuse at the **incisive foramen** to form the definitive palate.

Clinical Correlation

Cleft lip occurs when the maxillary prominence fails to fuse with the medial nasal prominence.

Cleft palate occurs when the palatine shelves fail to fuse with each other or the primary palate.

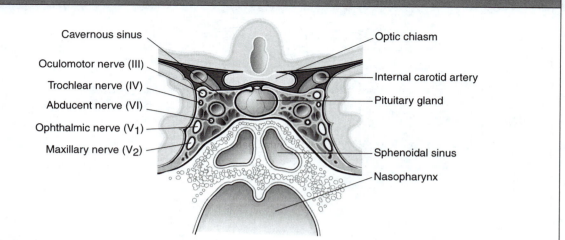

Cavernous sinus

Oculomotor nerve (III)

Trochlear nerve (IV)

Abducent nerve (VI)

Ophthalmic nerve (V$_1$)

Maxillary nerve (V$_2$)

Optic chiasm

Internal carotid artery

Pituitary gland

Sphenoidal sinus

Nasopharynx

The cavernous sinuses are located on either side of the body of the sphenoid bone. Each sinus receives blood from some of the cerebral veins, ophthalmic veins, and the sphenoparietal sinus. Each cavernous sinus drains into a transverse sinus via the superior petrosal sinus and into the internal jugular vein via the inferior petrosal sinus.

Cavernous Sinus Thrombosis

Infection can spread from veins of the face into the cavernous sinuses, producing a thrombosis that may involve the cranial nerves that course through the cavernous sinuses. Cranial nerves III, IV, and VI and the ophthalmic and maxillary divisions of CN V, as well as the internal carotid artery and its periarterial plexus of postganglionic sympathetic fibers, traverse the cavernous sinuses. All of these cranial nerves course in the lateral wall of each sinus, except for CN VI, which courses through the middle of the sinus. Initially, patients have an internal strabismus. Later, all eye movements are affected, along with with altered sensation in skin of the upper face and scalp.

EFFECTS OF LESIONS TO ROOTS AND NERVES OF THE BRACHIAL PLEXUS

The **brachial plexus** is formed by an intermingling of ventral rami from the C5 through T1 spinal nerves.

The ventral rami of the brachial plexus exhibit a proximal to distal gradient of innervation. Nerves that contain fibers from the superior rami of the plexus (C5 and C6) innervate proximal muscles in the upper limb (shoulder muscles). Nerves that contain fibers from the inferior rami of the plexus (C8 and T1) innervate distal muscles (hand muscles).

Five major nerves arise from the brachial plexus: the **musculocutaneous, median**, and **ulnar** nerves contain anterior division fibers and innervate muscles in the anterior arm, anterior forearm, and hand that act mainly as flexors. The **axillary** and **radial** nerves contain posterior division fibers, and innervate muscles in the posterior arm and posterior forearm that act mainly as extensors.

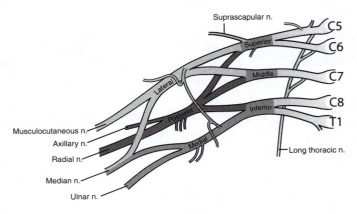

Lesioned Root	C5	C6	C7	C8	T1
Dermatome paresthesia	Lateral border of upper arm	Lateral forearm to thumb	Over triceps, midforearm, middle finger	Medial forearm to little finger	Medial arm to elbow
Muscles affected	Deltoid Rotator cuff Serratus anterior Biceps Brachioradialis	Biceps Brachioradialis Brachialis Supinator	Latissimus dorsi Pectoralis major Triceps Wrist extensors	Finger flexors Wrist flexors Hand muscles	Hand muscles
Reflex test	—	Biceps tendon	Triceps tendon	—	—
Causes of lesions	Upper trunk compression	Upper trunk compression	Cervical spondylosis Herniation of C6/C7 disk	Lower trunk compression	Lower trunk compression

Lesioned Nerve	Axillary (C5, C6)	Musculo-cutaneous (C5, C6, C7)	Radial (C5, C6, C7, C8)	Median (C6, C7, C8, T1)	Ulnar (C8, T1)
Altered sensation	Lateral arm	Lateral forearm	Dorsum of hand over first dorsal interosseous and anatomic snuffbox	Lateral 3 and 1/2 digits; lateral palm	Medial 1 and 1/2 digits; medial palm
Motor weakness	Abduction at shoulder	Flexion of forearm Supination	Wrist extension Metacarpo-phalangeal extension Supination	Wrist flexion Finger flexion Pronation Thumb opposition	Wrist flexion Finger spreading Thumb adduction Finger extension
Common sign of lesion	—	—	Wrist drop	Ape hand Hand of benediction Ulnar deviation at wrist	Claw hand Radial deviation at wrist
Causes of lesions	Surgical neck fracture of humerus Dislocated humerus	Rarely lesioned	Saturday night palsy Midshaft fracture of humerus Subluxation of radius Dislocated humerus	Carpal tunnel compression Supracondylar fracture of humerus Pronator teres syndrome	Fracture of medial epicondyle of humerus Fracture of hook of hamate Fracture of clavicle

CUTANEOUS INNERVATION OF THE HAND

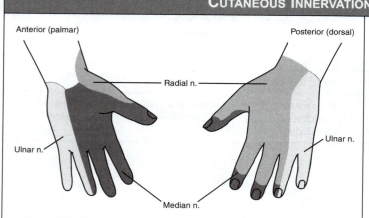

Anterior (palmar)   Posterior (dorsal)

Radial n.

Ulnar n.

Ulnar n.

Median n.

The palm is supplied mainly by the median and ulnar nerves. The median supplies the lateral 3½ digits and the adjacent area of the lateral palm and the thenar eminence. The ulnar supplies the medial 1½ digits and skin of the hypothenar eminence. The radial nerve supplies skin of the dorsum of the hand in the area of the first dorsal webbed space, including the skin over the anatomic snuffbox.

Back Muscles

Action	Muscles Involved	Innervation
Extend/Rotate vertebrae	1. Splenius capitis, splenius cervicis	Dorsal rami of spinal nerves
	2. Erector spinae: • Iliocostalis • Longissimus • Spinalis	Dorsal rami of spinal nerves
	3. Transversospinalis: • Semispinalis • Multifidus • Rotatores	Dorsal rami of spinal nerves

Movements of Pectoral (Shoulder) Girdle on Trunk

Action	Muscles Involved	Innervation	Major Segments of Innervation
Elevation	Levator scapulae Trapezius, upper part	Dorsal scapular Accessory	C4, C5 C1–C5
Depression	Pectoralis minor Trapezius, lower part	Medial pectoral Accessory	C7, C8
Protraction	Serratus anterior	Long thoracic	C5–C7
Retraction	Rhomboid major and minor Trapezius, middle fibers	Dorsal scapular Accessory	C5 C1–C5
Lateral (upward) rotation of scapula (in abduction)	Serratus anterior, lower half Trapezius, upper and lower parts	Long thoracic Accessory	C5–C7 C1–C5
Medial (downward) rotation of scapula (in adduction)	Rhomboid major and minor Levator scapulae	Dorsal scapular Dorsal scapular	C5 C4, C5

Movements at the Shoulder (Glenohumeral) Joint

Action	Muscles Involved	Innervation	Major Segments of Innervation
Flexion	Pectoralis major, clavicular head Deltoid clavicular part Biceps short head	Lateral pectoral Axillary Musculocutaneous	C5–C7 C5, C6 C5, C6
Extension	Deltoid, posterior fibers Latissimus dorsi Teres major	Axillary Thoracodorsal Lower subscapular	C5, C6 C6–C8 C6
Abduction	Deltoid, middle fibers Supraspinatus	Axillary Suprascapular	C5, C6 C5
Adduction	Pectoralis major, sternocostal part Latissimus dorsi Teres major	Medial and lateral pectoral Thoracodorsal Lower subscapular	C6–T1 C6–C8 C5, C6
Lateral rotation	Deltoid, posterior fibers Infraspinatus Teres minor	Axillary Suprascapular Axillary	C5, C6 C5, C6 C6
Medial rotation	Pectoralis major Latissimus dorsi Deltoid, clavicular part Teres major Subscapularis	Medial and lateral pectoral Thoracodorsal Axillary Lower subscapular Upper and lower subscapular	C5–T1 C6–C8 C5–C7 C5, C6 C5, C6

ROTATOR CUFF

The tendons of rotator cuff muscles strengthen the glenohumeral joint and include the **s**upraspinatus, **i**nfraspinatus, **t**eres minor, and **s**ubscapularis (the **SITS** muscles). The tendons of the muscles of the rotator cuff may become torn or inflamed. The tendon of the **supraspinatus** is most commonly affected. Patients with rotator cuff tears experience pain anteriorly and superiorly to the glenohumeral joint during abduction.

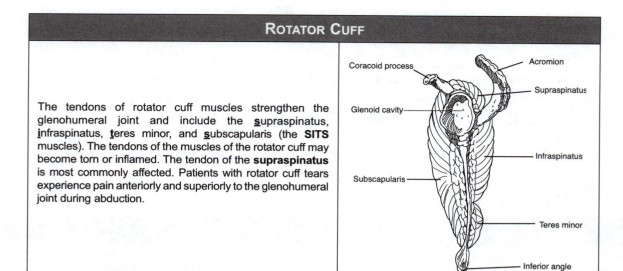

Labels: Coracoid process, Glenoid cavity, Subscapularis, Acromion, Supraspinatus, Infraspinatus, Teres minor, Inferior angle

MOVEMENTS AT THE ELBOW JOINT

Action	Muscles Involved	Innervation	Major Segments of Innervation
Flexion	Brachialis	Musculocutaneous	C5, C6
	Biceps brachii	Musculocutaneous	C5, C6
	Brachioradialis	Radial	C5, C6
Extension	Triceps	Radial	C7, C8

MOVEMENTS AT THE RADIOULNAR JOINTS

Action	Muscles Involved	Innervation	Major Segments of Innervation
Pronation	Pronator teres	Median	C6, C7
	Pronator quadratus	Median (anterior interosseous nerve)	C8, T1
Supination	Supinator	Radial (deep branch)	C6–C8
	Biceps brachii	Musculocutaneous	C5, C6

MOVEMENTS AT THE WRIST JOINT

Action	Muscles Involved	Innervation	Major Segments of Innervation
Flexion	Flexor carpi ulnaris Flexor carpi radialis	Ulnar Median	C8 C6, C7
Extension	Extensor carpi ulnaris Extensor carpi radialis longus Extensor carpi radialis brevis	Radial (deep br.) Radial Radial (deep br.)	C7, C8 C6, C7 C6, C7
Abduction	Extensor carpi radialis longus/brevis Flexor carpi radialis	Radial (deep br.) Median	C6, C7 C6, C7
Adduction	Flexor carpi ulnaris Extensor carpi ulnaris	Ulnar Radial (deep br.)	C8 C7, C8

MOVEMENTS OF THE FINGERS

Action	Muscles Involved	Innervation	Major Segments of Innervation
Flexion, All Fingers			
All joints and DIP	Flexor digitorum profundus	To index and middle: **median** (ant. interosseous n.)	C8
		To ring and little: **ulnar**	T1
MP and PIP, all	Flexor digitorum superficialis Lumbricals	Median Median—index and middle Ulnar—ring and little	C7, C8, T1 C8, T1 C8, T1
MP little finger	Flexor digiti minimi	Ulnar	C8, T1
Extension—MP Joints			
Index, middle, ring	Extensor digitorum	Radial (deep br.)	C6–C8
Index only	Extensor indicis	Radial (deep br.)	C7, C8
Little finger only	Extensor digiti minimi	Radial (deep br.)	C7, C8
Extension—IP Joints			
Through extensor expansion	Lumbricals	Median: index and middle Ulnar: ring and little	C8, T1 C8, T1
	Interossei	Ulnar	C8, T1
Abduction—MP Joints			
All fingers, except little	Dorsal Interossei Abductor digiti minimi	Ulnar Ulnar	C8, T1 C8, T1
Adduction—MP Joints			
All fingers, except middle	Palmar Interossei	Ulnar	C8, T1
Opposition little finger	Opponens digiti minimi	Ulnar	C8, T1

Definition of abbreviations: ant., anterior; br., branch; IP, interphalangeal joints; DIP, distal interphalangeal joints; MP, metacarpophalangeal joints; n, nerve; PIP, proximal interphalangeal joints.

Action	Muscles Involved	Innervation	Major Segments of Innervation
MOVEMENTS OF THE THUMB			
Flexion			
All joints, especially IP	Flexor pollicis longus	Median (ant. interosseous n.)	C8, T1
MP	Flexor pollicis brevis	Median (recurrent br.)	C8, T1
Extension			
All joints	Extensor pollicis longus	Radial (deep br.)	C7, C8
MP	Extensor pollicis brevis	Radial (deep br.)	C7, C8
Abduction			
	Abductor pollicis longus	Radial (deep br.)	C7, C8
	Abductor pollicis brevis	Median (recurrent br.)	C6–T1
Adduction			
	Adductor pollicis	Ulnar	C8, T1
Opposition			
	Opponens pollicis	Median (recurrent br.)	C6–T1

Definition of abbreviations: ant., anterior; br, branch; MP, metacarpophalangeal joints; IP, interphalangeal joints.

The **lumbosacral plexus** is formed by an intermingling of the ventral rami of the L2 through S3 spinal nerves. The ventral rami of the lumbosacral plexus exhibit a proximal to distal gradient of innervation. Nerves that contain fibers from the superior rami of the plexus (L2 through L4) innervate muscles in the anterior and medial thigh that act at the hip and knee joints. Nerves that contain fibers from the inferior rami of the plexus (S1 through S3) innervate muscles of the leg that act at the joints of the ankle and foot.

Four major nerves arise from the lumbosacral plexus:

The **obturator** and **tibial** nerves contain anterior division fibers and innervate muscles in the medial and posterior compartments of the thigh, the posterior compartment of the leg, and in the sole of the foot.

The **femoral** and **common fibular** nerves contain posterior division fibers and innervate muscles in the anterior compartment of the thigh, in the anterior and lateral compartments of the leg, and in the dorsum of the foot.

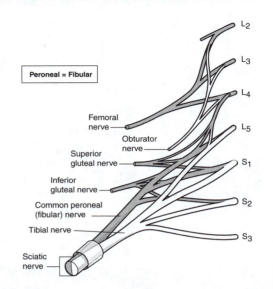

Lesioned Root	L3	L4	L5	S1
Dermatome paresthesia	Anterior thigh	Medial leg	Anterior leg, dorsum of foot	Lateral foot, sole
Reflex test	—	Patellar tendon	—	Achilles tendon
Muscles affected	Hip flexors Hip adductors	Knee extensors Hip adductors	Dorsiflexors Toe extensors	Plantar flexors Toe flexors
Causes of lesions	Osteoarthritis	Osteoarthritis	Herniation of L4/L5 disc	Herniation of L5/S1 disc
Lesioned Nerve	**Obturator (L2–L4)**	**Femoral (L2–L4)**	**Common Fibular (L4, L5, S1, S2)**	**Tibial (L4, L5, S1–S3)**
Altered sensation	Medial thigh	Anterior thigh, medial leg to medial malleolus	Anterior leg, dorsum of foot	Posterior leg, sole, and lateral border of foot
Reflex test	—	Patellar tendon	—	Achilles tendon
Motor weakness	Adduction of thigh	Extension of knee	Dorsiflexion, eversion of the foot	Plantar flexion Toe flexion
Common sign of lesion	—	—	Footdrop	—
Causes of lesions	Pelvic neoplasm Pregnancy	Diabetes Posterior abdominal neoplasm Psoas abscess	Compression at fibula neck Hip fracture/dislocation Misplaced gluteal injection Piriformis syndrome	Hip fracture/dislocation Penetrating trauma to buttock

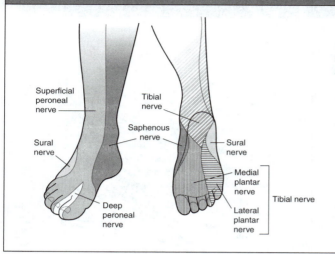

- The lateral leg and the dorsum of the foot are supplied mainly by the **superficial peroneal nerve**, with the exception of the first dorsal webbed space, which is supplied by the **deep peroneal nerve**.

- The sole of the foot is supplied by the lateral and medial plantar branches of the **tibial nerve**.

- The sural nerve (a combination of both peroneal and tibial branches) supplies the posterior leg and lateral side of the foot.

- The **saphenous nerve** (a branch of the femoral nerve) supplies the medial leg and medial foot.

MOVEMENTS AT THE HIP JOINT

Action	Muscles Involved	Innervation	Major Segments of Innervation
Flexion	Iliacus and psoas major	Lumbar ventral rami	L2, L3
	Rectus femoris	Femoral	L2–L4
	Sartorius	Femoral	L2, L3
	Tensor fasciae latae	Superior gluteal	L4, L5, S1
Extension	Gluteus maximus	Inferior gluteal	L5, S1, S2
	Semimembranosus	Sciatic (tibial)	L5, S1
	Semitendinosus	Sciatic (tibial)	L5, S1, S2
	Biceps femoris, long head	Sciatic (tibial)	S1, S2
	Adductor magnus, ischial part	Obturator	L3, L4
Adduction	Adductors longus, brevis, and magnus	Obturator	L2–L4
	Gracilis	Obturator	L2–L4
	Pectineus	Femoral	L2, L3
Abduction	Gluteus medius and minimus	Superior gluteal	L4, L5, S1
	Tensor fasciae latae	Superior gluteal	L4, L5, S1
Medial rotation	Gluteus minimus	Superior gluteal	L4, L5, S1
	Gluteus medius, anterior fibers	Superior gluteal	L4, L5, S1
	Tensor fasciae latae	Superior gluteal	L4, L5, S1
Lateral rotation	Gluteus maximus	Inferior gluteal	L5, S1, S2
	Sartorius	Femoral	L2–L4
	Obturator internus and superior gemellus	Nerve to obturator internus	L5, S1, S2
	Obturator externus	Obturator	L3, L4
	Quadratus femoris and inferior gemellus	Nerve to quadratus femoris	L4, L5, S1
	Piriformis	Nerve to piriformis	L5, S1, S2

MOVEMENTS AT THE KNEE JOINT

Action	Muscles Involved	Innervation	Major Segments of Innervation
Flexion	Semimembranosus	Sciatic (tibial)	L5, S1
	Semitendinosus	Sciatic (tibial)	L5, S1, S2
	Biceps femoris	Sciatic (tibial)	S1, S2
	—	Sciatic (common peroneal)	L5, S1, S2
	Gracilis	Obturator	L2–L4
	Sartorius	Femoral	L2, L3
	Popliteus	Tibial	L4, L5, S1
	Gastrocnemius	Tibial	S1, S2
Extension	Quadriceps femoris:		
	• Vastus medialis	Femoral	L2–L4
	• Vastus lateralis	Femoral	L2–L4
	• Vastus intermedius	Femoral	L2–L4
	• Rectus femoris	Femoral	L2–L4
Lateral rotation of leg	Gluteus maximus	Inferior gluteal	L5, S1, S2
	Biceps femoris	Sciatic (tibial and common peroneal)	L5, S1, S2
Medial rotation of leg	Popliteus ("unlocks" extended knee)	Tibial	L4, L5, S1
	Semimembranosus	Sciatic (tibial)	L5, S1
	Semitendinosus	Sciatic (tibial)	L5, S1, S2
	Gracilis	Obturator	L2–L4
	Sartorius	Femoral	L2, L3

COMMON KNEE INJURIES

The three **most commonly injured structures at the knee** are the tibial collateral ligament, the medial meniscus, and the ACL (**the terrible triad**).

A blow to the lateral aspect of the knee may sprain the tibial collateral ligament. The attached medial meniscus may also be torn.

Patients with a **medial meniscus tear** have pain when the leg is medially rotated at the knee. **ACL tears** may occur when the tibial collateral ligament and medial meniscus are injured. Patients with a torn ACL have an anterior drawer sign, in which the tibia may be displaced anteriorly from the femur in the flexed knee.

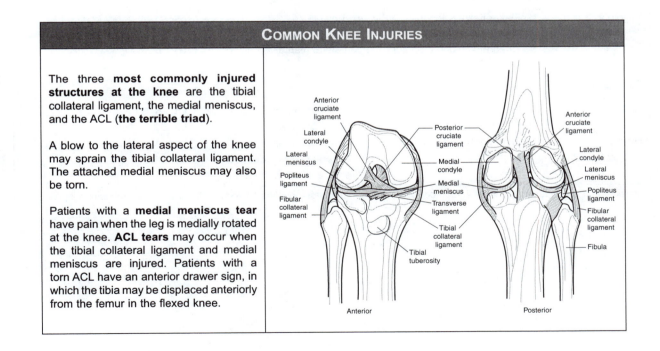

MOVEMENTS AT THE ANKLE JOINT			
Action	Muscles Involved	Innervation	Major Segments of Innervation
Plantar flexion	Gastrocnemius	Tibial	S1, S2
	Soleus	Tibial	S1, S2
	Plantaris	Tibial	L5, S1
Dorsiflexion	Tibialis anterior	Deep peroneal	L4, L5
	Extensor hallucis longus	Deep peroneal	L5, S1

MOVEMENTS AT THE TARSAL (TRANSVERSE TARSAL AND SUBTALAR) JOINTS			
Action	Muscles Involved	Innervation	Major Segments of Innervation
Inversion	Tibialis anterior	Deep peroneal	L4, L5
	Extensor hallucis longus	Deep peroneal	L5, S1
	Tibialis posterior	Tibial	L5, S1
Eversion	Peroneus longus	Superficial peroneal	L5, S1
	Peroneus brevis	Superficial peroneal	L5, S1

MOVEMENTS OF TOES			
Action	Muscles Involved	Innervation	Major Segments of Innervation
Flexion			
All joints	Flexor hallucis longus	Tibial	L5, S1
	Flexor digitorum longus	Tibial	L5, S1
	Quadratus plantae (flexor accessorius)	Lateral plantar	S1, S2
Extension			
All joints	Extensor digitorum longus	Deep peroneal	L4, L5, S1
Toes 2–4	Extensor digitorum brevis	Deep peroneal	L5, S1
Hallux	Extensor hallucis longus	Deep peroneal	L5, S1
IP only toes 2–5	Lumbricals	Lateral plantar, toes 3–5	L5, S1
		Medial plantar, toe 2	S1, S2

Definition of abbreviations: DIP, distal interphalangeal joints; MP, metatarsophalangeal joints; PIP, proximal interphalangeal joints.

MUSCULOSKELETAL DISORDERS

SKELETAL DISORDERS

Achondroplasia

- Autosomal dominant form of dwarfism; mutation of the fibroblast growth factor receptor 3 (FGFR3)
- Abnormal cartilage synthesis
- Decreased epiphyseal bone formation
- Short limbs, proportionately large body and head (disease spares the cranium and vertebral bones), "saddle nose"

Enchondromatosis

- Cartilaginous masses within the medullary cavity of bone
- **Ollier disease:** nonhereditary, multiple, most commonly hands and feet
- Patients present with pain and fractures; may undergo malignant transformation
- **Maffucci syndrome:** Familial; enchondromas and hemangiomas of the skin

Fibrous dysplasia

- Focal fibrous replacement of bone
- Incidence higher in male teenagers
- Usually monostotic; often asymptomatic or may lead to pathologic fracture
- Affects long bones, ribs, skull, and facial bones
- Fibrosis starts within the medullary cavity and remains encased in cortical bone
- **McCune-Albright syndrome:** Association of polyostotic fibrous dysplasia, café-au-lait spots, and sexual precocity in women

Hyperparathyroidism (osteitis fibrosa cystica)

- Osteoclasts resorb bone
- Kidney wastes calcium
- Osteitis fibrosa cystica more common in primary hyperparathyroidism
- Bone pain and fractures
- Fibrous replacement of marrow, causing cystic spaces in bone and "brown tumors"

Hypertrophic osteoarthropathy

- Idiopathic painful swelling of wrists, fingers, ankles, knees, or elbows
- Periosteal inflammation, new bone forms at the ends of long bones, metacarpals, and metatarsals
- Arthritis commonly seen, often with digital clubbing
- Etiology: Intrathoracic carcinoma, cyanotic congenital heart disease, and inflammatory bowel disease
- Regresses when underlying disease treated

Osteochondromatosis

- Bony metaphyseal projections capped with cartilage
- Gardner syndrome: Exostoses and colonic polyps—may become carcinomas

Osteogenesis imperfecta

Defect in type I collagen characterized by fragile bones, blue sclera, and lax ligaments
- *Type I*:   autosomal dominant mild-to-moderate disease
- *Type II*: autosomal recessive stillborn infant; generalized crumpled bones
- *Type III*: autosomal recessive progressive severe deformity; white sclera
- *Type IV:* autosomal dominant variable severity; normal sclera

Osteomalacia and rickets

- **Vitamin D deficiency** due to chronic renal insufficiency, intestinal malabsorption, or dietary deficiency; osteoid produced in normal amounts but not calcified properly (diffuse radiolucency on bone films); low calcium and phosphorus and high alkaline phosphatase
- *Rickets:* children, prior to closure of the epiphyses. Bone deformities, "rachitic rosary" (deformity of the chest wall), bowing of legs, and fractures
- *Osteomalacia:* impaired mineralization of normal osteoid matrix; fractures, deformities

(Continued)

SKELETAL DISORDERS (CONT'D.)

Osteomyelitis

- Spread by direct inoculation of bone or hematogenous seeding
- *Staphylococcus aureus, Streptococcus, Haemophilus influenzae*
- *Salmonella* (sickle cell disease); *Pseudomonas* (intravenous drug users and diabetics)
- *Mycobacterium tuberculosis* (Pott disease): tuberculous osteomyelitis of spine
- Patients present with fever, localized pain, erythema, and swelling
- X-ray may be normal for up to 2 weeks, then may show periosteal elevation
- **Specific findings** include:
  - Sequestrum, a necrotic bone fragment
  - Involucrum, new bone that surrounds the area of inflammation
  - Brodie abscess, localized abscess formation in the bone

Osteopetrosis

- Osteoclasts unable to resorb bone
- Increased density of cortex with narrowing of erythropoietic medullary cavities
- Brittle bones, anemia, blindness, deafness, hydrocephalus, cranial nerve palsies
- *Autosomal recessive:* affects children, causing early death due to anemia and infections (no bone marrow)
- *Autosomal dominant:* adults—fractures

Osteoporosis

- Decrease in bone mass; postmenopausal women
- Estrogen deficiency, low density of original bone, lack of exercise
- Bone formed normally but in decreased amounts (thinned cortical bone, enlarged medullary cavity)
- All bones are affected; x-ray shows generalized radiolucency
- Weight-bearing bones predisposed to fractures

Paget disease

- Excessive bone resorption with replacement by soft, poorly mineralized matrix (woven appearance microscopically); x-ray: enlarged, radiolucent bones
- Patients present with pain, deformity, fractures
- Laboratory tests: extremely elevated alkaline phosphatase
- Polyostotic: skull, pelvis, femur, and vertebrae
- Progresses from an osteolytic to an osteoblastic phase
- May cause bone hypervascularity with increased warmth of the overlying skin

MICROBIOLOGY OF OSTEOMYELITIS

Type Infection	Case Vignette/Key	Most Common Causative Agent	Mechanism of Pathogenesis	Diagnosis	Treatment
Fever, bone pain with erythema and swelling; some patients (particularly those with diabetes) may have associated cellulitis	Adults, children, and infants without major trauma or special conditions	*Staphylococcus aureus*	Hematogenous spread → lytic bone lesions, lytic toxins	Blood culture or bone biopsy	Nafcillin
	Sickle cell anemia	*Salmonella* spp.	HbS patients are functionally asplenic and cannot kill bloodborne pathogens	Gram ⊕, oxidase ⊖, nonlactose fermenting	Sensitivity testing necessary
	Trauma	*Pseudomonas aeruginosa*	Capsule protects against phagocytosis	Gram ⊕, oxidase ⊕, blue-green pigments; grape odor	Sensitivity testing necessary
	Spine, hip, knee, hands. Immigrants—Indian subcontinents	*Mycobacterium tuberculosis*	Tuberculous granuloma erodes into bone	Acid-fast bacilli or auramine stain	Multiple drug therapy

MUSCULOSKELETAL TUMORS	
Osteoblastic Tumors	
Osteoblastoma	Similar to an osteoid osteoma, but is large and painless; often involves vertebrae; may be malignant
Osteoid osteoma	Benign; affects diaphysis of long bones; often tibia or femur Causes pain that is worse at night and relieved by aspirin X-ray findings—central radiolucency surrounded by a sclerotic rim Pathology: brown nodule surrounded by dense sclerotic cortical bone
Osteoma	Benign; frequently involves skull *Hyperostosis frontalis interna*: osteoma that extends into the orbit or sinuses Pathology: dense normal bone
Osteosarcoma	Malignant; produces osteoid and bone **Most common bone tumor** Men are affected more often than women; usually second and third decade of life Associated with Paget disease in older patients Present with localized pain and swelling, weight loss, and anemia Classic x-ray findings—Codman triangle (periosteal elevation) and bone destruction Pathology: large, necrotic, and hemorrhagic mass Poor prognosis; patients are treated with amputation and chemotherapy Metastasis to the lungs common
Chondromatous Tumors	
Chondromyxoid fibroma	Benign, rare; affects young men Firm mass within the metaphyseal marrow cavity of the tibia or femur Contains fibrous and myxomatous tissue; must be differentiated from a malignant lesion
Chondrosarcoma	Malignant tumor; age range 30–60; men affected more than women May arise de novo or secondarily from pre-existing enchondroma Slower growing than osteosarcomas Typically presents with pain and swelling Involves the spine, pelvic bones, and upper extremities
Enchondroma	Solitary cartilaginous growth within the spongiosa of bone Solitary growths are similar to those in the multiple form (Ollier disease)
Osteochondroma	Benign metaphyseal growth; may be solitary; lesions identical to those in multiple form
Miscellaneous Tumors	
Ewing sarcoma	Malignant, rare; usually affects adolescents; often males Arises from mesenchymal cells Presents as pain, tenderness, and early widespread dissemination Commonly affects the pelvis and metaphysis of long tubular bones
Giant cell tumor	Malignant, uncommon; affects ages 20–50; arises in the epiphyseal region of long bones Presents as a bulky mass with pain and tenderness X-ray findings—expanding area of radiolucency without a sclerotic rim

JOINT PATHOLOGY	
Ankylosing spondylitis	Occurs predominantly in young men with HLA-B27 Also associated with inflammatory bowel disease Involves the sacroiliac joints and spine
Felty syndrome	Polyarticular rheumatoid arthritis associated with HLA-B27 Splenomegaly and leukopenia

Gout	**Hyperuricemia** leads to deposition of monosodium urate crystals (**needle-shaped and negatively birefringent**) in joints, leading to recurrent bouts of acute arthritis
	  • Caused by overproduction of uric acid (under 10%) or underexcretion of uric acid (over 90%)
	  • Joints are affected asymmetrically; **great toe** (first metatarsal joint) is classically affected (podagra)
	  • Later stages → chronic arthritis and **tophi** in affected joints
	  • Uric acid kidney stones develop in up to 25% of patients
	Primary gout (90% of cases): due to inborn error of purine metabolism, usually from an unknown enzyme deficiency (Lesch-Nyhan syndrome is a rare cause due to HGPRT deficiency)
	Secondary gout: hyperuricemia unrelated to purine metabolism

Juvenile rheumatoid arthritis (Still disease)	Peak incidence from 1–3 years; girls affected more frequently Often preceded by acute febrile illness Periarticular swelling, lymphadenopathy, hepatosplenomegaly, and absence of rheumatoid factor Variable course; resolution may occur
Osteoarthritis (degenerative joint disease)	Incidence ↑ with age; women more affected than men Affects 80% of people over 70 years old in at least one joint Aging or wear and tear (biomechanical) most important mechanism Insidious onset with joint stiffness, ↓ range of motion, and effusions X-ray findings—narrowing of the joint space due to loss of cartilage and osteosclerosis Joint fluid—few cells and normal mucin Most commonly affected joints—vertebrae, hips, knees, and distal interphalangeal (DIP) joints of fingers
Pseudogout (chondrocalcinosis)	Calcium pyrophosphate crystal deposition Associated with multiple diseases (e.g., Wilson disease, hypothyroidism, diabetes mellitus)
Psoriatic arthritis	Similar to rheumatoid arthritis, but absence of rheumatoid factor Associated with HLA-B27
Rheumatoid arthritis	Progressive arthritis More common in women, ages 20–60 years Autoimmune reaction with the formation of circulating antibodies (rheumatoid factor) Symptoms—low-grade fever, malaise, fatigue, and morning stiffness Physical examination—joint swelling, redness, and warmth Synovial fluid—increased cells (usually neutrophils) and poor mucin Elevated sedimentation rate and hypergammaglobulinemia X-ray findings—erosions and osteoporosis Starts in the small joints of the hands and feet but may involve any joint; usually symmetric involvement
Suppurative arthritis	Tender, red, swollen joint (e.g., "a hot knee") Monoarticular; high neutrophil count in joint fluid Due to *Staphylococcus*, *Streptococcus*, and gonococci **Reiter syndrome:** arthritis, uveitis, and conjunctivitis—possibly due to *Chlamydia*

	INFECTIOUS ARTHRITIS				
Presentation	Case Vignette/ Key Clues	Most Common Causative Agent	Mechanism of Pathogenesis	Diagnosis	Treatment
Pain, redness, low-grade fever, tenderness, swelling, reduced joint mobility	#1 overall, except in the 15–40 age group, where gonococcal is more prevalent	*Staphylococcus aureus*	Coagulase inhibits phagocytosis	Gram ⊕, coagulase ⊕ cocci, catalase ⊕	Nafcillin
	15–40 years; mono- or polyarticular	*Neisseria gonorrhoeae*	Pili mediate adherence and inhibit phagocytosis	Gram – diplococcus; does not ferment maltose or glucose	e.g., ceftriaxone
	Prosthetic joint	Coagulase-negative staphylococci	Biofilm allows adherence to Teflon®	Gram ⊕, catalase ⊕ cocci	Sensitivity testing necessary
	Viral	Rubella and hepatitis B, parvovirus	Immune complex mediated (type III hypersensitivity)	Detect immune complexes	Immunosuppressive therapy
	Chronic onset, monoarticular, weightbearing joints	*M. tuberculosis* or fungal	Granulomas erode into bone	Acid-fast bacillus or auramine stain, fungus stain	Multiple drug therapy

The rheumatoid arthritis (RA) **medications** can be divided into **three major classes**: antiinflammatory drugs, bridging therapy, and disease-modifying antirheumatic drugs (DMARDs). Pharmacologic goals of therapy are to decrease pain, maintain "normal" functional status, reduce inflammation, decrease disease progression, and facilitate healing.

Drug	Mechanism/Other Uses	Adverse Effects
Antiinflammatory Drugs		
Salicylates (aspirin)	**Irreversibly** inhibit COX-1 and -2, decreasing PG synthesis • Low dose: ↓ platelet aggregation • Intermediate dose: antipyretic, analgesic • High dose: antiinflammatory	• Chronic use associated with gastric ulcers, upper GI bleeding, acute renal failure, and interstitial nephritis • Large doses can produce tinnitus, vertigo, respiratory alkalosis • Overdose → metabolic acidosis, hyperthermia, dehydration, coma, death
NSAIDs (ibuprofen, naproxen, diclofenac, ketoprofen, indomethacin)	**Reversibly** inhibit COX-1 and -2, leading to decreased production of PGs Antiinflammatory, analgesic, antipyretic; indomethacin used to close PDA	• Abdominal distress, bleeding, ulceration • Renal damage (especially in patients with renal disease) due to clearance by kidney
COX-2 inhibitors (celecoxib)	Selectively inhibit COX-2 **COX-1 pathway:** produces PGs that protect the GI lining, maintain renal blood flow, and aid in blood clotting **COX-2 pathway:** produces PGs involved in inflammation and pain	• Beneficial because of reduced GI side effects • This drug class is under scrutiny due to ↑ incidence of stroke and MI. At this time, rofecoxib and valdecoxib have been taken off the market.
DMARDs	• May slow or reverse joint damage • Indicated for the treatment of RA when anti-inflammatory therapy insufficient to control patient's symptomatology • DMARDs usually do not show benefit for 6–8 weeks or longer; so, **bridging therapy** (corticosteroids) may be used until a full therapeutic effect is obtained. • DMARDs have severe and potentially fatal side effects.	
Hydroxychloroquine	• Stabilizes lysosomes, ↓ chemotaxis • Also an antimalarial	Ophthalmic abnormalities, dermatologic reactions, hematotoxicity, GI reactions
Methotrexate	• Inhibits dihydrofolate reductase, immunosuppressant • Also an antineoplastic	Hemotoxicity, ulcerative stomatitis, renal toxicity, elevated LFTs
Sulfasalazine	• Metabolized to 5-aminosalicylic acid (5-ASA) and sulfapyridine; parent drug and/or metabolites have anti-inflammatory and/or immunomodulatory properties • Used in inflammatory bowel disease	Rash, GI distress, headache, hematotoxicity
Gold compounds	• ↓ macrophage and lysosomal functions	Dermatitis, hematotoxicity, nephrotoxicity
Azathioprine	• ↓ purine metabolism and nucleic acid synthesis; immunosuppressant	Hematologic, GI disturbance, secondary infection, increased risk of neoplasia
Penicillamine	• ↓ T-cell activity and rheumatoid factor • Also a chelating agent	GI disturbances, proteinuria, bone marrow suppression, neurotoxicity
Etanercept	Binds TNF	Injection site reactions
Leflunomide	Inhibits cell proliferation and antiinflammatory	Hepatotoxicity, immunosuppression, GI disturbance, alopecia, rash, teratogen
Infliximab	• Monoclonal antibody to TNF-α • Also used in inflammatory bowel disease	Infusion reactions, infections, activation of latent TB

Definition of abbreviations: COX, cyclooxygenases; DMARDs, disease-modifying, slow-acting antirheumatic drugs; LFTs, liver function tests; PGs, prostaglandins; TNF, tumor necrosis factor; TB, tuberculosis.

DRUGS USED IN THE TREATMENT OF GOUT

There are **three** primary ways of treating gout: *1*) decreasing inflammation in acute attacks (NSAIDs, colchicine, intra-articular steroids), *2*) using uricosuric drugs to increase renal acceleration of uric acid, and *3*) decreasing conversion of purines to uric acid by inhibiting xanthine oxidase (allopurinol).

Agents	Mechanism	Comments
Acute treatment of gout	Acute treatment measures include NSAIDs (primarily indomethacin), colchicine, and corticosteroids (used only in resistant cases).	
NSAIDs	(*See* Rheumatoid Arthritis Drugs table.)	**Indomethacin** is drug of choice for acute gouty arthritis, although other NSAIDs also effective
Colchicine	**Binds tubulin and prevents microtubule assembly** Reduces the inflammatory response by decreasing leukocyte migration and phagocytosis	Previously considered drug of choice for gouty arthritis; however, its side effect profile limits its usage **Adverse effects:** severe diarrhea and abdominal distress, hematologic (bone marrow depression, aplastic anemia, or thrombocytopenia), renal failure, hepatic failure, peripheral neuropathy, alopecia
Chronic/prophylactic treatment of gout	These agents are used for the treatment and/or prevention of hyperuricemia with gout and gouty arthritis.	
Uricosuric agents (probenecid, sulfinpyrazone)	**Inhibits reabsorption of uric acid**, thus ↑ its excretion	Inhibits the secretion of many weak acids (e.g., penicillin, methotrexate) **Adverse reactions:** may precipitate acute gouty arthritis, which can be prevented by concurrent NSAIDs; cross-allergenicity with other sulfonamides
Allopurinol	**Inhibits xanthine oxidase**, the enzyme responsible for conversion of hypoxanthine and xanthine to uric acid	Also used as an adjunct to cancer chemotherapy Inhibits metabolism of 6-mercaptopurine and azathioprine (which are metabolized by xanthine oxidase) **Adverse reactions:** GI distress, rash

TUMORS INVOLVING JOINT SPACE

Malignant fibrous histiocytoma	Relatively common, affecting adult men > women Arise in soft tissue or bones Lower extremities > upper; also abdominal cavity
Pigmented villonodular synovitis	Villous proliferation of synovium colored brown by hemosiderin deposition Probably a reactive response to recurrent trauma or possibly a neoplastic process that does not metastasize
Synoviosarcoma	Rare tumor, early adulthood; affects males and females equally Slow growing, painless masses Aggressive, early metastases to the lung and pleura Two-thirds occur in lower extremities and one-third in upper extremities Arise from synovial lining cells of bursae and tendon sheaths

MUSCLE DISORDERS

Muscular Dystrophies

Becker muscular dystrophy	X-linked recessive inheritance or spontaneous Milder; patients may walk until age 20 or 25 Cardiac lesions are mild
Duchenne muscular dystrophy	Severe, **X-linked**, abnormal **dystrophin** protein, loss of muscle cell membrane stability Elevation of creatine kinase and histologic degeneration precedes clinical features Pelvic girdle weakness and ataxia Course is progressive; children unable to walk by the age of 10 Pseudohypertrophy of the calves characteristic Myocardial muscle involvement accompanies other muscle degeneration; may cause death Heterozygous female carriers have subclinical degeneration of muscle fibers
Facioscapulohumeral muscular dystrophy	Autosomal dominant, but spontaneous mutation relatively common Usually involves the face, neck, and shoulder muscles; pelvic muscles in later stages
Limb-girdle muscular dystrophy	Autosomal recessive Weakness begins in pelvic or shoulder girdle; may retain ambulation for 25 years
Myotonic dystrophy	Autosomal dominant pattern or spontaneous mutations Trinucleotide repeat (CAG) in a protein kinase Clinically unique: weakness, atrophy, and myotonia (tonic contractions) Head and neck muscles frequently weak and atrophic

Additional Muscular Disorders

Myasthenia gravis	**Autoimmune** disease; antibodies against **neuromuscular junction acetylcholine receptors** (nicotinic AChR) Typically affects young women with **fluctuating weakness** but **no sensory** abnormalities; worsens with increased use of muscles Diagnosis—decremental response on EMG or improvement with **edrophonium** May have **thymic abnormalities**, including thymoma (10–20%) or thymic hyperplasia (70–80%)
Myositides	**Polymyositis** and **dermatomyositis**; autoimmune or collagen vascular diseases Polymyositis more common in females Neck and proximal limb muscle weakness, dysphagia, and muscle pain Dermatomyositis: purple discoloration of the eyelids (heliotrope rash) and ↑ risk of internal malignancies
Myositis ossificans	Ossification at the site of traumatic hemorrhage Pain, swelling, and tenderness
Rhabdomyosarcoma	Most common soft tissue sarcoma in children 40% have metastases at the time of diagnosis **Embryonal rhabdomyosarcoma:** • Most often located in head and neck tissues • Sarcoma botryoides: embryonal rhabdomyosarcoma with a grape-like, soft, polypoid appearance usually located in the genitourinary or upper respiratory tract

Definition of abbreviation: EMG, electromyogram.

SKIN

SKIN AND SKIN APPENDAGES

The integument consists of the skin (epidermis and dermis) and associated appendages (sweat and sebaceous glands, hairs, and nails). The epidermis is devoid of blood vessels and contains a stratified squamous epithelium derived primarily from ectoderm.

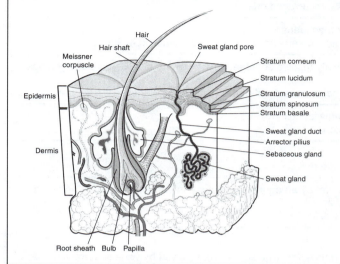

The **epidermis** is composed of five layers in thick skin:

- **Stratum basale:** a proliferative layer of columnar/cuboidal cells

- **Stratum spinosum:** a multilaminar layer of cuboidal/polygonal cells

- **Stratum granulosum:** has more flattened polygonal cells containing basophilic granules

- **Stratum lucidum:** a thin, eosinophilic layer of squamous cells

- **Stratum corneum:** a thick layer containing anucleate keratinized cells

- The **epidermis** contains four cell types: **keratinocytes**, which produce keratin; **melanocytes** (derived from neural crest) that produce melanin; **Langerhans cells**, which are antigen-presenting cells; and **Merkel cells**, associated with nerve fibers.
- The **dermis** is a connective tissue layer mainly of mesodermal origin.
- **Sweat glands** may be eccrine or apocrine.
- **Sebaceous glands** are branched, holocrine acinar glands that discharge their secretions onto hair shafts within hair follicles. They are absent in the palms and soles.
- **Hair** is composed of keratinized epidermal cells. Hair follicles and the associated sebaceous glands are known as pilosebaceous units.

SKIN PATHOLOGY	
Actinic keratosis	Premalignant and may develop into squamous cell carcinoma Fair-skinned people of middle age associated with chronic sun exposure
Basal cell carcinoma	Rough, crusty, red papules up to 1 cm in diameter Invasive, but rarely metastasizes Occurs on sun-exposed areas in middle-aged or elderly individuals with fair complexions Complete excision is usually curative; 50% recurrence rate
Bullous pemphigoid	Autoantibodies to dermoepidermal junction antigens Pemphigus vulgaris is due to autoantibodies to keratinocyte intercellular junction antigens
Capillary hemangiomas	Arise within the first weeks of life and usually resolve spontaneously; starting at 1–3 years of age; most completely gone by age 5 Soft, red, lobulated mass, 1–6 cm in diameter, composed of thick-walled capillaries
Dermatitis herpetiformis	Vesicular, pruritic disease often associated with celiac sprue IgA is found at the dermoepidermal junction
Erythema multiforme	Hypersensitivity reaction to drugs Stevens-Johnson syndrome is the severe form.
Kaposi sarcoma	Malignant mesenchymal tumor characterized by an aggressive course in patients with AIDS and by a slower course in elderly men without HIV Caused by human herpes virus type 8 (HHV8)
Malignant melanoma	Peaks by ages 40–60 **Lentigo maligna** melanoma grows horizontally first (radial growth), followed by vertical dermal invasion (nodular growth) and forms a large, brown-black patch Best prognosis of all forms of melanoma **Nodular** melanoma shows extensive dermal invasion and rapid growth Raised brown-black lesions may be found anywhere on skin or mucosa Worst prognosis of the melanomas Prognosis related to **depth of invasion**
Nevus flammeus (port wine stain)	Common congenital lesion; composed of telangiectatic vessels Usually located on the neck or face as a large, flat, irregular pink patch that tends to resolve spontaneously
Psoriasis	Silvery, scaly plaque that primarily affects knees, elbows, and the scalp
Squamous cell carcinoma	Malignant tumor; most frequently in sun-exposed areas with peak at 60 years of age Preponderance among women When on sun-exposed regions, rarely metastasizes When on unexposed skin, up to 50% metastasize

INFECTIOUS DISEASES OF THE SKIN, MUCOUS MEMBRANES, AND UNDERLYING TISSUES

Case Vignette/ Key Clues	Common Causative Agents	Mechanism of Pathogenesis	Diagnosis	Treatment
Furuncles, carbuncles				
Neck, face, axillae, buttocks	*Staphylococcus aureus*	Coagulase breaks fibrin clot Neutrophils + bacteria → pus	Catalase ⊕, coagulase ⊕, gram ⊕ cocci in grape-like clusters	Nafcillin for methicillin-sensitive *S. aureus* (MSSA); vancomycin for methicillin-resistant *S. aureus* (MRSA)
Inflamed follicles from neck down	*Pseudomonas aeruginosa* (hot tub folliculitis)	Capsule inhibits phagocytosis	Oxidase ⊕, gram ⊖ rod, blue-green pigment, grape odor	Susceptibility testing necessary
Acne vulgaris				
Inflammation of follicles and sebaceous glands; adolescent	*Propionibacterium acnes*	Fatty acids and peptides produced from sebum cause inflammation	Gram ⊕ rod, identified by clinical clues	Tetracycline, erythromycin
Cutaneous Lesions (scratching mosquito bites, cat scratches, etc.)				
Initially vesicular; skin erosion; honey-crusted lesions	*Streptococcus pyogenes*	Streptokinase A and B DNAse, hyaluronidase	Catalase ⊖, gram ⊕ cocci, bacitracin sensitive	Penicillin, erythromycin
Initially vesicular but with longer-lasting bullae	*Staphylococcus aureus*	Exfoliatins produce bullae	Catalase ⊕, coagulase ⊕, gram ⊕ cocci, in clusters	Nafcillin for MSSA; vancomycin for MRSA
Red, raised, butterfly-wing facial rash				
Dermal pain, edema, rapid spread	*Streptococcus pyrogenes* (erysipelas)	M protein inhibits phagocytosis, erythrogenic exotoxins, hyaluronidase	Catalase ⊖, gram ⊕ cocci, bacitracin-sensitive	Penicillin, erythromycin
Jaw area swelling with pain, sinus tract formation, yellow granules in exudate				
Carious teeth, dental extraction or trauma	*Actinomyces israelii*; "lumpy jaw"; actinomycosis	Unknown	Gram ⊕, anaerobic, filamentous branching rods, non-acid fast	Penicillin

(Continued)

Case Vignette/ Key Clues	Common Causative Agents	Mechanism of Pathogenesis	Diagnosis	Treatment
Vesicular lesions				
Sometimes preceded by neurologic pain	Herpes	Virus-rich vesicles ulcerate dsDNA, enveloped (nuclear membranes)	Cell culture, intranuclear inclusion, multinucleated cells	Acyclovir
Sometimes large	*Staphylococcus aureus*	Exfolatins produce bullae	Catalase ⊕, coagulase ⊕, gram ⊕ cocci, in clusters	Nafcillin for MSSA; vancomycin for MRSA
Subcutaneous granulomas/ulcers/cellulitis				
Tropical fish enthusiasts; granulomatous lesion (most commonly freshwater)	*Mycobacterium marinum*	Trauma + water exposure → granulomas form	Biopsy, slow growing acid-fast bacilli	Clarithromycin initially, then antimycobacterial therapy
Cellulitis following contact with saltwater or oysters	*Vibrio vulnificus*	Cytolytic compounds, antiphagocytic polysaccharides	Green colonies on TCBS agar (alkaline), gram ⊖ rod, oxidase ⊕	Tetracycline, aminoglycosides
Solitary or lymphocutaneous lesions; rose gardeners or florists; sphagnum moss	*Sporothrix schenckii* (rose gardener's disease)	Ulceration or abscess	Cigar-shaped yeast in pus	Potassium iodide, ketoconazole
Subcutaneous swelling (extremities, shoulders), sinus tract formation, granules (mycetoma)	*Actinomyces, Nocardia*	Unknown; granules are microcolonies	*Actinomyces*— Gram ⊕, anaerobic, filamentous branching non-acid fast rods *Nocardia*—partially acid-fast, branching filaments, aerobic	*Actinomyces*— penicillin *Nocardia*—sulfonamide
Malignant pustule				
Pustule → dark-red, fluid-filled, tumor-like lesion → necrosis → black eschar surrounded by red margin; postal worker or wool handler/ importer	*Bacillus anthracis*	Poly-D-glutamate capsule, exotoxin causes edema, cell death Three-component toxin	Gram ⊕, spore-forming, encapsulated rods	Ciprofloxacin, penicillin
Burns, cellulitis				
Blue-green pus; grape-like odor	*Pseudomonas aeruginosa*	Capsule inhibits phagocytosis	Oxidase ⊕, gram ⊖ rod, blue-green pigments, grape odor	Susceptibility testing necessary

(Continued)

INFECTIOUS DISEASES OF THE SKIN, MUCOUS MEMBRANES, AND UNDERLYING TISSUES (*CONT'D.*)

Case Vignette/ Key Clues	Common Causative Agents	Mechanism of Pathogenesis	Diagnosis	Treatment
Wounds				
Surgical wounds (clean)	*Staphylococcus aureus*	Same as above for *S. aureus*	Same as above for *S. aureus*	Nafcillin for MSSA, vancomycin for MRSA
Surgical wounds (dirty)	Enterobacteriaceae, anaerobes	Contamination from fecal flora	Gram ⊖ facultative anaerobes	Susceptibility testing necessary
Trauma with damage to blood supply	*Clostridium perfringens* and others	Alpha toxin (lecithinase) gas production, edema, cytotoxicity	Naegler reaction, anaerobic, gram ⊕ rod, spore forming	Debridement, penicillin
Animal bites	*Pasteurella multocida*	Capsule	Gram ⊖ rods	Amoxicillin/clavulanate
Cat scratches, resulting in lymphadenopathy with stellate granulomas	*Bartonella henselae*	Obligate intracellular	Gram ⊖ envelope	Various antibiotics (rifampin, ciprofloxacin, gentamicin, TMP-sulfamethoxazole)
Shallow puncture wound through tennis shoe sole	*Pseudomonas aeruginosa*	Capsule inhibits phagocytosis	Oxidase ⊕, gram ⊖ rod, blue-green pigments	Susceptibility testing necessary
Leprosy				
Blotchy, red lesions with anesthesia; facial and cooler areas of skin	*Mycobacterium leprae* (tuberculoid form)	Cell-mediated immunity kills intracellular organisms, damages nerves	Acid-fast, intracellular bacilli in punch biopsy, ⊕ lepromin test	Dapsone
Numerous nodular lesions; leonine facies	*Mycobacterium leprae* (lepromatous form)	Humoral immunity elicited does not stop growth of organisms	Acid-fast, intracellular bacilli in punch biopsy, ⊖ lepromin test	Dapsone
Keratinized area of skin (ringworm)				
Reddened skin lesion in growing ring shape, raised margin; infection nail bed or hair shaft	*Trichophyton* spp. (skin, hair, nails) *Epidermophyton* spp. (skin, nails) *Microsporum* spp. (skin, hair)	Fungi germinate in moist areas, invade	Wood's lamp (fluoresce), skin scraping and KOH; arthroconidia	Topical miconazole
Dermatitis				
Itching skin rash after swimming in fresh water lakes (swimmer's itch)	Bird schistosomes	Skin penetration by cercariae → death in skin → hypersensitivity	Clinical signs and history	Topical anti-inflammatory
Snake-like tracks on bare skin exposed to dog/cat feces (plumber's itch, cutaneous larva migrans)	Dog and cat hookworms (*Ancylostoma* spp.)	Skin penetration by larvae → death in skin → hypersensitivity	Clinical signs and history	Topical anti-inflammatory, thiabendazole

(Continued)

Case Vignette/ Key Clues	Common Causative Agents	Mechanism of Pathogenesis	Diagnosis	Treatment
Warts				
Plantar surfaces	HPV 1 and 4 (dsDNA, naked icosahedral)	Virus infects basal layers of skin, stimulates cells to divide	Intranuclear inclusion bodies	Cryotherapy
Umbilicated warts; wrestling teams; may be anogenital	*Molluscum contagiosum* (pox family, dsDNA, enveloped complex)	Infects epidermal cells to form fleshy lesion	Intracytoplasmic inclusions	Cryotherapy
Anogenital warts	HPV 6 and 11 (most common) HPV 16 and 18 (premalignant)	Virus stimulates cell division Cervical intraepithelial neoplasia Tumor suppressor gene inactivation	Intranuclear inclusion bodies	Cryotherapy
Mucocutaneous erosive lesions				
Foreign immigrant, ulcers; chronic facial disfiguration; sandfly vector	*Leishmania* spp.	Amastigotes intracellular in macrophages, proliferate and spread	Finding amastigotes with flagellar pocket inside phagocytic cells in biopsy	Antimonials pentamidine

			SELECTED RASHES			
Type of Rash	Progression	Other Symptoms	Causative Agent(s)	Pathogenesis	Diagnosis	Treatment
Scarlet fever						
Erythematous maculopapular (sandpaper-like)	Trunk and neck → extremities (spares palms and soles)	Sore throat, fever, nausea	*Streptococcus pyogenes*	Exotoxins A–C (superantigens)	Gram ⊕, catalase ⊖ cocci	Penicillin
Toxic shock syndrome						
Diffuse, erythematous, macular sunburn-like	Trunk and neck → extremities with desquamation on palms and soles	Acute onset, fever >102 F, myalgia, pharyngitis, vomiting, diarrhea; hypotension leading to multiorgan failure	*Staphylococcus aureus*	TSST-1 (superantigen)	Gram ⊕, catalase ⊕, coagulase ⊕ cocci	Nafcillin
Staphylococcal skin disease: scalded skin disease and scarlatina						
Perioral erythema, bullae, vesicles, desquamation	Trunk and neck → extremities, except tongue and palate; large bullae and vesicles precede exfoliation	Abscess or some site of infection	*Staphylococcus aureus*	Endotoxin	Gram ⊕, catalase ⊕, coagulase ⊕ cocci	Nafcillin

(*Continued*)

SELECTED RASHES (*CONT'D.*)

Type of Rash	Progression	Other Symptoms	Causative Agent(s)	Pathogenesis	Diagnosis	Treatment
Epidemic typhus						
Petechiae → purpura	Trunk → extremities; spares palms, soles, and face	Fever, rash, headache, myalgias, and respiratory symptoms	*Rickettsia prowazekii*	Endotoxin	Serology, Weil-Felix	Tetracycline, erythromycin
Rocky Mountain spotted fever (most common on East Coast)						
Petechiae	Ankles and wrists → generalized with palms and soles	Fever, rash, headache, myalgias, and respiratory symptoms	*Rickettsia rickettsii*	Endotoxin (overproduces outer membrane fragments)	Serology, Weil-Felix	Tetracycline, erythromycin
Early meningococcemia						
Petechiae → purpura	Generalized	Abrupt onset, fever, chills, malaise, prostration, exanthem → shock	*Neisseria meningitidis*	Endotoxin	Gram ⊖ diplococcus on chocolate agar; LPA for capsular antigens	Ceftriaxone
Secondary syphilis						
Skin: maculopapular; mucous membrane: condylomata lata	Generalized bronze rash involving the palms and soles	Fever, lymphadenopathy, malaise, sore throat, splenomegaly, headache, arthralgias	*Treponema pallidum*	Endotoxin	Serology: VDRL (nonspecific), FTA-ABS (specific)	Penicillin
Measles						
Confluent, erythematous, maculopapular rash, unvaccinated child	Head → entire body Koplik spots	Cough, coryza, conjunctivitis, and fever (prodrome); oral lesions, exanthem, bronchopneumonia, ear infections (unvaccinated individual)	Rubeola virus; negative sense RNA virus, non-segmented = Paramyxovirus	T-cell destruction of virus-infected cells in capillaries causes rash	Virus cultures, serology	Supportive

The Hematologic and Lymphoreticular System

HEMATOPOIESIS

All of the different blood cells are derived from stem cells in the bone marrow, as shown below.

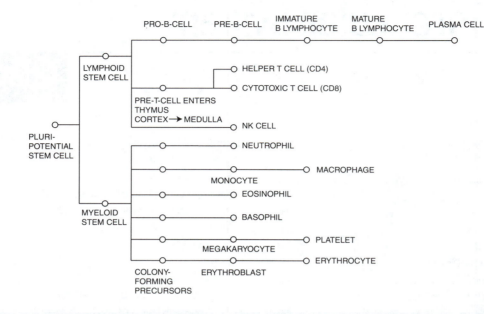

HEMOSTASIS

Hemostasis is the sequence of events leading to the cessation of bleeding by the formation of a stable fibrin-platelet plug. It involves the vascular wall, platelets, and the coagulation system.

Platelet Function and Dysfunction

Platelets are anuclear, membrane-bound cellular fragments derived from megakaryocytes in the bone marrow. They have a short lifespan of approximately 10 days. There are normally 150,000–400,000 platelets per mm^3 of blood. Platelet activity is measured by **template bleeding time**. Clinically, dysfunction is seen as **petechiae**. The platelet reaction consists of three steps. Dysfunction of each step is associated with different diseases:

- Adhesion (e.g., von Willebrand disease, Bernard-Soulier syndrome)
- Primary aggregation (e.g., thrombasthenia)
- Secondary aggregation and release (e.g., aspirin, storage pool disease)

FORMATION OF THE PLATELET PLUG	
Vascular wall injury	• Injury causes exposure of subendothelial extracellular collagen • Arteriolar contraction due to reflex neurogenic mechanisms, and the local release of **endothelin** occurs
Adhesion	• **von Willebrand factor (vWF)** binds exposed collagen fibers in the basement membrane • Platelets adhere to vWF via **glycoprotein Ib** and become **activated** (shape change, degranulation, synthesis of **thromboxane A_2, TxA_2**) • Deficiency of vWF → **von Willebrand disease**; deficiency of glycoprotein Ib receptor → **Bernard-Soulier syndrome**
Release reaction	• Release contents of platelet dense bodies (e.g., **ADP, calcium**, serotonin, histamine, epinephrine) and alpha granules (fibrinogen, fibronectin, factor V, vWF, platelet-derived growth factor) • Membrane expression of phospholipid complexes (important for coagulation cascade)
Aggregation	• **ADP** and **thromboxane A_2** (**TxA_2**) is released by **platelets** and **promote aggregation** (TXA_2 production is inhibited by **aspirin**) • Cross-linking of platelets by **fibrinogen** requires the **GpIIb/IIIa receptor**, which is deficient in **Glanzmann thrombasthenia** • Decreased endothelial synthesis of antithrombogenic substances (e.g., prostacyclin, nitric oxide, tissue plasminogen activator, thrombomodulin)

VON WILLEBRAND DISEASE
• Autosomal dominant defect • Impaired platelet adhesion • Spontaneous hemorrhage from mucous membranes; increases bleeding time and PTT (vWF stabilizes factor VIII)

DISORDERS OF PLATELET NUMBERS	
Thrombocytopenia	• **Decrease** in the platelet count (normal = 150,000–400,000/mm^3) • **Clinical features:** bleeding from small vessels, often skin, GI/GU tracts; **petechiae** and **purpura** are seen • **Classification:** decreased production (aplastic anemia, drugs, vitamin B$_{12}$ or folate deficiency); increased destruction, (e.g., DIC, TTP, ITP, drugs, malignancy); abnormal sequestration
Idiopathic thrombocytopenic purpura (ITP)	• Spleen makes antibodies against platelet antigens (e.g., GpIIb–IIIa, GpIb–IX); platelets destroyed in the spleen by macrophages • Acute form (children): self-limited, postviral • Chronic form (adults): ITP may be primary or secondary to another disorder (e.g., HIV, SLE) • Smear shows enlarged, immature platelets; normal PT and PTT • Treatment: corticosteroids, immunoglobulin therapy, splenectomy
Thrombotic thrombocytopenic purpura (TTP)	• **Clinical features:** pentad (thrombocytopenic purpura, fever, renal failure, neurologic changes, microangiopathic hemolytic anemia); usually in young women • Smear shows few platelets, schistocytes, and helmet cells • **Hemolytic uremic syndrome (HUS):** mostly in children after gastroenteritis with bloody diarrhea; organism: verotoxin-producing *E. coli* O157:H7; similar clinical triad
Thrombocytosis (reactive)	Increase in count due to bleeding, hemolysis, inflammation, malignancy, iron deficiency, stress, or postsplenectomy
Essential thrombocythemia	Increase in count due to primary myeloproliferative disorder

COAGULATION

Coagulation begins anywhere from a few seconds to 1–2 minutes after an injury.

Intrinsic Pathway

- **Factor XII** (Hageman factor) is activated on contact with the collagen

- "a" indicates activated form

Extrinsic Pathway

Initiated by exposure to tissue thromboplastin

Common Pathway

Factors IXa, VIIa, VIIIa, platelet phospholipids, and calcium activate factor X

Thrombin (IIa):

- Able to catalyze own activation

- Increases platelet aggregation

- Activates **factor XIII** (fibrin-stabilizing factor) and potentiates binding of factors V and VIII to phospholipid/Ca^{2+} complex

Fibrinogen (I):

- Split into self-polymerizing fibrin monomers

- Initially bind via loose hydrogen and hydrophobic bonds

- **Factor XIII** catalyzes formation of strong covalent bonds

Vitamin K–Dependent Factors

Factors II (prothrombin), VII, IX, X, protein C, and protein S

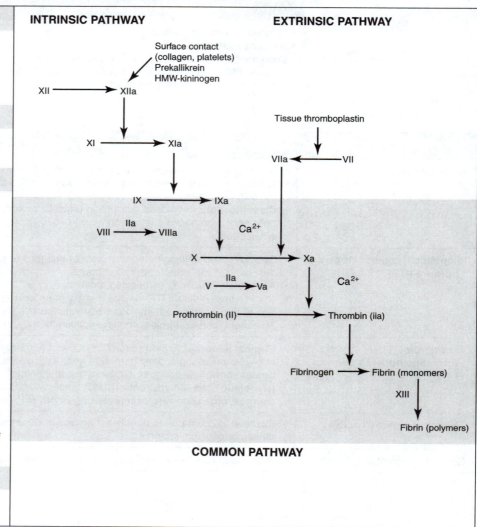

FINAL STEP: CLOT RETRACTION AND DISSOLUTION

- After the clot is formed, it begins to shrink.
- Edges of small wounds are pulled together by platelet actinomyosin.
- Fibrinolysis (dissolution) requires activation of plasminogen.
- Clot releases plasminogen activator, which converts plasminogen to plasmin, which in turn proteolyses fibrinogen and fibrin.
- Urokinase and streptokinase are exogenous sources of plasminogen activation. Tissue plasminogen activator (t-PA) is endogenously produced, but can also be administered as a drug in the setting of acute myocardial infarction.

Laboratory Tests of Coagulation System

Test	Measures	Specific Coagulation Factors Involved
Prothrombin time (PT)	Extrinsic and common coagulation pathways	VII, X, V, prothrombin, fibrinogen
Partial thromboplastin time (PTT)	Intrinsic and common coagulation pathways	XII, XI, IX, VIII, X, V, prothrombin, fibrinogen
Thrombin time (TT)	Fibrinogen levels	Fibrinogen
Fibrin degradation products (FDP)	Fibrinolytic system	—

Physiologic Regulation Of Clotting Cascade		Pathologic Dysregulation Of Clotting Cascade	
Fibrin	Adsorbs most of the thrombin, keeping it from spreading	**Factor VIII deficiency (hemophilia A)**	X-linked Severe cases bleed in infancy at circumcision or have multiple hemarthrosis Moderate cases have occasional hemarthrosis Mild cases may be missed until dental or surgical procedure Bleeding may require treatment with cryoprecipitate or lyophilized factor VIII
Antithrombin III	α-globulin that binds to and inactivates thrombin	**Factor IX deficiency (Christmas disease, hemophilia B)**	X-linked recessive Signs and symptoms same as hemophilia A
Laminar flow	Keeps platelets away from blood vessel walls	**Vitamin K deficiency**	Fat-soluble, produced by gut flora Essential in the post-translational modification of factors II, VII, IX, and X, as well as proteins C and S Vitamin K deficiency may result from fat malabsorption, diarrhea, antibiotics
Heparin	Polysaccharide produced by many cell types, promotes antithrombin inhibition of thrombin	**Liver disease**	Factors II, V, VII, IX, X, XI, and XII synthesized in the liver
Protein C and protein S	Vitamin K–dependent Endogenous anticoagulants Protein C is activated by thrombin bound to thrombomodulin In the presence of protein S, activated protein C promotes anticoagulation by inactivating factors V and VIII Protein C also promotes fibrinolysis by inactivating t-PA inhibitor, thereby promoting t-PA fibrinolytic activity	**Protein C deficiency** **Factor V Leiden (protein C resistance)**	Develop frequent deep venous and arterial thrombosis

Disseminated Intravascular Coagulation (DIC)

- Massive, persistent activation of both coagulation system and fibrinolytic system
- Consumption deficiency of clotting factors and platelets
- Morbidity/mortality from DIC may be related to either thrombosis or hemorrhage
- **Etiologies:** amniotic fluid embolism, infections (particularly gram-negative sepsis), malignancy, and major traumas, particularly head injury
- **Diagnosis:** low platelets, low fibrinogen, increased PT, increased PTT, and presence of fibrin degradation products

ANTICLOTTING AGENTS

Anticlotting agents are used in the treatment of ischemic stroke, deep venous thrombosis, myocardial infarction, and atrial fibrillation. Anticoagulants and thrombolytics work in arterial and venous circulations; antiplatelets act in the arterial circulation. Bleeding is the most important adverse effect of these agents.

CLASS	MECHANISM	COMMENTS/AGENTS
Anticoagulants	Decrease fibrin clot formation. Differ in pharmacokinetics/pharmacodynamics. **Heparin** is used when immediate anticoagulation is necessary (acute MI, DVT, pulmonary embolism, stroke, beginning therapy); **warfarin** is used chronically. LMWHs have a longer half-life than does heparin.	
Heparin (IV, SC) LMWHs	Binds **AT-III**; this complex inactivates **thrombin**, factors IXa, **Xa**, and XIIa	Acts in **seconds**; used acutely (days) aPTT used to monitor heparin, not LMWHs **Protamine** reverses heparin and LMWHs Used in pregnancy **LMWHs** (ardeparin, dalteparin, enoxaparin) inhibit **factor Xa** more and thrombin less than heparin
Warfarin (**PO**)	Interferes with the synthesis of the vitamin K–dependent clotting factors (II, VII, IX, X)	Takes 2–5 **days** to fully work; chronic use **PT** used to monitor **Vitamin K** reverses effect **Not** used in pregnancy **Cytochrome P450**–inducing drugs ↓ effect; cytochrome P450 inhibitors ↑ effect
Direct thrombin inhibitors	Bind directly to thrombin substrates and/or thrombin (ATIII not required) Bind to soluble thrombin and clot-bound thrombin	**Lepirudin**, bivalirudin, argatroban, hirudin
Antiplatelets	Platelets adhere to site of vascular injury, where they are activated by various factors to express a glycoprotein to which fibrogen binds, resulting in platelet aggregation and formation of a platelet plug. Antiplatelet drugs inhibit this process, thus reducing the chances of thrombi formation.	
COX inhibitors	Block COX-1 and COX-2, thereby inhibiting **thromboxane A_2**–mediated platelet aggregation	**Aspirin**—also antipyretic, antiinflammatory, analgesic Affected platelets are impaired for their lifespan (9–12 days) Side effects—tinnitus, ↓ renal function, GI ulceration/bleeding, Reye syndrome
ADP antagonists	Irreversibly inhibit ADP-mediated platelet aggregation	**Ticlopidine, clopidogrel**
Glycoprotein IIb/IIIa inhibitors	Reversibly inhibit binding of fibrin to platelet glycoprotein IIb/IIIa, preventing platelet cross-linking	**Abciximab**, eptifibatide, tirofiban
PDE/adenosine uptake inhibitors	Inhibit phosphodiesterase 2, thereby ↑ cAMP → inhibits platelet aggregation Block adenosine uptake → less adenosine A2 stimulation → ↑ cAMP	**Dipyridamole**, cilostazol
Thrombolytics	**Convert plasminogen → plasmin**, leading to fibrinolysis and breakdown of clots. Used IV for short-term emergency management of coronary thromboses in MI, DVT, pulmonary embolism, and ischemic stroke (t-PA).	
	t-PAs are thought to convert fibrin-bound plasminogen, thus targeting clots; others are not clot specific	Alteplase, reteplase (**t-PA derivatives**) Streptokinase, urokinase

Definition of abbreviations: ADP, adenosine diphosphate; aPTT, activated partial thromboplastic time; ATIII, antithrombin III; COX, cyclo-oxygenase; DVT, deep venous thrombosis; GI, gastrointestinal; IV, intravenous(ly); LMWH, low molecular weight heparin; MI, myocardial infarction; PO, by mouth; PT, prothrombin time; SC, subcutaneously; t-PA, tissue plasminogen activator.

DRUGS USED IN BLEEDING DISORDERS		
Antifibrinolytic (aminocaproic acid, tranexamic acid)	Inhibits fibrinolysis by inhibiting plasminogen-activating substances	Prevents and treats bleeding in hemophiliacs during dental and surgical procedures
Vitamin K	Plays a role in coagulation by acting as a cofactor for clotting factors II, VII, IX, and X	Indicated for treatment of warfarin overdose, as well as vitamin deficiency
Oprelvekin (IL-11)	Stimulates bone marrow platelet production via stimulation of IL-11 receptor	Used to prevent thrombocytopenia after antineoplastic therapy Edema commonly occurs
Desmopressin (DDAVP)	A synthetic analog of arginine vasopressin; causes a dose-related release of factor VIII and vWF from storage sites	Hemophilia A and von Willebrand disease

ERYTHROPOIESIS

Erythropoiesis is the process of RBC formation. Bone marrow stem cells (colony-forming units, CFUs) differentiate into proerythroblasts under the influence of the glycoprotein **erythropoietin**, which is produced by the kidney.

Proerythroblasts → **basophilic erythroblasts** → **normoblasts (nucleus extruded)** → **reticulocyte (still contains some ribosomes)** → **erythrocyte** (remain in the circulation approximately 120 days and are then recycled by the spleen, liver, and bone marrow)

DISORDERS OF RED BLOOD CELLS

POLYCYTHEMIA (INCREASE IN RED BLOOD CELL MASS)	
Polycythemia vera (primary)	• Myeloproliferative syndrome • Males age 40–60 • Vessels distended with viscous blood, congestive hepatosplenomegaly, and diffuse hemorrhages • Management is generally with therapeutic phlebotomy
Secondary polycythemia	• Increased erythropoietin levels • Etiologies: high altitude, cigarette smoking, respiratory, renal and cardiac disease and malignancies (e.g., renal cell carcinoma, hepatoma, leiomyoma, adrenal adenoma, cerebellar hemangioblastoma)
Relative polycythemia	Fluid loss with stable RBC mass (vomiting, diarrhea, burns)

Secondary to decreased production, increased destruction, sometimes both

Symptoms: palpitations, high-output heart failure, pallor, fatigue, dizziness, syncope, and angina

Decreased Production (Low Reticulocyte Count)	
Decreased production (low reticulocyte count) **Iron deficiency** (smear: hypochromic, microcytic)	• An important differential feature between the thalassemia traits and iron deficiency is that thalassemia traits result in an elevated number of microcytes, whereas iron deficiency results in a decreased number of microcytes. • Serum iron, total iron-binding capacity (TIBC), and ferritin confirm the diagnosis.
Megaloblastic—B_{12}/folate (smear: macrocytic, hypersegmented neutrophils)	• Impaired DNA synthesis • Vitamin B_{12} deficiency neurologic (subacute combined degeneration) and hematologic sequelae • **Vitamin B_{12}:** copious body stores, years to develop deficiency *Causes:* dietary deficiency, malabsorption, tapeworm, bacterial overgrowth, deficiency of intrinsic factor (pernicious anemia) • **Folate:** deficiency develops much more quickly (months) *Causes:* deficient intake (poor diet, alcoholism, malabsorption), increased need (pregnancy, malignancy, increased hematopoiesis), or impaired use (antimetabolite drugs) • Must treat patient with both folate and B_{12}. Folate may reverse anemia in a B_{12} deficiency but not neurologic complications
Aplastic	• Pancytopenia • *Multiple etiologies:* idiopathic, drugs, including alkylating agents, chloramphenicol, radiation, infections, and congenital anomalies (i.e., Fanconi anemia) • Prognosis is poor • Bone marrow transplant may be curative
Myelophthisic	Displacement of hematopoietic bone marrow by infiltrating tumor
Myeloid metaplasia with myelofibrosis	• Chronic myeloproliferative disorder with small numbers of neoplastic myeloid stem cells • Resultant bone marrow fibrosis leads to pancytopenia

Thalassemias		
Types	**Key Points**	**Clinical Picture**
ALPHA	Secondary to gene deletion: **four** genes can be deleted: **1 deleted:** silent carrier **3 deleted:** HbH disease **2 deleted:** trait **4 deleted:** hydrops fetalis, Bart Hb	• Variable clinical severity • Non α-chain aggregates less toxic • Mild hemolysis and anemia tend to be milder; Bart's in the neonate leads to anoxia and intrauterine death
BETA	• Defects in mRNA processing. • Homozygous: β-thalassemia major • Heterozygotes: β-thalassemia minor	• Mediterranean countries, Africa, and Southeast Asia • Relative excess of α chains; Hb aggregates and becomes insoluble • Intra- and extramedullary hemolysis • Extramedullary hematopoiesis • Secondary hemochromatosis
HB ELECTROPHORESIS	• α-Thalassemia: normal HbA_2 and HbF • β-Thalassemia minor (trait): elevated HbA_2, HbF	

Increased Destruction (Normal–High Reticulocyte Count)	
Blood loss	Loss rather than destruction
	Clinical features depend on rate and severity of blood loss
	Chronic loss better tolerated, regenerate by increasing erythropoiesis
	Acute blood loss: possible hypovolemia may lead to shock and death
	Hematocrit may be initially normal because of equal plasma and RBC loss; will decrease as interstitial fluid equilibrates
	Extravascular—premature RBC destruction, hemoglobin (Hb) breakdown, and a compensatory increase in erythropoiesis
	Intravascular—elevated serum and urinary Hb, jaundice, urinary hemosiderin, and decreased circulating haptoglobin. Bile pigment gallstones arise from chronic, not acute hemolysis
Warm hemolytic anemia	IgG
	Secondary to drugs, malignancy, and SLE
Cold hemolytic anemia	IgM
	Functions below body temperature in the periphery
	Associated with mononucleosis, *Mycoplasma* infection, idiopathic hemolytic anemia, and hemolytic anemia associated with lymphoma
Paroxysmal hemolytic anemia	IgG
	Functions in the periphery
Hereditary spherocytosis *Presplenectomy smear:* spherical cells lacking central pallor and reticulocytosis *Postsplenectomy smear:* more spherocytes and Howell-Jolly bodies	Autosomal dominant defect in spectrin
	Less pliable; vulnerable to destruction in the spleen
	Anemia, jaundice, splenomegaly, cholelithiasis
	Exhibit characteristically increased osmotic fragility
	Treatment: splenectomy
G6PD deficiency *Smear:* reticulocytosis and Heinz bodies (Hb degradation products)	X-linked deficiency of the enzyme (hexose monophosphate shunt)
	Decreased regeneration of NADPH, therefore glutathione
	Older cells unable to tolerate oxidative stress
	Associated with drugs (e.g., sulfa, quinine, nitrofurantoin), infections (particularly viral), or certain foods (fava beans)
Paroxysmal nocturnal hemoglobinuria	Acquired deficiency of a membrane glycoprotein
	Chronic intravascular hemolysis
	Predisposes to stem cell disorders (e.g., aplastic anemia, acute leukemia)
	Most frequently die of infection or venous thrombosis

Sickle Cell Disease		
Incidence	**Key Points**	**Clinical Picture**
• 2% of the U.S. African-American population has disease • 8% carry trait	• Substitution of valine for glutamic acid at position 6 of the beta chain • Sickle trait: 40% HbS-sickle in extreme conditions • "Sickle prep" is a blood sample treated with a reducing agent, such as metabisulfite; sickled cells may be seen • Definitive diagnosis made by Hb electrophoresis • HbS aggregates at low oxygen tension; leads to sickling • Heterozygote is protected from *Plasmodium falciparum* malaria	• Microvascular occlusion and hemolysis • Recurrent splenic thrombosis and infarction; autosplenectomy usually by age 5 • Also affects liver, brain, kidney, bones, penis (painful prolonged erection—priapism) • Vaso-occlusive crises ("painful crises") may be triggered by infection, dehydration, acidosis • Aplastic crises: Parvovirus • Functional asplenia: vulnerable to *Salmonella* osteomyelitis and infections with encapsulated organisms, such as *Pneumococcus* • Most patients die before age 30

Agents Used to Treat Anemia		
Class	**Mechanism**	**Indications**
Iron	Needed to form heme, the oxygen-carrying component of hemoglobin	Iron deficiency (microcytic hypochromic) anemia
Vitamin B$_{12}$ (cyanocobalamin, hydroxocobalamin)	Required for DNA synthesis, RBC production, and nervous system function	Pernicious anemia and anemia resulting from gastric resection
Folate	Essential for DNA synthesis and maintenance of normal erythropoiesis	Folic acid deficiency secondary to malabsorption syndrome and dietary insufficiency; macrocytic/megaloblastic anemias
Hydroxyurea (HU)	An antimetabolite that inhibits ribonucleotide reductase HU reactivates HbF synthesis and increases the number of reticulocytes containing HbF in sickle cell patients	Sickle cell anemia, polycythemia vera, and chronic myelogenous leukemia
Erythropoietin (EPO)	EPO is normally produced by the kidney Stimulates RBC production	Used for a variety of anemias, including anemia of renal failure Hypertension a common and severe side effect

WHITE BLOOD CELLS

Leukocytes can be divided into **granulocytes** and **agranulocytes** based on the presence of cytoplasmic granules.

GRANULOCYTES			
Granulocyte Type	**Features**	**Functional Role**	**Relative Abundance**
Neutrophils	• 3–5 nuclear lobes • Contain **azurophilic granules** (lysosomes) • Specific granules contain bactericidal enzymes (e.g., lysozyme)	First cells in **acute inflammation**	54–62% of leukocytes
Eosinophils	• Bilobed nucleus • Acidophilic granules contain hydrolytic enzymes and peroxidase	More numerous in the blood during **parasitic infections and allergic diseases**	1–3% of leukocytes
Basophils	Large basophilic and metachromatic granules, which contain proteoglycans, heparin, and histamine. Note that **mast cells are essentially tissue basophils.**	Degranulate in **type I hypersensitivity**, releasing granule contents and producing slow-reacting substance (SRS-A) = leukotrienes LTC_4, LTD_4, LTE_4	1% of leukocytes

GRANULOPOIESIS

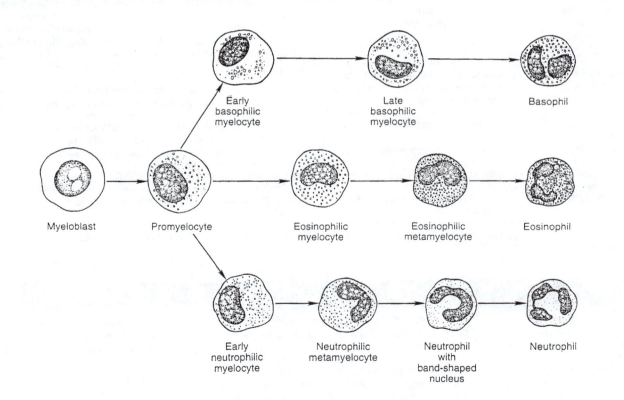

Early basophilic myelocyte → Late basophilic myelocyte → Basophil

Myeloblast → Promyelocyte

Eosinophilic myelocyte → Eosinophilic metamyelocyte → Eosinophil

Early neutrophilic myelocyte → Neutrophilic metamyelocyte → Neutrophil with band-shaped nucleus → Neutrophil

AGRANULOCYTES

Agranulocyte Type	Features	Functional Role	Relative Abundance
Lymphocytes	Dark blue, round nuclei; scant cytoplasm	T cells, B cells, null cells in immune system	25–33% of leukocytes
T cells	Differentiate in thymus	Helper and suppressor cells modulate the immune response	—
B cells	Differentiate in bone marrow	Humoral immunity—antibodies produced by plasma cells	—
Monocytes/macrophages	• Largest peripheral blood cells • Kidney-shaped nuclei, stain lighter than lymphocytes	Monocytes are precursors of tissue macrophages (histiocytes), osteoclasts, alveolar macrophages, and Kupffer cells of the liver	3–7% of leukocytes

DISORDERS OF LEUKOCYTES

NONNEOPLASTIC WHITE BLOOD CELL DISORDERS

Neutropenias: decreased production (most common)	• Megaloblastic anemia • Aplastic anemia • Leukemia/lymphoma • Autoimmune destruction of stem cells	• Lack of innate immune defense • Constitutional symptoms and a high susceptibility to infection, particularly gram-negative septicemia • Poor prognosis: death from overwhelming infection
Neutropenias: increased destruction	Splenic sequestration, often immune-mediated (e.g., Felty syndrome)	• Infected, necrotic ulcers may occur in mucosa (oral cavity, skin, vagina, anus, gastrointestinal tract) • Granulocyte-macrophage colony-stimulating factor (GM-CSF) and granulocyte-stimulating factor (GSF) are now used to treat postchemotherapy neutropenias
Drug-induced neutropenia	Alkylating agents, chloramphenicol, sulfonamides, chlorpromazine, and phenylbutazone	• Usually reversible • Chloramphenicol: dose-related marrow suppression in all patients; aplastic anemia in rare individuals
Polymorphonuclear leukocytosis (most common)	• Acute infection, tissue necrosis, and "stress" • Increased bands and left shift	• Döhle bodies (round, blue, cytoplasmic inclusions, product of rough endoplasmic reticulum) • Toxic granulations: coarse, dark, granules (lysosomes)
Monocytosis	Tuberculosis, endocarditis, malaria, brucellosis, rickettsiosis	
Lymphocytosis	Tuberculosis, brucellosis, pertussis, viral hepatitis, cytomegalovirus infections, infectious mononucleosis	
Eosinophilic leukocytosis	Neoplasms, allergy, asthma, collagen vascular diseases, parasitic infections, skin rashes	

HEMATOPOIETIC GROWTH FACTORS

Granulocyte colony-stimulating factor (G-CSF; filgrastim)	A glycoprotein that stimulates the bone marrow to produce granulocytes while promoting their survival and differentiation	Accelerates neutrophil recovery following chemotherapy; used for primary and secondary neutropenia
Granulocyte-macrophage colony-stimulating factor (GM-CSF, sargramostim)	A glycoprotein growth factor for erythroid megakaryocyte and eosinophil precursors. It also enhances the survival and function of circulating granulocytes, monocytes, and eosinophils	

NONNEOPLASTIC LYMPH NODE DISORDERS

Nonspecific lymphadenitis	Drugs, toxins, or infection	• In neck following dental or tonsillar infection • In axillary/inguinal regions after infections of the extremities • Enlarged abdominal lymph nodes (mesenteric adenitis) may cause abdominal pain resembling acute appendicitis
Generalized lymphadenopathy	Systemic viral or bacterial infections	• May be a precursor to AIDS • Associated with hyperglobulinemia and normal CD4 lymphocyte counts
Acute lymphadenopathy		• Swollen, red-gray nodes with prominent lymphoid follicles • Older patients have fewer germinal centers than children
Chronic lymphadenopathy		Most common in axillary and inguinal nodes; nodes large and nontender
Microscopic Findings: Three Basic Patterns		
Follicular hyperplasia B-cell antibody response		• Large germinal centers, containing mostly B cells, helper T cells, and histiocytes • Seen in bacterial infections or with exposure to new antigens
Paracortical hyperplasia T-cell reaction		• Reactive changes in cortex • Seen with phenytoin use, viral infections, or secondary immune responses
Sinus histiocytosis		• Lymphatic sinusoids prominent and distended with macrophages • Seen in nodes draining carcinomas or any chronic inflammation

NEOPLASTIC LEUKOCYTE DISORDERS

Hodgkin Disease

- Contiguous spread (from one node to the next) with spleen involved before liver
- High cure rate, rarely has leukemic component
- **Reed-Sternberg (RS)** cells (large, containing large "owl-eyed" nucleoli with a clear halo; abundant cytoplasm) are necessary, but not sufficient, to make diagnosis
- Bimodal age distribution (high peak: 15–35; low peak: 50+) in both men and women
- Clinical: painless cervical adenopathy +/– constitutional symptoms

Four Variants of Hodgkin Disease

Lymphocyte predominance		Sea of lymphocytes, few RS cells, variable number of histiocytes, little fibrosis, and no necrosis
Nodular sclerosis	*Worsening Prognosis*	• More common in women • Mediastinal, supraclavicular, and lower cervical nodes • Mixture of lymphocytes, histiocytes, a few eosinophils, plasma cells, and RS cells. Collagen bands create nodular pattern; RS cells called lacunar cells
Mixed cellularity		• Mixture of neutrophils, lymphocytes, eosinophils, plasma cells, and histiocytes • Large number of RS cells
Lymphocyte depletion		• Rare lymphocytes, many RS cells with variable eosinophils, plasma cells, and histiocytes • Diffuse fibrosis may be seen

NON-HODGKIN LYMPHOMAS (NHL)

- Lymphadenopathy and hepatosplenomegaly. In 30% of cases, initial involvement extranodal
- Usually discovered in only one chain of nodes—usually cervical, axillary, inguinal, femoral, iliac, or mediastinal
- Patients present with local or generalized lymphadenopathy, abdominal or pharyngeal mass, abdominal pain, or GI bleeding
- Involve lymph nodes or lymphoid tissue in the gut, oropharynx, liver, spleen, and thymus
- **Do not produce RS cells**, do not spread in contiguity, and frequently have a leukemic or blood-borne phase
- Occur in late 50s (rare and more aggressive in children and young adults)
- Weight loss common sign of disseminated disease
- Common in immunosuppressed patients

Two main categories: **nodular** (better prognosis) and **diffuse**

Staging similar to Hodgkin disease but staging less clinically significant in NHL because prognosis is more affected by histology, and the disease is often disseminated at time of diagnosis

Disease	Characteristics	Pathology
Well-differentiated lymphocytic lymphoma (diffuse)	Older patients Generalized lymphadenopathy, hepatosplenomegaly Often seeds the blood late in the disease similar to CLL Bone marrow almost always involved Survival: 5–7 years	Lymph nodes replaced by small round lymphocytes with scant cytoplasm, dark nuclei, and rare mitoses
Poorly differentiated lymphocytic lymphoma (PDLL) (nodular or diffuse)	Middle-aged or older Lymphadenopathy, infiltration of bone marrow, liver, and spleen at the time of diagnosis Prognosis is fair: nodular PDLL > diffuse PDLL	Atypical lymphocytes Nuclei are irregular and indented with coarse chromatin Mitoses are rare Leukemic phase less common
Histiocytic lymphoma (B cells) (diffuse >> nodular)	Nodal or extranodal involvement (skin, bone, gastrointestinal tract, brain); rarely, liver and spleen involvement; leukemic phase rare Prognosis poor if untreated, but combination chemotherapy may induce remission and occasionally a cure in lymphomas with a high mitotic rate	Large cells with vesicular nuclei and prominent nucleoli; may be pleomorphic
Mixed lymphocytic—histiocytic lymphoma (nodular)	Prognosis fair; remission may be achieved with combination chemotherapy	Cells with atypical lymphocytes and large histiocytes
Lymphoblastic lymphoma (diffuse) Cells similar to ALL	Bimodal—high peak: adolescents/young adults, low peak: 70s; male:female ratio, 2.5:1 Associated with a mediastinal mass, particularly in boys Often express T-cell markers Prognosis uniformly poor; T-cell lymphomas worse	Uniform size, scant cytoplasm, delicate chromatin, and absent nucleoli Nuclear membrane is loculated or convoluted Frequent mitoses
Burkitt undifferentiated lymphoma: **Epstein-Barr virus** (EBV) African Burkitt: translocation of 8;14, 2;8, or 8;22. Brings *c-myc* gene next to enhancers of heavy or light chain synthesis	Endemic in Africa and sporadic in the United States Children or young adults Lymphadenopathy is rare initial finding Africa: arises in the mandible or maxilla United States: arises in the abdomen (ovaries, GI tract, retroperitoneum) Sustained polyclonal activation of B cells Leukemic phase is rare; prognosis is fair	Sea of moderately large cells, round nuclei, multiple nucleoli, basophilic cytoplasm with lipid-containing vacuoles Many macrophages with ingested debris, producing the so-called **"starry sky"** pattern
Undifferentiated non-Burkitt lymphoma	Rare, usually adults, not associated with EBV Cells more variable than in Burkitt; may be multinucleate, have a single nucleolus and pale, scant cytoplasm	Cell markers show both B- and T-cell neoplasms Aggressive, as are all diffuse, large-cell lymphomas

CUTANEOUS T-CELL LYMPHOMAS

Mycosis fungoides	Three phases of skin lesions: inflammation, plaque, and tumor. Epidermal and dermal infiltrates by neoplastic T (CD4) cells with cerebriform nuclei. Nodules and fungating tumors may develop later in the disease. Nodal and visceral dissemination can occur.
Sézary syndrome	Rare chronic disease with progressive, pruritic erythroderma, exfoliation, and lymphadenopathy. "Sézary cells," T cells with cerebriform nuclei (similar to those seen in mycosis fungoides) infiltrate the peripheral blood. May be considered a preterminal phase of mycosis fungoides.

LEUKEMIAS

Disease	Characteristics	Pathology
Acute lymphocytic leukemia (ALL)	• 60–70% of cases occur in childhood; peak age 4; rare over 50 • Half the children are cured; prognosis for adults is very poor • Fatigue, fever, epistaxis, gingival petechiae, ecchymoses 2° to thrombocytopenia; may have subarachnoid or cerebral hemorrhage • Present with lymphadenopathy, bone pain, hepatosplenomegaly • Most likely leukemia to involve CNS • Prognosis: death often from infection or bleed • Most cells pre-B cells; T-cell variants occur, usually affecting boys and causing a thymic mass that may compress the trachea	Smear: lymphoblasts are prominent; mature WBCs rare **CD10 (CALLA)** is the diagnostic surface marker; terminal deoxynucleotidyl transferase (TDT) positive in both B-cell and T-cell ALL and negative in AML
Acute myelogenous leukemia (AML)	20% of acute leukemia in children, most common acute leukemia in adults Signs and symptoms resemble ALL, except usually also present with lymphadenopathy or splenomegaly	Primary cell type variable; see the French, American, and British (FAB) Classification of Myelogenous Leukemias, page 454.
Chronic myelogenous leukemia (CML)	• Middle age but may occur in children/young adults • Fatigue, fever, night sweats, and weight loss • Splenomegaly (up to 5 kg) giving abdominal discomfort • Variable remission period, may develop blast crisis • Two-thirds convert to AML; one-third to B-cell ALL • **Philadelphia chromosome (Ph1), t(9:22): *bcr:abl*** translocation is pathognomonic; present in 95% of cases • Prognosis in CML is worse in Ph1-negative patients	• Marked leukocytosis • Low-to-absent leukocyte alkaline phosphatase • Elevated serum vitamin B_{12} and vitamin B_{12}–binding proteins • High uric acid levels (due to rapid cell turnover.)
Chronic lymphocytic leukemia (CLL)	• Over 60 years of age • Asymptomatic or fatigue and weight loss; lymphadenopathy and hepatosplenomegaly later findings • Higher incidence of visceral malignancy • Median survival with treatment is 5 years but varies widely; prognostic factor is extent of disease	Lymph node histology indistinguishable from diffuse, well-differentiated lymphocytic lymphoma Classic cell: CD5 B cell Cells do not undergo apoptosis
Hairy cell leukemia	• Rare disease; cells express tartrate-resistant acid phosphatase • Present with hepatosplenomegaly; pancytopenia common • Prognosis: may now be cured with 2-chloro-deoxyadenosine (2CdA), an apoptosis inducer	Leukemic cells have "hair-like" cytoplasmic projections visible on phase-contrast microscopy Cells express some B-cell antigens
Adult T-cell leukemia/ lymphoma (CD4 T cell)	• Endemic in Japan • Lymphadenopathy, hepatosplenomegaly, skin involvement, and hypercalcemia • Poor prognosis; however, many infected patients do not progress to disease	Caused by human T-cell leukemia/lymphoma virus (HTLV1); exposure to the virus may be decades earlier
Myelodysplastic syndromes	Proliferative stem cell disorders—maturation defect Gray zone between benign proliferation and frank acute leukemias One-third of these patients later develop frank acute myelocytic leukemia	Presents as pancytopenia in elderly patients

Leukemia Clues	
Children	ALL
Myeloblasts	AML
Auer rods	AML, promyelocytic
DIC	Promyelocytic
Elderly	CLL
Splenomegaly	CML
Philadelphia chromosome	CML
Tartrate-resistant acid phosphatase	Hairy cell
HTLV-1	Adult T cell

THE FRENCH, AMERICAN, AND BRITISH (FAB) CLASSIFICATION OF MYELOGENOUS LEUKEMIAS

M0	Undifferentiated	—
M1	Myeloblasts without maturation	Myeloblasts have round-oval nuclei Auer rods
M2	Granulocyte maturation	—
M3	Promyelocytic	Auer rods DIC
M4	Mixed myeloid and monocytic	Features of both myelocytes and monocytes
M5	Monoblastic or monocytic	—
M6	Erythroid differentiation	Di Guglielmo disease Atypical multinucleated RBC precursors Usually converts to AML
M7	Megakaryocytic differentiation	—

PLASMA CELL DYSCRASIAS

Polyclonal hypergammaglobulinemia	1–2 weeks after an antigen stimulus (e.g., bacterial infection); also associated with granulomatous disease, connective tissue disorders, and liver failure Elevated serum globulins, elevated ESR Polyclonal Bence-Jones proteins in serum or urine Hyperviscosity of blood may lead to sludging and rouleaux formation with subsequent thrombosis, hemorrhage, renal impairment, and right-sided congestive heart failure
Waldenström macroglobulinemia	Age 60–70 years in both men and women Monoclonal IgM resembles lymphocytic lymphoma with M-protein spike on serum protein electrophoresis Symptoms due to hypergammaglobulinemia and tumorous infiltration Hepatosplenomegaly, lymphadenopathy, bone pain, and hyperviscosity Blindness and priapism due to hyperviscosity may be seen 2–5-year survival rate with chemotherapy
Monoclonal gammopathy of undetermined significance (MGUS)	Asymptomatic M-protein spike on serum electrophoresis Prognosis: initially thought benign, but approximately 2% may later develop myeloma, lymphoma, amyloidosis, or Waldenström macroglobulinemia
Multiple myeloma	Peak incidence is 50–60 years old; male = female Multifocal plasma cell neoplasms in the bone marrow, occasionally soft tissues Monoclonal immunoglobulin (IgG) Signs and symptoms result from excess abnormal immunoglobulins (causing hyperviscosity) and from infiltration of various organs by neoplastic plasma cells Proteinuria may contribute to progressive renal failure Infiltration of bone with plasma cell neoplasms may lead to bone pain and hypercalcemia Over 99% of patients have elevated levels of serum immunoglobulins or urine Bence-Jones proteins, or both Serum protein electrophoresis (SPEP) shows homogeneous peak or "spike" Marrow is infiltrated with plasma cells (usually over 30%) in various stages of maturation, called "myeloma cells"; contain cytoplasmic inclusions (acidophilic aggregates of immunoglobulin) called Russell bodies Multiple osteolytic lesions throughout the skeleton; appear as "punched-out" defects on x-ray Kidney: protein casts in distal tubules Prognosis: less than 2-year survival without therapy; death usually results from infection, bleeding, or renal failure **(Bruce Jones proteins)**

HEMATOLOGIC CHANGES ASSOCIATED WITH INFECTIOUS DISEASE

CHANGES IN BLOOD CELLS

Signs and Symptoms	Case Vignette/ Key Clues	Most Common Causative Agents	Pathogenesis	Diagnosis	Treatment
Anemia	Megaloblastic Ingestion of raw fish	*Diphyllobothrium latum*	Parasite absorbs B$_{12}$	Operculated eggs in stool	Niclosamide
	Normocytic	Chronic infections	Bacteria chelate iron	Culture, Gram stain	Depends on agent
	Microcytic and hypochromic (iron-deficiency anemia)	*Ancylostoma, Necator Trichuris*	Hookworms suck blood; trichuris damages mucosa	Golden brown, oval eggs; eggs with bipolar plugs	Mebendazole
Patient with cyclic or irregular fever, ↓ hemoglobin and hematocrit	Travel to tropics, parasites in RBCs	*Plasmodium* spp.	Parasite lyses RBC Autoimmune RBC destruction	Rings/trophozoites in blood film	Chloroquine, etc. (considerable drug resistance), followed by primaquine if *P. vivax* or *P. ovale*
↓ CD4 cell count	Lymphadenopathy Opportunistic infections	HIV	Virus infects and destroys CD4 ⊕ T cells, and macrophages	ELISA, Western blot	Reverse transcriptase inhibitors, protease inhibitors, fusion inhibitors
↑ PMNs (neutrophilia)	—	Generally found in many extracellular bacterial infections	*N*-formyl methionyl peptides are chemotactic for PMNs	Culture, Gram stain	Depends on agent
↑ eosinophils (eosinophilia)	—	Allergy	ECF-A released by mast cells attracts eosinophils	Skin testing: wheal and flare	Antihistamines
		Helminths during migrations	Parasites release allergens	Depends on agent	Depends on agent
↑ monocytes or lymphocytes	—	Intracellular organisms: viruses, *Listeria, Legionella, Leishmania, Toxoplasma*	Intracellular organisms elicit TH1 cells and CMI	Depends on agent	Depends on agent
↑ lymphocytes (mononucleosis) Fever, fatigue, lymphadenopathy, myalgia, headache	Infectious mononucleosis Heterophile ⊕, Downey type II cells (reactive T cells), sore throat, lymphadenopathy, young adult	Epstein-Barr virus	Virus infects B lymphocytes via CD21; CTLs respond to kill virus-infected cells	Monospot ⊕ Complete blood count	Supportive
	Heterophile ⊖	CMV	Virus infects fibroblasts; CTLs respond to kill virus-infected cells	Monospot ⊖ Virus culture	Ganciclovir (severe cases)
Lymphocytosis with hacking cough	Unvaccinated child, hypoglycemic	*Bordetella pertussis*	Tracheal cytotoxin, fimbrial antigen, endotoxin	Gram ⊖ rod Culture Bordet-Gengou agar or serology	Erythromycin, antitoxin

Section III

Appendices

ESSENTIAL EQUATIONS

BIOSTATISTICS			
Name	**Equations**	**Reasons for Use**	**Page**
Sample 2×2 table: test versus disease	**Disease** — Test Results / Positive: TP (a), FP (b); Negative: FN (c), TN (d); columns Present / Absent	*Note:* You should know the meanings of a, b, c, d. Data may be rotated in presentation. TP: true positive FP: false positive TN: true negative FN: false negative	
Sensitivity	$\text{Sensitivity} = \dfrac{a}{a + c} = \dfrac{TP}{TP + FN}$	Probability that test correctly identifies people with the disease	32
Specificity	$\text{Specificity} = \dfrac{d}{d + b} = \dfrac{TN}{TN + FP}$	Probability that test correctly identifies people without disease	32
Positive predictive value	$\text{PPV} = \dfrac{a}{a + b} = \dfrac{TP}{TP + FP}$	Probability that a person with a positive test is a true positive	32
Negative predictive value	$\text{NPV} = \dfrac{d}{d + c} = \dfrac{TN}{TN + FN}$	Probability that a person with a negative test is a true negative	32
Accuracy	$A = \dfrac{a + d}{a + d + b + c} = \dfrac{TP + TN}{TP + TN + FP + FN}$	Represents the true value of the measured attribute	32
Sample 2×2 table: risk factor versus disease	**Disease** — Risk Factor / Positive: a, b; Negative: c, d; columns Present / Absent	*Note:* You should know the meanings of a, b, c, d. The data may be rotated in presentation.	
Odds ratio	$\text{Odds ratio} = \dfrac{a/c}{b/d} = \dfrac{ad}{bc}$	Looks at odds of getting a disease with exposure to a risk factor versus nonexposure to risk factor	33
Relative risk	$RR = \dfrac{a/(a + b)}{c/(c + d)}$	"How much more likely?" Incidence rate of exposed group ÷ incidence rate of unexposed group	33
Attributable risk	$AR = \dfrac{a}{a + b} = \dfrac{c}{c + d}$	"How many more cases in one group?" Incidence rate in exposed group − incidence rate in unexposed group	33

GENETICS

Name	Equation	Reason for Use	Page
Hardy-Weinberg equilibrium	Allele frequencies: $p + q = 1$ Genotypic frequencies: $p^2 + 2pq + q^2 = 1$ p^2 = frequency of AA $2pq$ = frequency of Aa q^2 = frequency of aa	Used in population genetics. Assume no mutations, no selection against genotype, no migration or immigration of the population, random mating	75

CELL BIOLOGY AND NEUROPHYSIOLOGY

Name	Equation	Reason for Use	Page
Nernst equation	$E_x = \dfrac{60 \text{ mV}}{Z} \log_{10} \dfrac{[X]_o}{[X]_i}$ Z = electrical charge of ion; $[X]_o$ = extracellular ion concentration; $[X]_i$ = intracellular ion concentration	Calculation of equilibrium potential; effect of ion concentration on membrane potential	143
Estimated fluid volumes in liters	$TBW = 0.6 \times BW$ $ICF = 0.4 \times BW$ $ECF = 0.2 \times BW$ TBW = total body water; ICF = intracellular fluid volume; ECF = extracellular fluid volume; BW = body weight in kg	Assumes normal subject who is normally hydrated; starting point for evaluating changes of body fluids for diagnostic purposes or effects of administration of fluids	141

PHARMACOKINETICS

Name	Equation	Reason for Use	Page
Volume of distribution	$V_d = \dfrac{\text{Dose}}{C^0}$ C^0 = plasma concentration at time 0	Used to estimate the fluid volume into which a drug has distributed For 70 kg person: plasma vol. = 3 L; blood = 5 L; ECF = 12–14 L; TBW = 40–42 L	156
Clearance	$Cl = \dfrac{\text{Rate of drug elimination}}{\text{Plasma drug concentration}}$ $Cl = k_e \times V_d$ k_e = elimination constant	Used to measure the efficiency with which a drug is removed from the body	156
Half-life	$t_{1/2} = \dfrac{0.7 \times Vd}{Cl} = \dfrac{0.7}{k_e}$	Used to determine the time to decrease drug plasma concentration by 1/2	156
Bioavailability (F)	$F = \dfrac{AUC_{PO}}{AUC_{IV}}$ AUC = area under the curve	Used to estimate the fraction of administered drug to reach the systemic circulation	156
Maintenance dose	$MD = \dfrac{Cl \times C_P}{F}$	Used to calculate the dose to maintain a relatively constant plasma concentration	157

(Continued)

PHARMACOKINETICS (CONT'D.)

Name	Equation	Reason for Use	Page
Loading dose	$LD = \dfrac{V_d \times C_P}{F}$	Used to calculate drug dose to quickly achieve therapeutic levels	157
Therapeutic index	$TI = \dfrac{TD_{50}}{ED_{50}}$ or $\dfrac{LD_{50}}{ED_{50}}$ ED_{50}, TD_{50}, and LD_{50} are the effective, toxic, and lethal doses in 50% of the studied population	Used to determine the safety of a drug $\uparrow$ TI: safe drug $\downarrow$ TI: unsafe drug	157

CARDIOVASCULAR

Name	Equation	Reason for Use	Page
Stroke volume	$SV = EDV - ESV$ SV = stroke volume; EDV = end diastolic ventricular volume; ESV = end systolic ventricular volume	Basic formula for calculation of stroke volume from cardiac volumes	228
Ejection fraction	$EF = SV/EDV$ EF = ejection fraction (multiply by 100% to turn into percentage)	Ejection fraction is a common measure of cardiac contractility.	228
Cardiac output	$CO = SV \times HR$ CO = cardiac output; HR = heart rate	Calculation of cardiac output; used to explain or predict effects of changes of pumping ability or heart rate	228
Cardiac output (Fick method)	$CO = \dot{V}O_2/(Ca - Cv)$ $\dot{V}O_2$ = oxygen consumption, Ca = arterial oxygen content, Cv = venous oxygen content	Used to measure cardiac output; most accurate if Ca is pulmonary venous and Cv is pulmonary arterial	234
Resistance	$R = 8\,\eta l/\pi r^4$ η = viscosity, l = length, r = radius	Hydraulic resistance equation shows that dominant control of resistance is vessel radius.	234
Pressure gradient	$P_i - P_o = Q \times R$ P_i = input pressure P_o = output P; Q = flow, R = resistance	Predicts pressure gradient that results from fluid flow; can be rearranged to solve for R or Q	234
Total peripheral resistance (systemic vascular resistance)	$TPR = (MAP - RAP)/CO$ TPR = total peripheral resistance = systemic vascular resistance (Can ignore RAP in a normal person because RAP is usually small; it is important in disease, e.g., CHF)	Rearrangement of above; use to predict effects of changing input pressure or resistance on flow through a tissue; can also solve for resistance to evaluate its contribution to pathology or to compensatory mechanisms	234
Mean arterial pressure	$MAP = diastolic\ P + 1/3(pulse\ pressure)$ Pulse pressure = systolic P − diastolic P MAP = 1/3 systolic P + 2/3 diastolic P	Common method to calculate approximate mean arterial pressure	234
Series circuit	$R_T = R_1 + R_2 + R_3 \ldots + R_n$ R_T = total resistance	Adding resistor in series increases total resistance	234
Parallel circuit	$1/R_T = 1/R_1 + 1/R_2 + 1/R_3 \ldots + 1/R_n$	Adding in parallel decreases total resistance	234

(Continued)

CARDIOVASCULAR (CONT'D.)

Name	Equation	Reason for Use	Page
Compliance and elasticity	$C = \Delta V/\Delta P$ C = compliance; ΔV = change of volume; ΔP = change of pressure $E = \Delta P/\Delta V$ E = elasticity	Compliance measures flexibility of chamber; elasticity, its inverse, increases if it is stiff. Applied to heart in cardiomyopathy, to vessels with decreased compliance leading to isolated systolic hypertension ($\uparrow P_S$ but $\downarrow P_D$)	234
Wall tension (LaPlace law)	$T = P \times r$ T = wall tension P = transmural pressure; r = radius	LaPlace relationship for thin-walled chamber; shows that increased radius or transmural pressure increases wall tension and risk of rupture	237
Net filtration pressure (Starling equation)	Filtration = $K_f[(P_{cap} + \pi_{tissue}) - (\pi_{cap} + P_{tissue})]$ K_f = ultrafiltration coefficient P_{cap} = capillary blood pressure P_{tissue} = interstitial fluid pressure π_{cap} = plasma (capillary) protein oncotic pressure π_{tissue} = interstitial protein oncotic pressure	Used to evaluate balance of forces between filtration and reabsorption. Positive value is net filtration; negative is net reabsorption.	236

RESPIRATORY

Name	Equation	Reason for Use	Page
Compliance and elasticity	$C = \Delta V/\Delta P$ $E = \Delta P/\Delta V$ Specific compliance = C/V (corrects for body size)	Lung compliance increases in some diseases, such as emphysema; decreases in fibrosis, premature newborns, etc.	262
Total (minute) ventilation	$\dot{V} = V_T \times n$ $\dot{V}$ = minute ventilation; V_T = tidal volume; n = frequency	Measures total air movement into and out of lungs per minute	261
Alveolar ventilation	$\dot{V}_A = (V_T - V_D) \times n$ $\dot{V}_A$ = alveolar ventilation; V_T = tidal volume; V_D = dead space	Volume of air per minute that participates in gas exchange; the functional ventilation	261
Alveolar ventilation (Bohr method)	$\dot{V}_A = \dfrac{\dot{V}_{CO_2}}{P_{CO_2}} \times K$ $\dot{V}_{CO_2}$ = CO_2 production (mL/min) P_{CO_2} = partial pressure of CO_2 (mm Hg)	Bohr method to measure alveolar ventilation $\uparrow V_A \rightarrow \downarrow P_{aCO_2}$ $\downarrow V_A \rightarrow \uparrow P_{aCO_2}$	262
Physiologic dead space ratio	$\dfrac{V_D}{V_T} = \dfrac{P_{aCO_2} - P_{ECO_2}}{P_{aCO_2}}$ P_{aCO_2} = arterial CO_2, P_{ECO_2} = CO_2 in mixed expired gas	Measurement of physiologic dead space takes into account anatomic dead space and units with poor gas exchange.	262
Alveolar gas equation	$P_{AO_2} = P_{IO_2} - \dfrac{P_{ACO_2}}{R}$ *Note:* $P_{IO_2} = F_{IO_2} \times (P_B - P_{H_2O})$; F_{IO_2} = 0.21 on room air and 1.0 on pure O_2; P_B = 760 mm Hg, P_{H_2O} = 47 mm Hg; P_{IO_2} is 150 mm Hg at sea level	Calculation of alveolar oxygen for evaluation of alveolar-arterial gradient; allows differential diagnosis of arterial hypoxemia, e.g., diffusion barrier versus hypoventilation	266

(Continued)

Name	Equation	Reason for Use	Page
Forced vital capacity test	FEV_1/FVC FEV_1 = volume of air expelled in first second of forced expiration during forced vital capacity (FVC) maneuver	Clinical measure of airway resistance; reduced value indicates obstructive pulmonary disease; no change or increase in restrictive disease	265
Airway resistance	$R = \Delta P/Q = 8\,\eta l/\pi r^4$ Note: same factors as in blood flow, above.	Increased airway resistance is the hallmark of obstructive pulmonary disease.	263
LaPlace law for surface tension	$P = \dfrac{2T}{r}$ P = pressure due to surface tension; T = surface tension; r = radius	Shows that collapsing pressure is higher in smaller alveoli; surfactant $\downarrow$ tension	263
Fick's Law of Diffusion	$V_{gas} \propto D(P_1 - P_2) \times A/T$ D = diffusion constant; A = surface area; T = thickness	Identifies factors that change physiologically and pathologically to alter diffusion	267

RENAL AND ACID/BASE			
Name	**Equation**	**Reason for Use**	**Page**
Filtered load (FL)	$FL = GFR \times [solute]_{plasma}$ $[solute]_{plasma}$ = free, not bound solute	Filtered load is the critical parameter in formation of urine; comparison with excretion allows interpretation of renal transport.	288
Excretion	$E_x = \dot{V} \times [X]_{urine} = $ FL + transport $\dot{V}$ = urine flow; $[X]_{urine}$ = solute concentration in urine; transport is either secretion or reabsorption. If excretion > FL, there is net secretion. If excretion < FL, there is net reabsorption. If excretion = FL, there is no net transport.	Mass balance concept—urine formation involves up to three processes: filtration, secretion, and reabsorption. Excretion is the final result.	288
Clearance	$Clearance = \dot{V} \times \dfrac{[X]_{plasma}}{[X]_{urine}}$ • To calculate **GFR**: use **inulin, creatinine,** mannitol • To calculate **RPF**: use renal clearance of **para-aminohippuric acid (PAH)**	Relates excretion to plasma solute concentration; essential formula used in many ways	289
Renal blood flow	$RBF = \dfrac{RPF}{1 - hematocrit}$	Used to determine the volume of blood/plasma delivered to the kidneys per unit time	289
Free water clearance	$CH_2O = \dot{V} - C_{osm}$ C_{osm} = osmolar clearance; use urine osmolarity and plasma osmolarity in clearance equation	Evaluates balance between excretion of water and solutes; determines if kidneys are appropriately controlling solutes and water. Positive C_{osm}: hypotonic urine; negative C_{osm}: hypertonic urine.	289
Glomerular filtration rate (GFR)	$GFR = K_f [(P_{cap} + \pi_{BC}) - (\pi_{cap} + P_{BC})]$ (Same forces as in cardiovascular section, but specific to Bowman's capsule and glomerular capillaries).	Calculation of GFR from Starling forces: illustrates importance of glomerular capillary pressure and oncotic pressures.	291

(Continued)

Name	Equation	Reason for Use	Page
Filtration fraction (FF)	$FF = \dfrac{GFR}{RPF}$	Use for differential diagnosis of reduced GFR states.	291
Net acid excretion	$NAE = \dot{V} \times [NH_4^+]_u + \dot{V} \times [TA]_u - \dot{V} \times [HCO_3^-]$ TA = titratable acid (usually H_2PO_4)	Net acid excretion calculates the amount of acid excreted in the urine; more accurate but more difficult to measure than urinary anion gap.	303
Henderson-Hasselbalch equation	$pH = pKa + \log \dfrac{[base]}{[acid]}$ pKa = dissociation constant The main form used is: $pH = 6.1 \log \dfrac{HCO_3^-}{0.03\ P_{CO_2}}$	Calculates pH of solutions. Major physiologic use is to calculate pH in response to CO_2 and bicarbonate ion.	305
Plasma anion gap	$PAG = [Na^+] + ([Cl^-] + [HCO_3^-])$ Normal = 12 ± 2 (Concentrations are generally in plasma, but for bicarbonate specifically refers to arterial blood sample.) High PAG means excess acid in body.	Plasma anion gap measures amount of nonvolatile acid in blood to determine cause of (not whether they have) metabolic acidosis.	308
Urinary anion gap	$UAG = [Na^+] + [K^+] - [Cl^-]$ Negative UAG: kidneys are excreting acid Positive UAG: kidneys are excreting base	Urinary anion gap calculates amount of acid excreted; used to determine contribution of kidneys to acid/base status	308

	REFERENCE RANGE	SI REFERENCE INTERVALS

BLOOD, PLASMA, SERUM

* Alanine aminotransferase (ALT, GPT at 30°C)	8-20 U/L	8-20 U/L
Amylase, serum	25-125 U/L	25-125 U/L
* Aspartate aminotransferase (AST, GOT at 30°C)	8-20 U/L	8-20 U/L
Bilirubin, serum (adult) Total // Direct	0.1-1.0 mg/dL // 0.0-0.3 mg/dL	2-17 µmol/L // 0-5 µmol/L
* Calcium, serum (Total)	8.4-10.2 mg/dL	2.1-2.8 mmol/L
* Cholesterol, serum	140-250 mg/dL	3.6-6.5 mmol/L
Cortisol, serum	0800 h: 5-23 µg/dL // 1600 h: 3-15 µg/dL	138-635 nmol/L // 82-413 nmol/L
	2000 h: 50% of 0800 h	Fraction of 0800 h: ≤ 0.50
Creatine kinase, serum (at 30°C) ambulatory	Male: 25-90 U/L	25-90 U/L
	Female: 10-70 U/L	10-70 U/L
* Creatinine, serum	0.6-1.2 mg/dL	53-106 µmol/L
Electrolytes, serum		
Sodium	135-147 mEq/L	135-147 mmol/L
Chloride	95-105 mEq/L	95-105 mmol/L
* Potassium	3.5-5.0 mEq/L	3.5-5.0 mmol/L
Bicarbonate	22-28 mEq/L	22-28 mmol/L
Estriol (E_3) total, serum (in pregnancy)		
24-28 weeks // 32-36 weeks	30-170 ng/mL // 60-280 ng/mL	104-590 // 208-970 nmol/L
28-32 weeks // 36-40 weeks	40-220 ng/mL // 80-350 ng/mL	140-760 // 280-1210 nmol/L
Ferritin, serum	Male: 15-200 ng/mL	15-200 µg/L
	Female: 12-150 ng/mL	12-150 µg/L
Follicle-stimulating hormone, serum/plasma	Male: 4-25 mIU/mL	4-25 U/L
	Female: premenopause 4-30 mIU/mL	4-30 U/L
	midcycle peak 10-90 mIU/mL	10-90 U/L
	ostmenopause 40-250 mIU/mL	40-250 U/L
Gases, arterial blood (room air)		
pO_2	75-105 mm Hg	10.0-14.0 kPa
pCO_2	33-44 mm Hg	4.4-5.9 kPa
pH	7.35-7.45	[H^+] 36-44 nmol/L
Glucose, serum	Fasting: 70-110 mg/dL	3.8-6.1 mmol/L
	2-h postprandial: < 120 mg/dL	< 6.6 mmol/L
Growth hormone – arginine stimulation	Fasting: < 5 ng/mL	< 5 µg/L
	provocative stimuli: > 7 ng/mL	> 7 µg/L
Immunoglobulins, serum		
IgA	76-390 mg/dL	0.76-3.90 g/L
IgE	0-380 IU/mL	0-380 kIU/mL
IgG	650-1500 mg/dL	6.5-15 g/L
IgM	40-345 mg/dL	0.4-3.45 g/L
Iron	50-170 µg/dL	9-30 µmol/L
Lactate dehydrogenase (L → P, 30°C)	45-90 U/L	45-90 U/L
Luteinizing hormone, serum/plasma	Male: 6-23 mIU/mL	6-23 U/L
	Female: follicular phase 5-30 mIU/mL	5-30 U/L
	midcycle 75-150 mIU/mL	75-150 U/L
	postmenopause 30-200 mIU/mL	30-200 U/L
Osmolality, serum	275-295 mOsmol/kg	275-295 mOsmol/kg
Parathyroid hormone, serum, N-terminal	230-630 pg/mL	230-630 ng/L
* Phosphatase (alkaline), serum (p-NPP at 30°C)	20-70 U/L	20-70 U/L
* Phosphorus (inorganic), serum	3.0-4.5 mg/dL	1.0-1.5 mmol/L
Prolactin, serum (hPRL)	< 20 ng/mL	< 20 µg/L
* Proteins, serum		
Total (recumbent)	6.0-7.8 g/dL	60-78 g/L
Albumin	3.5-5.5 g/dL	35-55 g/L
Globulins	2.3-3.5 g/dL	23-35 g/L
Thyroid-stimulating hormone, serum or plasma	0.5-5.0 µU/mL	0.5-5.0 mU/L
Thyroidal iodine (^{123}I) uptake	8-30% of administered dose/24 h	0.08-0.30/24 h
Thyroxine (T_4), serum	5-12 µg/dL	64-155 nmol/L
Triglycerides, serum	35-160 mg/dL	0.4-1.81 mmol/L
Triiodothyronine (T_3), serum (RIA)	115-190 ng/dL	1.8-2.9 nmol/L
Triiodothyronine (T_3), resin uptake	25-35%	0.25-0.35
* Urea nitrogen, serum (BUN)	7-18 mg/dL	1.2-3.0 mmol urea/L
* Uric acid, serum	3.0-8.2 mg/dL	0.18-0.48 mmol/L

(*) Included in the Biochemical Profile (SMA-12)

	REFERENCE RANGE	SI REFERENCE INTERVALS
CEREBROSPINAL FLUID		
Cell count	0-5 cells/mm^3	0-5 x 10^6/L
Chloride	118-132 mmol/L	118-132 mmol/L
Gamma globulin	3-12% total proteins	0.03-0.12
Glucose	40-70 mg/dL	2.2-3.9 mmol/L
Pressure	70-180 mm H$_2$O	70-180 mm H$_2$O
Proteins, total	< 40 mg/dL	< 0.40 g/L
HEMATOLOGIC		
Bleeding time (template)	2-7 minutes	2-7 minutes
Erythrocyte count	Male: 4.3-5.9 million/mm^3	4.3-5.9 x 10^{12}/L
	Female: 3.5-5.5 million/mm^3	3.5-5.5 x 10^{12}/L
Hematocrit	Male: 41-53%	0.41-0.53
	Female: 36-46%	0.36-0.46
Hemoglobin, blood	Male: 13.5-17.5 g/dL	2.09-2.71 mmol/L
	Female: 12.0-16.0 g/dL	1.86-2.48 mmol/L
Hemoglobin, plasma	1-4 mg/dL	0.16-0.62 μmol/L
Leukocyte count and differential		
Leukocyte count	4500-11,000/mm^3	4.5-11.0 x 10^9/L
Segmented neutrophils	54-62%	0.54-0.62
Band forms	3-5%	0.03-0.05
Eosinophils	1-3%	0.01-0.03
Basophils	0-0.75%	0-0.0075
Lymphocytes	25-33%	0.25-0.33
Monocytes	3-7%	0.03-0.07
Mean corpuscular hemoglobin	25.4-34.6 pg/cell	0.39-0.54 fmol/cell
Mean corpuscular hemoglobin concentration	31-36% Hb/cell	4.81-5.58 mmol Hb/L
Mean corpuscular volume	80-100 μm^3	80-100 fl
Partial thromboplastin time (nonactivated)	60-85 seconds	60-85 seconds
Platelet count	150,000-400,000/mm^3	150-400 x 10^9/L
Prothrombin time	11-15 seconds	11-15 seconds
Reticulocyte count	0.5-1.5% of red cells	0.005-0.015
Sedimentation rate, erythrocyte (Westergren)	Male: 0-15 mm/h	0-15 mm/h
	Female: 0-20 mm/h	0-20 mm/h
Thrombin time	< 2 seconds deviation from control	< 2 seconds deviation from control
Volume		
Plasma	Male: 25-43 mL/kg	0.025-0.043 L/kg
	Female: 28-45 mL/kg	0.028-0.045 L/kg
Red cell	Male: 20-36 mL/kg	0.020-0.036 L/kg
	Female: 19-31 mL/kg	0.019-0.031 L/kg
SWEAT		
Chloride	0-35 mmol/L	0-35 mmol/L
URINE		
Calcium	100-300 mg/24 h	2.5-7.5 mmol/24 h
Chloride	Varies with intake	Varies with intake
Creatinine clearance	Male: 97-137 mL/min	
	Female: 88-128 mL/min	
Estriol, total (in pregnancy)		
30 weeks	6-18 mg/24 h	21-62 μmol/24 h
35 weeks	9-28 mg/24 h	31-97 μmol/24 h
40 weeks	13-42 mg/24 h	45-146 μmol/24 h
17-Hydroxycorticosteroids	Male: 3.0-10.0 mg/24 h	8.2-27.6 μmol/24 h
	Female: 2.0-8.0 mg/24 h	5.5-22.0 μmol/24 h
17-Ketosteroids, total	Male: 8-20 mg/24 h	28-70 μmol/24 h
	Female: 6-15 mg/24 h	21-52 μmol/24 h
Osmolality	50-1400 mOsmol/kg	
Oxalate	8-40 μg/mL	90-445 μmol/L
Potassium	Varies with diet	Varies with diet
Proteins, total	< 150 mg/24 h	< 0.15 g/24 h
Sodium	Varies with diet	Varies with diet
Uric acid	Varies with diet	Varies with diet

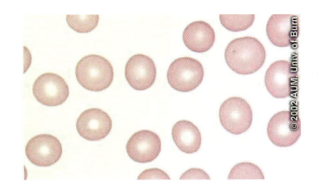

Normal red blood cell on peripheral smear

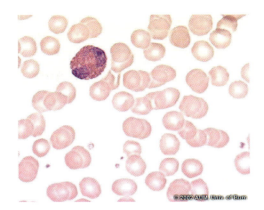

Eosinophil. These cells are most numerous in the blood during parasitic infections and allergic diseases.

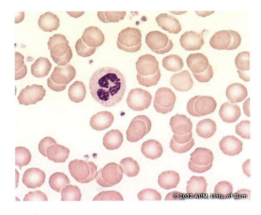

Segmented neutrophil. These are the first cells in acute inflammation and have two types of lysosomal granules: azurophilic (primary) granules and specific (secondary). An increase of these cells found on peripheral smear indicates bacterial infections, inflammation, trauma, and hemorrhage.

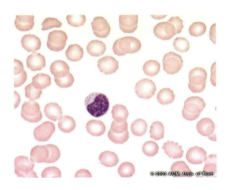

Lymphocyte on peripheral blood smear

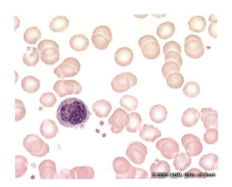

Monocyte. These are the precursors of phagocytic cells (macrophages, osteoclasts, Kupffer cells).

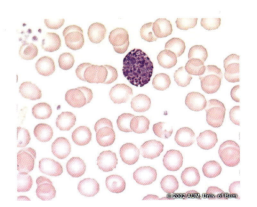

Basophil. These cells are involved in type I hypersensitivity and have large basophilic and metachromatic granules. An increase in basophils on a peripheral smear is seen in viral infections, urticaria, postsplenectomy, and hematologic malignancies.

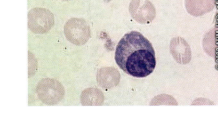

Plasma cell on peripheral blood smear

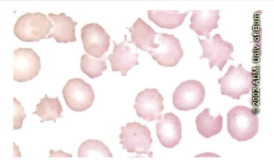

Acanthocytes. Red blood cells show many spicules on the surface of the cell. This can be seen in abetalipoproteinemia.

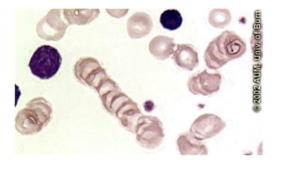

Rouleaux formation. Red blood cells appear to stack on each other in long chains. This occurs when there is a high erythrocyte sedimentation rate (ESR).

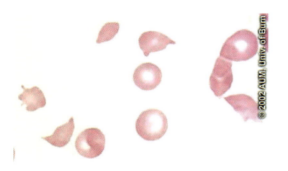

Schistocytes. These red blood cells are fragmented due to mechanical trauma (fibrin bands) and are seen in intravascular hemolysis.

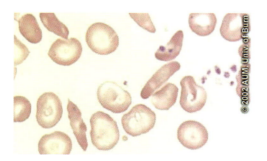

Sickle cells. Sickle cell anemia is an inherited blood disease in which the red blood cells produce abnormal pigment (hemoglobin). The abnormal hemoglobin causes crescent or sickle-shaped deformities.

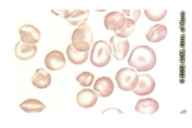

Spherocytes. These cells are near-spherical in shape and have no area of central pallor as seen in normal red blood cells. Spherocytes are found in hereditary spherocytosis, hemolytic anemia, and severe burns.

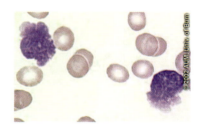

Target cells are erythrocytes with central staining and an inner ring and outer rim of pallor. They are seen in liver disease, thalassemia, or sickle cell disease.

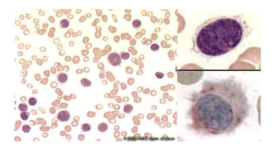

Smudge cells are leukocytes that have been damaged during preparation of the peripheral blood smear. This usually occurs because of the fragility of the cell and is seen in chronic lymphocytic leukemia (CLL).

Hairy cells are characterized by fine, irregular pseudopods at the cell surface and immature nuclear features. These cells are found only in hairy cell leukemia.

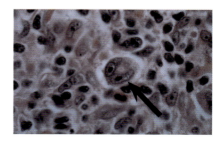

Hodgkin disease, Reed-Sternberg cell. A classic Reed-Sternberg cell has two nuclear lobes, large inclusion-like nucleoli, and abundant cytoplasm. These cells are essential in the histologic diagnosis of Hodgkin lymphoma.

ephrosclerosis of the kidney due to hypertension. Pinpoint petechial emorrhages can be seen on the surface of the kidney. This results from ptured arterioles, giving the kidney a "flea-bitten" appearance.

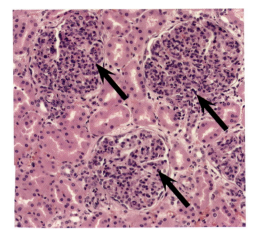

Poststreptococcal glomerulonephritis. Glomeruli are enlarged and hypercellular due to infiltration of leukocytes and endothelial and mesangial proliferation. Subepithelial humps would be seen on electron microscopy (*not shown here*).

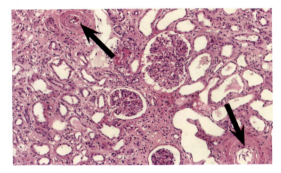

ibrinoid necrosis of arterioles in malignant hypertension. Injury to the enal arterioles results in fibrinogen and platelet deposition and focal necrosis f cells in the vessel wall. This is seen as eosinophilic granular changes occur affected blood vessel walls.

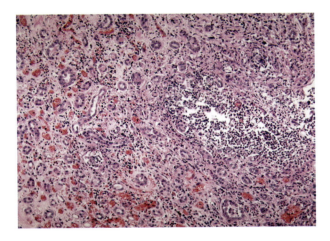

Acute pyelonephritis. Light microscopy is characterized by patchy interstitial suppurative inflammation, intratubular neutrophils, and tubular necrosis.

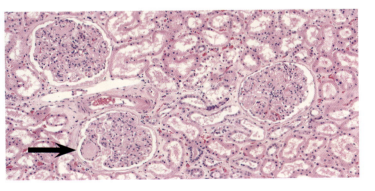

Nodular glomerulosclerosis in a diabetic patient. Also called Kimmelstiel-Wilson disease, this pathology results in PAS-positive glomerular nodules in ne peripheral capillary loops.

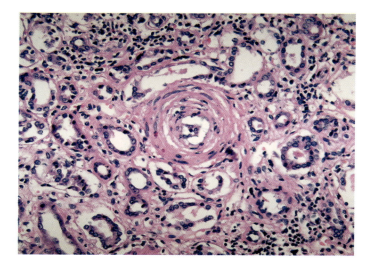

Hyperplastic arteriolitis of kidney in malignant hypertension. Smooth muscle cell proliferation and collagen deposition of arterioles and interlobular artery walls result in concentric intimal thickening. This is often referred to as "onion-skinning" because of the concentric appearance.

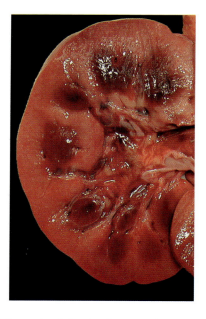

Color reversal of the cortex following hypotensive disease

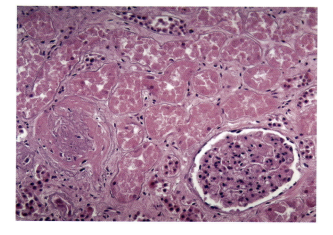

Papillary necrosis is mostly seen in diabetic patients and in those with urinary tract obstruction. Necrotic tissue shows coagulative necrosis with preservation of the tubule outline. Tubular lumens are necrotic as a result of an extension of infection along the tubular lumens.

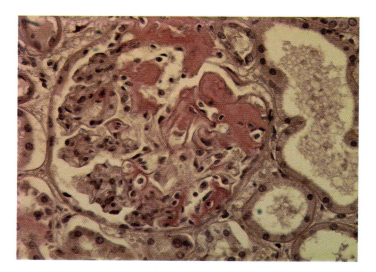

Kidney amyloid deposition, Congo red stain

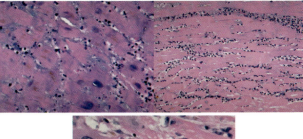

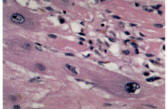

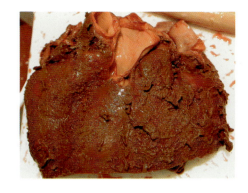

Fibrinous pericarditis is the most common form of pericarditis and is composed of fibrinous exudates. It is associated with myocardial infarction and uremia.

Microscopic features of myocardial infarction. A 1-day-old infarct (*top two images*) shows coagulative necrosis with wavy fibers, edematous tissue, and scattered neutrophils. A 7- to 10-day-old infarct (*bottom image*) reveals the absence of necrotic myocytes by phagocytosis.

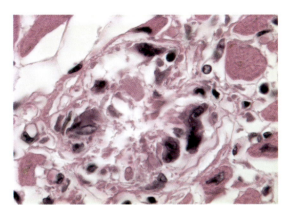

Rheumatic heart disease. The characteristic microscopic appearance is an Aschoff body, a focal lesion of eosinophilic collagen surrounded by inflammatory cells.

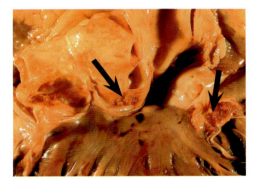

Infective (bacterial) endocarditis of the atrial valve. Bulky vegetations containing fibrin inflammatory cells and bacteria are deposited on the heart valves. Sometimes vegetations can erode into the myocardium and cause ring abscesses. Typically, subacute endocarditis has less valvular destruction than is found in acute endocarditis.

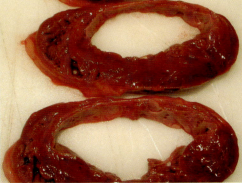

Dilated cardiomyopathy (DCM). In DCM, the heart is usually enlarged and flabby with dilatation of all chambers. The myocardial wall thins as the heart enlarges, resulting in impaired contractility (systolic dysfunction).

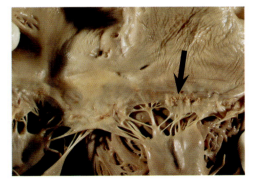

Nonbacterial thrombotic endocarditis (NBTE) is characterized by the deposition of small masses of fibrin platelets on the leaflets of the cardiac valves. In contrast to infective endocarditis, these vegetations contain no microorganisms. It is often related to cancer or sepsis and is significant because of the potential for embolization of the deposits, with resultant infarcts in secondary locations.

Cardiac Pathology

Amyloidosis of the heart. Cardiac amyloidosis produces restrictive hemodynamics, arrhythmias, or symptoms mimicking ischemic or valvular diseases.

Lines of Zahn. Alternating pale pink bands of platelets with fibrin and red bands of red blood cells form a true thrombus.

Gastrointestinal Pathology

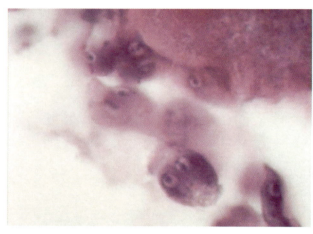

Giardia lamblia trophozoites are pear-shaped binucleated parasites. Trophozoites are noninvasive but can result in blunting of the intestinal villi.

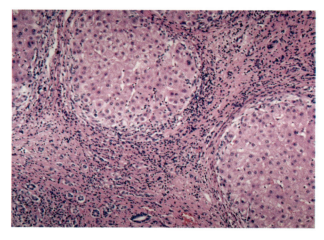

Chronic active hepatitis and cirrhosis from hepatitis C: inflammation in the portal tracts with predominantly lymphocytes and macrophages. There is bile duct damage and septal and bridging fibrosis.

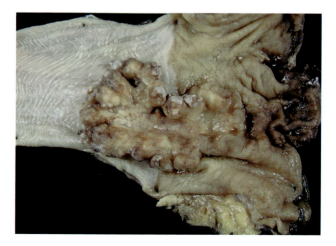

Adenocarcinoma of the esophagus. Adenocarcinomas arising from the distal esophagus are usually found in Barrett esophagus. Most of these tumors are mucin-producing, glandular tumors.

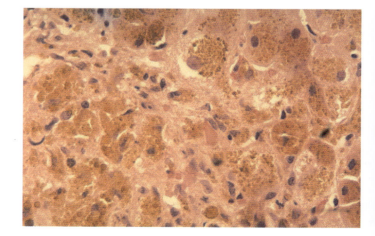

Hemochromatosis of the liver. Prominent hemosiderin deposition can be seen in the cytoplasm of these hepatocytes.

Gastrointestinal Pathology	Hematologic/Lymphoreticular

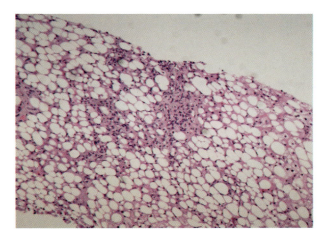

Fatty liver, nonalcoholic. Defects in any of the steps in uptake, catabolism, or secretion of fatty acids in the liver can result in steatosis. Fat vacuoles enlarge until the nucleus is displaced into the periphery of the hepatocyte.

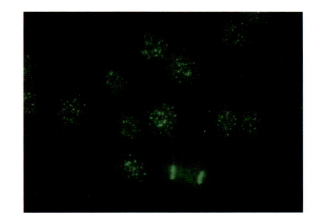

ANA immunofluorescence, centromere pattern. Antinuclear antibodies (ANA) are a sensitive (yet not specific) indicator of autoimmune diseases, such as SLE, scleroderma, and Sjögren's syndrome. The pattern of fluorescence suggests the type of antibody in the patient's serum, as each pattern is associated with specificity to different nuclear components.

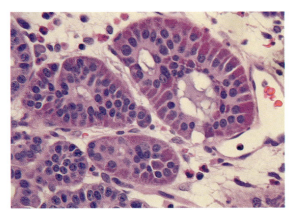

Carcinoid, small intestine. The small intestine is the second most common location for a carcinoid tumor (the appendix is the first). The tumor cells are uniform in appearance and have a scant pink granular cytoplasm and a round-to-oval stippled nucleus. Electron microscopy will reveal (*not shown here*) membrane-bound secretory granules with dense cores.

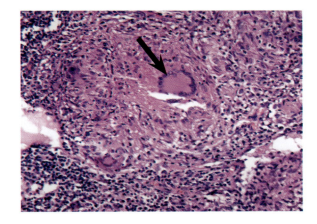

Lymph node, sarcoid. Classic lesions on microscopic appearance are noncaseating granulomas with epithelioid cells and occasional foreign body giant cells (Langhans cells).

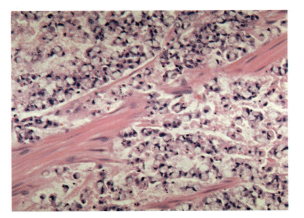

Invasive adenocarcinoma of the colon. The malignant cells have distinctive signet ring appearance from intracellular mucin vacuoles, which displace the nucleus to the side of the cell. This subtype is considered a more aggressive form of adenocarcinoma.

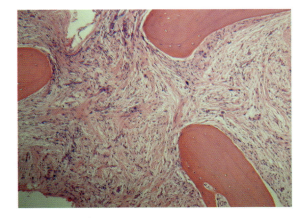

Bone marrow myelofibrosis. Marrow spaces becomes obliterated by fibrosis. This results in extensive extramedullary hematopoiesis principally in the spleen.

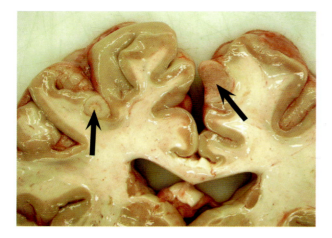

Metastatic disease to the brain. Metastatic lesions account for 25% of intracranial tumors. Metastases form sharply demarcated masses usually with surrounding edema. The most common location is at the gray matter–white matter junction.

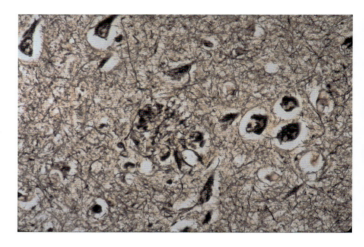

Neurofibrillary tangles within a neuron in Alzheimer disease. These tangles are bundles of paired filaments in the cytoplasm (abnormally hyperphosphorylated *tau* proteins).

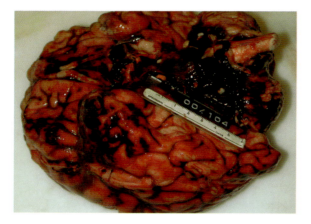

Subarachnoid hemorrhage. This kind of hemorrhage may result from a ruptured intracranial aneurysm, trauma, or other vascular malformation. Irrespective of the etiology, there is an increased risk of injury after the hemorrhage due to vessel spasm in surrounding vessels that may involve the circle of Willis.

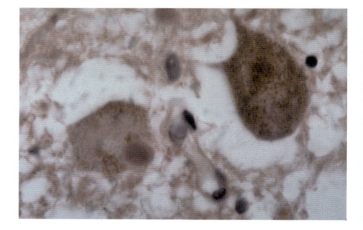

Lewy Bodies in a substantia nigra neuron of Parkinson disease. These eosinophilic cytoplasmic filament inclusions are composed of α-synuclein. Lewy bodies may also be found in cholinergic cells of the basal nucleus of Meynert.

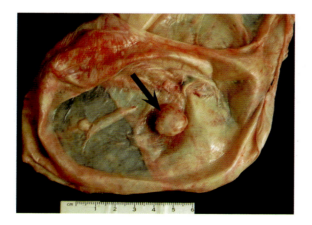

Dural meningioma. Meningiomas are well-defined, rounded masses that compress the underlying brain. The tumor may extend into the overlying bone. Characteristic microscopic features include a whorled pattern of cell growth and psammoma bodies.

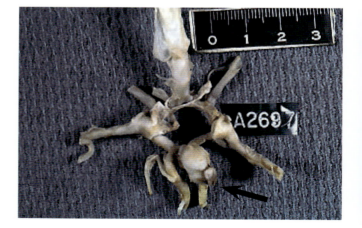

Berry aneurysm of the circle of Willis. Aneurysms occur on the anterior Circle of Willis in 80% of cases. The anterior communicating artery and middle cerebral artery trifurcation are the most common locations. Sudden onset of severe headache is often the first symptom of aneurysm rupture.

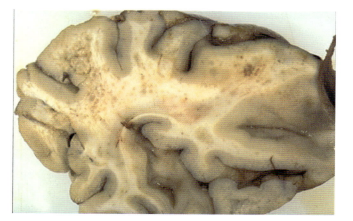

Progressive multifocal leukoencephalopathy is caused by the JC polyomavirus, which primarily infects oligodendrocytes and results in demyelination. Lesions or patchy white matter destruction has affected the entire lobe of this brain.

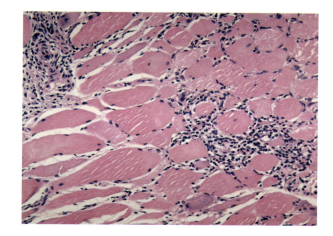

Muscle polymyositis. Inflammatory cells are found in the endomysium, and both necrotic and regenerating muscle fibers are scattered throughout the fascicle.

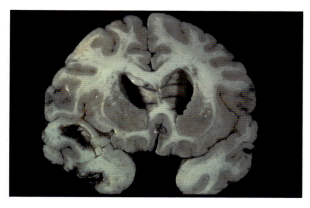

Temporal lobe abscess. A cerebral abscess is seen here on the right temporal lobe.

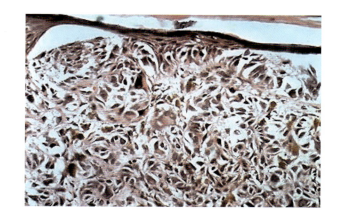

Melanoma cells are larger than normal nevus cells. They contain large nuclei with irregular contours, clumped chromatin, and prominent red nucleoli.

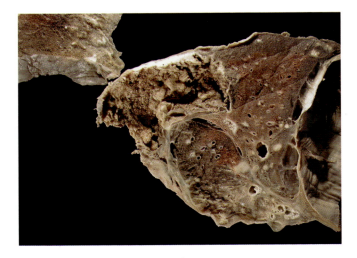

Cavitary lung abscess in the setting of prior tuberculosis scar tissue

Pulmonary infarction. Pale infarcted lung tissue is shown in comparison with normal lung tissue.

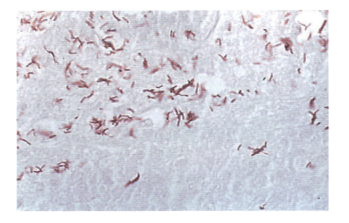

***Mycobacterium tuberculosis*, acid fast stain.** An acid fast stain is used to diagnose the presence of mycobacteria in tissue and cytologic preparations. Many thin, red, rod-like *M. tuberculosis* organisms are shown here.

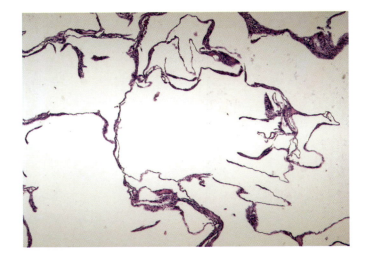

Panacinar emphysema. Emphysema is characterized by abnormally large alveoli separated by thin septa. These alveoli are permanently enlarged due to alveolar wall destruction. This type of emphysema more commonly affects the lower zones and anterior margins of the lung and is associated with α-1 AT deficiency.

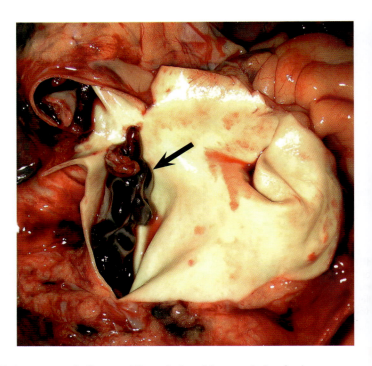

Pulmonary embolism, saddle embolus. A large majority of pulmonary emboli arise from deep venous leg thrombi. They pass through larger vascular channels until they lodge in smaller arteries of the lung. In this case, a large embolus occludes the bifurcation of the pulmonary artery (saddle embolus) and has caused sudden death in the patient.

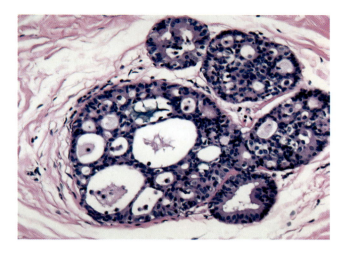

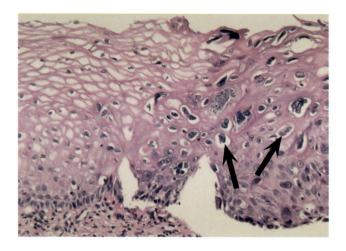

Atypical ductal hyperplasia of the breast. The duct is filled with columnar and rounded cells. The appearance is similar to lobular carcinoma in situ (LCIS), except that the atypia is limited in extent and the cells do not completely fill the ductal spaces. There is an increased risk of developing breast carcinoma when these lesions are identified.

Condyloma acuminata is a benign sexually transmitted tumor of stratified squamous epithelium. Characteristic histologic features are acanthosis, parakeratosis, hyperkeratosis, and nuclear atypia in surface cells with vacuolization (koilocytes).

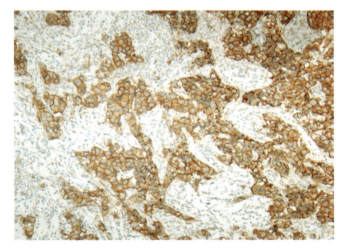

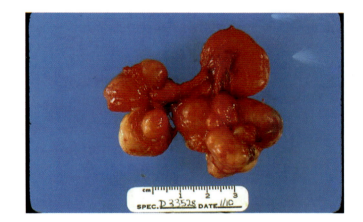

HER2-positive breast carcinoma. Breast cancers are routinely assayed for the HER2/neu gene using fluorescent in situ hybridization (FISH) and protein using immunohistochemistry (brown stain). These tests predict the clinical responses to antibodies targeted to the protein. Carcinomas that are HER2-positive tend to be poorly differentiated.

Fibroadenomas of the breast are sharply demarcated mobile masses within the breast. It is the most common benign tumor of the female breast and is more common in women under 30 years old.

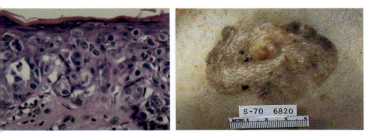

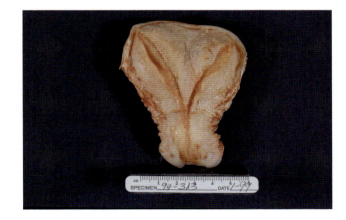

Paget disease of the nipple. Presents as an erythematous scaly crust in a unilateral nipple. Malignant ("Paget") cells extend from the ductal system into the skin of the nipple. There is an increased incidence of underlying invasive carcinoma.

Bicornuate uterus. A heart-shaped uterus results from an incomplete fusion of the Müllerian or paramesonephric ducts. This abnormality is the most common type of uterine malformation.

Hydatidiform mole, gross specimen. Numerous swollen (hydropic) villi are shown here.

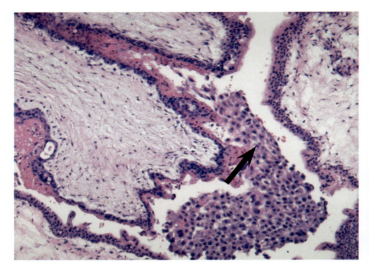

Complete hydatidiform mole. A complete hydatidiform mole shows hydropic swelling of most chorionic villi, trophoblast hyperplasia, and little-to-no vascularization of the villi. The majority of complete moles result from the fertilization by a single sperm of an egg that has lost its chromosomes.

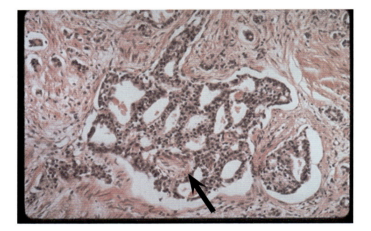

Prostate cancer. Small malignant cells with enlarged nuclei and dark cytoplasm make up this abnormal prostate gland. Perineural invasion by malignant cells is shown here (*arrow*).

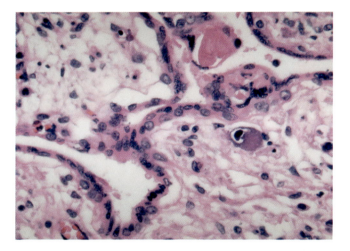

CMV infection of the placenta. Placental villitis occurs with hydropic change within the placenta with congenital cytomegalovirus (CMV) infection. An enlarged cell with mauve intranuclear inclusions is seen here, which is typical for congenital cytomegalovirus infection. Congenital infection with CMV is a common cause for hydrops fetalis.

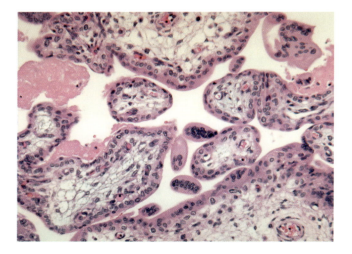

Normal placental villi

ESSENTIAL DISEASES AND FINDINGS

ESSENTIAL EPONYMS (DISEASES AND FINDINGS)	
Name	**Description**
Addison disease	Primary adrenocortical insufficiency
Albright syndrome	Young girls with short stature, polyostotic fibrous dysplasia, precocious puberty, café-au-lait spots
Alport syndrome	Progressive hereditary nephritis with sensorineural deafness
Argyll-Robertson pupil	Small, irregular pupils that react poorly to light in neurosyphilis (accommodation is preserved)
Arnold-Chiari malformation	Congenital herniation of cerebellar tonsils and vermis through the foramen magnum; may compress medulla or cervical cord
Aschoff bodies	Painless nodules in rheumatic fever
Auer rods	Intracytoplasmic inclusions in acute myelogenous leukemia
Babinski sign	Upward moving great toe when sole stroked; indicates upper motor neuron lesion
Baker's cyst	Popliteal fossa cyst in rheumatoid arthritis
Bartter syndrome	Hypokalemia, metabolic alkalosis, elevated renin and aldosterone, normal to low blood pressure
Becker muscular dystrophy	Less severe than Duchenne, also due to defective dystrophin
Bell's palsy	Facial paralysis due to lower motor neuron CN VII palsy
Bence Jones protein	Kappa or lambda immunoglobin light chains in urine of patients with multiple myeloma or Waldenström macroglobulinemia
Berger disease	IgA nephropathy; most common form of primary glomerulonephritis
Bernard-Soulier disease	Thrombocytopenia, large platelets; defect in platelet adhesion
Birbeck granules	Intracellular "tennis racket"–shaped structures in histiocytosis X (eosinophilic granuloma)
Bouchard's nodes	PIP swelling in osteoarthritis secondary to osteophytes
Brushfield spots	Ring of iris spots in Down syndrome
Bruton disease	X-linked agammaglobulinemia; mature B cells absent
Budd-Chiari syndrome	Posthepatic venous thrombosis causing occlusion of hepatic vein or inferior vena cava
Buerger disease	Small/medium artery vasculitis, especially in young male smokers
Burkitt lymphoma	EBV-associated lymphoma with 8:14 translocation (starry sky appearance)
Burton's lines	Blue discoloration of gums in lead poisoning

(Continued)

ESSENTIAL EPONYMS (DISEASES AND FINDINGS) (CONT'D.)

Name	Description
Caisson disease	Gas emboli in divers
Call-Exner bodies	Small spaces with eosinophilic material in granulosa-theca cell tumor of ovary
Chagas disease	Infection with *Trypanosoma cruzi* (Central and South America)
Charcot's triad #1	Nystagmus, intention tremor, and scanning speech; suggests multiple sclerosis
Charcot's triad #2	Jaundice, RUQ pain, and fever; suggests cholangitis
Charcot-Leyden crystals	Crystals in sputum made of eosinophil membranes; suggests bronchial asthma
Chediak-Higashi disease	Phagocyte deficiency related to abnormally large granules in neutrophils
Cheyne-Stokes respirations	Terminal pattern of respirations with increasing breaths followed by apnea; indicates central apnea in coronary heart disease and increased intracranial pressure
Chvostek's sign	Facial musical spasm on tapping; indicates hypocalcemia
Codman's triangle on x-ray	Subperiosteal new bone formation; suggests osteosarcoma
Cori disease	Liver and muscle glycogen storage disease due to debranching enzyme deficiency
Councilman bodies	Eosinophilic intracytoplasmic balls in hepatocytes; suggests toxic or viral hepatitis
Cowdry type A bodies	Intranuclear inclusions; suggests herpesvirus infection
Crigler-Najjar syndrome	Mild (type 2) to life-threatening (type 1) congenital unconjugated hyperbilirubinemia
Curling ulcer	Acute gastric ulcer secondary to severe burns
Curschmann's spirals	Coiled mucinous fibrils found in sputum in bronchial asthma
Cushing ulcer	Gastric ulcer produced by increased intracranial pressure
Donovan bodies	Intracellular bacteria in granuloma inguinale
Dressler syndrome	Fibrinous pericarditis developing after myocardial infarction
Dubin-Johnson syndrome	Benign black liver secondary to congenital conjugated hyperbilirubinemia
Duchenne muscular dystrophy	X-linked recessive muscle dysfunction secondary to deleted dystrophin gene
Edwards syndrome	Trisomy 18; causes "rocker bottom" feet, low-set ears, and heart disease
Eisenmenger's complex	Uncorrected left-to-right cardiac shunt causes late right-to-left shunt with late cyanosis
Erb-Duchenne palsy	"Waiter's tip" hand secondary to superior trunk brachial plexus injury
Fanconi syndrome	Kidney dysfunction secondary to proximal tubular reabsorption defect
Gardner syndrome	Constellation of colon polyps with osteomas and soft tissue tumors
Gaucher disease	Glucocerebrosidase deficiency leading to potentially fatal glucocerebroside accumulation in multiple organs, notably spleen, liver, marrow, and brain
Ghon focus	Small lung lesion of early tuberculosis
Gilbert syndrome	Benign congenital unconjugated bilirubinemia (mostly just scares doctors)
Goodpasture syndrome	Anti-basement membrane antibodies; causes pulmonary and kidney bleeding

(Continued)

ESSENTIAL EPONYMS (DISEASES AND FINDINGS) *(CONT'D.)*

Name	Description
Gower's maneuver	Child using arms to help with leg weakness when trying to stand; suggests Duchenne muscular dystrophy
Guillain-Barré syndrome	Autoimmune peripheral nerve damage causing life-threatening paralysis
Hand-Schüller-Christian disease	Chronic, progressive, potentially fatal histiocytosis in which macrophages attack a child's body
Heberden's nodes	Osteophytes at DIP; suggests osteoarthritis
Heinz bodies	Red cell inclusions in G6PD deficiency
Henoch-Schönlein purpura	Hypersensitivity vasculitis causing hemorrhagic urticaria and arthritis
Homer-Wright rosette	Microscopic finding of a ring of neural cells suggesting neuroblastoma
Horner syndrome	Dysfunction of oculosympathetic pathway; ptosis, miosis, hemianhidrosis, apparent enophthalmos; causes include Pancoast tumor, lateral medullary syndrome
Howell-Jolly bodies	Red cell inclusions of DNA suggesting hyposplenism
Huntington disease	Autosomal-dominant caudate degeneration causing chorea and psychiatric problems
Janeway lesions	Hemorrhagic nodules in palms or soles; suggest endocarditis
Jarisch-Herxheimer reaction	Overaggressive treatment of infection causing endotoxin release with possible shock; classic example is syphilis
Job syndrome	Poor delayed hypersensitivity with neutrophil chemotaxis abnormality causing hyper-IgE with skin abscesses and other infections
Kaposi sarcoma	HHV-8 infection in AIDS patients causing vascular sarcoma
Kartagener syndrome	Dynein defect causes defective cilia, leading to bronchiectasis
Kayser-Fleischer rings	Green to golden copper deposits in iris around pupil; suggest Wilson disease
Kimmelstiel-Wilson nodules	Acellular glomerular nodules; suggest diabetic nephropathy
Klüver-Bucy syndrome	Bilateral amygdala lesions causing bizarre behavior with tendency to put anything in the mouth
Koplik spots	Minute white specks in buccal mucosa that may be first sign of measles
Krukenberg tumor	Gastric adenocarcinoma with ovarian metastases
Kussmaul ventilation	Diabetic ketoacidosis causes rapid, deep breathing to blow off CO_2
Lesch-Nyhan syndrome	X-linked HGPRT deficiency causing high uric acid levels with risk of brain damage
Lewy bodies	Round intracytoplasmic inclusions in neurons; seen in Parkinson disease
Libman-Sacks disease	Noninfectious endocarditis in SLE
Lines of Zahn	White streaks in arterial thrombus
Lisch nodules	Brown iris lesions in neurofibromatosis
Mallory bodies	Ropy cytoplasmic inclusions in hepatocytes in alcoholic liver disease

(Continued)

Name	Description
Mallory-Weiss syndrome	Esophagogastric lacerations with profuse bleeding secondary to heavy vomiting, forcing part of stomach into esophagus
McArdle disease	Muscle phosphorylase deficiency causing glycogen storage disease with prominent muscular symptoms
McBurney's point	Appendicitis is suggested by tenderness on palpation on a line between the anterior superior spine of the ilium and the umbilicus
Negri bodies	Neuron inclusions on electron microscopy in rabies
Niemann-Pick disease	Potentially fatal sphingomyelinase deficiency causing sphingomyelin deposition in brain and other organs, cherry-red macula spot, and neurologic problems
Osler's nodes	Pea-sized nodules on palms and soles suggesting endocarditis
Pancoast tumor	Apical lung cancer causing Horner syndrome
Parinaud syndrome	Dorsal midbrain syndrome often caused by compression by pineal gland; paralysis of upward gaze, may compress cerebral aqueduct → noncommunicating hydrocephalus
Parkinson disease	Motor disorder (resting tremor, rigidity) secondary to nigrostriatal dopamine depletion
Peutz-Jeghers syndrome	Benign autosomal-dominant colon polyposis syndrome
Peyronie disease	Penis deviates on erection secondary to fibrosis
Pick bodies	Round, silver-staining cytoplasmic structures in neurons in Pick disease; contain tau protein
Pick cells	Swollen (balloon) cells found in Pick disease; may contain Pick bodies
Pick disease	Frontal and temporal atrophy; progressive dementia; similar to Alzheimer disease but has a shorter course
Plummer-Vinson syndrome	Esophageal webs with iron deficiency anemia
Pompe disease	Lysosomal glucosidase deficiency causing cardiomegaly
Pott disease	Tuberculosis of the vertebrae
Raynaud syndrome	Recurrent vasospasm in extremities causing hand or foot color changes
Reed-Sternberg cells	Large binucleate tumor cells in Hodgkin disease
Reid index	Increased Reid index means thick mucous glands in bronchus and suggests chronic bronchitis
Reinke crystals	Crystals seen in Leydig cell tumors on microscopy
Reiter syndrome	Nongonococcal urethritis causes immune response, leading to conjunctivitis and arthritis
Roth spots	Retinal hemorrhages; suggest endocarditis
Rotor syndrome	Fairly benign congenital conjugated hyperbilirubinemia
Russell bodies	Round plasma cell inclusions that suggest multiple myeloma
Schiller-Duval bodies	Glomerulus-like microscopic structures in yolk sac tumors

(Continued)

Name	Description
Sézary syndrome	Cutaneous form of T-cell lymphoma with marked generalized erythema
Sheehan syndrome	Postpartum pituitary necrosis leading to massive hormonal deficits
Sipple syndrome	MEN type IIa; medullary thyroid carcinoma, pheochromocytoma, and parathyroid disease
Sjögren syndrome	Autoimmune attack on salivary glands with dry eyes, dry mouth, and arthritis
Spitz nevus	Childhood spindle cell lesion that looks like melanoma but has better prognosis
Trousseau's sign of hypocalcemia	Carpal spasm
Trousseau's sign of malignancy	Migratory thrombophlebitis suggesting visceral (pancreatic) carcinoma
Virchow's node	Left supraclavicular node enlargement suggesting metastatic gastric carcinoma
Virchow's triad	Combination of blood stasis, endothelial damage, and hypercoagulation causes venous clots with risk of pulmonary embolism
von Recklinghausen neurologic disease	Neurofibromatosis
von Recklinghausen bone disease	Osteitis fibrosa cystica
Wallenberg syndrome	Lateral medullary syndrome caused by PICA occlusion; causes contralateral pain/temperature deficits in body, ipsilateral pain/temperature deficits in face, dysphagia, vestibular dysfunction, ipsilateral Horner syndrome
Waterhouse-Friderichsen syndrome	Adrenal hemorrhage complicating meningococcemia
Weber syndrome	Medial midbrain syndrome; ipsilateral oculomotor paralysis, contralateral spastic paralysis, contralateral lower facial weakness
Wermer syndrome	MEN type I; parathyroid tumors, endocrine pancreatic tumors, and pituitary gland tumors
Whipple disease	*Tropheryma whippelii* causes malabsorption syndrome
Wilson disease	Altered copper metabolism causes damage to liver and brain; Kayser-Fleischer rings
Zenker's diverticulum	Lower esophageal diverticulum
Zollinger-Ellison syndrome	Gastrin-secreting tumor causing peptic ulcers

	EYE FINDINGS ON PHYSICAL EXAMINATION	
Finding	**Classic Disease Association (Notes)**	
Argyll Robertson pupil	Tertiary (neuro) syphilis; loss of light reflex constriction; accommodation is preserved; classic form bilateral	
Blue sclera	Osteogenesis imperfecta, types I and II (fatal) Also may be seen in Ehlers-Danlos syndrome, pseudoxanthoma elasticum, Marfan syndrome	
Brushfield spots	Down syndrome (ring of white spots around periphery of iris; trisomy 21)	
Charcot's triad #1	Multiple sclerosis (nystagmus, intention tremor, scanning speech; triad #2 is for cholangitis: jaundice, fever, rigors, pain)	

(Continued)

EYE FINDINGS ON PHYSICAL EXAMINATION *(CONT'D.)*

Finding	Classic Disease Association (Notes)
Cherry-red spot	Tay-Sachs, Niemann-Pick, central retinal artery occlusion (retinal pallor contrasting with strikingly red macular spot)
Cotton-wool spots	Chronic hypertension (small areas of yellowish-white discoloration in the retina)
Horner syndrome	Impaired sympathetic innervation to eye (ptosis, miosis, anhidrosis, and apparent enophthalmos; numerous causes, including vascular, traumatic, congenital, Pancoast tumor, other tumors)
Internuclear ophthalmoplegia (INO)	Multiple sclerosis (disorder of lateral conjugate gaze; affected eye cannot adduct and nystagmus occurs in the abducting eye; convergence is intact)
Kayser-Fleischer rings	Wilson disease (greenish or golden copper deposits in crescent or ring in Descemet's membrane)
Lens dislocation	Marfan syndrome (can be accompanied by aortic dissection and joint hyperflexibility)
Lisch nodules	Neurofibromatosis type I (tan hamartomas on the iris)
Roth spots	Bacterial endocarditis (hemorrhage in retina with a white center; also seen in leukemia, diabetes, collagen-vascular diseases)

SKIN FINDINGS

Finding	Classic Disease Association (Notes)
Adenoma sebaceum	Tuberous sclerosis (raised, erythematous papules on the face, especially around the nose)
Anesthesia	Leprosy (skin may be blotchy, red, or thickened)
Bullae (tense)	Bullous pemphigoid
Bullae (flaccid, rupturing)	Pemphigus
Brown-black lesion with fuzzy edge	Melanoma (depth of lesion most important prognostic indicator)
Butterfly rash	Systemic lupus erythematosus (nose and cheeks)
Café-au-lait spots	Neurofibromatosis (light brown spots, often over 1 cm)
Chancre	Primary syphilis (pain**less** ulcer, usually on genitalia)
Chancroid	*Haemophilus ducreyi* (pain**ful** ulcer, usually on genitalia)
Condylomata lata	Secondary syphilis (smooth, flat, painless genital lesions; scrapings may show spirochetes with darkfield microscopy)
Dermatitis, dementia, diarrhea	Pellagra caused by niacin deficiency
Dog or cat bite	*Pasteurella multocida*
Elastic skin	Ehlers-Danlos syndrome
Erythema chronicum migrans	Lyme disease (expanding red ring with central clearing at tick bite site)
Generalized hyperpigmentation	Addison disease (primary adrenal insufficiency)
Kaposi sarcoma	AIDS (usually slightly raised violaceous papules or plaques)

(Continued)

SKIN FINDINGS (CONT'D.)

Finding	Classic Disease Association (Notes)
Port wine stain	Hemangioma (large, purplish lesion on face)
Rash on palms and soles	Secondary syphilis, Rocky Mountain spotted fever
Silvery, scaly plaques	Psoriasis (knees, elbows, scalp)
Slapped cheeks	Erythema infectiosum (fifth disease, parvovirus B19)
Vesicles, small painful	Herpes, dermatitis herpetiformis

EXTREMITY FINDINGS ON PHYSICAL EXAMINATION

Finding	Classic Disease Association (Notes)
Arachnodactyly	Marfan syndrome (very long fingers and toes)
Babinski sign	Upper motor neuron lesion (stimulation of sole of foot → upgoing great toe)
Baker's cyst	Rheumatoid arthritis (cyst in popliteal fossa)
Bouchard's node	Osteoarthritis (PIP osteophytes)
Boutonniere deformity	Rheumatoid arthritis (finger flexed at PIP and hyperextended at DIP)
Calf pseudohypertrophy	Duchenne muscular dystrophy (replacement of muscle with fat and connective tissue)
Heberden's nodes	Osteoarthritis (DIP enlargement because of osteophytes)
Janeway lesions	Endocarditis (hemorrhagic nodules in palms or soles)
Osler's nodes	Endocarditis (tender nodules on palms and soles)
Palpable purpura	Henoch-Schönlein purpura (legs and buttocks)
Rash affecting palms and soles	Secondary syphilis, Rocky Mountain spotted fever
Raynaud syndrome	Recurrent vasospasm (pale to blue to red on hands or feet)
Simian crease	Down syndrome (single long crease across palm; trisomy 21)
Splinter hemorrhage	Infective endocarditis, trauma (found under fingernails)
Tendon xanthomas	Familial hypercholesterolemia (classically Achilles tendon)
Tophi	Gout (hard nodules composed of uric acid)

RADIOLOGIC FINDINGS

Finding	Classic Disease Association (Notes)
Bamboo spine	Ankylosing spondylitis (rigid spine with fused joints)
Boot-shaped heart	Right ventricular hypertrophy; tetralogy of Fallot (upturned ventricular apex and large pulmonary artery make the "boot")
Codman's triangle	Osteosarcoma (new subperiosteal bone lifts periosteum)

(Continued)

RADIOLOGIC FINDINGS *(CONT'D.)*	
Finding	**Classic Disease Association (Notes)**
Double-bubble sign	Duodenal atresia, also duodenal stenosis, duodenal webs, annular pancreas, malrotation of the gut (two air-filled structures in upper abdomen, with little or no air distally)
"Hair on end" or "crew-cut"	Beta thalassemia, sickle cell anemia (extramedullary hematopoiesis below periosteum leads to formation of bony spicules = "hair" on outside of bone)
Mammillary body atrophy	Wernicke encephalopathy (memory loss)
Periosteal elevation	Pyogenic osteomyelitis (elevation due to subperiosteal inflammation; this may be the earliest radiologic sign of osteomyelitis)
"Punched out" (lytic) lesions of bone	Multiple myeloma
Rib notching	Coarctation of aorta (dilated aorta before coarctation puts chronic pressure on ribs)
Soap bubble	Giant cell tumor of bone (lytic expansile lesion)
String sign	Crohn disease (small bowel follow-through shows very narrow lumen, typically in terminal ileum)

AUSCULTATION FINDINGS	
Sound	**Possible Causes**
Systolic Murmurs	
Soft systolic ejection murmurs	May be normal in infants, children, pregnancy
Systolic ejection murmur (right 2nd interspace)	Aortic stenosis
Systolic ejection murmur (mid to lower left sternal border)	Hypertrophic obstructive cardiomyopathy
Systolic ejection murmur (left 2nd interspace)	Pulmonic stenosis
Systolic ejection murmur (apex, can increase through systole)	Mitral regurgitation
Systolic ejection murmur (lower left sternal border, increases with inspiration)	Tricuspid regurgitation
Holosystolic ejection murmur (left fourth interspace)	Ventricular septal defect
Diastolic Murmurs	
Diastolic murmur (apex)	Mitral stenosis
Diastolic murmur (left 4th interspace)	Tricuspid stenosis
Decrescendo diastolic murmur (left 4th interspace)	Aortic regurgitation (see also Austin-Flint murmur)
Austin-Flint murmur (mid-to-late-diastolic rumble/low-frequency murmur over apex)	Severe aortic regurgitation
Decrescendo diastolic murmur (right sternal edge and left 2nd interspace)	Pulmonic regurgitation

(Continued)

AUSCULTATION FINDINGS (CONT'D.)	
Sound	**Possible Causes**
Continuous Murmurs	
Continuous murmur (left 2nd interspace below median end of clavicle)	Patent ductus arteriosus
Continuous murmur (centrally at 3rd interspace level)	Aorticopulmonary window defect
Continuous murmur (peripheral body sites)	Systemic arteriovenous connections
Miscellaneous Findings	
Loud S_1	Mitral stenosis
Soft or absent S_1	Mitral regurgitation if valve is stiff
Late aortic valve closure in S_2	Left bundle branch block, aortic stenosis
Late pulmonic valve closure in S_2	Atrial septal defect, right bundle branch block
Fixed split S_2 during respiration	Atrial septal defect
Paradoxical splitting of S_2	Left bundle branch block (also some cases of aortic stenosis and patent ductus)
Single S_2	Badly damaged aortic valve (regurgitation, stenosis, or atresia)
Early systolic click	Congenital aortic or pulmonic valve stenosis, severe pulmonary hypertension
Changing systolic clicks with position	Myxomatous degeneration of mitral or tricuspid valves
S_3 (pericardial knock)	Dilated and noncompliant left (strongest on expiration) or right (strongest on inspiration) ventricle, normal in kids
S_4	Right (strongest on inspiration) or left (strongest on expiration) ventricular dysfunction (myocardial ischemia or early myocardial infarction)
Summation gallop (combined S_3 and S_4)	Tachycardic patient with right or left ventricular dysfunction
Diastolic knock	Constricting pericardium
Mitral opening snap	Mitral stenosis

GENETIC ASSOCIATIONS	
Finding	**Classic Disease Association (Notes)**
5p–	Cri-du-chat syndrome (cat-like cry, feeding problems, abnormal mental development)
45,XO	Turner syndrome (infertile female, webbed neck, coarctation of aorta)
47,XXY	Klinefelter syndrome (male with small testes and eunuchoid habitus)
CFTR	Cystic fibrosis (chloride channel gene, chromosome 7, recurrent pneumonia, pancreatic exocrine insufficiency)
FBN1 gene (codes for fibrillin)	Marfan syndrome (chromosome 15, tall stature, hyperextensible joints, dissecting aortic aneurysm)

(Continued)

GENETIC ASSOCIATIONS (CONT'D.)

Finding	Classic Disease Association (Notes)
NF1	Neurofibromatosis type I (von Recklinghausen disease, chromosome 17, neurofibromas, café-au-lait spots)
NF2	Neurofibromatosis type II (bilateral acoustic neurofibromatosis, chromosome 22)
t(8;14)	Burkitt lymphoma (c-myc)
t(9;22)	CML and occasionally AML (Philadelphia chromosome, bcr-abl hybrid)
t(14;18)	Many follicular lymphomas (bcl-2)
Trisomy 13	Patau syndrome (microcephaly, mental retardation, cleft palate, polydactyly, heart malformations)
Trisomy 18	Edwards syndrome (rocker bottom feet, microcephaly, mental retardation, multiple organ defects)
Trisomy 21	Down syndrome (most common chromosomal disorder, older maternal age, mental retardation, early Alzheimer disease)
VHL	von Hippel-Lindau (chromosome 3, hemangioblastomas, renal cell carcinoma)
XYY	XYY syndrome (very tall male with increased risk of behavior problems)

MICROSCOPIC FINDINGS

Finding	Classic Disease Association (Notes)
Auer rods	Acute myelogenous leukemia, particularly promyelocytic (rods in white blood cell cytoplasm)
Basophilic stippling	Lead poisoning (dots in erythrocytes)
Birbeck granules on EM	Histiocytosis X (eosinophilic granuloma)
Call-Exner bodies	Granulosa-theca cell tumor of ovary (ring of cells with pink fluid in center)
Cerebriform nuclei	Mycosis fungoides (cutaneous T-cell lymphoma)
Clue cells	Gardnerella vaginitis (bacteria on epithelial cells)
Councilman bodies	Toxic or viral hepatitis (pink, round cytoplasmic inclusion in hepatocytes)
Cowdry type A bodies	Herpes (intranuclear eosinophilic inclusions)
Crescents in Bowman's capsule	Rapidly progressive crescentic glomerulonephritis
Curschmann's spirals	Bronchial asthma (coiled mucinous fibrils found in sputum)
Depigmentation of neurons in substantia nigra	Parkinson disease (degeneration of dopaminergic nigrostriatal neurons)
Donovan bodies	Granuloma inguinale (oval, rod-shaped organisms in cells)
Ferruginous bodies	Asbestosis (rod-shaped structures with crystals on them)
Heinz bodies	G6PD deficiency (red cell inclusions)
Homer Wright rosettes	Neuroblastoma (ring of neural cells)
Howell-Jowell bodies	Splenectomy or nonfunctioning spleen (blue-black erythrocyte inclusions)
Hypersegmented neutrophils	Macrocytic anemia (vitamin B_{12} or folate deficiency)

(Continued)

MICROSCOPIC FINDINGS (CONT'D.)	
Finding	**Classic Disease Association (Notes)**
Hypochromic microcytosis	Iron deficiency anemia, lead poisoning
Keratin pearls	Squamous cell carcinoma (concentric layers of keratin)
Kimmelsteil-Wilson nodules	Diabetic nephropathy (acellular nodules in glomerulus)
Koilocytes	HPV infections such as condyloma, cervical dysplasia (look for perinuclear halo)
Lewy bodies	Parkinson disease (round, pink nodules in neuronal cytoplasm)
Mallory bodies	Alcoholic liver disease (ropy, pink cytoplasmic structures in hepatocytes)
Needle-shaped, negatively birefringent crystals	Gout (uric acid)
Negri bodies	Rabies (large viral inclusions in neurons, see on Emergency Medicine)
Neurofibrillary tangles	Alzheimer disease (tangles of fibers in neuron cytoplasm)
Owl's eye nuclei	Cytomegalovirus (due to virus particles in nucleus)
Pick bodies	Pick disease (silver protein deposits in neurons)
Pseudopalisading tumor cell arrangement	Glioblastoma multiforme (foci of necrosis surrounded by intact tumor cells)
Pseudorosettes	Ewing sarcoma (rings of cells with central vessel)
Reed-Sternberg cells	Hodgkin lymphoma (large binucleate cell with large nucleoli)
Reinke crystals	Leydig cell tumor (rectangular crystals, ovary or testes)
Renal epithelial casts in urine	Acute toxicity/viral (epithelial casts reflect tubular damage)
Rhomboid crystals in joint fluid, positively birefringent	Pseudogout (calcium pyrophosphate crystals)
Rouleaux	Multiple myeloma (stacked erythrocytes)
Russell bodies	Multiple myeloma (hyaline spheres in plasma cells)
Schiller-Duval bodies	Yolk sac tumor (look like glomeruli)
Senile plaques	Alzheimer disease (extracellular amyloid)
Signet ring cells	Gastric carcinoma (have nucleus compressed to one side of cell)
Smudge cells	Chronic lymphocytic leukemia (smashed lymphocyte)
Spike and dome on EM	Membranous glomerulonephritis (irregular dense deposits with basement membrane material between deposits)
"Starry sky" pattern	Burkitt lymphoma (sheets of small lymphocytes with scattered histiocytes as "stars")
Subepithelial humps on Emergency Medicine	Poststreptococcal glomerulonephritis
Sulfur granules	*Actinomyces israeli* (clusters of bacteria)
Tram track appearance on light microscopy	Membranoproliferative glomerulonephritis (double contour capillary loops)
Waxy casts in urine	Chronic end-stage renal disease
WBC casts in urine	Acute pyelonephritis
WBCs in urine	Acute cystitis (heavy neutrophilic infiltrate)
"Wire loop" lesion	Lupus nephritis (thickened capillary basement membrane)

Classic Antibody Findings

Finding	Classic Disease Association (Notes)
Anti-basement membrane	Goodpasture syndrome
Anticentromere	Scleroderma (CREST syndrome)
Anti-double stranded DNA (ANA antibodies)	Systemic lupus erythematosus (type III hypersensitivity-immune complexes)
Antiepithelial cell	Pemphigus vulgaris
Antigliadin	Celiac disease
Antihistone	Drug-induced SLE
Anti-IgG	Rheumatoid arthritis (rheumatoid factor)
Antimitochondrial	Primary biliary cirrhosis
Antineutrophil	Vasculitis
Antiplatelet	Idiopathic thrombocytopenic purpura
C-ANCA, P-ANCA	Wegener granulomatosis (C-ANCA), polyarteritis nodosa (mostly P-ANCA, but can have both)
CLL	*Mycoplasma pneumoniae*, mononucleosis, lymphoma, CLL

Abnormal Erythrocytes on Peripheral Smear

Finding	Classic Disease Association (Notes)
Acanthocytes (spur cells)	Abetalipoproteinemia (severe burns, liver disease, hypothyroidism)
Basophilic stippling	Lead poisoning (thalassemia)
Bite cells and Heinz bodies	Glucose-6-phosphate dehydrogenase deficiency (spleen removes Heinz bodies, leading to "bitten" appearance of RBCs)
Dacrocytes (teardrop cells)	Scarring of bone marrow (myelophthisis), splenic dysfunction
Echinocytes (burr cells)	Often drying artifact, uremia
Elliptocytes (ovalocytes)	Hereditary elliptocytosis (iron deficiency, thalassemia, myelophthisis)
Howell-Jolly bodies and Cabot rings	Splenic dysfunction (thalassemia)
Macrocytes (large cells)	Vitamin B_{12} and folate deficiency (myelodysplastic syndromes, liver disease)
Microcytes (small cells)	Iron deficiency anemia (thalassemia and some cases of anemia of chronic disease)
Pappenheimer bodies	Sideroblastic anemia (splenic dysfunction)
Rouleaux formation	Multiple myeloma (RBCs stacked like coins)
Schistocytes	Intravascular hemolysis (fragmented cells)
Spherocytes	Hereditary spherocytosis (extravascular hemolysis)
Stomatocytes	Hereditary stomatocytosis (alcoholism)
Target cells	Liver disease, thalassemia (HbC, occasionally in iron deficiency)

ABNORMALITIES OF WHITE BLOOD CELLS AND PLATELETS ON PERIPHERAL SMEAR	
Finding	**Classic Disease Association (Notes)**
Bilobed neutrophil nuclei	Pelger-Huet anomaly
Cerebriform nuclei (convoluted appearance to nucleus)	Mycosis fungoides (cutaneous T-cell lymphoma)
Dohle bodies	Sepsis, May-Hegglin anomaly (pale blue, oval cytoplasmic inclusions that can be near cytoplasmic membrane of neutrophils)
Giant platelets	Bernard-Soulier syndrome
Hypersegmented neutrophil nuclei	Megaloblastic (macrocytic) anemia
Large blue granules in cytoplasm of all white blood cells	Alder-Reilly anomaly
Large eosinophilic granules in neutrophil cytoplasm	Chediak-Higashi syndrome
Toxic granulation	Sepsis (medium-to-large sized dark blue granulations in neutrophil cytoplasm)

SERUM ENZYMES	
Enzyme	**Classic Associated Conditions**
Alanine aminotransferase (ALT)	Liver damage
Alkaline phosphatase (Alk phos)	Bone, biliary, and placental disease
Amylase	Pancreatic and salivary disease
Angiotensin-converting enzyme (ACE)	Sarcoidosis (also primary biliary cirrhosis, Gaucher disease, leprosy)
Aspartate aminotransferase (AST)	Acute myocardial infarction, liver disease
Creatinine kinase (CK) CK-MB	Myocardial infarction (early 2–8 h), severe skeletal muscle injury
Elastase-1	Pancreatic disease

Lactate dehydrogenase (LDH)
    LD1>LD2
    High LD4 and LD5
    High LD1 And LD5
	Acute myocardial infarction (early), hemolysis, renal infarction
	Liver damage (also skeletal muscle damage)
	Acute myocardial infarction complicated by liver congestion; alcoholic liver disease complicated by megaloblastic anemia

Lipase	Pancreatic disease
Myoglobin	Myocardial infarction (early, but nonspecific)
Troponin I	Myocardial infarction (elevates as early as 3 h post MI, then stays elevated up to 9 days after MI)

DRUG LIST

This drug table is designed for reference. Do not attempt to memorize it; we suggest you use this as a starting point to create your own personal drug list. Many of the most commonly used drugs are presented, but the list is not exhaustive. Also remember that most drugs have more side effects than noted in this table. We have included brand names in addition to the generic names—even though brand names are **not** tested on the USMLE—because you will be exposed to many brand names during your clinical years.

Generic Name (Brand Name) • Primary Use	Therapeutic Class and Mechanism	Most Common Adverse Effects
Acebutolol (Sectral®) • Hypertension, ventricular arrhythmias	β_1-adrenoreceptor blocker with mild intrinsic sympathomimetic activity	Heart failure, hypoglycemic unawareness, bradycardia, hypotension, potential bronchospasm in asthmatics (not completely β_1 selective), impotence
Acetaminophen (Tylenol®) • Pain, fever, headache	Nonopiate, nonsalicylate, non-NSAID analgesic/antipyretic	Hepatic failure in overdose situation (treat with *N*-acetylcysteine)
Acetazolamide (Diamox®) • Glaucoma, high altitude sickness, edema if accompanied by metabolic alkalosis, urinary alkalization	Carbonic anhydrase inhibitor	Hypochloremic metabolic acidosis, renal stones, hypokalemia, paresthesias, hyperammonemia/hepatic encephalopathy in cirrhotic patients
Acyclovir (Zovirax®) • Herpes simplex	Antiviral (inhibits viral DNA polymerases)	Nausea/vomiting, neurotoxicity (agitation, headache, confusion, seizures in overdose), nephrotoxicity (crystalluria)
Albuterol (Proventil®) • Asthma	Antiasthma (β_2-receptor agonist)	Tremor, tachycardia, CNS stimulation, hypertension
Alendronate (Fosamax®) • Osteoporosis	Bisphosphonate	Esophageal ulcers, esophagitis, abdominal pain, gastric reflux, dysphagia
Allopurinol (Zyloprim®) • Gout	Xanthine oxidase inhibitor (irreversible suicide inhibitor)	Rash that can progress to Stevens-Johnson syndrome, and/or generalized vasculitis, irreversible hepatotoxicity
Alprazolam (Xanax®) • Anxiety	Benzodiazepine, sedative/hypnotic (increases frequency of $GABA_A$-receptor opening)	Drowsiness, dizziness, amnesia, decreased motor skills, dependence, respiratory depression with high doses (can be reversed with flumazenil)
Alteplase (t-PA; Activase®) • Acute myocardial infarction, stroke, pulmonary embolism	Tissue-plasminogen activator	Bleeding
Amiloride (Midamor®) • Hypertension, congestive heart failure	Potassium-sparing diuretic (blocks Na^+ channels in cortical collecting tubules)	Hyperkalemia

(Continued)

Generic Name (Brand Name) • Primary Use	Therapeutic Class and Mechanism	Most Common Adverse Effects
Amiodarone (Cordarone®) • Cardiac arrhythmias	Antiarrhythmic (classes IA, III)	Pulmonary fibrosis, deposits in skin, photosensitivity, thyroid dysfunction, can worsen arrhythmias
Amitriptyline (Elavil®) • Depression, anxiety	Tricyclic antidepressant (blocks norepinephrine [NE] and serotonin [5HT] reuptake)	Strong anticholinergic side effects (e.g., urinary retention, tachycardia, increased intraocular pressure), cardiac arrhythmias on overdose
Amlodipine (Norvasc®) • Hypertension, coronary artery disease	Calcium channel blocker	Dizziness, edema, somnolence, palpitations
Amoxicillin (Trimox®) • Respiratory tract infections, otic infections, urinary tract infections	Beta-lactam antibiotic (penicillin)	Diarrhea, maculopapular rash (especially in patients with mononucleosis), pseudomembranous colitis, anaphylactic reactions
Amoxicillin/potassium clavulanate (Augmentin®) • Respiratory tract infections, otic infections, urinary tract infections	Beta-lactam antibiotic (penicillin)/ beta-lactamase inhibitor	Diarrhea, maculopapular rash (especially in patients with mononucleosis), pseudomembranous colitis, anaphylactic reactions
Amphetamine mixed salts (Adderall®) • Treatment of attention deficit hyperactivity disorder	Stimulant	CNS stimulation, tachycardia, cardiac arrhythmias, dependence
Amphotericin B • Systemic mycoses	Antifungal (binds ergosterol)	Chills and fevers, hypotension, nephrotoxicity (dose-limiting)
Ampicillin (Omnipen®) • Urinary tract infections, upper respiratory tract infections	Beta-lactam antibiotic (penicillin)	Diarrhea, maculopapular rash (especially in patients with mononucleosis), pseudomembranous colitis, anaphylactic reactions
Anastrozole (Arimidex®) • Estrogen-dependent breast cancer in postmenopausal women	Aromatase inhibitor (decreases estrogen synthesis)	Hot flushes, fatigue
Aripiprazole (Abilify®) • Schizophrenia, bipolar disorder	Atypical antipsychotic	Fewer extrapyramidal side effects than typical antipsychotics
Aspirin (many name brands) • Pain/fever/headache, prevention of clotting with myocardial infarction/ transient ischemic attack	NSAID, salicylate; analgesic, antipyretic, antiplatelet, antiinflammatory (irreversibly inhibits COX-1/COX-2)	Gastric ulcers/bleeding, hypersensitivity, bronchoconstriction, nephrotoxicity, Reye syndrome; high doses: tinnitus, hyperventilation, acid/base disorders
Atenolol (Tenormin®) • Hypertension, angina pectoris due to coronary atherosclerosis, acute myocardial infarction	Antihypertensive (β_1 antagonist)	Heart failure, hypoglycemic unawareness, potential bronchospasm in asthmatics (not completely β_1 selective), bradycardia, hypotension, impotence
Atomoxetine (Strattera®) • Attention deficit hyperactivity disorder	Norepinephrine (NE)–reuptake inhibitor	CNS stimulation, agitation, mood swings, potential increase in suicidal ideation, hepatotoxicity (rare)
Atorvastatin (Lipitor®) • Hyperlipidemia, hypertriglyceridemia	HMG-CoA reductase inhibitor	Hepatic dysfunction, rhabdomyolysis, myalgia, myopathy

(Continued)

Generic Name (Brand Name) • Primary Use	Therapeutic Class and Mechanism	Most Common Adverse Effects
Azithromycin (Zithromax®) • Respiratory tract infections	Macrolide (azalide) antibiotic	Gastrointestinal distress, does not inactivate P450
Baclofen (Lioresal®) • Muscle spasticity secondary to multiple sclerosis, spinal cord injury	Muscle relaxant/spasmolytic ($GABA_B$ agonist)	Drowsiness, dizziness, mental confusion, incoordination
Benazepril (Lotensin®) • Hypertension, congestive heart failure, diabetic nephropathy	ACE inhibitor	Cough, angioedema, hyperkalemia, neutropenia (rare)
Benztropine (Cogentin®) • Parkinsonism, extrapyramidal disorders due to neuroleptics	Anticholinergic (muscarinic antagonist)	Strong anticholinergic side effects (e.g., dry mouth, tachycardia, urinary retention, worsening of glaucoma, paralytic ileus, hyperthermia)
Bleomycin (Blenoxane®) • Hodgkin disease; testicular, ovarian, and bladder cancers	Antineoplastic (antibiotic)	Pulmonary fibrosis, hypersensitivity reactions, mucocutaneous reactions
Botulinum toxin (Botox®) • Spastic disorders, local muscle spasms, cosmetic (wrinkle reduction)	Spasmolytic (prevents ACh release)	Weakness of injected and adjacent muscles
Brimonidine (Alphagan P®) • Open-angle glaucoma, ocular hypertension	Antiglaucoma agent (α_2 agonist; decreases aqueous humor secretion)	Conjunctivitis, ocular itching
Bromocriptine (Parlodel®) • Parkinsonism, hyperprolactinemia	Dopamine agonist	Dyskinesias, nausea/vomiting, behavioral effects, postural hypotension
Budesonide (Pulmicort®) • Asthma	Corticosteroid	Oral candidiasis, may retard growth rate in children
Budesonide nasal spray (Rhinocort Aqua®) • Allergic rhinitis	Corticosteroid	Epistaxis (nosebleed), may retard growth rate in children
Bupivacaine (Marcaine®) • Local anesthesia	Local anesthetic (amide)	Cardiovascular toxicity, various CNS symptoms (excitation or depression, dizziness, seizures), allergic reactions
Bupropion (Wellbutrin®) • Depression, smoking cessation	Antidepressant (heterocyclic)	Seizures, anxiety, insomnia, mania
Buspirone (BuSpar®) • Generalized anxiety disorder	Nonbenzodiazepine, nonbarbiturate anxiolytic; partial agonist at 5-HT_{1A} receptors	Dizziness, nervousness
Butalbital (with acetaminophen/caffeine; Fioricet®; with aspirin/caffine, Fiorinal®) • Tension headaches	Antiheadache; barbiturate	Drowsiness, may be habit forming
Candesartan (Atacand®) • Hypertension, heart failure	Angiotensin II–receptor (type AT_1) antagonist	Hypotension, increased BUN and potassium, contraindicated in pregnancy

(Continued)

Generic Name (Brand Name) • Primary Use	Therapeutic Class and Mechanism	Most Common Adverse Effects
Captopril (Capoten®) • Hypertension, congestive heart failure, diabetic nephropathy	ACE inhibitor (prototype; others in class include benazepril, enalapril, lisinopril, quinapril, ramipril)	Cough, angioedema, hyperkalemia, neutropenia (rare)
Carbamazepine (Tegretol®) • Seizures, trigeminal neuralgia	Anticonvulsant	Ataxia, diplopia, blood dyscrasias, P450 inducer, teratogen
Carisoprodol (Soma®) • Painful musculoskeletal conditions	Skeletal muscle relaxant	Tachycardia, postural hypotension, mental confusion, drowsiness, incoordination
Carvedilol (Coreg®) • Heart failure, hypertension	Mixed α_1/β receptor antagonist	Heart failure, hypoglycemic unawareness, bronchospasm in asthmatics, bradycardia, hypotension, impotence
Celecoxib (Celebrex®) • Pain and inflammation secondary to a variety of conditions (osteoarthritis, rheumatoid arthritis, others)	NSAID (specific COX-2 inhibitor)	Increased risk of serious cardiovascular thrombotic events (myocardial infarction and stroke), gastrointestinal bleeding, ulceration, hepatic and renal dysfunction
First-generation cephalosporins Cefadroxil (Duricef®), cefazolin (Ancef®, Kefzol®), cephalexin (Keflex®)	Beta-lactam antibiotic (gram-positive infections [except *Enterococci* and *Listeria*], some enterics; not for CNS infections)	Anaphylaxis, serum sickness, rashes, diarrhea, pseudomembranous colitis; may potentiate renal toxicity of aminoglycosides; the *N*-methylthiotetrazole side chain found in cefamandole, cefotetan, and cefoperazone is associated with hypoprothrombinemia and intolerance to ethanol
Second-generation cephalosporins Cefaclor (Ceclor®), cefonicid (Monocid®), cefotetan (Cefotan®), cefoxitin (Mefoxin®), cefprozil (Cefzil®) and cefuroxime (Ceftin®, Zinacef®)	Beta-lactam antibiotic (less gram-positive activity and more gram-negative activity than first generation; not for CNS infections [except cefuroxime])	
Third-generation cephalosporins Cefdinir (Omnicef®), cefixime (Suprax®), cefotaxime (Claforan®), cefpodoxime (Vantin®), ceftazidime (Fortaz®, Tazidime®, Tazicef®), ceftibuten (Cedax®), ceftizoxime (Cefizox®) and ceftriaxone (Rocephin®)	Beta-lactam antibiotic (less gram-positive activity and more gram-negative activity than second generation; usually reserved for serious infections; ceftriaxone is drug of choice for penicillin-resistant gonococcal infections; also used for late-stage Lyme disease)	
Fourth-generation cephalosporins Cefepime (Maxipime®)	Beta-lactam antibiotic (more gram-negative activity and same gram-positive activity as first generation)	
Cetirizine (Zyrtec®) • Seasonal allergic rhinitis	Histamine H_1-receptor antagonist (second generation)	Fewer CNS side effects than first-generation antihistamines
Cholestyramine (Questran®) • Hyperlipidemia	Antihyperlipidemic	Constipation
Chloroquine (Aralen®) • Malaria	Antimalarial	Gastrointestinal distress, rash, visual and auditory impairment, peripheral neuropathy

(Continued)

Generic Name (Brand Name) • Primary Use	Therapeutic Class and Mechanism	Most Common Adverse Effects
Cimetidine (Tagamet®) • Peptic ulcer disease, gastroesophageal reflux disease, Zollinger-Ellison	Histamine H_2-receptor antagonist	Potent hepatic enzyme inhibitor, gynecomastia, decreased libido
Ciprofloxacin (Cipro®) • Urinary tract infections, chronic bacterial prostatitis, respiratory tract infections, many others	Fluoroquinolone antibiotic (bacteriocidal inhibitor of topoisomerases)	Gastrointestinal distress, CNS dysfunction, superinfection, collagen dysfunction, pregnancy category D
Cisplatin (Platinol®) • Testicular, bladder, lung, and ovarian cancers	Antineoplastic (alkylating agent)	Nausea/vomiting, neurotoxic, nephrotoxic
Citalopram (Celexa®) • Depression	Selective serotonin reuptake inhibitor (SSRI) antidepressant	CNS stimulation, sexual dysfunction, gastrointestinal distress, serotonin syndrome, seizures in overdose; drug interactions with MAOIs, TCAs, meperidine, dextromethorphan
Clarithromycin (Biaxin®) • Respiratory tract infections	Macrolide antibiotic	Potent hepatic enzyme inhibitor, pseudomembranous colitis
Clomiphene (Clomid®) • Infertility	Fertility agent (blocks estrogen receptors in pituitary, induces ovulation)	Multiple births
Clomipramine (Anafranil®) • Obsessive-compulsive disorder, depression	Tricyclic antidepressant; norephinephrine (NE) and serotonin (5HT) reuptake inhibitor	Strong anticholinergic side effects (e.g., cardiac arrhythmias, urinary retention, tachycardia, increased intraocular pressure, cognitive impairment)
Clonidine (Catapres®) • Hypertension, opioid withdrawal	Antihypertensive (α_2-agonist)	Sedation, rebound hypertension if stopped suddenly
Clonazepam (Klonopin®) • Seizures, panic disorder	Benzodiazepine, sedative/hypnotic, anticonvulsant (increases frequency of opening of $GABA_A$ receptor)	Drowsiness, dizziness, amnesia, respiratory depression
Clopidogrel (Plavix®) • Reduction of antithrombotic events	Antiplatelet agent, blocks ADP receptors on platelets	Bleeding, thrombotic thrombocytopenic purpura, neutropenia
Clozapine (Clozaril®) • Schizophrenia in patients unresponsive to other agents	Atypical antipsychotic	Agranulocytosis (requires weekly WBC count), seizures
Codeine/Acetaminophen (Tylenol® #2, #3 and #4 [least codeine in #2, most in #4]) • Moderate-to-severe pain	Opioid analgesic/acetaminophen combination	Respiratory depression, euphoria, constipation, pruritus, dependence
Colchicine (Colchicine®) • Gout	Inhibits microtubule assembly	Gastrointestinal distress, hepatic and renal damage
Cromolyn (intranasal: NasalCrom®, inhalational: Intal®, oral: Crolom®, ophthalmic: Opticrom®) • Asthma, allergies	Mast cell stabilizer	Cough, throat irritation when inhaled
Cyclobenzaprine (Flexeril®) • Treatment of muscle spasm	Skeletal muscle relaxant	Anticholinergic side effects, drowsiness

(Continued)

Generic Name (Brand Name) • Primary Use	Therapeutic Class and Mechanism	Most Common Adverse Effects
Cyclophosphamide (Cytoxan®) • Lymphomas, ovarian and breast cancer, neuroblastoma	Antineoplastic (alkylating agent)	Bone marrow suppression, hemorrhagic cystitis (use mesna), gastrointestinal distress, alopecia
Cyclosporine (Restasis®) • Immunosuppressant for organ transplants	Immunosuppressant (binds cyclophilin)	Nephrotoxicity, peripheral neuropathy, hypertension, hirsutism
Dantrolene (Dantrium®) • Malignant hyperthermia, neuroleptic malignant syndrome (unlabeled use)	Skeletal muscle relaxant (blocks Ca^{2+} release from sarcoplasmic reticulum by blocking the ryanodine receptor)	Related to skeletal muscle relaxation
Desmopressin (DDAVP®) • Central diabetes insipidus, primary nocturnal enuresis	Synthetic vasopressin	Hyponatremia, decreased plasma osmolality, seizures
Dextroamphetamine (Dexedrine®) • ADHD, narcolepsy	Stimulant	CNS stimulation, tachycardia, cardiac arrhythmias, dependence
Diazepam (Valium®) • Status epilepticus, anxiety disorders, acute alcohol withdrawal, muscle spasms	Benzodiazepine; sedative/hypnotic, anticonvulsant (increases frequency of opening of $GABA_A$ receptor)	Respiratory depression, somnolence, dizziness, dependence
Digoxin (Lanoxin®) • Heart failure, atrial arrhythmias	Cardiac glycoside, antiarrhythmic, inhibits Na^+/K^+-ATPase	Arrhythmias, visual defects (green-yellow halos), nausea
Diltiazem (Cardizem®) • Hypertension, arrhythmias, angina	Calcium channel blocker	Peripheral edema, dizziness, bradycardia, AV block, hypotension
Diphenhydramine (Benadryl®) • Allergies, motion sickness	Antihistamine (first generation)	Antimuscarinic side effects, sedation
Diphenoxylate/Atropine (Lomotil®) • Diarrhea	Antidiarrheal (diphenoxylate: weak opioid; atropine: antimuscarinic)	Atropine is added to prevent abuse; side effects related to constipation, some CNS effects
Donepezil (Aricept®) • Mild-to-moderate dementia of Alzheimer disease	Anti-Alzheimer disease (reversible cholinesterase inhibitor)	Gastrointestinal (diarrhea, nausea, vomiting, increased gastric acid secretion), bradycardia or heart block
Dopamine • Shock	Sympathomimetic amine vasopressor (low dose: increases renal blood flow; moderate dose: positive inotropic effects)	Multiple (careful monitoring of patient's vitals required)
Doxazosin (Cardura®) • Benign prostatic hypertrophy, hypertension	α_1 antagonist	Orthostatic hypotension and syncope, particularly as a "first-dose effect," tachycardia
Doxepin (Sinequan®) • Depression, resistant pruritus	Tricyclic antidepressant (norephineprhine [NE] and serotonin [5HT] reuptake blocker)	Strong anticholinergic side effects (urinary retention, tachycardia, increased intraocular pressure, cognitive impairment), cardiac arrhythmias
Doxorubicin (Doxil®) • Cancer	Antineoplastic (anthracycline antibiotic)	Cardiotoxicity (dexrazoxane may protect), myelosuppression, alopecia, gastrointestinal distress

(Continued)

Generic Name (Brand Name) • Primary Use	Therapeutic Class and Mechanism	Most Common Adverse Effects
Doxycycline (many name brands) • Prostatitis, sinusitis, *Chlamydia*, pelvic inflammatory disease, acne, prophylaxis against anthrax	Tetracycline antibiotic	Photosensitivity and skin reactions, gastrointestinal distress, dental enamel dysplasia
Duloxetine (Cymbalta®) • Major depressive disorder, diabetic peripheral neuropathic pain, generalized anxiety disorder	Serotonin and norepinephrine reuptake inhibitor (SNRI)	Nausea, sleep disorders, dizziness, dry mouth, anxiety, hypomania
Edrophonium (Enlon®) • Diagnosis of myasthenia gravis	Cholinesterase inhibitor (reversible, short-acting)	Bradycardia
Efavirenz (Sustiva®) • HIV infection	Nonnucleoside, reverse transcriptase inhibitor (NNRTI); used in combination regimens	CNS dysfunction, skin rash, elevated plasma cholesterol
Enalapril (Vasotec®) • Hypertension, congestive heart failure, diabetic nephropathy	ACE inhibitor	Cough, angioedema, hyperkalemia, neutropenia (rare)
Enoxaparin (Lovenox®) • Prevention of thrombosis	Anticoagulant; enhancer of antithrombin III activity; low molecular weight (LMW) heparin	Bleeding, much lower incidence of thrombocytopenia than heparin
Entacapone (Comtan®) • Parkinson disease	Antiparkinson (COMT inhibitor)	Exacerbates the effects of levodopa
Erythromycin (E-Mycin®) • Upper respiratory tract infections (including *Mycoplasma* and *Legionella*), skin infections, *Chlamydia*	Macrolide antibiotic	Potent hepatic enzyme inhibitor, gastrointestinal distress, arrhythmia
Escitalopram (Lexapro®) • Depression, anxiety disorders, obsessive-compulsive disorder	Selective serotonin reuptake inhibitor (SSRI) antidepressant	Serotonin syndrome, somnolence, insomnia, tachycardia, postural hypotension, paresthesias, sexual dysfunction
Esomeprazole (Nexium®) • Peptic ulcer disease, gastroesophageal reflux disease, Zollinger-Ellison	Proton pump inhibitor	Gastrointestinal side effects, dizziness, headache
Estrogens (various preparations and combinations) • Contraception, hormone-replacement therapy, osteoporosis, female hypogonadism, dysmenorrhea	Estrogen-receptor agonist	Nausea, breast tenderness, endometrial hyperplasia, biliary disease, clot formation
Etanercept (Enbrel®) • Rheumatoid arthritis, ankylosing spondylitis, psoriatic arthritis	Tumor necrosis factor (TNF) inhibitor, immunosuppressant, DMARD (disease-modifiying antirheumatic drug)	Infections, injection site infections
Ethosuximide (Zarontin®) • Absence seizures	Anticonvulsant (blocks T-type Ca^{2+} channels)	Gastrointestinal distress

(Continued)

Generic Name (Brand Name) • Primary Use	Therapeutic Class and Mechanism	Most Common Adverse Effects
Ezetimibe (Zetia®) • Hyperlipidemia	Antihyperlipidemic (inhibits absorption of dietary cholesterol)	Diarrhea, myalgia, myopathy (rare)
Famciclovir (Famvir®) • Herpes simplex	Antiviral (inhibits viral DNA polymerases)	Nausea/vomiting, fatigue, CNS symptoms
Famotidine (Pepcid®) • Peptic ulcer disease, gastroesophageal reflux disease, Zollinger-Ellison	Histamine H_2-receptor antagonist	Headache, dizziness, gastrointestinal symptoms
Felodipine (Plendil®) • Hypertension	Calcium channel blocker	Headache, dizziness, reflex tachycardia, gingival hyperplasia
Fentanyl (Duragesic®) • Moderate-to-severe pain	Analgesic (opioid agonist)	Respiratory depression, constipation, miosis, emesis, pruritus, dependence
Fenofibrate (TriCor®) • Hypertriglyceridemia, hypercholesterolemia	Antihyperlipidemic (fibric acid derivative; ligand for peroxisome proliferator-activated receptor-alpha [PPAR-α])	Gastrointestinal distress, gallstones, myopathy (especially in combination with statins), elevated liver enzymes
Fexofenadine (Allegra®) • Seasonal allergic rhinitis	Histamine H_1-receptor antagonist (second generation)	Fewer CNS side effects than first-generation antihistamines
Filgrastim (Neupogen®) • Neutropenia (e.g., chemotherapy, bone marrow transplant)	Granulocyte colony-stimulating factor (G-CSF), cytokine	Bone pain, splenomegaly, splenic rupture (rare)
Finasteride (Proscar®) • Benign prostatic hyperplasia, male pattern baldness	5α-reductase inhibitor	Pregnancy category X, impotence, hypotension
Fludrocortisone (Flonase®) • Allergic rhinitis	Corticosteroid	Epistaxis, pharyngitis, angioedema, upper respiratory infection
Fluconazole (Diflucan®) • Esophageal and invasive candidiasis, coccidiomycosis, cryptococcal meningitis	Conazole antifungal (inhibits 14-α-demethylase, preventing the conversion of lanosterol to ergosterol)	Hepatic dysfunction, decreased steroid synthesis, inhibits CYP3A4
Fluticasone (Flovent®) • Asthma	Corticosteroid; antiasthmatic	Epistaxis, pharyngitis, angioedema, upper respiratory infection
Flumazenil (Romazicon®) • Benzodiazepine overdose	Benzodiazepine-receptor antagonist	Seizures
Fluoxetine (Prozac®) • Depression, obsessive-compulsive disorder, anxiety disorders, bulimia	Selective serotonin reuptake inhibitor (SSRI) antidepressant	CNS stimulation, sexual dysfunction, gastrointestinal distress, serotonin syndrome, seizures in overdose; drug interactions with MAOIs, TCAs, meperidine, dextromethorphan
Flutamide (Eulexin®) • Prostatic carcinoma	Androgen-receptor antagonist	Hepatotoxicity
Fluvastatin (Lescol®) • Hypercholesterolemia	HMG-CoA reductase inhibitor; antihyperlipidemic	Myalgia, myopathy, rhabdomyolysis, hepatic dysfunction, elevated transaminases

(Continued)

Generic Name (Brand Name) • Primary Use	Therapeutic Class and Mechanism	Most Common Adverse Effects
Fluvoxamine (Luvox®) • Depression, obsessive-compulsive disorder	Selective serotonin reuptake inhibitor (SSRI) antidepressant	CNS stimulation, sexual dysfunction, serotonin syndrome seizures in overdose
Fosfomycin (Monurol®) • UTIs	Broad-spectrum, bactericidal antibiotic	Diarrhea
Fosinopril (Monopril®) • Hypertension, heart failure, diabetic nephropathy	ACE inhibitor	Cough, angioedema, hyperkalemia, neutropenia (rare)
Furosemide (Lasix®) • Edema and hypertension	Loop diuretic (blocks $Na^+/K^+/2Cl^-$ transporter in thick ascending limb)	Hypokalemia, hypocalcemia, hyperuricemia, hyponatremia, glycosuria, tinnitus, and hearing loss
Gabapentin (Neurontin®) • Epilepsy, postherpetic neuralgia, diabetic peripheral neuropathy	Anticonvulsant	Dizziness, somnolence
Ganciclovir (Cytovene®) • CMV, HSV, VZV infections	Antiviral (inhibits viral DNA polymerases)	Myelosuppression, fever, rash
Gatifloxacin (Tequin®) • UTIs, chronic bacterial prostatitis, respiratory tract infections, many others	Fluoroquinolone antibiotic (bacteriocidal inhibitor of topoisomerases)	Gastrointestinal distress, CNS dysfunction, superinfection, collagen dysfunction, pregnancy category D
Gemfibrozil (Lopid®)	Antihyperlipidemic (fibric acid derivative; ligand for peroxisome proliferator-activated receptor-alpha [PPAR-α])	Gastrointestinal distress, gallstones, myopathy (especially in combination with statins), elevated liver enzymes
Gentamicin (Garamycin®) • Severe gram-negative infections	Aminoglycoside antibiotic	Ototoxicity, nephrotoxicity, CNS stimulation
Glatiramer (Copaxone®) • Relapsing-remitting multiple sclerosis	Immune-modifying agent	Injection site reaction, chest pain
Glimepiride (Amaryl®) • Type 2 diabetes mellitus	Oral hypoglycemic agent, sulfonylurea	Hypoglycemia, weight gain, rash
Glipizide (Glucotrol®) • Type 2 diabetes mellitus	Oral hypoglycemic agent, sulfonylurea	Hypoglycemia, weight gain, rash
Glyburide (Micronase®, DiaBeta®, Glynase®) • Type 2 diabetes mellitus	Oral hypoglycemic agent, sulfonylurea	Hypoglycemia, weight gain, rash
Granisetron (Kytril®) • Nausea/vomiting	Antiemetic ($5HT_3$ antagonist)	Headache, dizziness
Haloperidol (Haldol®) • Schizophrenia, Tourette syndrome	Antipsychotic, butyrophenone (blocks dopamine D_2 receptors; high potency)	Extrapyramidal symptoms, tardive dyskinesia, hyperprolactinemia, neuroleptic malignant syndrome, fewer autonomic side effects than low-potency neuroleptics

(Continued)

Generic Name (Brand Name) • Primary Use	Therapeutic Class and Mechanism	Most Common Adverse Effects
Halothane (Fluothane®) • General anesthesia	General inhalational anesthetic	Cardiovascular and respiratory depression, sensitizes heart to catecholamines, hepatitis
Heparin (many brand names) • Prevention of thrombosis	Anticoagulant (enhances antithrombin III activity)	Bleeding, thrombocytopenia; antidote is protamine
Hydrochlorothiazide (HydroDIURIL®) • Edema and hypertension	Antihypertensive and thiazide diuretic (inhibits Na^+/Cl^- transporter in distal convoluted tubule)	Hypokalemia, hypercalcemia, hyperuricemia, hyperglycemia, hyperlipidemia, possible sulfonamide allergenicity
Hydralazine (Apresoline®) • Hypertension	Antihypertensive (vasodilator; releases nitric oxide from endothelial cells)	Systemic lupus erythematosus–like syndrome, tachycardia, salt/H_2O retention
Hydrocodone (Vicodin®) • Moderate-to-severe pain	Opioid analgesic	Respiratory depression, euphoria, constipation, nausea, pruritus, dependence
Ibuprofen (Motrin®) • Osteoarthritis, rheumatoid arthritis, inflammatory conditions, mild-to-moderate pain, antipyretic	NSAID (nonselective COX inhibitor)	Increased risk of serious cardiovascular thrombotic events, bleeding, gastrointestinal ulceration
Imipenem-cilastatin (Primaxin®) • For severe infections, e.g., respiratory, intraabdominal, others	Imipenem: carbapenem antibiotic; cilastatin: renal dehydropeptidase inhibitor (prevents inactivation of imipenem)	Allergy (cross-allergenicity with penicillins), gastrointestinal distress, seizures
Imipramine (Tofranil®) • Depression	Tricyclic antidepressant (norepinephrine [NE] and serotonin [5HT] reuptake blocker)	Strong anticholinergic side effects (e.g., urinary retention, tachycardia, increased intraocular pressure), cardiac arrhythmias on overdose
Indinavir (Crixivan®) • HIV infection	Protease inhibitor	Nephrolithiasis, hematologic abnormalities, inhibition of P450
Indomethacin (Indocin®) • Arthritis, acute inflammation	Antiinflammatory, NSAID (nonspecific COX inhibitor)	Gastrointestinal bleeding, increased risk of thrombotic events, renal toxicity
Interferon-α (INF-α; Roferon-A®, Intron-A®) • Hepatitis B and C, leukemias, melanoma, Kaposi sarcoma	Interferon	Flu-like symptoms, depression, hematologic disturbances
Interferon-β (INF-β; Avonex®, Refib®) • Multiple sclerosis	Interferon	Flu-like symptoms, depression, hematologic disturbances
Interferon-γ (INF-γ; Actimmune®) • Chronic granulomatous disease	Interferon	Flu-like symptoms, depression, hematologic disturbances
Ipratropium (Atrovent®) • Bronchospasm associated with chronic obstructive pulmonary disease	Anticholinergic bronchodilator (muscarinic antagonist)	Quaternary amine, so there is little systemic absorption
Irbesartan (Avapro®) • Hypertension, heart failure, diabetic neuropathy	Angiotensin II–receptor (type AT_1) antagonist	Hypotension, increased BUN and potassium, contraindicated in pregnancy

(Continued)

Generic Name (Brand Name) • Primary Use	Therapeutic Class and Mechanism	Most Common Adverse Effects
Isoniazid (INH; Nydrazid®) • Tuberculosis	Antimycobacterial	Hepatotoxicity, hemolysis (in G6PD deficiency, peripheral neuropathy; reversed by pyridoxine)
Isoproterenol (Isuprel®) • Heart block, bronchospasm	Nonspecific β agonist	Tremor, angina, arrhythmia
Isosorbide (dinitrate [Isordil®]; mononitrate [Imdur®]) • Angina pectoris	Nitrate vasodilator	Hypotension, tachycardia, headache
Isotretinoin (Accutane®) • Severe cystic acne	Retinoid	Pregnancy category X, depression, suicidal ideation, decreased night vision, dry mouth
Itraconazole (Sporanox®) • Blastomycoses, sporotrichoses, others	Conazole antifungal (inhibits 14-α-demethylase, preventing the conversion of lanosterol to ergosterol)	Hepatic dysfunction, decreased steroid synthesis, inhibits CYP3A4
Ivermectin (Stromectol®) • *Strongyloides*, onchocerciasis	Anthelmintic	Hypotension, headache, muscle aches
Ketoconazole (Nizoral®) • *Blastomyces, Histoplasma, Candida*, other	Conazole antifungal (inhibits 14-α-demethylase, preventing the conversion of lanosterol to ergosterol)	Hepatic dysfunction, decreased steroid synthesis, inhibits CYP3A4
Lamivudine (3TC) (Epivir®) • HIV infection, hepatitis B	Antiretroviral, nucleoside reverse transcriptase inhibitor (NRTI)	Least toxic of the NRTIs, some headache, gastrointestinal distress; all NRTIs may cause lactic acidemia and hepatomegaly with steatosis
Lamotrigine (Lamictal®) • Partial seizures, adjunctive for other seizure types, bipolar disorder	Anticonvulsant	Stevens-Johnson syndrome, life-threatening rash, sedation, ataxia
Lansoprazole (Prevacid®) • Ulcers, gastroesophageal reflux disease, Zollinger-Ellison	Proton pump inhibitor (irreversible blocker of H^+/K^+ ATPase on parietal cells)	Gastrointestinal side effects, dizziness, headache
Latanoprost (Xalatan®) • Open-angle glaucoma, ocular hypertension	$PGF_{2\alpha}$ agonist	Eyelash changes, iris pigmentation changes
Leflunomide (Arava®) • Rheumatoid arthritis	DMARD, pyrimidine synthesis inhibitor (inhibits dihydroorotate dehydrogenase)	Diarrhea, elevated hepatic enzymes, alopecia, rash
Leuprolide (Lupron Depot®) • Advanced prostatic cancer	Gonadotropin-releasing hormone (GnRH) analog (others in class include goserelin, nafarelin)	Bone pain, gynecomastia, impotence, testicular atrophy, hematuria
Levodopa-carbidopa (Sinemet®) • Parkinsonism	Levodopa: dopamine precursor; carbidopa: peripheral decarboxylase inhibitor)	Dyskinesias, behavioral changes, hypotension, on-off phenomena
Levofloxacin (Levaquin®) • Urinary tract infections, chronic bacterial prostatitis, respiratory tract infections, many others	Fluoroquinolone antibiotic (bacteriocidal inhibitor of topoisomerases)	Gastrointestinal distress, CNS dysfunction, superinfection, collagen dysfunction, pregnancy category D

(Continued)

Generic Name (Brand Name) • Primary Use	Therapeutic Class and Mechanism	Most Common Adverse Effects
Levothyroxine (Synthroid®) • Hypothyroidism	Synthetic T_4	Symptoms of hyperthyroidism
Lisinopril (Prinivil® and Zestril®) • Hypertension, congestive heart failure, diabetic nephropathy	ACE inhibitor	Cough, angioedema, hyperkalemia, neutropenia (rare)
Lithium (Eskalith®) • Bipolar disease	Antimanic	Nephrogenic diabetes insipidus, tremor, goiter, seizures, teratogen
Loratadine (Claritin®) • Seasonal allergic rhinitis	Histamine H_1 receptor antagonist (second generation)	Fewer CNS side effects than first-generation antihistamines
Lorazepam (Ativan®) • Anxiety	Benzodiazepine, sedative/hypnotic (increases frequency of $GABA_A$ receptor opening)	Drowsiness, dizziness, amnesia, respiratory depression
Losartan (Cozaar®) • Hypertension, diabetic neuropathy, heart failure	Angiotensin II–receptor (type AT_1) antagonist (prototype; others in this class include candesartan, eprosartan, irbesartan, olmesartan, telmisartan, valsartan)	Hypotension, increased BUN and potassium, contraindication in pregnancy
Lovastatin (Mevacor®) • Hypercholesterolemia	HMG-CoA reductase inhibitor, antihyperlipidemic (prototype; others in this class include atorvastatin, fluvastatin, pravastatin, rosuvastatin, simvastatin)	Myalgia, myopathy, rhabdomyolysis, hepatic dysfunction, elevated transaminases
Mannitol (Osmitrol®) • Increased intracranial pressure, to promote diuresis in renal failure, increased intraocular pressure (narrow-angle glaucoma), to promote excretion of renal toxins	Osmotic diuretic	Extracellular fluid volume expansion causing hyponatremia, nausea, headache
Mebendazole (Vermox®) • Whipworm, pinworm infections	Anthelminthic	Gastrointestinal distress
Meclizine (Antivert®) • Motion sickness	Antiemetic (H_1 antagonist)	Dizziness, drowsiness
Medroxyprogesterone (Provera®) • Contraceptive injection, hormone-replacement therapy	Progestin	Thromboembolic disorders, myocardial infarction, galactorrhea
Memantine (Namenda®) • Alzheimer disease	NMDA-receptor antagonist	Dizziness
Meperidine (Demerol®) • Moderate-to-severe pain	Opioid analgesic	Seizures, typical opioid side effects, dangerous in combination with SSRIs and MAOIs, anticholinergic
Mesalamine (Canasa®) • Inflammatory bowel disease	Antiinflammatory	Gastrointestinal distress, dizziness
Metaproterenol (Alupent®) • Asthma	Antiasthmatic (β_2-receptor agonist)	CNS stimulation, hypertension, tachycardia

(Continued)

Generic Name (Brand Name) • Primary Use	Therapeutic Class and Mechanism	Most Common Adverse Effects
Metformin (Glucophage®) • Type 2 diabetes mellitus	Antidiabetic, biguanide	Lactic acidosis
Methadone (Dolophine®) • Maintenance treatment and detoxification of opioid addiction, moderate-to-severe pain	Opioid analgesic	Respiratory depression, euphoria, constipation, pruritus, dependence
Methotrexate (Trexall®) • Neoplastic disease, arthritis, psoriasis	Antineoplastic, immunosuppressant (inhibits dihydrofolic reductase)	Myelosuppression, gastrointestinal distress, crystalluria (leucovorin rescue used to lower toxicity)
Methylphenidate (Ritalin®) • Attention deficit hyperactivity disorder	Stimulant	CNS stimulation, tachycardia, cardiac arrhythmias
Metoclopramide (Reglan®) • Gastroesophageal reflux disease, diabetic gastroparesis, nausea/vomiting	Antiemetic, prokinetic agent, dopamine antagonist	Extrapyramidal side effects, hyperprolactinemia
Metoprolol (Lopressor®, Toprol XL®) • Hypertension, angina pectoris, heart failure	Antihypertensive (β_1-anatgonist)	Heart failure, hypoglycemic unawareness, potential bronchospasm in asthmatics (not completely β_1 selective), bradycardia, hypotension, impotence
Metronidazole (Flagyl®) • Trichomoniasis, amebiasis, anaerobic bacterial infections, numerous other infections	Trichomonacide, antiprotozoal, and antibacterial agent	Disulfiram-like reaction, neuropathy, metallic taste, reversible neutropenia, seizures
Miconazole (Monistat-3® and -7®) • Vulvovaginal candidiasis, topical fungal infections	Conazole antifungal	Allergic contact dermatitis
Mifepristone (RU486®) • Abortifacient, postcoital contraceptive	Progestin and glucocorticoid antagonist/abortifacient	Vaginal bleeding, infection, sepsis
Mirtazapine (Remeron®) • Major depressive disorder	Antidepressant	Weight gain, sedation
Misoprostol (Cytotec®) • Prevention of NSAID-induced ulcers	Antiulcer medication (prostaglandin E_1 agonist)	Diarrhea, miscarriage
Monometasone (Elocon®) • Inflammatory and pruritic manifestations of corticosteroid-responsive dermatoses	Topical corticosteroid, antiinflammatory	HPA-axis suppression, increased topical infection (bacterial, viral, and fungal)
Monometasone (Nasonex®) • Allergic rhinitis	Corticosteroid	Epistaxis, pharyngitis, angioedema, upper respiratory tract infection
Montelukast (Singulair®) • Asthma	Antiasthma (for prevention, not to reverse acute attacks), selective antagonist of leukotriene D_4 (LTD_4) receptors	Gastrointestinal disturbances, hypersensitivity reactions

(Continued)

Generic Name (Brand Name) • Primary Use	Therapeutic Class and Mechanism	Most Common Adverse Effects
Morphine (MS Contin®) • Moderate-to-severe pain	Opioid analgesic/narcotic analgesic	Respiratory depression, euphoria, constipation, pruritus, dependence
Mupirocin (Bactroban®) • Impetigo, methicillin-resistant *Staphylococcus aureus* (MRSA)	Topical antibiotic	Contact dermatitis
Mycophenolate mofetil (CellCept®) • Prophylaxis of organ rejection in patients receiving allogenic renal, cardiac, or hepatic transplants	Immunosuppressant (inosine monophosphate dehydrogenase [IMPDH] inhibitor)	Gastrointestinal distress, myelosuppression
Nafcillin (Unipen®) • *Staphylococcal* infections	Penicillinase-resistant penicillin	Penicillin allergy
Nalbuphine (Nubain®) • Pain	Opioid, mixed agonist/antagonist (stimulates kappa, weak mu antagonist)	Sedation, CNS effects; less respiratory depression, less analgesia, and less abuse potential than strong mu agonists
Naltrexone (ReVia®) • Decreases alcohol cravings, used in opioid dependence	Opioid antagonist	Longer half-life than naloxone, can cause abstinence symptoms
Naloxone (Narcan®) • Used to reverse acute opioid overdose	Opioid antagonist	Short half-life may necessitate multiple doses
Naproxen (Naprosyn®, Naprelan®) • Osteoarthritis, inflammatory conditions, rheumatoid arthritis, pain	NSAID	Increased risk of serious cardiovascular thrombotic events, bleeding, gastrointestinal ulceration
Nedocromil (Tilade®) • Asthma	Mast cell stabilizer	Coughing, airway irritation
Nefazodone (Serzone®) • Depression	Antidepressant (heterocyclic)	Hepatotoxicity, P450 inhibitor
Nelfinavir (Viracept®) • HIV infection	Protease inhibitor	Diarrhea, P450 interactions
Neostigmine (Prostigmin®) • Myasthenia gravis, reversal of neuromuscular blockade	Cholinesterase inhibitor (quaternary amine)	Excess cholinomimetic effects
Nevirapine (Viramune®) • HIV infection	Antiretroviral, nonnucleoside reverse transcriptase inhibitor (NNRTI)	Fatal hepatotoxicity, Stevens-Johnson syndrome, toxic epidermal necrolysis
Niacin (Niaspan®) • Hypercholesterolemia	Antihyperlipidemic	Flushing, hepatotoxicity
Nifedipine (Procardia®, Adalat CC®) • Angina, hypertension	Dihydropyridine calcium channel blocker	Orthostatic hypotension, tachycardia, dizziness, peripheral edema, syncope
Nitrofurantoin (Macrodantin®, Macrobid®) • Urinary tract infections	Urinary antiseptic	Gastrointestinal distress, hypersensitivity pneumonitis

(Continued)

Generic Name (Brand Name) • Primary Use	Therapeutic Class and Mechanism	Most Common Adverse Effects
Nitroglycerin (Nitro-Dur®, Nitro-Bid®, Nitrostat®) • Angina	Antianginal vasodilator, nitrate	Tachycardia, hypotension, headache
Olanzapine (Zyprexa®) • Schizophrenia	Atypical antipsychotic (blocks $5HT_2$ receptors)	Increased mortality in elderly with dementia-related psychosis, postural hypotension
Omeprazole (Prilosec®) • Ulcers, gastroesophageal reflux disease, Zollinger-Ellison	Proton pump inhibitor (irreversible blocker of H^+/K^+-ATPase on parietal cells; prototype, others in this class include esomeprazole, lansoprazole, pantoprazole, rabeprazole)	Gastrointestinal side effects, dizziness, headache
Ondansetron (Zofran®) • Nausea/vomiting	Antiemetics, ($5HT_3$ antagonist; prototype, others in class include granisetron, dolasetron)	Headache, dizziness
Orlistat (Xenical®) • Obesity	Antiobesity, pancreatic lipase inhibitor	Oily spotting, flatulence, bloating
Oxazepam (Serax®) • Anxiety, alcohol withdrawal	Benzodiazepine; sedative/hypnotic, anticonvulsant (increases frequency of opening of $GABA_A$ receptor)	Respiratory depression, somnolence, dizziness
Oxybutynin (Ditropan XL®) • Urinary incontinence	Genitourinary smooth muscle relaxant, antimuscarinic	Typical antimuscarinic side effects
Oxycodone (sustained-release, OxyContin®; with aspirin: Percodan®, with acetaminophen: Percocet®) • Moderate to severe pain	Opioid analgesic	Respiratory depression, euphoria, constipation, pruritus, dependence
Pantoprazole (Protonix®) • Ulcers, gastroesophageal reflux disease, Zollinger-Ellison	Proton pump inhibitor (irreversible blocker of H^+/K^+-ATPase on parietal cells)	Gastrointestinal side effects, dizziness, headache
Paroxetine (Paxil®) • Depression, obsessive-compulsive disorder, anxiety disorders, bulimia	Selective serotonin reuptake inhibitor (SSRI) antidepressant	CNS stimulation, sexual dysfunction, gastrointestinal distress, serotonin syndrome, seizures in overdose; drug interactions with MAOIs, TCAs, meperidine, dextromethorphan
Penicillin (many brand names) • Numerous bacterial infections	Beta-lactam antibiotic	Allergic reactions, anaphylaxis, drug fever, Stevens-Johnson syndrome, pseudomembranous colitis
Phenelzine (Nardil®) • Depression	Antidepressant, irreversible and nonselective monoamine oxidase (MAO) inhibitor	Malignant hypertension with tyramine-containing foods and indirect-acting sympathomimetics, serotonin syndrome with serotonergic drugs, e.g., SSRIs
Phenobarbital (Pb®) • Seizures, preanesthetics, insomnia	Sedative hypnotic, anticonvulsant, long-acting barbiturate (increases duration of $GABA_A$-receptor opening)	Sedation, P450 induction, dependence, additive with other CNS depressants
Phenoxybenzamine (Dibenzyline®) • Pheochromocytoma	Irreversible α-adrenergic antagonist	Hypotension, gastrointestinal distress

(Continued)

Generic Name (Brand Name) • Primary Use	Therapeutic Class and Mechanism	Most Common Adverse Effects
Phenytoin (Dilantin®) • Generalized tonic-clonic and complex partial seizures	Anticonvulsant (hydantoin)	Gingival hyperplasia, sedation, diplopia, hirsutism, teratogen
Physostigmine (Antilirium®) • Anticholinergic overdose, glaucoma	Cholinesterase inhibitor (tertiary amine)	Cholinomimetic effects (diarrhea, urination, miosis, bronchoconstriction, bradycardia, excitation, lacrimation, salivation, sweating [DUMBBELSS])
Pilocarpine (Isopto Carpine®) • Glaucoma	Antiglaucoma, (muscarinic agonist)	Cholinomimetic effects
Pindolol (Visken®) • Hypertension	Nonselective β-adrenergic antagonist with intrinsic sympathomimetic activity	Heart failure, hypoglycemic unawareness, bronchospasm in asthmatics, bradycardia, hypotension, impotence
Pioglitazone HCl (Actos®) • Type 2 diabetes mellitus	Thiazolidinedione; stimulates peroxisome proliferator-activator receptors (PPARs)	Less side effects (hypoglycemia, weight gain) than sulfonylureas, cardiovascular toxicity
Piroxicam (Feldene®) • Osteoarthritis, inflammatory conditions, rheumatoid arthritis	NSAID	Increased risk of serious cardiovascular thrombotic events, bleeding, gastrointestinal ulceration
Pravastatin (Pravachol®) • Hypercholesterolemia	HMG-CoA reductase inhibitor, antihyperlipidemic	Myalgia, myopathy, rhabdomyolysis, hepatic dysfunction, elevated transaminases
Prednisone (Deltasone®) • Inflammatory conditions, immunosuppressive	Antiinflammatory, corticosteroid, glucocorticosteroid, immunosuppressant	Sodium retention, fluid retention, potassium loss, hypokalemic alkalosis, peptic ulcer disease, cushingoid state, osteoporosis
Pregabalin (Lyrica®) • Neuropathic pain associated with diabetic peripheral neuropathy, seizures	GABA analog	Somnolence
Procainamide (Procanbid®) • Ventricular arrhythmias	Class IA antiarrhythmic (Na^+ channel blocker)	Lupus erythematosus–like syndrome, hematoxicity, hypotension, cardiovascular effects (torsades)
Prochlorperazine (Compazine®) • Nausea/vomiting	Phenothiazine antiemetic	Extrapyramidal side effects, lowers seizure threshold, neuroleptic malignant syndrome
Propranolol (Inderal®) • Hypertension, angina, arrhythmias, hyperthyroidism, migraine, benign essential tremor	Nonselective β-adrenergic antagonist	Heart failure, hypoglycemic unawareness, bronchospasm in asthmatics, bradycardia, hypotension, impotence
Propylthiouracil (PTU) (generic) • Hyperthyroidism	Antithyroid agent (blocks tyrosine iodination, inhibits coupling)	Rash, immune reactions (rare)
Quetiapine (Seroquel®) • Schizophrenia, bipolar disorder	Atypical antipsychotic	Increased suicidal risk, somnolence, hypotension, tachycardia

(Continued)

Generic Name (Brand Name) • Primary Use	Therapeutic Class and Mechanism	Most Common Adverse Effects
Quinidine (Quinaglute®, Quinidix®) • Atrial and ventricular arrythmias	Class IA antiarrythmic	Cinchonism (Gastrointestinal symptoms, tinnitus, visual disturbances, CNS excitation), distress, torsade
Rabeprazole (AcipHex®) • Ulcers, gastroesophageal reflux disease, Zollinger-Ellison	Proton pump inhibitor (irreversible blocker of H^+/K^+-ATPase on parietal cells)	Gastrointestinal side effects, dizziness, headache
Raloxifene (Evista®) • Osteoporosis	Selective estrogen-receptor modulator (SERM)	Hot flashes, leg cramps, blood clots
Ramipril (Altace®) • Hypertension, congestive heart failure, diabetic nephropathy	ACE inhibitor	Cough, angioedema, hyperkalemia, neutropenia (rare)
Ranitidine (Zantac®) • Peptic ulcer disease, gastroesophageal reflux disease, Zollinger-Ellison	Histamine H_2-receptor antagonist	Headache, dizziness, gastrointestinal symptoms
Rifampin (Rifadin®) • Tuberculosis	Antitubercular agent (inhibits DNA-dependent RNA polymerase)	Hepatotoxicity, induces P450
Risedronate (Actonel®) • Osteoporosis	Bisphosphonate	Esophageal ulcers, esophagitis, abdominal pain, gastric reflux, dysphagia
Risperidone (Risperdal®) • Schizophrenia	Atypical antipsychotic	Fewer extrapyramidal side effects than typical neuroleptics, postural hypotension, dizziness, stroke
Ropinirole (Requip®) • Parkinson disease, restless legs syndrome	Dopamine-receptor agonist	Sedation, dyskinesias, nausea/vomiting
Rosiglitazone (Avandia®) • Type 2 diabetes mellitus	Thiazolidinedione, stimulates peroxisome proliferator-activator receptors (PPARs)	Fewer side effects than sulfonylureas; hypoglycemia and weight gain may occur, cardiovascular toxicity
Rosuvastatin (Crestor®) • Hyperlipidemia, hypertriglyceridemia	HMG-CoA reductase inhibitor	Hepatic dysfunction, rhabdomyolysis, myalgia, myopathy
Salmeterol (Serevent®) • Asthma, chronic obstructive pulmonary disease	Bronchodilator (β_2-receptor agonist; long acting)	CNS stimulation, hypertension, tachycardia
Selegiline (Eldepryl®) • Parkinson disease	Antiparkinson (MAO_B inhibitor)	CNS stimulation, dyskinesias, can cause serotonin syndrome in combination with SSRIs, hypertension (especially with higher doses)
Sertraline (Zoloft®) • Depression, obsessive-compulsive disorder, anxiety disorders, bulimia	Selective serotonin reuptake inhibitor (SSRI) antidepressant	CNS stimulation, sexual dysfunction, gastrointestinal distress, serotonin syndrome, seizures in overdose; drug interactions with MAOIs, TCAs, meperidine, dextromethorphan

(Continued)

Generic Name (Brand Name) • Primary Use	Therapeutic Class and Mechanism	Most Common Adverse Effects
Sildenafil (Viagra®) • Erectile dysfunction	Cyclic guanosine monophosphate (cGMP)–specific phosphodiesterase type 5 (PDE5) inhibitor	Postural hypotension, tachycardia, myocardial infarction, priapism, vision loss
Simvastatin (Zocor®) • Hyperlipidemia, hypertriglyceridemia	HMG-CoA reductase inhibitor, antihyperlipidemic	Myalgia, myopathy, rhabdomyolysis, hepatic dysfunction, elevated transaminases
Spironolactone (Aldactone®) • Primary hyperaldosteronism, edematous conditions, hypertension, hypokalemia, hypertension in pregnancy	Potassium-sparing diuretic, aldosterone receptor antagonist	Gynecomastia, hyperkalemia, dilutional hyponatremia
Stavudine (d4T) (Zerit®) • HIV Infection	Antiretroviral, nucleoside reverse transcriptase inhibitor (NRTI)	Peripheral neuropathy (dose-limiting), all NRTIs may cause lactic acidemia and hepatomegaly with steatosis
Succinylcholine (Anectine®) • Muscle relaxation (adjunct to surgery, intubation)	Depolarizing muscle relaxant (short duration, metabolized by plasma cholinesterases)	May have role in malignant hyperthermia, muscle pain, hyperkalemia
Sulfasalazine (Azulfidine®) • Inflammatory bowel disease	Antiinflammatory (derivative of mesalazine)	Gastrointestinal distress, dizziness
Sumatriptan (Imitrex®) • Migraine	Antimigraine (abortive); selective 5-hydroxytryptamine$_{1D}$ (5-HT$_{1D}$)–receptor agonist	Coronary artery vasospasm, hypertension, tachycardia, chest or throat pain/pressure, myocardial infarction, stroke, cerebral hemorrhage, asthenia
Tadalafil (Cialis®) • Erectile dysfunction	Cyclic guanosine monophosphate (cGMP)–specific phosphodiesterase type 5 (PDE5) inhibitor	Postural hypotension, tachycardia, myocardial infarction, priapism, vision loss
Tamoxifen (Nolvadex®) • Metastatic breast cancer, prevention of breast cancer in high-risk patients	Selective estrogen-receptor modulator (SERM)	Hot flushes, increased risk of venous thrombosis
Tamsulosin (Flomax®) • Benign prostatic hypertrophy	α_1-adrenergic antagonist	Orthostatic hypotension, syncope (first-dose response), hypotension, tachycardia
Temazepam (Restoril®) • Insomnia	Benzodiazepine; sedative/hypnotic (increases frequency of GABA$_A$-receptor opening)	Drowsiness, dizziness, amnesia, respiratory depression
Terazosin (Hytrin®) • Benign prostatic hypertrophy, hypertension	α_1-adrenergic antagonist	Orthostatic hypotension and syncope, particularly as a "first-dose effect," tachycardia
Terbinafine (Lamisil®) • Onychomycosis	Antifungal (inhibits squalene epoxidase)	Gastrointestinal distress, headache, hepatotoxicity
Tetracycline (Achromycin®) • Acne, Chlamydia, numerous sexually transmitted infections, Rocky Mountain spotted fever, many others	Tetracycline antibiotic	Teratogenicity (tooth developmental problems, hepatic failure), photosensitivity, pseudomembranous colitis, renal toxicity, maculopapular and erythematous rashes

(Continued)

Generic Name (Brand Name) • Primary Use	Therapeutic Class and Mechanism	Most Common Adverse Effects
Theophylline (Theo-Dur®) • Chronic asthma, chronic obstructive pulmonary disease	Bronchodilator, methylxanthine, phosphodiesterase inhibitor, adenosine antagonist	Insomnia, tremor, gastrointestinal distress
Timolol (ophthalmic: Timoptic®, Betimol®; oral: Blocadren®) • Glaucoma, hypertension	Antiglaucoma, antihypertensive; nonselective β-adrenergic antagonist	Heart failure, hypoglycemic unawareness, bronchospasm in asthmatics, bradycardia, hypotension, impotence
Tolterodine tartrate (Detrol®) • Urinary incontinence	Muscarinic antagonist	Anticholinergic side effects (e.g., tachycardia, dry mouth, urinary retention)
Topiramate (Topamax®) • Epilepsy, migraine	Anticonvulsant, antimigraine	Cognitive deficits, fatigue, renal stones, anorexia
Tramadol (Ultram®) • Moderate-to-moderately severe pain	Centrally acting synthetic opioid analgesic, inhibits serotonin (5HT) and norepinephrine reuptake	Seizures, dizziness, constipation
Trazodone (Deseryl®) • Depression	Antidepressant (heterocyclic)	Priapism, sedation, cardiac arrhythmias
Tretinoin (Retin-A®) • Acne vulgaris	Antiacne (vitamin A derivative)	Irritation, erythema, peeling, dryness, burning/stinging
Triamterene (Dyrenium®) • Edema, hypertension,	Potassium-sparing diuretic (Na^+ channel blocker in distal tubule)	Hyperkalemia
Trihexyphenidyl (Artane®) • Control of extrapyramidal disorders, Parkinson disease	Anticholinergic (muscarinic antagonist)	Strong anticholinergic side effects (e.g., dry mouth, tachycardia, urinary retention, worsening of glaucoma, paralytic ileus, hyperthermia)
Trimethoprim/sulfamethoxazole (Bactrim®, Septra®) • Urinary tract infections, *Pneumocystic carinii* infections, many gram-negative bacteria	Combination blocks folic acid synthesis	Toxicity primarily due to sulfonamide; hypersensitivity, hematologic disorders, kernicterus, competes for plasma proteins
Valacyclovir (Valtrex®) • Herpes simplex	Antiviral (inhibits viral DNA polymerases)	Confusion, hallucinations, seizures, thrombotic thrombocytopenic purpura/hemolytic uremic syndrome, especially with high doses in AIDS patients
Valproic acid (Depakote®) • Epilepsy, mania, migraine prophylaxis	Anticonvulsant/antimanic (inhibits T-type Ca^{2+} channels)	Gastrointestinal distress, hepatic failure (rare but can be fatal), teratogenicity (neural tube defects), inhibits drug metabolism
Valsartan (Diovan®) • Hypertension, heart failure	Angiotensin II–receptor (type 1 AT_1) antagonist	Hypotension, increased BUN and potassium, contraindicated in pregnancy
Vancomycin (Vancocin®) • Severe infections caused by susceptible strains of methicillin-resistant (beta-lactam–resistant) staphylococci and other serious gram-positive infections	Antibiotic (glycopeptide bacteriocidal; inhibits cell wall synthesis)	Red man syndrome, ototoxicity, nephrotoxicity, hypersensitivity

(Continued)

Generic Name (Brand Name) • Primary Use	Therapeutic Class and Mechanism	Most Common Adverse Effects
Venlafaxine (Effexor®) • Depression	Antidepressant (heterocyclic)/inhibits norepinephrine [NE] and serotonin [5HT] uptake	Somnolence, nausea, impotence, tachycardia, CNS stimulation
Verapamil (Calan®, Verelan®) • Hypertension, arrhythmias, angina, prophylaxis of paroxysmal supraventricular tachycardia (PSVT)	Vasodilator and cardiac depressant, calcium channel blocker (blocks L-type calcium channels)	Strong negative inotropic effects, hypotension, atrioventricular block, heart failure, constipation
Vinblastine (Velban®) • Lymphomas, neuroblastoma, testicular carcinoma, Kaposi sarcoma	Antineoplastic/M phase–specific agent (inhibits mitotic spindle formation)	Myelosuppression, alopecia, gastrointestinal distress
Vincristine (Oncovin®) • Leukemias, lymphomas, Wilms tumor	Antineoplastic/M phase–specific agent (inhibits mitotic spindle formation)	Peripheral neuropathy, alopecia, gastrointestinal distress
Warfarin (Coumadin®) • Coagulation disorders, venous thrombosis, pulmonary embolism, atrial fibrillation, stroke, systemic embolism after myocardial infarction	Anticoagulant (vitamin K–dependent clotting factor inhibitor)	Bleeding, contraindicated in pregnancy, multiple drug interactions with P450 inducers or inhibitors
Zafirlukast (Accolate®) • Asthma	Antiasthma (for prevention, not to reverse acute attacks), selective antagonist of leukotriene D_4 and E_4 (LTD_4 and LTE_4) receptors	Hepatic failure
Zidovudine (ZDV; Retrovir®) • HIV infection	Nucleoside reverse transcriptase inhibitor (NRTI); formerly called azidothymidine (AZT)	Bone marrow suppression leading to anemia and neutropenia (may require transfusions), headache, asthenia, myalgia, gastrointestinal distress; all NRTIs may cause lactic acidemia and hepatomegaly with steatosis
Zileuton (Zyflo®) • Asthma (prophylaxis, chronic treatment)	5-lipoxygenase inhibitor	Dyspepsia, elevation of liver function tests
Zolmitriptan (Zomig®) • Migraine	Antimigraine (abortive)/selective 5-hydroxytryptamine$_{1D}$ (5-HT$_{1D}$)–receptor agonist	Coronary artery vasospasm, hypertension, tachycardia, chest or throat pain/pressure, myocardial infarction, stroke, cerebral hemorrhage, asthenia
Zolpidem (Ambien®) • Insomnia	Nonbenzodiazepine hypnotic; binds BZ_1 site on the $GABA_A$ receptor; can be reversed by flumazenil	Daytime drowsiness, dizziness, abnormal behaviors

Calmodulin, 406
Caloric test, 196
Calves, pseudohypertrophy, 430
Calyces, 284
cAMP (cyclic adenosine monophosphate), 158, 381
Campylobacter jejuni, 348
Canal of Schlemm, 192
C-ANCA, 249
Cancer. *See* Carcinoma
Candesartan, 255
Candida spp., 110, 181, 395, 402
Candida albicans, 131, 133, 273, 274
    in AIDS patients, 100
Candidiasis, 131, 395
    in AIDS patients, 100
Cannabis, 14
Capacitation, 384, 391
Capillary(ies)
    filtration and reabsorption in, 236
    flow and pressure changes in, factors affecting, 237
    hemangioma of, 432
    hydrostatic pressure in, 236
    oncotic pressure in, 236
    peritubular, 290
    pulmonary, 269
Capsules, 112
Captopril, 164, 254
Caput medusa, 324, 344
Carbachol, 175, 193
Carbamazepine, 211
Carbamoyl phosphate synthase I, 47
Carbapenems, 114
Carbenicillin, 113
Carbidopa, 202
Carbon dioxide transport, 269
Carbon monoxide, 38, 267
    changes after heart failure, 229
Carbon monoxide poisoning, 159, 268, 271
    antidote for, 161
Carbonic anhydrase, 334
Carbonic anhydrase inhibitor, 193, 301, 309, 310
    electrolyte changes caused by, 310
Carbonic anhydrase reaction, 305
Carboplatin, 166
Carboxypeptidase, 334
Carbuncles, 433
Carcinoembryonic antigen, 154
Carcinoembryonic antigen tumor, 342
Carcinogenesis, mechanisms, 152
Carcinoid, 280
Carcinoid syndrome, 44, 154, 280
Carcinoid tumor, 154
Carcinoma
    adrenal, 361
    anaplastic, 373
    basal cell, 432
    bile duct, 345, 347
    breast. *See* Breast cancer
    bronchogenic, 280
    cervical, 153
    colorectal, hereditary nonpolyposis, 62
    defined, 151
    embryonal, 386
    esophageal, 339
    follicular, 373
    gallbladder, 347
    hepatocellular, 153, 154, 345
    large cell, 280
    lung, 355
    medullary. *See* Medullary carcinoma
    nasopharyngeal, 153
    ovarian, 154
    pancreatic, 154, 343
    papillary, 373, 374

penile, 381
    prostatic, 154, 382
    renal cell, 153, 315
    risk factors for, 151
    small cell. *See* Small cell carcinoma
    squamous cell, 432
    stomach, 340
    transitional cell, of the bladder, 316
Carcinoma in situ, 151
    penile, 381
Cardia, 327
Cardiac cycle, 230
Cardiac enzymes, after myocardial infarction, 243
Cardiac function curve, 228
    examples of, 229
Cardiac glycosides, 254
Cardiac ion channels, 223
Cardiac output, 228
    changes after heart failure, 229
    integrated control, 305
    integrated control of, 239
Cardiac performance
    definitions, 228
    mechanical, 228
Cardiac pressure-volume loops, 231–232
Cardiac tamponade, 247
Cardiac valves, 232
    disorders of, 233–239
Cardiogenic shock, 251
Cardiomyopathies, 246
Cardiovascular system. *See also* Cardiac *entries*; Heart
    anatomy of, 218–222
    embryology of, 216–218
    pathology of, 240–251
    pharmacology of, 252–256
    physiology of, 223–239
Carmustine, 165
Carnitine acyltransferases, 36, 48
Carnitine shuttle, 48
Carnitine transporter, 48
Carpal tunnel syndrome, 414
Carrier-mediated diffusion, 140
Carvedilol, 179
Caseation, 147
Case-control studies, 33
Caseous necrosis, 147
Caseous pericarditis, 247
Caspofungin, 134
Castor oil, 351
CAT (carnitine acyltransferase), 36, 48
Cat scratches, 435
CAT-1 (carnitine actyltransferase-1), 48
CAT-2 (carnitine actyltransferase-2), 48
Catalase, 112, 146, 433
Catecholamines, 44, 178
Catechol-O-methyltransferase, 178
    inhibitors, 180, 202
Cats, as reservoir hosts, feces, 122
Cauda equina, 186
Caudate, 201
Caudate nucleus, 201
Cavernous sinus, 183
    thrombosis of, 412
CCD (cortical collecting duct), 290
CCK. *See* Cholecystokinin
CCR5 (chemokine receptor 5), 100
CD markers, 91
CD2, 91
CD3, 91
CD4, 89, 91, 100
CD8, 86, 88, 89, 90, 91
CD10 (CALLA) surface marker, 453
CD14, 90, 91
CD16, 90, 91

CD18 absence, 96
CD19, 91
CD20, 91
CD21, 91
CD28, 91
CD40, 91
CD40L, 86
CD56, 90, 91
CDK4 oncogene, 152
cDNA, 67
CEA. *See* Carcinoembryonic antigen *entries*
Cecum, 329
Cefazolin, 114
Cefepime, 114
Cefoperazone, 114
Cefotaxime, 403
Cefotetan, 114
Cefoxitin, 114
Ceftazidime, 114
Ceftriaxone, 273, 274, 402, 403
Cefuroxime, 114
Celecoxib, 428
Celiac artery, 318, 319, 322
Celiac circulation, 322
Celiac sprue, 341
Cell adhesion, 80
Cell body, 184
Cell cycle, 81
    proteins and, 152
Cell death, 147
    programmed. *See* Apoptosis
Cell injury
    causes of, 146
    irreversible, 147
    mechanisms of, 146
    reversible, 147
Cell signaling, 82–83
Cell transport, 140
Cell wall, 108
Cell wall synthesis inhibitors, 113–114
    carbapenems, 114
    cephalosporins, 114
    monobactams, 114
    non-beta lactam, 114
    penicillins, 113
Cell-cycle regulatory proteins, 152
Cell-mediated immunity, 403
Cells, 108
    B cells, 88
    chief, 320, 332
    chromaffin, 361
    of immune system, 87–88
    natural killer, 86, 88
    regeneration and repair, 149
    response in acute inflammation, 93
    T cells, 86
    types, in nervous system, 184
Cellular membrane, 108
Cellularity, mixed, in Hodgkin disease, 451
Cellulitis, 434
Central artery, retinal, 209
Central canal, 182
Central nervous system, 170, 184
    adult derivatives, 170
    depressants, 13
    stimulants of, 13
    trauma to, 207
Central sulcus, 204, 205
Centriacinar (centrilobular) emphysema, 277
Cephalexin, 114
Cephalosporins, 109, 113, 114
Ceramidase, 52
Cerebellar tonsillar herniation, 207
Cerebellum, 199
Cerebral amyloid angiopathy, 206
Cerebral aqueduct, 170, 182, 199, 204

Cerebral cortex, 204–207
Cerebral hemispheres, 170
Cerebral herniations, 207
Cerebral infarcts, 210
Cerebrospinal fluid, 182
    parameters, in meningitis, 182
    production of and barriers, 183
    sinuses and, 183
Cerebrovascular disorders, 210
Ceruloplasmin, 344
Cervical intraepithelial neoplasia, 395
Cervical spondylosis, 413
Cervicitis, 402
Cervix, 378, 379
    carcinoma, 153, 395
    enlargement of, 186
Cestodes, 122, 124
Cetirizine, 162
CFC. See Cardiac function curve
CFTR protein, 343
CGD (chronic granulomatous disease), 96
cGMP, 82, 381
CGRP (calcitonin gene-related polypeptide), 328
Chagas disease, 121, 122, 339
Chancre, 403
Chancroid, 403
Chaperones, molecular, 65
ChAT (choline acetyltransferase), 175
Chediak-Higashi syndrome, 79, 96
Chemical injury, 146
Chemokine, 94
Chemokine receptors, 100
Chemoreceptors, 272
    trigger zone for, 329
Chenodeoxycholic acid, 335
Chenodiol, 351
Chest wall
    disorders of, 279
    elastic properties of, 263
CHF (congestive heart failure), 244
Chief cells, 320, 332
Child abuse, 8
Child development, 6–8
    milestones in, 7–8
Chinese liver fluke, 123
Chi-square, 34
Chlamydia spp., 395, 396, 402–403, 426
Chlamydia spp., infectious arthritis and, 427
Chlamydia psittaci, 276
Chlamydia trachomatis, 402
Chlamydiae, 117
Chloramphenicol, 64, 113, 115, 450
Chlordiazepoxide, 22
Chloroquine, 120, 455
Chlorpheniramine, 162
Chlorpromazine, 17
Cholangiocarcinoma, 345, 347
Cholangitis, sclerosing, 344
Cholecalciferol. See Vitamin D
Cholecystokinin, 326, 327, 330, 335
Cholelithiasis, 347
Cholera toxin, 111, 338
Cholestasis, 343
Cholesterol, 50, 51
    synthesis of, 50
Cholesterol esters, 50
Cholesterol stones, 347
Cholestyramine/Colestipol, 51
Cholic acid, 335
Choline acetyltransferase, 175
Choline uptake, 175
Cholinergic agonists, 175
Cholinergic pharmacology, 175–177
Cholinergic transmission, 175
Cholinesterases, plasma, 213
Chondrocalcinosis, 426

Chondromatous tumors, 425
Chondromyxoid fibroma, 425
Chondrosarcoma, 425
Chordae tendineae, 219
Chordee, 381
Chordoma, 138
Choriocarcinoma, 154, 386, 398
Choriomeningitis, lymphocytic, 128
Chorion, 137
Chorionic plate, 392
Choroid plexus, 182, 183
Christmas disease, 443
Chromaffin cells, 361
Chromatin, 58
Chromium, as cancer risk, 151
Chromosomal abnormalities, 72–74
Chromosomal deletions, 73
Chromosomal inversions, 73
Chromosomal translocations, 73
Chronic granulomatous disease, 96
Chronic obstructive pulmonary disease, 264, 265, 277
Chronic passive congestion, 343
Churg-Strauss syndrome, 248
Chylomicrons, 48, 51, 337
Chyme, 327
Chymotrypsin, 334
Cigarette smoke, as cancer risk, 151
Cilastatin, 114
Ciliary body epithelium, 193
Ciliary ganglion, 172
Ciliary muscles, 172, 192, 193
Ciliates, 117
Cilostazol, 444
Cimetidine, 162, 333
CIN (cervical intraepithelial neoplasia), 395
Cingulate gyrus, 200, 204
Cingulate herniation, 207
Cingulate sulcus, 204
Cingulum, 203
Ciprofloxacin, 116, 434
Circadian rhythms, 200
Circle of Willis, 208
    berry aneurysms of, 311
Circulation
    autonomic control, 238
    celiac, 322
    cerebrospinal fluid, ventricles and, 182
    fetal, 218
    hepatic portal, 324
    parasympathetic regulation of, 238
    pulmonary circulation, 235
    sympathetic regulation of, 238
    systemic, 235
Circumcision, 381
Circumflex artery, 219
Cirrhosis, 344
Cis (forming) face, Golgi apparatus, 77
Cisapride, 351
Cisplatin, 166
Citalopram, 20, 163
Citrate, 37
Citrate shuttle, 48
Citrate synthase, 37
Citric acid cycle, stoichiometry of, TCA, 37
Citrulline, 47
CJD. See Creutzfeldt-Jakob disease
CK-MB cardiac enzyme, 243
Clarithromycin, 64, 115, 434
Clarke's nucleus, 186
Classical conditioning, 4, 5
Classical pathway, in complement cascade, 96
Clathrin-coated pits, 77
Clavicle, 414
Clavulanate, 275, 435
Claw hand, 414

Clearance
    of drug, 156
    renal, 289
Cleavage, of zygote, 136
Cleft lip, 411
Cleft palate, 411
Climbing fibers, 199
Clindamycin, 64, 115
Clitoris, 378, 379
CLL (chronic lymphocytic leukemia), 453
Clomiphene, 394
Clonazepam, 22, 210
Cloned DNA, 68
Clonidine, 13
Clonidine methyldopa, 179
Clonorchis spp., 122
Clonorchis sinensis, 123, 345
Clostridium botulinum, 111
Clostridium difficile, 114, 348
    superinfection, 115
Clostridium perfringens, 111, 112, 349, 350, 435
Clotting cascade, 442
    pathologic dysregulation in, 443
    physiologic regulation in, 443
Clozapine, 18
CMI (cell-mediated immunity), 403
CML (chronic myelogenous leukemia), 74, 152, 453
CMV. See Cytomegalovirus
CMV retinitis, 129
c-myc oncogene, 152, 153
CO. See Carbon monoxide
CO2 transport, 269
CoA (coenzyme A), 39
Coagulase, 112, 433
Coagulation
    disseminated intravascular, 443
    pathways of, 442. See also Clotting cascade
    tests of, 443
Coagulative necrosis, 147
Cocaine, 13, 180, 213
Coccidioides spp., 132
Coccidioides immitis, 132, 276
    in AIDS patients, 100
Coccidioidomycosis, 132
Coccygeus, 380
Coccyx, 379
Cochlea, 197
Cochlear nucleus, 197
    VIII fibers, 198
Codeine, 212
Codman triangle, 425
Codon, 62
Coelom, 318
Coenzyme Q, 38
Cohort studies, 33
Colchicine, 79, 429
Cold hemolytic anemia, 447
Colestipol, 51
Colitis, ulcerative, 347
Collagen, 80
    synthesis of, 66
    type I, 423
    types of, 149
Collagenase, 112
Collecting duct, 295, 297, 298, 299
Collecting tubule, 284
Colles fascia (superficial perineal fascia), 380
Colloid carcinoma, of the breast, 401
Colon. see Large intestine
Colorectal cancer, hereditary nonpolyposis, 62
Coma, 13
Common coagulation pathway, 442
Common cold, 273
Common peroneal (fibular) nerve, 419
Common variable deficiency, 98
Communicating hydrocephalus, 183

Communicating rami, 186
Compensation, in acid/base regulation, 305
Competitive inhibitor, 53
Complement
    deficiencies of, 96
    split product C5a, 94
Complement cascade, 96
Complementary DNA, 67
Complementation, 128
Complete androgen insensitivity, 378
Complete atrioventricular conduction block, 226
Complete endocardial cushion defect, 240
Complete mole, 398
    partial mole versus, 398
Complex I (NADH dehydrogenase), 38
Complex II (succinate dehydrogenase), 38
Complex III (cytochrome b/c$_1$), 38
Complex seizure, 210
Compliance, 234, 262, 263
COMT. See Catechol-O-methyltransferase
Concentrating segment, in loop of Henle, 294
Concentration, drug, 157
Concentration gradients, 140
Concussion, 207
Conditioning, 4, 5
Conduction, in heart, 222
Conduction blocks, atrioventricular, 226
Conduction deafness, 197
Condyloma acuminatum, 395, 403
Cone bug, 121
Confidence intervals, 34
Confluence of sinuses, 183
Confounding bias, 33
Congenital adrenal hyperplasia, 359, 361, 378
Congenital anomalies, 341
    VACTERL, 138
    VATER, 138
Congenital enzyme deficiency syndromes, 360
Congenital heart disease
    acyanotic, 240
    cyanotic, 240–241
    obstructive, 241
Congenital hepatic malformations, 343
Congenital malformations, of nervous system, 171
Congenital reproductive anomalies, 378
Congestive heart failure, 244
Congestive myopathy, 246
Congo red stain, 150
Conidia, 131
Conjugated bilirubin, 335
Conjugated hyperbilirubinemia, 343
Conjugation, 113
Conjugation phase, 77
Conn syndrome, 359, 361
Connective tissue diseases, 149
Connexon, 80
Constrictor pupillae, 192
Contact dermatitis, 102
Contraception, 393
Contractility, cardiac, 228
Contraction, isovolumic, 231
Contralateral hemianopia, 209
Contusion, 207
Conus arteriosus, 216
Conus medullaris, 186
Convergence, 194
Conversion disorder, 23
Cooper ligaments, 400
COPD. See Chronic obstructive pulmonary disease
Copper poisoning, antidote for, 161
Coprophilia, 26
Cor pulmonale, 244
Cori cycle, 39
Cori disease, 41
Corona radiata, 388
Coronary arteries, 219

Coronaviruses, 127, 273
Corpus albicans, 389
Corpus callosum, 201, 204
Corpus cavernosum, 379, 380
Corpus luteum, 388, 389, 390
Corpus spongiosum, 379, 380
Corpus striatum, 201
Cortex, 285
    blood supply to, 208
Cortical adenomas, of kidney, 315
Cortical collecting duct, 290
Cortical reaction, 384
Corticobulbar tract, 199
Corticospinal tract, 198, 199
Corticosteroids, 52, 105, 278, 428
Corticotropin-releasing hormone, 354
Cortisol, 356, 364
    excess versus deficiency, 357
Corynebacterium spp., 110
Corynebacterium diphtheriae, 111, 273
Coumarin poisoning, antidote for, 161
Councilman body, 148
Countercurrent mechanism
    in absence of ADH, 299
    in presence of ADH, 298
Cowper gland, 380
COX. See Cyclooxygenase(s)
Coxsackie A virus, 273
Coxsackie B virus, 245
CPM (progressive multifocal leukoencephalopathy), 184
Cranial nerves, 190
    and brain stem, 190–191
    skeletal muscle innervated by, 410
Craniopharyngioma, 185
Creatine, 44
Creatinine clearance, 289
Cremaster muscle and fascia, 383
Cremasteric reflex, 383
CREST syndrome, 103
Cretinism, 372
Creutzfeldt-Jakob disease, 73, 207
CRH (corticotropin-releasing hormone), 354
Cribriform plate, 191
Cricothyroid, 259
Cri-du-chat syndrome, 74
Crigler-Najjar syndrome, 44, 343
Crista terminalis, 219
Crohn disease, 347
Cromolyn, 278
Crossbridge cycle, 407
Cross-sectional studies, 33
Croup, 274
Cruise ship agent (virus), 127
Crura
    of clitoris, 379
    of penis, 380
Crus cerebri, 187
Cryotherapy, 436
Crypt abscesses, 347
Cryptococcus spp., 181
Cryptococcus neoformans, 133
    in AIDS patients, 100
Cryptorchidism, 383
Cryptosporidiosis, 118
Cryptosporidium spp., 117, 118
Cryptosporidium parvum, 350
    in AIDS patients, 100
CSF. See Cerebrospinal fluid
Cumulus oophorus, 388
Cuneate fasciculus, 188
Cuneate nucleus, 188
Cuneus gyrus, 192, 204
Curling ulcers, 340
Currant jelly sputum, 275
Cushing disease, 355, 361

Cushing syndrome, 357, 361
Cushing ulcers, 340
Cutaneous larva migrans, 126, 435
Cutaneous leishmaniasis, 121
CXCR4 (α-chemokine receptor), 100
Cyanide poisoning, 38
Cyanocobalamin (B$_{12}$), 54
Cyanosis, 217
Cyanotic congenital heart disease, 240–241
Cyclic adenosine monophosphate, 158, 381
Cyclin-dependent kinases, 81
Cyclins, 81
Cyclobenzaprine, 409
Cyclooxygenase(s), 52, 428
    COX-1 pathway, 428
    COX-2 inhibitors, 428
    COX-2 pathway, 428
    as inflammation mediator, 95
    inhibitors, 428, 444
Cyclopentolate, 176
Cyclophosphamide, 105, 165
Cyclosporine, 105
Cyclothymia, 18, 19
Cystadenocarcinoma, 397
Cystadenoma, 397
Cystathionine synthase, 45, 46
Cysteine, 43
Cystic disease, 399
    renal, 311
Cystic fibrosis, 70, 71, 278, 343
    genetic testing in, 69
Cystic fibrosis transmembrane conductance
        regulator protein, 343
Cysticerci, 124
Cysticercosis, 124
Cystine, 46
Cystine stones, 314
Cystinuria, 46, 314
Cystitis
    hemorrhagic, 316
    infectious, 316
Cystitis emphysematosa, 316
Cystosarcoma phyllodes, 399
Cytarabine, 165
Cytochrome a/a$_3$, 38
Cytochrome b/c$_1$, 38
Cytochrome c, 38
Cytochrome c oxidase, 112
Cytochrome P450, 77
Cytokeratin stain, 150
Cytokines, 90, 91. See also Granulocyte colony-
        stimulating factor; Granulocyte-macrophage
        colony-stimulating factor; Interferon
        entries; Interleukins; Tumor necrosis factor;
        individual cytokines
    in cell regeneration, 149
    receptors, 158
    recombinant, clinical uses of, 104
Cytomegalovirus, 126
    in AIDS patients, 100
    hematologic changes caused by, 455
Cytoplasmic pathway, 36
Cytosine, 58
Cytosine arabinoside, 61
Cytoskeleton, 79
Cytosol, 387
Cytosolic enzymes, 42
Cytotoxic hypersensitivity reaction, 102
Cytotoxic T cells, 86, 88, 89
Cytotoxicity, antibody-dependent cell-mediated, 86
Cytotrophoblast, 136

D

D cells, 331
D receptors, in cell signaling, 83
d4T (stavudine), 101
DA agonists, 202

Dracunculus spp., 122, 125
DRG (dorsal root ganglia), 186, 188
Dronabinol, 14, 330
Droperidol, 214
Drug-induced disorders
    of bone, 369
    of minerals, 369
    neutropenia, 450
Drugs. *See also individual drugs by name or class*
    of abuse, 13–14
    pharmacodynamics of, 157–158
    pharmacokinetics of, 156–157
    volume distribution, 156
Dry eyes (keratoconjunctivitis sicca), 102
Dry mouth (xerostomia), 102
DTH (delayed type hypersensitivity), 102, 403
DTL. *See* Descending thin loop of Henle
DTs (delirium tremens), 12
Dubin-Johnson syndrome, 343
Duchenne muscular dystrophy, 70, 430
Duct of Gartner, 378
Ductal cells, 334
Ductus arteriosus, 218
Ductus deferens, 378, 379, 383
    artery to, 383
Duodenal atresia, 341
Duodenum, 320, 328
Dura, 181
Dura mater, 183
Duret hemorrhage, 207
Dwarfism, 375, 423
Dyes, as cancer risk, 151
Dynamic compression, 264
Dyneins, 79, 384
Dyscrasias, 454
Dysdiadochokinesia, 199
Dysentery, 348
Dysgerminoma, 397
Dyspareunia, 27
Dysplasia
    defined, 148, 151
    tooth enamel, 115
Dysthymia, 18, 19
Dystonia, 18
Dystrophin, 430

E

EA (efferent arteriole), 290, 292
Ear infections, 273–274
Early distal tubule, 290
Eating disorders, 21
Ebola virus, 128
EBV. *See* Epstein-Barr virus
ECF (extracellular fluid) volume, 141
Echinocandin, 134
Echinococcus spp., 122
Echinococcus granulosus, 124
Echinococcus multilocularis, 124
Echothiophate, 177, 193
ECT (electroconvulsive therapy), 20
Ectasia, mammary duct, 401
Ectoderm, 138
    derivatives, 138
    neural, 170
Ectopic pregnancy, 136
Ectopic thyroid nests, 372
Edema, 251
    pulmonary, 281
Edema factor, 111
Edetate calcium disodium, for lead poisoning, 160, 161
Edinger-Westphal nuclei, 193
Etidocaine, 213
Edrophonium, 176
EDT (early distal tubule), 290
EDTA (edetate calcium disodium), for lead poisoning, 160, 161

EDV (end diastolic volume), 228
Edwards syndrome, 72
EE (enteroendocrine) cells, 320
EF (edema factor), 111
EF (ejection fraction), 228
Efavirenz, 101
Efferent arteriole, 290, 292
Efferent limb, 188
Efficacy, drug, 157
EGF. *See* Epidermal growth factor
EHEC (enterohemorrhagic *E. coli*), 111
Ehlers-Danlos syndrome, 66, 149
Eicosanoids, 52
    metabolism of, 52
Einthoven's triangle, 227
Eisenmenger complex, 217
Eisenmenger syndrome, 240
Ejaculation disorders, 27
Ejaculatory duct, 378, 379, 380
Ejection fraction, 228
Elasticity, 262
Elastin, 80
Elbow joint, movement at, 416
Elder abuse, 8
Electrocardiogram, principles of, 224–226
Electrochemical gradients, 140
Electroconvulsive therapy, 20
Electrogenic pump, 144
Electrolytes
    abnormalities of, 287
    diuretic-induced changes in, 310
Electron shuttles, 38
Electron transport chain, 37, 38
Elimination, drug, 156
ELISA. *See* Enzyme-linked immunosorbent assay
Elongation, in protein translation, 64
Embolic cerebral infarcts, 210
Embryoblast, 136
Embryology
    early, 136
    week 2, 137
    weeks 3 through 8, 138
Embryonal carcinoma, 386
Embryonal rhabdomyosarcoma, 395, 430
Embryonic disk, bilaminar, 137
Emetics, 330
Emphysema, 262, 265, 267, 277
Empty sella syndrome, 355
Enalapril, 164, 254
Encainide, 252
Encephalitis
    amebic, 119
    bacterial, 119
    fungal, 181
    viral, 127, 182
Encephalopathy, 203
Enchondromatosis, 423, 425
End diastolic volume, 228
End systolic volume, 228
Endocarditis, 245
    acute, 245
    Libman-Sacks, 102, 245
Endocrine pancreas, 363–365
    disorders of, 365
Endoderm, 138, 318
    derivatives, 138
    development of, 284
    neural, 170
Endometrial adenocarcinoma, 396
Endometriosis, 396
Endometritis, 396
Endometrium, 391
Endomysium, 407
Endosomes, 77
Endospores, 131
Endotoxin, 109, 110

Enflurane, 214
Enfuvirtide, 101
Entacapone, 180, 202
Entamoeba spp., 117
Entamoeba histolytica, 118, 348
Enterobacteriaceae, 435
Enterobius spp., 122, 125
Enterochromaffin cells, 330, 331
Enterococcus faecalis, 110
Enteroendocrine cells, 320
Enteroglucagon, 331
Enterohemorrhagic *E. coli,* 111, 349
Enteroinvasive *E. coli,* 348
Enterokinase, 334
Enteropathogenic *E. coli,* 349
Enterotoxic *E. coli,* 111
Enterotoxigenic *E. coli,* 349
Enuresis, 10
Enzyme-linked immunosorbent assay, 69
    in AIDS diagnosis, 100
Enzyme-linked receptors, 82
Enzymes, 54. *See also individually named enzymes*
    deficiency syndromes of, 360
    kinetics of, 53
    ligand-regulated transmembrane, 158
Eosin stain, 150
Eosinophilic leukocytosis, 450
Eosinophils, 87, 449
    in chronic inflammation, 97
Eotaxin, in chronic inflammation, 97
Ependymal cells, 183, 184
Ependymoma, 185
Ephedrine, 180
Epiblast, 137
Epidemic typhus, 437
Epidermal growth factor, 149
    receptors, 83
Epidermis, 431
Epidermophyton spp., 131, 435
Epididymis, 378, 379, 380
Epidural hematoma, 181, 210
Epidural space, 181
Epiglottitis, 274
Epilepsy, myoclonic, 70
Epileptic seizures, 210, 211
Epimysium, 407
Epinephrine, 41, 44, 178, 193, 278, 364
Epispadias, 381
Epithalamus, 170, 200
Epithelial cells, 258
Epithelial foot processes, loss of, 311
Epithelium
    of digestive tract, 319
    hyperplasia of, 399
    tumors of, 397
Eplerenone, 310
EPO. *See* Erythropoietin
EPS (extrapyramidal side effects), of antipsychotics, 17, 18
Epstein-Barr virus, 126, 153, 273
    hematologic changes caused by, 455
    in non-Hodgkin lymphoma, 452
Eptifibatide, 444
Equilibrium, 140
Equilibrium potential, 143
Equine encephalitis, viruses causing, 127
Equivalence zone, in Ab-Ag complexes, 93
erb oncogenes, 152
Erectile dysfunction, 27, 381
    treatment of, 381
Erection, penile. *See* Penile erection
Erector spinae muscle, 415
Ergonovine, 163
Ergosterol, 108
Ergot alkaloids, 163
Ergotamine, 163

Ergotism, 163
ERT (estrogen replacement therapy), 393
Erysipelas, 433
Erythema marginatum, 243
Erythema multiforme, 432
Erythrocytic schizont, 119
Erythromycin, 64, 115, 275, 402, 403, 433
Erythroplakia, 339
Erythropoiesis, 445
Erythropoietin, 104, 445
    for anemia, 448
Escherichia spp., 110
Escherichia coli
    in bacterial meningitis, 181
    enterohemorrhagic, 349
    enteroinvasive, 348
    enterotoxic, 111
    enterotoxigenic, 349
E-selectin, 94
Esmolol, 179
    as antidote, 161
Esomeprazole, 333
Esophageal varices, 324, 339, 344
Esophagus, 318, 320
    carcinoma of, 339
    pathology of, 339–340
    ulceration of, 369
Essential amino acids, 46
Essential thrombocythemia, 441
Esterases, 334
Esters, 213
Estradiol, 387
    in feedback examples, 140
Estrogen replacement therapy, 393
Estrogens, 389, 390, 392, 393
ESV (end systolic volume), 228
Eszopiclone, 22
Etanercept, 428
ETC (electron transport chain), 37, 38
Ethacrynic acid, 310
Ethanol, 12, 13
    as antidote, 161
Ethanol poisoning, 159
Ethical issues, 29–31
Ethinyl estradiol, 393
Ethosuximide, 211
Ethylene glycol poisoning, antidote for, 161
Etidronate, 369
Etomidate, 214
Etoposide, 166
Euchromatin, 58
Eukaryotes, 58, 108
Eukaryotic chromatin structure, 58
Ewing sarcoma, 425
Excitation-contraction coupling, 406
Excretion, renal regulation of, 296
Excretion of X (E_X), 288
Exfoliatins, 433
Exhibitionism, 26
Exocrine pancreas, 343
Exophthalmos, 372
Exotoxins, 110, 111, 436
Experimenter expectancy bias, 33
Expiration, 264
Expiratory reserve volume, 261
Exposure, classic conditioning and, 5
Exstrophy
    bladder, 316
    of bladder, 381
Extensor carpi radialis brevis, 417
Extensor carpi radialis longus, 417
Extensor carpi ulnaris, 417
Extensor digitorum brevis, 422
Extensor digitorum longus, 422
Extensor hallucis longus, 422
Extensor pollicis brevis, 418
Extensor pollicis longus, 418

External anal sphincter, 379
External auditory meatus, 411
External intercostal muscles, 262
External laryngeal nerve, 259
External oblique fascia, 383
External spermatic fascia, 383
Extinction, 5
Extracellular fluid volume, 141
Extracellular pathogens, 86
Extraembryonic mesoderm, 137
Extrahepatic biliary atresia, 343
Extramammary Paget disease, of the vulva, 395
Extraocular muscles, 195
Extrapyramidal nervous system, 201
Extrapyramidal side effects, of antipsychotics, 17, 18
Extrinsic asthma, 278
Extrinsic coagulation pathway, 442
Eye
    anatomy of, 192
    pharmacology of, 193
Eye movement, control of, 195
Eyeworm, 122

F

F cells, 331
F (filtered load), 288
F-1, 6-BP, 36
F-2, 6-BP, 36
FAb, in globulin structure, 92
F(Ab)$_2$, in globulin structure, 92
Fabry disease, 52
Face, development of, 411
Facial nerve (VII), 191, 196
    skeletal muscle innervated by, 410
Facial nucleus and fibers, 198
Facilitated diffusion, 78, 140, 141
Facioscapulohumeral muscular dystrophy, 430
Factitious disorders, 23
Factor II, 442
Factor IIa, 442
Factor III, 442
Factor V, 112
Factor V Leiden, 443
Factor VII, 442
Factor VIIa, 442
Factor VIII deficiency. *See* Hemophilia A
Factor VIIIa, 442
Factor IX, 442
Factor IX deficiency, 443
Factor IXa, 442
Factor X, 112, 442
Factor XII. *See* Hageman factor
Facultative intracellular parasites, 117
FAD, 39
FADH, 387
FADH$_2$, 37
Fading, 5
Falx cerebri, 183
Famciclovir, 129
Familial hypercholesterolemia, 70
Familial polyposis coli, 151
Famotidine, 162, 333
Fanconi syndrome, 115
Farber disease, 52
Fas ligand, 148
Fasciculation, 409
Fasciculi, 186, 407
Fasciola spp., 122
Fasciola hepatica, 123
Fasciolopsis spp., 122
Fasciolopsis buski, 123
Fat necrosis, 147
Fatty acids
    free, 51
    metabolism of, 48
    oxidation of, 48

synthesis of, 37, 39, 48, 54
Fatty acyl CoA synthetase, 54
Fatty change, cell injury and, 147
Fatty liver, 344
Fatty streak, 249
Fava beans, 40
FDP (fibrin degradation products), 442, 443
Feedback, negative and positive, 140
Feedback control, in differential diagnosis of cortisol
    excess, 357
Feeding center, 326
Felbamate, 210, 211
Felty syndrome, 426, 450
Female
    inhibited orgasm in, 27
    sexual arousal disorder in, 27
Female reproductive system, 387–394
    anatomy of, 379–380
    congenital anomaly of, 378
    development of, 378
    pathology of, 395–398
    pharmacology of, 393–394
    physiology of, 387–392
Femoral nerve, 419, 420, 421
Fentanyl, 212, 214
Ferrochelatase, 44
Fertilization, 136, 384, 391
Fetal alcohol syndrome, 240
Fetal circulation, 218
Fetishism, 26
FEV$_1$ (forced expiratory volume in 1 s), 223, 265
Fexofenadine, 162
FGF (fibroblast growth factor), 149
Fibrates, 51
Fibrin, 443
Fibrin degradation products, 443
Fibrinogen, 442
Fibrinoid necrosis, 147
Fibrinolysis, 442
Fibrinopeptides, 94
Fibrinous pericarditis, 247
Fibroadenoma, 399
Fibrocystic disease, 399
    versus breast cancer, 401
Fibroma
    chondromyxoid, 425
    ovarian, 398
Fibronectin, 80
Fibrosis, 262, 265, 267, 399
Fibrous dysplasia, 423
Fibula, 421
Fibular collateral ligament, 421
Fick's law of diffusion, 141, 267
Filgrastim. *See* Granulocyte colony-stimulating
    factor
Filovirus, 128
Filtered load, 288
Filtration, in urine formation, 288, 291
Filtration fraction, 291
Filum terminale, 186
Fimbria, 391
Finasteride, 382
Finger, movement of, 417
Finger flexors, 413
First degree atrioventricular conduction block, 226
First-order elimination, 156
First-pass effect, 157
Fish tapeworm, 124
Fistulas, 347
Fitz-Hugh-Curtis syndrome, 395
Flagellates, 117
Flagellum, 384
Flat worms, 122
Flavivirus, 127
Flecainide, 252
Flexor carpi radialis muscles, 417

Flexor carpi ulnaris muscles, 417
Flexor digiti minimi muscles, 417
Flexor digitorum longus muscles, 422
Flexor digitorum profundus muscles, 417
Flexor digitorum superficialis muscles, 417
Flexor hallucis longus muscles, 422
Flexor pollicis brevis muscles, 418
Flexor pollicis longus muscles, 418
Flocculonodular lobe, 196
Flora, normal, 110
Flow cytometry, 104
Fluconazole, 134
Flucytosine, 113, 134
Fluid abnormalities, 287
Fluid balance, estimation of fluid volumes, 286
Fluid volume
    changes in, 142
    compartments and, 141
    distribution and, 141
    estimation and, 286
    extra- and intracellular, 141
    measurement of, 141
    normal values of, 286
Flukes. *See* Trematodes
Flumazenil, 13
    as antidote, 161, 214
Fluorescent treponemal antibody-absorption test,
    403
5-Fluorodeoxyuridine, 60
Fluoroquinolones, 113, 116
5-Fluorouracil, 165
Fluoxetine, 20, 163
Fluphenazine, 17
Flurazepam, 22
Flutamide, 382
Fluvoxamine, 20, 163
FO (foramen ovale), 216
Focal proliferative glomerulonephritis, 312
Focal segmental glomerulosclerosis, 311, 312
Folate, for anemia, 448
Folic acid, 54
Folic acid synthesis inhibitors, 116
Folinic acid, 116
Follicles, 378
    antrum of, 388
    carcinoma of, 373
    development of, 388
    Graafian, 388, 389
    hyperplasia of, 451
Follicle-stimulating hormone, 354, 385, 387, 393,
    394
Follicular phase, in menstrual cycle, 390
Folliculitis, hot tub, 433
Folliculogenesis, and ovulation, 388
Fomepizole, as antidote, 161
Food poisoning, 350
Foot, sensory innervation of, 420
Foramen lacerum, 191
Foramen magnum, 191
Foramen ovale, 191, 216, 240
Foramen rotundum, 191
Foramen spinosum, 191
Foramen/Foramina
    incisive, 411
    jugular, 183, 191
    of Luschka, 182
    of Magendie, 182
    of Monro, 182
Forced expiratory volume in 1 s, 223, 265
Forced vital capacity, 223, 265
Foregut, 318, 319
Formoterol, 278
Formyl methionyl peptides, 94
Fornix, 203, 204
Forward motility factor, 384
Foscarnet, 129

Fosphenytoin, 210
Fourth ventricle, 170, 182, 190, 204
Fracture(s)
    midshaft humeral, 414
        vessel and nerve damage associated with, 222
Fragile X syndrome, 70
Frameshift point mutations, 62
Francisella spp., 112
Francisella tularensis, 117
Free energy, 53
Free fatty acids, 51
Free radicals, protection against, 146
Free water clearance, 289
Freudian defense mechanisms, 11
Frontal eye field, 195, 205
Frontal lobe, 204, 205
Frontal lobe syndrome, 205
Frontonasal prominence, 411
Frotteurism, 26
Fructokinase deficiency, 36
Fructose-1,6-bisphosphatase, 42
Fructosuria, 36
FSH. *See* Follicle-stimulating hormone
FTA-ABS test, 403
5-FU (5-fluorouracil), 165
Fulminant hepatitis, 345
Functional residual capacity, 261
Fundus, 320, 327, 379
Fungal infections, 131–133
    nonsystemic, 131
    opportunistic, 133
    systemic, 132
    treatment of, 134
Fungal meningoencephalitis, 181
Fungemia, systemic agents for, 134
Fungi, types of, 131
Funiculi, 186
Furazolidone, 122
Furosemide, 301, 310
Furuncles, 433
Fusion inhibitor, 101, 455
Fusobacterium spp., 110, 275
FVC (forced vital capacity), 223, 265

G

G cells, 330, 332
G protein, 158
G protein–coupled receptor systems, 83
G6PD. *See* Glucose-6-phosphate dehydrogenase
GABA. *See* γ-*aminobutyric acid*
Gabapentin, 211
GAE (granulomatous amebic encephalitis), 119
Gal-1-P uridyltransferase deficiency, 36
Galactokinase deficiency, 36
Galactosemia, 36
α-Galactosidase
    A, 52
    inhibitors, 366
Galantamine, 206
Gall bladder, 318, 335
Gallstones, 347
Gametocytes, 119
Gametogony, 119
γ-aminobutyric acid, 44
    receptors, 158
Ganciclovir, 129, 455
Ganglion blockers, 175
    predominant tone and effects of, 177
Ganglion cells, 342
Gangrenous necrosis, 147
Gap junctions, 80
Gardnerella spp., 396
Gartner, duct of, 378
Gas exchange, 266–273
    diffusion-limited, 267
    perfusion-limited, 267

Gastric H⁺ secretion, 332
Gastric inhibitory peptide, 330, 331, 363
Gastric reflux, 327
Gastric secretions, 332
    mechanism of, 332
    phases of, 333
Gastric veins, 324
Gastrin, 330, 331, 332, 333
Gastrinoma. *see* Zollinger-Ellison syndrome
Gastrin-releasing peptide, 331
Gastritis
    acute, 340
    chronic, 340
Gastrocnemius muscle, 421, 422
Gastrocolic reflex, 329
Gastroduodenal artery, 322
Gastroepiploic artery, 322
Gastroesophageal reflux disease, 327, 333
Gastroileal reflex, 328
Gastrointestinal system
    cestodes in, 124
    embryology of, 318–319
    gross anatomy of, 321–324
    histology of, 319–320
    hormones in, 330–331
    microbiology of, 348–350
    pathology of, 339–347
    pharmacology of, 351
    physiology of, 326–328
Gastrointestinal tract
    cross-sectional anatomy of, 325
    development of, 318
Gastroparesis, diabetic, 328
Gastrulation, 138
Gaucher disease, 52
GBM (glomerular basement membrane), 312
GC (glomerular capillaries), 290, 291
G-CSF (granulocyte colony-stimulating factor), 91,
    104
Gel electrophoresis, 69
Gender identity, 26
Gene disorders, 71
Gene flow, and equilibrium, 75
General anesthesia, 210, 213, 214
Generalized anxiety disorder, 21
Generalized seizure, 210
Genetic code, 64
Genetic drift, 128
    and equilibrium, 75
Genetic shift, 128
Genetic testing, 69
Genetics, population, 75
Genital warts, 395, 403
Genitofemoral nerve, 383
Genitourinary system disease, 402–403
Genomic imprinting, 202
Gentamicin, 64, 115, 275
GERD (gastroesophageal reflux disease), 327, 333
Germ cell tumors, 386, 397
Germ layers, 138. *See also individually named*
    layers
Germ tube test, 131, 402
German measles. *See* Rubella
Gerstmann syndrome, 205, 209
Gestational trophoblastic disease, 137, 398
GFAP (glial fibrillary acidic protein), 185
GFR. *See* Glomerular filtration rate
GH. *See* Growth hormone
Ghon complex, 277
GHRH (growth hormone-releasing hormone), 354
Giant cell arteritis, 249
Giant cell tumor, 425
Giant intestinal fluke, 123
Giardia spp., 117
Giardia lamblia, 118, 350
    in AIDS patients, 100

Giardiasis, 118, 122
Gigantism, 355, 375
Gilbert syndrome, 44, 343
GIP. See Gastric inhibitory peptide
Glanzmann thrombasthenia, 440
Glaucoma, 192
    and diuretics, 310
    treatment of, 193
Glenohumeral joint, movement at, 415
Glia, 184
Gliadin, 341
Glial fibrillary acidic protein, 185
Glial fibrillary acidic protein stain, 150
Glioblastoma multiforme, 185
Glipizide, 366
Globus pallidus, 201
Glomerular capillaries, 290, 291
Glomerular diseases, 311–312
Glomerular filtration rate, 291
    autoregulation of, 292
    filtration regulation and, 292
Glomeruli, hyalinized, 312
Glomerulonephritis
    chronic, 312
    focal proliferative, 312
Glomus tumor, 251
Glossopharyngeal nerve (IX), 191, 410
Glottis, 327
Glucagon, 41, 331, 363, 364, 366
    as antidote, 161
Glucagon receptors, 83
Glucocorticoids, 361
Glucogenic conversion, 45, 46
Glucokinase, 36, 42
Gluconeogenesis, 37, 39, 42
Glucose
    counter-regulation of, 364
    integrated control, 364
Glucose transport, 36
Glucose-6-phosphatase, 41, 42
Glucose-6-phosphate, 40
Glucose-6-phosphate dehydrogenase, 40, 44
Glucose-6-phosphate dehydrogenase deficiency,
    40, 44, 70, 447
Glucuronosyl transferase, 343
GLUT-1 and 3, 36
GLUT-2, 36
GLUT-2 transporter, 336
GLUT-4, 36
GLUT-5 transporter, 336
Glutamate, 43, 44, 45, 385
Glutamate decarboxylase, 44
Glutamine, 43
Glutathione peroxidase, 40, 146
Glutathione reductase, 40
Gluteus maximus, 379, 420, 421
Gluteus medius, 420
Gluteus minimus, 420
Glyburide, 366
Glycerin, 351
Glycerol kinase, 49
Glycerol-3, 38
Glycerol-3-P, 42
Glycerol-3-P dehydrogenase, 49
α-Glycerol-3-P shuttle, 38
Glycine, 43, 44
Glycocalyx, 109
Glycogen
    formation of, 41
    metabolism of, 41
Glycogen debranching enzyme, 41
Glycogen phosphorylase, 41
Glycogen storage diseases, 41
Glycogen synthase, 41
Glycogenolysis, 41
Glycolysis, 36
    irreversible, 36

Glycoprotein IIb/IIIa
    inhibitors, 444
    receptor, 440
Glycopyrrolate, 176
Glycosylation, N-linked, 76, 78
GM-CSF (granulocyte-macrophage colony-
    stimulating factor), 91, 104
GnRH. See Gonadotropin-releasing hormone
Goblet cells, 320, 328
God compounds, 428
Golgi apparatus, 76, 77
Gonadotropin-releasing hormone, 354, 385, 387,
    390
    analog of, 382
    in feedback examples, 140
Gonococci, 426
Gonorrhea, 385
Goodpasture syndrome, 102, 312
Gout, 60, 426
    treatment of, 429
Gouty nephropathy, 313
Gp. See Glycoprotein IIb/IIIa
gp41, in acquired deficiency syndrome, 100
Graafian follicle, 388, 389
Gracile fasciculus, 188
Gracile nucleus, 188
Gracilis muscle, 420, 421
Grade, of tumor, 154
Graded dose-response curve, 157
Gradients
    concentration, 140
    electrochemical, 140
Graft versus host rejection, 103
Grafts
    rejection types and, 103
    types of, 103
Gram characteristics, of bacteria, 109
Gram reaction, 109
Gram stain, 150
Granisetron, 330
Granules
    in acute inflammation, 93
    azurophilic, 449
    enzymes in, 449
Granulocyte colony-stimulating factor, 91, 104
Granulocyte-macrophage colony-stimulating factor,
    91, 104
Granulocytes, 449
Granulomatous amebic encephalitis, 119
Granulomatous diseases, 277
Granulopoiesis, 449
Granulosa cell tumor, 398
Granulosa cells, 388
Granulovacuolar degeneration, 206
Graves disease, 371, 372, 373
Gravity, 196
Gray baby syndrome, 115
Gray communicating rami, 186
Gray matter, 186
Great vessels, transposition of, 217, 241
Greater peritoneal sac, 321
Greater vestibular gland, 379, 380
Grief, 19
Griseofulvin, 134
Group transferases, 115
Growth curve, bacterial, 108
Growth factors
    in cell regeneration, 149
    receptors, 158
Growth hormone, 355, 364, 374–375
    biologic actions of, 374
    control of, 374
    disorders of, 375
    receptors, 158
    treatment options and, 375
Growth hormone-releasing hormone, 354

GRP (gastrin-releasing peptide), 331
Guanethidine, 180
Guanine, 58
Guanylate cyclase, 82, 83
Gubernaculum, 382
Guillain-Barré syndrome, 184
Gummas, 385
Gut tube, 318
GVD (granulovacuolar degeneration), 206
Gynecomastia, 386, 401
Gyri, 204

H

H band, 407
H^+ secretion, gastric, 332
H_1 antagonists, 162
H_1 receptor, 162
H_2 antagonists, 162, 333
H_2 receptor, 162
H_2O_2 (hydrogen peroxide), 146
H_3 receptor, 162
Haemophilus ducreyi, 403
Haemophilus influenzae, 110, 273, 274, 275
    in bacterial meningitis, 181
Hageman factor (factor XII)
    in coagulation, 442
    as inflammation mediator, 95
Hair, 431
Hairy cell leukemia, 154, 453
Hairy leukoplakia, 339
    as AIDS complication, 101
Half-life, of drugs, 156
Hallucinogens, 14
Haloperidol, 17
Halothane, 214
Hamate, 414
Hand
    innervation of, 414
    muscles in, 413
Hantavirus, 128, 276
Hardy-Weinberg equilibrium, 75
Hartnup disease, 46, 337
Hashimoto thyroiditis, 372
Haustra, 329
Hay fever, 102
HBs (Hirano bodies), 206
HBeAg, 346
HbH disease, 446
Hb-O_2 dissociation curve, 268
HBsAg, 346
HBV. See Hepatitis B virus
hCG. See Human chorionic gonadotropin
HCl, 332
HDL (high density lipoprotein), 51
Head and neck, embryology and anatomy, 410–412
Heart. See also Cardiac entries; Cardiovascular
    system
    autonomic control of, 238
    borders of, 220
    conduction in, 222
    congenital abnormalities of, 240–241
    mechanical performance of, 228
    muscle of, 406
    neoplasms of, 247
    parasympathetic regulation of, 238
    sympathetic regulation of, 238
    valves of, 232. See also individually named valves
    valvular disorders of, 233
Heart disease
    congenital. See Congenital heart disease
    ischemic, 242
    valvular, 246
Heart failure
    cardiac output changes after, 229
    dilated, 237
    drugs used in, 254–255
    progressive, 232

Heart rate, 228
  estimation of, 225
Heart rhythms, 226
Heart sounds, 230
Heart tube, 216
Heavy chain domains, in globulin structure, 92
Heavy metal poisoning, 160
Heinz bodies, 40
Helicobacter pylori, 333, 340
Heliotrope rash, 430
Helper T cells, 89
Hemangioblastoma, 251
Hemangioma, 251
  capillary, 432
Hematoma, 181
  epidural and subdural, 210
  lens-shaped biconvex, 181
Hematopoiesis, 440
Hematopoietic growth factors. *See* Granulocyte
  colony-stimulating factor; Granulocyte-
  macrophage colony-stimulating factor
Hematoxylin stain, 150
Heme synthesis, 37
Hemiballism, 200, 201, 202
Hemicholinium, 175, 177
Hemidesmosomes, 80
Hemisection, 189
Hemisphere lesions, 199
Hemochromatosis, 344
Hemodynamics, 234
  in acute inflammation, 93
Hemoflagellates, 121
Hemoglobin. *See* Hb entries
Hemolytic anemia, 40, 447
Hemolytic crisis, 44
Hemophilia A, 70, 443
  treatment of, 445
Hemophilia B, 70, 443
Hemorrhage
  cerebrovascular, 210
  Duret, 207
  splinter, 245
  subarachnoid, 181, 210
Hemorrhagic cystitis, 316
Hemorrhagic pancreatitis, acute, 343
Hemorrhagic pericarditis, 247
Hemostasis, 440
Henderson-Hasselbalch equation, 305
Henle, loop of. *See* Descending thin loop of Henle;
  Loop of Henle
Hepadnavirus, 126
Heparin, 444
Heparin poisoning, antidote for, 161
Heparinase, 112
Hepatic ducts, 335
Hepatic excretion, 335
Hepatic glycogen phosphorylase, 41
Hepatic portal circulation, 324
Hepatitis
  acute, 345
  alcoholic, 344
  chronic, 345
  fulminant, 345
  halothane, 214
Hepatitis A, 346
Hepatitis B virus, 126, 153, 346
  infectious arthritis and, 427
Hepatitis C, 344, 346
Hepatitis D, 346
Hepatitis E virus, 127, 346
Hepatoblastoma, 345
Hepatocellular carcinoma, 153, 154, 345
Hepatolenticular degeneration. *See* Wilson disease
Hereditary angioedema, 96
Hereditary nonpolyposis colorectal cancer, 62
Hereditary spherocytosis, 447
Hernias, 339, 341

Heroin, 13, 212
Herpes simplex virus, 126, 402, 403, 434
  in AIDS patients, 100
Herpesviruses, 126, 153, 251, 426, 432
Hers disease, 41
Heterochromatin, 58
Hexamethonium, 175
Hexokinase, 36
Hexosaminidase A, 52
Hexose monophosphate shunt, 40
HGPRT (hypoxanthine guanine phosphoryl
  pyrophosphate transferase), 60
HHV8 (human herpesvirus type 8), 251, 426, 432
Hiatal hernia, 339
High altitude disease, 271, 272
High density lipoprotein, 51
High molecular weight kininogen, 95
Hilum, 285
Hindgut, 318, 319
Hinge region, in globulin structure, 92
Hip joint, movements at, 420
Hippocampus, 203, 205
Hirano bodies, 206
Hirschsprung disease, 342
Hirsutism, 382
Hirudin, 444
Histamine, 44, 162, 331, 332
  as inflammation mediator, 95
Histamine receptors, 162
Histidine, 43, 44
Histidine decarboxylase, 44, 162
Histiocytes, in chronic inflammation, 97
Histology, 258
Histones, 58
Histoplasma spp., 132
Histoplasma capsulatum, 117, 132, 276
  in AIDS patients, 100
Histrionic disorder, 24
HIV. *See* Human immunodeficiency virus
H+/K+-ATPase, 332, 333
HLA (human leukocyte antigen), 89, 426
HMG (human menopausal gonadotrophin)-CoA
  reductase, 50
HMP (hexose monophosphate), 40
HMWK (high molecular weight kininogen), 95
HNPCC (hereditary nonpolyposis colorectal
  cancer), 62
Hodgkin disease, 451
Holoprosencephaly, 171
Homatropine, 176
Homeostasis, 200
Homocysteine methyltransferase, 54
Homocystinuria, 45, 46
Homogentisate oxidase, 45
Homogentisic acid, 46
Homosexuality, 26
Homovanillic acid, 361
Hookworms, 126, 435
Hormonal regulation
  of calcium and phosphate, 367
  of spermatogenesis, 385
  of steroidogenesis, 385
Hormone replacement therapy, 393
Hormones, 44, 166
  adrenal, 356
  characteristics of, 354
  gastrointestinal, 330–331
  lipase sensitivity to, 48, 49
Horner syndrome, 194, 198, 280
Horseshoe kidney, 285
Hot tub folliculitis, 433
HPV (human papilloma virus), 381, 395, 403
HRT (hormone replacement therapy), 393
hst-1-int-2 oncogene, 152
HSV. *See* Herpes simplex virus
5HT. *See* Serotonin

HTLV-1 (human T-cell leukemia virus), 153
HU. *See* Hydroxyurea
Human chorionic gonadotropin, 137, 154, 388, 392
Human immunodeficiency virus, 127. *See also*
  Acquired immunodeficiency syndrome
  detection of, 69
  hematologic changes caused by, 455
  nephropathy in, 312
  therapeutic approaches to, 101
Human leukocyte antigens, 89, 426
Human menopausal gonadotrophin-CoA reductase,
  50
Human papilloma virus, 381, 395, 403
Human T-cell leukemia virus, 153
Humerus, midshaft fracture, 414
Humor, 11
Humoral immunity, defects, 98
Hunter syndrome, 52
Huntington disease, 70, 201, 202
Hurler syndrome, 52
Hürthle cells, 372
HVA (homovanillic acid), 361
Hyaline membrane formation, 279
Hyalinized glomeruli, 312
Hyaluronidase, 112, 384
Hybridization, 69
Hydatid cyst disease, 124
Hydatidiform mole, 398
  dilated villi and, 138
  hCG levels and, 137
Hydralazine, 255
Hydraulic resistance equation, 234
Hydrocele, 382, 383
Hydrocephalus, 171, 183
Hydrocephalus ex vacuo, 183
Hydrochlorothiazide, 310
Hydrocodone, 212
Hydrogen peroxide, 146
Hydronephrosis, 314, 315
Hydrophobic amino acids, 43
Hydropic swelling, cell injury and, 147
Hydrops fetalis, 446
Hydroureter, 315
Hydroxychloroquine, 120, 428
Hydroxylase deficiency, 359
Hydroxylation phase, 77
Hydroxylysine, 66
Hydroxyproline, 66
Hydroxyurea, 60
  for anemia, 448
Hydroxyzine, 162
Hymenolepis spp., 122
Hyperacute rejection, 103
Hyperaldosteronism, 359
Hypercalcemia, 368n, 369
Hypercholesterolemia
  familial, 70
  type II, 51
Hypergammaglobulinemia, polyclonal, 454
Hyperglycemic agents, 366
Hyperkinetic movement disorders, 201
Hyperlipidemias, 51
Hyperosmolar nonketotic coma, 365
Hyperosmotic volume, contraction and expansion,
  142
Hyperostosis frontalis interna, 425
Hyperparathyroidism, 368, 423
  primary, 369
  secondary, 369
Hyperplasia, 148
  atypical, 151
  congenital adrenal, 359
  follicular, 451
  paracortical, 451

Hyperpolarization, 143
Hyperprolactinemia, 355
   antipsychotics and, 17
Hypersegmental neutrophils, anemia and, 446
Hypersensitivity reactions, 102
    type I (immediate), 102, 278, 449
    type II (cytotoxic/noncytotoxic), 102
    type III (immune complex), 102
    type IV (delayed), 102, 403
Hypertension, 250
   cerebral infarcts caused by, 210
   malignant, 250
   portal, 344
   pulmonary, 281
Hyperthermia, malignant, 214
Hyperthyroidism, 372
   primary, 371
   treatment of, 373
Hypertriglyceridemia, type I, 51
Hypertrophic cardiomyopathy, 246
Hypertrophic osteoarthropathy, 423
Hypertrophy, 148
Hyperuricemia, 426
Hypervitaminosis, 146
Hyphae, 131
Hypnozoites, 119
Hypoactive sexual disorder, 27
Hypoaldosteronism, 360
Hypoblast, 137
Hypocalcemia, 368n
Hypochondriasis, 23
Hypogammaglobulinemia, Bruton X-linked, 98
Hypoglossal canal, 191
Hypoglossal nerve (XII), 191, 410
Hypokinetic movement disorders, 201
Hypoparathyroidism, 368, 369
Hypophosphatemic rickets, 70
Hypophysis, 204
Hyposmotic volume, contraction and expansion, 142
Hypospadias, 378, 381
Hypotension, cerebral infarcts and, 210
Hypothalamic hypothyroidism, 371
Hypothalamus, 170, 200, 204, 354–355
   nuclei of, 200
   supraoptic and paraventricular nuclei of, 362
Hypothalamus-anterior pituitary system, 354–355
Hypothyroidism, 372
   hypothalamic, 371
   pituitary, 371
   primary, 371
   treatment of, 373
Hypoventilation, 271
Hypovolemic shock, 251
Hypoxanthine guanine phosphoryl pyrophosphate
    transferase, 60
Hypoxia, 146
   alveolar, 269
Hypoxyphilia, 26

I

I band, 407
I cells, 330
^{131}I (radioactive iodine), 373
Ia sensory neuron, 188
Ibuprofen, 428
Ibutilide, 253
I-cell disease, 65
ICF (intracellular fluid) volume, 141
ICP (inferior cerebellar peduncle), 198, 199
IDDM (insulin-dependent diabetes mellitus), 365
Idiopathic hypertrophic subaortic stenosis, 246
Idiopathic rapidly progressive glomerulonephritis,
   312
Idiopathic thrombocytopenic purpura, 441
Idiotypes, 88
IDL, 51
L-Iduronate-2-sulfatase, 52

α-L-Iduronidase, 52
IF (inferior rectus) nerve, 190
IFN. *See* Interferon *entries*
Ig. *See* Immunoglobulin(s)
IGF (insulin-like growth factor) receptors, 83
Ileocecal valve, 329
Ileum, 320
Iliacus muscle, 420
Iliocostalis muscle, 415
Ilioinguinal nerve, 383
Illness, children's conceptions of, 7
ILs. *See* Interleukins
Imipenem, 114
Imipenem/meropenem, 113
Imipramine, 20, 180
Immature teratoma, 397
Immediate hypersensitivity reaction, 102, 278, 449
Immune complex hypersensitivity reaction, 102
Immune responses, 98
Immune system
   cells of, 87–88
   innate versus adaptive, 86
   response by, 86
Immunity, humoral, defects of, 98
Immunization, forms of, 98
Immunodeficiency(ies)
   acquired. *See* Acquired immunodeficiency
     syndrome
   common variable, 98
   severe combined, 99
Immunoglobulin(s)
   basic structure of, 92
   chronic inflammation and, 97
   IgA, 92
   IgA deficiency, 98
   IgA nephropathy, 312
   IgA proteases, 112
   IgD, 92
   IgE, 92
   IgG, 92
   IgM, 92
   thyroid-stimulating, 371
Immunology, techniques in diagnosis, 104
Immunostaining, 69
Immunosuppressants, 105
Imperforate anus, 342
Implantation, and pregnancy, 392
Impotence, 26
Imprinting, in single-gene disorders, 71
In situ hybridization, 69
Incidence, in biostatistics, 32
Incisive foramen, 411
Indinavir, 101
Indirect-acting sympathomimetics, 180
Indomethacin, 428, 429
Infant development, 6
Infarction, evolution of, 226
Infections
   bacterial. *See individual pathogens by name*
   of ear, 273–274
   fungal. *See* Fungal infections
   hepatic, 345
   opportunistic, in AIDS patients, 100
   parasitic, 345. *See also individual parasites by*
     name
   respiratory tract, 273–276
   viral. *See individually viruses by name*
Infectious arthritis, 427
Infectious cystitis, 316
Infectious diseases
   hematologic changes associated with, 455
   of skin, mucosa, and underlying tissues,
     433–436
Inferior cerebellar peduncle, 198, 199
Inferior colliculus, 190, 197
Inferior epigastric artery, 383

Inferior epigastric vein, 383
Inferior frontal gyrus, 204
Inferior gemellus muscle, 420
Inferior gluteal nerve, 419, 421
Inferior mediastinum, 218
Inferior mesenteric artery, 318, 319, 323
Inferior mesenteric vein, 324
Inferior oblique muscle, 190, 195
Inferior pancreaticoduodenal artery, 322
Inferior parathyroid gland, 411
Inferior parietal lobule, 204, 205
Inferior petrosal sinus, 183
Inferior rectus muscle, 190, 195
Inferior sagittal sinus, 183
Inferior temporal gyrus, 204
Inferior vena cava, 324
Infiltrating ductal carcinoma, 401
Inflammation
   acute, 93–97
   chemical mediators of, 95
   chronic, 97
   transmural, 347
Inflammatory diarrhea, 348
Infliximab, 105, 428
Influenza, 128
Influenza virus, 276
Infraspinatus muscle, 415
Infraspinatus tendon, 416
Infundibulum, 219, 391
Inguinal canal, 383
Inhalants, 14
Inheritance patterns, 70
Inhibin, 387
Inhibited male orgasm, 27
Inhibitors, classes of, 53
Initiation, in protein translation, 64
Injuries, knee, 421
Innate immunity, 86
Inner ear, 197
Inner mitochondrial membrane, 38
Innervation
   foot and leg, 420
   hand and palm, 414
   pelvic, 380
   skeletal muscle, 410
   sympathetic, 222
INO (internuclear ophthalmoplegia), 184, 195
Inorganic lead, antidote for, 161
Inositol triphosphate, 158
   in adrenergic transmission, 178
   in cholinergic transmission, 175
Insomnia, 10
Inspiration, 264
Inspiratory capacity, 261
Inspiratory reserve volume, 261
Instrumental conditioning, 4
Insulin, 41, 331, 363, 364, 366
   in diabetes treatment, 366
   exocytosis of, 363
   pathophysiology associated with, 365
Insulin receptors, 82, 83, 158
Insulin-dependent diabetes mellitus, 365
Insulin/glucagon ratio, 364
Insulin-like growth factor receptors, 83
Integral proteins, 78
Integrins, 94
Intellectualization, 11
Intention tremor, 199
Interferon-α, 91, 104, 130
Interferon-β, 91, 104, 130
Interferon-γ, 91, 104, 130
   cell-mediated immunity and, 90
   T-helper cells and, 90
Interleukins
   IL-1, 91, 110, 149
   IL-2, 90, 91, 104

IL-3, 91
IL-4, 90, 91
IL-5, 90, 91
IL-6, 90, 91, 110
IL-7, 91
IL-8, 91
IL-10, 90, 91
IL-11, 91, 104, 445
IL-12, 90
Intermaxillary segment, 411
Intermediate filaments, 79
Intermediate gray horn, 186
Intermediate zone, 186
Intermittent porphyria, acute, 44
Internal arcuate fibers, 188
Internal auditory meatus, 191
Internal capsule, 187, 201
Internal carotid artery, 208, 412
Internal intercostal muscles, 262
Internal jugular veins, 183
Internal oblique muscle, 383
Internal spermatic fascia, 383
Internuclear ophthalmoplegia, 184, 195
Interossei muscles, 417
Interstitial (atypical) pneumonia, 275
Interstitial fluid, 141
Interthalamic adhesion, 204
Interval scale, 34
Interventricular foramen of Monro, 182, 204
Intestinal fluke, giant, 123
Intestinal schistosomiasis, 123
Intoxication. See also Poisoning
    diarrhea by, 350
Intracellular fluid volume, 141
Intracellular pathogens, 86
Intracellular receptors, 158
Intracerebral hemorrhage, 210
Intraductal papilloma, 399
Intrahepatic biliary atresia, 343
Intraocular pressure, 192
Intrauterine devices, 393
Intrinsic asthma, 278
Intrinsic coagulation pathway, 442
Intrinsic factor, 332
Introjection, 11
Intussusception, 341
Inulin clearance, 289
Inversions, chromosomal, 73
Involucrum, 424
IO (inferior oblique) muscle, 190, 195
IOC (intraocular pressure), 192
Iodides, 373
Iodination, 370
Iodine, radioactive, 373
Iodine deficiency, 371
Iodoquinol, 118
Ion-channel–linked receptors, 82
Ionizing radiation, as cancer risk, 151
IP (inferior parathyroid gland), 411
IP$_3$. See Inositol triphosphate
Ipecac, 330
Ipratropium, 176, 278
Ipsilateral gaze, 195
IR (inferior rectus) muscle, 190, 195
Iris, 192
Iron, for anemia, 448
Iron deficiency, 446
Iron poisoning, 160
    antidote for, 161
Ischemia, 146
    myocardial, 147, 242
    renal, 314
Ischemic acute tubular necrosis, 313
Ischemic bowel disease, 341
Ischemic heart disease, 242
Ischial tuberosity, 379

Ischioanal fossa, 380
Ischiocavernosus muscle, 379, 380
Isethionate, 119
Islets of Langerhans, hormones of, 363
Isocarboxazid, 20, 179
Isocitrate dehydrogenase, 37
Isoflurane, 214
Isolation of affect, 11
Isoleucine, 43
Isomaltase, 336
Isoproterenol, 179, 278
Isosmotic volume, contraction and expansion of, 142
Isosorbide, 254
Isosorbide dinitrate, 83, 255
Isospora spp., 117
Isovolumic contraction and relaxation, 231
Isthmus, fallopian tube, 391
ITP (idiopathic thrombocytopenic purpura), 441
Itraconazole, 134
IUD (intrauterine devices), 393
Ixodes tick, 122

J
Janeway lesions, 245
Janus kinases, 158
Jaundice, 44
JC virus, 184
    in AIDS patients, 100
Jejunum, 320, 328
JGA (juxtaglomerular apparatus), 290, 291
Joint space tumors, 429
Joints. See also individually named joints
    pathology of, 426
Jones criteria, 243
Jugular foramen, 183, 191
Juvenile rheumatoid arthritis, 426
Juxtaglomerular apparatus, 290, 291

K
K$^+$, 253
K$^+$ channel blockers, 253
K$^+$ excretion, 303
    increased, 302
    metabolic acidosis and, 303
    metabolic alkalosis and, 303
K$^+$ secretion
    volume contraction and, 302
    volume expansion and, 302
K$^+$ sparing diuretics
    electrolyte changes caused by, 310
    mechanism of, 309
K cells, 330
Kala-azar, 121
Kallikrein, as inflammation mediator, 95
Kaposi sarcoma, 153, 251, 432
    as AIDS complication, 101
κ receptors, 212
Kartagener syndrome, 70, 79, 278, 384
Karyolysis, 147
Karyorrhexis, 147
Kawasaki disease, 248
Kayser-Fleischer rings, 202, 344
K$_d$ (drug concentration), 157
Keloids, in wound healing, 149
Keratin, 79
Keratinocytes, 431
Keratitis, 119
Keratoconjunctivitis sicca, 102
Ketamine, 14, 214
Ketoacidosis. See Diabetic ketoacidosis
Ketoconazole, 134, 276, 361, 382, 434
Ketogenesis, 364
Ketogenic conversion, 45
α-Ketoglutarate, 37, 46
α-Ketoglutarate dehydrogenase, 37, 54
Ketone body metabolism, 50

Ketoprofen, 428
K$_f$ (ultrafiltration coefficient), 236
Kidney. See also Renal entries; Renal system
    cystic disease of, 311
    development of, 284
    function of, 286
    gross anatomy of, 285
    horseshoe, 285
    pelvic, 285
    relationship to abdominal wall, 285
    tubular diseases and, 313
    tubulointerstitial diseases of, 313
    vascular diseases of, 314
Kinases, cyclin-dependent, 81
Kinesins, 79
Kininogen, high molecular weight, 95
Ki-ras oncogene, 152
Kissing bug, 121
Klebsiella pneumoniae, 275
Klinefelter syndrome, 72, 401
Klüver-Bucy syndrome, 203, 205
Knee injuries, 421
Knee joint, movements at, 421
Koilocytosis, 395
Koilocytotic atypia, 403
Koplik spots, 275
Korsakoff syndrome, 203
K-ras, 280
Kupffer cells, in chronic inflammation, 97

L
L cells, 331
LAAM, 13
Labetalol, 179
Labia majora, 378
Labia minora, 378
Labile cells, 149
Labile toxin, 111
Labioscrotal swelling, 378
Labyrinthine artery, 209
Lactase, 336
Lactase deficiency, 336
Lactate, in anaerobic conditions, 36, 42
Lactate dehydrogenase, 39
Lactation, 392
Lactic acid, 39
Lactic acidosis, 39
Lactobacillus, 110
Lactoferrin, in phagocytosis, 95
Lactulose, 351
LAD (left anterior descending artery), 219
Lag phase, bacterial, 108
Lamina, basal and reticular, 80
Lamina propia, digestive tract, 319
Lamina terminalis, 204
Laminin, 80
Lamivudine, 101
Lamotrigine, 210, 211
Langerhans cells, 431
Lansoprazole, 333
Laplace's law, 237, 263
Large cell carcinoma, 280
Large intestine, 320, 329, 342
Laryngopharynx, 259
Laryngotracheitis, 274
Laryngotracheobronchitis, 274
Larynx, 259
    intrinsic muscles of, 259
Lassa fever, 128
Latanoprost, 193
Late distal tubule, 290
Late-look bias, 33
Lateral condyle, 421
Lateral corticospinal tract, 187
Lateral cricoarytenoid muscle, 259
Lateral geniculate body, 192

Lateral gray horn, 186
Lateral hypothalamic area, 326
Lateral hypothalamic nucleus, 200
Lateral lemniscus, 197
Lateral medullary syndrome, 198
Lateral meniscus, 421
Lateral nasal prominence, 411
Lateral pectoral nerve, 415
Lateral plantar nerve, 420, 422
Lateral pontine syndrome, 198
Lateral rectus, 195
Lateral spinothalamic tract, 189
Lateral sulcus, 204
Lateral ventricle, 170, 182, 201
    body of, 182
Latissimus dorsi muscle, 413, 415
Laxatives, 351
LCAT (lecithin cholesterol acyltransferase), 51
LDH cardiac enzyme, 243
LDL (low density lipoprotein), 51
L-dopa, 202
LDT (late distal tubule), 290
Lead poisoning, 44, 160
    antidotes for, 161
Lead time bias, 33
Learning, 4–5
Learning-based therapies, 5
Leber hereditary optic neuropathy, 70
Lecithin cholesterol acyltransferase, 51
Lecithinase, 111, 112, 435
Leflunomide, 428
Left anterior descending artery, 219
Left atrium, 219
    pressure in, 230
Left axis deviation, 227
Left coronary artery, 219
Left gastric artery, 322
Left testicular vein, 383
Left ventricle, 220
    pressure in, 228, 230
Leg, sensory innervation of, 420
Legal issues, 29–31
Legionella spp., 112, 276
Legionella pneumophila, 117
Leiomyoma, 396
Leishmania spp., 117, 436
Leishmania braziliensis, 121
Leishmania donovani, 121
Leishmaniasis, 121, 122
Lente insulin, 366
Lenticulostriate artery, 209
Lentiform nucleus, 201
Lentigo maligna melanoma, 432
Lepirudin, 444
Leprosy, 435
LES (lower esophageal sphincter), 327
Lesch-Nyhan syndrome, 60, 70, 426
Lesser peritoneal sac, 321
Lethal factor, 111
Leucine, 43
Leukemia(s), 152, 453
    adult T-cell, 153, 453
    classification of, 454
    clues for, 454
    hairy cell, 154
Leukocyte adhesion deficiency, 96
Leukocyte disorders, 450–454
    neoplastic, 451
Leukocytosis
    eosinophilic, 450
    polymorphonuclear, 450
Leukodystrophies, 184
Leukoplakia, 339
Leukotrienes, 52, 94
    antagonists, 278
Leuprolide, 382

Levator ani muscle, 379, 380
Levator scapulae muscle, 415
Levodopa, 202
Levofloxacin, 116
Levorphanol, 212
Lewy bodies, 202
Leydig cell, 384
Leydig cell tumor, 386
LF (lethal factor), 111
LFT (liver function test), 428
LGB (lateral geniculate body), 192, 200
LH. See Luteinizing hormone
Libman-Sacks endocarditis, 102, 245
Lichen planus, 339
Lidocaine, 213, 252
Ligament(s)
    anococcygeal, 379
    anterior cruciate, 421
    Cooper, 400
    fibular collateral, 421
    median umbilical, 284
    popliteus, 421
    posterior cruciate, 421
    round, 379
    suspensory, 379
    tibial collateral, 421
    transverse, 421
    of Treitz, 322
Ligand-gated channels, 158
Ligand-regulated transmembrane enzymes, 158
Light chain domains, in globulin structure, 92
Limb leads, 225
Limb-girdle muscular dystrophy, 430
Limbic system, 203
Limited scleroderma, 103
Linear acceleration, 196
Lineweaver-Burk equation, 53
Lineweaver-Burk plot, 53
Linezolid, 64, 115
Lingual gyrus, 192, 204
Linitis plastica, 340
Linkage disequilibrium, 75
Lipase, 343
    hormone-sensitive, 49
Lipids, 51
    absorption of, 337
    amphipathic, 78
    derivatives of, 52
    synthesis and metabolism of, 48–49
    type A, 109
Lipid-soluble AChE inhibitors, 177
Lipid-soluble vitamins, 55
Lipoic acid, 39
Lipoid nephrosis, 311
Lipopolysaccharide, 109, 110
Lipoprotein, 48
    transport and metabolism, 51
Lipoprotein lipase, 48, 51
Lipoteichoic acid, 112
Lipoxygenase, 52
    as inflammation mediator, 95
Lipoxygenase inhibitors, 278
Liquefactive necrosis, 147
Lisinopril, 254
Listeria monocytogenes, 117
    in bacterial meningitis, 181
Lithium, in bipolar disorder, 20, 310
Liver. See also Hepatic and Hepato- entries
    failure of, 343
    infections of, 345
    nutmeg type, 244
    pyogenic abscess of, 345
    tumors of, 345
Liver cell adenoma, 345
Liver diseases
    acquired, 344
    alcoholic, 344

Liver fluke, Chinese, 123
Liver function test, 428
LMWH (low molecular weight heparin), 444
Loa loa, 122
Loading dose, 157
Lobar pneumonia, 275
Lobes, of brain
    atrophy of, 207
    key features of, 205
Lobular carcinoma, of the breast, 401
Log phase, bacterial, 108
Lomustine, 165
Long thoracic nerve, 413, 415
Longissimus muscle, 415
Loop diuretics, 301, 309, 310
    electrolyte changes caused by, 310
Loop of Henle, 284, 294
    ascending. See Ascending thin loop of Henle;
        Thick ascending loop of Henle
    and countercurrent mechanism, 298, 299
    descending. See Descending thin loop of Henle
Loperamide, 212, 351
Lopinavir, 101
Loratadine, 162
Lorazepam, 22, 210
Losartan, 164, 255
Lovastatin, 50
Low density lipoprotein, 51
Low molecular weight heparin, 444
Lower esophageal sphincter, 327
Lower extremities, musculoskeletal anatomy of,
    420–422
Lower medulla, 190
Lower motor neuron, 188
    facial nerve lesion and, 196
Lower scapular nerve, 415
LPS (lipopolysaccharide), 109, 110
LSD (lysergic acid diethylamide), 14, 163
LT (labile toxin), 111
Lubricant, stool, 351
Lumbar enlargement, 186
Lumbar nodes, 383, 386
Lumbar puncture, 181
Lumbar splanchnic nerves, 380
Lumbar ventral rami, 420
Lumbosacral plexus, lesions in, 419
Lumbricals, 417, 422
Lumpy jaw, 433
Lung
    capacity of, 261
    changes in compliance, 262
    diseases of, 264, 277–279
    elastic properties of, 262–263
    small cell carcinoma of, 154
    structure of, 260
    tumors of, 280
    vascular disorders of, 281
Lung disease, 265
    intrinsic, 279
Lung fluke, 123
Luteal phase, 387
    in menstrual cycle, 390
Luteinizing hormone, 354, 385, 387, 390, 393, 394
    in feedback examples, 140
Lymph node disorders, nonneoplastic, 451
Lymphadenitis, nonspecific, 451
Lymphadenopathy, types, 451
Lymphatic vessels, 383
Lymphocyte depletion, in Hodgkin disease, 451
Lymphocyte predominance, in Hodgkin disease,
    451
Lymphocytes, 88, 450. See also B cells; T cells
    B- and T-cell antigen receptors, characteristics
        of, 88
    in chronic inflammation, 97
    receptor diversity of, 88
Lymphocytic choriomeningitis, 128

Metastasis, 151
  osteoblastic, 382
  in TNM staging, 154
Metastatic tumors, CNS and PNS, 185
Metazoans, 122
Metencephalon, 170
Metformin, 366
Methacholine, 175
Methadone, 13, 212
Methanol poisoning, antidote for, 161
Methemoglobin, 38
Methicillin, 113
Methimazole, 373
Methionine, 43, 44, 64
Methionine synthase, 46
Methohexital, 214
Methotrexate, 60, 165, 428
Methoxamine, 179
Methoxyflurane, 214
1-Methyl-4-phenyl-1,2,3,6-tetrahydropyridine, 202
Methylcellulose, 351
N-methyl-D-aspartate antagonist. See NMDA
Methyl-malonyl CoA mutase, 54
Methyl-malonyl CoA mutase deficiency, 45, 46
Methylphenidate, 16, 180
α-Methyltyrosine, 180
Methylxanthines, 278
Methysergide, 163
Metoclopramide, 328, 330, 351
Metolazone, 310
Metoprolol, 179, 252
Metronidazole, 116, 118, 122, 402
Metyrapone, 361
Metyrosine, 180
Mexiletine, 252
Meyer loop, 192, 205
Mezlocillin, 113
Mg²⁺, 253
MGB (medial geniculate body), 197
Mg[OH]₂, 351
MGUS (monoclonal gammopathy of undetermined significance), 454
MHC. See Major histocompatibility complex
Micelles, 335, 337
Michaelis-Menten equation, 53
Michaelis-Menten plot, 53
Miconazole, 119, 273, 274, 402, 435
Microbial diarrhea
  inflammatory, 348
  noninflammatory, 349–350
Microcytic sideroblastic anemia, 44
Microfilaments, 79
Microglia, 184
  in chronic inflammation, 97
Microphallus, 378
Microsporum spp., 131, 435
Microtubules, 79
  assembly of, 429
Midazolam, 22, 214
Midbrain, 170, 190, 199, 201
Middle cerebellar peduncle, 198, 199
Middle cerebral artery, 208, 209, 210
Middle ear cavity, 411
Middle frontal gyrus, 204
Middle mediastinum, 218
Middle meningeal artery, 181, 210
Middle respiratory tract infections, 274
Middle temporal gyrus, 204
Midgut, 318, 319
Midline/intralaminar nucleus, 200
Midshaft fracture of humerus, 414
Midsystolic click, 246
MIF (Müllerian-inhibiting factor), 378
Mifepristone, 393, 394
Miglitol, 366
Migrating motor complexes, 327

Migratory polyarthritis, 243
Migratory thrombophlebitis, 154, 343
Mikulicz syndrome, 102
Mineral disorders, drug-induced, 369
Mineral oil, 351
Mineralocorticoids, 361
Minimum alveolar anesthetic concentration (MAC), 214
Minocycline, 64, 115
Miosis, 13, 213
Mirtazapine, 20, 179
Misoprostol, 333
Missense point mutations, 62
MIT (monoiodotyrosine), 370
Mitochondria, 48, 76, 77
Mitochondrial encephalomyelopathy, lactic acidosis, and stroke-like episodes, 70
Mitochondrial enzymes, 42
Mitochondrial inheritance pattern, 70
Mitochondrial membrane, inner, 38
Mitochondrial pathway, 37
Mitosis
  in cell cycle, 81
  phases of, 81
Mitral valve, 219, 232
  prolapse of, 246
  regurgitation of, 233
  stenosis of, 233, 246
Mivacurium, 409
Mixed agonist-antagonist agents, 212
Mixed cellularity, in Hodgkin disease, 451
Mixed stones, 347
MLCK (myosin light chain kinase), 408
MLF (medial longitudinal fasciculus), 195
MMC (migrating motor complexes), 327
Mobitz I atrioventricular block, 226
Mobitz II atrioventricular block, 226
Moderate agonists, 212
Molar pregnancy, 398
Molecular chaperones, 65
Molluscum contagiosum, 436
Mönckeberg medial calcific sclerosis, 250
Monoamine oxidase, 163, 178
Monoamine oxidase inhibitors, 20, 163, 180, 202
Monobactams, 114
Monocistronic RNA, 108
Monoclonal antibodies, 105
Monoclonal gammopathy of undetermined significance, 454
Monocytes, 87, 450
  in chronic inflammation, 97
Monocytosis, 450
Monodeiodinase, 371
Monoiodotyrosine, 370
Mononuclear phagocyte system, 184
Monosodium urate, 426
Monospot test, 273
Montelukast, 278
Mood disorders, 18–21
Moraxella catarrhalis, 273
Morphine, 13, 212, 214
Mortality rates, 32
Mosaicism, 72
Mossy fibers, 199
Motilin, 330
Motor neuron lesions, upper versus lower, 187
Movement disorders, 201
6-MP (6-mercaptopurine), 60
M-phase/maturation promoting factor, 81
M-protein spike, 454
MPSI. See Hurler syndrome
MPSII. See Hunter syndrome
MPTP (1-methyl-4-phenyl-1,2,3,6-tetrahydropyridine), 202
MR (medial rectus) muscle, 190, 195
mRNA, 36, 63, 108

MRSA (methicillin-resistant S. aureus), 433
MS (multiple sclerosis), 184
MSSA (methicillin-sensitive S. aureus), 433
Mucocutaneous leishmaniasis, 121
Mucor spp., 133, 181
Mucormycosis, 133
  sinus, 365
Mucosa, digestive tract, 319
Mucosal protective agents, 333
Mucous cells, 320, 332
Mucous membrane, infectious diseases of, 433–434
Mucus, 328, 332
Müllerian-inhibiting factor, 378
Multidrug exporters, 115
Multifidus muscle, 415
Multiple endocrine neoplasia, 152
  type I, 365
  type IIa, 365
  type IIb/III, 365
Multiple myeloma, 313, 454
  classic clues for, 454
Multiple sclerosis, 184
μ receptors, 212
Mumps, 128, 385
Murmurs, 220
Muromonab, 105
Muscarinic acetylcholine receptors, 83
Muscarinic antagonists, 176, 278
Muscarinic blocker poisoning, 159
Muscarinic cholinergic receptor, 193
Muscle glycogen phosphorylase, 41
Muscle relaxants, 409
Muscle spindle receptor, 188
Muscle stretch reflexes, 188
Muscles
  of breathing, 262
  characteristics of, 406–409
  disorders of, 430
  fiber types I and II, 407
  laryngeal, 259
  pharyngeal, 259
Muscular dystrophies, 430
Muscularis externa, digestive tract, 319
Muscularis mucosa, digestive tract, 319
Musculocutaneous nerve, 413, 414, 415, 416
Musculoskeletal system
  disorders of, 423–430
  head and neck, 410–412
  lower extremities, 420–422
  muscle structure and function in, 406–409
  skin in, 431–437
  tumors of, 424
  upper extremities and back, 413–419
Mutations, 62
  somatic hypermutation, 88
Myasthenia gravis, 430
Myasthenic syndrome, 154
myc oncogenes
  L-myc, 152, 280
  N-myc, 152, 361
Mycobacteria, nontuberculous, 117
Mycobacterial meningoencephalitis, 181
Mycobacterium avium-intracellulare, 181
  in AIDS patients, 100
Mycobacterium leprae, 117, 435
Mycobacterium marinum, 434
Mycobacterium tuberculosis, 117, 181, 276
  in AIDS patients, 100
  infectious arthritis and, 427
  in osteomyelitis, 424
Mycolic acids, 109
Mycophenolate, 105
Mycoplasma pneumoniae, 274, 275
Mycosis fungoides, 453
Myelencephalon, 170
Myelin, 184

Myelination, disorders of, 184
Myelodysplastic syndromes, 453
Myelofibrosis, myeloid metaplasia with, 446
Myelogenous leukemias, 453
  acute, 453
  chronic, 74, 152, 453
  classification of, 454
Myeloid metaplasia with myelofibrosis, 446
Myeloma, multiple. *See* Multiple myeloma
Myeloperoxidase, in phagocytosis, 95
Myelophthisic anemia, 446
Myenteric plexus, 319
Myocardial infarction, 219, 242
  myocardium appearance after, 243
Myocardial ischemia, 147, 242
Myocarditis, viral, 245
Myoclonic epilepsy, 70
Myoclonic seizure, 210
Myofilaments, 407
Myogenic response, 292
Myometrium, 391, 392
Myopathic CAT/CPT deficiency, 48
Myosin, 407
Myosin light chain kinase, 408
Myositis, 430
Myositis ossificans, 430
Myotatic reflex, 188
Myotonic dystrophy, 430
N-Myristoylation, 78
Myxedema, 372
Myxoma, 247

N

Na$^+$ channel blockers, 252
Na$^+$-dependent coporter, 336
Na$^+$-K$^+$ pump, 78, 144
Na$^+$/glucose symporter, 78
NADH dehydrogenase, 38
NAD/NADH, 36, 37, 39
Nadolol, 179, 373
NADPH, 36, 37, 39, 40
NADPH oxidase, in phagocytosis, 95
NADPH oxidase deficiency, 96
NAE (net acid excretion), 303
Naegleria spp., 117, 119
Nafcillin, 113, 424, 433, 436
Nalbuphine, 212
Nalmefene, 212
Naloxone, 212
  as antidote, 161
Naltrexone, 12, 212
Naphthylamine, as cancer risk, 151
Naproxen, 428
Naratriptan, 163
Narcissistic disorder, 24
Narcolepsy, 10
Narrow-angle glaucoma, 192
Nasopharynx, 259, 412
  carcinoma of, 153
Nateglinide, 366
Natural killer cells, 86, 88, 90
Natural selection, and equilibrium, 75
Necator spp., 122, 125
  hematologic changes caused by, 455
Neck. *See* Head and neck
Necrophilia, 26
Necrosis, 147
  acute tubular, 313
Nedocromil, 278
Nefazodone, 20
Negative feedback, 140
Negative predictive value, 32
Negative-sense RNA viruses, 128
Negri bodies, 182
Neisseria gonorrhoeae, 395, 402
  infectious arthritis and, 427
  pili of, 112

Neisseria meningitidis
  in bacterial meningitis, 181
  in early meningococcemia, 437
Nelfinavir, 101
Nemathelminthes, 122
Nematodes. *See* Roundworms
Neocortex, 204
Neomycin, 64, 115
Neonatal respiratory distress syndrome, 279
Neoplasia, 151
Neoplasms
  adrenal, 361
  cardiac, 247
  testicular, 386
  thyroid, 373
Neostigmine, 176
Neostriatum, 202
Nephroblastoma, 315
Nephrons, 284
  blood vessels associated with, 290
  structure of, 290
Nephropathy, 312, 313
Nephrotic syndrome, 311
Nephrotoxic acute tubular necrosis, 313
Nernst equation, 143
Nerve damage, associated with fractures, 222
Nerves. *See individual nerves by name*
Nervous system
  and cell types, 184
  cell types of, 184
  congenital malformations of, 171
  development of, 170–171
Net acid excretion, 303
Neural crest, 138, 170
Neural folds, 170
Neural tube, 170
Neuroectoderm, 138, 170
Neurofibrillary tangles, 206
Neurofibromatosis, 70
  type 1, 71
  type 2, 71
Neurofilament, 79
Neurohistology, and pathology correlates, 184–185
Neuroleptanesthesia, 214
Neuroleptic malignant syndrome, 17
Neuromuscular blockers, 409
Neuron, 184
Neuron specific enolase stain, 150
Neurosyphilis, 194
Neurotoxicity, anesthetics, 213
Neurotransmitters, 44
Neurulation, 170
Neutral lipids, 51
Neutropenia, 450
Neutrophils, 87, 449
  granules, primary and secondary, 93
  hypersegmental, anemia and, 446
  margination and extravasation, 94
  migration/chemotaxis of, 94
Nevirapine, 101
Nevus flammeus, 432
Newborn, diseases in, 44, 279
NF. *See* Neurofibromatosis
NF-1 gene, 153
NF-2 gene, 153
NFT (neurofibrillary tangles), 206
NHL. *See* Non-Hodgkin lymphoma
Niacin, 39, 54
Nickel, as cancer risk, 151
Niclosamide, 455
Nicotinamide adenine dinucleotide. *See* NADPH entries
Nicotine, 14, 175
Nicotinic AChR, 430
Nicotinic acid, 51
Nicotinic agonists/antagonists, 175
Nicotinic receptors, 158

Nicotinamide-adenine dinucleotide phosphate, 95
NIDDM (noninsulin-dependent diabetes mellitus), 365
Niemann-Pick disease, 52
Nifedipine, 254
Nifurtimox, 121
  in Chagas disease, 122
Night terrors, 10
Nightmares, 10
Nigrostriatal pathway, and antipsychotics, 17
Nitrates, 83, 254
Nitric oxide, 44, 328, 380
Nitric oxide receptors, 83
Nitric oxide synthase, 44, 83
Nitrous oxide, 214
Nitroglycerin, 83, 254, 255
Nitroprusside, 83, 255
Nitrosamines, as cancer risk, 151
Nitrosoureas, 165
Nizatidine, 162, 333
NK (natural killer) cells, 86, 88, 90
NMDA antagonist, 206
NMDA receptor, 158
NNRTIs (nonnucleoside reverse transcriptase inhibitors), 101
NO. *See* Nitric oxide
Nocardia spp., 117, 434
Nodular hyperplasia, 345
Nodular melanoma, 432
Nodular non-Hodgkin lymphoma, 452
Nodular sclerosis, in Hodgkin disease, 451
Nominal scale, 34
Nonbacterial chronic prostatitis, 382
Nonbacterial thrombotic endocarditis, 245
Nonbacterial verrucous endocarditis, 245
Noncommunicating hydrocephalus, 183
Noncompetitive antagonist, 157
Noncompetitive inhibitor, 53
Noncytotoxic hypersensitivity reaction, 102
Nondepolarizing blockers, 409
Nondisjunction, during meiosis, 72
Nonessential amino acids, precursors, 46
Non-germ cell tumors, 386
Non-Hodgkin lymphoma, 341, 452
  as AIDS complication, 101
Noninfiltrating intraductal carcinoma, 401
Noninflammatory diarrhea, 349–350
Noninsulin-dependent diabetes mellitus, 365
Nonnucleoside reverse transcriptase inhibitors, 101
Nonpolar aliphatic side chains, 43
Non-selective β agonists, 278
Nonsense point mutations, 62
Nonsteroidal antiinflammatory drugs, 52, 428, 429
Norepinephrine, 178
Norethindrone, 393
Norgestrel, 393
Normal pressure hydrocephalus, 183
Normetanephrine, 178
Nortriptyline, 20, 180
Norwalk virus, 127, 349
Nose, infection of, 273
Notochord, 170
NPH (neutral protein Hagedorn) insulin, 366
NRDS (neonatal respiratory distress syndrome), 279
NRTIs (nucleoside reverse transcriptase inhibitors), 101
NSAIDs, 52, 428, 429
Nucleic acids, 58
  structure of, 58
  synthesis and salvage of, 59–60
Nucleoside reverse transcriptase inhibitors, 101
Nucleosides, 58
Nucleosomes, 58
N-Nucleotide addition, 88
Nucleotides, 58, 59
  synthesis of, 40

Nucleus, 76
Nucleus ambiguus, 198
Null Hypothesis, 33
Nutmeg liver, 244, 343
Nutrasweet®, 46
Nystatin, 134, 273, 274, 402

O

O_2, 146
O_2 capacity, 268
O_2 content, 268
Oat cell carcinoma. *See* small cell carcinoma
Obligate intracellular parasites, 117
Oblique and transverse arytenoids, 259
Observational studies, 33
Obsessive-compulsive disorder, 21, 24
Obstruction, ureteral, 315
Obstructive congenital heart disease, 240
Obstructive lung disease, 264, 265, 277–278
Obstructive uropathy, 314
Obturator externus muscle, 420
Obturator internus muscle, 420
Obturator nerve, 419, 420, 421
Occipital lobe, 204, 205
Octreotide, 375
Oculomotor nerve (III), 190, 412
    skeletal muscle innervated by, 410
Oculomotor nucleus, 195
Oddi, sphincter of, 330, 335
Ofloxacin, 116
OH (hydroxyl) radical, 146
1,25-$(OH)_2$-vitamin D_3, 367
Olanzapine, 18
    in bipolar disorder, 20
Olfactory bulb, 205
Olfactory nerve (I), 190
Olfactory tract, 205
Oligoclonal bands, 184
Oligodendrocytes, 184
Oligodendroglia, 185
Oligomycin, 38
Ollier disease, 423, 425
Omental bursa, 321
Omeprazole, 333
Omphalocele, 341
Onchocerca spp., 122, 125
Oncogenes, 152, 361
Oncogenic viruses, 153
Ondansetron, 163, 330
One-way ANOVA, 34
Oocyte, 389
Open-angle glaucoma, 192
Opening snap, 246
Operant conditioning, 4, 5
Operculated eggs, 123
Ophthalmic artery, 209
Ophthalmic nerve (V_1), 190, 412
Opioid poisoning, 159
    antidote for, 161
Opioid receptors, 212
Opioids, 13, 212–213
    characteristics, 213
Opisthorchis spp., 122
Opponens digiti minimi muscles, 417
Opponens pollicis muscles, 13, 418
Opportunistic infections
    in AIDS patients, 100
    fungal, 133
Oprelvekin, 445
Opsonization, 95
Optic canal, 191
Optic chiasm, 192, 204, 412
Optic nerve (II), 190
Optic tract, 192
Oral cavitary disease, 273
Oral contraceptives, 345

Oral hyperglycemic agents, 366
Ordinal scale, 34
Organ blood flow, control of, 238
Organ of Corti, 197
Organ systems, autonomic effects on, 173–174
Organ transplantation, immunology of, 103
Organelles, subcellular, 40–41
Organophosphates, 177
Orgasm disorders, 27
Ornithine, 47
Ornithine transcarbamoylase deficiency, 385
Oropharynx, 259
Orotic acid, 47
Orthomyxovirus, 128
Osmotic diuresis, 301
Osmotic diuretics, 301, 309, 310
Osmotic laxatives, 351
Osteitis fibrosa cystica, 369, 423
Osteoarthritis, 426
Osteoarthropathy, hypertrophic, 423
Osteoblastic metastases, 382
Osteoblastic tumors, 425
Osteoblastoma, 425
Osteochondromatosis, 423, 425
Osteoclasts, in chronic inflammation, 97
Osteogenesis imperfecta, 66, 149, 423
Osteoid osteoma, 425
Osteomalacia, 338, 423, 425
Osteomyelitis, 424
    microbiology of, 424
    Salmonella, 448
Osteopetrosis, 424
Osteoporosis, 424
Osteosarcoma, 153, 425
Osler nodes, 245
Ostium primum defects, 240
Ostium secundum defects, 240
Otic ganglion, 172
Otitis externa, 274
    malignant, 365
Otitis media, acute, 273
Outer cortical artery, 209
Outer membrane, 109
Ovary, 378
    cancer of, 154
    diseases of, 397
    fibroma of, 398
Overdose. *See also* Poisoning
    of opioid analgesics, 213
Oviduct, 379
Ovulation, and folliculogenesis, 388
Ovulatory phase, in menstrual cycle, 390
Oxaloacetate, 37, 39
Oxazepam, 22
Oxazolidinones, 115
Oxidative phosphorylation, 36, 37, 38
Oxycodone, 13, 212
Oxygen, as antidote, 161
Oxygen transport, 268
Oxygen-dependent killing, in phagocytosis, 95
Oxygen-independent killing, in phagocytosis, 95
Oxytocin, 392

P

P wave, 224
p21, 81
p53, 81
p-53 gene, 148, 153, 280
PA (protective antigen), 111
Paclitaxel, 166
PAG (plasma anion gap), 308
Paget disease, 424
    of the breast, 401
    extramammary, of the vulva, 395
PAH (para-aminohippuric acid), 289
Paired helical filaments, 206

Palate, development of, 411
Palatine tonsil, 411
Palatoglossus muscle, 259
Palatopharyngeus muscle, 259
Pale infarct, 210
Palivizumab, 105
Palm, innervation of, 414
Palmar interossei muscles, 417
Palmitoylation, 78
Palmitoyl-CoA, 48
2-PAM (pralidoxime), 161
PAM (primary amebic meningoencephalitis), 119
Pamidronate, 369
Pampiniform plexus, 383
Panacinar emphysema, 277
P-ANCA, 248
Pancoast tumor, 280
Pancreas, 363–366
    annular, 343
    carcinoma of, 154
    secretions of, 334
Pancreatic amylase, 336
Pancreatic duct, 334
Pancreatic enzymes, 334
Pancreatic polypeptide, 331
Pancreatic proteases, 337
Pancreatic secretions, 334
Pancreatitis
    acute hemorrhagic, 343
    chronic, 343
Pancrelipase, 351
Pancuronium, 409
Paneth cells, 320
Panic disorder, 21
PANS (parasympathetic autonomic nervous
    system), 172, 173–174, 193
Pantoprazole, 333
Pantothenic acid, 54
Papanicolaou (Pap) smear, 395
Papez circuit, 200, 203
Papillary carcinoma, 374
Papillary hidradenoma, 395
Papillary muscles, 219, 220
Papilloma, 126
    intraductal, 399
Papilloma viruses, 342
Papovavirus, 126
Para-aminohippuric acid, 289
Paracentral lobule, 204
Paracortical hyperplasia, 451
Paraesophageal hernia, 339
Parafollicular cells, of the thyroid, 367
Paragonimus spp., 122
Paragonimus westermani, 123
Parainfluenza, 128
Parainfluenza virus, 274
Parallel circuits, 234
Paralytic ileus, 328
Paramedial pontine reticular formation, 195
Paramesonephric ducts, 284, 378
Paramyxovirus, 128
Paraneoplastic syndromes, 154
Paranoid disorder, 24
Paraphilias, 26
Paraphimosis, 381
Parasites
    facultative intracellular, 117
    obligate intracellular, 117
    protozoan, 118. *See also* Protozoal infections
Parasitic infections, 345
Parasympathetic autonomic nervous system, 172,
    173–174, 193, 222
Parasympathetic neurons, 172
Parasympathetic outflow, 173
Parasympathetic regulation, of heart and circulation,
    238

Parasympathetic stimulation, for penile erection, 380
Parathion, 177
Parathyroid gland, 367
Parathyroid hormone, 296, 367
Paraumbilical veins, 324
Paraventricular nuclei, hypothalamic, 362
Paraventricular nucleus, 200
Parietal cells, 320, 332
Parietal lobe, 204, 205
Parietooccipital sulcus, 204
Parinaud syndrome, 199
Parkinson disease, 129, 201, 202
    treatment of, 202
Parkinsonism, 18
Parotid salivary glands, 326
Paroxetine, 20, 163
Paroxysmal hemolytic anemia, 447
Paroxysmal nocturnal hemoglobinuria, 447
Partial agonist, 157
Partial mole, 398
    versus complete mole, 398
Partial seizure, 210
Partial thromboplastin time, 443
Parvovirus, 126
    infectious arthritis and, 427
PAS (periodic acid-Schiff) stain, 150
Passive-aggressive, 11
Pasteurella spp., 112
Pasteurella multocida, 435
Patellar tendon, 419
Patent ductus arteriosus, 218, 240
Patent foramen ovale, 240
Patent urachus, 285, 316
Paternity testing, 69
Pathogens
    extracellular and intracellular, 86
    factors and diagnostic enzymes for, 112
    unusual growth requirements of, 112
Pavlovian conditioning, 4
PBPs (penicillin binding proteins), 109, 113
P_{cap} (capillary hydrostatic pressure), 236
PCL (posterior cruciate ligament), 421
PCP ("angel dust"), 14
PCR (polymerase chain reaction), 67, 69
PDA (patent ductus arteriosus), 218, 240
PDE (phosphodiesterase) inhibitors, 381
PDE/adenosine uptake inhibitors, 444
PDGF. *See* Platelet-derived growth factor
Pearson correlation, 34
Pectineus muscle, 420
Pectoral girdle, movements of, 415
Pectoralis major muscle, 413, 415
Pectoralis minor muscle, 415
Pedophilia, 26
Peduncle(s)
    cerebellar, 190, 199
    cerebral, 190
    inferior cerebellar, 198
    middle cerebellar, 198
Pellagra, 54
Pelvic diaphragm, 380
Pelvic floor, and perineum, 380
Pelvic inflammatory disease, 136, 395
Pelvic innervation, 380
Pelvic kidney, 285
Pelvic splanchnic nerves, 172, 380
Pemoline, 16
Pemphigus vulgaris, 80, 432
Penciclovir, 129
Penicillamine, 202, 428
    for heavy metal poisoning, 160, 161
Penicillin G, 113
Penicillin V, 113
Penicillin-binding proteins, 109, 113
Penicillins, 109, 113, 273, 403, 433, 434, 435, 436

Penile erection
    dysfunctional, 27, 381
    physiology of, 380
Penis, 378, 379
    bulb of, 380
    carcinoma, 381
    diseases of, 381
Pentamidine, 122, 276, 436
Pentazocine, 212
Pentose phosphate shunt, 40
Pepsin, 332, 337
Pepsinogen, 332
Peptic ulcer disease, treatment of, 333
Peptic ulcers, 340
Peptidoglycan, 108, 109, 113
Peptidyltransferase, 115
Peptococcus spp., 275
Peptostreptococcus spp., 396
Perforin, 90
Pergolide, 163, 202
Pericardial disease, 247
Pericardial effusion, 247
Pericarditis, 247
Perimetrium, 391
Perimysium, 407
Perineal pouches, 380
Perineum, 380
    and pelvic floor, 380
Periodic acid-Schiff stain, 150
Peripheral nervous system, 170
Peripheral proteins, 78
Periplasmic space, 109
Peristalsis, 328
Peritoneal organs, 321
Peritoneum, 379
Peritubular capillaries, 290
Permanent cells, 149
Permeability, selective, 143
Pernicious anemia, 54, 338, 340, 448
Peroneus brevis muscle, 422
Peroneus longus muscle, 422
Peroxisomes, 76, 77
Persistent truncus arteriosus, 217, 241
Personality disorders, 24
Pertussis toxin, 111
Petechiae, 440, 441
Petit mal seizure, 210
Peyer patches, 320
PFK-1 (phosphofructokinase), 36
PGs. *See* Prostaglandins
pH control mechanisms, 306
Phagocytic cells, defects of, 96
Phagocytosis, 95
Phallus, 378
Pharmacodynamics, 157–158
Pharmacokinetics, 156–157
Pharyngeal arch, muscles derived from, 410
Pharyngeal pouches, 318, 411
Pharynx, 259
Phencyclidine, 14
Phenelzine, 20, 163, 179
Phenobarbital, 22, 211
Phenolphthalein, 351
Phenothiazine, 330
Phenotypic masking, 128
Phenotypic mixing, 128
Phenoxybenzamine, 179
Phentolamine, 179
Phenylalanine, 43, 46
Phenylalanine hydroxylase, 45
Phenylephrine, 179
Phenylethanolamine-*N*-methyl transferase, 44
Phenylketonuria, 45, 46, 70
Phenytoin, 211
Pheochromocytoma, 361, 365
PHF (paired helical filaments), 206

Philtrum, 411
Phimosis, 381
Phobias, 21
Phosphate regulation, 368
    disorders of, 368
    endocrine, 367–369
Phosphofructokinase, 36
6-Phosphogluconate, 40
Phospholipases
    A_2, 52
    A and B, 334
    C, 158
Phospholipids, 52
Physical injury, 146
Physician-patient relationships, 28–29
Physiologic dead space, 262
Physiologic jaundice, of newborn, 44
Physostigmine, 176, 193
    as antidote, 161
Pia mater, 181, 183
PICA (posterior inferior cerebellar artery), 198, 208, 209
Pick disease, 207
Picornavirus, 127
PID (pelvic inflammatory disease), 136, 395
Pigment stones, 347
Pigmented villonodular synovitis, 429
PIH (prolactin-inhibiting factor), 354
Pili, 112
Pilocarpine, 175, 193
Pilocystic astrocytoma, 185
Pilosebaceous units, 431
Pindolol, 179
Pineal body, 190, 200, 204
Pineal gland, 170
Pineal region tumor, 199
"Pink puffers," 265
Pinworms, 125
Pioglitazone, 366
Piperacillin, 113
Piriformis muscle, 420
Piriformis syndrome, 419
Pituitary gland, 354–355, 412
    anterior, hyperfunction of, 355
    characteristics of, 354
    hypofunction, 355
    in hypothalamus-anterior pituitary system, 354–355
Pituitary hyperthyroidism, 371
Pituitary hypothyroidism, 371
Pityriasis, 131
PKU (phenylketonuria), 45, 70
Placenta, 388, 392
Placental alkaline phosphatase, 154
Placental transport, 92
Plant alkaloids, 166
Plantaris muscle, 422
Plaques
    complicated, 249
    mature, 249
    senile, 206
Plasma, 141
Plasma anion gap, 308
Plasma cell dyscrasias, 454
Plasma cell mastitis, 401
Plasma cells, 88
Plasma flow, renal, 289
Plasma membrane, 78
Plasma osmolarity, regulation by ADH, 300
Plasminogen, 442
Plasminogen activator, 442
Plasmodium spp., 117, 120
    hematologic changes caused by, 455
    life cycle of, 119
Plasmodium falciparum, 120
Plasmodium malariae, 120

Plasmodium ovale, 120
Plasmodium vivax, 120
Platelet-derived growth factor, 149
Platelet-derived growth factor receptors, 83
Platelets, 440
   disorders of, 441
Platyhelminthes, 122
Pleura, 260
   diseases of, 281
   tumors of, 280
Pleural effusion, 281
Plummer-Vinson syndrome, 340
PMN (polymorphonuclear leukocyte), 403
PNET (primitive neuroectodermal tumor), 185
Pneumocystis carinii, 122, 133, 276
   in AIDS patients, 100
Pneumocystis jiroveci. See Pneumocystis carinii
Pneumocystosis, 122
Pneumonia, 275–276
Pneumotaxic center, 272
Pneumothorax, 263, 281
PNMT (phenylethanolamine-*N*-methyltransferase), 44
Podagra, 426
Podocytes, 291
Poiseuille's equation, 234
Poisoning. *See also* Intoxication
   antidotes for, 161
   common toxic syndromes, 159
   food, 350
   heavy metal, 160
Polio, 189
Polio virus, 127
Poliomyositis, 430
Polyarteritis nodosa, 248
Polycistronic mRNA, 108
Polyclonal hypergammaglobulinemia, 454
Polycyclic aromatic hydrocarbons, as cancer risk, 151
Polycystic disease
   in adults, 311
   in childhood, 311
   ovarian, 397
Polycythemia, 268, 445
Polycythemia vera, 445
Poly-D-glutamate, 434
Polydipsia, 301
   primary, 362
Polyene antifungal agents, 113
Polymerase chain reaction, 67
Polymorphonuclear leukocytes, 403
Polymorphonuclear leukocytosis, 450
Polymyalgia rheumatica, 249
Polyoma, 126
Polyps, 342
Polysaccharidase, 334
Polysome, 64, 76
POMC (proopiomelanocortin), 356
Pompe disease, 41
Pons, 170, 187, 190, 198, 204
Popliteus ligament, 421
Popliteus muscle, 421
Population genetics, 75
Pork tapeworm, 124
Porphyria, acute intermittent, 44
Porphyria cutanea tarda, 44
Port wine stain, 432
Portacaval anastomoses, 324
Portal hypertension, 324, 344
Portal vein, 321
Positive feedback, 140
Positive predictive value, 32
Positive-sense RNA viruses, 127
Postcentral gyrus, 204
Postcoital contraceptives, 393
Postductal coarctation, 241

Posterior cerebral arteries, 208, 209
Posterior communicating artery, 209
Posterior cricoarytenoid, 259
Posterior cruciate ligament, 421
Posterior fornix, 379
Posterior funiculus, 186
Posterior inferior cerebellar artery, 208, 209
Posterior interventricular artery, 219
Posterior mediastinum, 218
Posterior nucleus, 200
Posterior pituitary, 354–355
Poststreptococcal glomerulonephritis, 311
Postsynthetic gap phase, in cell cycle, 81
Post-translational modifications, 65
Potassium. *See* K$^+$ *entries*
Potassium iodide, 434
Potency, drug, 157
Pott disease, 424
Potter sequence, 285
Pouch of Douglas, 379
Poxvirus, 126
PP (pulse pressure), 234
PPRF (paramedial pontine reticular formation), 195
PR interval, 225
Prader-Willi syndrome, 74
Pralidoxime, 161
Pramipexole, 202
Pravastatin, 50
Praziquantel, 123, 124
Prazosin, 179
Precentral gyrus, 204
Predictive value, 32
Prednisolone, 278
Prednisone, 166, 278
Preductal coarctation, 241
Prefrontal cortex, 205
Pregnancy
   ectopic, 136
   and implantation, 392
   molar, 398
Prekallikrein, 95
Preload, cardiac, 228
Premature ejaculation, 27
Premature infants, and jaundice, 44
Premature ventricular contraction, 226
Premenstrual phase, in uterine cycle, 389
Premenstruation, 389
Premotor cortex, 205
Prenylation, 78
Preoptic nucleus, 200, 387
Presenilin-1 gene, 206
Presenilin-2 gene, 206
Presynthetic gap phase, in cell cycle, 81
Pretectal nuclei, 193
Prevalence, 32
Prevotella spp., 110
Priapism, 381
Prilocaine, 213
Primary active transport, 140
Primary adrenocortical insufficiency, 360
Primary amebic meningoencephalitis, 119
Primary amyloidosis, 150
Primary auditory cortex, 205
Primary bile acids, 335
Primary biliary cirrhosis, 344
Primary cell type variable, acute myelogenous leukemia and, 453
Primary follicle, 388
Primary hyperaldosteronism, 359
Primary hyperparathyroidism, 368, 369
Primary hypoparathyroidism, 368
Primary hypothyroidism, 371
Primary motor cortex, 205
Primary palate, 411
Primary polydipsia, 362
Primary premotor cortex, 205

Primary sclerosing cholangitis, 345
Primary somatosensory cortex, 205
Primary spermatocyte, 384
Primary tumors, CNS and PNS, 185
Primary union, in wound healing, 149
Primary visual cortex, 192, 205
Primary yolk sac, 137
Primitive atrium, 216
Primitive gut tube, 318, 319
Primitive neuroectodermal tumor, 185
Primitive streak, 138
Primitive ventricle, 216
Primordial follicle, 388
Prinzmetal angina, 242
Prion protein, 207
Probenecid, 429
Procainamide, 252
Procaine, 213
Procarbazine, 165
Processus vaginalis, 382
Prochordal plate, 137
Progesterone, 389, 390, 392
Progestins, 393
Proglottid, 124
Progressive multifocal leukoencephalopathy, 184
Progressive systemic sclerosis. *See* Scleroderma
Projection, 11
Prokaryotic cells, 108
Prokaryotic chromosomes, 61
Prolactin, 354, 392
Prolactin-inhibiting factor, 354
Proliferative phase, in uterine cycle, 389
Proline, 43, 66
Prolonyl CoA carboxylase deficiency, 45
Promethazine, 162
Pronator quadratus muscles, 416
Pronator teres muscle, 416
Pronator teres syndrome, 414
Proopiomelanocortin, 356
Propafenone, 252
Propamidine, 119
Prophase, in mitosis, 81
Propionibacterium acnes, 433
Propionyl-CoA carboxylase, 45, 54
Propionyl-CoA carboxylase deficiency, 46
Propofol, 214
Propoxyphene, 212
Propranolol, 179, 254, 373
Propylthiouracil, 373
Prostaglandins, 52, 428
   PGE_1, 381
   PGE_2, 52
   $PGF_{2\alpha}$, 52
   PGI_2, 52
Prostate, 379, 380
   cancer of, 154, 382
   diseases of, 382
Prostate specific antigen stain, 150, 154
Prostatic acid phosphatase, 154
Prostatic urethra, 284
Prostatitis, 382
   acute, 382, 401
   chronic, 382
Protamine, 444
   as antidote, 161
Protease inhibitors
   in AIDS treatment, 100
   as anti-HIV therapy, 101, 455
Proteases, IgA, 112
Protective antigen, 111
Protein translation, 64
   modifications after, 65
Protein(s), 65
   apoproteins, 51
   C type, 442, 443
   cell cycle and, 152

CFTR, 343
chronic inflammation and, 97
digestion of, 337
integral, 78
M type, 112
in plasma membrane, 78
post-translational modifications to, 65
S type, 442, 443
structure of, 65
synthesis inhibition, 115
tau, 206
A type, 112
Proteins, peripheral, 78
Proteoglycans, 80
Proteosomes, 65
Proteus spp., 274
in urolithiasis, 314
Prothrombin (factor II), 442
Prothrombin time, 443
Proton pump inhibitors, 333
Proto-oncogenes, 152
Protozoal infections, 117, 118, 121
major, 122
Proximal convoluted tubule, 284
Proximal nephron, 284
Proximal penile urethra, 284
Proximal tubule, 290, 293–294
Prozone phenomenon, 93
PRPP aminotransferase, 60
Prussian blue stain, 150
PSA (prostate specific antigen) stain, 150, 154
Psammoma bodies, 185, 373, 397
P-selectin, 94
Pseudocysts, 343
Pseudoephedrine, 180
Pseudogout, 426
Pseudohyperparathyroidism, 369
Pseudohypertrophy, of the calves, 430
Pseudohyphae, 131
Pseudointersexuality
female, 378
male, 378
Pseudomonas spp., 274, 275
in osteomyelitis, 424
Pseudomonas aeruginosa, 111, 274, 343, 433, 434, 435
Pseudomyxoma peritonei, 397
Pseudopolyps, 347
Psilocybin, 14
Psoas abscess, 419
Psoas major muscle, 420
Psoriasis, and antimalarial drugs, 432
Psoriatic arthritis, 426
Psychopathology, 15–25
Psyllium, 351
PT (prothrombin time), 443
PT (proximal tubule), 290, 293–294
Pterygopalatine ganglion, 172
PTH (parathyroid hormone), 296, 367
PTT (partial thromboplastin time), 443
PTU (propylthiouracil), 373
Pudendal nerve, 329, 380
Pulmonary arteries, 260
Pulmonary blood flow, 269
Pulmonary capillary, 267
Pulmonary circulation, 235
Pulmonary edema, 281
Pulmonary emboli, 281
Pulmonary hypertension, 281
Pulmonary trunk, 217
Pulmonary veins, 260
Pulmonic valve, 232
stenosis or atresia of, 241
Pulse pressure, 234
Pulvinar nucleus, 200
Pupillary light reflex pathway, 193

Pupillary light-near dissociation, 194
Pupillary sphincter, 172, 193
Pupils
abnormalities of, 194
constriction of, 13, 194
Purine, 58
analogs of, 60
synthesis of, 59–60
Purkinje cells, 199
Purkinje fibers, 222
Purpura, 441
Purulent meningitis, acute, 181
Pustule, malignant, 434
Putamen, 201
PV loops (cardiac pressure-volume loops), 231–232
PVC (premature ventricular contraction), 226
Pyelonephritis, 313
Pyknosis, 147
Pylorus, 320, 327
stenosis of, 340
Pyogenic liver abscesses, 345
Pyramidal decussation, 187
Pyramids, 187, 198
Pyridostigmine, 176
Pyridoxine, 54
Pyrimethamine, 60, 113, 116, 122
Pyrimidine, 58
analogs of, 60, 61
synthesis of, 59
Pyruvate carboxylase, 39, 42, 54
Pyruvate dehydrogenase, 39, 54
Pyruvate kinase, 36, 42
Pyruvate kinase deficiency, 36
Pyruvate metabolism, 39

Q

Q waves, 226
QRS complex, 224
QRS duration, 225
QT interval, 225
Quadratus femoris muscle, 420, 421
Quadratus plantae muscles, 422
Quantal does-response curve, 157
Quaternary amines, 175
Quetiapine, 18
Quinidine, 252
Quinine, 120
Quinupristin, 115

R

R Groups, 43
R (reabsorption), 288
p-value, 33
using for decision-making, 33
Rabeprazole, 333
Rabies, 128
Radial dilator muscles, 193
Radial nerve, 413, 414, 416, 417
Radiation, ionizing, as cancer risk, 151
Radioactive iodine, 373
Radioulnar joints, movement at, 416
Raloxifene, 394
Ranitidine, 162, 333
Rapidly progressive glomerulonephritis, idiopathic, 312
Rashes, 436–437
Rathke pouch, 185
Ratio scale, 34
Rationalization, 11
Raynaud disease, 250
Rb gene, 153
RBC (red blood cell), 36
RBF. *See* Renal blood flow
Reabsorption, 288
Reaction formation, 11
Recall bias, 33
Receptive relaxation, 327

Receptors. *See also individual receptor types by name*
in cell signaling, 83
in cholinergic transmission, 175
diversity of, 88
enzyme-linked, 83
within ion channels, 158
in parasympathetic autonomic nervous system, 173–174
spare, for drug binding, 157
in sympathetic autonomic nervous system, 173–174
T cell, 86
transmembrane, tyrokinase activation and, 158
Reciprocal translocations, chromosomal, 73
Recombinant cytokines, clinical uses, 104
Recombinant DNA, 67–68
Rectouterine pouch, 379
Rectovesical pouch, 379
Rectum, 329
Rectus femoris muscle, 420, 421
Recurrent laryngeal branch, 259
Recurrent laryngeal nerve, 280
Red blood cells, 36
disorders of, 445–448
Red man syndrome, 114
Red muscle fibers, 407
Red nucleus, 199
5α-Reductase 2 deficiency, 378
5α-Reductase 2 gene, 378
5α-Reductase inhibitor, 382
Reduviid bug, 121
Reed-Sternberg cells, 451
Reflex tests
brachial plexus, 413
lumbosacral plexus, 419
Reflex(es)
cremasteric, 383
deep tendon, 188
defecation, 329
gastrocolic, 329
gastroileac, 328
muscle stretch, 188
myotatic, 188
pupillary light, 193
Reflexes, vestibuloocular, 196
Reflux nephropathy, 313
Refractory periods, 224
absolute and relative, 144
Regression, 11
Regular insulin, 366
Reinforcement, 4
Reiter syndrome, 426
Rejection
acute, 103
chronic, 103
Relative afferent pupil, 194
Relative polycythemia, 445
Relative refractory periods, 144, 224
Relaxation
isovolumic, 231
receptive, 327
Remifentanil, 214
Renal agenesis, 285
Renal blood flow, 289
autoregulation of, 292
filtration regulation and, 292
Renal caliculi, 285
Renal cell carcinoma, 153, 315
Renal failure, 368
Renal pelvis, 284
Renal plasma flow, 289
Renal sympathetic nerves, 300
Renal system
acid/base regulation and, 303
embryology and anatomy of, 284–285

pathology of, 311–316
pharmacology of, 309–310
physiology of, 286–309
water and solutes regulation in, 296
Renal vein, 324
thrombosis of, 314
Renin, 164, 358
Renin secretion, autoregulation of, 291
Renin-angiotensin-aldosterone, 300
blood pressure control by, 358
Reovirus, 127
Repaglinide, 366
Repeated measures ANOVA, 34
Repolarization, 144
Repression, 11
Reproductive system
female. See Female reproductive system
male. See Male reproductive system
RER (rough endoplasmic reticulum), 76
Reserpine, 180
Residual volume, 261
Respiratory acidosis, 307
Respiratory alkalosis, 307
Respiratory bronchioles, 258
Respiratory depression, 13
Respiratory distress syndromes, 262, 279
Respiratory syncytial virus, 128, 274
Respiratory system
anatomy of, 259–260
embryology of, 258
histology of, 258
pathology of, 273–281
physiology of, 261–272
Respondent conditioning, 4
Responses, cellular (adaptive), 148
Resting membrane potential, 143
Restriction endonucleases, 67, 68
Restriction fragment length polymorphisms, 69
Restrictive (infiltrative) myopathy, 246
Restrictive lung disease, 265, 279
ret oncogene, 152
Retarded ejaculation, 27
Rete ovarii, 378
Rete testes, 378
Reteplase, 444
Reticular lamina, 80
Reticulin stain, 150
Retinoblastoma, 81, 153, 185
Retinoblastoma susceptibility protein, 81
Retrolental fibroplasia, 279
Retroperitoneal organs, 321
Retrovirus, 127
Reuptake, adrenergic transmission and, 178
Reuptake inhibitors, 180
Reverse transcriptase inhibitors
in AIDS treatment, 100
as anti-HIV therapy, 101, 455
Reye syndrome, 344, 444
RFLP (restriction fragment length polymorphisms), 69
Rh disease, of newborn, 44
Rhabdomyoma, 247
Rhabdomyosarcoma, 430
embryonal, 395, 430
Rhabdovirus, 128
RhD immune globulin, 105
Rheumatic fever, 102
acute, 243
Rheumatic heart disease, 243
Rheumatoid arthritis, 426
treatment of, 428
Rheumatoid factor, 426
Rhinoviruses, 273
Rhizopus spp., 133
RhoGAM™, 105
Rhomboid major muscle, 415
Rhomboid minor muscle, 415

Ribavirin, 129, 274, 276
Riboflavin (B$_2$), 54
Ribonuclease, 334
Ribonucleic acid, 58, 108
Ribonucleotide reductase, 59
Ribonucleotides, 59
Ribose, 58
Ribose-5-phosphate, 59
Ribosomal RNA, 63
Ribosomes, 64
Ribosylation, 111
Ribulose-5-P, 40
Rickets, 55, 338, 423
hypophosphatemic, 70
Rickettsia spp., 117
Rickettsia prowazekii, 437
Rickettsia rickettsii, 437
Rifampin, 113
Right and left bundle branches, 222
Right atrium, 219
Right axis deviation, 227
Right coronary artery, 219
Right testicular vein, 383
Right ventricle, 219
Rimantadine, 129, 276
Ringworm, 435
Rinne test, 197
Risedronate, 369
Risperidone, 18
Ritonavir, 101
Rituximab, 105
Rivastigmine, 206
RM (resting membrane) potential, 143
RNA, 58, 108
processing and transcription of, 63
types of, 63
RNA viruses
double-stranded, 127
negative-sense, 128
positive-sense, 127
RNA-dependent DNA polymerase, 127
Robertsonian translocations, 73
formation and consequences of, 74
Robin sequence, 410
Rocky Mountain spotted fever, 437
Rocuronium, 409
Rolando sulcus, 205
Romaña sign, 121
Romberg sign, 188
Ropinirole, 202
Ropivacaine, 213
Rose gardener's disease, 434
Rosenthal fibers, 185
Rosiglitazone, 366
Rotator cuff, 413, 416
Rotatores muscle, 415
Rotaviruses, 127, 349
Roth spots, 245
Rotor syndrome, 343
Rough endoplasmic reticulum, 76
Round ligament, 379
Roundworms, 122
transmitted by eggs, 125
transmitted by larvae, 126
RPF (renal plasma flow), 289
RPGN (rapidly progressive glomerulonephritis), idiopathic, 312
rRNA, 63
RS (Reed-Sternberg) cells, 451
RSV (respiratory syncytial virus), 128, 274
RU-486 (mifepristone), 393, 394
Rubella, 127
infectious arthritis and, 427
Rubeola, 128, 275, 437
Rugae, 320
Russell bodies, 454

S

S cells, 330
S phase, in cell cycle, 81
S-100, 154
S-100 stain, 150
Saccule, 196
Sacrococcygeal teratoma, 138
SAD (seasonal affective disorder), 19
Saddle nose, 423
Sadism, 26
Salicylates, 428
poisoning by, 159
Saliva, 326
amylase in, 336
Salivary glands, 326
Salmeterol, 179, 278
Salmonella spp., 348
in osteomyelitis, 424
Salmonella O antigen, 113
Salmonella osteomyelitis, 448
Salmonella typhi, 117
Salvage pathways, 59–60
SAM (S-adenosylhomocysteine), 44
SAM (S-adenosylmethionine), 45
San Joaquin Valley fever, 132
Sandfly, and leishmaniasis transmission, 121
SANS (sympathetic autonomic nervous system), 172, 173–174, 193
Saphenous nerve, 420
Saquinavir, 101
Sarcoidosis, 277
Sarcoma
defined, 151
Kaposi. See Kaposi sarcoma
Sarcoma botryoides, 395, 430
Sarcomeres, 407
Sarcoplasmic reticulum, 77
Sargramostim. See Granulocyte-macrophage colony-stimulating factor
Sarin, 177
SARS virus, 127, 276
Sartorius muscle, 420, 421
Satiety center, 326
Saturday night palsy, 414
Scalded skin disease, 436
Scales, statistical, 34
Scarlatina, 436
Scarlet fever, 436
Scarpa fascia, 380
Schatzki rings, 340
Schaumann bodies, 277
Schistosoma spp., 122
Schistosoma haematobium, 123
Schistosoma japonicum, 123
Schistosoma mansoni, 123
Schistosomiasis, 123, 345
Schizogony, 119
Schizoid disorder, 24
Schizophrenia, 16
Schizotypal disorder, 24
Schwann cells, 184
Schwannoma, 185
bilateral acoustic, 185
Sci-70 (anti-DNA topoisomerase I antibodies), 103
Sciatic nerve, 419, 420, 421
Scleroderma, 102
diffuse, 103
limited, 103
Sclerosing adenosis, 399
Sclerosing cholangitis, 344
Sclerosis
amyotrophic lateral, 189
Mönckeberg medial calcific, 250
multiple, 184
nodular, in Hodgkin disease, 451
tuberous, 247

"Squamous pearls," 280
SR (superior rectus) muscle, 190, 195
SS (septum secundum), 216
SSRIs. *See* Selective serotonin reuptake inhibitors
ST elevation, 242
ST segment, 224
    depression of, 242
Stable angina pectoris, 242
Stable cells, 149
Stage, of tumor, 154
Staining methods, 150
Standard limb leads, 225
Staphylococci, coagulase-negative, infectious
    arthritis and, 427
Staphylococcus spp., 426
Staphylococcus aureus, 110, 111, 112, 274, 350,
    401, 433, 435, 436
    infectious arthritis and, 427
    methicillin-resistant, 433
    methicillin-sensitive, 433
    in osteomyelitis, 424
Staphylococcus epidermidis, 110
"Starry sky" pattern, in non-Hodgkin lymphoma, 452
Starvation, and osmotic diuresis, 301
Statins, and cholesterol synthesis, 50
Stationary phase, bacterial, 108
Statistical scales and tests, 34
Status epilepticus seizure, 210
Stavudine, 101
STDs (sexually transmitted diseases), 402–403
Steady state, 140, 156
Stein-Leventhal syndrome, 397
Steroid receptors, 158
Steroidogenesis, hormonal control of, 385
    female, 387
Stibogluconate, 122
Still disease, 426
Stimulant laxatives, 351
Stimulants, CNS, 13
Stimulus control, 5
Stomach, 318, 327, 337
    body and fundus of, 320
Stool-softener, 351
Straight sinus, 183
Stranger anxiety, 6
Stratum basale, 431
Stratum corneum, 431
Stratum granulosum, 431
Stratum lucidum, 431
Stratum spinosum, 431
Streptococcus spp., 401, 426
    group A, 112
    group B, 181, 396
Streptococcus mutans, 110
Streptococcus pneumoniae, 273, 275
    in bacterial meningitis, 181
Streptococcus pyogenes, 111, 273, 433, 436
    erythrogenic toxin of, 113
Streptococcus viridans, 110, 245
Streptogramins, 113
Streptokinase, 433, 442, 444
Streptomycin, 64, 115
Stretch reflex, 188
Striatum, 201
String sign, 347
Stroke volume, 228
Stroke work, 231
Strong agonists, 212
Strongyloides spp., 122, 125
Subacute bacterial endocarditis, 245
Subacute combined degeneration, 189
Subarachnoid hemorrhage, 181, 210
Subarachnoid space, 181, 182
Subcellular organelles, 40–41
Subcutaneous granulomas, 434
Subcutaneous nodules, 243

Subcutaneous tissue, infectious diseases of,
    433–436
Subdural hematoma, 181, 210
Subdural space, 181
Subendothelial deposits, 311
Subepithelial humps and spikes, 311
Subfalcine herniation, 207
Sublimation, 11
Sublingual salivary glands, 326
Submandibular salivary glands, 326
Submandibular VI ganglion, 172
Submucosal layer, digestive tract, 319
Submucosal plexus, 319
Subscapularis muscle, 415
Subscapularis tendons, 416
Substance abuse, 12–14
Substance P, 328
Substantia nigra, 199, 201
Substrate-level phosphorylation, 36
Subtalar joint, movements at, 422
Subthalamic nucleus, 201, 202
Subthalamus, 170, 200
Succimer, for heavy metal poisoning, 160, 161
Succinate dehydrogenase, 38
Succinyl CoA, 37
Succinylcholine, 214, 409
Sucralfate, 333
Sucrase, 336
Sudden acute respiratory syndromes, 276
Sudden infant death syndrome, 10
Sulci, 204
Sulcus limitans, 170
Sulfasalazine, 428
Sulfinpyrazone, 429
Sulfonamides, 113, 116, 434
Sulfonylureas, 366
Sumatriptan, 163
Superantigens, 89, 111, 436
Superficial inguinal nodes, 386
Superficial inguinal ring, 383
Superficial perineal (Colles) fascia, 380
Superficial perineal pouch, 380
Superficial peroneal nerve, 420, 422
Superficial transverse perineal muscle, 379
Superinfection, with *C. difficile,* 115
Superior cerebellar artery, 209
Superior cerebellar peduncle, 199
Superior cerebral artery, 208
Superior colliculus, 190, 199
Superior colliculus/pretectal area, 199
Superior frontal gyrus, 204
Superior gemellus muscle, 420
Superior gluteal nerve, 419, 420
Superior mediastinum, 218
Superior mesenteric artery, 318, 319, 322, 323,
    324, 341
Superior mesenteric veins, 324
Superior oblique muscle, 195
Superior olivary nucleus, 197
Superior orbital fissure, 191
Superior parathyroid gland, 411
Superior parietal lobule, 204, 205
Superior petrosal sinus, 183
Superior rectal veins, 324
Superior rectus muscle, 190, 195
Superior sagittal sinus, 182, 183
Superior temporal gyrus, 197, 204
Superior vena cava syndrome, 280
Superoxide, 146, 268
Supinator muscle, 413, 416
Suppression, 11
Suppurative arthritis, 426
Suppurative pericarditis, 247
Suprachiasmatic nucleus, 200
Supramarginal gyrus, 204
Supraoptic nuclei, hypothalamic, 362
Supraoptic nucleus, 200

Suprascapular nerve, 413, 415
Supraspinatus tendon, 416
Sural nerve, 420
Suramin, 121, 122
Surface tension, 263
Surfactant, 258, 263
    deficiency of, 279
Suspensory ligament, 379
SV (stroke volume), 228
Swallowing, 327
Sweat glands, 431
Sweating, fluid and electrolyte abnormalities in, 287
Swelling
    hydropic, cell injury and, 147
    labioscrotal, 378
Sydenham chorea, 243
Sylvius, aqueduct of. *See* Cerebral aqueduct
Sympathetic autonomic nervous system, 172,
    173–174, 193
Sympathetic chain, 172
Sympathetic innervation, 222
Sympathetic neurons, 172
Sympathetic regulation, of heart and circulation, 238
Sympathetic (thoracolumbar) outflow, 173
Sympathomimetics, indirect-acting, 180
Syncytiotrophoblast, 136, 392
Syndrome of inappropriate ADH secretion, 154,
    301, 355, 362
Syngeneic grafts, 103
Synoviosarcoma, 429
Syphilis, 385
    primary, 403
    secondary, 403, 437
    tertiary, 403
Syringomyelia, 171, 189
Systematic desensitization, 5
Systemic circulation, 235
Systemic lupus erythematosus, 102
Systole, 230

T

T cells, 86, 450
    antigen receptor, characteristics of, 88
    cytotoxic (CD8+), 89
    defects, 99
    receptor diversity, 88
    receptors, 86
T tubules, 406
T wave, 224
T_3. *See* Triiodothyronine
T_4 (thyroxine), 44, 370
Tabes dorsalis, 189
Tachycardia, ventricular, 226
Tacrine, 176, 206
Tacrolimus, 105
Tadalafil, 381
Taenia spp., 122
Taenia saginata, 124
Taenia solium, 124
Takayasu arteritis, 248
TAL. *See* Thick ascending loop of Henle
Tamoxifen, 166, 394
Tamsulosin, 179
Tapeworms, 122, 124
Tardive dyskinesia, 18
Tarsal joints, movements at, 422
Tartrate-resistant acid phosphatase, 154
tau protein, 206
Taxol, 79
Tay-Sachs disease, 52
TB (tuberculosis), 428
TBW (total body water), 141
3TC (lamivudine), 101
TCA (tricarboxylic acid), 37
    cycle for, 38, 39
T-cell lymphoma, 453
    cutaneous, 153

TCR (T cell receptor), 86
TD (tardive dyskinesia), 18
Tectorial membrane, 197
Teeth grinding, 10
Teichoic acids, 109
Telencephalon, 170
Telophase, in mitosis, 81
Temazepam, 22
Temporal arteritis, 249
Temporal lobe, 204, 205
Teniae coli muscle bands, 329
Tensor fasciae latae muscle, 420
Tentorium cerebelli, 183
Teratoma, 386
    immature, 397
    sacrococcygeal, 138
Terazosin, 179
Terbinafine, 134
Terbutaline, 179, 278
Teres major muscle, 415
Teres minor muscle, 415
Teres minor tendon, 416
Terminal bronchioles, 258
Termination, in protein translation, 64
Tertiary amines, 175
Testes, 382
    inflammatory lesions of, 385
    neoplasms of, 386
Testicle, 379
Testicular artery, 383
Testicular feminization syndrome, 378
Testosterone, 378, 381, 385
Tetanus toxin, 111
Tetracaine, 213
Tetracycline, 275, 276
Tetracyclines, 64, 113, 115, 118, 402, 403, 433, 434
Tetraiodothyronine, 370
Tetralogy of Fallot, 217, 240
Tetrodotoxin, 144
TGF-α (transforming growth factor α), 149
TH1 cells, 90
TH2 cells, 90
Thalamus, 170, 200, 201, 203, 204
Thalassemia-α, 446
Thalassemia-β, 446
Thayer-Martin agar, 402
Theca cell, 387
Theca externa, 388
Theca interna, 388
T-helper cells, 89–100
Theophylline, 278
    poisoning by, antidote for, 161
Therapeutic index, 157
Thiabendazole, 126
Thiamine, 39, 54
Thiamine pyrophosphate, 39
Thiazide diuretics, 301, 309, 310
    electrolyte changes caused by, 310
Thiazolidinediones, 366
Thick ascending loop of Henle, 290, 294, 295
Thioamides, 373
Thiopental, 22, 214
Thioridazine, 17
Third degree atrioventricular conduction block, 226
Third ventricle, 170, 182, 201, 204
    cerebral aqueduct of, 182
THO cells, 90
Thoracic splanchnic nerves, 172
Thoracodorsalis nerve, 415
Thorax, cross-sectional anatomy of, 221
Threadworm, 126
Threonine, 43
Threshold, 144
Throat, infection of, 273
Thrombasthenia, Glanzmann, 440
Thrombin (factor IIa), 442

Thrombin time, 443
Thromboangiitis obliterans, 248
Thrombocythemia, essential, 441
Thrombocytopenia, 441
Thrombocytosis, 441
Thrombolytics, 444
Thrombophlebitis, migratory, 154
Thrombopoietin, 104
Thrombosis
    cavernous sinus, 412
    renal vein, 314
Thrombotic cerebral infarcts, 210
Thrombotic thrombocytopenic purpura, 441
Thromboxanes, 52
    TxA$_2$, 440
Thumb, movements of, 418
Thymidine, 58
Thymidine kinase, 129
Thymidylate synthase, 54
Thymine dimer repair, 62
Thymoma, 154, 430
Thymus, 411
    abnormalities of, 430
Thyroarytenoid, 259
Thyroepiglotticus, 259
Thyroglobulin, 370
Thyroglossal duct, 411
Thyroglossal duct cyst, 372
Thyroid gland, 370–373
    activity regulation in, 371
    disorders of, 371–372
    medullary carcinoma of, 150, 154, 366
    neoplasms of, 373
    treatment options and, 373
Thyroid hormones, 364. See also Thyroxine; Triiodothyronine
    control, 370
    physiologic actions of, 370
    secretion of, 371
    synthesis and storage of, 370
Thyroid receptors, 158
Thyroiditis
    de Quervain granulomatous subacute, 372
    Hashimoto, 372
Thyroid-stimulating hormone, 354, 370
Thyroid-stimulating immunoglobulins, 371
Thyrotropin-releasing hormone, 354, 370
Thyroxine, 44, 370
TI (therapeutic index), 157
Tiagabine, 211
Tibial collateral ligament, 421
Tibial nerves, 419, 420, 421, 422
Tibial tuberosity, 421
Tibialis anterior muscle, 422
Tibialis posterior muscle, 422
Ticarcillin, 113
Ticlopidine, 444
Tidal volume, 261
Tight junction (zonula occludens), 80
Timolol, 179, 193
Tinea barbae, 131
Tinea capitis, 131
Tinea corporis, 131
Tinea cruris, 131
Tinea pedis, 131
Tinea versicolor, 131
Tiotropium, 278
Tirofiban, 444
Tissue hydrostatic pressure, 236
Tissue oncotic pressure, 236
Tissue plasminogen activator, 442
    inhibitor, 443
Tizanidine, 409
T$_{max}$. See Transport maximum
TMP-SMX (trimethoprim-sulfamethoxazole), 122
TNF. See Tumor necrosis factor
TNM staging, 154

Tobramycin, 115
Tocainide, 252
Toes, movements of, 422
Togavirus, 127
Tolcapone, 180, 202
Tonic-clonic seizure, 210
Tooth enamel dysplasia, 115
Topiramate, 210, 211
Topoisomerase, 58
Torsion, 383
Total body water, 141
Total lung capacity, 261
Total peripheral resistance, 234
Tourette syndrome, 202
Toxic shock syndrome, 436
Toxic syndromes, common, 159
Toxicity, cardiovascular, 213
Toxicology, 159–161
Toxins, bacterial, 110, 111
Toxocara spp., 122
Toxocara canis, 125
Toxocara cati, 125
Toxoplasma spp., 117
Toxoplasma gondii, 117, 122
    in AIDS patients, 100
Toxoplasmosis, 122
t-PA. See Tissue plasminogen activator
TPP (thiamine pyrophosphate), 39
TPR (total peripheral resistance), 234
Trabeculae carneae, 219, 220
Tracheobronchial nodes, 260
Tracheoesophageal fistula, 258, 340
Tracheoesophageal septum, 258
Traction diverticula, 339
Tracts, spinal cord, 186
Tranexamic acid, 445
Trans (maturing) face, Golgi apparatus, 77
Transaminase, 39
Transamination, of amino groups, 45–46
Transcription, and RNA processing, 63
Transduction, in bacterial genetics, 113
Transfer RNA, 63, 64
Transformation, 113
Transforming growth factor α, 149
Transitional cell carcinoma, of the bladder, 316
Transketolase, 54
Translation, of protein. See Protein translation
Translocations
    chromosomal, 73
    Robertsonian. See Robertsonian translocations
Transmembrane receptors, tyrosine kinase activation and, 158
Transplantation immunology, 103
Transport, 140
    placental, 92
    types of, 78
Transport maximum (T$_{max}$), 292
    estimation of, 293
Transposition of the great vessels, 217, 241
Transposon, 113
Transtentorial (uncal) herniation, 194, 207
Transversalis fascia, 383
Transverse colon, 329
Transverse ligament, 421
Transverse sinuses, 183
Transverse tarsal joint, movements at, 422
Transversospinalis muscle, 415
Transvestite fetishism, 26
Tranylcypromine, 20, 163, 179
TRAP (tartrate-resistant acid phosphatase), 154
Trapezius muscle, 415
Trapezoid body, 197
Trastuzumab, 105
Trauma, to central nervous system, 207
Trazodone, 20
Treacher-Collins syndrome, 410

Trematodes, 122
  diseases caused by, 123
Treponema pallidum, 403, 437
TRH (thyroid-releasing hormone), 354, 370
Triacylglycerol lipases, 334
Triacylglycerols, 49, 51
Triamterene, 310
Triazolam, 22
Tricarboxylic acid cycle, 37
Triceps muscle, 413, 416
Triceps tendon, 413
Trichinella spp., 122, 125
Trichinosis, 126
Trichomonas vaginalis, 118, 402
Trichomoniasis, 118, 122
Trichophyton spp., 131, 435
Trichrome stain, 150
Trichuris spp., 122, 125
  hematologic changes caused by, 455
Tricuspid valve, 219, 232
Tricyclic antidepressants, 20, 180
  poisoning by, 159
Trigeminal nerves (V), 190, 196
  skeletal muscle innervated by, 410
Triglyceride metabolism and regulation, 49
Trihexyphenidyl, 176, 202
Triiodothyronine, 44, 370
  reversal, 371
Trimeprazine, 123
Trimethaphan, 175
Trimethoprim, 60, 113, 116
Trimethoprim-sulfamethoxazole, 122, 276
Trinucleotide repeat, 430
Trisomy 13 (Patau syndrome), 72
Trisomy 18 (Edwards syndrome), 72
Trisomy 21 (Down syndrome), 72, 240, 241
tRNA, 63, 64
Trochlear nerve (IV), 190, 412
  skeletal muscle innervated by, 410
Tropheryma whippelii, 341
Trophoblast, 136
Trophoblastic tumors, 154
Trophozoite, 119
Tropical sprue, 341
Tropicamide, 176
Troponins, 243, 406
Trousseau syndrome, 343
Truncoconal septum, 241
Truncus arteriosus, 216
Trypanosoma spp., 117
Trypanosoma b. rhodesiense, 121
Trypanosoma brucei gambiense, 121
Trypanosoma cruzi, 117, 121, 245, 339
Trypanosomiasis, 122
Trypomastigotes, 121
Trypsin, 334
Tryptophan, 43, 44
Tryptophan hydroxylase, 44, 163
Tsetse fly, 121
TSH (thyroid stimulating hormone), 354, 370
TSI (thyroid-stimulating immunoglobulin), 371
TSST-1, 111, 436
TT (thrombin time), 443
t-test, 34
TTP (thrombotic thrombocytopenic purpura), 441
Tuber cinereum, 204
Tuberculin test, 102
Tuberculosis, 277, 385, 428
Tuberoinfundibular pathways, and antipsychotics, 17
Tuberous sclerosis, 247
Tubocurarine, 409
Tubular adenoma, 342
Tubular diseases, renal, 313
Tubulin, 79
Tubuloglomerular feedback, 292

Tubulointerstitial diseases, renal, 313
Tubulovillous adenomas, 342
Tumor markers, 154
Tumor necrosis factor, 148, 428
  TNF-α, 89, 91, 110, 149
  TNF-β, 90, 91
Tumor suppresser genes, 153
  breast cancer and, 400
Tumors
  benign, 339
  borderline, 24, 397
  of breast, 399
  of CNS and PNS, 185
  epithelial, 397
  germ cell, 386
  giant cell, 425
  grade and stage of, 154
  hepatic, 345
  joint space, 429
  of joint space, 429
  of lung and pleura, 280
  malignant. *See* Malignant tumors
  metastatic, 185
  musculoskeletal, 424, 425
  non-germ cell, 386
  osteoblastic, 425
  Pancoast, 280
  in paraneoplastic syndromes, 154
  pineal region, 199
  renal, 315
  trophoblastic, 154
  vascular, 251
Tunica vaginalis, 382
Turner syndrome, 72, 241
T-wave inversion, 242
TX (thromboxanes), 52, 440
Tympanic membrane, 197, 411
Type I error, 33
Type II error, 33
Typhus, epidemic, 437
Tyramine, 163
Tyrosine, 43, 44
Tyrosine hydroxylase, 44
Tyrosine kinase, 158
  receptor, 82
  transmembrane receptors activating, 158
Tyrosine transporter, 44
Tzanck smear, 402

U

UAG (urinary anion gap), 308
UB (ultimobranchial body), 411
Ubiquitin, 65
UDP-glucose, 41
UDP-glucuronyl transferase, 44
UDP-glucuronyl transferase deficiency, 44
UES (upper esophageal sphincter), 327
Ulceration, 347
Ulcers, 434
  curling, 340
  Cushing, 340
  esophageal, 369
  peptic, 333, 340
Ulnar nerve, 413, 414, 416, 417, 418
Ultimobranchial body, 411
Ultrafiltration coefficient, 236
Ultralente insulin, 366
Ultraviolet exposure, as cancer risk, 151
Umbilical artery, 392
Umbilical vein, 392
UMN. *See* Upper motor neuron
Uncal herniation, 194, 207
Unconjugated hyperbilirubinemia, 343
Undoing (defense mechanism), 11
Union, in wound healing, 149
Unipolar depression, 19

Unithiol, for heavy metal poisoning, 161
Unstable angina, 242
Upper esophageal sphincter, 327
Upper extremities, musculoskeletal anatomy, 413–419
Upper medulla, 190
Upper motor neuron, 187
  facial nerve lesion and, 196
Upper respiratory tract infections, 273–274
Urachus, 285
  patent, 316
Uracil, 47, 58, 62
Urate nephropathy, acute, 313
Urea cycle, 47
Ureaplasma spp., 396
Ureaplasma urealyticum, 402
Urease, 112
Ureteric bud, 284
Ureters, 379
  anomalies of, 315
  development of, 284
  double, 285, 315
  obstruction of, 315
Urethra, 379
  congenital abnormalities of, 285
  development of, 284
Urethritis, 402
Uric acid, 59
Uric acid stones, 314
Uricosuric agents, 429
Uridine 5′-diphosphate. *See* UDP *entries*
Urinary anion gap, 308
Urinary bladder, 379
Urine
  extravasation of, 380
  formation processes, 288
Urine flow, 297
Urine osmolarity, 297, 300
Urobilinogens, 336
Urodilatin, 300
Urogenital diaphragm, 379, 380
Urogenital folds, 378
Urogenital sinus, 284
Urokinase, 442, 444
Urolithiasis, 314
Uroporphyrinogen decarboxylase deficiency, 44
Uroporphyrinogen-I synthase, 44
Uroporphyrinogen-I synthase deficiency, 44
Urorectal septum, 284
Urothelia, 26
Ursodiol, 351
Uterine cycle, 389
Uterine tubes, 378
  fertilization in, 136
Uterus, 378, 379, 391
  diseases of, 396
Utricle, 196

V

V receptors, in cell signaling, 83
VA (ventral anterior nucleus), 200
Vaccinia, 126
VACTERL congenital anomalies, 138
Vagina, 378, 379
  diseases of, 395
Vaginal adenosis, 395
Vaginismus, 27
Vaginosis, bacterial, 402
Vagus nerve (X), 191
  skeletal muscle innervated by, 410
Valacyclovir, 129
Valine, 43
Valproic acid
  in bipolar disorder, 20
  for seizure, 210, 211
Valsalva maneuver, 329
Valsartan, 164

Valvular disorders, 233–239
Valvular heart disease, 246
Vancomycin, 113, 114, 433
Vanillylmandelic acid, 178, 361
Vardenafil, 381
Variant CJD, 207
Varicella-zoster virus, 126
Varicocele, 383
Varicose veins, 251
Variola, 126
Vas deferens, 380
Vasa recta, 290, 298, 299
Vascular diseases, renal, 314
Vascular disorders, pulmonary, 281
Vascular function curve, 228
   examples of, 229
Vascular tumors, 251
Vasculitides, 248–249
Vasoactive inhibitory peptide, 327, 328, 331
Vasodilation, metabolic, 238
Vasodilators, 255
Vasopressin, 362. See also Antidiuretic hormone
   receptors, 83
Vastus intermedius muscle, 421
Vastus lateralis muscle, 421
Vastus medialis muscle, 421
VATER congenital anomalies, 138
VA/VL thalamic nuclei, 201
VDJ recombination, 88
VDRL test, 403
Vector cardiogram, 227
Vectors
   DNA, 68
   viral, 128
Veins. See individual veins by name
Venlafaxine, 20
Venous disease, 251
Venous drainage, 181–183
   of lungs, 260
   ventricular system and, 182–183
Ventilation, 261–262
   control of, 272
Ventilation-perfusion relationships, 270
Ventral anterior nucleus, 200
Ventral gray horn, 186
Ventral horn synapse, 187
Ventral lateral nucleus, 199, 200
Ventral pancreatic bud, 318
Ventral root, 186
Ventral white commissure, 189
Ventricular fibrillation, 226
Ventricular septal defect, 217, 240
Ventricular septum, 217
Ventricular system, 181–183
   and CSF circulation, 182
   and venous drainage, 182–183
   ventricles in, 170, 182, 190, 204, 219
Ventricular tachycardia, 226
Ventromedial nucleus, 200, 326
Ventroposterolateral nucleus, 188, 189, 200
Ventroposteromedial nucleus, 196, 200
Verapamil, 253, 254
Vermis, 199
   lesions of, 199
Verotoxin, 111, 349
Vertebrae, 171
Vertebral arteries, 208, 209
Vertigo, 196
Very low density lipoprotein, 48, 51
Vesamicol, 177
Vecuronium, 409
Vesicouterine pouch, 379
Vesicular lesions, 434
Vesicular stomatitis virus, 128
Vessel damage, associated with fractures, 222
Vestibular bulb, 379, 380

Vestibular nuclei, 196, 198
Vestibular system, 196
Vestibulocochlear nerve (VIII), 191
Vestibuloocular reflex, 196
VFC. See Vascular function curve
VHL gene, 153
Vibrio cholerae, 111, 349
Vibrio parahaemolyticus, 349
Vibrio vulnificus, 434
Vigabatrin, 211
Villous adenoma, 342
Villus/Villi, 320, 328, 392
Vimentin, 79
Vimentin stain, 150
Vinblastine, 79, 166
Vincristine, 79, 166
Vinyl chloride, as cancer risk, 151
VIP (vasoactive inhibitory peptide), 327, 328, 331
VIPoma, 331
V/Q mismatch, 271
Viral encephalitis, 182
Viral genetics, 128
Viral hepatitides, characteristics of, 346. See also
   Hepatitis
Viral myocarditis, 245
Viral vectors, 128
Virchow node, 340
Viridans streptococci, 110, 245
Virology, 126–130
Viruses, 117. See also individually named viruses
   oncogenic, 153
Visceral larva migrans, 125
Visceral leishmaniasis, 121
Visual association cortex, 205
Visual field defects, 19256
Visual system, 192–197
   lesions of, 192
Vital capacity, 261
Vitamin A, 55
Vitamin B_1, 39, 54
Vitamin B_2, 54
Vitamin B_3, 39, 54
Vitamin B_6, 54
Vitamin B_{12}, 54, 448
Vitamin C, 54, 66
Vitamin D, 55, 338
   in regulation of calcium and phosphate, 367
Vitamin D deficiency, 368, 423
Vitamin D excess, 368
Vitamin D_3, 367
Vitamin E, 55
Vitamin K, 55, 329
   as antidote, 161
   coagulation and, 442, 445
Vitamin K deficiency, 443
Vitamins. See also individually named vitamins
   deficiencies in, 146
   lipid soluble, 55
   water-soluble, 54
Vitelline duct, 318
Vitelline fistula, 341
VL (ventral lateral nucleus), 200
VLDL (very low density lipoprotein), 48, 51
VMA (vanillylmandelic acid), 178, 361
Voltage-gated channels, Na+, 144
Volume
   drug distribution, 156
   fluid distribution, 141
Voluntary contralateral horizontal gaze, 205
Voluntary motor system, 187
Volvulus, 341
Vomiting, 329
von Gierke disease, 41, 42
von Hippel-Lindau disease, 70, 71, 153, 251, 315
von Recklinghausen disease, 71
   of bone, 369

von Willebrand disease, 440, 441
   treatment of, 445
von Willebrand factor, 440
Voriconazole, 134
Voyeurism, 26
VPL (ventroposterolateral nucleus), 188, 189, 200
VPM (ventroposteromedial nucleus), 196, 200
VSD (ventricular septal defect), 217
VSV (vesicular stomatitis virus), 128
Vulva, diseases of, 395
Vulvovaginitis, 402
   Candida, 395
vWF (von Willebrand factor), 440
VX, 177
VZV (varicella-zoster virus), 126

W

Waldenström macroglobulinemia, 454
"Walking pneumonia," 275
Wall tension, 237
Wallenberg syndrome, 198
Warfarin, 444
   poisoning by, antidote for, 161
Warm hemolytic anemia, 447
Warts, 436
   genital, 395, 403
Water deprivation, 301
Water regulation
   disorders of, 301
   renal, 296
Waterhouse-Friderichsen syndrome, 360
Water-induced diuresis, 299
Watershed areas, 210
Water-soluble vitamins, 54. See also individually
   named vitamins
Weak agonists, 212
Weber syndrome, 199
Weber test, 197
Wegener granulomatosis, 249
Wernicke encephalopathy, 203
Wernicke-Korsakoff syndrome, 200
Wernicke aphasia, 205
Wernicke area, 205
West Nile virus, 127
Western blot technique, 69
   in AIDS diagnosis, 100
Whipple disease, 341
Whipworm, 125
White blood cell disorders, 449–450
   nonneoplastic, 450
White blood cells, 449
White matter, 186
White muscle fibers, 407
Wigger's diagram, 230
Wilms tumor, 74, 153, 315
Wilson disease, 202, 344
   antidote for, 161
Window period, in Ab-Ag complexes, 93
Withdrawal, 12, 213
Worms. See individual types of worm
Wound healing, 149
Wrist
   extensor muscles of, 413
   flexor muscles of, 413
   movement at, 417
WT-1 gene, 153
WT-2 gene, 153
Wuchereria spp., 122, 125

X

Xanthine oxidase, 60, 429
Xenogeneic grafts, 103
Xeroderma pigmentosum, 62
Xerostomia, 102
XII nucleus, 198
X-linked hyper-IgM syndrome, 98
X-linked inheritance patterns, 70
XYY syndrome, 72

Y

Yeasts, 131
Yersinia enterocolitica, 348
Yersinia pestis, 117
Yohimbine, 179
Yolk sac, 318
    primary, 136
    tumor of, 386
Yolk stalk, 318

Z

Z lines, 407
Zafirlukast, 278
Zalcitabine, 101
Zaleplon, 22
ZDV (zidovudine), 101, 130
Zenker diverticula, 339
Zero-order elimination, 156
Zidovudine, 101, 130
Zileuton, 52, 278
Ziprasidone, 18
Zollinger-Ellison syndrome, 331, 333, 365
Zolpidem, 22
    poisoning by, antidote for, 161
Zona fasciculata, 356
Zona glomerulosa, 356
Zona pellucida, 388, 391
Zona reticularis, 356
Zonal reaction, 384
Zoophilia, 26
Zygote, 136

4 Practice Tests for the

TOEFL®

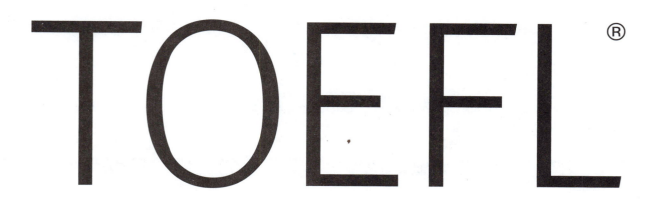

Second Edition

TABLE OF CONTENTS

How To Use This Book

WELCOME TO KAPLAN TOEFL PRACTICE TESTS

Congratulations on your decision to improve your English proficiency, and thank you for choosing Kaplan for your TOEFL preparation. You've made the right choice in acquiring this book—you're now armed with four full-length TOEFL practice tests, produced as a result of decades of researching the TOEFL and similar tests and teaching many thousands of students the skills they need to succeed.

This book is guaranteed to help you to score higher—let's start by walking through what you need to know to take advantage of this book and the Audio Tracks.

Your Book

This book contains four TOEFL practice tests, which include full-length Listening, Reading, Writing, and Speaking sections.

Review the listening scripts and answers at the back of this book to better understand your performance. Look for patterns in the questions you answered correctly and incorrectly. Were you stronger in some areas than others? This analysis will help you to target specific areas when you practice and prepare for the TOEFL.

Your Online Center

Your Online Center lets you access additional materials to reinforce your learning and sharpen your skills. Resources include the following:

- Online audio tracks of sample conversations and lectures to provide you with realistic practice for the Listening, Speaking, and Writing sections of the test
- Materials to help you evaluate and improve your Speaking and Writing score

Getting Started

Register your Online Center using these simple steps:

1. Go to **kaptest.com/booksonline.**
2. Follow the on-screen instructions. Make sure you have your book with you.

You can then listen to the audio online on your computer or on your mobile device through the Kaplan Mobile Prep app, which can be downloaded in the App Store from your iOS device or the Google Play Store from your Android device.

Access to the Online Center is limited to the original owner of this book and is nontransferable. Kaplan is not responsible for providing access to the Online Center to customers who purchase or borrow used copies of this book. Access to the Online Center expires one year after you register.

TOEFL Test Updates

In August 2019, ETS revised the TOEFL iBT in order to create a shorter test. The TOEFL follows the same format and contains the same question types, but there are fewer questions overall. The TOEFL iBT is now 30 minutes shorter than the previous test. It now takes 3 hours to complete.

Alongside these changes, a new feature, MyBest scores, was released. MyBest scores allows test takers to combine their highest scores for each section across all valid TOEFL iBT test scores received in the past 2 years. For the most up-to-date TOEFL news and specifications, visit **ets.org/toefl**.

Practice
Test 1

TEST DIRECTIONS

This test is designed to measure your ability to understand and use English in an academic context. The test has four sections.

In the **Reading** section, you will read three passages and answer questions about them.

In the **Listening** section, you will listen to two dialogues and three talks and answer questions about them.

In the **Speaking** section, there are four tasks. The first task asks you to speak based on your own personal experience. In the other three, you will read passages and/or listen to dialogues and talks, then speak based on what you have read and/or heard.

In the **Writing** section, there are two tasks. In the first task, you will read a passage, listen to a talk, then write based on what you have read and heard. The second task asks you to write based on your own personal experience and ideas.

There is a 10-minute break after the **Listening** section.

At the beginning of each section, there are directions that explain how to answer the questions or respond to the tasks in the section.

In the **Reading** and **Listening** sections, you should work carefully but quickly. You should try to answer every question to the best of your ability. Make an educated guess on questions that you are unsure of. In the **Speaking** and **Writing** sections, each task is separately timed. In each case, you should try to respond to the task as completely as possible in the given time.

READING SECTION

Directions: In this section of the test, you will read three passages. You will be tested on your ability to understand them by answering several questions on each passage.

While you read, you may take notes. You can then use your notes when answering questions.

Most questions are worth 1 point. Questions that are worth more than 1 point have a special note telling you how many total points they are worth.

You will have 54 minutes to read the three passages and answer all the questions. If you finish the questions before 54 minutes is up, you can go back and review your work in this section.

Passage 1

Nathaniel Hawthorne: His Life and Work

1   Nathaniel Hawthorne was born on the United States' birthday, July 4th, in 1804 to a prominent colonial family in Salem, Massachusetts. Hawthorne deliberately set out to create an American voice in literature. Believing that American authors of his time were mimicking the style of the British Romantics, Hawthorne refused to imitate others and developed a new style of writing using distinctly American themes and settings.

2   Hawthorne's most critically acclaimed and popular novel was *The Scarlet Letter*, but his body of work reaches far beyond this classic to include children's books, essays, short stories, and a comedy. Hawthorne often complained that America lacked literary subject matter equal to Europe's, which had inspired its Romantics. In his personal life and family history, however, Hawthorne did find a deep well of inspiration. Many critics have suggested that Hawthorne's central concern, the dark side of morality, was informed by a sense of guilt over the roles his ancestors had played in early America. He was a descendant of John Hawthorne, one of the infamous judges of the Salem witchcraft trials of 1692. His family had also participated in the persecution of the Quakers earlier in the 17th century.

3   His time at Bowdoin College in Maine (1821–1825) proved to have great significance in his life, for he formed lifelong political and literary friends there. Those years provided subject matter for his first novel, *Fanshawe*, which he published at his own expense in 1828. (Legend holds that the author, ashamed of the work, burned the unsold copies.) While Hawthorne did not believe that his writing had yet achieved eloquence, his experiences at Bowdoin brought him into companionship with such men as Henry Wadsworth Longfellow, Horatio Bridge, and Franklin Pierce, who would become the 14th president of the United States. After college, Hawthorne dabbled briefly in the transcendentalist movement, an experience that would give him a taste of communal living and inspire the setting for *The Blithedale Romance*, written in 1852. It was around this time that Hawthorne befriended and won the respect of Herman Melville, who would later dedicate *Moby-Dick* to him.

4   **A** Hawthorne next tried his hand at children's books: *Grandfather's Chair* (1841), *Famous Old People* (1841), *Liberty Tree* (1841), and *Biographical Stories for Children* (1842) were little known but critically acclaimed. **B** It was not until the publishing of his story of the victims of Puritan obsession and intolerance, *The Scarlet Letter*, that Hawthorne reached his greatest renown. **C** The book is credited with influencing Henry James's *The Portrait*

of a Lady, Kate Chopin's *The Awakening*, and William Faulkner's *As I Lay Dying.* **D** In Hawthorne's own words, "*The Scarlet Letter* is positively a hellfired story, into which I found it almost impossible to throw any cheering light."

5 *The House of the Seven Gables*, published the following year in 1851, was a farcical tale in which Hawthorne attempted to shine a redemptive light on some of the dark themes of *The Scarlet Letter*. Also based in Puritan New England, this book is considered a refutation of the notions of sin, the anguish wrought by guilt, and the lack of confession or forgiveness found in *The Scarlet Letter*. Rather, this light comedy has a theme of redemption* and features the Pynchon and Maule families overcoming sin and its consequences through renewal. In *The House of the Seven Gables*, Hawthorne conveys hope for the human cycle of sin, repentance, forgiveness, and restoration.

6 There is much legend attached to Hawthorne's life. Some reports characterize him as a brooding recluse who seldom went out. In fact, he was more social and urbane than is often assumed. Hawthorne married Sophia Amelia Peabody of Salem in 1842, and the couple settled in Concord, Massachusetts, in his mother's family home, referred to as the "Old Manse." When unable to provide for his family through his writing, he always took other work while continuing to write. Many of these positions were in government service, including an appointment from President Franklin Pierce, his old college friend, as consul in Liverpool, England. It was in Europe in 1860 that Hawthorne wrote his last novel, *The Marble Faun*, again taking up the subject of sin and guilt.

7 Hawthorne is considered the first American novelist to create dynamic characters with hidden motivations. Through symbolism, allegory, and character development, Hawthorne gave his readers psychological insight into the minds of the prideful, the secretive, and the guilty. In the process, he added to the respect given to American literature from the Old World.

redemption: the act of being saved from the power of evil and its consequences

1 The word mimicking in paragraph 1 is closest in meaning to

Ⓐ mocking.

Ⓑ ignoring.

Ⓒ disputing.

Ⓓ copying.

2 According to paragraph 2, Hawthorne published all of the following EXCEPT

Ⓐ poetry.

Ⓑ novels.

Ⓒ expository writing.

Ⓓ humorous works.

3 Which of the following sentences most closely expresses the essential information in the highlighted sentence in paragraph 2?

 (A) Hawthorne's obsession with morality and sin certainly came from a sense of guilt over his family's ignoble history.

 (B) Many critics believe that Hawthorne learned about issues of sin and morality from his ancestors, who played a prominent role in New England history.

 (C) For some scholars, the guilt Hawthorne felt over the role his ancestors played in some of the darker chapters in American history explains the author's focus on sin and morality.

 (D) Numerous critics have argued that Hawthorne's central concern with his ancestors' shameful deeds comes from the writer's deeply conflicted moralistic nature.

4 It can be inferred from paragraph 3 that Herman Melville was a

 (A) famous politician.

 (B) writer.

 (C) transcendentalist.

 (D) professor.

5 The word renown in paragraph 4 is closest in meaning to

 (A) fame.

 (B) respect.

 (C) knowledge.

 (D) wealth.

6 In paragraph 4 of the passage, there is a missing sentence. Look at the four letters (**A**, **B**, **C**, and **D**) in paragraph 4 that show where the following sentence could be added.

The title of the book refers to the letter A, a shameful symbol that women accused of adultery were forced to wear in Puritan New England.

Where would the sentence best fit? Choose the letter for the place where the sentence should be added.

 (A) Option A

 (B) Option B

 (C) Option C

 (D) Option D

7   According to paragraph 5, which novel of Hawthorne's is noted for its comparatively lighthearted tone?

Ⓐ *The Scarlet Letter*

Ⓑ *Biographical Stories for Children*

Ⓒ *The House of the Seven Gables*

Ⓓ *Fanshawe*

8   Contrary to what might be assumed about his personality, according to paragraph 6, which of these best describes Hawthorne?

Ⓐ Someone who rarely went out

Ⓑ Engaged in society and sophisticated activities

Ⓒ Involved in local and international politics

Ⓓ Someone fond of parties

9   It can be inferred from paragraph 6 that Hawthorne's writing

Ⓐ made him very wealthy.

Ⓑ did not make him rich.

Ⓒ was his sole source of income.

Ⓓ earned him almost no money in his lifetime.

10 **Directions:** Find the phrases in the answer choices list that relate to the Hawthorne novel listed. Write your answers in the appropriate place. TWO of the answer choices will NOT match either category. *This question is worth 4 points.*

Answer Choices	*The Scarlet Letter*
A. Puritan morality without redemption	
B. Hope for the human condition	
C. Hawthorne's most famous work	
D. Published in 1842	*The House of the Seven Gables*
E. The Pynchon and Maule families	
F. Marital infidelity	
G. Dark themes lightened with humor	
H. Influenced other well-known authors	
I. Little known but critically acclaimed	

Passage 2

The Biological Effects of Ionizing Radiation

1   Energy transported by electromagnetic waves or by atomic particles is called radiation*. Our bodies are continuously bombarded with radiation from many directions. Radiation sources include: infrared, ultraviolet, and visible radiation from the sun; radio waves from radio and television stations; microwaves from microwave ovens; and x-rays from various medical procedures. In addition, natural and man-made radioactive materials are present in the soil and in many building materials.

2   When radiation is absorbed by biological systems, a number of things may happen. Electrons in the material may remain in the parent atom but be promoted to higher energy states. Molecules absorbing this radiation may increase their vibration, also called their rotation energies. Another possibility is that the radiation carries enough energy to break chemical bonds and remove an electron from the parent atom or molecule, forming an ion. This process is called ionization. In general, radiation that causes ionization (ionizing radiation) is far more harmful to biological systems than radiation that does not cause ionization (nonionizing radiation). Ionizing radiation cannot be detected with any of the five senses.

3   Most living tissue contains at least 70 percent water by mass. The chemistry of radiation is primarily due to the effects of ionizing radiation on water. It is common to define ionizing radiation as radiation that can ionize water, a process requiring a minimum energy of 1,216 kilojoules per mole (18 grams) of water. Most alpha, beta, and gamma rays (as well as higher-energy ultraviolet rays) possess sufficient energies to ionize water. As ionizing radiation passes through living tissue, it removes electrons and forms highly reactive H_2O+ ions. These charged ions can react with other water molecules to form H_3O+ ions and a neutral but highly unstable and reactive OH (oxygen-hydrogen) molecule. This OH molecule is an example of a free radical, a substance with one or more unpaired electrons. In cells and tissues, free radicals can attack various biomolecules to form other free radicals, which, in turn, can attack other compounds. Thus, formation of a single free radical can initiate a large number of chemical reactions that are ultimately able to disrupt the normal operation of cells.

4   **A** The damage to cells produced by radiation depends on the length of time that the body is exposed and the energy of the radiation. **B** Biological effects are also influenced by the type of radiation and the location of the radiation in relation to the body. **C** The primary types of ionizing radiation—alpha particles, beta particles, and gamma rays—are most commonly found in radioactive and medical waste and certain natural elements, including uranium. **D**

5   Gamma rays are particularly harmful because they penetrate human tissue very easily. Consequently, the damage that they cause is not limited to the skin. The skin surface usually acts as a barrier to radiation from outside the body and stops most alpha particles. Beta particles are only able to penetrate about one centimeter beneath the skin surface. Hence, alpha and beta particles are not as dangerous as gamma rays unless the radiation source somehow enters the body. Ingestion of certain radioactive substances such as radon or plutonium can be very dangerous because these

substances' chemical nature causes them to concentrate in the body organs or the bones and produce intense localized damage to the surrounding tissue.

6   In general, the tissues that show the greatest damage from radiation are those that reproduce rapidly, such as bone marrow, blood-forming tissues, and lymph nodes. The principal damaging effect of extended exposure to low doses of ionizing radiation is an onset of cancer, which is an uncontrolled reproduction of cells due to damage to the cells' growth-regulation mechanism. Leukemia, characterized by excessive growth of white blood cells, is one of the major cancer problems associated with radiation.

radiation: a type of energy radiated or transmitted in the form of rays, waves, or particles

11   The words bombarded with in paragraph 1 are closest in meaning to

A   shocked by.

B   hit with.

C   invaded by.

D   filled with.

12   According to paragraph 2, all of the following are true about ionizing radiation EXCEPT

A   it can sometimes be smelled.

B   it is more dangerous than non-ionizing radiation.

C   it can result in the production of free radicals.

D   it can cause cancer.

13   The author discusses ionizing radiation in paragraph 3 in order to

A   explain its effects in comparison to non-ionizing radiation.

B   provide a scientific description of the process.

C   give examples of its negative health consequences.

D   emphasize the role water plays in its creation.

14   Based on information in paragraph 3, which of the following best explains the term free radical?

A   A potentially harmful molecule that is a by-product of radiation

B   A charged atom that reproduces biomolecules rapidly

C   An H3O+ ion formed as a consequence of ionizing radiation

D   A neutral but highly stable and reactive molecule

15 Which of the following sentences most closely expresses the essential information in the highlighted sentence in paragraph 3?

(A) Just one free radical can thus be the impetus for a chemical process that may eventually lead to cellular damage.

(B) In this way, a single free radical will ultimately disrupt the chemical structure and normal behavior of cells.

(C) Nevertheless, the normal operation of cells can, in time, be negatively affected due to the chemical process that one free radical can begin.

(D) Hence, free radicals can eventually disturb the normal activity of cells, unless the radiation victim is given chemical treatment.

16 There is a sentence missing from paragraph 4. Look at the four letters (**A**, **B**, **C**, and **D**) in the passage that show where the following sentence could be added.

X-rays, another potential source of ionizing radiation, are emitted by medical scanning devices, and, in much smaller quantities, by the cathode tubes in television screens and computer monitors.

Where would the sentence best fit? Choose the letter for the place where the sentence should be added.

(A) Option A

(B) Option B

(C) Option C

(D) Option D

17 The word penetrate in paragraph 5 is closest in meaning to

(A) scar.

(B) impale.

(C) puncture.

(D) enter.

18 According to paragraph 5, which source of ionizing radiation is potentially harmful, even in small doses?

(A) The sun

(B) Building materials

(C) Radon

(D) Radio waves

19 According to paragraph 6, what is the main reason that ionizing radiation is considered particularly dangerous?

Ⓐ It cannot be detected by the five senses.

Ⓑ It can lead to uncontrolled cell reproduction.

Ⓒ It increases cell rotation energy.

Ⓓ It can penetrate the skin and damage organs.

20 **Directions:** Below is an introductory sentence for a short summary of the passage. Complete the summary by choosing the THREE answer choices that express key ideas in the passage. Sentences that express ideas that are NOT in the passage or mention minor details do NOT belong in the summary. *This question is worth 2 points.*

Though we are surrounded by many forms of radiation, it is ionizing radiation that poses the greatest health risks.

Answer Choices	
A. The ionization of water produces free radicals that can destroy the normal operation of cells.	D. The harm caused by ionizing radiation depends on the nature of the exposure and the type of radiation.
B. Ionized water molecules can produce H3O+ ions and OH molecules, which are known as free radicals.	E. Although ionizing radiation is present in small quantities in everyday life, if not ingested, its potential for harm is negligible.
C. The primary adverse effect of extended exposure to ionizing radiation is cancer.	F. The most harmful rays can penetrate matter easily, including human tissue.

Passage 3
The Social Cognitive Theory of Learning

1   Learning is an important aspect of virtually all areas of life. From infancy through old age people must learn to talk, read, play, work, and get along socially in society. Due to its pervasive nature, learning has long been a topic of intense study within psychology. While psychologists tend to agree that learning plays a vital role in human functioning, they have developed very different perspectives, or theories, on its causes, processes, and consequences.

2   The learning theories that dominated the first half of the 20th century came predominantly from the behavioral school of psychology. Behaviorists view learning as a function of environmental factors that promote associations between stimuli and responses. Drawing on the animal experiments of Pavlov, who showed how dogs could learn to associate the sound of a bell with food, early behaviorists saw learning as a product of conditioning—that is—the repeated performance of an act, usually in the interest of some external reward. From the behavioral perspective, learning is essentially the repetition of externally reinforced behaviors.

3   Alfred Bandura began his research on observational learning in the early 1960s as a reaction to the behaviorist viewpoint on learning. The early research findings of Bandura and his colleagues challenged the prevailing view of learning by demonstrating that it is not necessary to perform a behavior in order to learn the behavior and that reinforcement·is not a necessary component of learning. Social cognitive theory was developed by Bandura in order to provide a comprehensive explanation of observational learning.

4   Bandura's social cognitive theory is based on the assumption that the majority of learning done by humans occurs within a social environment. Modeling is a major construct of the theory and refers to the fact that people learn by observing the behavior of others and the response that the behaviors elicit from those around them. When people observe the consequences of modeled behaviors, they gain information regarding the appropriateness of these behaviors. Research on modeling has been used to explain how people learn a variety of skills, beliefs, strategies, and knowledge.

5   The three functions of modeling proposed by Bandura's social cognitive theory are response facilitation, inhibition/disinhibition, and observational learning. Response facilitation involves the modeling of socially acceptable behavior. The modeled behavior tends to include social prompts that motivate the observer to perform the modeled behavior. Inhibition/disinhibition involves the modeling of socially unacceptable behavior. During inhibition, the model receives punishment as a consequence for performing a prohibited behavior and the observer is discouraged from performing the behavior. On the other hand, during disinhibition the prohibited behavior being modeled does not result in a negative consequence for the model, and the observer is encouraged to perform the unacceptable behavior. Observational learning occurs when an observer performs a new behavior that they would not have performed prior to observing the behavior modeled.

6   The four sub processes involved in observational learning are attention, retention, production, and motivation. In order for observational learning to occur, a person must be exposed to the behaviors of models within their daily lives and be capable of and willing to pay attention to these behaviors. **A** The specific characteristics of the model will influence how effective a model is at attracting attention. **B** People tend to attend to models that they regard as similar to themselves, models that they view as having power and status, and models that they view as kind and nurturing. **C** Features of the task being modeled are another variable that influences attention. **D** Thus, teachers will often use bright colors, music, or odd shapes to encourage children to attend to their lessons.

7   Once the behavior of a model is observed, the input received must be cognitively processed and retained in the form of a general rule. This general rule undergoes constant revision based on future observations of others as well as the input received from others regarding the performer's behavior. Production occurs when the observer translates the modeled behavior into overt behavior and performs the new behavior. Another sub process, motivation, plays an important role in production; behaviors viewed as important, ethical, or advantageous to the observer are the ones most often produced.

8   Bandura's research marked the beginning of a movement toward a view of learning that emphasizes cognitive rather than behavioral processes. Social cognitive theory has become one of the major cognitive learning theories dominating the psychological field today.

21   Based on the information in paragraph 1, which of the following best defines the term theories?

(A) Sets of ideas that try to explain something about life or the world

(B) Experiments that scientists carry out to determine if their ideas are true or false

(C) Treatments that are intended to help people with learning disabilities

(D) Types of psychological therapy that have not been proven to be helpful

22   According to paragraph 2, which idea is associated with stimulus/response?

(A) Modeling

(B) Behaviourism

(C) Social cognitive theory

(D) Observational learning

23   Which of the following sentences most closely expresses the essential information in the highlighted sentence in paragraph 5?

(A) Likewise, disinhibition involves the encouragement of behavior that is not socially acceptable.

(B) Disinhibition, however, occurs when the model receives a negative reaction for performing an act of conformity.

(C) Conversely, through the process of disinhibition, a behavior that is not considered socially acceptable can be encouraged.

(D) At the same time, if an observer is rewarded for an illicit behavior, which is known as disinhibition, he/she will not necessarily learn the behavior.

24   According to the information in paragraph 5, all of the following are aspects of the modeling component of the social cognitive theory EXCEPT

(A) the promotion of actions that society approves of.

(B) the discouragement of actions that society frowns upon.

(C) the acquisition of new behaviors.

(D) the repeated performance of a behavior.

25 According to the information in paragraph 6, which is a necessary condition for observational learning to take place?

   (A) Learners must witness the model's behavior on a regular basis.
   (B) Learners must see the models as similar to themselves.
   (C) Learners must be rewarded for paying attention to the model.
   (D) Learners must regard the model as kind and nonthreatening.

26 There is a sentence missing from paragraph 6. Look at the four letters (**A**, **B**, **C**, and **D**) in paragraph 6 that show where the following sentence could be inserted.

   It is therefore not surprising that for children, parents are among the earliest and most important models.

   Where would the sentence best fit? Choose the letter for the place where this sentence should be added.

   (A) Option A
   (B) Option B
   (C) Option C
   (D) Option D

27 The author describes teachers' lessons in paragraph 6 in order to

   (A) demonstrate the production sub process of observational learning.
   (B) show how presentation can be used to promote attention.
   (C) provide an example of modeling a person with power or status.
   (D) refute the behavioral view of learning.

28 The word overt in paragraph 7 is closest in meaning to

   (A) noticeable.
   (B) prohibited.
   (C) cognitive.
   (D) proper.

29 According to paragraph 7, how does motivation influence the production of learned behavior?

- (A) Only behaviors considered of benefit to the model will be produced.
- (B) Behaviors will only be produced when the learner believes he/she will receive a physical reward.
- (C) Motivation plays a small role in determining what behaviors will be produced.
- (D) Observers are more likely to produce behaviors that satisfy personal goals or moral standards.

30 **Directions:** Below is an introductory sentence for a short summary of the passage. Complete the summary by choosing the THREE answer choices that express key ideas in the passage. Sentences that express ideas that are NOT in the passage or mention minor details do NOT belong in the summary. *This question is worth 2 points.*

Much research into the psychology of learning today is guided by social cognitive theory.

Answer Choices	
A. The social cognitive theory maintains that a great deal of human learning occurs through modeling, of which observational learning is an important part.	D. Early behavioral theory was based on the canine experiments of Pavlov, who found the ringing of a bell could be associated with food.
B. Alfred Bandura proposed the social cognitive theory based on research that found a great deal of learning occurs through observation.	E. The social cognitive theory arose in response to behaviorism, which emphasizes the primacy of behavior over thought in learning.
C. Teachers use bright colors and odd shapes in their lessons to promote attentiveness on the part of their students.	F. Disinhibition is the encouragement and adoption of behaviors that are not considered socially acceptable.

LISTENING SECTION

Directions: In this section of the test, you will hear dialogues and academic talks, and you will be tested on your ability to understand them. You will hear each dialogue and academic talk only once, and then answer some questions after each is finished. The questions ask about the main idea, supporting details, and the way the speakers use language. Answer each question based on what is stated or implied by the speakers. You cannot go back to a question once you have answered it. Answer every question in the order that it appears.

While you listen, you may take notes. You can then use your notes when answering questions.

You will see the following headphones icon next to some questions: 🎧 This icon indicates that you will hear part of the dialogue or academic talk repeated for the question.

You will be given 14 minutes to answer all the questions in this section. This does not include the time to listen to the dialogues and academic talks.

Dialogue 1

🎧 **Track 1**

Directions: Now use your notes to help you answer the questions.

1 Why does the student meet with the professor?

   Ⓐ To join him for lunch

   Ⓑ To ask for help with her homework

   Ⓒ To inquire about earning extra credit

   Ⓓ To discuss her grade on the 401 midterm

2 Does the professor normally accept extra credit projects?

   Ⓐ Yes, he understands that students sometimes blank under pressure.

   Ⓑ He sometimes does, but only if he develops the project ahead of time.

   Ⓒ He usually does if the project is related to the coursework.

   Ⓓ He usually doesn't, but may be open to a project that demonstrates the concept in depth.

3 Listen to part of the dialogue again, and then answer the question. Why does the professor say this?

   Ⓐ To encourage the student to explain what happened during the test

   Ⓑ To inquire where the student was during the midterm

   Ⓒ To indicate that he thought the test was difficult

   Ⓓ To demonstrate that he remembered the student's grade

4 What will the student do for extra credit?

  (A) Retake the exam

  (B) Retake the part of the exam she did poorly on

  (C) Write an explanation of why she did poorly on the test

  (D) Research concepts not covered in the book

5 What will the student probably do that afternoon?

  (A) She will meet the professor in his office to discuss the project.

  (B) She will work on her proposal for an extra credit assignment.

  (C) She will study for the part of the exam she will retake.

  (D) She will hand in a revision of her term paper.

Dialogue 2

Track 2

Directions: Now use your notes to help you answer the questions.

6 What is the professor referring to when he says WS?

  (A) The Women's Shelter

  (B) A Women's Seminar

  (C) Women's Studies

  (D) Women's Sociology

7 What else is required in addition to the coursework?

  (A) Completing an internship

  (B) Writing a term paper

  (C) Starting a community organization

  (D) Joining the National Organization for Women

8 What can be inferred about cross-disciplinary courses?

  (A) Students can take the same course many times in different departments.

  (B) Students can have the same professor for all their courses.

  (C) Students are permitted to skip some courses and still complete their major.

  (D) Students can take courses from different fields to complete their major.

9 Listen to part of the dialogue again, and then answer the question. What does the student's answer mean?

(A) She remembers the details of the requirements.

(B) She read the information too long ago to remember it.

(C) She already registered for all the courses she needs.

(D) She discussed the requirements with the professor months ago.

10 Why is the student looking forward to joining a women's organization?

(A) She wants to start her own organization.

(B) She hopes to bring some of her classmates to participate.

(C) She hopes to find a job by working there.

(D) She needs the money that she will receive from the organization.

Academic Talk 1: Art History

Track 3

Directions: Now use your notes to help you answer the questions.

11 What is the professor mainly discussing?

(A) The difference between public art and art in museums

(B) What famous critics have said about public art

(C) The characteristics of a work of public art

(D) Graffiti in the New York City subway system

12 Listen to part of the talk again, and then answer the question. Why does the professor say this:

(A) To encourage the student to expand on his answer

(B) To express uncertainty about the facts

(C) To emphasize how important museums are to the public

(D) To criticize the student's answer

13 What are two of the key elements that are shared by most works of public art?

Choose two answers.

A They are found in large cities.

B They are found in public places.

C They are controversial.

D They are on display for a short period of time.

14 Listen to part of the talk again, and then answer the question. What does the professor mean when she says this: 🎧

(A) The artists were unable to complete the project.

(B) The artists were unable to relocate the project.

(C) The project was on hold.

(D) The project dates had to be changed.

15 Listen to part of the talk again, and then answer the question.

How does the professor emphasize the fact that public art is considered controversial?

(A) By asking a series of questions

(B) By repeating the word "controversial"

(C) By citing how much money was spent on The Gates

(D) By reading the opinion of a well-known critic

16 Listen to part of the talk again, and then answer the question. What can be said about the professor?

(A) She assumes that the class has done the reading.

(B) She does not remember what the homework topic was.

(C) She expects to spend class time discussing the reading.

(D) She will not be asking about the topic again.

Academic Talk 2: Archaeology

🎧 **Track 4**

Directions: Now use your notes to help you answer the questions.

17 What is the talk mainly about?

(A) Animal mummies in ancient Egypt

(B) Egyptian beliefs about the afterlife

(C) The treatment of organs in mummification

(D) The process of making mummies

18 According to the talk, what did the Egyptians consider the most important organ?

(A) The brain

(B) The spleen

(C) The heart

(D) The lungs

19 According to the talk, which of the following can be inferred about Egyptian society?

    (A) All Egyptians mummified their animals.

    (B) Rich and poor were given the same advantages.

    (C) A definite class structure was in place.

    (D) Egyptians worshipped rich people.

20 Listen to part of the talk again, and then answer the question. Why does the professor say this: 🎧

    (A) To show how little some people think about their brains

    (B) To emphasize the importance of the brain

    (C) To make a connection between movies and real life

    (D) To introduce a famous experiment involving the brain

21 Listen to part of the talk again, and then answer the question. Why does the professor say this: 🎧

    (A) He thinks some students will think this information is unpleasant.

    (B) He knows this is a large amount of information to cover in one day.

    (C) He wants the students to ask questions about embalming.

    (D) He believes some of the students will find the information funny.

22 In the lecture, the professor describes the steps for mummification. Indicate whether each of the following is a step in this process.

	Yes	No
A. Removing the brain		
B. Wrapping all organs together		
C. Sealing cuts with cloth		
D. Massaging the body with oils		
E. Bandaging the body with linen		

Academic Talk 3: Literature

🎧 **Track 5**

Directions: Now use your notes to help you answer the questions.

23 What is the lecture mainly about?

    (A) The works of Edgar Allan Poe

    (B) Effective literary devices

    (C) The importance of reading a work more than once

    (D) Common types of symbolism

24 Why does the professor talk about symbolism?

   (A) To introduce the concept of implied meaning

   (B) To compare it to point of view

   (C) To explain the qualities of a good poem

   (D) To give an example of a literary device that is often misunderstood

25 According to the professor, how do symbolism and foreshadowing differ?

   (A) Symbolism is easier to see than foreshadowing.

   (B) Symbolism is harder to use than foreshadowing.

   (C) Symbolism is less effective than foreshadowing.

   (D) Symbolism makes a work more difficult to read than foreshadowing.

26 Listen to part of the talk again, and then answer the question. What does the professor imply?

   (A) It is not always necessary for the reader to understand everything to enjoy a work of literature.

   (B) By reading widely, it is possible to become more skilled at finding hidden references in literature.

   (C) It is much better for an author not to reveal too much to the reader in the early stages of a work.

   (D) Works often require more than one reading for full understanding.

27 What does the professor say about the work *A Jury of Her Peers*?

   (A) It uses foreshadowing more extensively than a play does.

   (B) It demonstrates that authors can create several different effects from one idea.

   (C) The title makes the author's use of foreshadowing more explicit.

   (D) The students should become familiar with the work.

28 Listen to part of the talk again, and then answer the question. What can be inferred from the professor's statement?

   (A) Poe used foreshadowing better than his contemporaries did.

   (B) Many authors use foreshadowing successfully.

   (C) Poe created the device known as foreshadowing.

   (D) Other authors have learned from Poe's example.

SPEAKING SECTION

Directions: In this section, you will be asked to respond to a variety of tasks and topics. There are four tasks. Respond to each task as completely as you can, always speaking clearly.

For task 1, you will speak about a topic that is familiar to you. Your response will be graded on your ability to speak about the topic clearly.

For tasks 2 and 3, you will be asked to read a short text. The text will then go off the screen and you will hear a talk or dialogue on the same topic. For each task, you will be asked a question about what you have read and heard. You will need to use information from the text and the talk to answer the questions. Your responses will be graded on your ability to speak clearly and accurately about what you have read and heard.

For task 4, you will hear part of an academic talk. You will then answer a question about what you have heard. Your response will be graded on your ability to speak clearly and accurately about what you have heard.

You are allowed to take notes during the reading and listening. You are allowed to use your notes to help you respond. Listen closely to the directions for each task.

For each task, you will be given a short time to prepare your response. You will be given a certain amount of time to speak. Use a watch or clock to time yourself.

Task 1

Directions: For this task, you will give your opinion about a topic that is familiar to you. You will hear a question. You will then have 15 seconds to prepare your response and 45 seconds to speak.

🎧 **Track 6**

It is better to study for exams alone rather than with a group of friends. Do you agree or disagree with the statement? Give details and examples in your explanation.

> 15 seconds to prepare
> 45 seconds to speak

Task 2

Directions: For this task, you will read a short text and then listen to a dialogue about the same topic. You will hear a question about what you have read and heard. You will then have 30 seconds to prepare your response and 60 seconds to speak.

City University has hired a new president. Read the announcement from the board of trustees. You have 45 seconds to read the passage. Begin reading now.

An Announcement from the Board of Trustees

The Board of Trustees is pleased to announce that the university has selected Victor C. Mullins to be the university's 25th president. Mullins will succeed Dr. James White, who announced his retirement in July.

Victor Mullins comes to City University after having served 16 years in the United States Senate. Prior to becoming a senator, he worked in his family's real estate business.

In a statement released yesterday, the Board of Trustees cited Mullins's "extensive administrative and financial experience" as the primary reason for selecting him to head the institution.

🎧 Track 7

The woman expresses her opinion of a recent decision made by the university. State her opinion and explain the reasons she gives for holding that opinion.

> 30 seconds to prepare
> 60 seconds to speak

Task 3

Directions: For this task, you will read a short text and then hear a talk about the same topic. You will hear a question about what you have read and heard. After you hear the question, you will have 30 seconds to prepare your response and 60 seconds to speak.

Now read the passage about the Bretton Woods conference. You have 45 seconds to read the passage. Begin reading now.

A Meeting at Bretton Woods

In July 1944, the leaders of 44 nations gathered in a small New England town to set the rules for monetary relations between the major industrialized powers. The most influential countries at Bretton Woods, led by the United States, were united in the belief that a strong international economic system would lead to economic security, which would, in turn, help ensure peace.

As part of their effort to achieve economic stability, the nations gathered at Bretton Woods agreed to maintain fixed exchange rates for their currencies, anchored by the United States' guarantee to redeem international dollar holdings at the rate of $35 per ounce of gold. The Bretton Woods system remained in place relatively unchanged until the early 1970s.

🎧 Track 8

The professor talked about the end of the Bretton Woods system. Explain what the purpose of the Bretton Woods system was and how and why it ended. Give details and examples to support your answer.

> 30 seconds to prepare
> 60 seconds to speak

Task 4

Directions: For this task, you will hear a short academic talk. You will hear a question about it. You will then have 20 seconds to prepare your response and 60 seconds to speak.

🎧 **Track 9**

Using points and examples from the talk, explain how a price war between two competing retail stores reflects the principles of game theory.

20 seconds to prepare
60 seconds to speak

WRITING SECTION

Directions: You will need your headphones for this section.

This section is designed to measure your ability to write in English. There are two tasks.

For the first task, you will read a short text and listen to an academic talk. You will answer a question about what you have read and heard. For the second task, you will use your knowledge and experience to answer a question.

Task 1

Directions: For this task, you will have 3 minutes to read a short text. You may take notes if you wish. Then you will hear an academic talk on the same topic. You may take notes while you listen.

You will then read a question that asks about the relationship between the text and the talk. You will have 20 minutes to write a response. Using information from the text and talk, answer the question as completely as you can. You will **not** be asked to give your opinion. You will be able to review the text while you write. You may use your notes to help you write your response.

You should try to write 150 words or more. Your response will be graded on the quality, completeness, and accuracy of your writing. If you finish early, you may move on to the second task.

You now have 3 minutes to read the passage. After you read the passage, listen to the talk.

The movement against plastic bags is gaining support in many countries. However, there are multiple benefits to plastic bags that legislators are both overlooking and underestimating. Careful consideration of these benefits is crucial for ensuring that consumers are equipped to make educated decisions.

First, plastic bag manufacturing and disposal actually has a lower environmental impact than many alternative bags offered at our supermarkets. Cotton tote bags, a popular alternative to plastic bags, would have to be used thousands of times in order to compensate for the environmental impact of their production. Additionally, washing them requires water, and the chemicals found in most detergents have the potential to pollute waterways. Paper bags actually take up more space in landfills than plastic bags do, and they are less convenient, as they cannot be repurposed for other household needs, like lining trash bins.

In addition to this, the plastic industry is always evolving. Manufacturers are responding to consumer demand for alternatives by creating a variety of plant-based and alternative plastics. These substitutes for traditional plastic bags are more environmentally friendly while still providing all of the same benefits.

The final consideration is that plastic bags can easily be recycled. Most grocery stores provide receptacles in which used plastic bags can be collected and taken to special recycling facilities that are equipped to process them. These bags are then turned into new bags or even other useful plastic items, like bottles and boxes.

Track 10

Summarize the points made in the lecture you just heard, explaining how they cast doubt on points made in the reading.

Task 2

For this task, you will be asked to write an essay in which you state, explain, and support your opinion on an issue. You will have 30 minutes to complete your essay.

You should try to write 300 words or more. Your essay will be graded on how well you use language, organize your essay, and develop your ideas.

Do you agree or disagree with the following statement?

> People have a healthier lifestyle when they live in the countryside than in the city.

Use specific reasons to support your answer.

Practice Test 2

TEST DIRECTIONS

This test is designed to measure your ability to understand and use English in an academic context. The test has four sections.

In the **Reading** section, you will read three passages and answer questions about them.

In the **Listening** section, you will listen to two dialogues and three talks and answer questions about them.

In the **Speaking** section, there are four tasks. The first task asks you to speak based on your own personal experience. In the other three, you will read passages and/or listen to dialogues and talks, then speak based on what you have read and/or heard.

In the **Writing** section, there are two tasks. In the first task, you will read a passage, listen to a talk, then write based on what you have read and heard. The second task asks you to write based on your own personal experience and ideas.

There is a 10-minute break after the **Listening** section.

At the beginning of each section, there are directions that explain how to answer the questions or respond to the tasks in the section.

In the **Reading** and **Listening** sections, you should work carefully but quickly. You should try to answer every question to the best of your ability. Make an educated guess on questions that you are unsure of. In the **Speaking** and **Writing** sections, each task is separately timed. In each case, you should try to respond to the task as completely as possible in the given time.

READING SECTION

Directions: In this section of the test, you will read three passages. You will be tested on your ability to understand them by answering several questions on each passage.

While you read, you may take notes. You can then use your notes when answering questions.

Most questions are worth 1 point. Questions that are worth more than 1 point have a special note telling you how many total points they are worth.

You will have 54 minutes to read the three passages and answer all the questions. If you finish the questions before 54 minutes is up, you can go back and review your work in this section.

Passage 1

How Satellites Have Revolutionized Communication

1 A satellite is any object that orbits a celestial body. The moon is considered to be the earth's largest natural satellite. Artificial satellites at one time were perceived as top-secret devices used by spies, military agents, and science fiction characters. But today, there are many practical uses for modern satellites, including weather forecasting, television transmission, global positioning systems (GPS), astronomy, and accurate mapping of the earth.

2 Prior to the advent of satellites, electronic communication was primarily accomplished via wires and cables strung between high towers and run underground. Science fiction writer Arthur C. Clarke was the first to envision using man-made satellites as communication devices. In an article released in a 1945 edition of *Wireless World* magazine, he described a worldwide coverage network using three satellites placed 120 degrees apart in Earth's orbit. Of course, Clarke's vision wasn't entirely science fiction. Today's technology allows communication to occur regularly between all parts of the world via wireless satellite transmissions.

3 Most satellites fall into one of two orbital categories, GEO or non-GEO. Satellites in a GEO (Geostationary Earth Orbit) maintain 24-hour synchronization with the earth's orbit and appear in a fixed spot above the earth at all times. These satellites orbit higher than 22,000 miles (36,000 km), cover entire hemispheres at once, and are generally used for weather forecasting and communications. Non-GEO satellites generally travel lower than the GEO satellites and have an asynchronous orbit, meaning they move independently of the earth's orbit. As a result, at various times they can be seen passing overhead as they move across the sky. Non-GEO satellites have a shorter range and footprint area and are generally used for observation, photography, scientific studies, and navigation.

4 On October 4, 1957, under extreme secrecy, the Soviets launched the *Sputnik 1* satellite into orbit. It was a very simple 184-pound ball that only lasted 92 days before burning up in the earth's atmosphere. The apparent superiority of the Soviet space program both embarrassed and frightened U.S. citizens. The event fueled America's race to space, which led to the historical U.S. moon landing and the subsequent creation of the International Space Station.

5 Satellites are used for various aspects of everyday life, from live cable news coverage to military intelligence monitoring. The military uses satellites to track enemy movement, monitor nuclear activity, provide early warnings of missile launching, and photograph

inaccessible areas of foreign lands. Scientists have been able to use satellite technology to study global warming, monitor plants and animals, and—by putting observational satellites in orbit, like the Hubble Space Telescope—open windows to the universe. A network of Global Positioning System (GPS) satellites is used to determine exact locations of cars, planes, trains, ships, and humans. Right now, there isn't very much of the earth's soil that isn't monitored by thousands of orbiting satellites.

6   Satellite technology has made the world a much smaller and, arguably, a safer place to live. Through satellite tracking, meteorologists can provide early warnings about large storms or tornados, which saves hundreds of lives every year. **A** Knowing when and where a missile may be launched helps the military warn civilians of impending danger and enables soldiers to destroy the missile before it reaches its intended target. **B** What once took days or weeks of travel—for example, a face-to-face conversation with a long-distance relative—can now be achieved in seconds with satellite communication technology. **C**

7   Satellites are even sent as probes to distant planets so we can explore our solar system and its complexity. **D** The galaxy is extremely large, and due to the current limitations of space travel technology, it is impossible to send manned missions to distant locations. Satellites act as human eyes and ears, monitoring distant planets for signs of life outside of Earth. If humans ever do find new life-forms in space, it is likely that satellites will establish our first contact. Unfortunately, this is still science fiction.

1   According to paragraph 2, how did Arthur C. Clarke play an important role in the development of artificial satellites?

   (A) He conceived of a global system of satellites used for communication.

   (B) He imagined the possibility of sending a satellite into orbit around the earth.

   (C) He published *Wireless World*, which elevated satellites above science fiction.

   (D) He was the first person to envision the development of artificial satellites.

2   The word envision in paragraph 2 is closest in meaning to

   (A) see.

   (B) imagine.

   (C) engineer.

   (D) propose.

3   According to paragraph 2, satellites are useful in the transmission of information mainly because

   (A) they do not rely on wires and cables strung between high towers.

   (B) they can receive and send data over large areas of the earth.

   (C) they can transmit information in an inefficient but affordable manner.

   (D) they can transmit data from the earth to distant parts of the universe.

4   According to the information in paragraph 3, GEO satellites differ from non-GEO satellites in all of the following ways EXCEPT

    (A) GEO satellites are further from the earth.

    (B) GEO satellites are more commonly used for scientific studies.

    (C) GEO satellites move along with the earth's orbit and appear stationary.

    (D) GEO satellites cover a larger geographic area of the earth.

5   The author discusses the Soviet space program in paragraph 4 in order to

    (A) show how it spurred innovation in the United States' own space program.

    (B) compare Soviet science education with that of the United States.

    (C) justify the premise that satellite technology need not be very sophisticated.

    (D) provide an example of a satellite that could only stay aloft for a short time.

6   According to paragraph 6, which of the following statements most accurately reflects the author's opinion about artificial satellites?

    (A) While satellites have served many useful purposes, their proliferation may pose problems in the future.

    (B) What is most valuable about satellites is their potential to discover other life-forms in the universe.

    (C) Satellites have greatly increased our knowledge of the world and our ability to communicate with each other.

    (D) Without satellites, long-distance communication and meteorological forecasting would be impossible.

7   The word impending in paragraph 6 is closest in meaning to

    (A) horrible.

    (B) military.

    (C) awaiting.

    (D) coming.

8 There is a sentence missing from paragraph 6 or 7. Look at the four letters (**A**, **B**, **C**, and **D**) in the passage that show where the following sentence could be inserted.

Moreover, satellites have enabled developing countries to make use of modern communication technologies without having to construct costly wire and cable infrastructures.

Where would the sentence best fit in the passage? Choose the letter for the place where this sentence should be added.

(A) Option A

(B) Option B

(C) Option C

(D) Option D

9 Which of the following sentences most closely expresses the essential information in the highlighted sentence in paragraph 7?

(A) For now, the galaxy's size and the inadequacy of technology prevents manned missions to remote parts of the galaxy.

(B) Because of the galaxy's size and mankind's present technological shortcomings, sending a satellite far into the galaxy is not possible.

(C) Since the galaxy is huge and our technology limited, it will be a while before we will be able to travel to faraway locations in the cosmos.

(D) The great size of the galaxy makes sending a human to distant parts of the universe technically very difficult.

10 **Directions:** Below is an introductory sentence for a short summary of the passage. Complete the summary by choosing the THREE answer choices that express key ideas in the passage. Sentences that express ideas that are NOT in the passage or mention minor details do NOT belong in the summary. *This question is worth 2 points.*

Satellites have revolutionized our ability to communicate with each other and observe our world, as well as worlds beyond.

Answer Choices	
A. Before the development of artificial satellites, the idea of long-distance communication without wires was only the stuff of science fiction.	D. Among the most important uses for satellites today are mass communi-cations, meteorological forecasting, and scientific study.
B. Arthur C. Clarke envisioned satellites long before we were technologically capable of sending them into space.	E. Scientists are confident that one day soon a satellite will discover other intelligent life-forms in outer space.
C. There are two kinds of satellites: GEO, which follow the earth's orbit, and non-GEO, which move independently of the earth's orbit.	F. In 1957, the Soviets launched *Sputnik*, a 184-pound ball that spent three months in space before burning up in the earth's atmosphere.

Passage 2

Women's Suffrage

1   Over the past 200 years, the fight for the right of women to vote, known as women's suffrage, has spanned the globe, encompassing multiple movements and including groups of women and men who fought against government-sanctioned circumscriptions on voting rights, based on gender, race, and class.

2   Which country was the first to grant women suffrage? In Sweden, women initially secured the right to vote in 1718, but this only covered members of city guilds who paid tax, not all women. This right was rescinded in 1772. When Corsica was declared a sovereign nation in 1755, its constitution included one of the earliest implementations of women's suffrage. However, this too was revoked in 1769 when the island was claimed by the French. Female inhabitants of the Pitcairn Islands, a British territory comprised of four islands in the South Pacific Ocean, were granted suffrage in 1838.

3   These women, originally descended from mutineers of the *HMS Bounty*, took this right with them when they resettled on Norfolk Island, now an Australian territory, in 1856. Their neighbor, New Zealand, was the first self-governing country in the world to grant women of all races the right to vote in parliamentary elections after ratification of the Electoral Act in September 1893. They were followed closely by South Australia, a self-governing British Colony in which women gained suffrage in 1895. This right was extended to a majority of women in the remaining Australian states in the years prior to World War I, although restrictions on voting rights for indigenous women were only completely abolished by the Commonwealth Electoral Act of 1962.

4   On the other side of the Pacific Ocean, seeds were planted in the mid 19th century for what would be a 70-year-long struggle in the United States to secure women's right to vote. Activists Lucretia Mott and Elizabeth Cady Stanton met at an anti-slavery convention held in London in 1840. Mott and Stanton, along with other female delegates from the U.S., were refused seats at the convention. This was the first in a series of incidents which motivated Mott and Stanton to establish a movement. As a result, they joined forces with a group of Christians, the Quakers, in Seneca Falls, New York, and organized the Seneca Falls Convention. This was the first women's rights convention, which took place over two days in 1848. Susan B. Anthony, an activist and social reformer, joined them in 1852, and in the 1860s she became a vocal advocate for working women in the sewing and print trades in New York, encouraging the formation of the Working Women's Association. Anthony also fought for equal pay for working women during her tenure as a delegate to the National Labor Conference in 1868. Early victories for women's suffrage came in the western territories of Utah and Wyoming in the late 1860s, although it wasn't until 1919 that the Senate approved the Nineteenth Amendment to the U.S. Constitution, which prohibited sex-based voting restrictions. Race-based voting restrictions, however, remained in place in the United States until passage of the Voting Rights Act of 1965.

5   The last western republic to grant women suffrage was Switzerland. Modern Switzerland's initial constitution was written in 1848 and established legal equality for all human beings. Unfortunately, it did not explicitly include women, meaning that multiple laws were devised that placed women in a legally inferior position in Swiss society.

6   The first feminist movements in Switzerland were organized in the 1860s, at the same time that women's suffrage in the United States was starting to be victorious. Meta von Salis, a Swiss feminist and historian, organized meetings in Switzerland's major cities on the theme of voting rights for women. Despite the fact that her efforts were generally met with hostility, when the first congress of Swiss women was held in Geneva in 1896, numerous male speakers called for cooperation between men and women, which brought even further attention to the cause.

7   Although the fight for Swiss women's suffrage continued into the beginning of the 20th century, it's progress was halted by the World Wars and their aftermath. A referendum on the issue was held in 1959, but 67% of Swiss men voted against it. Nevertheless, in some of the French-speaking member-states, called cantons, women did obtain the right to vote in local elections. After a second referendum in 1971, all Swiss women gained the right to vote in federal elections. The first female president of the Swiss Confederation, Micheline Calmy-Rey, was elected in 2007. She was the first of seven female presidents elected in Switzerland throughout the early 21st century.

11 The word circumscriptions in paragraph 1 is closest in meaning to

    (A) prejudices.

    (B) considerations.

    (C) restraints.

    (D) propensities.

12 In paragraph 1, the author mentions gender, race, and class in order to

    (A) give examples of groups that were discriminated against by government policies.

    (B) explain how most feminist movements were inclusive during the 19th and 20th centuries.

    (C) acknowledge the exclusion of some women from voting rights acts in various countries.

    (D) illustrate several factors that limited women's access to certain rights.

13 In paragraph 3, what does the author mention about voting rights for women?

    (A) Some countries did not grant all women the right to vote at the same time.

    (B) Men were often at the forefront of the fight for women's voting rights.

    (C) Women acted violently in their campaign to get the vote.

    (D) All women in Australia were granted the right to vote before World War One.

14 The word indigenous in paragraph 3 is closest in meaning to

    (A) local.

    (B) remote.

    (C) natural.

    (D) native.

15 According to paragraph 4, what incident was the initial catalyst for the women's suffrage movement in the United States?

    (A) The establishment of the Seneca Falls Convention

    (B) Women being refused seats at a convention in London

    (C) The formation of the Working Women's Association

    (D) Early victories in some Western states

16 All of the following are mentioned in paragraph 4 as a significant factor in the women's suffrage movement in the United States EXCEPT

(A) the labor movement.

(B) the support of men.

(C) discrimination in other countries.

(D) alliances with religious groups.

17 To what does the cause refer in paragraph 6?

(A) Cooperation between men and women

(B) The first congress of Swiss women

(C) Women's right to vote

(D) Reducing working hours

18 According to paragraph 7, what was the main reason for all Swiss women being able to vote?

(A) The outcome of the Second World War

(B) Local elections in French-speaking areas

(C) The election of a female president

(D) The results of a second referendum

19 It can be inferred from paragraph 7 that women's voting rights in Switzerland were

(A) aided by campaigns by women in the United States.

(B) attained quickly and easily.

(C) stopped by the government who disapproved of von Salis.

(D) delayed because of war.

20 Directions: An introductory sentence for a brief summary of the passage is provided below. Complete the summary by selecting the THREE answer choices that express the most important ideas in the passage. Some sentences are incorrect because they contain information that was not in the passage or they contain minor details. *This question is worth 2 points.*

The struggle for women's suffrage has a complex and circuitous history.

Answer Choices	
A. Some feminist movements occurred simultaneously in different parts of the world.	D. Switzerland was one of the last countries to grant women voting rights.
B. Many early victories for women's rights were reversed due to various social and political conflicts.	E. The first women's rights convention was held in upstate New York.
C. Women in the South Pacific were able to transfer their rights to another country.	F. Significant achievements for women's rights movements occurred in the late 19th and early 20th centuries.

Passage 3

The Incandescent Lightbulb

1   The active component of a "normal" lightbulb, properly referred to as an incandescent bulb, consists of a thin wire made of a hard metallic element, tungsten, housed inside a glass container. The tungsten wire is called the filament.

2   The basic idea behind these bulbs is simple. When the bulb is used, electricity flows through the filament, which is so thin that it offers considerable resistance to the flow of electricity, and this resistance turns electrical energy into heat. The heat produced is enough to make the filament emit light. The emission of visible light by any hot object is called incandescence. Some examples of incandescent objects are hot coals in a campfire or barbecue grill, the sun, and a red, glowing burner on an electric stove when the temperature is high. The higher the temperature of the incandescent object, the brighter the light that is given off.

3   To optimize the visible light emitted and the longevity of a filament, the material used for the filament must withstand high temperatures without melting or reacting. Many filament materials were evaluated in the attempt to create optimum visible-light emission and filament longevity. Early lightbulbs used filaments of carbon. However, a carbon filament will not last long at temperatures higher than 2,100°C before it vaporizes. At lower filament temperatures, a carbon-filament bulb gives off only dim light. The tungsten filament used in today's lightbulb does not melt because tungsten has a very high melting point (6,100°F, or 3,370°C). Because most of the air has been sucked out of a glass lightbulb, there is no oxygen to react with, or oxidize, the filament. Consequently, tungsten filaments last a comparatively long time.

4   Although tungsten filaments offer the best combination of high melting point and low vapor pressure of any known elemental filament material, they eventually fail because of evaporation. The heat causes the tungsten to slowly evaporate, thus narrowing the diameter of the filament. This increases the electrical resistance (due to the smaller cross-section of the wire) and causes the filament to heat up more, which in turn increases the evaporation rate even further. Eventually, the filament fails. The black on the inside of a burned-out lightbulb is tungsten vapor returned to solid form. Besides their limited life spans, incandescent lightbulbs also waste a lot of electricity. Heat is not light, so all of the energy consumed by resistance is wasted.

5   A fluorescent bulb, however, uses a completely different method to produce light. This bulb consists of a glass tube with an electrode at each end. Inside the tube is a gas containing argon and mercury vapor. As electricity flows through the tube, a stream of electrons flows through the gas from one electrode to the other. These electrons collide with the mercury atoms and raise them to a higher-energy, or "excited," state. As the mercury atoms move from the excited state back to the unexcited state, they emit this acquired energy in the form of packets of light—photons—in the ultraviolet region of the spectrum. These ultraviolet photons hit a phosphor coating on the inside of the tube and cause this phosphor to emit visible light, to "fluoresce," in other words. Since in a fluorescent bulb the emission of light is caused by electricity and not by heat, the bulb can be much cooler than an incandescent bulb. Since a fluorescent bulb is cooler, there is nothing to vaporize, and therefore the bulb lasts longer.

6   Since fluorescent bulbs produce less heat than incandescent bulbs do, they are much more efficient. **A** A fluorescent bulb produces between four and six times as much light per watt as an incandescent bulb does. **B** This is why a 15-watt fluorescent bulb and a 60-watt incandescent bulb produce the same amount of light. **C** Still, as efficient and economical as they may be, fluorescent bulbs have not supplanted incandescent ones. **D**

21   The word emit in paragraph 2 is closest in meaning to

   (A) cause.

   (B) give off.

   (C) circulate.

   (D) reflect.

22   Based on information in paragraph 2, which of the following best describes the term incandescence?

   (A) The light released by burning of heat-resistant material

   (B) The release of light as a consequence of heat

   (C) The heat produced by electricity as it flows through resistance

   (D) The generation of heat due to an increase in light intensity

23 Which of the following sentences most closely expresses the essential information in the highlighted sentence in paragraph 2?

Ⓐ The heat of the object is influenced by its brightness.

Ⓑ The object's brightness rises in proportion to its temperature.

Ⓒ The heat of the incandescent object corresponds to its dimness.

Ⓓ Raising the temperature of the object creates a warmer light.

24 The word withstand in paragraph 3 is closest in meaning to

Ⓐ produce.

Ⓑ uphold.

Ⓒ endure.

Ⓓ maintain.

25 According to paragraph 3, what is the main reason tungsten filaments were deemed superior to carbon ones?

Ⓐ tungsten never burns out.

Ⓑ carbon gives off a dimmer light.

Ⓒ tungsten is more resistant to heat.

Ⓓ carbon requires more energy to illuminate.

26 According to paragraph 5, what is the main difference between an incandescent bulb and a fluorescent bulb?

Ⓐ An incandescent bulb is housed in a glass container.

Ⓑ An incandescent bulb produces light more efficiently.

Ⓒ A fluorescent bulb produces light from electricity, not heat.

Ⓓ A fluorescent bulb produces light without generating heat.

27 Fluorescent bulbs are described in paragraph 5 in order to

Ⓐ contrast them to less efficient tungsten bulbs.

Ⓑ show how they are less efficient than incandescent bulbs.

Ⓒ provide an example of a more sophisticated incandescent bulb.

Ⓓ conclude that they are superior to incandescent bulbs.

28 There is a sentence missing from paragraph 6. Look at the four letters (**A**, **B**, **C**, and **D**) in paragraph 6 that show where the following sentence could be inserted.

Whether for sentimental or aesthetic reasons, tungsten-filament bulbs remain popular.

Where would the sentence best fit? Choose the letter for the place where this sentence should be added.

(A) Option A
(B) Option B
(C) Option C
(D) Option D

29 It can be inferred in paragraph 6 that incandescent bulbs today

(A) are preferred by consumers.
(B) produce inferior quality light.
(C) cost more than fluorescent bulbs.
(D) are becoming increasingly uncommon.

30 **Directions:** Find the phrases in the answer choices list that relate to the type of bulb listed. Write your answers in the appropriate place. TWO of the answer choices will NOT match either category. *This question is worth 3 points.*

Answer Choices	Incandescent bulbs
A. Have filaments	
B. Produce ultraviolet light	
C. Form photons	
D. Convert heat energy to light	**Fluorescent bulbs**
E. Use chemical reactions to generate light	
F. Are similar to the glowing of red-hot metal	
G. Generate light without electricity	
H. Use electrodes	
I. Are able to withstand very high temperatures	

LISTENING SECTION

Directions: In this section of the test, you will hear dialogues and academic talks, and you will be tested on your ability to understand them. You will hear each dialogue and academic talk only once, and then answer some questions after each is finished. The questions ask about the main idea, supporting details, and the way the speakers use language. Answer each question based on what is stated or implied by the speakers. You cannot go back to a question once you have answered it. Answer every question in the order that it appears.

While you listen, you may take notes. You can then use your notes when answering questions.

You will see the following headphones icon next to some questions: 🎧 This icon indicates that you will hear part of the dialogue or academic talk repeated for the question.

Most questions are worth 1 point. Questions that are worth more than 1 point have a special note telling you how many total points they are worth.

You will be given 14 minutes to answer all the questions in this section. This does not include the time to listen to the dialogues and academic talks.

Dialogue 1

 Track 11

Directions: Now use your notes to help you answer the questions.

1 How did the student learn about the peer advisement program?

    Ⓐ From a sign on the door

    Ⓑ From a flyer on campus

    Ⓒ From an open house

    Ⓓ From an email

2 Why should the student attend the open house?

    Ⓐ To meet her professors

    Ⓑ To earn a credit toward her degree

    Ⓒ To see where she would be working

    Ⓓ To get more information about the program

3 What can be inferred about the peer advisor?

    Ⓐ He is a transfer student.

    Ⓑ He is a licensed counselor.

    Ⓒ He is ready to leave the program.

    Ⓓ He is enthusiastic about the program

4 Listen to part of the dialogue again, and then answer the question. What does the peer advisor mean when he says this: 🎧

  Ⓐ He wants to know if the student would like a snack.

  Ⓑ He wants to offer some counseling to the student.

  Ⓒ He plans to summarize the program for the student.

  Ⓓ He does not know much about the program himself.

5 Listen to part of the dialogue again, and then answer the question. What does the student mean when she says this: 🎧

  Ⓐ She wonders if she might have to deal with serious cases.

  Ⓑ She thinks the courses will be too intense for her.

  Ⓒ She wants to know if the counselors also have weekend duties.

  Ⓓ She hopes she will meet many experienced counselors.

Dialogue 2

🎧 **Track 12**

Directions: Now use your notes to help you answer the questions.

6 Why does the manager think the student looks familiar?

  Ⓐ She has seen him in a restaurant many times.

  Ⓑ She had worked with him in the past.

  Ⓒ He frequently visits the bookstore.

  Ⓓ He brought her his résumé a few days earlier.

7 What can be inferred about the manager?

  Ⓐ She thinks the student is overqualified for the job.

  Ⓑ She does not feel like making dinner after working all day.

  Ⓒ She is unhappy about having to work late.

  Ⓓ She has to work at the cash registers during the busy time.

8 Why does the student offer to go home and get his résumé?

  Ⓐ He is afraid someone else will get the job.

  Ⓑ He knows the manager is too busy to see him now.

  Ⓒ He forgot to bring it with him and is sorry.

  Ⓓ He thinks the manager will eat at the diner later.

9 Listen to part of the dialogue again, and then answer the question. What does the manager mean when she says this: 🎧

(A) The store will also be very busy.

(B) The store staff will be tired from all the work.

(C) The bookstore will be messy because of renovation work.

(D) The customers will not know where the books will be.

10 Listen to part of the dialogue again, and then answer the question. Why is the student surprised?

(A) He cannot understand why students waste money buying unnecessary books.

(B) He cannot understand why students return books right after starting class.

(C) He thinks the manager must be mistaken about the timing.

(D) He thinks the store should not accept returns until later in the semester.

Academic Talk 1: Music

🎧 **Track 13**

Directions: Now use your notes to help you answer the questions.

11 What is the talk mainly about?

(A) How recorded music eventually came to replace live performances

(B) How recording techniques and music performance styles have changed

(C) How Edison's original concept of the phonograph had to change

(D) How classical music helped the phonograph industry to become profitable

12 Why does the professor talk about Edison's attempts to market the phonograph as a dictation machine?

(A) To explain why it took a long time for music recording to get established

(B) To criticize Edison and show that even great inventors can make mistakes

(C) To illustrate the relationship of big business to the success of inventions and demonstrate that without the support of business, the phonograph would never have developed

(D) To give an example of an invention that, over time, changed its function

13 Listen to part of the talk again, and then answer the question. What does the professor imply?

    Ⓐ It would be hard to hear classical music clearly in saloons and fairgrounds.

    Ⓑ The first recordings of Bach and Beethoven were surprisingly successful.

    Ⓒ Fairground and saloon owners wanted music of wide appeal.

    Ⓓ Fairground and saloon patrons had sophisticated musical taste.

14 What does the professor say about Caruso?

    Ⓐ He was one of the loudest singers ever.

    Ⓑ His performing style was introverted and refined.

    Ⓒ He began his career performing in fairgrounds and saloons.

    Ⓓ He helped to give the phonograph credibility.

15 What does the professor say about Edison and music?

    Ⓐ He enjoyed opera, coronet solos, and Caruso's performances.

    Ⓑ He was not very musical but did his best to learn more about it.

    Ⓒ He investigated the commercial potential of music systematically.

    Ⓓ He built up a very important archive of recordings of classical music.

16 According to the talk, which of the following are true of sound recording?

Choose three answers.

    A It was quickly accepted by classical musicians.

    B It has allowed musicians to become more self-critical.

    C It led to the spread of international styles in performing.

    D Studio and live performances are often very different.

    E There was a huge demand for music recordings at first.

Academic Talk 2: Film History

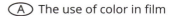 **Track 14**

Directions: Now use your notes to help you answer the questions.

17 What is the talk mainly about?

    Ⓐ The use of color in film

    Ⓑ Film as truth and art

    Ⓒ The impact of edited images

    Ⓓ Acting methods in film

18 What is the overall effect of combining images in a montage?

  (A) Combining multiple images can create new meanings for the viewer.

  (B) Using many images indicates the filmmaker's inability to tell a clear story.

  (C) Combining multiple images makes the viewer suspend judgment about content.

  (D) Combining many different images creates new color associations in the mind's eye.

19 Listen to part of the talk again, and then answer the question. What can be inferred from this comment by the professor: 🎧

  (A) Chemicals in the film work together to merge the images.

  (B) The images interact rapidly to create something new.

  (C) It is helpful if filmmakers are familiar with the science of color.

  (D) The images create a chemical reaction in the viewer's brain.

20 Listen to part of the talk again, and then answer the question. Why does the professor say this: 🎧

  (A) To express uncertainty about the judgment of the viewers

  (B) To prompt students to pay attention and answer the question

  (C) To introduce the definition of dialectical filmmaking

  (D) To suggest that what seems obvious is in fact the opposite

21 Listen to part of the talk again, and then answer the question. What does the professor mean when she says this: 🎧

  (A) She believes that watching films too often can hurt one's eyes.

  (B) She thinks that the brain functions as an eye, but sees colors differently.

  (C) She thinks the brain and the eye work together to create a new impression.

  (D) She means that the eye is not affected by contrasting colors.

22 Which of the following does the professor compare film to in the lecture?

Choose two answers.

  [A] Art

  [B] Arrogance

  [C] Sadness

  [D] Truth

Academic Talk 3: Physics

Track 15

Directions: Now use your notes to help you answer the questions.

23 What is the main topic of the lecture?

   (A) The role of physics in the development of batteries
   (B) The invention of the dry cell or flashlight battery
   (C) How to increase the power available from batteries
   (D) How batteries produce portable power

24 What does the professor imply?

   (A) Batteries are essential in spite of their high environmental cost.
   (B) Batteries will never be cost-effective for use in electric vehicles.
   (C) The convenience of batteries justifies their higher cost.
   (D) The cost of batteries needs to be reduced.

25 Listen to part of the talk again, and then answer the question. Why does the professor refer to givers and takers?

   (A) To make an abstract concept easier to understand
   (B) To find out if students have understood the lecture
   (C) To correct a misunderstanding
   (D) To summarize his conclusions so far

26 According to the professor, why is the dry cell battery better than earlier batteries?

   (A) It is easier to transport.
   (B) It uses less zinc.
   (C) It is cheaper to manufacture.
   (D) It is more powerful.

27 Why does the professor use the example of the water pipe?

- Ⓐ To introduce the work of James Watt
- Ⓑ To clarify the meaning of voltage and current
- Ⓒ To demonstrate that water can also provide power
- Ⓓ To show how current in a battery flows in only one direction

28 According to the lecture, which of the following are true of batteries?

Choose three answers.

- ☐A The only way to increase electrical power in a circuit is to connect several batteries.
- ☐B The electrolyte in a battery does not have to be a liquid.
- ☐C Power depends on both current and voltage.
- ☐D Three different materials are needed to create a battery.
- ☐E Batteries stop working because the electrolyte gets used up.

SPEAKING SECTION

Directions: In this section, you will be asked to respond to a variety of tasks and topics. There are four tasks. Respond to each task as completely as you can, always speaking clearly.

For task 1, you will speak about a topic that is familiar to you. Your response will be graded on your ability to speak about the topic clearly.

For tasks 2 and 3, you will be asked to read a short text. The text will then go off the screen and you will hear a dialogue or talk on the same topic. For each task, you will be asked a question about what you have read and heard. You will need to use information from the text and the talk to answer the questions. Your responses will be graded on your ability to speak clearly and accurately about what you have read and heard.

For task 4, you will hear part of an academic talk. You will then answer a question about what you have heard. Your response will be graded on your ability to speak clearly and accurately about what you have heard.

You are allowed to take notes during the reading and listening. You are allowed to use your notes to help you respond. Read the directions for each task closely.

For each task, you will be given a short time to prepare your response. You will be given a certain amount of time to speak. Use a watch or clock to time yourself.

Task 1

Directions: For this task, you will give your opinion about a topic that is familiar to you. You will hear a question. You will then have 15 seconds to prepare your response and 45 seconds to speak.

🎧 **Track 16**

Some people prefer to rent their home, while others prefer to buy a property. Which would you prefer and why? Include details and examples in your explanation.

15 seconds to prepare
45 seconds to speak

Task 2

Directions: For this task, you will read a short text and then listen to a dialogue about the same topic. You will hear a question about what you have read and heard. You will then have 30 seconds to prepare your response and 60 seconds to speak.

Eastern State University is planning to change its parking policy. Read the announcement about the change from the Department of Parking Management. You will have 45 seconds to read the announcement. Begin reading now.

An Announcement from the Department of Parking Management

Eastern State University has announced a new parking policy, which will go into effect in September 2023. This policy is intended to ensure that the very limited number of parking spaces available on campus are allocated as fairly as possible. Up to now, preference was given to faculty and staff and then to commuting students. Any remaining parking spaces were offered to students living on campus on the basis of seniority. Beginning with the coming academic year, the university will give out parking spaces by means of a lottery. Details about the lottery are available on the DPM website.

🎧 **Track 17**

The woman expresses her opinion about a new university policy. State her opinion and explain the reasons she gives for holding that opinion.

> 30 seconds to prepare
> 60 seconds to speak

Task 3

Directions: For this task, you will read a short text and then hear a talk about the same topic. You will hear a question about what you have read and heard. After you hear the question, you will then have 30 seconds to prepare your response and 60 seconds to speak.

Now read the passage about the British Corn Law. You have 45 seconds to read the passage. Begin reading now.

The Corn Law

While Great Britain fought the Napoleonic Wars with France from 1803 to 1815, it had not been possible for the English to import corn and other cereals from Europe. This led to higher bread prices and to more British landowners planting wheat. When the war with France ended in 1815, the landowners feared that cheaper imported grains would affect their profits. So Parliament, dominated by landowners, introduced legislation that became known as the Corn Law. The purpose of the law was to continue to regulate the importing of cereals and protect the profits of domestic farmers and landowners. The law stated that cereals could not be imported into Britain until the domestic price reached 80 shillings a quarter bushel. This meant that the cost of cereals and bread were kept artificially high.

🎧 **Track 18**

The professor discusses the Corn Law. Using information from the lecture and the reading, explain why the Corn Law was enacted and why some people opposed it.

> 30 seconds to prepare
> 60 seconds to speak

Task 4

Directions: For this task, you will hear a short academic talk. You will hear a question about it. You will then have 20 seconds to prepare your response and 60 seconds to speak.

🎧 **Track 19**

Using points and examples from the talk, explain how economic factors contributed to the Harlem Renaissance in New York City in the early 1900s.

> 20 seconds to prepare
> 60 seconds to speak

WRITING SECTION

Directions: You will need your headphones for this section.

This section is designed to measure your ability to write in English. There are two tasks.

For the first task, you will read a short text and listen to an academic talk. You will answer a question about what you have read and heard. For the second task, you will use your knowledge and experience to answer a question.

Task 1

Directions: For this task, you will have 3 minutes to read a short text. You may take notes if you wish. Then you will hear an academic talk on the same topic. You may take notes while you listen.

You will then read a question that asks about the relationship between the text and the talk. You will have 20 minutes to write a response. Using information from the text and talk, answer the question as completely as you can. You will not be asked to give your opinion. You will be able to review the text while you write. You may use your notes to help you write your response.

You should try to write 150 words or more. Your response will be graded on the quality, completeness, and accuracy of your writing. If you finish early, you may move on to the second task.

You now have 3 minutes to read the passage. After you read the passage, listen to the talk.

As dairy-free diets become increasingly trendy, it is important to examine the benefits of dairy and how dairy products can be incorporated into a healthy lifestyle.

First, dairy products are excellent sources of essential nutrients. Depending on the product, dairy offers, in varying degrees, calcium, protein, and vitamins A, D, and B12, as well as niacin and riboflavin. These nutrients support bone growth and density and promote muscle development. The protein found in dairy products provides sustained energy to the body naturally; and yogurt, a natural probiotic, enhances the functionality of the immune system and encourages healthy digestion.

Futhermore, despite the fact that many people say humans are not built to digest dairy products, evidence shows that milk has been a part of the human diet for thousands of years. When inhabitants of Northern Europe began transitioning from a nomadic to a more structured way of life, they discovered the many health benefits of fermented dairy products, like cheese and yogurt. The fermentation process that they developed encouraged bacteria to deplete the lactose carbohydrates in milk, which enabled people who could not digest lactose to enjoy the many benefits of dairy.

Finally, there is a range of organic dairy products available in stores that cater to consumers who prefer a more eco-friendly approach to grocery shopping. Organic international farming standards ensure animal welfare and sustainable farming practices. Therefore, organic dairy products come from cows that graze outdoors on a natural diet of grass. Their manure is often reused as natural fertilizer for crops, and the result is more delicious products that are better for both our bodies and for the environment.

🎧 **Track 20**

Summarize the main points in the lecture you just heard, explaining how they cast doubt on the points made in the reading.

Task 2

For this task, you will be asked to write an essay in which you state, explain, and support your opinion on an issue. You will have 30 minutes to complete your essay.

You should try to write 300 words or more. Your essay will be graded on how well you use language, organize your essay, and develop your ideas.

> In our modern world, there are too many cars in our cities. This has a negative effect on the air we breathe. What do you think is the best way to reduce the number of cars in cities?
>
> • Ban all cars from the center of the city
>
> • Reduce ticket prices on public transport
>
> • Encourage people to use bikes
>
> • Introduce congestion charges in the city center

Use specific reasons and examples to support your answer.

Practice Test 3

TEST DIRECTIONS

This test is designed to measure your ability to understand and use English in an academic context. The test has four sections.

In the **Reading** section, you will read three passages and answer questions about them.

In the **Listening** section, you will listen to two dialogues and three talks and answer questions about them.

In the **Speaking** section, there are four tasks. The first task asks you to speak based on your own personal experience. In the other three, you will read passages and/or listen to dialogues and talks, then speak based on what you have read and/or heard.

In the **Writing** section, there are two tasks. In the first task, you will read a passage, listen to a talk, then write based on what you have read and heard. The second task asks you to write based on your own personal experience and ideas.

There is a 10-minute break after the **Listening** section.

At the beginning of each section, there are directions that explain how to answer the questions or respond to the tasks in the section.

In the **Reading** and **Listening** sections, you should work carefully but quickly. You should try to answer every question to the best of your ability. Make an educated guess on questions that you are unsure of. In the **Speaking** and **Writing** sections, each task is separately timed. In each case, you should try to respond to the task as completely as possible in the given time.

READING SECTION

Directions: In this section of the test, you will read three passages. You will be tested on your ability to understand them by answering several questions on each passage.

While you read, you may take notes. You can then use your notes when answering questions.

Most questions are worth 1 point. Questions that are worth more than 1 point have a special note telling you how many total points they are worth.

You will have 54 minutes to read the three passages and answer all the questions. If you finish the questions before 54 minutes is up, you can go back and review your work in this section.

Passage 1

Acid Rain

1   Recently, the concentration of sulfur-containing compounds in the atmosphere has increased in urban and industrial environments. The problem originates with the burning of fossil fuels—such as coal, natural gas, and oil—in power plants for the purpose of making electricity. In the burning process, also called combustion, oxygen from the air combines with carbon and sulfur in the substance being burned to form gases called oxides. When sulfur is present in the fuel, reaction with oxygen produces sulfur dioxide (SO_2). In the United States, 80 percent of the sulfur dioxide in the atmosphere comes from power plants that burn coal or oil. The extent to which SO_2 emissions is a problem in the burning of coal and oil depends on the level of their sulfur concentrations.

2   In the atmosphere, SO_2 can be oxidized to sulfur trioxide (SO_3) by reaction with oxygen (O). When SO_3 dissolves in water, it produces sulfuric acid (H_2SO_4). Many of the environmental effects ascribed to SO_2 are actually due to the reaction product H_2SO_4. The sulfuric acid eventually returns to the ground by way of rain, snow, or fog; this phenomenon is known as acid rain.

3   Rainwater is naturally acidic and generally has a pH value in the range of 5 to 6. The term pH, which stands for potential of hydrogen, measures the acidity of a substance. The pH scale ranges from zero (the most acidic) to 14 (the most alkaline). A change of one unit on the pH scale represents a tenfold change in acidity. Living organisms generally thrive near pH 7, the neutral point, and function less successfully toward either end of the scale. When pH levels of rainwater drop below 5.6, the rainwater is considered acid rain.

4   The primary source of rainwater's natural acidity is carbon dioxide (CO_2), well known to us as the gas that we exhale. Carbon dioxide reacts with water to form carbonic acid (H_2CO_3). Acid rain, however, is more acidic than normal rainwater and typically has a pH of about 4. Its corrosive nature causes widespread damage to the environment and affects other parts of the ecological network.

5   In soil, acid rain dissolves and washes away useful nutrients needed by plants. This slows the plants' growth, especially that of affected trees. The acid rain also attacks trees by eating holes in the waxy coatings of their leaves and needles and leaving brown dead spots. If many such spots form, a tree loses some of its ability to make food through photosynthesis. Also, organisms that cause disease can infect the tree through its

injured leaves. Once weakened, trees are more vulnerable to other stresses, such as insect infestations, drought, and cold temperatures.

6   Acid rain can also release toxic substances that are naturally present in some soils, such as aluminum and mercury, freeing these toxins to pollute water or to poison plants that absorb them. In cities, acid pollutants accelerate natural wear on buildings and statues.

7   Water with a pH below 4.5 is unable to support wildlife. If one plant or animal population is adversely affected by acid rain, animals that feed on that organism may also suffer, and the entire ecosystem is likely to be affected. In the air, acids join with other chemicals to produce urban smog, which can irritate the lungs and make breathing difficult, especially for people who already have respiratory diseases.

8   Acid rain can best be curtailed by reducing the amount of sulfur dioxide released by power plants, vehicles, and factories. **A** The simplest ways to cut these emissions are to use less energy from fossil fuels and to lessen emissions of sulfur dioxide by switching to cleaner-burning fuels. **B** Using cleanable coals and low-sulfur fuels will enable electric-utility companies and other industrial businesses to lower their pollution emissions. **C** Auto-emission pollution can be reduced by using clean-burning fuels such as natural gas, which contains almost no sulfur and is being used more often in vehicles. **D**

9   Unfortunately, natural gas and the less-polluting coals tend to be more expensive, and this puts them out of the reach of poorer nations.

1   According to paragraph 1, what is the main source of acid rain-causing chemicals in the United States?

   Ⓐ Gasoline

   Ⓑ Coal

   Ⓒ Power plants

   Ⓓ Factories

2   Based on information in paragraph 2, which of the following best explains the term "acid rain"?

   Ⓐ Rain that contains excess sulfur trioxide

   Ⓑ Sulfur dioxide that is present in rain

   Ⓒ Rain that contains unhealthy levels of oxygen

   Ⓓ Rain that contains sulfuric acid

3   The word thrive in paragraph 3 is closest in meaning to

   Ⓐ do well.

   Ⓑ struggle.

   Ⓒ survive.

   Ⓓ give up.

4   Paragraph 3 discusses the potential of hydrogen (pH) scale in paragraph 3 in order to

  (A) show how acidity can be present at healthy or unhealthy levels.

  (B) describe the relationship of acidity to the composition of acid rain.

  (C) explain how the sulfur content of acid rain is measured on a scale.

  (D) illustrate the negative consequences of high acid-content rain.

5   According to paragraph 4, where does the acidity of normal rainwater come from?

  (A) Sulfur dioxide

  (B) A toxic gas in the atmosphere

  (C) Carbon dioxide

  (D) The breathing of humans

6   The word adversely in paragraph 7 is closest in meaning to

  (A) especially.

  (B) negatively.

  (C) fatally.

  (D) unusually.

7   The word curtailed in paragraph 8 is closest in meaning to

  (A) lessened.

  (B) solved.

  (C) exacerbated.

  (D) suspended.

8   According to paragraph 8, all of the following would most likely reduce the amount of acid rain-causing chemicals EXCEPT

  (A) converting car engines to run on electricity.

  (B) using more solar and wind power.

  (C) installing sulfur dioxide filters on power plants.

  (D) drilling for new sources of fossil fuels.

9 There is a sentence missing from paragraph 8. Look at the four letters (**A**, **B**, **C**, and **D**) that show where the following sentence could be inserted.

For instance, some coal contains sulfur in a form that can be washed out easily before the coal is burned.

Where would the sentence best fit in the passage? Choose the letter for the place where this sentence should be added.

- (A) Option A
- (B) Option B
- (C) Option C
- (D) Option D

10 Directions: Below is an introductory sentence for a short summary of the passage. Complete the summary by choosing the THREE answer choices that express key ideas in the passage. Sentences that express ideas that are NOT in the passage or mention minor details do NOT belong in the summary. *This question is worth 2 points.*

Acid rain is a serious environmental problem affecting industrialized countries.

Answer Choices	
A. People with respiratory problems are particularly vulnerable to the negative health effects of acid rain.	D. The most effective way of reducing acid rain is to cut back on the use of fossil fuels and to use cleaner fuel alternatives.
B. Acid rain is caused by the emission of sulfur dioxide, most of which comes from oil- and coal-fueled power plants.	E. Acid rain hurts trees by damaging their leaves, which impedes their ability to manufacture food through photosynthesis.
C. Acid rain washes away soil and slows plant growth due to absorption of toxic substances that are released.	F. Sulfur dioxide reacts with oxygen in the atmosphere to produce sulfuric acid, which falls to the earth in the form of precipitation.

Passage 2

Prohibition

1 Between 1920 and 1933, the sale, transportation, importation, and production of alcoholic beverages was banned in the United States. This era in the country's history, known as Prohibition, had complex repercussions and a significant impact on the social and economic well-being of the population.

2 Congress passed the Wartime Prohibition Act in 1918, a temporary ban on the sale of alcoholic beverages intended to save grain for the war effort. One year later, the Volstead—or National Prohibition—Act was passed, despite President Woodrow Wilson having vetoed the measure. This act legally defined "intoxicating liquors" and

the penalties for producing them. The result was the ratification of the Eighteenth Amendment to the U.S. Constitution, which established prohibition as a nationwide law. On January 17, 1920, the United States went dry. However, the federal government lacked the means to enforce the Volstead Act, which gave rise to multiple illegal enterprises.

3   Despite this, there is evidence to show that Prohibition did have a positive social impact. As there was a reduction in the amount of liquor consumed in the United States, alcohol-related health issues, arrests for public drunkenness, and admissions to state psychiatric facilities all fell significantly during this time. But the development of an organized black market meant that alcohol was still widely available. By 1925, anywhere from 30,000 to 100,000 speakeasy clubs were operating in New York City. These illegal clubs flourished during the Prohibition era. Also called "blind pigs" or "blind tigers," some of the earliest speakeasies offered customers the opportunity to consume alcohol, often under false pretenses. The operator of a saloon or bar would charge customers to see an attraction, such as an animal or a variety show, and then serve *complimentary* alcoholic beverages. The speakeasies that thrived during the 1920s and 30s initiated social changes in American culture including increased opportunities for women, who took advantage of the circumstances to start their own business. Speakeasies also encouraged the coming together of people of different races, giving everyone the chance to meet and socialize.

4   During this period of Prohibition, the production and sale of alcohol was still legal in four neighboring countries and as a result, breweries and distilleries in the Caribbean, Mexico, and Canada flourished. Their products were either consumed in vast quantities by American tourists or smuggled across borders into the United States. The Detroit Rover, which forms part of the border between Canada and the U.S., proved especially difficult for law enforcement to control. Industrial-scale smuggling took place across the U.S.-Canada border, with Canadian beer and whiskey flowing in large quantities into the United States, undermining support for Prohibition and creating insurmountable issues for authorities.

5   As well as smuggling alcohol into the U.S., the illegal production of alcohol within the country also took off. The term "bootlegging" is thought to have originated during the American Civil War, when soldiers snuck liquor into their camps in small flasks tucked into their boots beneath their trousers. During the Prohibition era in the 20th century, it came to refer to people making their own alcohol, which took place in many places including household bathtubs and factories. Home-distilled hard liquor, called bathtub gin in the North and moonshine in the South, became increasingly accessible. In the first six months of 1920, the federal government processed 7,291 violations of the Volstead Act. Over the next 13 years, violations continued to rise, as smuggling operations expanded and bootleggers continued to find loopholes and exploit them.

6   One such loophole was the production of dehydrated grape juice blocks, which was not illegal during Prohibition, despite the fact that if rehydrated and left to sit for a few weeks, they would ferment and turn into wine. This led to a fourfold increase in the production of grape juice blocks between 1920 and 1933. Bootleggers were able to hire chemists to return the substance to its original drinkable form. Another loophole was through the medical industry. After only six months of prohibition, over 15,000 doctors

and 57,000 pharmacists applied for and received licenses to prescribe and sell medicinal alcohol, which remained legal at the time. Over 11 million prescriptions a year were written for medicinal alcohol in the 1920s, and counterfeit prescriptions were easily forged across the nation.

7   Although the Eighteenth Amendment was repealed in 1933, to this day, there are numerous dry counties and townships in the United States that restrict or prohibit the sale of liquor.

11 The word repercussions in paragraph 1 is closest in meaning to

Ⓐ consequences.

Ⓑ restrictions.

Ⓒ advantages.

Ⓓ influences.

12 The word ratification in paragraph 2 is closest in meaning to

Ⓐ consideration.

Ⓑ authorization.

Ⓒ deliberation.

Ⓓ contention.

13 According to paragraph 2, why was law enforcement unable to control illegal activity during Prohibition?

Ⓐ The president did not support the Volstead Act.

Ⓑ The United States has multiple borders.

Ⓒ They lacked the resources to supervise the amount of crime taking place.

Ⓓ Entrepreneurs came up with new ways to make alcoholic beverages.

14 According to paragraph 3, which of the following was NOT a positive consequence of Prohibition?

Ⓐ A reduction in alcohol-related illness

Ⓑ The growth of the entertainment industry

Ⓒ The coming together of people of different races.

Ⓓ Opportunities for industrious women

15 To what do the circumstances refer in paragraph 3?

Ⓐ False pretenses

Ⓑ Arrests

Ⓒ Integration

Ⓓ Illegal operations

16 According to paragraph 5, where did people produce their own alcohol during Prohibition?

- Ⓐ In their bathroom
- Ⓑ In their backyard
- Ⓒ In the local park
- Ⓓ In their car

17 From information in paragraph 6, the following were illegal ways of obtaining alcohol EXCEPT

- Ⓐ home brewing.
- Ⓑ international transportation.
- Ⓒ in clubs called "speakeasies."
- Ⓓ from medical professionals.

18 What can be inferred from paragraph 6 about prescriptions for medicinal alcohol?

- Ⓐ There were few alternative medicines available.
- Ⓑ There was an increase in alcohol-related illness.
- Ⓒ They were often obtained under false pretenses.
- Ⓓ Doctors gave out more prescriptions than pharmacists.

19 In paragraph 6, the author discusses grape juice in order to

- Ⓐ explain why grape production increased during Prohibition.
- Ⓑ illustrate common alternatives to alcoholic beverages.
- Ⓒ give an example of a legal exception people took advantage of.
- Ⓓ provide recommendations for home brewing methods.

20 Directions: An introductory sentence for a brief summary of the passage is provided below. Complete the summary by selecting the THREE answer choices that express the most important ideas in the passage. Some sentences are incorrect because they contain information that was not in the passage or they contain minor details. *This question is worth 2 points.*

The Prohibition era in the United States between 1920 and 1933 gave rise to multiple shifts in the social and economic landscape of the country.

Answer Choices	
A. Some organized crime syndicates smuggled alcohol across the U.S.-Canadian border.	D. Bootlegging started during the American Civil War.
B. There was a reduction in alcohol-related health issues.	E. Prohibition lacked both political and widespread popular support.
C. Illegal businesses both large and small flourished throughout the United States.	F. People who had been discriminated against in the past saw opportunities to prosper.

Passage 3
Attention Deficit/Hyperactivity Disorder

1   In the past, Attention Deficit/Hyperactivity Disorder (ADHD) was defined by the presence of motor restlessness, or excessive activity. Although hyperactivity was associated with impulsivity and attention deficits, the latter were never emphasized. Some past labels used in place of the more modern term ADHD, such as "hyperkinesis," attest to this oversight. Today, however, ADHD focuses not only upon motor activity, but also upon attention deficits, which are then associated with hyperactivity.

2   ADHD has a complex etiology, or set of causes, although most psychiatrists ascribe it to biological factors. While evidence supports the hypothesis that ADHD may be genetically transmitted, research has yet to identify the vehicle of transmission. Other possible causes that have been cited include brain dysfunction, and complications experienced during pregnancy and at birth. In addition, there have been studies examining the link between ADHD and diet, namely sugar. However, diet has not been found to play an important causative role.

3   In order to be classified as ADHD, an individual must display the following diagnostic features. First, the onset of the disorder must occur before the age of seven. This can sometimes prove difficult, as children below the age of five vary greatly in their development and thus symptoms may be difficult to identify. Second, the symptoms must be present for at least six months. Third, the symptoms must be found in at least two different surroundings, like home, school, or work. Finally, the inattention and/or hyperactivity needs to be more than what one would normally expect from an individual at a similar stage of development. The issue of normative development is often controversial because its boundaries can be so unclear. In diagnosing ADHD, mental health professionals must be sensitive to differences in age, culture, and gender.

4   ADHD consists of three subtypes. The subtypes are used to identify the dominant behavioral patterns that are indicated in their titles. The three subtypes, as noted in the *Diagnostic and Statistical Manual IV* (DSM) are: Predominantly* Inattentive, Predominantly Hyperactive-Impulsive, and Combined Type. The first subtype, Predominantly Inattentive, focuses on different aspects of attention. Individuals in this category may shift from task to task without finishing one or the other, make careless mistakes, and not listen to others. This may lead to frequent conversational shifts and inattention to detail. An individual's sustained attention, which examines the ability to focus on a task over time, and selective attention, which explores the ability to focus on a relevant task or stimulus without being distracted by unrelated elements, are often analyzed. Individuals with ADHD-Predominantly Inattentive tend to have fewer behavioral problems than those individuals with ADHD-Hyperactive-Impulsive.

5   On the other hand, the second subtype, Predominantly Hyperactive-Impulsive, emphasizes motor movement and impatience, concerning issues of motivation and self-regulation. This subtype is often seen at its earlier stages and then often progresses into the Combined Type. Individuals who exhibit this subtype may demonstrate difficulty remaining seated, fidgetiness, difficulty awaiting one's turn, and disorganized and haphazard behavior. Those with this subtype always appear to be on the move and show the greatest difficulty with tasks that are sedentary or highly structured.

6   The final subtype, the Combined Type, is the most common. It includes inattention, hyperactivity, and impulsivity. It is associated with being in constant motion, not following through on requests, getting sidetracked, interrupting, inability to participate in organized sports, and impulsivity impairing social interactions. The Combined Type includes a number of behaviors found in the two subtypes previously discussed, and thus widely affects functioning.

7   The treatment an individual receives for ADHD may vary. Methods used include Cognitive Behavioral Therapy (CBT), pharmacological treatment, individual counseling, and parent training. **A** In the U.S., the most popular form of treatment is pharmacological, or the use of medication. However, while research has found it to be effective in reducing impulsivity and increasing attention, there is still concern over side effects and the inability of medication to help all children. **B** Alternative treatments like behavioral interventions and CBT have been tried. **C** Unfortunately, they are only successful in certain domains, and the positive results are nowhere near as impressive as those found with the use of stimulant medication. **D**

predominantly: mostly or mainly

21   The author mentions the term "hyperkinesis" in paragraph 1 in order to

(A) show how in the past people had a more narrow view of ADHD.

(B) provide an example of a typical manifestation of ADHD.

(C) demonstrate the role excited vision plays in ADHD.

(D) suggest that ADHD was thought to only consist of a lack of attention.

22   Which of the following sentences most closely expresses the important information in the highlighted sentence in the passage?

(A) Research indicates that ADHD may be passed on genetically, although it has not been determined precisely how.

(B) Though they are uncertain about whether ADHD has a genetic origin, scientists are confident that they will discover its means of transmission.

(C) Research has proven the theory that ADHD is spread genetically, but the spread of the disorder remains a mystery.

(D) Research has determined how ADHD is spread, although it has not verified whether it has a genetic origin.

23 According to paragraph 2, all of the following are thought to be major factors in the development of ADHD EXCEPT

(A) genes.

(B) brain disorder.

(C) prenatal problems.

(D) diet.

24 Based on the information in paragraph 3, all of the following would support a diagnosis of ADHD EXCEPT

(A) a child showing symptoms of ADHD before age seven.

(B) ADHD symptoms that are present for three months.

(C) symptoms of the disorder observed at home and school.

(D) inability to sit still in an 18-year-old.

25 The word onset in paragraph 3 is closest in meaning to

(A) symptoms.

(B) development.

(C) peak.

(D) features.

26 It can be inferred from the information in paragraph 3 that children's normative development

(A) is essentially the same regardless of culture and gender.

(B) is impossible to determine accurately due to genetics.

(C) varies depending on biological and cultural factors.

(D) depends on the income of their parents.

27 According to paragraph 5, all of the following are primary indicators of the Predominantly Hyperactive-Impulsive subtype EXCEPT

(A) an inability to stay seated for an extended period of time.

(B) making careless mistakes.

(C) difficulty participating in organized sports.

(D) impatience.

28 The word in paragraph 6 is closest in meaning to

(A) lost.

(B) in trouble.

(C) distracted.

(D) aggressive.

29 There is a sentence missing from paragraph 7. Look at the four letters (**A**, **B**, **C**, and **D**) in the passage that show where the following sentence could be inserted.

Critics argue that this type of treatment simply supplies a quick and easy answer to the problems faced by many schools and parents.

Where would the sentence best fit in the passage? Choose the letter for the place where this sentence should be added.

(A) Option A

(B) Option B

(C) Option C

(D) Option D

30 Directions: Below is an introductory sentence for a short summary of the passage. Complete the summary by choosing the THREE answer choices that express key ideas in the passage. Sentences that express ideas that are NOT in the passage or mention minor details do NOT belong in the summary. *This question is worth 2 points.*

Attention Deficit/Hyperactivity Disorder is a condition characterized by impulsive behavior and difficulties maintaining concentration.

Answer Choices	
A. To be diagnosed with ADHD, a person must show symptoms in different settings before the age of seven. B. Some psychiatrists suspect that sugar and other dietary factors may contribute to ADHD. C. The disorder consists of three sub-types: Predominantly Inattentive, Predominantly Hyperactive-Impulsive, and Combined.	D. Treatment of ADHD may include counseling and skills training, although in America there is a preference for pharmacological remedies. E. The causal factors of ADHD are thought to be largely biological; scientists speculate that it may derive from genes or natal conditions. F. Combined Type ADHD involves the exhibition of both hyperactive and inattentive behaviors and is the least common type.

LISTENING SECTION

Directions: In this section of the test, you will hear dialogues and academic talks, and you will be tested on your ability to understand them. You will hear each dialogue and academic talk only once, and then answer some questions after each is finished. The questions ask about the main idea, supporting details, and the way the speakers use language. Answer each question based on what is stated or implied by the speakers. You cannot go back to a question once you have answered it. Answer every question in the order that it appears.

While you listen, you may take notes. You can then use your notes when answering questions.

You will see the following headphones icon next to some questions: 🎧 This icon indicates that you will hear part of the dialogue or academic talk repeated for the question.

Most questions are worth 1 point. Questions that are worth more than 1 point have a special note telling you how many total points they are worth.

You will be given 14 minutes to answer all the questions in this section. This does not include the time to listen to the dialogues and academic talks.

Dialogue 1

🎧 **Track 21**

Directions: Now use your notes to help you answer the questions.

1 How does the professor know the student?

- (A) He recently read an article she had published.
- (B) She worked for him the previous semester.
- (C) He heard about her from one of his colleagues.
- (D) She was a student in one of his classes.

2 Why does the professor think the student could work well with him?

- (A) She is available every day.
- (B) She is bilingual and can help him translate.
- (C) She is very precise in her research.
- (D) She knows how to use several spreadsheet programs.

3 What does the professor want the student to do first?

- (A) Check databases for journal articles
- (B) Enter data from questionnaires
- (C) Distribute 200 questionnaires
- (D) Read his book prospectus on test taking

4 What can be inferred about most of the work the student will have to do?

(A) It has to be done on a computer.

(B) It will be tedious.

(C) It will involve talking to bilingual students.

(D) It will be done mainly on the weekends.

5 Listen to part of the dialogue again, and then answer the question. What does the professor imply when he says this: 🎧

(A) That the student is not qualified for the job

(B) That the student should look for a research position

(C) That the student might not have time for the job

(D) That the student has time now that she lives on campus

Dialogue 2

🎧 **Track 22**

Directions: Now use your notes to help you answer the questions.

6 What is the student's main concern with the course he wants to drop?

(A) He thinks there are too many assignments.

(B) He thinks his fellow students are not taking their work seriously.

(C) He wants to do extra work because he failed the midterm exam.

(D) He feels the course is not being as well taught as it should be.

7 Why did the student think the midterm exam was unusual?

(A) It covered only four points from the professor's lectures.

(B) It included material that was never covered in class.

(C) It was not mandatory.

(D) It was 65 percent of the final grade.

8 Why does the advisor say the student can drop the course now?

(A) Because the student agreed to audit the course instead

(B) Because he will substitute the course with another

(C) Because he can do so without being penalized

(D) Because he is an honors student and has the privilege

9 What can be inferred as the main reason the student asked about dropping the course?

 Ⓐ He realized he would spoil his 4.0 GPA.

 Ⓑ He has a habit of not finishing what he started.

 Ⓒ He just learned the course is not a requirement.

 Ⓓ He wanted to file a formal complaint about the professor.

10 Listen to part of the dialogue again, and then answer the question. What does the advisor mean?

 Ⓐ The student obviously works hard in his courses.

 Ⓑ The student cannot get A grades all the time.

 Ⓒ The student needs to reduce his working hours.

 Ⓓ The student should try harder in the class.

Academic Talk 1: Women's Studies

🎧 **Track 23**

Directions: Now use your notes to help you answer the questions.

11 What is the talk mainly about?

 Ⓐ Historical background of the Indian women's movement

 Ⓑ The impact of the women's movement on government

 Ⓒ Comparisons between the U.S. and Indian constitutions

 Ⓓ Parallels between rural and urban women in India

12 How did Indian village women show their support for demonstrators?

 Ⓐ They represented their villages at conferences.

 Ⓑ They participated in women's cultural presentations.

 Ⓒ They made loud noises using household objects.

 Ⓓ They stopped doing chores for their husbands and sons.

13 What can be inferred about the Indian women's movement from the 1970s to 1980s?

 Ⓐ It solved all the social problems facing Indian women up to that time.

 Ⓑ It brought Indian women together.

 Ⓒ It paralleled the U.S. feminist movement on exactly the same issues.

 Ⓓ It initiated a global feminist movement supported by the United Nations.

14 Listen to part of the talk again, and then answer the question. Why does the professor say this: 🎧

    (A) To ask permission to discuss a different topic

    (B) To prompt students to pay attention to the next point

    (C) To compare and contrast two countries side by side

    (D) To introduce a point that is not under discussion

15 Listen to part of the talk again, and then answer the question. What does the student mean when she says this: 🎧

    (A) She believes it is time for the women's movement to change.

    (B) She also used to hold the belief she is describing.

    (C) She once was an angry demonstrator.

    (D) She agrees with those perceptions.

16 In the talk, the professor describes a number of facts that are part of the Indian women's movement. Indicate which of the following were mentioned in the talk.

	Yes	No
A. Marches through villages		
B. Effective use of the media		
C. Theatrical presentations		
D. Concerns over land rights		
E. Elections to political office		

Academic Talk 2: Music

🎧 **Track 24**

Directions: Now use your notes to help you answer the questions.

17 What is the talk mainly about?

    (A) A singer who writes songs about the importance of water in society

    (B) Songs that express women's anger against society

    (C) A singer whose songs deal with emotional reactions to life

    (D) Songs that focus on a fast-paced lifestyle

18 What can be inferred about the singer's attitude toward nature?

(A) She feels it is unpredictably destructive.

(B) She feels its changes come in predictable waves.

(C) She feels it helps people to converse with each other.

(D) She feels it is a source of personal healing.

19 Listen to part of the talk again, and then answer the question. Why does the professor say this: 🎧

(A) To indicate he is using a different meaning for the word "crash"

(B) To encourage students to look up the definition of "crash"

(C) To question the singer's original meaning of "crash"

(D) To justify his misuse of the word "crash" in this context

20 Listen to part of the talk again, and then answer the question. What does the student mean when he says this: 🎧

(A) He thinks his classmate is completely wrong.

(B) He is trying to get his classmate to change her mind.

(C) He is reminding his classmate there's more to consider.

(D) He forgot the point his classmate was making.

21 Listen to part of the talk again, and then answer the question. Why does the professor say this: 🎧

(A) He is about to start singing for the students.

(B) He is about to read from a new set of notes.

(C) He wants the students to talk about something personal.

(D) He is about to share his thoughts with the class.

22 In the lecture, the professor discusses several themes covered in the songs. Indicate which of the following themes are considered by the singer.

	Yes	No
A. Gender issues		
B. Fast-paced living		
C. Loneliness		
D. Death		
E. Environmental pollution		

Academic Talk 3: History

🎧 **Track 25**

Directions: Now use your notes to help you answer the questions.

23 What is the talk mainly about?

(A) Jefferson's presidency

(B) French perceptions of Virginia

(C) Jefferson's philosophy of government

(D) Jefferson's interpretation of his home state

24 What is the logical progression of Jefferson's description of Virginia?

(A) From physical to philosophical

(B) From ancient to modern

(C) From animals to people

(D) From small towns to large cities

25 How do the two parts of Jefferson's book reflect his personality?

(A) They show he has not traveled widely throughout the state.

(B) They show he is a scientist above all other occupations.

(C) They show that he is objective as well as subjective.

(D) They show that he likes to argue both sides of a subject.

26 Listen to part of the talk again, and then answer the question. What does the professor mean when he says this: 🎧

(A) He thinks Jefferson presents full details of each topic he addresses.

(B) He thinks Jefferson passes over the topics very broadly.

(C) He thinks Jefferson was disorganized in his presentation of lists.

(D) He thinks Jefferson included too many facts and details in his book.

27 Listen to part of the talk again, and then answer the question. Why does the professor say this: 🎧

  Ⓐ To tell the students that he will need to leave the class early

  Ⓑ To encourage the students to think out the question themselves

  Ⓒ To test students' ability to infer concepts from their notes

  Ⓓ To suggest that Jefferson did not know much about biology

28 Listen to part of the talk again, and then answer the question. What does the professor imply when he says this: 🎧

  Ⓐ He thinks Jefferson says nothing new in his conclusion.

  Ⓑ He thinks Jefferson presents the most impressive material at the end.

  Ⓒ He thinks Jefferson tries to pack in a lot of information at the end.

  Ⓓ He thinks Jefferson holds back information so he can write another book.

SPEAKING SECTION

Directions: In this section, you will be asked to respond to a variety of tasks and topics. There are six tasks. Respond to each task as completely as you can, always speaking clearly.

For task 1, you will speak about a topic that is familiar to you. Your response will be graded on your ability to speak about the topic clearly.

For tasks 2 and 3, you will be asked to read a short text. The text will then go off the screen and you will hear a talk or dialogue on the same topic. You will be asked a question about what you have read and heard. You will need to use information from the text and the talk to answer the questions. Your response will be graded on your ability to speak clearly and accurately about what you have read and heard.

For task 4, you will hear part of an academic talk. You will then answer a question about what you have heard. Your response will be graded on your ability to speak clearly and accurately about what you have heard.

You are allowed to take notes during the reading and listening. You are allowed to use your notes to help you respond. Read the directions for each task closely.

For each task, you will be given a short time to prepare your response. You will be given a certain amount of time to speak. Use a watch or clock to time yourself.

Task 1

Directions: For this task, you will give your opinion about a topic that is familiar to you. You will hear a question. You will then have 15 seconds to prepare your response and 45 seconds to speak.

🎧 **Track 26**

> The television, the internet, and other electronic media are causing printed books to become obsolete as a source of information or entertainment. Do you agree or disagree with the statement? Give details and examples in your explanation.

> 15 seconds to prepare
> 45 seconds to speak

Task 2

Directions: For this task, you will read a short text and then listen to a dialogue about the same topic. You will hear a question about what you have read and heard. You will then have 30 seconds to prepare your response and 60 seconds to speak.

> North Park University is planning to build new athletic facilities. Read the announcement about the plans from the Office of Alumni Relations. You will have 45 seconds to read the announcement. Begin reading now.

> **An Announcement from the Office of Alumni Relations**

> North Park University is pleased to announce that construction of a new sports facility will commence this spring. Among the features of the new state-of-the-art

sports complex will be a basketball court and an Olympic-size swimming pool. The new center, which will be used for competitions as well as for recreation, is made possible by a generous grant from Thomas C. Watson, a 1969 alumnus of the university. It is thanks to the generous support of alumni like Mr. Watson that we can make improvements to the campus for the benefit of the whole university community.

Track 27

The man expresses his opinion about the announcement made by the alumni office. State his opinion and explain the reasons he gives for holding that opinion.

> 30 seconds to prepare
> 60 seconds to speak

Task 3

Directions: For this task, you will read a short text and then hear a talk about the same topic. You will hear a question about what you have read and heard. After you hear the question, you will then have 30 seconds to prepare your response and 60 seconds to speak.

Now read the passage about wolves. You have 45 seconds to read the passage. Begin reading now.

Wolves in Yellowstone Park

Wolves once roamed the North American continent from Mexico to the Arctic Circle. However, by 1973, when they were placed on the endangered species list, hunting and trapping had eliminated them from every U.S. state except Alaska and Minnesota. Even the massive Yellowstone National Park was no longer home to wolves. That changed in 1995 when 14 wolves were reintroduced to the park. Though environmentalists cheered the return of this natural predator to the park, ranchers and farmers whose lands abutted the park protested. They claimed that the wolves would leave the park to prey on their herds. They demanded the right to protect their property and animals from wolves. They even went to court to demand that the wolves be removed.

Track 28

The professor talks about the results of wolves being brought back to Yellowstone National Park. Explain what those results are and how those results are contrary to what people living near the park expected.

> 30 seconds to prepare
> 60 seconds to speak

Task 4

Directions: For this task, you will hear a short academic talk. You will hear a question about it. You will then have 20 seconds to prepare your response and 60 seconds to speak.

🎧 Track 29

Using points and examples from the talk, explain why Gideon's case was important and what values are reflected in the Supreme Court's decision.

> 20 seconds to prepare
>
> 60 seconds to speak

WRITING SECTION

Directions: You will need to use your headphones for this section.

This section is designed to measure your ability to write in English. There are two tasks.

For the first task, you will read a short text and listen to an academic talk. You will answer a question about what you have read and heard. For the second task, you will use your knowledge and experience to answer a question.

Task 1

Directions: For this task, you will have 3 minutes to read a short text. You may take notes if you wish. Then you will hear an academic talk on the same topic. You may take notes while you listen.

You will then read a question that asks about the relationship between the text and the talk. You will have 20 minutes to write a response. Using information from the text and talk, answer the question as completely as you can. You will not be asked to give your opinion. You will be able to review the text while you write. You may use your notes to help you write your response.

You should try to write 150 words or more. Your response will be graded on the quality, completeness, and accuracy of your writing. If you finish early, you may move on to the second task.

You now have 3 minutes to read the passage. After you read the passage, listen to the talk.

The availability of electric vehicles has recently increased, and more and more consumers are starting to explore alternatives to the petroleum-powered cars we've been driving for the last century. And for good reason.

The first major point in support of electric cars is that you can charge them in your home and avoid going to gas stations entirely. Charging stations can be easily installed in most homes and garages, and many electric companies offer discounts and incentives for those choosing to forego gas-fueled vehicles. The convenience of plugging in your car at night and waking up the next morning to a car that's ready to go for the day should not be underestimated.

Additionally, electric cars are generally cheaper to operate than cars that rely on gas. In most parts of the world, electricity is cheap and ubiquitous—it can even be extracted from the sun and converted to solar power, which can then be used to charge electric vehicles. Due to the considerable efficiency of electric vehicles compared to those with internal combustion engines, the cost per mile of the former is significantly less. Electric cars also don't need oil changes, and they don't have exhaust systems, so maintenance costs are significantly reduced.

Finally, electric cars have a much smaller environmental impact than conventional vehicles. They do not emit exhaust, which releases carbon emissions that contribute to climate change. Instead, electric cars contribute to an improvement in air quality, and they don't deplete natural resources, like oil. Especially in areas where renewable energy is readily available, the environmental benefits of electric cars are dramatic.

Track 30

Summarize the points made in the talk you just heard, explaining how they cast doubt on the points made in the reading.

Task 2

For this task, you will be asked to write an essay in which you state, explain, and support your opinion on an issue. You will have 30 minutes to complete your essay.

You should try to write 300 words or more. Your essay will be graded on how well you use language, organize your essay, and develop your ideas.

> Some people prefer to socialize in a group of people. Others prefer to spend time alone. Which do you prefer?

Use specific reasons to support your answer.

Practice
Test 4

TEST DIRECTIONS

This test is designed to measure your ability to understand and use English in an academic context. The test has four sections.

In the **Reading** section, you will read three passages and answer questions about them.

In the **Listening** section, you will listen to two dialogues and three talks and answer questions about them.

In the **Speaking** section, there are four tasks. The first task asks you to speak based on your own personal experience. In the other three, you will read passages and/or listen to dialogues and talks, then speak based on what you have read and/or heard.

In the **Writing** section, there are two tasks. In the first task, you will read a passage, listen to a talk, then write based on what you have read and heard. The second task asks you to write based on your own personal experience and ideas.

There is a 10-minute break after the **Listening** section.

At the beginning of each section, there are directions that explain how to answer the questions or respond to the tasks in the section.

In the **Reading** and **Listening** sections, you should work carefully but quickly. You should try to answer every question to the best of your ability. Make an educated guess on questions that you are unsure of. In the **Speaking** and **Writing** sections, each task is separately timed. In each case, you should try to respond to the task as completely as possible in the given time.

READING SECTION

Directions: In this section of the test, you will read three passages. You will be tested on your ability to understand them by answering several questions on each passage.

While you read, you may take notes. You can then use your notes when answering questions.

Most questions are worth 1 point. Questions that are worth more than 1 point have a special note telling you how many total points they are worth.

You will have 54 minutes to read the three passages and answer all the questions. If you finish the questions before 54 minutes is up, you can go back and review your work in this section.

Passage 1

Hubble's "Tuning Fork" Galaxy Diagram

1 **A** In the 1920s, the American astronomer Edwin Hubble devised the first classification system for galaxies*. **B** Based on observations that he had made from the Mount Wilson Observatory in California, he created a classification system, identifying four galaxy "families": spiral, barred spiral, elliptical, and irregular.
C Hubble then organized this classification system into a chart known as the "tuning fork" galaxy diagram. This diagram is still used today by astronomers to classify and compare newly discovered galaxies. **D**

2 Our solar system is a member of the Milky Way galaxy, which is thought to be a magnificently gigantic spiral galaxy. Such galaxies are easily identified by their beautiful spiral arms, which curve out from a bulging nucleus. Rich in gases and dust, spiral galaxies often give birth to new stars. On the Hubble tuning fork diagram, spiral galaxies are classified with the uppercase letter *S* (for "spiral") followed by a lowercase *a*, *b*, or *c*. The letter represents the size and density of the galaxy, with *a* signifying the densest, largest galaxies and *c* the least dense, smallest galaxies.

3 Barred spiral galaxies are close cousins of spiral galaxies. The only real visible difference is a bar-shaped formation of stellar and interstellar material running directly through the galactic center. This bar has a strong gravitational pull that causes the galaxy to elongate across its center. Barred spiral galaxies are classified by the letters *SB* and the same lowercase letter system described previously. Recent discoveries have led to the theory that our Milky Way galaxy may actually be a barred spiral because of its elongated center.

4 An elliptical galaxy differs greatly from a spiral galaxy, even though—strangely—it is believed to be a product of an interaction between two spiral galaxies. When spiral galaxies collide or pass too close to each other, a great realignment occurs and an elliptical galaxy is formed. This kind of galaxy has no visible spiral arms and no surrounding disk, only a weak nucleus with no internal structure. It contains only a small amount of dust and gas and shows no evidence of star formation. Elliptical galaxies are classified by the capital letter *E*, followed by a number on a scale from zero to seven. The number pertains to the density and shape of the galaxy, with zero indicating the densest and most spherical galaxy and seven being the loosest and least formed.

5 Near the intersection of the three branches of Hubble's tuning fork galaxy diagram is a subgroup of galaxies—sometimes referred to as lenticular galaxies—that appear

elliptical in form, but which have characteristics of spiral galaxies, most notably strong gravitational centers. For this reason, depending on whether they show spiral or barred spiral tendencies, lenticular galaxies are classified as either SO or SBO galaxies, respectively. They are clean visually, containing very little debris, but unlike elliptical galaxies, they have solid nuclei. An SBO galaxy has a bar-like formation stretching through the center that slightly elongates its shape. The visible difference is a lack of a halo or any surrounding debris. Lenticular galaxies are sometimes described as spiral galaxies without the arms.

6   Hubble's last category consists of the irregular galaxies, so named because of their asymmetrical and varied shapes. They are thought to be either the remnants of collisions between spiral galaxies or very young galaxies that have not yet reached a symmetrical, rotating state. These galaxies are classified as Irr (for *irregular)*, coupled with a Roman numeral I or II. Irr I galaxies look like misshapen spirals, and Irr II galaxies have very abstract shapes.

7   The Hubble Telescope, which was launched into space in 1990, was dedicated to discoveries made by Edwin Hubble and his contributions to world astronomy and science. It helps today's scientists observe and analyze galaxies that Hubble could only have dreamed of seeing. Until different shapes and sizes of galaxies are discovered, the tuning fork chart that Hubble created will continue to be used to identify and classify all of our future galactic discoveries.

galaxies: the large groups of stars and associated matter that the universe is made out of

1   According to paragraph 1, where did Edwin Hubble make his galactic observations?

    Ⓐ Through the Hubble Telescope
    Ⓑ From a California observatory
    Ⓒ Using a tuning fork diagram
    Ⓓ With his own telescope

2   There is a sentence missing from paragraph 1. Look at the four letters (A, B, C, and D) in the passage that show where the following sentence could be inserted.

Resembling the shape of the tool musicians use to tune their instruments, the system consists of a stem (elliptical galaxies) and two branches (the two kinds of spiral galaxies).

Where would the sentence best fit in the passage? Choose the letter for the place where this sentence should be added.

    Ⓐ Option A
    Ⓑ Option B
    Ⓒ Option C
    Ⓓ Option D

3 The phrase close cousins of in paragraph 3 is closest in meaning to

    Ⓐ descendents of.

    Ⓑ intimately related to.

    Ⓒ in relative proximity to.

    Ⓓ situated next to.

4 According to paragraph 3, what kind of galaxy would the tuning fork classification SBc represent?

    Ⓐ A large elliptical galaxy

    Ⓑ A dense spiral galaxy

    Ⓒ A massive irregular galaxy

    Ⓓ A small barred spiral galaxy

5 According to information in paragraph 3, what do astronomers today believe about the Milky Way galaxy?

    Ⓐ It is probably not a spiral galaxy.

    Ⓑ It is probably a barred spiral galaxy.

    Ⓒ It could be a barred spiral galaxy.

    Ⓓ It could be an elliptical galaxy.

6 The word debris in paragraph 5 is closest in meaning to

    Ⓐ scattered material.

    Ⓑ small galaxies.

    Ⓒ asteroids.

    Ⓓ energy.

7 According to the information in paragraph 5, what do lenticular galaxies resemble?

    Ⓐ Elliptical galaxies

    Ⓑ Barred spiral galaxies

    Ⓒ A subgroup of galaxies

    Ⓓ A halo

8 It can be inferred from paragraph 6 that irregular galaxies

(A) often end up disintegrating in huge explosions.

(B) are the most common form of galaxies.

(C) have several nuclei that create irregularity.

(D) may sometimes form into spiral or elliptical galaxies.

9 The author discusses the Hubble Telescope in paragraph 7 in order to

(A) provide background about the telescope Hubble used for his research.

(B) introduce the idea that today's scientists may disprove Hubble's discoveries.

(C) suggest that Hubble had a very limited idea of the size of the universe.

(D) emphasize the importance of Hubble's contributions to astronomy.

10 Directions: Find the phrases in the answer choices list that relate to spiral or elliptical galaxies. Write your answers in the appropriate place. TWO of the answer choices will NOT match either category. *This question is worth 4 points.*

Answer Choices	Spiral galaxies
A. Have arms that radiate out from a nucleus	
B. Contain little dust or gas	
C. Include the "tuning fork" classification E7	**Elliptical galaxies**
D. Are similar to SB galaxies	
E. Have varied and asymetrical shapes	
F. Include the Milky Way galaxy	
G. Are not believed to produce new stars	
H. Resemble lenticular galaxies	
I. Are usually relatively small	

Passage 2

Ellis Ruley, Folk Artist

1   Like many artists, folk artist Ellis Ruley received virtually no recognition for his unique talent during his lifetime. He began to paint late in life, in an unreceptive and unnurturing environment. Nevertheless, he possessed a fiercely independent spirit and a highly creative impulse. Born on December 3, 1882, in Norwich, Connecticut, Ruley received little schooling and began working at a very early age. His family was one of only a handful of African American families in Norwich, none of which were prosperous. Ruley's family moved a total of 18 times in as many years from the time he was born, and both he and his father worked as laborers in coal yards and construction sites. His life proved unexceptional until the age of 42 when, while driving from work with a coworker one day, they were struck by a runaway truck, and Ruley ultimately received $25,000 in compensation for his injuries. This incident proved to be a pivotal event in Ruley's life, as the money enabled him to change his economic conditions overnight. He purchased three acres of land in a suburban area of Norwich, on which stood a small, antiquated house, bought a car, and married the divorced wife of his brother, a woman several years his junior named Wilhelmina. It was about this time, it is thought, that he first began to paint, although none of his work is actually dated.

2   Ruley had an intuitive sense of design and a strong sense of color. He seems to have started painting in order to decorate windows and wallpaper in his home, but he eventually switched his medium and for most of his career as an artist painted almost exclusively on posterboard, using ordinary house paints. Ruley's paintings were deeply connected to nature, a fact not only noticeable in his work but one that was reflected in his daily life. He called himself a "naturalist" and tried to be as self-sufficient as possible, growing vegetables and fruit trees on his land. He made a pond so that animals could come and drink from it and swim. **A** These backyard scenes from nature were reproduced by Ruley throughout his work, metamorphosing on his ubiquitous posterboard into jungles and forests. **B** He painted birds and flowers and animals, waterfalls, his own versions of hunters and hula dancers and pop stars and famous Americans. **C** He painted horses, canoes, zebras, farmhouses, and Adam and Eve—but with a unique style that created a strangely unsettling, dreamlike effect. **D** Ruley was painting his own visions of paradise, but there was almost always a sense of danger or foreboding even in the most bucolic scenes.

3   Ruley's paintings have been compared to those of 19th-century French painter Henri Rousseau or 20th-century Haitian artist Philomé Obin, but Ruley's work falls into the category of folk art inspired in part by African folklore. In African myth, animals are spirits, with the ability to change form and help people escape bondage. Hence much of Ruley's work fits into a tradition of African American artists identifying spirits in nature. In Ruley's painting *Waterfall*, ghostly mask-like forms seem to beckon from the water. In *See How Pretty*, running water forms skull-like shapes, representing spirits in the water, as two skeletal young girls approach a stream. *Waterfall* and *See How Pretty* are representative of the fact that in African cultures, works of art have often been used as a means of channeling the forces of spirits and nature and protecting oneself from them.

4   At the age of 77, Ruley died as the result of mysterious wounds to his head. A racist extremist group was suspected, although the culprits were never identified. At the time of his death, many of his own neighbors did not even know he was an artist. The only exhibition of his work during his lifetime was on December 2, 1952, at a show at the Norwich Art School, which received a brief, though positive, review in the *Norwich Bulletin-Record*. In spite of its lack of visibility during Ruley's lifetime, his primitive work possesses, as that review of his show pointed out, a "directness of approach, sincerity and a love for his work" that many still appreciate today. Joseph Gualtieri, curator of the Slater Museum, and producer of Ruley's one show, later remarked, "He was a painter of the exotic . . . he brings to his work a freshness of vision, full of stimulating surprises and unexpected happenings."

11   Based on information in paragraph 1, it can be inferred that

    (A) during Ruley's childhood, there were many African American families in Norwich.

    (B) Ruley displayed artistic creativity while still a child, but developed it only later.

    (C) Ruley's work received considerable recognition after his death.

    (D) after the age of 42, Ruley was no longer able to perform manual labor.

12   The phrase pivotal event in paragraph 1 is closest in meaning to

    (A) turning point.

    (B) surprising outcome.

    (C) hopeful circumstance.

    (D) likely prospect.

13   According to paragraph 1, all of the following are true of Ellis Ruley EXCEPT

    (A) he married a woman who was younger than himself.

    (B) he divorced his first wife to marry Wilhelmina.

    (C) he moved house after his accident.

    (D) he and his father held similar jobs.

14 There is a sentence missing from paragraph 2. Look at the four letters (**A**, **B**, **C**, and **D**) in the passage that show where the following sentence could be inserted.

This gave him an opportunity to observe them close up.

Where would the sentence best fit in the passage? Choose the letter for the place where this sentence should be added.

(A) Option A

(B) Option B

(C) Option C

(D) Option D

15 According to paragraph 2, why did Ruley refer to himself as a naturalist?

(A) He often included themes from nature in his work.

(B) He preferred to use paint that was made from natural materials.

(C) He painted primarily out-of-doors.

(D) He believed that consuming natural foods improved his work.

16 In paragraph 3, how does the author describe Ruley's art?

(A) The author explains how it was affected by his medium.

(B) The author shows how it became more and more sophisticated over time.

(C) The author argues that his work is superior to that of more famous folk artists.

(D) The author identifies the influence of myth on his painting.

17 Which of the following sentences most closely expresses the essential information in the highlighted sentence in paragraph 4?

(A) Ruley's work, though not well known while he was alive, is now admired for qualities that were originally pointed out in a newspaper article about his show.

(B) Despite the primitiveness of Ruley's work, one newspaper reviewer who attended his show particularly appreciated his artistic talent and unique vision.

(C) According to one newspaper reviewer who attended his show, Ruley's work, which was not appreciated for many years, would have been better received had it demonstrated more directness and honesty.

(D) Even though the people of Ruley's day felt that his work lacked vision, one newspaper reviewer who attended his show pointed out some of its remarkable characteristics.

18 The word curator in paragraph 4 is closest in meaning to

Ⓐ director.

Ⓑ founder.

Ⓒ teacher.

Ⓓ neighbor.

19 It can be inferred from information in paragraph 4 that

Ⓐ Ruley's first show received both favorable and unfavorable reviews.

Ⓑ Ruley's neighbors had little interest in art and culture.

Ⓒ Ruley's talent was appreciated by the leaders of the Norwich Art School.

Ⓓ Ruley died before he could fully develop his artistic vision.

20 **Directions:** Below is an introductory sentence for a short summary of the passage. Complete the summary by choosing the THREE answer choices that express key ideas in the passage. Sentences that express ideas that are NOT in the passage or mention minor details do NOT belong in the summary. *This question is worth 2 points.*

Ellis Ruley was a folk artist with a primitive yet compelling style.

Answer Choices	
A. The first half of his life was not an easy one, but a midlife change in his circumstances made it possible for him to discover and develop his artistic talent.	D. Ruley included a wide variety of every-day subjects in his paintings, treating them in a way that gave the viewer a sense of peace and safety.
B. Ruley was probably killed by a group of extremists who resented the attention his work had gained.	E. Ruley based much of his work on themes derived from African folklore.
C. Ruley started life as a laborer, but spent his last few decades living as a farmer while painting in his spare time.	F. Ruley only had one exhibition of his work in his lifetime, which received a positive review, and died before many even knew he was an artist.

Passage 3

The Pinta Island Tortoise

1 Endemism is the term used to describe the state of a species that is unique to one singular geographic location. **A** Biological, climatic, and physical features are all significant factors in endemism. **B** These singular species, also called endemic types, are especially likely to live in biologically and geographically isolated areas, such as highlands, lakes, and islands. **C** But endemic species are extremely vulnerable: if their restricted habitat is threatened or new organisms are introduced to their environment, they can easily become endangered or extinct. **D** One example of this is the Pinta Island tortoise.

2   The Pinta Island tortoise, or *Chelonoidis abingdonii*, is a species of giant tortoise native to Ecuador's Pinta Island in the Galapagos. This endemic species was first identified in 1877, when specimens arrived in London for inspection by British taxonomists. Prior to that, the population had been plundered by whalers and pirates, who kept the tortoises on their ships as a low-maintenance food source that they consumed during long journeys. By the end of the 19th century, most of the Pinta Island tortoises had been killed by hunters. The endemic species was thought to be extinct until the last known individual of the species, known as Lonesome George, was discovered in 1971 on the island of Pinta by an Hungarian scientist. Although hunting was illegal by this time, the introduction in 1958 of feral goats had decimated the island's vegetation, and the population of Pinta Island Tortoises had been reduced to one single male. For his own safety, George was relocated to the Charles Darwin Research Center on a neighboring island. Over the following decades, biologists scoured the islands and zoos worldwide for a suitable mate for George, in order to keep the species alive. But all breeding attempts proved unsuccessful, and in 2012 he died of natural causes. The entire species was believed to have been rendered extinct by his death.

3   However, subsequent discoveries threw this assumption into doubt. The same year that Lonesome George passed away, researchers were able to identify 17 first-generation hybrid tortoises that were partially descended from the same species. This led to speculation that Pinta Island tortoises were still surviving on other Galapagos Islands. In 2015, researchers from Yale University discovered another species with a 90% DNA match to *Chelonoidis abingdonii* on Wolf Volcano, the highest peak in the Galapagos, and speculated that this could be used to resurrect the species. In December 2018, researchers published a paper in which they described the sequencing of George's genome. In it, they identified some of his ageing-related genes and estimated that *Chelonoidis abingdonii* had actually been in decline for the past 1 million years.

4   Research into the remaining Galapagos tortoise species shows just how unique and important these endemic types are to their native habitat. In the wild, these animals usually spend a majority of the day at rest. They are herbivores and drink large quantities of water, which they are able to store in their bodies for extended periods of time. Their most active breeding period occurs when the weather is hottest, from January to May. During most of the remaining year, the females migrate to nesting zones, where they lay and tend to their eggs. These giant tortoises are an essential component of the island ecosystem. They act as ecological engineers and nutrient recyclers and are responsible for spreading seeds across the island. The extinction of the Pinta Island tortoise has had a major impact on the functionality of the local environment.

5   In addition to the *Chelonoidis abingdonii* dying out, several of the remaining species of Galapagos tortoises are listed as endangered. But conservation attempts are underway; there has been a concerted effort by conservationists to revive multiple species of Galapagos tortoise through captive breeding in zoos and other research facilities. Due to conservation interventions, the decline of giant tortoise populations has been halted in the Galapagos Islands. Invasive species such as goats, rodents, and cats have been eliminated from several islands, which has given the native ecosystem a chance

to recover. Once all of the remaining pests are removed and the environment has been restored, conservationists are hopeful that the tortoise species endemic to the Galapagos Islands can be returned to their native habitats.

21 There is a sentence missing from paragraph 1. Look at the four letters (**A**, **B**, **C**, and **D**) in the passage that show where the following sentence could be inserted.

This excludes artificial confinement in zoos, research facilities, or other man-made environments.

Where would the sentence best fit? Choose the letter for the place where this sentence should be added.

(A) Option A

(B) Option B

(C) Option C

(D) Option D

22 In paragraph 1, each of the following is mentioned as a feature of endemic species EXCEPT

(A) they are vulnerable.

(B) they are unique.

(C) they are exploited.

(D) they are isolated.

23 According to paragraph 2, which of the following is NOT true of the Pinta Island tortoise?

(A) They were bred successfully.

(B) Goats ate all their food.

(C) They were believed to have died out in 2012.

(D) They were eaten on boats.

24 According to paragraph 3, what has recent research into Lonesome George's DNA shown?

(A) Tortoises are resistant to cancer.

(B) Tortoises cannot experience stress.

(C) His species cannot survive at high altitudes.

(D) His species was slowly deteriorating.

25 The word plundered in paragraph 2 is closest in meaning to

(A) conserved.

(B) ransacked.

(C) assaulted.

(D) liberated.

26 What can be inferred from paragraph 2 about Pinta Island tortoises before 1877?

(A) Humans had not seen them before.

(B) The locals let them live in peace.

(C) They were already at risk of becoming endangered.

(D) Their numbers were flourishing on the island.

27 To what does this assumption refer in paragraph 3?

(A) Lonesome George died of natural causes.

(B) Pinta Island tortoises had been wiped out.

(C) Lonesome George had produced offspring.

(D) Pinta Island tortoises are the longest living species of tortoise.

28 Concerted effort in paragraph 5 is closest in meaning to

(A) serious attempt.

(B) lengthy relationship.

(C) ulterior motive.

(D) thorough investigation.

29 Which of the sentences below best expresses the essential information in the highlighted sentence in paragraph 5?

Due to conservation interventions, the decline of giant tortoise populations has been halted in the Galapagos Islands.

(A) Scientists have intervened with the giant tortoise populations of the Galapagos Islands.

(B) Interventions in conservation of giant tortoises have declined in the Galapagos Islands.

(C) Conservationists have been able to prevent further losses of giant tortoises in the Galapagos Islands.

(D) Giant tortoise populations are declining in the Galapagos Islands.

30 Directions: An introductory sentence for a brief summary of the passage is provided below. Complete the summary by selecting the THREE answer choices that express the most important ideas in the passage. Some sentences are incorrect because they contain information that was not in the passage or they contain minor details. *This question is worth 2 points.*

Galapagos tortoises are an endemic species whose existence and decline demonstrates how crucial it is that unique animals are protected.

Answer Choices	
A. They were discovered by pirates and whalers in the 19th century. B. The story of Lonesome George illustrates the vulnerability of endemic species. C. Tortoises are not the only endemic species that live on the Galapagos Islands.	D. Hunting and invasive pests are some of the factors contributing to the deterioration of unique species like the Pinta Island tortoise. E. Lonesome George is thought to have been the last of his species. F. Research and conservation efforts are necessary for preserving endemic species and the environments they need to survive.

LISTENING SECTION

Directions: In this section of the test, you will hear dialogues and academic talks, and you will be tested on your ability to understand them. You will hear each dialogue and academic talk only once, and then answer some questions after each is finished. The questions ask about the main idea, supporting details, and the way the speakers use language. Answer each question based on what is stated or implied by the speakers. You cannot go back to a question once you have answered it. Answer every question in the order that it appears.

While you listen, you may take notes. You can then use your notes when answering questions.

You will see the following headphones icon next to some questions: 🎧 This icon indicates that you will hear part of the dialogue or academic talk repeated for the question.

Most questions are worth 1 point. Questions that are worth more than 1 point have a special note telling you how many total points they are worth.

You will be given 14 minutes to answer all the questions in this section. This does not include the time to listen to the dialogues and academic talks.

Dialogue 1

🎧 **Track 31**

Directions: Now use your notes to help you answer the questions.

1 What is the focus of the professor's class project?

- Ⓐ Ways to teach a five-part lesson
- Ⓑ How to teach a grammar lesson
- Ⓒ The experience of student teaching
- Ⓓ The demographics of a particular school

2 Why did the student need to talk with the professor?

- Ⓐ To get an extension on his project
- Ⓑ To clarify the parts of the project
- Ⓒ To explain why he was so late
- Ⓓ To turn in the first part of the project

3 What subject does the student teach?

- Ⓐ Math
- Ⓑ Spanish
- Ⓒ Physical education
- Ⓓ European history

4 Listen to part of the dialogue again, and then answer the question. What is the professor implying?

(A) It is not always obvious that a student is in class.

(B) She has trouble remembering all of the students' names.

(C) She has caught the student sleeping in class.

(D) It is difficult to answer all the students' questions in a large class.

5 Listen to part of the dialogue again, and then answer the question. What can be inferred about the student?

(A) He is going to quit his job.

(B) He is upset about missing class.

(C) He does not like to drive when it rains.

(D) He was having a difficult day.

Dialogue 2

Track 32

Directions: Now use your notes to help you answer the questions.

6 Why does the student go to the administrative office?

(A) To pay her student fees

(B) To resolve a problem

(C) To register for a class

(D) To translate wire instructions

7 What has happened with the bank transfer?

(A) An overpayment was made.

(B) It was not received by the school.

(C) It was sent to the correct account.

(D) It was returned to the sender.

8 Listen to part of the dialogue again, and then answer the question. What does the administrator mean when he says this:

(A) He is asking if the student understands the policy.

(B) He is telling the student not to go to Monday classes.

(C) He is asking the student to pay the school fees.

(D) He wants the student to come back on Monday.

9 What does the administrator offer to do?

(A) Extend the payment deadline

(B) Refund the incorrect payment

(C) Set up a meeting with his manager

(D) Send the student a copy of the receipt

10 What will the administrator probably do?

(A) Ask the student to speak to the manager in person

(B) Report his decision to his manager

(C) Place an immediate call to his manager

(D) Ask his manager to confirm his decision

Academic Talk 1: Biology

🎧 **Track 33**

Directions: Now use your notes to help you answer the questions.

11 What is the discussion mainly about?

(A) What diabetes is

(B) How diabetes causes disease

(C) What diabetics should do

(D) How to prevent diabetes from occurring

12 Which of the following facts about diabetes does the professor mention?

(A) It is common in overweight people.

(B) Many diabetics are never diagnosed.

(C) It can cause problems like kidney failure and heart disease.

(D) Six percent of the U.S. population has diabetes.

13 Listen to part of the talk again, and then answer the question. What does the student suggest?

(A) People with diabetes are unfortunate.

(B) There are no known cures for diabetes.

(C) Reducing sugar intake can cure diabetes.

(D) Diabetes cannot be cured if left untreated.

14 Listen to part of the talk again, and then answer the question. What does the professor mean when he says this: 🎧

    (A) Diabetics should eliminate sweets from their diets.

    (B) Diabetics actually need to eat more sweets than the average person.

    (C) Diabetics and nondiabetics who want to eat sweets should check with their doctors first.

    (D) Diabetics and nondiabetics can eat sweets if they want to.

15 Listen to part of the talk again, and then answer the question. What is the purpose of the professor's comment?

    (A) To emphasize the danger of diabetes

    (B) To describe a focus of scientific research

    (C) To demonstrate how diabetes can be managed

    (D) To illustrate his concern for people with diabetes

16 Which of the following are diabetics required to do regularly?

    (A) Consume foods that are high in sugar

    (B) Consume excess fats and starches

    (C) Donate blood on a weekly basis

    (D) Measure the amount of glucose in their blood

Academic Talk 2: Film Studies

🎧 **Track 34**

Directions: Now use your notes to help you answer the questions.

17 What is the talk mainly about?

    (A) Adapting a book into a film

    (B) A novelist who became a screenwriter

    (C) Why books are better than movies

    (D) A book that was made into an unpopular movie

18 Why does the professor mention the first scene in the film *Bonfire of the Vanities*?

    (A) It replicates the opening episode in the book exactly.

    (B) It shows the director's careful selection of character.

    (C) It shows a very different perspective from the book's.

    (D) It is the only scene that is effective in both book and film.

19 According to the talk, what can be inferred about film adaptations?

(A) They are often better than the original books.

(B) They are often inferior to the original books.

(C) They are usually just as good as the original books.

(D) They are sometimes written by the books' authors.

20 Listen to part of the talk again, and then answer the question. Why does the professor say this: 🎧

(A) To let the students know it is time to be quiet

(B) To help introduce the day's subject

(C) To find out how many people know the expression

(D) To give the students some time to think

21 Listen to part of the talk again, and then answer the question. What does the student mean by this: 🎧

(A) Movies adapted from books rarely make a profit.

(B) A movie is usually shorter than the book from which it was adapted.

(C) Movies adapted from books cannot really compare to the original.

(D) A movie is really just a short version of the original book.

22 In the talk, the professor describes a number of things that can be affected by an adaptation. Choose three of the answer choices below that were mentioned in the talk.

	Yes	No
A. Number of characters		
B. Works of art		
C. Politics		
D. Details in the book		
E. Dialogue		

Academic Talk 3: Astronomy

🎧 **Track 35**

Directions: Now use your notes to help you answer the questions.

23 What is the main topic of this talk?

(A) Two space probes sponsored by the European Space Agency

(B) How space probes may resolve mysteries about Mercury

(C) Similarities between the planet Mercury and the moon

(D) Einstein's predictions about Mercury's eliptical orbit

24 Why does the professor begin by discussing how difficult it is to see Mercury from Earth?

  (A) To remind students of the main idea of the previous talk

  (B) To suggest that Mercury is too close to the sun to explore

  (C) To explain why students may be unfamiliar with Mercury

  (D) To emphasize how little we know about Mercury

25 What can be inferred about Mercury?

  (A) A space probe has never been put in orbit around the planet.

  (B) It has a dense atmosphere because it orbits so close to the sun.

  (C) It has held little interest for scientists since the mid-1970s.

  (D) It is the most mysterious planet in the solar system.

26 Why are the *Mariner 10* pictures all of one side of Mercury?

  (A) The camera broke down halfway through the mission due to extreme heat.

  (B) The probe left Mercury before the planet had turned to reveal the other side.

  (C) The sun's rays were too bright to allow pictures to be taken of the other side.

  (D) The probe's camera focused on the side of Mercury not visible from Earth.

27 What will spectrometry determine about Mercury?

  (A) Whether Einstein's general theory of relativity explains its orbit

  (B) Whether the volcanoes on the far side of the planet are active

  (C) The reasons for the planet's unusually strong magnetic field

  (D) The reasons for the planet's present size and composition

28 What is true of Mercury's magnetic field?

  (A) It is similar to those of the other inner planets.

  (B) It will present danger to the BepiColombo probe.

  (C) It exists because the planet is so close to the sun.

  (D) It cannot work in the same way as that of Earth.

SPEAKING SECTION

Directions: In this section, you will be asked to respond to a variety of tasks and topics. There are six tasks. Respond to each task as completely as you can, always speaking clearly.

For task 1, you will speak about a topic that is familiar to you. Your response will be graded on your ability to speak about the topic clearly.

For tasks 2 and 3, you will be asked to read a short text. The text will then go off the screen and you will listen to a dialogue or talk about the same topic. For each task, you will be asked a question about what you have read and heard. You will need to use information from the text and the talk to answer the questions. Your responses will be graded on your ability to speak clearly and accurately about what you have read and heard.

For task 4, you will hear part of an academic talk. You will then answer a question about what you have heard. Your response will be graded on your ability to speak clearly and accurately about what you have heard.

You are allowed to take notes during the reading and listening. You are allowed to use your notes to help you respond. Read the directions for each task closely.

For each task, you will be given a short time to prepare your response. You will be given a certain amount of time to speak. Use a watch or clock to time yourself.

Task 1

Directions: For this task, you will give your opinion about a topic that is familiar to you. You will hear a question. You will then have 15 seconds to prepare your response and 45 seconds to speak.

🎧 Track 36

> Some people believe that the best way to reduce carbon emissions is to restrict air travel. Do you think this is a good idea? Give details and examples in your explanation.

15 seconds to prepare
45 seconds to speak

Task 2

Directions: For this task, you will read a short text and then listen to a dialogue about the same topic. You will hear a question about what you have read and heard. You will then have 30 seconds to prepare your response and 60 seconds to speak.

> South Shore University's Business School Club is looking for a person to be its coordinator in the upcoming academic year. You will have 45 seconds to read the announcement. Begin reading now.
>
> **Get Involved!**
>
> Are you a senior in the School of Business? Are you looking for a way to make a contribution to your school in your last year? Are you interested in making great

contacts with business owners in the local community? The South Shore University Business School Club seeks a dynamic graduating senior with great organizational skills to be its coordinator for the coming academic year. The coordinator has overall responsibility for planning and implementing all club activities for the year. For more information about this exciting position, please refer to the Student Services website.

🎧 Track 37

The man tries to persuade the woman to do something. Say what he tries to persuade her to do and explain the reasons he gives.

> 30 seconds to prepare
>
> 60 seconds to speak

Task 3

Directions: For this task, you will read a short text and then hear a talk about the same topic. You will hear a question about what you have read and heard. After you hear the question, you will then have 30 seconds to prepare your response and 60 seconds to speak.

Now read the passage about computer hacking. You have 45 seconds to read the passage. Begin reading now.

Hacking: Crime or Service to Society?

There exist two divergent views on hacking. The definition of the term itself shows that divergence; a standard dictionary will tell you that two of the term's meanings are: a) to create computer programs for fun and b) to gain illegal access to a computer.

So which is it? Are hackers simply people with inquisitive minds who wish to probe the limits of computer systems—and thereby show where things can be improved? Or are they devious criminals who have taken simple crude vandalism to a higher—and much farther reaching—level? The answer to that question, like so many others, probably depends on who you speak to. Those with a knack for computers and a rebellious spirit will probably tell you that hacking is all in good fun. But those on the other side of that "fun"—people who have had their finances scrambled or personal information released to the world—will probably take offense at such a description of the act of hacking.

🎧 Track 38

Two opinions on computer hacking are given in the reading. Explain which of these views the professor holds and how she supports her opinion.

> 30 seconds to prepare
>
> 60 seconds to speak

Task 4

Directions: For this task, you will hear a short academic talk. You will hear a question about it. You will then have 20 seconds to prepare your response and 60 seconds to speak.

🎧 **Track 39**

Using points and examples from the talk, explain the factors that contributed to the loss of Holland's colony of New Amsterdam.

> 20 seconds to prepare
>
> 60 seconds to speak

WRITING SECTION

Directions: You will need to use your headphones for this section.

This section is designed to measure your ability to write in English. There are two tasks.

For the first task, you will read a short text and listen to an academic talk. You will answer a question about what you have read and heard. For the second task, you will use your knowledge and experience to answer a question.

Task 1

Directions: For this task, you will have 3 minutes to read a short text. You may take notes if you wish. Then you will hear an academic talk on the same topic. You may take notes while you listen.

You will then read a question that asks about the relationship between the text and the talk. You will have 20 minutes to write a response. Using information from the text and talk, answer the question as completely as you can. You will not be asked to give your opinion. You will be able to review the text while you write. You may use your notes to help you write your response.

You should try to write 150 words or more. Your response will be graded on the quality, completeness, and accuracy of your writing. If you finish early, you may move on to the second task.

You now have 3 minutes to read the passage. After you read the passage, listen to the talk.

There are good reasons why inhabitants of many continents, including Asia, Africa, and South America, incorporate insects into their diets. They benefit both our bodies and the planet in multiple ways.

The first consideration is that they are a substantial and efficient source of nutrients. Insects like ants, crickets, beetles, and caterpillars can provide a considerable amount of protein and iron. These nutrients increase muscle mass and strength while providing nourishment and energy to our bodies. Just one small serving of these animals contains as much protein as a significantly larger portion of beef or chicken.

Eating insects is also incredibly resource efficient. Crickets and mealworms, for example, require less water, feed, and soil than any of the conventional livestock animals like chickens, pigs, and cows. Additionally, they require less energy per kilogram of protein than they provide, and their production emits markedly less greenhouse gas than the alternatives. Insect farming also requires much less agricultural space than conventional livestock farming, which leaves land free for conservation or other uses.

Lastly, the population continues to expand and the systems currently in place for producing and distributing food often fail to accommodate many of the world's inhabitants. A significant amount of people do not have access to the nutritious food they need in order to live a healthy life. The large-scale farming and eating of insects has the potential to provide cheap, accessible nourishment to people around the world who are experiencing hunger and malnutrition. Children especially can benefit from edible insects, which require relatively few natural resources but can provide considerable sustenance, especially for those in need.

🎧 **Track 40**

Summarize the points made in the lecture you just heard, and then compare the speaker's opinion with the opinion stated in the reading.

Task 2

Directions: For this task, you will be asked to write an essay in which you state, explain, and support your opinion on an issue. You will have 30 minutes to complete your essay.

You should try to write 300 words or more. Your essay will be graded on how well you use language, organize your essay, and develop your ideas.

Some people believe that technological innovations are creating a less communicative and interactive society.

Do you agree or disagree with the statement? Use specific reasons to support your answer.

Listening
Scripts

PRACTICE TEST 1

LISTENING SECTION

Dialogue 1

Track 1

NARRATOR:	Listen to a dialogue between a professor and a student.
STUDENT:	Professor Smith! I was planning to drop by your office later on today to, uh, to discuss my midterm. Will you, ah, have a few minutes for me a little bit later?
PROFESSOR:	Actually, the 401 midterm is tomorrow, so I have several appointments this afternoon—but if you have a few minutes now, I'd be more than happy to discuss the midterm with you right here.
STUDENT:	I don't have class until 2:15, but I wouldn't want to interrupt your lunch ...
PROFESSOR:	No, it's no problem. Please, take a seat. So, what's up?
STUDENT:	I wanted to talk to you about my midterm ... I didn't do as well as I expected to. I studied but I just blanked on the second part. Is there anything I can do for extra credit to boost my grade a little bit?
PROFESSOR:	You know, I was wondering what happened to you.
STUDENT:	I just completely blanked on it. I knew it so well the night before, but I just lost it all during the test. I really do understand it ... I'm, I'm not sure what happened ...
PROFESSOR:	I really don't believe in extra credit projects, because they're usually done at home. It's not fair to the other students who've had to answer questions under pressure in class, and with time limits too. But what did you have in mind?
STUDENT:	Oh. I hadn't really thought about it ... maybe I could retake the part of the test I messed up on? Or write a paper?
PROFESSOR:	To be honest, I think you'd need to do something a little, uh, more involved than either of those. You'd really need to put some thought into a project and come up with something that demonstrates that you understand the concept, but also show that you can take it a step further than what we did in class and what was tested on the exam. I suppose, if you're able to do that, I could consider giving you some extra credit for it.
STUDENT:	Great! Thanks so much!
PROFESSOR:	I'm not guaranteeing that I'll accept your project, though. It has to be something really extraordinary to qualify for extra credit. Remember, it has to be more in-depth than what we've covered in class. I want this project to be a, um, a learning experience for you, so it should also synthesize some material that we haven't yet covered in class, not just reiterate what we've already discussed.

STUDENT:	Okay … Maybe I can do an analysis of the more involved structures that the book doesn't cover? I can do some extra research …
PROFESSOR:	Sure, something like that might work. Wow, is it five to 2 already? I have to run to class. Why don't you email me your proposal for the project, and I'll get back to you to let you know if it will work.
STUDENT:	Great! Thanks so much. I'll have a proposal to you by tomorrow morning.
NARRATOR:	Now use your notes to help you answer the questions.
	Why does the student meet with the professor?
	Does the professor normally accept extra credit projects?
	Listen to part of the dialogue again, and then answer the question.
PROFESSOR:	You know, I was wondering what happened to you.
NARRATOR:	Why does the professor say this?
	What will the student do for extra credit?
	What will the student probably do that afternoon?

Dialogue 2

Track 2

NARRATOR:	Listen to a dialogue between a student and a professor.
PROFESSOR:	Please come in, Molly. I'm sorry to keep you waiting.
STUDENT:	No problem, Professor Warren. Thanks for seeing me.
PROFESSOR:	Uh, you said on the phone that you wanted to speak with me about majoring in women's studies.
STUDENT:	Yes, um … actually, I'll be double-majoring.
PROFESSOR:	Oh? In … ?
STUDENT:	Sociology as well as women's studies.
PROFESSOR:	That's a good combination since sociology offers lots of courses that are cross-disciplinary with WS, like, uh … let me get the catalogue here.
STUDENT:	Like Sociology of Women?
PROFESSOR:	That's right … here's the catalogue.
STUDENT:	I'm taking Sociology of Women now with Professor Davis.
PROFESSOR:	Mmm, that would serve as an elective for both WS and sociology.
STUDENT:	Sort of like the "two birds with one stone" thing, right?
PROFESSOR:	Uh, you could say that. Are you familiar with the requirements?
STUDENT:	No. I mean, I must have seen them in the catalogue when I registered, but that was a couple of months ago.
PROFESSOR:	Well, basically, you'll need to take the introductory course, followed by Feminist Theories and Women's History—those are required, plus five electives.
STUDENT:	That could be from any department?

PROFESSOR:	Oh, any department that's cross-referenced with WS—meaning that the course will fulfill an elective requirement in both departments.
STUDENT:	That seems easy enough. I could finish the coursework in less than a year, going full-time.
PROFESSOR:	But we have other requirements for the major, besides the courses.
STUDENT:	Oh? I, uh, I don't remember reading about that.
PROFESSOR:	I'm sure it's in the book. Let's see, uh, yes. You'll need to complete an internship at a women's organization.
STUDENT:	You mean like the, the National Organization for Women?
PROFESSOR:	No—well, I suppose, if you found an opportunity to intern there, or rather at your local chapter, of course you could do that. But we'd prefer something more community-oriented, like a women's shelter or a women's health clinic.
STUDENT:	Would this be volunteer or paid?
PROFESSOR:	Oh, no, no pay here. This is purely for the experience, about 3 hours a week, of helping a small nonprofit organization that focuses on important women's issues. Then you'd come back to the school each week and report on your experience to your classmates in the Women's Seminar.
STUDENT:	It sounds like, like a lot of work, but I think it's a wonderful thing to do. I may even make connections there for a future job.
PROFESSOR:	It's quite possible. Some of our students who've interned at some of these places have actually gone back to work there.
NARRATOR:	Now use your notes to help you answer the questions.
	What is the professor referring to when he says WS?
	What else is required in addition to the coursework?
	What can be inferred about cross-disciplinary courses?
	Listen to part of the dialogue again, and then answer the question.
PROFESSOR:	Uh, you could say that. Are you familiar with the requirements?
STUDENT:	No. I mean, I must have seen them in the catalogue when I registered, but that was a couple of months ago.
NARRATOR:	What does the student's answer mean?
	Why is the student looking forward to joining a women's organization?

Academic Talk 1: Art History

Track 3

NARRATOR:	Listen to part of a talk in an art history class.
PROFESSOR:	Okay, let's get started. Today, we're going to continue our discussion by talking about public art. Who can sum up the textbook's definition of public art for the class?
STUDENT A:	I think the book says that it's, ah, it's basically any work of art that's readily

available to the general population—it's either mounted in an outdoor space or in a building that's accessible to the public.

PROFESSOR: So by that definition, wouldn't an exhibit at a museum be public art, because the building is somewhat open to the public? Or is there more to it than that?

STUDENT A: No ... it doesn't really apply to art that can be found in museums or galleries. It's more like art that uses the public space as part of the exhibit. One of the examples in the book was Michelangelo's painting on the ceiling of the Sistine Chapel. I guess it sort of applies to buildings where you wouldn't expect to see art ... like in churches or Keith Haring's graffiti in New York City's subways ...

PROFESSOR: That's it. You hit it right on the head. The distinction between public art and most other forms of art is that public art turns up in places where it's least expected—painted church ceilings, statues in parks, subway graffiti ...

Does anyone remember the Cow Parade exhibit we had in the city a few summers ago? I see some of you shaking your heads. Well, during Cow Parade, there were about 250 life-size cows made out of plaster that were on exhibit throughout the city. Local artists had the opportunity to purchase a cow, decorate it in any way they wanted to, and exhibit it on the streets of the city. Each individual cow had a theme, and the cows were put up on streets all throughout Manhattan for a few months. During that time, anyone and everyone had access to the cows. In my opinion, Cow Parade is a great example of public art, as well as one of the most exciting and innovative ideas I've seen recently.

Okay ... so we've established that public art is a piece of art that uses its surroundings and is readily available to the public. There's more information on that topic in last night's reading, so we won't review it now. But what else is distinctive about public art?

STUDENT B: Well, artists can put up works outside and use that space to create big works of art that would never fit in a gallery ... like when Christo and Jeanne-Claude put up *The Gates* in Central Park. They hung that saffron-colored material from big doorways—or gates—along 23 miles of the park, and tons of people went to the park to see them. The whole point was that the sunlight would hit the material and it would billow in the wind and it would be beautiful. They could never have found an indoor space that would have created the same effect.

PROFESSOR: I'm glad you brought that up. *The Gates* exhibit is a good example, because it exemplifies a lot of the elements of public art. Something we've already discussed is how public art takes the natural surroundings into account and works with them. Do you guys know that it took over 20 years for *The Gates* to be approved by New York City, in part because the artists needed to find a way to build the gates without any adverse impact on the environment? That was one of the stipulations of the artists' contract with the city, and they couldn't move the project forward until they solved that dilemma.

Just like *The Gates*, much of the public art we see is controversial. Many people wonder, is it really art to drape a million square yards of fabric across poles in Central Park? Is it really art to spray-paint figures on subway station billboards? Or to paint a couple of plaster cows and park them on street corners in New York City? Or does art need to be more cultured, more refined, more thoughtful than that? We'll get into that discussion a little later though.

So now we've mentioned a few of the factors that need to be present for a work to be called public art. The work has to be fully, and easily, available to the public, either on display outdoors or in an accessible building. The piece should have a synergistic relationship with its surroundings, and it's usually contemporary. Okay, let's go to our books and see what some of our more well-known critics have to say about this subject.

NARRATOR:	Now use your notes to help you answer the questions.
	What is the professor mainly discussing?
	Listen to part of the talk again, and then answer the question.
STUDENT A:	… it's basically any work of art that's readily available to the general population—it's either mounted in an outdoor space or in a building that's accessible to the public.
PROFESSOR:	So by that definition, wouldn't an exhibit at a museum be public art, because the building is somewhat open to the public? Or is there more to it than that?
NARRATOR:	Why does the professor say this:
PROFESSOR:	Or is there more to it than that?
NARRATOR:	What are two of the key elements that are shared by most works of public art?
	Listen to part of the talk again, and then answer the question.
PROFESSOR:	… that was one of the stipulations of the artists' contract with the city, and they couldn't move the project forward until they solved that dilemma.
NARRATOR:	What does the professor mean when she says this:
PROFESSOR:	… they couldn't move the project forward …
NARRATOR:	Listen to part of the talk again, and then answer the question.
PROFESSOR:	Just like *The Gates*, much of the public art we see is controversial. Many people wonder, is it really art to drape a million square yards of fabric across poles in Central Park? Is it really art to spray-paint figures on subway station billboards? Or to paint a couple of plaster cows and park them on street corners in New York City?
NARRATOR:	How does the professor emphasize the fact that public art is considered controversial?
	Listen to part of the talk again, and then answer the question.
PROFESSOR:	There's more information on that topic in last night's reading, so we won't review it now.
NARRATOR:	What can be said about the professor?

Academic Talk 2: Archaeology

Track 4

NARRATOR:	Listen to part of a talk in an archaeology class.
PROFESSOR:	Okay, yesterday we spoke about how the ancient Egyptians believed in the afterlife. As a result, they wanted to preserve the dead body because they believed the soul would return to it one day and it would need to recognize its own body. The more the dead body looked lifelike, the easier the soul could find it. As you all probably know from TV and the movies, these bodies are called mummies.

So yeah, we all know mummies, but how many of you really understand how complex the process was? Before 1500 B.C., mummification was experimental. It only became more refined between the 18th and 21st Dynasty … about 1500 to 1000 B.C. Um, don't forget the numbers go backwards when we're talking B.C., okay? After that … say, 1000 B.C., the process declined. Fortunately, in the fifth century B.C., the Greek historian Herodotus recorded the embalming methods of the Egyptians. Oh, you know the word "embalming," right? Preserving the body—and yeah, we have that even today, although not to the degree I'm about to describe.

The first step in mummifying was—and I hope this won't spoil your lunch—removing the brain. The embalmers pulled the brain out through the nose with an iron hook—okay, okay, I know this is a little gross—and then they poured drugs into the skull to preserve it. Archeologists have actually found holes in the bones of a mummy's skull because of this procedure.

Now why did they do that? We all think the brain is the seat of wisdom and knowledge. What would we do without our brain, like the Scarecrow from *The Wizard of Oz*, right? Well, for the ancient Egyptians, the brain was never preserved since they considered it useless. The heart, not the brain, for them was the seat of the soul. Then, as if that weren't enough, the Egyptians would open up the body and remove more organs … the lungs, intestines, stomach, liver, and spleen. Imagine, all of these were more important than the brain. The heart was always left in place. Because it was the core of a person's character, they believed it was vital for eternal life.

Once the organs were removed, they washed the inside of the body with water and wine. The organs were each wrapped separately in linen and then placed in jars capped with the heads of gods. You remember how many gods the Egyptians worshipped. The jars would later be buried with the body.

Then the body was, was dehydrated for 40 days and washed off with towels. So, because the body was all dried out, it became hard and stiff. The Egyptians actually massaged … the dry skin with sweet oils and grease. Any cuts were sealed with hot wax. The mouth and nose were filled with cloth, while the body was painted red for men and yellow for women. The arms were arranged across the chest or along the side of the body.

Then, for the next two weeks—imagine, two weeks—the Egyptians would bandage the body with linen strips. Three thousand years later, archeologists discovered the skeletons of two mice that had accidentally nestled inside the bandages and got wrapped up too! Even they got preserved.

Some of the high-ranking mummies had elaborate gold funerary masks placed over their head and shoulders. You've all seen these in books. The poor guys, well they only had cardboard covers. As you can tell, the mummification process was pretty expensive. Only rich people were buried in pyramids—those incredible buildings that housed all the treasures that would then follow them on their final journey. The poor had to accept simple burials, but we can assume they too made the same trip as the rich guys.

That's kind of it in a nutshell. I want to show you some pictures now and review some of the details. Oh, and I also wanted to mention that deliberate embalming of animals was also very common in ancient Egypt—not like the accidental burial of the two mice! Thousands of mummified animals were buried, including sacred animals such as bulls, rams, cats, dogs, ibises, crocodiles, and lots of other species. While animals were honored by the Egyptians—and I'll spend more time tomorrow on the significance of animals in Egyptian mythology—animal mummies haven't always been as venerated as King Tut's was, let's say. In fact, in 1859, a whole graveyard with 300,000 mummified cats was excavated and shipped to Great Britain. Why? To be used as fertilizer.

Okay, so now I'm going to show you some slides of mummies. Could someone turn off the lights, please?

NARRATOR:	Now use your notes to help you answer the questions.
	What is the talk mainly about?
	According to the talk, what did the Egyptians consider the most important organ?
	According to the talk, which of the following can be inferred about Egyptian society?
	Listen to part of the talk again, and then answer the question.
PROFESSOR:	We all think the brain is the seat of wisdom and knowledge. What would we do without our brain, like the Scarecrow from *The Wizard of Oz*, right?
NARRATOR:	Why does the professor say this:
PROFESSOR:	What would we do without our brain …
NARRATOR:	Listen to part of the talk again, and then answer the question.

PROFESSOR:	The embalmers pulled the brain out through the nose with an iron hook—okay, okay, I know this is a little gross—
NARRATOR:	Why does the professor say this:
PROFESSOR:	—okay, okay, I know this is a little gross—
NARRATOR:	In the lecture, the professor describes the steps for mummification. Indicate whether each of the following is a step in this process.

Academic Talk 3: Literature

Track 5

| NARRATOR: | Listen to part of a talk in a literature class. |
| PROFESSOR: | Um … If I could have your attention … uh, let's start today by considering how an author's diction and syntax—or word choice and order—are deliberately chosen in any particular work of literature. Of course, authors, poets, playwrights have a choice of many literary devices. The author creates the structure, and an interpreter—or reader—must investigate in order to draw inferences and conclusions. |

Some common literary devices include: symbolism, foreshadowing, characterization, irony, point of view, tone … and so on.

Symbolism and foreshadowing, which we'll talk about today, require the audience … er … reader to be a bit of a detective … Greater inferencing skills are necessary … you know, reading between the lines, understanding what is implied rather than stated. In symbolism, objects seem to stand for something other than themselves. Springtime symbolizes new birth … a tire pump in a garden symbolizes a snake in Eden. Symbolism requires connotation rather than denotation … or figurative rather than literal meaning, as I said, implying rather than stating directly. Typically, to the trained reader, symbolism is easier to see than its not-so-distant cousin, foreshadowing.

Detecting foreshadowing requires locating suggestions—that's what connotations are—locating suggestions that will appear later in the text. Identifying foreshadowing is particularly satisfying to the reader. The use of foreshadowing creates suspense which is then resolved when the expectation is met. Potentially, though, the reader may not be aware of the evidence and clues until the first reading is complete. In other words, the resolution of the plot helps the audience grasp foreshadowing during a subsequent—a second—reading. When a reader rereads, which is expected at the interpretation level, foreshadowing becomes more visible, contributing to the meaning and purpose … plot and … uh … theme of the work.

Now, let's apply this literary device of foreshadowing to specific works. Even the title of a work may indicate foreshadowing. In the case of Susan Glaspell's play entitled *Trifles*, oh, she also created a short work of prose based on the same plot and theme entitled *A Jury of Her Peers*. The titles alone foreshadow how the tale will be told of a woman being judged by other women based on what appear to be trifles, or insignificant details.

Beyond the title, many works demonstrate foreshadowing in their first lines. How about this? From *A Tale of Two Cities* by Dickens: "It was the best of times, it was the worst of times." The first line gives the reader a glimpse ... er, foreshadowing ... of the happy and tragic events that will be the subject of the novel. In Edgar Allan Poe's "The Tell-Tale Heart," the word choice, sentence length, structure, and repetition provide foreshadowing, even in the speech patterns of the narrator. And Poe also clearly uses foreshadowing in another short story, "The Cask of Amontillado." In that story, a character quite literally declares his intent to seek revenge on his enemy. And since we, as the readers, have already been told what is to happen, given, if you like, ... the, uh ... "whodunit" information, the focus and suspense of the story is thrown onto how the revenge is to be carried out.

There are several examples of foreshadowing here: The revenge takes place in the catacombs, we know that the moment of revenge is approaching as the main character assures his enemy that he will not die of a cough ... Poe is certainly a master of foreshadowing, but he's not the only one who was skilled at using it.

The character of the grandmother in Flannery O'Connor's *A Good Man Is Hard to Find* is a good example. It's almost as if she had a warning, a premonition if you like. The first line, uh, again, is suggestive of bad things to come: "The grandmother didn't want to go to Florida." It is as though she had prophetic knowledge of the events to come.

NARRATOR: Now use your notes to help you answer the questions.

What is the lecture mainly about?

Why does the professor talk about symbolism?

According to the professor, how do symbolism and foreshadowing differ?

Listen to part of the talk again, and then answer the question.

PROFESSOR: Potentially, though, the reader may not be aware of the evidence and clues until the first reading is complete.

NARRATOR: What does the professor imply?

What does the professor say about the work *A Jury of Her Peers*?

Listen to part of the talk again, and then answer the question.

PROFESSOR: Poe is certainly a master of foreshadowing, but he's not the only one who was skilled at using it.

NARRATOR: What can be inferred from the professor's statement?

SPEAKING SECTION

Task 1

Track 6

NARRATOR: For this task, you will give your opinion about a topic that is familiar to you. You will hear a question. You will then have 15 seconds to prepare your response and 45 seconds to speak.

NARRATOR: It is better to study for exams alone rather than with a group of friends. Do you agree or disagree with the statement? Give details and examples in your explanation.

Task 2

Track 7

NARRATOR: Listen to two students as they discuss the announcement.

STUDENT A: Well, at least they're honest.

STUDENT B: How d'you mean?

STUDENT A: I mean it's incredible—absolutely unbelievable—that they'd choose someone who has not, uh, no teaching experience whatsoever. But it just proves that universities today are being run more like businesses than like educational institutions.

STUDENT B: That may not be all bad. I mean, large universities are a lot like businesses. So it's probably good to have someone at the top who understands about budgets and finance and, uh, that stuff. Think of all the, the fund-raising a university president has to do ... Senator Mullins's experience in politics and public relations will probably come in handy.

STUDENT A: Senator Mullins's name is sure to raise a lot of money, but I doubt we'll ever see any of it. I hear they're building a new faculty dining room ...

STUDENT B: Well, my friend who works in the financial aid office says they're talking about adding new scholarships. So ... if Mullins can raise enough money, maybe we'll finally get the new science lab they've been talking about for so long. And maybe having a famous president will attract top faculty to the school. That would be a real plus.

NARRATOR: Now get ready to answer the question.

NARRATOR: The woman expresses her opinion of a recent decision made by the university. State her opinion and explain the reasons she gives for holding that opinion.

Task 3

Track 8

NARRATOR: Listen to part of a talk in an economics class.

PROFESSOR: There are several reasons why the Bretton Woods system eventually broke down. The success of the system depended to a great extent on the presence of a dominant player who would be largely responsible for making the rules of the game and making sure those rules were followed. For many years, the United States was that dominant player. Then the 1960s saw Europe and Japan gaining in economic strength, while the United States' economy, in contrast, got steadily weaker. With inflation rising at home, the United States could no longer claim its, uh, leadership role, and, uh, eventually, well, the system collapsed when Richard Nixon removed the gold backing from the U.S. dollar in 1971.

But I wouldn't characterize Bretton Woods as a complete failure. It did bring stability to world markets and facilitate increased trade among nations. Indeed, there are some who support a return to the Bretton Woods system in some modified form. Of course, the world is a much different place than it was in 1944. Sixty years ago, no one could have predicted the birth of the euro and the dominant effect its 450-plus million users would have on the world economy. Nevertheless, the fact that Bretton Woods continues to be discussed attests to the very important role that it played in fashioning the world economy after World War II.

NARRATOR: Now get ready to answer the question.

NARRATOR: The professor talked about the end of the Bretton Woods system. Explain what the purpose of the Bretton Woods system was and how and why it ended. Give details and examples to support your answer.

Task 4

Track 9

NARRATOR: For this task, you will hear a short academic talk. You will hear a question about it. You will then have 20 seconds to prepare your response and 60 seconds to speak. Listen to part of a talk in a marketing class.

PROFESSOR: Now, the reason that game theory is of interest to so many people is that it combines several different disciplines: mathematics, economics, statistics, and psychology. When you're playing a game, let's say … um, chess … well, you, uh, you try to come up with a strategy that will result in your winning the game. And part of your strategy will involve trying to outsmart your opponent, trying to guess which move he will make next. Competing businesses operate on the same principle. When two companies are competing for the same objective, they try to guess what the competition's next move will be. In other words, when a company makes decisions—when it tries to choose a strategy to follow—it has to constantly consider what the competition might do in response. And the competition is doing the same thing—constantly trying to figure out what the other side is thinking. Using game-theory terminology, we'd say that when there are exactly two players and Player A's loss results in Player B's gain … in game theory, we call that "zero sum." Of course, things get much more complicated when there are more than two players involved. This all may sound very complex, but the beauty of game theory is that—in principle anyway—it's actually quite simple. In fact, a number of people, among them John Nash, whose name you might be familiar with from the movie *A Beautiful Mind*, people like Nash have come up with mathematical formulas that support the idea that many aspects of game theory are, in fact, predictable. And what's exciting is, once you begin to understand what game theory is all about, you begin to see it at work in everyday life and you see it has applications in so many different and unrelated areas ... in sports, in business, in diplomacy. The list is endless.

NARRATOR: Using points and examples from the talk, explain how a price war between two competing retail stores reflects the principles of game theory.

WRITING SECTION

Task 1

Track 10

NARRATOR: Now listen to part of a talk on the topic you just read about.

PROFESSOR: Across the world, federal governments, including those of Italy, China, Bangladesh, Rwanda, and South Africa, have banned disposable plastic bags. In fact, bans have been introduced in over 70 countries, with varying degrees of enforcement, and 33 countries have imposed a fee for bags in stores. Some local governments and jurisdictions, such as those in California and Hawaii in the U.S., have also banned these enemies of the ecosystem. And for good reason. Disposable plastic bags are a threat to the environment, and they deplete numerous resources.

The first major issue is that plastic bags are usually only used once and then thrown away. This means that all of the resources that go into producing them are exploited and then disposed of after a single use. These days, there are many viable alternatives that consumers can use multiple times. For example, cotton tote bags can be easily stashed in a purse or backpack and taken out for use at a grocery or drugstore. Some of them even bear logos and patterns that give shopping a personalized touch. Paper bags can also be reused, and then easily recycled with other paper waste.

Another important point is that plastic bags, even the so-called "eco-friendly" versions, can take multiple lifetimes to biodegrade. When plastic bags become litter, they pollute cities, neighborhoods, rivers, and farmlands. This causes long-term damage to ecosystems around the world. Additionally, they can last for thousands of years in trash sites, which disrupts the natural biodegradation of other waste.

Finally, plastics bags are incredibly difficult to recycle. They have become an ecological burden because, while production and use have increased over the years, we have failed to implement efficient recycling systems that can sufficiently process the vast amount of plastic waste that results from our dependence on this product. Unlike glass bottles or paper bags, plastic bags can't be sorted from other materials by machinery at most recycling facilities. They get stuck in conveyor belts and jam equipment. Some grocery stores provide receptacles for collecting and recycling used plastic bags, but most shoppers don't remember to use them.

PRACTICE TEST 2

LISTENING SECTION

Dialogue 1

Track 11

NARRATOR:	Listen to a dialogue between a student and a peer advisor.
STUDENT:	I'm not sure if I'm in the right office. Is this the peer advisement?
PEER ADVISOR:	It is. Hi, I'm Matt. I'm one of the peer advisors.
STUDENT:	Oh? I didn't see a sign on the door.
PEER ADVISOR:	We're getting a new one. I was just about to stick up a temporary one when you walked in. So, how can I help you?
STUDENT:	Uh, I saw this flyer … here it is … I think I might be interested in the peer advisement program, but I don't know what it is exactly.
PEER ADVISOR:	Well, I can explain. By the way, do you know we have an open house in about three weeks? We started putting up flyers about it.
STUDENT:	Mmm, I only found this general one.
PEER ADVISOR:	Okay. Well, in a nutshell, peer advisement is a great program—for psych majors especially—but anyone can participate since this program trains you. It has coursework to supplement what you get in another major. So what are you majoring in?
STUDENT:	Psych, as a matter of fact.
PEER ADVISOR:	Great. You'll be able to, to overlap some of your classes then with ours. We've got some general courses on counseling methods and a series of seminars, and you'll have an internship for a year.
STUDENT:	Where would that be?
PEER ADVISOR:	Everything's done directly on campus. So you'd work right in this office, or maybe in another student-centered office like admissions or the bursar.
STUDENT:	Doing what?
PEER ADVISOR:	Mainly answering students' questions about the college … helping them feel comfortable here … making it easy to understand the requirements. The majority of students who come here are transfers, especially from overseas. Many don't know exactly what to expect from an American college.
STUDENT:	Sounds like a valuable service.
PEER ADVISOR:	It sure is. I actually finished up my program already, but I'm volunteering to help out and I even run one of the seminars now.
STUDENT:	Is there any, uh, like heavy-duty counseling? Like students who might have more, say, major problems?
PEER ADVISOR:	Well, sometimes. You can't avoid that, of course. But if a student needs more in-depth help, we can certainly refer them to someone who can

	help them. We have access to lots of resources both on and off campus.
STUDENT:	And when did you say the open house was?
PEER ADVISOR:	In about three weeks. Come! If you give me your email address, I can send you a reminder.
NARRATOR:	Now use your notes to help you answer the questions.
	How did the student learn about the peer advisement program?
	Why should the student attend the open house?
	What can be inferred about the peer advisor?
	Listen to part of the dialogue again, and then answer the question.
PEER ADVISOR:	Okay. Well, in a nutshell, peer advisement is a great program—for psych majors especially—but anyone can participate since this program trains you. It has coursework to supplement what you get in another major.
NARRATOR:	What does the peer advisor mean when he says this:
PEER ADVISOR:	Well, in a nutshell …
NARRATOR:	Listen to part of the dialogue again, and then answer the question.
STUDENT:	Is there any, uh, like heavy-duty counseling? Like students who might have more, say, major problems?
PEER ADVISOR:	Well, sometimes. You can't avoid that, of course. But if a student needs more in-depth help, we can certainly refer them to someone who can help them.
NARRATOR:	What does the student mean when she says this:
STUDENT:	Is there any, uh, like heavy-duty counseling?

Dialogue 2

Track 12

NARRATOR:	Listen to a dialogue between a student and a bookstore manager.
STUDENT:	May I please speak to, uh, someone in charge of the bookstore?
MANAGER:	That's me. I'm Regina Watson, the manager. What can I do for you?
STUDENT:	I'm a freshman and I'm, I'm looking for work at the college. I was wondering if maybe there's any part-time work available?
MANAGER:	Well, uh, yes, there is, there's a part-time position open at the moment.
STUDENT:	What kind of position is it?
MANAGER:	Mostly cash register work. You've had experience working at a register?
STUDENT:	Yeah, this summer I've been working full-time as a cashier at the Five Star Diner downtown.
MANAGER:	Oh, you did? Why, hmm, I thought you looked familiar. I eat there all the time.
STUDENT:	Well, now that you mention it, I do remember that you used to come in around five—
MANAGER:	Yeah, 5, 5:30. Usually I'd stop by for dinner after work. So, you know

	what it's like to be working the register at a busy time then …
STUDENT:	Yeah, that I do. Dinner hour gets pretty crowded.
MANAGER:	I'll say. Well, then you can imagine that next week, what with classes starting, this place'll be a madhouse.
STUDENT:	But you only have three registers. How do you manage?
MANAGER:	For about a week and a half, we set up twice as many registers to handle the crowd. Plus, we have a returns desk with two registers.
STUDENT:	Sounds like a valuable service.
STUDENT:	Returns? So soon in the semester?
MANAGER:	Oh yes, sometimes students pick up the wrong book by accident, or they decide to drop the course after a couple of classes.
STUDENT:	When things die down, what else would the, uh, job involve?
MANAGER:	Well, we always need somebody at the register, of course, but then there are other responsibilities like inventory, and book orders for the next semester, and sweeping up. Everybody at the register rotates and pitches in.
STUDENT:	I wouldn't mind any of that.
MANAGER:	Well, I'd be happy to consider you. No question we need to hire somebody soon. Could you stop by with a résumé later on today?
STUDENT:	I'm on my way home now and then headed off to work. It's my last week at the diner since my classes are starting next week. Say, maybe I could bring a copy of my résumé to the diner if you're going to stop by?
MANAGER:	Actually, tonight I have to work late to check the stock. Tomorrow'd be just fine, if you could stop by here in the morning.
STUDENT:	No problem. I'll bring my résumé in around 11.
NARRATOR:	Now use your notes to help you answer the questions.
	Why does the manager think the student looks familiar?
	What can be inferred about the manager?
	Why does the student offer to bring in his résumé tomorrow in the end?
	Listen to part of the dialogue again, and then answer the question.
MANAGER:	… So, you know what it's like to be working the register at a busy time then …
STUDENT:	Yeah, that I do. Dinner hour gets pretty crowded.
MANAGER:	I'll say. Well, then you can imagine that next week, what with classes starting, this place'll be a madhouse.
NARRATOR:	What does the manager mean when she says this:
MANAGER:	… this place'll be a madhouse.
NARRATOR:	Listen to part of the dialogue again, and then answer the question.
MANAGER:	For about a week and a half, we set up twice as many registers to handle the crowd. Plus we have a returns desk with two registers.

STUDENT:	Returns? So soon in the semester?
NARRATOR:	Why is the student surprised?

Academic Talk 1: Music

Track 13

NARRATOR:	Listen to part of a talk in a music class.
PROFESSOR:	Today I'm going to talk about one of the major influences on musical performance in the 20th and 21st centuries. I mean, of course, the development of sound recording.
	Prior to Edison's invention of the phonograph in 1877, musical performances could only be, be described or remembered. They couldn't be reproduced. When sound recording developed, musicians were suddenly able to study the performances of famous musicians in great detail and even to copy them. Musicians who lived outside the major performance centers, such as London, Vienna, Berlin, and Paris, could now hear on records how Melba sang or how Kreisler played the violin. Also, minor flaws in the performance that would've been passed over in the concert hall became much more apparent on a recording that could be played over and over again. All of this led performers to concentrate on technical accuracy. And it eroded local performance traditions in favor of a more international style.
	Of course, uh, Edison's first idea for exploiting his new invention had nothing to do with music. He saw the phonograph as a dictation machine that would revolutionize the business world. Unfortunately for Edison, many of the office workers who'd painstakingly built up shorthand note-taking skills weren't so keen on the idea … and sabotaged the new dictation machines whenever they could. As a result, very few major firms adopted them.
STUDENT A:	So, how'd the phonograph come to be used for recording music?
PROFESSOR:	Well, there was a demand from operators of fairgrounds and saloons. They wanted recorded music to entertain customers. And eventually Edison was forced to change direction. Now, given the places where phonograph music was played, it's hardly surprising that the first recordings weren't of Bach and Beethoven. The bestsellers of the day included humorous whistling, cornet solos, and comic dialogues.
STUDENT A:	I've heard it said that one of the problems was that Edison wasn't very musical.
PROFESSOR:	That is a common view, but I think it does him a bit of an injustice. Although his musical tastes were certainly not highbrow … um … once he was committed to music recording, Edison spent a great deal of time and money building up a collection of American sheet music with an eye to assessing it for its recording potential. His collection runs to tens of thousands of items and is now archived at the University of Michigan.

STUDENT B:	So, uh, how did recordings of serious music get started?
PROFESSOR:	Well, it took a while. Edison preferred sentimental ballads to opera or chamber music. Plus, the early phonograph had two limitations. One was the poor quality of reproduction and the other was its association with fairgrounds and saloons. Classical artists regarded it as a, um, toy. They simply never took it seriously. However … one artist changed all that … Caruso.
STUDENT A:	But wasn't the sound of Caruso's recordings still really terrible? I mean … I've heard a few of those old records and they sound kind of comic.
PROFESSOR:	By today's standards that's certainly true, but you've got to remember that people were judging by the standard of cylinder recordings, which were so, so faint that you had to listen through rubber tubes … a bit like today's earphones … to hear anything at all. By 1902, when Caruso made his first recordings, reproduction had improved considerably. Caruso had two great advantages … First, his voice recorded very clearly. Remember, the range of that primitive recording apparatus was very limited, and many famous artists' voices just didn't suit the equipment.
	The other reason was that his interpretations had a certain melodramatic quality … that today we might call larger than life or maybe even exaggerated. Anyway, his style was perfect for overcoming the, uh, limitations of the recording mechanism and for creating the illusion that he was performing in the room rather than on a machine.
STUDENT B:	But that style isn't popular now, is it? These days I don't think artists try to overcome the impersonality of the machine. Most musicians try hard to communicate in concert, but they tend to be much more reserved on CDs.
PROFESSOR:	That's a very good point. As recording techniques got more realistic, people I think began to see particular performing conventions as "over the top." Styles that worked well in the heat of the moment in the concert hall, where you had to project and communicate with the person in the back row, maybe started to seem exaggerated when heard repeatedly in the calm of the listener's home. Although it's true that many performers adopt a more extrovert style in the concert hall, I think it's also true that some of the perfectionism and "inwardness" of studio performance has spilled over into live performance. We now expect people in concerts to sound like the CD.
NARRATOR:	Now use your notes to help you answer the questions.
	What is the talk mainly about?
	Why does the professor talk about Edison's attempts to market the phonograph as a dictation machine?
	Listen to part of the talk again, and then answer the question.
PROFESSOR:	Now, given the places where phonograph music was played, it's hardly surprising that the first recordings weren't of Bach and Beethoven.
NARRATOR:	What does the professor imply?
	What does the professor say about Caruso?

What does the professor say about Edison and music?

According to the talk, which of the following are true of sound recording?

Academic Talk 2: Film History

Track 14

NARRATOR: Listen to part of a talk in a film history class.

PROFESSOR: Okay ... We're going to see some clips today from Russian silent cinema, and, uh, we're going to use these clips to help us understand the art of montage. Montage? If you have never heard of that, I might use the word editing instead. But it's much more than that. Let's see what the great Russian filmmaker from the silent era said about, uh, what can be really called the art of silent film. Film should reflect the truths of life. Maybe you've heard of that concept. Film as truth, film as art. But how does this happen? Eisenstein believed that film was supposed to make ... visual connections ... connections between contradictory opposites. And this, this would create conflict. And for him, for Eisenstein, conflict was the essence of art. That tension, that sense of problem, to make an important statement. An important message, if you will.

Eisenstein's famous book, it's called *Film Form*, uh, in it, Eisenstein refers to vibrations of color. He wasn't referring to color in film, because he worked in black and white. But colors in general. Have you ever noticed how when you put a blue and green swatch of color next to each other, the colors seem to change? There's a new visual effect going on. Well, the colors don't actually change, but it's the effect on the mind's eye. What Eisenstein would call their energy or vibrations, interacting with light, plus the receptive eye, and how the brain translates all this stuff ... that creates new impressions and new meanings.

Eisenstein's colleague, Kuleshov, applied this same principle. He took a picture of an expressionless actor and juxtaposed it—matched it—to a happy image, like, uh, a puppy or a baby. When he showed the two images to a bunch of people, they thought the actor was reacting happily even though, of course, the picture of the actor showed absolutely no emotion! Then he took the same picture of the same actor and put it next to a sad image, like of a baby crying. What happened? Everybody thought the actor was sad too. But what's really going on? It was the people's association that sad images must mean sad reactions that led them to read into the actor's face.

So, what does all that have to do with editing, or as I mentioned earlier, uh, montage? Eisenstein's controversial principle of montage insists upon the element of conflict arising from this juxtaposition of two or more images. And how one image can lay its meaning on another. The amazing part of this—and the part that's hard to understand in some ways—is that the images colliding editorially do not even have to make sense. You can have a picture of an old person, say, cutting back and forth with a picture of a clock, and that's telling you something about the significance of time to that person ... maybe that time is running out ... or maybe that the person is waiting for someone. Even though you might never associate the person with the clock right off. The final combination lifts the viewer to a new message of life. A new truth. A new idea. Film as truth, film as art—you're starting to get the idea now, aren't you?

Now, I'll have to throw in another word here. Dialectical. It sounds tough, but if you say a film has a dialectic approach, then, well, what is that? It just means that nothing in life is isolated. Deeper layers of meaning can be extracted from all combined forms. How does this get, um, get translated into film? Dialectical montage ... and you hear, now I'm combining those two words, dialectical and montage. This creates a new "other" from every image that passes before the eye. It's, uh, kind of like a chain reaction of images that build to the film's conclusion.

When you see the clip in a few minutes, for example ... there's a peacock. What do we associate with a peacock? Vanity, arrogance, and the image following it is a man. But what does a peacock have to do with anything? The man lives in the city. How many peacocks live in the city? It's, it's a statement. The man is vain, the man is arrogant. And Eisenstein's driving home the point visually. Let's look at some of these examples on film now.

NARRATOR:	Now use your notes to help you answer the questions.
	What is the talk mainly about?
	What is the overall effect of combining images in a montage?
	Listen to part of the talk again, and then answer the question.
PROFESSOR:	This creates a new "other" from every image that passes before the eye. It's, uh, kind of like a chain reaction of images that build to the film's conclusion.
NARRATOR:	What can be inferred from this comment by the professor:
PROFESSOR:	It's, uh, kind of like a chain reaction of images ...
NARRATOR:	Listen to part of the talk again, and then answer the question.
PROFESSOR:	Everybody thought the actor was sad too. But what's really going on?
NARRATOR:	Why does the professor say this:
PROFESSOR:	But what's really going on?
NARRATOR:	Listen to part of the talk again, and then answer the question.
PROFESSOR:	Well, the colors don't actually change, but it's the effect on the mind's eye.
NARRATOR:	What does the professor mean when she says this:
PROFESSOR:	... but it's the effect on the mind's eye.
NARRATOR:	Which of the following does the professor compare film to in the lecture?

Academic Talk 3: Physics

Track 15

NARRATOR:	Listen to a part of a talk in a physics class.

PROFESSOR: Okay, today, we're going to talk about batteries. Now, as you know, uh, batteries are used throughout the world as portable sources of electrical power in products such as, uh, CD players, laptop computers, power tools, and, uh, even electric vehicles. In fact, anytime the need for portability outweighs the higher cost of portable energy, people turn to batteries. Now, the downside to batteries is their higher cost—batteries currently cost over a thousand times the price of the power you get from the wall sockets in your home. Yet these higher costs don't seem to stop people from buying more and more batteries.

So ... okay, let's get to the important stuff ... how does a battery work? Now, uh, a battery is made up of one or more devices known as red-ox cells. That's R-E-D dash O-X, short for "reduction and oxidation," which is what happens inside.

Okay, so, what's a red-ox cell? Well, you've heard the saying, "There're two kinds of people in this world—givers and takers." This may help describe what red-ox cells are and how they work. In red-ox cells, what is being given and taken are electrons—those are, of course, the tiny negatively charged particles that fly around the nucleus of all atoms. Commonly used red-ox cells contain two different electrodes. The first is an electron donor—uh, it releases electrons. The second electrode accepts these electrons. The material giving up electrons is called the anode, you spell that A-N-O-D-E, while the, uh, the material that takes these electrons is called the cathode. Cathode is spelled C-A-T-H-O-D-E.

So, a red-ox cell consists of three basic materials: an anode and a cathode in one container and a conducting substance between them. This conducting substance is called an electrolyte—it carries the electrons from anode to cathode. A number of substances can act as the electrolyte. In the earliest batteries, the electrolyte was a liquid, such as sulfuric acid. You can still see this in today's car batteries. Later, in order to make batteries more convenient and portable, this liquid was replaced by a paste—that's how we got the dry cell or flashlight battery, which was first patented in 1866. The main advantage of a dry cell battery is that it's a lot easier to transport than a battery that uses a liquid as its electrolyte.

Regardless of what is used as the electrolyte, the process inside a battery is the same. The electrons flow from the anode to the cathode through the electrolyte and back to the anode through a wire or other connector outside the cell. All you need to do is connect this wire—complete the circuit outside the battery so that the electrons can get back to the anode.

So how much power do you get from a battery? Well that depends on two important concepts, current and voltage. The current is the number of electrons that flow around the circuit, whereas the voltage is the pressure with which they flow. The pressure of the electron flow in the circuit depends on the materials used for the anode and cathode. These materials determine how fast the anode can get rid of electrons and how fast the cathode can accept them.

An easy way to imagine the potential difference in a battery is to think of a water pipe. In a water pipe the power depends both on how strong the pressure is and how much water is flowing through the pipe, and it's exactly the same with an electric current. To determine the total power, you multiply the pressure by the amount of current. This power is measured in watts, named after the British scientist James Watt. You can increase the power by increasing the current in one cell—that is, by increasing the surface area of cathode and anode available to exchange electrons or simply by connecting several cells together.

NARRATOR: Now use your notes to help you answer the questions.

What is the main topic of the lecture?

What does the professor imply?

Listen to part of the talk again, and then answer the question.

PROFESSOR: Okay, so, what's a red-ox cell? Well, you've heard the saying, "There're two kinds of people in this world—givers and takers."

NARRATOR: Why does the professor refer to givers and takers?

According to the professor, why is the dry cell battery better than earlier batteries?

Why does the professor use the example of the water pipe?

According to the lecture, which of the following are true of batteries?

SPEAKING SECTION

Task 1

Track 16

NARRATOR: For this task, you will give your opinion about a topic that is familiar to you. You will hear a question. You will then have 15 seconds to prepare your response and 45 seconds to speak.

NARRATOR: Some people prefer to rent their home, while others prefer to buy a property. Which would you prefer and why? Give details and examples in your explanation.

Task 2

Track 17

NARRATOR: Listen to two students as they discuss the change in policy.

STUDENT A: Why is it that the commuters are always getting discriminated against?

STUDENT B: I think the new system's a good idea. At least everyone'll have a fair shot. The faculty won't get special treatment.

STUDENT A: It's the commuters who deserve special treatment. Most of the professors live pretty close by. For those of us who live far away from campus, convenience is a necessity. Now, we'll have to waste precious study time driving around in circles. Or worse yet, we'll have to pay some garage.

STUDENT B: You can't really say we don't get special treatment. The annual fee we pay for a permit's a lot lower than what the faculty pays.

STUDENT A: At least, under the old system, we were guaranteed spots till they ran out. Now, I'll be competing with everyone, including people who live on campus. Under this new policy, I'll just have to hope I get lucky.

STUDENT B: You know, my brother's school instituted a similar system last year. For some reason, a lot of people didn't even bother entering. So who knows? Maybe we'll actually have a better chance than before …

NARRATOR: Now get ready to answer the question.

NARRATOR: The woman expresses her opinion about a new university policy. State her opinion and explain the reasons she gives for holding that opinion.

Task 3

Track 18

NARRATOR: Listen to part of a talk in an economics class.

PROFESSOR: The 19th-century Corn Law of Britain is interesting to look at because it mirrors some of the trade issues that continue to affect politics today. As you will recall from your reading, bread prices went way up in England during the wars with France. But even though people weren't fond of paying high prices for their daily bread, there was a war on, difficulties were expected, and the people shrugged and bore it. But when the war ended, and Parliament acted to keep those prices up, the reaction was very different. In fact, as the legislation was being passed, Parliament had to be defended by troops against a crowd that had gathered to express their, uh, opposition to the law.

This law was opposed by different segments of the population for different reasons. At this point in British history, towns were growing, and the former farmers who moved to the towns to work in industry no longer had access to their own fresh food. They were increasingly dependent on bread—and the more money they spent on bread, the less they had for their rent and everything else.

Now, the manufacturers who created the jobs in the towns hated the law because they thought higher bread prices would lead to demands for higher wages—and they saw it as a symbol of the political dominance of the landowners. That is to say, Parliament was listening to the landowners, and not to the new manufacturers.

Opposition to the law did not let up, and it went through a series of reforms. But despite the size of the first opposition group, and the wealth of the second, it wasn't repealed until the 1840s.

NARRATOR: Now get ready to answer the question.

NARRATOR: The professor discusses the Corn Law. Using information from the lecture and the reading, explain why the Corn Law was enacted and why some people opposed it.

Task 4

Track 19

NARRATOR: For this task, you will hear a short academic talk. You will hear a question about it. You will then have 20 seconds to prepare your response and 60 seconds to speak.

Listen to part of a talk in an urban history class.

PROFESSOR: Usually, when people talk about the Harlem Renaissance—the period extending from the end of World War I to the Great Depression in the mid-1930s—they focus on the cultural aspects, and particularly on the great black writers of the period who produced an extensive body of literature of all types: drama, poetry, fiction, and nonfiction.

Certainly, culture was an important part of the rebirth of this New York neighborhood. But there's another element of the Harlem Renaissance that can't be ignored, and without which this rebirth would never have come about, and that is the economic aspect. Blacks began settling in the northern cities of the United States soon after the end of the Civil War. This migration to the North was the result of a variety of factors. Blacks were eager to escape the racism and discrimination they suffered in the South. At the same time, with the South in the midst of an economic depression, blacks saw the North as the land of opportunity.

Before it became the social and cultural center of black America, Harlem was a white, upper-class neighborhood inhabited by a large number of Jews and Italians. Thanks in large part to huge improvements in public transportation—the advent of the bus and the elevated train—Harlem enjoyed a real estate boom, which spurred a big surge in construction. Then, suddenly, between 1903 and 1905, an economic crisis brought a sudden end to the construction, leaving many homes and apartment buildings abandoned and unfinished. At about this same time, the subway line that connected Harlem to downtown Manhattan was completed. The existence of convenient public transportation and the availability of affordable housing were two factors that paved the way for blacks to move into Harlem in large numbers.

NARRATOR: Now get ready to answer the question.

NARRATOR: Using points and examples from the talk, explain how economic factors contributed to the Harlem Renaissance in New York City in the early 1900s.

WRITING SECTION

Task 1

Track 20

NARRATOR: Listen to part of a talk on the topic you just read about.

PROFESSOR: There is a legitimate reason why dairy-free diets are becoming more and more popular in some parts of the world.

First of all, dairy products tend to be high in saturated fat. Although fat is a necessary part of our diets, some dairy products, like butter, milk, and cheese contain excessive amounts of saturated fats, which are best avoided, as they can contribute to increased cholesterol levels and heart disease. Plant-based fats, on the other hand, such as those found in olive oil, nuts, and avocados, are more easily digestible and ultimately a more nourishing way to get the right amount of healthy fat that your body needs throughout the day.

Additionally, studies have shown that a majority of the planet's population has some degree of lactose intolerance. Lactose is an enzyme found naturally in our bodies, which breaks down the sugar in dairy so that it can be properly digested. For a majority of adults, this process is compromised, which results in a range of symptoms and health issues. Why run the risk of such symptoms when there are so many healthy, delicious alternatives? Soy and nut milks are nutritious substitutes for dairy milk, and easily accessible foods like almonds, broccoli, beans, and seeds provide many of the nutrients found in dairy products.

Lastly, the dairy industry is responsible for making a significant impact on the environment. Millions of farmers worldwide tend to millions of cows, which puts a heavy burden on natural resources, including water and soil. Dairy cows and their manure produce greenhouse gas emissions, which contribute to climate change, and insufficient management of waste and fertilizers damage water sources and land. By consuming dairy products, people are supporting an industry that often causes serious damage to the environment.

NARRATOR: Summarize the main points in the lecture you just heard, explaining how they cast doubt on the points made in the reading.

PRACTICE TEST 3

LISTENING SECTION

Dialogue 1

Track 21

NARRATOR:	Listen to a dialogue between a student and a professor.
PROFESSOR:	Well, Marie, I appreciate you coming in on such short notice.
STUDENT:	It's no problem, Professor Chen. I spend almost every day here on campus. I … I practically feel like I live here.
PROFESSOR:	Hmm, then you might not want to take on this research position after all.
STUDENT:	Oh! Oh, no, I didn't mean it that way, Professor Chen. I just meant I'm around the college a lot between classes … and now, working for you … hopefully.
PROFESSOR:	I put in long hours myself as an undergrad, you know, back in the Dark Ages. Anyway, so do you think you'll be able to devote about 10 hours a week to being my research assistant?
STUDENT:	Yes, of course. I'm looking forward to it … I was very grateful when you called to ask if I'd be interested in the job.
PROFESSOR:	Well, I was looking through the papers that your class did for me last semester, and yours was outstanding. You really paid attention to detail with your research. That's the kind of precision work I'm looking for.
STUDENT:	So, what would my responsibilities be?
PROFESSOR:	First off, I'm working on a textbook on bilingual education, so I'd need you to check the databases for every current journal article that's out there … I'll let you read the book prospectus before you start, and you'll see exactly what focus I'm after.
STUDENT:	I can definitely manage that. I love doing database searches and checking out websites.
PROFESSOR:	Good. Although I mention that first, it's not my number-one priority. A more pressing project is entering the data I just collected from my study on students' attitudes toward test taking—I assume you remember the spreadsheet program that you used in my class last year?
STUDENT:	Oh, yeah. I use that program in two of my classes this semester.
PROFESSOR:	Well, then, I'll be giving you about 200 questionnaires and you'll need to enter those data, according to the codes I indicate.
STUDENT:	When would you like me to start doing the data entry?
PROFESSOR:	I'm expecting the first batch of 50 questionnaires this afternoon, and you could start—well, we need to set up your schedule, don't you think? Can we do that tomorrow during my office hours? I have to run to a meeting now.
STUDENT:	That sounds fine.

PROFESSOR:	Great. And I'll have a key made for you at some point. I'm here every day, but sometimes I go out of town.
STUDENT:	Every day, like me.
PROFESSOR:	Yes, sometimes I feel like I live here too!
NARRATOR:	Now use your notes to help you answer the questions.
	How does the professor know the student?
	Why does the professor think the student could work well with him?
	What does the professor want the student to do first?
	What can be inferred about most of the work the student will have to do?
	Listen to part of the dialogue again, and then answer the question.
STUDENT:	I spend almost every day here on campus. I . . . I practically feel like I live here.
PROFESSOR:	Hmm, then you might not want to take on this research position after all.
NARRATOR:	What does the professor imply when he says this:
PROFESSOR:	Hmm, then you might not want to take on this research position after all.

Dialogue 2

Track 22

NARRATOR:	Listen to a dialogue between a first-year student and his advisor.
STUDENT:	I really appreciate your taking the time to see me.
ADVISOR:	Let's see if I can help. What's this about?
STUDENT:	I . . . I think I really need to drop a course, but I feel bad.
ADVISOR:	Why's that?
STUDENT:	I feel bad because I hate giving up . . . it's just not my nature to quit in the middle of something.
ADVISOR:	I understand. But what makes you want to drop it?
STUDENT:	I . . . I don't like the way the professor's teaching . . . I hate to say that.
ADVISOR:	Tell me what's going on.
STUDENT:	It sounds like I'm complaining, but I mean, look at my grades. I have all A's, a 4.0 GPA. It's not like I'm trying to weasel out of work.
ADVISOR:	Not with all A's, I wouldn't think.
STUDENT:	I mean, the professor rambles a lot, gets off-topic, you know. He starts with one idea, and 10 minutes later he's somewhere else.
ADVISOR:	That can be disconcerting.
STUDENT:	And he gave us a list of stuff for the midterm, but practically nothing from the list was on the test. In fact, there were questions I swear he never talked about in class.
ADVISOR:	Hmm, I see the problem, but my question is, is this a required course?
STUDENT:	No, that's the irony. I was just taking it because I wanted to learn more

about the topic. It's like a personal interest.

ADVISOR: Well, this is a little easier to handle because it's not a requirement. As an elective, you're free to drop it.

STUDENT: There's no penalty for dropping, is there?

ADVISOR: No. That is, not yet, because fortunately, you're just under the wire for the deadline. It will go on your record as a WD—a withdrawal—but that won't affect your GPA.

STUDENT: Whew.

ADVISOR: So go to the Registrar and ask for the form. Or better yet—since you don't want to wait too long—drop it online.

STUDENT: I'm gonna go to the library now and do it. Like I said, I really wanted to stick with this course to the end, but when I saw that 65 on my midterm, I said forget it.

ADVISOR: Well, maybe you could audit the course?

STUDENT: Oh, I, I—no, I just can't take it with this guy!

ADVISOR: Well, maybe you can take the course in the future with a professor whose teaching style is more in tune with your learning style.

STUDENT: Yeah, I've got three more semesters to go, so I guess that's a possibility.

NARRATOR: Now use your notes to help you answer the questions.

What is the student's main concern with the course he wants to drop?

Why did the student think the midterm exam was unusual?

NARRATOR: Now use your notes to help you answer the questions.

Why does the advisor say the student can drop the course now?

What can be inferred as the main reason the student asked about dropping the course?

Listen to part of the dialogue again, and then answer the question.

STUDENT: … It's not like I'm trying to weasel out of work.

ADVISOR: Not with all A's, I wouldn't think.

NARRATOR: What does the advisor mean?

Academic Talk 1: Women's Studies

Track 23

NARRATOR: Listen to part of a talk in a women's studies class.

PROFESSOR: Sometimes, in order to understand the development of the feminist movement in one culture, it's useful to compare and contrast it with that in another culture. By taking two very different cultures—the U.S. and India, for example—we can see some of the motivations behind their respective feminist movements. First, let me ground you in a little background of India's history as it relates to women's issues.

One researcher called the Indian women's movement a complicated process. It was born out of the country's independence, declared in 1947.

	Its constitution called for equality between men and women. Let me make an aside here … although I'm not focusing on the U.S. now—
STUDENT A:	I was just gonna say, it reminds me of the U.S. Constitution. Even though it was written in the 18th century, it didn't even really mention women's rights until the women's voting amendment was added in the 20th century.
PROFESSOR:	You just made my point, and I'll let you all think about that one for a moment. Getting back to India though, uh, India established a number of administrative bodies designed to create opportunities for women. So with this, India established a promising foundation for equality that, that facilitated women's activism, especially in the 1970s. Can anyone tell me why that decade's so important to feminism?
STUDENT B:	I seem to remember that in the '70s, as we spoke about in, uh, was it last week? The United Nations declared 1975 International Women's Year.
STUDENT A:	Could you also say that in the '70s the women's movement became known all around the globe?
PROFESSOR:	Yes, and we'll be looking at other countries to see some interesting parallels. Early feminism in India was rooted in social conditions that affected quality of life for both men and women. People often forget that women were concerned for the welfare of their sons and husbands too. When people think of quote "women's lib" in the U.S., for example, we often get strong—and may I add, misleading—images that don't accurately portray the women's movement.
STUDENT B:	I think most people—and me too, once upon a time—most people think of tough, angry women screaming for equality.
PROFESSOR:	And for many people, that became the stereotypical women's libber, at least in the U.S. But that's far from the truth. In India and elsewhere, women were indeed concerned about equality in general and challenged exploitative, extortionist practices by landowners, for example. Of course, they also turned to critical issues affecting women's safety and health. Concerned about the effects of alcohol in the home environment, Indian women sometimes took the law into their own hands. Like, they would destroy liquor stores that contributed to drinking problems.
	Very important—Indian women participated in numerous episodes of mass solidarity. This suggests that they'd developed effective campaigns for, for communication and shared belief. For example, as demonstrations of women marched through a village, women in the homes would come out beating their utensils, like metal plates with rolling pins, in a nonverbal outcry of support.
STUDENT B:	Better to beat plates than people!
PROFESSOR:	Good point. The Indian women's movement matured during the 1980s. Sisterhood was celebrated in a specifically Indian context, emphasizing positive aspects of women's creativity and potential. A national workshop featured feminists and artists who explored important women's topics through theater, song and dance, and fine arts. They tapped many

traditions … religion, mythology, and Indian culture … for symbols of women's power.

STUDENT A: They must have chosen a lot of women warriors and goddesses, all of them pretty powerful figures.

PROFESSOR: And these images represented their struggles and, uh, vitality. One writer called the reach of the Indian women's movement both vertical and horizontal. In other times, rather, in other words, the movement spanned a variety of organizations on the foundational level and also reached up into the highest echelons of governance. Equally important to the movement was the representation of women from rural and urban settings at conferences. Today, Indian women's groups are joining movements in the U.S. and Britain because many Indian women are resettling in those countries.

Later this week, I'll describe some of the more controversial social traditions unique to India that seriously challenged the women's movement for two decades, and continue to do so. Although I already made some parallels to the U.S. feminist movement, I'll synthesize the comparison of both countries after we address more aspects of Indian culture. Please jot down in your notes any parallels you might see between the two countries, based on our previous discussions of the U.S. women's movement.

NARRATOR: Now use your notes to help you answer the questions.

What is the talk mainly about?

How did Indian village women show their support for demonstrators?

What can be inferred about the Indian women's movement from the 1970s to 1980s?

Listen to part of the talk again, and then answer the question.

PROFESSOR: Let me make an aside here … although I'm not focusing on the U.S. now—

NARRATOR: Why does the professor say this:

PROFESSOR: Let me make an aside here …

NARRATOR: Listen to part of the talk again, and then answer the question.

STUDENT B: I think most people—and me too, once upon a time—most people think of tough, angry women screaming for equality.

NARRATOR: What does the student mean when she says this:

STUDENT B: —and me too, once upon a time—

NARRATOR: In the talk, the professor describes a number of facts that are part of the Indian women's movement. Indicate which of the following were mentioned in the talk.

Academic Talk 2: Music

Track 24

NARRATOR:	Listen to part of a talk in a music class.
PROFESSOR:	Perhaps not many of you've heard of Joules Graves, but I hope you listened to her songs, for that was part of the homework. Her CD, *A Sacred Tantrum*, specifically addresses women's perceptions. Both how women are perceived and how they should be perceived. At the same time, though, Graves talks about the human condition. Loving, healing, dancing, contemplating. Being lost and being found. Anger and loneliness.
STUDENT A:	Sounds like she just about covers everything a person could go through in life … both men and women.
PROFESSOR:	Yes, you hit the nail on the head. Graves depicts a realistic emotional journey for everyone. She thinks people shouldn't be afraid to look at themselves. Even if they feel angry, they can rediscover something sacred about themselves in relation to nature. Graves uses the metaphor of water to help convey her nature theme. But why water?
STUDENT B:	Water is soothing and calming. And it cleans.
STUDENT A:	And it's used a lot in literature, as a symbol for life. Like, aren't people always searching for signs of water on other planets as evidence of life?
PROFESSOR:	Exactly. And aren't babies born in water? And life was said to spring from water? We equate water with life. So Graves is saying how water can heal someone who's angry or been hurt by negative social constructs. She uses the water idea as a way to crash—not literally, of course—through such social constructs as fashion, gender, and the prim-and-proper way society thinks women should behave.
STUDENT B:	Well, I heard that people refer to the women's movement over the last 150 years as happening in waves, like the first wave, second wave, third wave.
STUDENT A:	What do waves have to do with it?
STUDENT B:	Think about waves on a beach and how they come crashing down with force …
PROFESSOR:	And the women's movement did just that. It crashed down—so to speak—on some of those social constructs. Graves makes no small connection between the feminist movement and the water in her songs. And we hear the final songs on the CD repeat the major themes she weaves throughout the CD: anger giving way to self-affirmation, which gives way to anger again, which finally yields to self-affirmation. In fact, one of her songs is called "What Comes Around Goes Around."
STUDENT A:	Well, if you're talking about the women's movement, a lot of women were angry about things that weren't fair or equal in society. Maybe Graves is referring to that anger in her songs?
STUDENT B:	But don't forget, there's the affirming part too.
PROFESSOR:	It's all a cycle. Ebbs and flows—like water—and always changing. Maybe starting angry, but turning into something positive. Notice how her voice reflects this: it's rough and filled with raw energy. You almost expect

her voice to veer off into dissonance, be purposefully off-key, like a person shouting. But then she'll control her singing and always return to pitch. And that delicate guitar and percussion … how they support and contrast with her vocal moods. Her songs have the form of speak-singing at times.

STUDENT A: I don't know about speak-singing. Whenever I hear that term, I always feel the singer is, like, lecturing to the listener. I don't really think of that as entertainment.

PROFESSOR: Well, it may not be to everyone's taste. But just consider objectively what the singer is trying to accomplish with these songs. Graves maybe wants to simply tell you her experiences. Like the song "Alone and All One" calls out for solidarity, belonging to the world, even while accepting that this fast-food, high-tech, everyone's-busy-all-the-time world can be crazy. To become "all one," like she says, one must know what it is to be "alone."

STUDENT B: That's both ironic and true. Everybody wants to escape the craziness, but it's also important to reach out to someone who's lost.

PROFESSOR: Well, as she says, being open is "Not for Cowards"—the title of yet another song. In opening up to emotions, one affirms life. The experience becomes almost a ritual bathing in nature—and there you go, back to the water theme again.

On a personal note, I think one of Graves's lyrics especially captures the human condition: "There's only just a fine line/between alone and all one." That line's hard to see and hard to cross. But Graves seems to think that when both men and women find a common ground, they can come together to fill a need all people have. Wouldn't that outcome be worth throwing a tantrum for?

NARRATOR: Now use your notes to help you answer the questions.

What is the talk mainly about?

What can be inferred about the singer's attitude toward nature?

Listen to part of the talk again, and then answer the question.

PROFESSOR: She uses the water idea as a way to crash—not literally, of course—through such social constructs as fashion, gender, and the prim-and-proper way society thinks women should behave.

NARRATOR: Why does the professor say this:

PROFESSOR: … not literally, of course …

NARRATOR: Listen to part of the talk again, and then answer the question.

STUDENT A: Well, if you're talking about the women's movement, a lot of women were angry about things that weren't fair or equal in society. Maybe Graves is referring to that anger in her songs?

STUDENT B: But don't forget, there's the affirming part too.

NARRATOR: What does the student mean when he says this:

STUDENT B: But don't forget, there's the affirming part too.

NARRATOR: Listen to part of the talk again, and then answer the question.

PROFESSOR: On a personal note, I think one of Graves's lyrics especially captures the human condition.

NARRATOR:	Why does the professor say this:
PROFESSOR:	On a personal note …
NARRATOR:	In the lecture, the professor discusses several themes covered in the songs. Indicate which of the following themes are considered by the singer.

Academic Talk 3: History

Track 25

| NARRATOR: | Listen to part of a talk in a history class. |
| PROFESSOR: | By now, I hope you've all read Jefferson's book, *Notes on the State of Virginia*. Thomas Jefferson, uh, who most of you probably know as the third president of the United States, was a man of many talents. Musician, inventor, diplomat, writer. As you may recall, he wrote this book to answer questions posed to him by the French. They wanted to, to better understand the state of Virginia … Jefferson's home state. Now, he had quite a number of questions to answer, but he doesn't just answer them randomly. I hope you noted something of a structure to his material. We'll discuss this in greater depth later. |

First, though, I want to point out that by sorting out the questions into specific categories, Jefferson got the chance to write essays that would allow him to elaborate on many issues. He wasn't just going to focus on facts and figures on the state of Virginia. Instead, he was going to take the opportunity—articulate as he was—to find a platform for his philosophy and his knowledge. So, I'd like you to keep this question in mind as we look at these different essays, or, or chapters. Where does the objective scientist and writer begin … as Jefferson is asked to be? And where does a very subjective and opinionated human being come in? I'd like you to think about this … that both personas are reflected in his essays.

So, uh, what does Jefferson do from the outset? Well, logically, he needs to introduce the place he wants to talk about. So in fact, he starts out by presenting a map of the state's topography and brings his readers on a tour of the concrete elements of nature for about, oh, about the, the first half of the book.

According to the questions he's been given, he creates a logical succession of answers. First, there's the land, then there's all the aspects of nature: rivers, mountains, mines, trees, animals, birds, people. He loads each discussion with as many "hard facts" as he can assemble from truly varied sources: established geographic measurements, documents and charters, personal calculations and astute personal observations, foreign and ancient sources, firsthand witnesses and practitioners, like uh, the miners themselves. And Jefferson throws in some entertainment … anecdotes from Indian folklore and curious facts that a "tourist" would love to hear.

He also liked to create comparisons as a way of making a point. For example, he compares the Mississippi River with the Nile River! Now, everybody knew a good deal about the Nile in Jefferson's day, and so, because they were familiar with the nature of that ancient river, the French could transfer that understanding to a river they knew nothing about. Curiously, though, Jefferson is still selective, even though he has massive amounts of information to share. He just sort of sweeps over multitudes of facts with functional lists … lists of trees, lists of birds, whatever. Obviously, he didn't find it as important, for some reason, to describe leaves and birds in such minute detail as when he talked about the rivers and minerals. I'll leave you to figure out why he did that.

Speaking from his distinction as a key figure in the American fight for Independence … the writer of the Declaration of Independence, as I hope you all recall … you'll see that Jefferson saves the best stuff for last. By laying out the land of Virginia—that is, physically … the land and its nature—he now moves into discussing the larger and more conceptual issues that make up the state. Notice a big difference. He begins to talk more forcefully in the "I" voice. It's, it's almost as if his own life, now, becomes a source of knowledge. He's an authority on politics, economics, trade, human relations, government, history. And now he speaks in broader terms, in powerful rhetoric. Here's our chance for deeper discussion the next time we meet. What's Jefferson accomplished by doing this? His shift in voice is significant, even though his style seems to clash with the first half of the book. Let's look at specific sections now, to see if we can understand Jefferson's ulterior motives behind these notes.

NARRATOR: Now use your notes to help you answer the questions.

What is the talk mainly about?

What is the logical progression of Jefferson's description of Virginia?

How do the two parts of Jefferson's book reflect his personality?

Listen to part of the talk again, and then answer the question.

PROFESSOR: Curiously, though, Jefferson is still selective, even though he has massive amounts of information to share. He just sort of sweeps over multitudes of facts with functional lists …

NARRATOR: What does the professor mean when he says this:

PROFESSOR: He just sort of sweeps over multitudes of facts …

NARRATOR: Listen to part of the talk again, and then answer the question.

PROFESSOR: Obviously, he didn't find it as important, for some reason, to describe leaves and birds in such minute detail as when he talked about the rivers and minerals. I'll leave you to figure out why he did that.

NARRATOR: Why does the professor say this:

PROFESSOR: I'll leave you to figure out …

NARRATOR: Listen to part of the talk again, and then answer the question.

PROFESSOR: … you'll see that Jefferson saves the best stuff for last. By laying out the land of Virginia—that is, physically … the land and its nature—he now moves into discussing the larger and more conceptual issues that make up the state.

NARRATOR: What does the professor imply when he says this:

PROFESSOR: … Jefferson saves the best stuff for last.

SPEAKING SECTION

Task 1

Track 26

NARRATOR: The television, the internet, and other electronic media are causing printed books to become obsolete as a source of information or entertainment. Do you agree or disagree with the statement? Give details and examples in your explanation.

Task 2

Track 27

NARRATOR: Listen to two students as they discuss the announcement.

STUDENT A: Why is it that the athletes always get all the money? It's so unfair!

STUDENT B: Have you seen the swimming pool we have now? Can you believe we've had the same pool since 1904?

STUDENT A: And can you believe I live in the only dorm on campus that doesn't have internet access? And that the bio labs haven't been renovated since my dad was a student here? I have nothing against sports. I'm only saying that the university should spend its limited resources in ways that'll do the most good for the largest number of people.

STUDENT B: Athletics are important. They help students relieve stress and keep their bodies in good shape. And our sports teams help foster school spirit.

STUDENT A: That's all very nice, but I just think the administration has its priorities all wrong. They should put academics first. Talk about stress! I could use a new language lab to improve my grades. That'd help my stress.

STUDENT B: Look at the bright side. Maybe our fancy new sports center will earn so much money in ticket sales that they'll be able to add several labs.

NARRATOR: Now get ready to answer the question.

NARRATOR: The man expresses his opinion about the announcement made by the alumni office. State his opinion and explain the reasons he gives for holding that opinion.

Task 3

Track 28

NARRATOR: Now listen to part of a talk in a zoology class.

PROFESSOR: People who lived near Yellowstone raised a lot of fuss when wolves were returned there by scientists in the mid-'90s. The old prejudices and fears came right to the surface again. The "big bad wolf" coming to get you. It's a lot of nonsense really, and the Yellowstone Wolf Project has helped prove that. The wolves are not a problem—in fact, a lack of wolves, or an absence of wolves is the problem. How many of you have heard of someone being attacked by a wolf? No one, right? Now how many of you know someone who got into a car accident because deer were on the roads or highways? Or have neighbors who can't grow flowers or vegetables because the deer eat everything? Yeah, a lot more of you. We have a serious deer problem in this country because we have no predators to control the deer population. The deer numbers are out of control, but we have people worried about a couple of dozen wolves in Yellowstone. Well, the wolves haven't been causing problems to the neighbors of Yellowstone. Cattle and sheep and horses simply aren't being attacked. The wolves have plenty of deer in the park to keep them busy. We need more wolves—not less.

NARRATOR: Now get ready to answer the question.

NARRATOR: The professor talks about the results of wolves being brought back to Yellowstone National Park. Explain what those results are and how those results are contrary to what people living near the park expected.

Task 4
Track 29

NARRATOR: For this task, you will hear a short academic talk. You will hear a question about it. You will then have 20 seconds to prepare your response and 60 seconds to speak.

Listen to part of a talk in an American government class.

PROFESSOR: In the 1960s, the United States Supreme Court handed down a landmark decision that affirmed the legal rights of persons accused of a crime. Gideon v. Wainwright centered on a man named Clarence Gideon, who was arrested for breaking into a bar in 1961. When Gideon asked the court to appoint a lawyer to defend him, the court denied his request, saying that state law required the court to provide defendants with an attorney only in capital cases, that is to say, cases involving a person's death or the death penalty. As Gideon was too poor to afford a lawyer, he defended himself at his trial and—perhaps not surprisingly— was sentenced to jail. While he was in prison, Gideon studied law books on his own and eventually wrote a petition asking the Supreme Court to hear his case. In its decision the Supreme Court ruled that Gideon's right to a fair trial—guaranteed under the Fourth Amendment to the Constitution—had been violated. The Supreme Court ruled that every state must provide a lawyer for any person who's accused of a crime and cannot afford to pay for his or her own legal defense. Gideon was given a second trial. This time, he was represented by a defense attorney and he was declared innocent.

You might be asking yourself why the Fourth Amendment was relevant to Gideon's case. In considering the case, the Supreme Court focused on what exactly is meant by "a fair trial." And what the Supreme Court decided was that forcing a man with no legal expertise to defend himself in court, simply because he did not have the means to pay for a lawyer, put the defendant at an unfair disadvantage.

NARRATOR: Now get ready to answer the question.

NARRATOR: Using points and examples from the talk, explain why Gideon's case was important and what values are reflected in the Supreme Court's decision.

WRITING SECTION

Task 1

Track 30

NARRATOR: Listen to part of a talk on the topic you just read about.

PROFESSOR: Despite the fact that more and more electric vehicles are becoming available to consumers, they present significant drawbacks, despite what manufacturers and many environmentalists want us to think.

First, electric vehicles are not especially convenient. While gas stations are ubiquitous, charging stations are not. And you can't run down to the gas station and refuel your electric car in a matter of minutes. Instead, it can take hours to recharge your car so that it's at the point of real usefulness. If you forget to plug in your car before you go to bed, you're stuck the next day without access to transportation.

Furthermore, the current electric cars that are most widely available are generally much more expensive than conventional cars. Despite the fact that they may offer a luxury feel and multiple amenities intended to offset the high cost of these alternative vehicles, their price range makes them inaccessible to most consumers. When it comes to electric cars, sustainability is a luxury that many people cannot afford.

The final consideration is that, although some say electric vehicles have a lower environmental impact than conventional cars, buying a new car—electric or not—will always have a detrimental effect on the environment. It is widely known that one of the best ways to support sustainability is to reduce consumerism. If your petroleum-fueled car is perfectly functional, it is environmentally irresponsible to get rid of it and purchase a new car. Even if your replacement model is electric, the production and delivery of electric cars still make a significant environmental footprint, which driving it around will not undo.

NARRATOR: Summarize the points made in the talk you just heard, explaining how they cast doubt on the points made in the reading.

PRACTICE TEST 4

LISTENING SECTION

Dialogue 1

Track 31

NARRATOR:	Listen to a dialogue between a student and a professor.
PROFESSOR:	Oh, Jerry, come in. My office hours have just started.
STUDENT:	Hi, Professor Wright. I, uh, needed to clarify something on the project you gave out yesterday. You said it, uh, the project, should have five parts, but I only see one here.
PROFESSOR:	Yes, I mentioned in class I'd be giving out the other parts as we go along because I, I want you to just develop one part at a time.
STUDENT:	I don't remember that—oh, I came in late.
PROFESSOR:	Yes, right, you were about 15 minutes late.
STUDENT:	I'm really sorry. I got stuck at work, then I got stuck in traffic, and then I got stuck trying to park! When it rains, it pours.
PROFESSOR:	I marked you down as present when I saw you. But if that happens again, please come to me after class and let me know. It's a big class, and if you're just slipping in and out, I might mark you absent when you aren't.
STUDENT:	Thanks.
PROFESSOR:	Now, did you have questions on the part I handed out?
STUDENT:	To be honest, I haven't gone over it since class. We're supposed to describe the school we're teaching in, right?
PROFESSOR:	The school, the students, the demographics. Anything to help me understand where you're student teaching.
STUDENT:	Okay. Uh, what's coming up in the other parts?
PROFESSOR:	Well, I explain that in the handout too. But basically, for the second part, I want you to describe a topic you'll be teaching this semester to your students. You're teaching math, right?
STUDENT:	No, I teach Spanish.
PROFESSOR:	Oh, okay. So then pick a topic in Spanish, like, um, teaching a particular verb, and tell me how you'd carry out that lesson.
STUDENT:	Oh, I can do like going to the park and teach the verb "play" or "run" in different tenses.
PROFESSOR:	That's right, and you could delve into maybe popular sports in Spain—some aspect of the culture. I want details about how you'd carry that out in the classroom.
STUDENT:	And the other parts?

PROFESSOR:	I expect you to write test questions for the students, as well as how you'd evaluate their quest—I mean their answers. That's parts three and four. And in part five, I want you to write a reflection paper.
STUDENT:	Like what I learned?
PROFESSOR:	And how you could improve what you did, things like that.
STUDENT:	That's a lot of work. But if I'm going to be a teacher someday, this is how I learn.
PROFESSOR:	That's the point, Jerry.
NARRATOR:	Now use your notes to help you answer the questions.
	What is the focus of the professor's class project?
	Why did the student need to talk with the professor?
	What subject does the student teach?
	Listen to part of the dialogue again, and then answer the question.
PROFESSOR:	I marked you down as present when I saw you. But if that happens again, please come to me after class and let me know. It's a big class, and if you're just slipping in and out, I might mark you absent when you aren't.
NARRATOR:	What is the professor implying?
	Listen to part of the dialogue again, and then answer the question.
STUDENT:	I'm really sorry. I got stuck at work, then I got stuck in traffic, and then I got stuck trying to park! When it rains, it pours.
NARRATOR:	What can be inferred about the student?

Dialogue 2

Track 32

NARRATOR:	Listen to a dialogue between a student and an administrator.
STUDENT:	Hi, I got this letter saying there's a problem with my activity fees?
ADMINISTRATOR:	Umm … Oh yes, we thought it'd be easier to clear everything up if you came in. We don't seem to have received your activity fees payment. I know there's never been a problem before, but … umm, I'm afraid it's university policy that we have to receive the first installment of fees before the semester starts. The fees are normally deposited by wire transfer into the university's account, aren't they?
STUDENT:	That's right, my dad wires the money from Taiwan. I've got a copy of the wire instructions here. It's in both Chinese and English.
ADMINISTRATOR:	Excellent. Let me just check this against our records. Well … this all seems okay … No, look … two digits of our account number have been reversed.
STUDENT:	So does that mean the money's gone to someone else's account?
ADMINISTRATOR:	Well, that's possible. Or the other account number might not actually exist. Then the bank would try to find the account where

it's supposed to go, and if that's not possible, they'd send it back … though that could take some time … possibly a few weeks.

STUDENT: Well, my dad didn't say anything about the money being returned. But I can ask him to check it out with the bank back home.

ADMINISTRATOR: Right. In the meantime, though, as I said, it's actually university policy that fees need to be paid before the semester starts on Monday. Would you be able to … um … ?

STUDENT: Wow, that's a lot of money. I don't have that. I mean, I'd need to wait till my dad could wire it, which wouldn't really be any faster, would it?

ADMINISTRATOR: No, that's true. Okay … well, your fees have always been paid on time up to now, and we do have evidence that the funds were actually sent. I think I'd better take a copy of this, if you don't mind … Okay, I'll need to get this confirmed by my manager … She'll be in

Monday … but I don't think there'll be a problem extending the payment deadline by, say, two weeks. That should give your dad time to sort out the payment error and make a new payment. Is there a phone number where we can reach you on Monday in case my manager needs to ask you more questions?

STUDENT: Yes, I'll be at 555-6789 most of the day. I do hope this gets sorted out quickly. And thanks for being so understanding.

NARRATOR: Now use your notes to help you answer the questions.

Why does the student go to the administrative office?

What has happened with the bank transfer?

Listen to part of the dialogue again, and then answer the question.

ADMINISTRATOR: … as I said, it's actually university policy that fees need to be paid before the semester starts on Monday. Would you be able to … um … ?

NARRATOR: What does the administrator mean when he says this:

ADMINISTRATOR: Would you be able to … um … ?

NARRATOR: What does the administrator offer to do?

What will the administrator probably do?

Academic Talk 1: Biology

Track 33

NARRATOR: Listen to part of a talk in a biology class.

PROFESSOR: All right, today's topic is diabetes. Diabetes is a disease marked by high levels of glucose in the blood. Now, can someone tell me what blood glucose is?

STUDENT A: It's blood sugar, right?

PROFESSOR: Yes, the cells of our bodies use blood glucose, blood sugar, as a source of energy. However, before our bodies can use this blood glucose, it must move from the bloodstream into our individual cells. And this process requires a protein called insulin, which is produced by the pancreas. Insulin helps blood glucose move from the bloodstream into individual cells, so your body can use it for energy. Questions … ? Okay, so what is diabetes? Diabetes occurs when the body doesn't produce enough insulin or when the body is unable to use insulin properly. With low insulin levels, it becomes very difficult for your body to use blood glucose for energy. And when the body cannot convert blood glucose into energy, what does it do? Any ideas … ? Okay, it begins to break down stored fat to use for fuel. And this can cause problems because using too much fat for fuel can lead to high blood pressure and strokes. So high blood sugar really is a killer—

STUDENT B: Excuse me, um … how exactly does high blood sugar damage you?

PROFESSOR: Lots of ways. First, your kidneys. Your kidneys remove impurities from the blood—that's their job. When you have extra glucose in the blood, this glucose passes through the kidneys, but the kidneys can't get rid of it all. Since not all of the extra glucose is removed by the kidneys, this excess glucose—accompanied by water—spills into the urine. The body tries to get rid of this glucose and water mix, and this causes frequent urination, excessive thirst, and hunger. If diabetes isn't treated, it can cause further complications, including kidney failure … and there are other things, like blindness and heart disease. Now presently, there is no cure for diabetes, but—yes, Margaret?

STUDENT A: But they say that foods with high sugar contents can cause diabetes. So, so wouldn't cutting down on sweets help get rid of diabetes?

PROFESSOR: Actually, that's a myth. Diabetes is caused by a combination of genetic and environmental factors. Sweets are no more out of bounds to people with diabetes than they are to the rest of us, especially if they are eaten as part of a healthy diet and exercise plan. On top of that, people who take insulin to treat their diabetes may sometimes need to eat high-sugar foods to prevent their blood glucose levels from falling too low. Now as I was saying, there is no cure for diabetes. So a person with diabetes must control the amount of glucose in their blood through regular physical exercise, a carefully controlled diet, and medication. They may require insulin injections a few times a day to provide the body with the insulin it doesn't produce.

And this can be tricky! You see, our bodies don't require a *constant* amount of insulin, the amount we need actually *varies*. So diabetics typically have to measure the level of glucose in a drop of their blood several times each day. If the blood glucose level is too high or too low, they can adjust the amount of insulin injected, as well as the amount of physical exercise they do, or their food intake to maintain a normal blood glucose level.

STUDENT B: What happens if a person with diabetes injects too much insulin?

PROFESSOR: If a person with diabetes injects too much insulin, it can produce low blood sugar levels. This can lead to hypoglycemia, a condition characterized by shakiness, confusion, and anxiety.

STUDENT B: So low insulin levels mean blood sugar levels get too high, but overly high insulin levels means your blood sugar level drops too low.

PROFESSOR: That's right. You want insulin levels that are neither too high, nor too low.

STUDENT A: So let's say a diabetic injects too much insulin, and now they drop to where their blood sugar is too low. What should they do?

STUDENT B: You said it earlier: they should eat sweets … try to boost their blood sugar levels, right?

PROFESSOR: Yes, by consuming foods with sugar, such as fruit juice or sugar candy, many diabetics can eliminate hypoglycemic symptoms.

Okay, so to recap, even today, scientists are unsure of the exact cause of diabetes. It continues to be a mystery, although both genetics and environmental factors such as obesity and the lack of exercise appear to play roles. But the basic steps all diabetics have to follow are the same: eat right, manage your weight, stay physically active, stop smoking, and take the diabetes medicines if prescribed by your doctor.

NARRATOR: Now use your notes to help you answer the questions.

What is the discussion mainly about?

Which of the following facts about diabetes does the professor mention?

Listen to part of the talk again, and then answer the question.

PROFESSOR: Now presently, there is no cure for diabetes, but—yes, Margaret?

STUDENT A: But they say that foods with high sugar contents can cause diabetes. So, so wouldn't cutting down on sweets help get rid of diabetes?

NARRATOR: What does the student suggest?

Listen to part of the talk again, and then answer the question.

PROFESSOR: Diabetes is caused by a combination of genetic and environmental factors. Sweets are no more out of bounds to people with diabetes than they are to the rest of us, especially if they are eaten as part of a healthy diet and exercise plan.

NARRATOR: What does the professor mean when he says this:

PROFESSOR: Sweets are no more out of bounds to people with diabetes than they are to the rest of us …

NARRATOR: Listen to part of the talk again, and then answer the question.

PROFESSOR: Now as I was saying, there is no cure for diabetes. So a person with diabetes must control the amount of glucose in their blood through regular physical exercise, a carefully controlled diet, and medication.

NARRATOR: What is the purpose of the professor's comment?

Which of the following are diabetics required to do regularly?

Academic Talk 2: Film Studies

Track 34

NARRATOR: Listen to part of a discussion in an American Studies class.

PROFESSOR:	Does anyone know the old saying, "One action can speak a thousand words"? Well, keep this proverb in mind as we consider our topic today. How a book gets adapted into a movie. Today, I'll be referring to Tom Wolfe's gigantic book—over 700 pages—called *Bonfire of the Vanities*. It was turned into a, oh, roughly two-hour movie of the same name by director Brian De Palma.
	Imagine sitting down to the task of reading lots of descriptive detail, more characters than you can shake a stick at, and numerous twists and turns in the plot, and digging out only the essence that you should include in a film—a totally different medium—to get the author's point across, capture the quality of the book, and yet create a completely different work of art. A filmmaker's work of art, compared with the author's work of art.
STUDENT A:	It seems to me that it's too hard to make the structures of each art form mesh.
STUDENT B:	Yeah, but it happens all the time. Books are always being adapted into movies.
STUDENT A:	Well, maybe it happens all the time, but it doesn't always work out. Lots of movies fall really short of the book.
PROFESSOR:	Yes, we'll need to address that issue. Of course, a novel follows structures that distinguish it from other literary forms, like a short story, a poem, or a play. So too a film based on a novel must draw upon its own defining cinematic structures and techniques to convey story, emotion, and message. Skilled novelists rely on the energy of the printed word to create an intimate bond with the reader. In a film, the printed word rarely factors in.
STUDENT A:	Film's purely visual and audio. So the novel has to be re-created through a lot of things that the book doesn't even worry about. Image, sound, music, and action.
STUDENT B:	Yeah, and the book has the leisure to describe all that in hundreds of words, while the film has to get its point across quickly in a limited number of shots.
PROFESSOR:	That's the dilemma. It's hard to make a worthy film adaptation for an audience who knows the book. One criticism about the Bonfire film was that it digressed from the novel in significant ways instead of remaining faithful to the book's satiric humor, rich detail, and linear development. Don't worry, we'll go through the film and examine key sequences to see what I mean. I'm just giving you a thumbnail sketch of what to keep in mind.
	But I'll describe one example right now from the opening before we see anything. The book and the film both wanted to convey the hypocrisy and tension that society creates. Wolfe starts out with a chaotic scene describing the mayor and included a lot of punctuation—exclamation points, dashes, ellipses—and wordplay, all very verbal mechanisms. It's all intended to show the mayor getting hit on the head with a mayonnaise jar ... remember that from the book? Well, De Palma opens his film with a newspaper reporter about to receive an award for his book. But the reporter doesn't even appear in the book until much later. What is De Palma doing?

STUDENT A:	I guess he's forcing us to see the story through the reporter's eyes instead of just an objective set of eyes looking at life in general.
STUDENT B:	That's a radical choice, isn't it? I mean, I'd think he would have to ask himself if that's what the author really wanted.
PROFESSOR:	Of course. And as the audience, you'd have to ask yourself, was that an effective choice? And, of course, always ask my favorite question: why or why not? Those who adapt books into films have to take liberties sometimes, but are those liberties in the best interest of the book? Characters are dropped, new ones are added. Dialogue is omitted or rewritten. All the details that a novelist luxuriates in might go out the window. Tough choices.
STUDENT A:	Like, somehow I always feel like I'm missing something from a film adaptation. I'm expecting a lot more after I've read the book. I think I'd prefer to read the book after the movie to see what I missed.
PROFESSOR:	That's why lots of times, audiences do leave the film adaptation … disappointed. It's hard to separate the film from the book, especially when the book really grabbed you. And that reminds me of another saying you've all probably heard or used: "Don't bother going to the movie. Read the book instead." Right? Okay, let's begin to examine why a film adaptation, which should capture the book, would motivate someone to say that.
NARRATOR:	Now use your notes to help you answer the questions.
	What is the talk mainly about?
	Why does the professor mention the first scene in the film?
	According to the talk, which can be inferred about film adaptations?
	Listen to part of the talk again, and then answer the question.
PROFESSOR:	Does anyone know the old saying, "One action can speak a thousand words"? Well, keep this proverb in mind as we consider our topic today.
NARRATOR:	Why does the professor say this:
PROFESSOR:	… "One action can speak a thousand words"?
NARRATOR:	Listen to part of the talk again, and then answer the question.
STUDENT A:	It seems to me that it's too hard to make the structures of each art form mesh.
STUDENT B:	Yeah, but it happens all the time. Books are always being adapted into movies.
STUDENT A:	Well, maybe it happens all the time, but it doesn't always work out. Lots of movies fall really short of the book.
NARRATOR:	What does the student mean by this:
STUDENT A:	Lots of movies fall really short of the book.
NARRATOR:	In the talk, the professor describes a number of things that can be affected by an adaptation. Choose three of the answer choices below that were mentioned in the talk.

Academic Talk 3: Astronomy

Track 35

NARRATOR: Listen to part of a talk in an astronomy class.

PROFESSOR: Today we're going to talk about the planet Mercury. Okay ... it's not easy to see Mercury—it's so close to the sun that it's only visible during, uh ... around dawn and dusk, never in darkness. It's also close to the horizon when it is visible to the naked eye, so we're seeing it through the maximum thickness of the atmosphere. When it's higher in the sky, it can be seen through telescopes, but you can't actually make out any, any detail, since there's no real contrast against the bright daytime sky.

So far, we've only sent one probe to Mercury, um ... that was in 1963, oh, sorry, I meant 1973. So the first probe went up in '73 and *Mariner 10* flew by the planet three times in 1974 and '75 and sent back a lot of information. A lot of that information was in the form of pictures of about half of Mercury's surface. Because Mercury's so close to the sun, it's really hard to get *to* Mercury and even harder to put a probe in orbit around it. That's because of the sun's tremendous gravitational field. Recently though, a new form of propulsion ... called an ion engine, has opened up new possibilities for exploring Mercury. It'll make a probe less dependent on picking up thrust from other planets to counteract the gravitational pull of the sun, as is currently necessary with conventional rockets.

Two missions to Mercury are actually being planned right now. NASA is sending a probe called *Messenger*, planned to arrive in 2008, for three flybys, and will enter Mercury's orbit in 2011.

The European Space Agency is sending a larger mission known as BepiColombo. This mission will have three spacecraft, including a landing module and a module designed to investigate the magnetic field. It's planned for launch in 2008 or '9, so about the same time NASA's mission reaches Mercury.

One interesting thing is that the *Mariner*'s pictures of Mercury, about 1,800 in total, all show only one side of the planet. Of course, this is because the planet rotates very slowly ... about once every 58 and a half Earth days. Radar pictures taken from the earth suggest that the other side of Mercury has large mountains. There may, um ... be volcanoes, though it's unlikely that they're still active.

Scientists are hoping to get answers to several unsolved mysteries with the *Messenger* and BepiColombo missions. One is why Mercury is so dense ... over 70 percent iron, twice as much as the other inner planets ... Venus, Earth, the moon, and Mars. Maybe when the planets were formed, there was more dense material like iron close to the sun, or maybe Mercury was originally a much larger planet whose surface was blasted off into space leaving the iron core, or maybe the heat from the sun in the early days of the solar system boiled away the lighter elements from the planet's surface.

Spectrometers carried by the probes should be able to tell us which, if any, of these three theories is correct, depending on what elements they find. If Mercury's composition is similar to the moon, it's unlikely that heavy elements were concentrated near the sun. If Mercury's surface was blasted away, elements like aluminum would float to the surface and solidify, confirming the second theory. Finally, the absence of lighter, volatile elements like sodium on the surface might confirm the third theory … that Mercury has had part of its surface evaporated away by the sun's heat.

Hopefully the probes may also tell us something about Mercury's, um … magnetic field. The earth's magnetic field protects us from dangerous radiation from the sun. Venus and Mars have hardly any magnetic field, but Mercury has one, and we're not quite sure how. We guess it's generated in the iron core, but because Mercury has no atmosphere to speak of, and so no … no ionosphere to complete the circuit, and allow the magnetic field to be sustained like it is here on Earth, it's a bit of a mystery.

One last thing that the BepiColombo mission will test has to do with Einstein's general theory of relativity. Mercury has quite an elliptical orbit, which Einstein explained in terms of a curvature of the time-space continuum close to the sun. The BepiColombo probe will be traveling through the presumed curvature, so the readings on its instruments will provide a powerful test of Einstein's predictions.

NARRATOR: Now use your notes to help you answer the questions.

What is the main topic of this talk?

Why does the professor begin by discussing how difficult it is to see Mercury from Earth?

What can be inferred about Mercury?

Why are the *Mariner 10* pictures all of one side of Mercury?

What will spectrometry determine about Mercury?

What is true of Mercury's magnetic field?

SPEAKING SECTION

Task 1

Track 36

NARRATOR: Some people believe that the best way to reduce carbon emissions is to restrict air travel. Do you think this is a good idea? Give details and examples in your explanation.

Task 2

Track 37

NARRATOR: Now listen to two students as they discuss the announcement.

STUDENT A: You should apply, Sarah.

STUDENT B: Me? No way! I'm swamped as it is. I couldn't possibly take on something like this. I actually know the person who did it last year. That position's a lot of work.

STUDENT A: It doesn't have to be. Remember that leadership skills seminar we took last semester? Rule number one: A great leader is someone who knows how to delegate. The trick is to find other people to do all the work and then make sure they get the job done.

STUDENT B: Look, it's not that I don't want to do it. I'm sure it would have its benefits, but I really need to concentrate on looking for a job. Graduation's right around the corner and I haven't even gotten a résumé together.

STUDENT A: Yeah, but just think how good that position would look on your résumé. And the club would be a great way to make connections. You'd meet lots of local business leaders, socialize with them. Next thing you know, they ask you to come by the office for an interview ...

STUDENT B: No wonder you want to go into sales.

NARRATOR: Now get ready to answer the question.

NARRATOR: The man tries to persuade the woman to do something. Say what he tries to persuade her to do and explain the reasons he gives.

Task 3

Track 38

NARRATOR: Now listen to part of a talk in a computer science class.

PROFESSOR: A very real—and growing—problem that most, if not all of you will face if you continue in the technology field, is hacking. Some of you might wish otherwise, but simply put, hacking is a felony in the United States and most other countries. Now, when it's done by request and under a contract between an ethical hacker and an organization, it's okay. But that's not really what we're talking about when we're talking about hacking. Hacking is entering a person's or organization's computer without permission. This is unethical and a serious crime. No matter what your reasons are, how you might claim to be serving a higher good, it's really the same thing as breaking into someone's office or home. That's a crime. Everyone knows that. What baffles me is that in this day and age people still are trying to create a distinction between entering someone's home and entering someone's computer. If they haven't asked you to do it, you're in the wrong. Period. End of discussion. Even the so-called "joyriders" are in the wrong. Those are the hackers who say they're just rising to the challenge of breaking into a company's supposedly secure system, only to leave without doing anything or causing any harm. If you break into this computer lab, do you think the police wouldn't arrest you just because you didn't take anything?

NARRATOR: Now get ready to answer the question.

NARRATOR: Two opinions on computer hacking are given in the reading. Explain which of these views the professor holds and how she supports her opinion.

Task 4

Track 39

NARRATOR: Now listen to part of a talk in an urban history class.

PROFESSOR: The written history of what is today New York City traces its roots to 1626, when a group of colonists arrived from the Netherlands to establish a settlement they called New Amsterdam. The story of how the Dutch purchased the island of Manhattan from the Indians for the equivalent of $24 is legendary. But beyond that, relatively little is known about the early settlers. It bears noting that Holland at that time was a very prosperous and desirable place to live. As a result, few Dutch people had any incentive to cross the ocean. Rather, those who came to New Amsterdam were people of many different nationalities who were searching for economic opportunities. From its inception then, the town that would one day become New York was a melting pot.

In the countryside, outside of New Amsterdam, the situation was markedly different. Intent on consolidating their control of the area, the Dutch instituted a system of "patroonships." Anyone who could finance the settlement of 50 adults was named a "patroon," or landowner, and was granted large parcels of land and feudal rights. Land ownership was denied to common workers, who had little choice but to labor on the land of their patroons. In many ways, this system bears a striking resemblance to Europe in the Middle Ages, with large blocks of land and exclusive political power centered in the hands of a very few.

Understandably, the colony's governors, whose role it was to implement and maintain this system, were unpopular with the people and got little support from them. Given the climate in which they lived, it's perhaps not surprising that when the British soldiers arrived in the harbor of New

Amsterdam prepared for battle, the Dutch settlers surrendered to them without a fight.

NARRATOR: Now get ready to answer the question.

NARRATOR: Using points and examples from the talk, explain the factors that contributed to the loss of Holland's colony of New Amsterdam.

WRITING SECTION

Task 1

Track 40

NARRATOR: Now listen to part of a talk on the topic you just read about.

PROFESSOR: Although some might argue that a diet of ants, crickets, and grasshoppers can be both nutritious and provide some relief for depleted natural resources, there are multiple reasons why it's best to proceed with caution.

First of all, there is a little-known class of nutrients that can interfere with the body's ability to absorb and process protein. The exoskeleton of some insects has been found to contain these anti-nutrients, such as phytic acid, tannins, and lectins. These substances compromise the nutritional value of foods, especially those made from plants, like rice, wheat, and flour.

Furthermore, the use of pesticides in edible insect production is essentially unregulated. Agricultural areas dedicated to the raising and harvesting of insects have been found to be polluted by harmful chemicals from pesticides, which can find their way into the groundwater and pollute the surrounding land and waterways. In some areas, this has led to health problems as a result of eating dead insects raised on land that was disinfested through the use of pesticides.

Finally, many insects feed on decaying matter, like rotting food and waste, which are ripe with bacteria. Even insects that are grown and harvested on farms are subject to microbial fauna and spore-bearing bacteria. It has been found that insects are capable of carrying parasites which can be harmful or even deadly, especially for children. Unless insect production takes place under strict hygienic conditions, eating these animals can pose a serious threat to populations. Much more research is required before insects are introduced as a potential solution for worldwide hunger.

Answers and Explanations

PRACTICE TEST 1

Reading Section

Passage 1: Nathaniel Hawthorne: His Life and Work

1 (D)

2 (A)

3 (C)

4 (B)

5 (A)

6 (C)

7 (C)

8 (B)

9 (B)

10 *The Scarlet Letter*: (A), (C), (F), (H); *The House of the Seven Gables*: (B), (E), (G)

Passage 2: The Biological Effects of Ionizing Radiation

11 (B)

12 (A)

13 (B)

14 (A)

15 (A)

16 (D)

17 (D)

18 (C)

19 (B)

20 (A), (C), (D)

Passage 3: The Social Cognitive Theory of Learning

21 (A)

22 (B)

23 (C)

24 (D)

25 (A)

26 (C)

27 (B)

28 (A)

29 (D)

30 (A), (B), (E)

Listening Section

Dialogue 1

1 (C)

2 (D)

3 (A)

4 (D)

5 (B)

Dialogue 2

6 (C)

7 (A)

8 (C)

9 (B)

10 (C)

Academic Talk 1: Art History

11 (C)

12 (A)

13 (B), (C)

14 (C)

15 (A)

16 (A)

Academic Talk 2: Archaeology

17 (D)

18 (C)

19 (C)

20 (B)

21 (A)

22 *yes*: (A), (D), (E); *no*: (B), (C)

Academic Talk 3: Literature

23 (B)

24 (A)

25 (A)

26 (D)

27 (C)

28 (B)

Speaking Section

1   Answers will vary. **Skill tested:** Express and support an opinion based on a familiar experience

2   Answers will vary. **Skill tested:** Summarize and compare information gleaned from multiple sources

3   Answers will vary. **Skill tested:** Summarize and compare information gleaned from multiple sources

4   Answers will vary. **Skill tested:** Summarize and compare information gleaned from a lecture

Writing Section

1   Answers will vary. **Skill tested:** Summarize and compare information gleaned from multiple sources

2   Answers will vary. **Skill tested:** Express and support an opinion based on a familiar experience

PRACTICE TEST 2

Reading Section

Passage 1: How Satellites Have Revolutionized Communication

1   (A)

2   (B)

3   (B)

4   (B)

5   (A)

6   (C)

7   (D)

8   (C)

9   (A)

10   (A), (C), (D)

Passage 2: Women's Suffrage

11   (C)

12   (A)

13   (A)

14   (D)

15   (B)

16   (B)

17   (C)

18   (D)

19   (D)

20   (A), (B), (F)

Passage 3: The Incandescent Lightbulb

21   (B)

22   (B)

23   (B)

24   (C)

25   (C)

26   (D)

27   (A)

28   (D)

29   (A)

30   *Incandescent bulbs:* (A), (D), (F), (I); *Fluorescent bulbs:* (C), (E), (H)

Listening Section

Dialogue 1

1   (B)

2   (D)

3   (D)

4   (C)

5   (A)

Dialogue 2

6   (A)

7   (B)

8   (D)

9   (A)

10   (B)

Academic Talk 1: Music

11   (B)

12   (A)

13   (C)

14 (D)

15 (C)

16 (B), (C), (D)

Academic Talk 2: Film History

17 (C)

18 (A)

19 (B)

20 (D)

21 (C)

22 (A), (D)

Academic Talk 3: Physics

23 (D)

24 (C)

25 (A)

26 (A)

27 (B)

28 (B), (C), (D)

Speaking Section

1 Answers will vary. **Skill tested:** Express and support an opinion based on a familiar experience

2 Answers will vary. **Skill tested:** Summarize and compare information gleaned from multiple sources

3 Answers will vary. **Skill tested:** Summarize and compare information gleaned from multiple sources

4 Answers will vary. **Skill tested:** Summarize and compare information gleaned from a lecture

Writing Section

1 Answers will vary. **Skill tested:** Summarize and compare information gleaned from multiple sources

2 Answers will vary. **Skill tested:** Express and support opinion based on a familiar experiences.

PRACTICE TEST 3

Reading Section

Passage 1: Acid Rain

1 (C)

2 (D)

3 (A)

4 (A)

5 (C)

6 (B)

7 (A)

8 (D)

9 (B)

10 (B), (D), (F)

Passage 2: Prohibition

11 (A)

12 (B)

13 (C)

14 (B)

15 (D)

16 (A)

17 (D)

18 (C)

19 (C)

20 (C), (E), (F)

Passage 3: Attention Deficit/Hyperactivity Disorder

21 (A)

22 (A)

23 (D)

24 (B)

25 (B)

26 (C)

27 (B)

28 (C)

29 (B)

30 (C), (D), (E)

Listening Section

Dialogue 1

1 (D)

2 (C)

3 (B)

4 (A)

5 (C)

Dialogue 2

6 (D)

7 (B)

8 (C)

9 (A)

10 (A)

Academic Talk 1: Women's Studies

11 (A)

12 (C)

13 (B)

14 (D)

15 (B)

16 (A), (C), (D)

Academic Talk 2: Music

17 (C)

18 (D)

19 (A)

20 (C)

21 (D)

22 (A), (B), (C)

Academic Talk 3: History

23 (D)

24 (A)

25 (C)

26 (B)

27 (B)

28 (B)

Speaking Section

1 Answers will vary. **Skill tested:** Express and support an opinion based on a familiar experience

2 Answers will vary. **Skill tested:** Summarize and compare information gleaned from multiple sources

3 Answers will vary. **Skill tested:** Summarize and compare information gleaned from multiple sources

4 Answers will vary. **Skill tested:** Summarize and compare information gleaned from a lecture

Writing Section

1 Answers will vary. **Skill tested:** Summarize and compare information gleaned from multiple sources

2 Answers will vary. **Skill tested:** Express and support an opinion based on a familiar experience

PRACTICE TEST 4

Reading Section

Passage 1: Hubble's "Tuning Fork" Galaxy Diagram

1 (B)

2 (D)

3 (B)

4 (D)

5 (C)

6 (A)

7 (A)

8 (D)

9 (D)

10 *Spiral galaxies*: (A), (D), (F); *Elliptical galaxies*: (B), (C), (G), (H)

Passage 2: Ellis Ruley, Folk Artist

11 (C)

12 (A)

13 (B)

14 (A)

15 (A)

16 (D)

17 (A)

18 (A)

19 (C)

20 (A), (E), (F)

Passage 3: Pinta Island Tortoises

21 (A)

22 (C)

23 (A)

24 (D)

25 (B)

26 (C)

27 (B)

28 (A)

29 (C)

30 (B), (D), (F)

Listening Section

Dialogue 1

1 (C)

2 (B)

3 (B)

4 (A)

5 (D)

Dialogue 2

6 (B)

7 (B)

8 (C)

9 (A)

10 (D)

Academic Talk 1: Biology

11 (A)

12 (C)

13 (C)

14 (D)

15 (C)

16 (D)

Academic Talk 2: Film Studies

17 (A)

18 (C)

19 (B)

20 (B)

21 (C)

22 (A), (D), (E)

Academic Talk 3: Astronomy

23 (B)

24 (D)

25 (A)

26 (B)

27 (D)

28 (D)

Speaking Section

1 Answers will vary. **Skill tested:** Express and support an opinion based on a familiar experience

2 Answers will vary. **Skill tested:** Summarize and compare information gleaned from multiple sources

3 Answers will vary. **Skill tested:** Summarize and compare information gleaned from multiple sources

4 Answers will vary. **Skill tested:** Summarize and compare information gleaned from a lecture

Writing Section

1 Answers will vary. **Skill tested:** Summarize and compare information gleaned from multiple sources

2 Answers will vary. **Skill tested:** Express and support an opinion based on a familiar experience